Lecture Notes in Computer Science 5098

Commenced Publication in 1973
Founding and Former Series Editors:
Gerhard Goos, Juris Hartmanis, and Jan van Leeuwen

Francisco J. Perales   Robert B. Fisher (Eds.)

Articulated Motion and Deformable Objects

5th International Conference, AMDO 2008
Port d'Andratx, Mallorca, Spain, July 9-11, 2008
Proceedings

 Springer

Volume Editors

Francisco J. Perales
UIB, Dept. of Computer Science and Mathematics
Computer Graphics and Vision Group
C/ Valldemossa Km. 7.5, PC 07122, Palma de Mallorca, Spain
E-mail: paco.perales@uib.es

Robert B. Fisher
University of Edinburgh
School of Informatics
James Clerk Maxwell Building, The King's Buildings
Mayfield Road, Edinburgh EH9 3JZ, UK
E-mail: rbf@inf.ed.ac.uk

Library of Congress Control Number: 2008930132

CR Subject Classification (1998): I.4, I.5, I.2.10, I.3, I.6

LNCS Sublibrary: SL 6 – Image Processing, Computer Vision, Pattern Recognition, and Graphics

ISSN 0302-9743

ISBN 978-3-540-70516-1 Springer Berlin Heidelberg New York

Springer is a part of Springer Science+Business Media

springer.com

© Springer-Verlag Berlin Heidelberg 2008

Typesetting: Camera-ready by author, data conversion by Scientific Publishing Services, Chennai, India
Printed on acid-free paper   SPIN: 12327829   06/3180   5 4 3 2 1 0

Preface

The AMDO2008 conference took place at the Hotel Mon Port, Port d'Andratx (Mallorca), July 9–11, 2008, institutionally sponsored by the International Association for Pattern Recognition (IAPR), the MEC (Ministerio de Educación y Ciencia, Spanish Government), the Conselleria d'Economia, Hisenda i Innovació (Balearic Islands Government), the Consell de Mallorca, the AERFAI (Spanish Association in Pattern Recognition and Artificial Intelligence), the EG (Eurographics Association) and the Mathematics and Computer Science Department of the UIB. In addition, important commercial sponsors collaborated with practical demonstrations; the main contributors were: VICOM Tech, ANDROME Iberica, Ndigital (NDI), Robot S.A, DAT.

The subject of the conference was ongoing research in articulated motion on a sequence of images and sophisticated models for deformable objects. The goals of these areas are to understand and interpret the motion of complex objects that can be found in sequences of images in the real world. The main topics considered as priority are: geometric and physical deformable models, motion analysis, articulated models and animation, modelling and visualization of deformable models, deformable model applications, motion analysis applications, single or multiple human motion analysis and synthesis, face modelling, tracking, recovering and recognition models, virtual and augmented reality, haptics devices, biometrics techniques. The conference topics were grouped into the following tracks: Track 1: Computer Graphics (Human Modelling and Animation), Track 2: Human Motion (Analysis, Tracking, 3D Reconstruction and Recognition), Track 3: Multimodal User Interaction (VR and AR, Speech, Biometrics) and Track 4: Advanced Multimedia Systems (Standards, Indexed Video Contents).

This conference was the natural evolution of the previous editions and was consolidated as a European reference symposium in the topics mentioned above. The new goal of this conference was to promote interaction and collaboration among researchers working directly in the areas covered by the main tracks. New perceptual user interfaces and the emerging technologies increase the relation between areas involved with human–computer interaction. The new perspective of the AMDO 2008 conference was to strengthen the relationship between the many areas that have as their key point the study of the human body using computer technologies as the main tool. The response to the call of papers for this conference was very good. From 64 full papers submitted, 36 were accepted for oral presentation and 7 as posters. The review process was carried out by the Program Committee, each paper being assessed by at least two reviewers. The conference included several parallel sessions of oral presented papers, poster sessions and three tutorials. Also, the conference benefited from the collaboration of the invited speakers covering various aspects of the main topics. These invited speakers were: M. Pantic (Imperial College London, UK / University of Twente, Netherlands), E. Boyer (LJK / UJF / INRIA Rhone-Alpes, France) and J. Abascal (University of the Basque country Spain).

July 2008

F.J. Perales
R. Fisher

Organization

AMDO 2008 was organized by the Computer Graphics, Vision and Artificial Intelligence team of the Department of Mathematics and Computer Science, Universitat de les Illes Balears (UIB) in cooperation with IAPR (International Association for Pattern Recognition), AERFAI (Spanish Association for Pattern Recognition and Image Analysis) and EG (Eurograhics Association).

Executive Committee

General Conference Co-chairs	F. J. Perales, Mathematics and Computer Science Department, UIB (Spain)
	R. Fisher, University of Edinburgh (UK)
Organizing Chairs	M.J. Abasolo, D. Arellano, J.M. Buades, A. Delgado, G. Fiol, M. González, A. Jaume, A. Igelmo, C. Manresa, R. Mas, M. Mascaró P., M. Miró, G. Nicolau, P. Palmer, J. Rossi, X. Varona
	Dept. of Mathematics and Computer Science (UIB, Spain)
Tutorial Chairs	M. González, J. Varona, F.J. Perales UIB (Spain)

Program Committee

Abásolo, M.J.	Universitat Illes Balears, Spain
Badler, N.I.	University of Pennsylvania, USA
Baldasarri, S.	University of Zaragoza, Spain
Bartoli, A.	CNRS - LASMEA, France
Baumela, L.	Technical University of Madrid, Spain
Boulic, R.	EPFL, Switzerland
Bowden, R.	University of Surrey, UK
Boyer, E.	LJK / UJF / INRIA Rhone-Alpes, France
Brunet, P.	UPC, Spain
Buades, J.M.	Universitat Illes Balears, Spain
Campilho, A.	University of Oporto, Portugal
Caplier, A.	GIPSA-lab/DIS, France
Cerezo, E.	University of Zaragoza, Spain
Cohen, I.	University of Southern California, USA
Coll, T.	Universitat Illes Balears, Spain
Davis, L.S.	University of Maryland, USA

Del Bimbo, A.	Univ. di Firenze, Italy
Dogan, S.	I-Lab/centre CCSR, University of Surrey, UK
Dugelay, J.L.	EURECOM, France
Fiol-Roig, G.	Universitat Illes Balears, Spain
Fisher, R.	University of Edinburgh, UK
Flerackers, E.	Hasselt University, Belgium
Flores, J.	Mar-USC, Spain
Garcia, E.	Universidad de la Rioja, Spain
Göbel, M.	FleXilution, Germany
Gong, S.	QM Westfield Coll, UK
Gonzàlez, J.	IRI, CSIC-UPC, Spain
González-Hidalgo, M.	Universitat Illes Balears, Spain
Hilton, A.	University of Surrey, UK
Jorge, Joaquim A.	Technical University of Lisbon, Portugal
Komura, T.	IPAB, University of Edinburgh, UK
Mas, R.	Universitat Illes Balears, Spain
Matey, L.	CEIT, Spain
Medioni, G.	University of Southern California, USA
Metaxas, D.	University of Pennsylvania, USA
Mir, A.	Universitat Illes Balears, Spain
Miró-Julià, M.	Universitat Illes Balears, Spain
Murino V.	University of Verona, Italy
Natal, J.	IDMEC, University of Porto, Portugal
Pantic M.	Imperial College London, UK / Univ. of Twente, Netherlands
Perales, F.J.	Universitat Illes Balears, Spain
Pérez de la Blanca, N.	University of Granada, Spain
Pla, F.	University of Jaume I, Spain
Qin, H.	Stony Brook University, New York, USA
Radeva, P.	UAB-CVC, Spain
Sanfeliu, A.	IRI, CSIC-UPC, Spain
Santos-Victor, J.	IST, Portugal
Serón, F.	University of Zaragoza, Spain
Shirai, Y.	University of Osaka, Japan
Skala, V.	University of Plzen, Czech Republic
Susin, A.	UPC, Spain
Tavares, J.	University of Porto, Portugal
Terzopoulos, D.	University of Toronto, Canada
Thalmann, D.	EPFL, Switzerland
Varona, J.	Universitat Illes Balears, Spain
Vetter, T.	University of Basel, Switzerland
Villanueva, J.	UAB-CVC, Spain
Wang, L.	University of Melbourne, Australia
Xiao, Y.	University of Edinburgh, UK

Sponsoring Institutions

IAPR (International Association for Pattern Recognition)
AERFAI (Spanish Association for Pattern Recognition and Image Analysis)
EG (Eurograhics Association)
MEC (Ministerio de Educación y Ciencia, Spanish Government)
Conselleria d'Economia, Hisenda i Innovació (Balearic Islands Government)
Consell de Mallorca
Mathematics and Computer Science Department, Universitat de les Illes Balears
(UIB)
Ajuntament d'Andratx. Sol de Ponent
Ajuntament de Palma
Sa Nostra. Caixa de Balears

Commercial Sponsoring Enterprises

VICOM-Tech S.A., www.vicomtech.es
ANDROME Iberica S.A, www.androme.es
Robot, www.robotmallorca.com
Ndigital (NDI), www.ndigital.com
DAT (Development Advanced Technology), www.dat-inf.com/home.html

Table of Contents

Inverse Kinematics Using Sequential Monte Carlo Methods

Nicolas Courty[1] and Elise Arnaud[2]

[1] SAMSARA/VALORIA, European University of Brittany, Vannes, France
[2] Université Joseph Fourier, INRIA Rhône-Alpes, LJK, Grenoble, France

Abstract. In this paper we propose an original approach to solve the Inverse Kinematics problem. Our framework is based on Sequential Monte Carlo Methods and has the advantage to avoid the classical pitfalls of numerical inversion methods since only direct calculations are required. The resulting algorithm accepts arbitrary constraints and exhibits linear complexity with respect to the number of degrees of freedom. Hence, the proposed system is far more efficient for articulated figures with a high number of degrees of freedom.

1 Introduction

Given a kinematic chain described by a fixed number of segments linked by joints in 3D space, the forward and inverse kinematics problems can be derived. The first amounts to computing the pose of the figure given the values of the joint angles. The second is the process of determining the parameters of the kinematic chain in order to obtain a desired configuration. The latter has been extensively studied in computer animation due to its large number of applications, such as connecting characters to the virtual world, as well as in robotics, where manipulator arms are commanded in terms of joint velocities.

Classical approaches for solving inverse kinematics require numerical inversion operations that may have singularities and exhibit the classical problems encountered in numerical inversion.

In this paper, we propose to solve the problem with sequential Monte Carlo methods (SMCM), that are based on the importance sampling principle. The main advantage of using a sampling approach is that we solve the inverse kinematics using the direct kinematics, hence avoiding numerical inversion of the forward operator. To do so, we cast the problem into a hidden Markov model (HMM), whose hidden state is given by all the parameters that define the articulated figure. Hence, the state space consists of all the possible configurations of the state. The inverse kinematics is then re-formulated in a filtering framework. This allows us to derive a simple and efficient algorithm. The sequential aspect of the procedure is one of its keypoints. The algorithm produces a complete motion, satisfying all the required constraints, from the initial position to the target position as a result of an optimization procedure. Each intermediate pose corresponds to an optimization step of a sequential algorithm, not requiring any batch calculations. The contributions of our method to the domain of

F.J. Perales and R.B. Fisher (Eds.): AMDO 2008, LNCS 5098, pp. 1–10, 2008.
© Springer-Verlag Berlin Heidelberg 2008

articulated character control are threefold: (i) our method does not require any explicit numerical inversion, (ii) any type of constraints can be added to the system in an intuitive manner, (iii) this method can be implemented in a few lines of codes without the need of complex optimization algorithms.

The paper is organized as follows. Next section provides a short related work on human figure animation. In section 3, we propose the Bayesian formulation of motion control, and explain how HMMs can be advantageouly used in that framework. An analogy with filtering formulation is done. In section 4, we focus on the specific statistical model we propose for inverse kinematics. Finally, results are presented in section 5.

2   Related Work

Creating realistic and plausible motions remains an open challenge within the animation community. Pure synthesis models like inverse kinematics have been well studied and used as a support in several other problems such as motion reconstruction in presence of missing markers, or retargetting [6,12,3]. Nevertheless, the fact that most of the time its solution is undetermined implies that several constraints need to be added to the produced motion [15,1,13]. The types of those constraints and the way to handle them in the resolution of the inverse problem is a critical part of the existing algorithms. Recent works propose to use motion capture data to constraint the motion [10,4,5]. Our approach uses a statistical description of the problem, similarly to [14] and [5]. This first addresses the motion-editing problem using a non linear Kalman Filter, while the second uses a learned statistical dynamic model in a constrained-based motion optimization framework. However, our methodology differs significantly from these works since it is not data-driven, and uses a sampling approach. To the best of our knowledge, no SMCM have been applied yet for inverse kinematics. Let us note that SMCM have been used to address the markerless motion capture problem in the computer vision community [8,7]. The problem is then over-constrained by image features, and SMCM are used to explore efficiently local minima. The problem adressed here is different since we aim at generating plausible motion trajectories by exploring an under-constrained state space. Finally, it is possible to outline some similarities with recent works in the domain of motion planning like [2] where a stochastic search is used to find a clear path in obstructed area. Again, our work differ from these because of the sequential aspect of our method that allows to adapt dynamically to changes in goals or environment.

3   Inference Problem and SMCM

Formulation overview. In this paper, we propose a statistical inverse kinematics solver. It is based on a Bayesian formulation of the problem, that enables us to combine motion priors, skeleton constraints (e.g. joint limits) and kinematic constraints. We denote $\mathbf{x} = \mathbf{x}_{0:F} = \{\mathbf{x}_0, \mathbf{x}_1, \cdots, \mathbf{x}_F\}$ the sequence of poses from the initial pose of the chain $\mathbf{x}_0$ to its final pose $\mathbf{x}_F$ satisfying the kinematic constraints. We denote $\mathbf{z}$ as the set of variables that we are interested to control and that takes into account the various constraints. The goal is to infer the most likely trajectory $\hat{\mathbf{x}}$ given $\mathbf{z}$. We have:

$$\hat{\mathbf{x}} = \arg\max_{\mathbf{x}} p(\mathbf{x}|\mathbf{z}) = \arg\max_{\mathbf{x}} \frac{p(\mathbf{z}|\mathbf{x})\ p(\mathbf{x})}{p(\mathbf{z})}, \tag{1}$$

where $p(\mathbf{z})$ is a normalizing constant. The involved components are the motion prior $p(\mathbf{x})$ and the likelihood $p(\mathbf{z}|\mathbf{x})$. The motion prior carries the *a priori* knowledge about the very nature of the motion ; whereas the likelihood $p(\mathbf{z}|\mathbf{x})$ gives an evaluation on how good the motion is with respect to the set of constraints.

In this paper, we propose to use *sequential* Monte Carlo techniques. The formulation (1) has to be modified to suit a sequential approximation of $p(\mathbf{x}|\mathbf{z})$. Let $\mathbf{z}$ be given by a desired trajectory of the controlled variables, i.e. $\mathbf{z} = \mathbf{z}_{0:F}$. Each $\mathbf{x}_k$ should satisfy all the constraints at time k. Using Bayes' theorem $p(\mathbf{x}_k|\mathbf{z}_{0:k})$ may be expressed using $p(\mathbf{x}_{k-1}|\mathbf{z}_{0:k-1})$, $k \leq F$:

$$p(\mathbf{x}_k|\mathbf{z}_{0:k}) = \frac{p(\mathbf{z}_k|\mathbf{x}_k)\ p(\mathbf{x}_k|\mathbf{z}_{0:k-1})}{\int p(\mathbf{z}_k|\mathbf{x}_k)\ p(\mathbf{x}_k|\mathbf{z}_{0:k-1})\ d\mathbf{x}_k}, \tag{2}$$

$$\text{where}\ \ p(\mathbf{x}_k|\mathbf{z}_{0:k-1}) = \int p(\mathbf{x}_k|\mathbf{x}_{k-1})\ p(\mathbf{x}_{k-1}|\mathbf{z}_{0:k-1})\ d\mathbf{x}_{k-1}. \tag{3}$$

The new involved components are : the motion prior, now described as an *evolution prior* $p(\mathbf{x}_k|\mathbf{x}_{k-1})$ and a *likelihood* $p(\mathbf{z}_k|\mathbf{x}_k)$. Those two densities define the *model* of the system. This leads us to consider an HMM to model the motion control problem.

Sequential Monte Carlo methods. [9] The filtering recursion (2-3) does not yield closed-form expressions for general non-linear non-Gaussian models. To calculate this recursion, SMCMs propose to implement recursively an approximation of the sought filtering distribution $p(\mathbf{x}_k|\mathbf{z}_{0:k})$. This approximation consists of a finite weighted sum of N delta-Diracs centered on the hypothesized locations in the state space, called particles. These particles are instances, or copies of the system. A weight $w_k^{(i)}$ is assigned to each particle $\mathbf{x}_k^{(i)}$, $i = 1 : N$ to describe its relevance. Hence, the approximation is:

$$\hat{p}(\mathbf{x}_k|\mathbf{z}_{0:k}) = \sum_{i=1:N} w_k^{(i)} \delta_{\mathbf{x}_k^{(i)}}(\mathbf{x}_k). \tag{4}$$

Assuming that the approximation of $p(\mathbf{x}_{k-1}|\mathbf{z}_{0:k-1})$ is known, the recursive implementation of the filtering distribution is done by propagating the swarm of weighted particles $\{\mathbf{x}_{k-1}^{(i)}, w_{k-1}^{(i)}\}_{i=1:N}$. The estimate of the state is obtained by maximizing the estimated distribution given by (4), i.e. $\hat{\mathbf{x}}_k$ is the *maximum a posteriori* (MAP) estimate. At each iteration the algorithm can be decomposed in three steps :

1. *exploration of the state space:* The set of new particles $\{\mathbf{x}_k^{(i)}\}_{i=1:N}$ is obtained using the importance sampling method. The particles are drawn from the *importance function* denoted by $\pi(\mathbf{x}_k|\mathbf{x}_{0:k-1}^{(i)}, \mathbf{z}_{0:k})$.
2. *calculation of the new weights:* To maintain a consistent sample, the weights are updated according to a recursive evaluation:

$$w_k^{(i)} \propto w_{k-1}^{(i)} \frac{p(\mathbf{z}_k|\mathbf{x}_k^{(i)})\, p(\mathbf{x}_k^{(i)}|\mathbf{x}_{k-1}^{(i)})}{\pi(\mathbf{x}_k^{(i)}|\mathbf{x}_{0:k-1}^{(i)}, \mathbf{z}_{0:k})}, \qquad \sum_{i=1:N} w_k^{(i)} = 1. \tag{5}$$

3. *mutation/selection of the particles:* As soon as the number of significant particles is too small, it is necessary to perform a resampling step. This procedure aims at removing particles with weak weights, and reproducing particles associated to strong weights

These three steps constitute the general framework of SMCMs. Different instances of this general algorithm can be defined. The simple method we use is built with the following rules: (i) the importance function coincides with the evolution law, i.e. $\pi(\mathbf{x}_k|\mathbf{x}_{0:k-1}^{(i)}, \mathbf{z}_{0:k}) = p(\mathbf{x}_k|\mathbf{x}_{k-1}^{(i)})$; (ii) this implies that the resulting weights are $w_k^{(i)} \propto w_{k-1}^{(i)}\, p(\mathbf{z}_k|\mathbf{x}_k^{(i)})$. The application of this algorithm for the inverse kinematics problem is described in the next section.

4 SMCM for Inverse Kinematics

Notations. Let us consider a kinematic chain $\mathcal{C}$ composed of n joints. $\mathcal{C}$ is parameterized by the rotation vector $\mathbf{Q} = \{\mathbf{q}_1, \ldots, \mathbf{q}_n\} \in$ the *articular space* $SO(3)^n$. Each joint of $\mathcal{C}$ is expressed as an unitary quaternion $\in S^3$. We define the forward kinematic operator $\mathbf{H}$ that computes the configuration of the end effector of the chain $\mathbf{P}$. $\mathbf{P}$ is defined by a position and an orientation, *i.e.* $\mathbf{P} \in$ the *task space* $SE(3)$. The forward kinematics equation is given as:

$$\mathbf{P} = \mathbf{H}(\mathbf{Q}) \tag{6}$$

The goal of inverse kinematics is to find a vector $\mathbf{Q}$ such that $\mathbf{P}$ is equal to a given desired configuration $\mathbf{P}_d$: $\mathbf{Q} = \mathbf{H}^{-1}(\mathbf{P}_d)$. $\mathbf{H}$ is a highly non linear operator difficult to invert.

We denote $\phi(\mathbf{q}\,; \mathbf{m}, \mathbf{\Sigma})$ as the generalized Gaussian density for quaternion variable $\mathbf{q}$, called QuTem distribution [11]. It corresponds to the Gaussian distribution of covariance Σ in the tangent space at the quaternion mode $\mathbf{m}$ wrapped onto a hemisphere of S^3. For each joint, an associated quaternion and its QuTem distribution is defined. The covariance matrix describes the kinematic properties of the joint. For simplicity, we take a diagonal covariance matrix. A very small value of an element of the diagonal with respect to the others, may be assimilated to a degree of freedom with very small variability. This allows us to control the effective number of degrees of freedom of a given joint. The distribution of the vector of quaternions $\mathbf{Q}$ is denoted $\Phi(\mathbf{Q}\,; \mathbf{M}, \Gamma)$. We assume that this last distribution defines a generalized Gaussian distribution over the pose space $SO(3)^n$, where n is the number of joints, and $\mathbf{M}$ and Γ are deduced from the QuTem parameters.

Model design. The goal of inverse kinematics is to estimate the value of the vector $\mathbf{Q}$ such that the resulting kinematic chain satisfies the kinematic constraints and other user-defined constraints. The rotation vector is now seen as a hidden random variable evolving in time until the final task is reached. The notation $\mathbf{Q}_k$ describes the random vector of quaternions at iteration k, corresponding to the state of the filter at time k. The notion of time refers to the iterated convergence steps toward the achievement of the goal *wrt.* the constraints.

In an operational IK system, it is desirable to be able to add several constraints to ensure particular effects. In our framework, those constraints can be handled either in the definition of the *evolution prior*, either in the *likelihood* characterization. Specifically, the nature of the kinematic structure (encoded in the Σ matrix) and hard constraints like joint limits or self-intersection avoidance are part of the sampling process (evolution prior), whereas soft or numerical constraints (such as minimizing a given function) are included in the likelihood.

Evolution prior. The evolution prior $p(\mathbf{Q}_k|\mathbf{Q}_{k-1})$ carries the *a priori* knowledge about the intrinsic nature of the motion, as well as biomechanical constraints and other binary constraints. A sample of this density is constructed by sampling from $\Phi(\mathbf{Q}_k \; ; f(\mathbf{Q}_{k-1}) \; , \; \Sigma)$, until $\mathbf{Q}_k$ is accepted, i.e. satisfies the binary constraints, including the joint limit constraints. This rejection/acceptance process guarantees that no impossible configurations will be generated. The mean of this density $f(\mathbf{Q}_{k-1})$ may describe any *a priori* knowledge on the kinematic chain motion. In case of motion control, it may be inferred from a learning phase. In this paper, we aim at demonstrating the advantages of our framework for the simple inverse kinematics problem where no *a priori* motion has to be verified. Hence, our model can be expressed as $f(\mathbf{Q}_{k-1}) \equiv \mathbf{Q}_{k-1}$. The main advantage of the algorithm proposed here is that it deals with inequality constraints in a very simple manner, using an acceptance/reject procedure.

Likelihood. The likelihood calculation $p(\mathbf{z}_k|\mathbf{Q}_k)$ gives an evaluation of how good the configuration is with respect to the desired task. If a unique kinematic constraint is imposed, the likelihood of a given state $\mathbf{Q_k}$ is evaluated by calculating the distance between the end effector configuration – obtained from equation (6) – and the desired configuration $\mathbf{P}_d$. The likelihood model used here is:

$$p(\mathbf{z}_k|\mathbf{Q}_k) \propto \exp \; [-d_{\Sigma_z}(\mathbf{P}_d \; , \; \mathbf{H}(\mathbf{Q}_k)) \,] , \qquad (7)$$

where d_{Σ_z} is the Mahalanobis distance with respect to the diagonal measurement noise covariance Σ_z, given by:

$$d_{\Sigma_z}(\mathbf{P}_d \; , \; \mathbf{H}(\mathbf{Q}_k)) = (\mathbf{P}_d \; - \; \mathbf{H}(\mathbf{Q}_k))^t \Sigma_z^{-1}(\mathbf{P}_d \; - \; \mathbf{H}(\mathbf{Q}_k)). \qquad (8)$$

To guide the optimization towards the final pose, we propose to iteratively reduce the value of Σ_z.

Other non-binary constraints may be added to the model. The methodology to do so is the following: each constraint has to be expressed in terms of a cost function whose value is 0 if the constraint is satisfied and large otherwise.

Supposing that j different constraints, assumed to be independent, are modeled by the cost functions $C_1 \ldots C_j$, associated to noise covariances $\Sigma_1 \ldots \Sigma_j$ then the likelihood is defined as:

$$p(\mathbf{z}_k|\mathbf{Q}_k) \propto \exp[-d_{\Sigma_z}(\mathbf{P}_d \, , \, \mathbf{H}(\mathbf{Q}_k))\,] \ \prod_i \exp \ [-C_i^t \, \Sigma_i \, C_i] \qquad (9)$$

Let us finally note here that setting the amplitude of the noises with respect to each constraint can be seen as a classifier between *important* and *optional* constraints. This is related in a sense to the weighted scheme of standard inverse kinematics. Enforcing strict priority levels within this framework is part of our future work.

Algorithm. A synopsis of the inverse kinematics filter is described in algorithm 1. Because of the jittered trajectories obtained if using directly the SMCM algorithm as previously described, an additional interpolation step is used to smooth the trajectory in $SO(3)$. This step is a Kalman-like interpolation step, controlled by a parameter α.

Algorithm 1. Inverse Kinematics filter

---

1. exploration of the state space using N copies of the system, i.e.
   for $i = 1...N$, draw $\mathbf{Q}_k^{(i)} \sim p(\mathbf{Q}_k|\mathbf{Q}_{k-1}^{(i)})$
2. calculation of the weights:
   - for $i = 1...N$, calculate $w_k^{(i)} \propto w_{k-1}^{(i)} p(\mathbf{z}_k|\mathbf{Q}_k^{(i)})$
   - do weight normalization
3. calculation of the pose estimate:
   - obtain the first estimate as the MAP estimate, i.e.
     $\tilde{\mathbf{Q}}_k = \mathbf{Q}_k^{(j)}$ such as $w_{k-1}^{(j)} = \max \left(w_k^{(1)}...w_k^{(N)} \right)$
   - obtain the final estimate as the smoothed estimate, i.e.:
     $\hat{\mathbf{Q}}_k = \text{interpolate} \left(\hat{\mathbf{Q}}_{k-1}, \tilde{\mathbf{Q}}_k, \alpha \right)$
4. if necessary, mutation/selection of the particles

---

5   Results

Simple positioning task. The first example is a simple positioning task for a kinematic model of an arm constituted of 4 segments with 4 pivot articulations, i.e. there are 3 rotational DOFs. The target is a point in $3D$ space. Figure 1.a shows the initial and the final configuration at convergence. Figure 1.b describes the convergence of our algorithm to the solution (distance to target) along several trials. Figure 1.c is a plot of the $3D$ trajectories of the end effector of the arm. Figure 1.d shows the evolution of the particles along the first frames of the animation. We then apply a similar task to a chain composed of 90 DOFs, i.e. 30 segments with 3 rotational degrees of freedom each. The center of mass of this chain is constrained to lie on a vertical line passing through the root of the chain. Another constraint is introduced to smooth the overall aspect of the

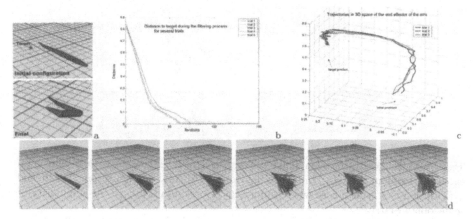

Fig. 1. Convergence of the algorithm (a) 3D view of the articular chain and the target (b) Distance to target. One can observe that the nature of the convergence does not change along the different trials (c) Trajectories of the end effector i $3D$ space. (d) **Importance sampling** along 6 iterations. Each particle is displayed as colored linked segments. This color is a function of the weights: the lighter the greater the weight.

chain. This constraint can be seen as a regularization function. It is expressed using the following energy function C:

$$C = \sum_{i=1}^{n} \sum_{j=-k}^{k} ||Log(\mathbf{q}_i^{-1}\mathbf{q}_{i+j})||. \qquad (10)$$

This function aims at minimizing the differences, using geodesical distance, between successive rotations in the chain. We run this example at an approximate speed of 60 frames per second. Figure 2 shows the initial and final configurations. Let us note that this particular initial configuration stands for a typical singularity that lead numerical schemes to fail. In our case, efficiently sampling around this initial configuration provides pretty good solutions for an inferior computation time.

Computational performances. From a computational point of view, there are two major questions that arise in our framework. The first is, which is the number of particles that the simulation requires to be correct. Second, how this method compares to classical numeric inversion schemes. In figure 3, we investigate this first issue with the following setup: given a kinematic chain whose number of degrees of freedom is parameterizable, we perform a simple positioning task one thousand times, and report the percentage of success. In this case, the task is considered successful if the distance between the end effector and the target is below a certain threshold within a given number of iterations. This threshold is set to 0.001 unit for a 2 units original distance to target within 200 iterations. One can remark that with 30 particles the percentage of successful realizations is almost always 100 percent, which gives an idea of the minimal

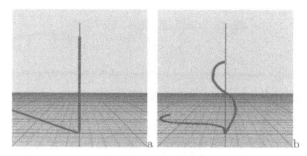

Fig. 2. Chain example. This chain is composed of 30 segments with 3 rotational degrees of freedom each (a) Initial configuration (b) final configuration. The initial configuration is a typical case where numerical inversion fails due to the singularity of the Jacobian matrix.

number of particles needed for a robust use. Another interesting issue is that this minimal percentage diminishes with the number of degrees of freedom. One may explain this behavior by the fact that, when there are more degrees of freedom, redundancy increases, as well the size of the solution state space, so that the sampled particles are more likely to be in the solution space of the task.

In Figure 3.b we compare the average time per iteration of two different numerical IK solutions. the Jacobian transpose method and the damped pseudo-inverse methods, and our method with 50 and 20 particles are compared. In both numerical methods the Jacobian is evaluated with a finite difference scheme. This scheme is very time costly at each iteration and tempers the intrinsic advantages of the Jacobian transpose method. By nature, our method leads to a linear complexity $o(kN)$ where k is the number of DOFs and N the number of particles. This makes our framework far more efficient for structures with large number of DOFs.

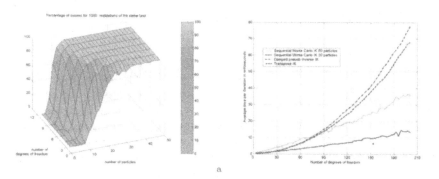

Fig. 3. Performances of our method (a) Relations between number of particles, number of degrees of freedom and task success. (b) Comparison with state-of-the-art IK methods. Note the linear nature of the complexity of our method (instead of exponential with numeric IK).

Human figure. As a first exemple, we consider a complete human figure with 40 joints. Snapshots of the resulting animation are shown in Figure 4. For this example, we add to the state the root position, that is the pelvis, so that the whole figure can move in the $3D$ space. The feet are constrained to stay on the floor, while the left and the right arms are given two different targets. The feet constraint is enforced by the acceptance/rejection strategy.

Fig. 4. Human figure animation In this animation, feet are constrained to lie on the floor, the right hand is linked with the yellow dot while the left arm has the blue dot as target. Notice how the knees bend to achieve the task.

Hand animation. As a second example, the considered chain is a forearm with a hand. In this animation, each fingertip is given a target empirically determined. Two sets of targets are chained during the animation. Figure 5 shows images from this animation. In order to increase the realism of the produced animation, we add a biomechanical constraint linking the last two joints of each fingers. Note the difficulty of handling such a kinematic configuration if a classical inverse kinematics scheme was used.

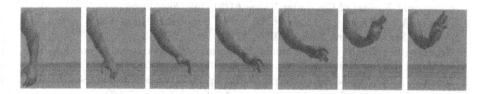

Fig. 5. Hand animation In this animation the fingers were given a target position represented as colored dots in the images

6 Conclusion and Future Work

In this article we introduced Sequential Monte Carlo Methods in the context of computer animation to solve inverse kinematics problem. We proposed a new modelization of the motion control problem in terms of hidden Markov models. Our inverse kinematics filter is very simple to implement and test. It runs very fast and provides a totally original alternative to solve this classical problem.

Only direct calculations of the kinetic model are needed. The validation of our model has been done under several different situations ranging from simple positioning tasks to hand animation, with convincing results. Future work will follow two main directions: evaluating the cost of adding constraints *wrt.* the number of needed particles, and adding more complex evolution priors (eventually learnt from motion capture data).

Acknowledgement. This work is part of the ARC Fantastik, supported by INRIA France. The authors would like to thank B. Cernuschi-Frías, L. Reveret and M. Tournier for fruitful discussions and suggestions on this work.

References

1. Baerlocher, P., Boulic, R.: An inverse kinematics architecture enforcing an arbitrary number of strict priority levels. The Visual Computer 20(6), 402–417 (2004)
2. Bertram, D., Kuffner, J., Dillmann, R., Asfour, T.: An integrated approach to inverse kinematics and path planning for redundant manipulators. In: ICRA, pp. 1874–1879 (2006)
3. Le Callennec, B., Boulic, R.: Interactive motion deformation with prioritized constraints. Graphical Models 68(2), 175–193 (2006)
4. Carvalho, S., Boulic, R., Thalmann, D.: Interactive Low-Dimensional Human Motion Synthesis by Combining Motion Models and PIK. Computer Animation & Virtual Worlds 18(4–5), 493–503 (2007)
5. Chai, J., Hodgins, J.K.: Constraint-based motion optimization using a statistical dynamic model. ACM Tra. on Graphics (Proc. SIGGRAPH) 26(3), 686–696 (2007)
6. Choi, K.J., Ko, H.S.: Online motion retargetting. Journal of Visualization and Computer Animation 11, 223–235 (2000)
7. Sminchisescu, C., Triggs, B.: Fast mixing hyperdynamic sampling. Image and Vision Computing (2006)
8. Deutscher, J., Reid, I.: Articulated body motion capture by stochastic search. International Journal of Computer Vision 61(2), 185–205 (2005)
9. Doucet, A., de Freitas, N., Gordon, N. (eds.): Sequential Monte Carlo methods in practice. Springer, New York (2001)
10. Grochow, K., Martin, S., Hertzmann, A., Popovic, Z.: Style-based inverse kinematics. ACM Tra. on Graphics (Proc. SIGGRAPH) 23(3), 522–531 (2004)
11. Johnson, M.P.: Exploiting quaternions to support expressive interactive character motion. PhD thesis, Massachusetts Institute of Technology (2003)
12. Monzani, J.-S., Baerlocher, P., Boulic, R., Thalmann, D.: Using an intermediate skeleton and inverse kinematics for motion retargetting. Computer Graphics Forum 19(3) (2000)
13. Sentis, L., Khatib, O.: Synthesis of whole-body behaviors through hierarchical control of behavioral primitives. Int. Journal of Humanoid Robotics 2(4) (2005)
14. Tak, S., Ko, H.-S.: A physically-based motion retargeting filter. ACM Tra. On Graphics (TOG) 24(1), 98–117 (2005)
15. Yamane, K., Nakamura, Y.: Natural motion animation through constraining and deconstraining at will. IEEE Tra. on Visualization and Computer Graphics 09(3), 352–360 (2003)

Estimation of Dense, Non-rigid Motion Fields from a Multi-camera Array Using a Hierarchical Mixture Model

Adam Bowen, Andrew Mullins, Roland Wilson, and Nasir Rajpoot*

Department of Computer Science
University of Warwick, UK
rgw@dcs.warwick.ac.uk

Abstract. The problem of modelling objects of arbitrary complecity for video based rendering has been much studied in recent years, with the growing interest in 'free viewpoint' video and similar applications. Typical approaches fall into two categories: those which approximate surfaces from dense depth maps obtained by generalisations of stereopsis methods and those which employ an explicit geometric representation such as a mesh. While the former has generality with respect to geometry, it is inevitably limited in terms of viewpoint; the latter, on the other hand, sacrifices generality of object geometry for freedom to pick an arbitary viewpoint. The purpose of the work reported here is to bridge this gap in object representation, by employing a surface element model, but one which is freed from the restrictions of a mesh. Estimation of the model and tracking it through time from multiple cameras is achieved by novel multiresolution stochastic simulation methods. After a brief outline of the method, its use in modelling human motions using data from the Warwick multi-camera studio is presented to illustrate its effectiveness compared to the current state of the art.

1 Introduction

The problem of modelling and tracking 3D objects from one or more video sequences has received considerable attention over recent years, as interest in 'free viewpoint' video has grown and computational and capture costs have fallen. Techniques range from straightforward adaptation of stereo vision algorithms, eg. [2] to meshes and visual hulls [1]. Although the former, requiring no explicit model of the object to be tracked, is general in that respect, it suffers from the restriction on viewing point and the positioning of cameras. On the other hand, techniques based on meshes inevitably make assumptions about the shapes of the objects and may constrain the motions. The problem is that, without such constraints, a mesh or voxel representation simply has too many degrees of freedom to represent any plausible motion. What is needed is a way of constraining the motion to conform to the sorts of movements that, for example, dancers

---

* This work was supported by the UK EPSRC.

F.J. Perales and R.B. Fisher (Eds.): AMDO 2008, LNCS 5098, pp. 11–21, 2008.

or similarly complex figures might undergo, while retaining the flexibility to represent arbitrary objects and their movements. This naturally suggests a hierarchical model and indeed there have been attempts to use such structures in motion estimation, notably [1] and [3], in which the motion of the trunk is used to constrain movements of limbs.

In this paper, we present a generalisation of these ideas, which is capable of representing objects of arbitrarily complex shapes undergoing smooth motions. It is capable of dealing with articulated objects, but shows the potential to cope with more complex scenes, involving multiple objects. In order to achieve this goal, it is necessary to construct a model which is flexible, yet stable enough to track coherent motions over time. The method we present is based on a general approach to the statistical modelling of data, Gaussian mixtures, which can be combined with a clustering process to group elements on the basis of their visual properties, such as colour, texture and motion, to form a hierarchy of mixture models representing the objects in the scene. This in turn serves to reduce the complexity of motion estimation and to constrain the degrees of freedom, without being tied to a particular model, such as a mesh or voxel representation. It represents an extension of the work reported in [7] to deal with moving 3D data. The approach has been tested on a number of sequences, both publicly available ones, such as the Microsoft Research data [9], and some captured using the Warwick camera array, a studio with 48 fire-wire digital video cameras. Further details of the set-up are available at [11].

After a brief introduction to the theory behind the mixture model and an outline of the algorithms for constructing it and tracking it, we present a series of results to show its efficacy in a number of sequences. Although the results presented here are based on a locally planar surface representation, using patch estimates derived using a particle filter from sets of neighbouring cameras, which we have used throughout our work on free viewpoint video (eg. [5],[4]), the mixture model is capable of being used with arbitrary input data - from point clouds to voxels, with appropriate attributes. Moreover, the resulting motion estimates define a smooth motion field, which may be used to animate arbitrary objects [5]. These are features shared by no other representation of which we are aware. The paper is concluded with a discussion of the advantages and limitations of the model, as well as some possible extensions. Full details of the methods can be found in [5], [6].

2   Construction and Tracking of Gaussian Mixtures

In previous work, it was shown that a Gaussian mixture can be constructed in a top-down fashion, starting with a single component and splitting components when their fit to the data was poor, as judged by either a Bayesian or other criterion, such as AIC [7]. As noted in that paper, the Gaussians have the considerable advantage of forming a closed set under affine transformations, making the motion computations simpler. In the work reported here, a bottom-up process was used, to allow greater control over the number of levels in the tree and number of components/level, which were important in the formulation of the motion estimator. We regard the feature vectors as a set, $\{\boldsymbol{f}_i \in R^n, 1 \le i \le N\}$, of points in R^n. Normally, $\boldsymbol{f}_i$ would represent the position, orientation, colour and possibly motion of a 3D surface or volume element, giving up to 9 dimensions, but this is a matter of utility in a particular application: surface texture might also be included. The aim is to represent the data density by a normal mixture with, say, M_l components at level l, where $0 \le l \le L$ and $M_l < M_{l-1}$. To ensure a tree structure, components at level l, rather than data, are used as input to the next level, $l + 1$, of the tree. Correspondingly, the covariance of the data assigned to any component is carried forward in the clustering at the next level of the tree.

A Bayesian approach to clustering is used, based on the conjugate priors for the Gaussian mixture problem, namely a Dirichlet prior on the mixture weights, a normal on the means and a Wishart density on the covariances [8]. This has the considerable advantage of allowing a Gibbs sampler to be used and, in this application, is not overly restrictive. The complete algorithm is as follows [8]:

1. Simulate from the full conditionals:

$$\pi \sim D(\alpha^*) \tag{1}$$
$$\Sigma_i^{-1} \sim W(W_i^*, r_i^*) \tag{2}$$
$$\boldsymbol{\mu}_i \sim N(\mathbf{y}_i^*, \tau_i^* \Sigma_i) \tag{3}$$

where

$$\alpha^* = \alpha + n \tag{4}$$
$$r_i^* = r + n_i \tag{5}$$
$$\tau_i^* = \frac{\tau}{\tau n_i + 1} \tag{6}$$
$$\mathbf{y}_i^* = \frac{n_i \bar{\mathbf{x}}_i + 1/\tau \mathbf{y}_i}{n_i + 1/\tau} \tag{7}$$
$$W_i^* = \left(W_i^{-1} + n_i \boldsymbol{S}_i + \frac{n_i}{\tau n_i + 1} (\bar{\mathbf{x}}_i - \mathbf{y}_i)(\bar{\mathbf{x}}_i - \mathbf{y}_i)^T \right)^{-1} \tag{8}$$

$\bar{\mathbf{x}}_i$ is the sample mean of the ith component, $\boldsymbol{S}_i$ the sample covariance and n_i is the number of data points assigned to it. W_i, α, r, τ_i and $\mathbf{y}_i$ are parameters on the prior distributions for each component. $D(\alpha)$ is a Dirichlet distribution with parameter α and $W(V, n)$ is a Wishart distribution with parameters V and n.

2. Derive the cluster assignments:
   Assign the class label of the ith data point, $\boldsymbol{x}_j$, randomly to one of the components $k \in 1..K$ proportionally to $N(\mathbf{x}_j - \boldsymbol{\mu}_k, \Sigma_k)$ and update the sample means $\bar{\boldsymbol{x}}_k$ and covariances $\boldsymbol{S}_k$ according to

$$\bar{x}_k = \frac{1}{n_k} \sum_{i \in \{j|z_j=k\}} x_i \tag{9}$$

$$S_k = \frac{1}{n_k} \sum_{i \in \{j|z_j=k\}} (x_i - \bar{x}_k)(x_i - \bar{x}_k)^T \tag{10}$$

Note that, for levels $l > 0$, the covariances of the components must be included in both the covariance estimate (10) and the classifications. This process is iterated until convergence is achieved at a given level, l. Data are then assigned to cluster i on level l using a MAP rule and the clusters on level l, characterised by their estimated means and covariances, are used as data in the process at level $l + 1$.

Once the MGM model has been constructed, it can be tracked through time in various ways, including extended Kalman filtering or by particle filtering, the latter being the method adopted in the experiments [5]. In both cases, the key idea is to use a sequential, Bayesian approach, in which the estimate for level l can be used as a prior for level $l - 1$. Because of the hierarchical nature of the representation, it is sufficient to employ a rigid motion model for each component, requiring estimation of a 6-parameter vector θ per component and maximising the posterior

$$P(\theta_{l,i}|Y_j, j \in \Lambda_{l,i}) \propto \int_{\theta_{l+1,p(i)}} d\theta \prod_{j \in \Lambda_{l,i}} P(Y_j|\theta_{l,i}\theta)P(\theta_{l,i}|\theta) \tag{11}$$

where $p(i)$ is the parent of component (l, i) at level $l + 1$ and Y_k are the data, which in the experiments consisted of the average colour in each of a set of S patches selected at random from the set associated with component (l, i). Elimination of the 'nuisance' variable $\theta_{l+1,p(i)}$ is impractical, but can be avoided by using the MAP estimate $\hat{\theta}_{l+1,p(i)}$, with no obvious degradation in the quality of the estimates. At the top level of the MGM tree, the prior is derived instead from the estimate at the previous time. The particle filter employs a Gaussian approximation to the posterior and used the prior as the importance density, greatly simplifying the computations [10]. A summary of the main steps in the algorithm is:

For levels $L > l \geq 0$,

1. Sample from importance density, $P(\theta_{l,i}|\hat{\theta}_{l-1,p(i)})$, to get weights $w_{l,i}, 1 \leq i \leq M_l$.
2. Compute likelihoods at current estimate $\theta_{l,i}$, $P(Y_j|\theta_{l,i})$.
3. Use weighted likelihoods to estimate posterior mean and covariance.

To understand how the motion field is constructed from the Gaussian components, note that at the finest level, we have a motion for each component $(0, i)$, consisting of two elements: a translation vector $t_{0,i}$ and a rotation matrix $R_{0,i}$. Now, given an arbitary point in 3D, x, say, there are corresponding probabilities $P(i|x)$ that it belongs to the ith component,

$$P(i|x) = w_i N(x - \mu_i, \Sigma_i) / \sum_j w_j N(x - \mu_i, \Sigma_i) \tag{12}$$

where $N(.,.)$ is the 3D normal density with parameters μ_i, Σ_i for the ith component and w_i is a weight representing the population of the ith component. Where the MGM model uses additional data, such as colour or velocity, the projection onto the three spatial dimensions remains Gaussian. Now the translation at x is simply the conditional mean

$$t(x) = \sum_i P(i|x)t_i \tag{13}$$

and the rotation may be similarly interpolated, in common axes, using the exponential form

$$R(x) = \prod_i R_i^{P(i|x)} \tag{14}$$

These are used to update the positions of the individual data elements from the estimated motion at the highest resolution in the MGM tree.

3   Experiments

Experiments were carried out on a number of sequences captured in the Warwick studio, as well as two from the Microsoft Research site. All were captured at 1024×768 pixel resolution, the Warwick ones at 30 fps. Unlike the Microsoft camera arrangement, which has eight cameras arrayed in a line, with a maximum disparity of 150 pixels, the Warwick cameras are arranged to provide full coverage of the room in a non-uniform way: 32 cameras are arranged in a recatngular array on one wall and the remainder in the corners and mid-points of each of the remaining three walls, with one in the ceiling space. The maximum overlap between cameras is only 50%, resulting in disparities of up to 400 pixels. Consequently, accurate modelling and rendering is a far more challenging problem for the Warwick data than for the Microsoft array.

Table 1. Energy of the final clustering in thousands; lower values indicate a better fit

	K-Means	Hierarchical Clustering	MGMM
'Kate' sequence	327	394	131
'Hamutal' sequence	179	200	119
'Breakdancers' sequence	132	124	73
'Ballet' sequence	117	113	66

Table 2. Clustering time using the three algorithms on several data sets. The tim es were computed on an Intel Xeon 3.2GHz, the K-Means clustering was 1 level only and the MGMM was run for 200 iterations.

	K-Means	Hierarchical Clustering	MGMM
'Kate' (34934 patches)	13m 09s	130m 39s	1m 46s
'Hamutal' (17022 patches)	2m 57s	13m 22s	56s
'Breakdancers' (9617 patches)	2m 01s	5m 40s	24s
'Ballet' (3210 patches)	30s	14s	20s

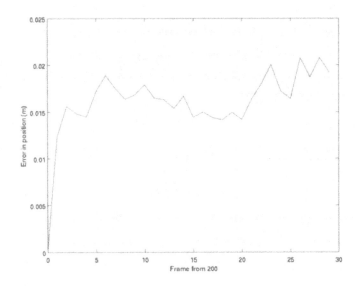

Fig. 1. Plot of the error in position vs frame number for the tracked index finger in 'Kate'

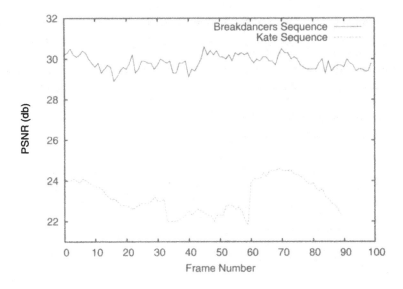

Fig. 2. Plot of the PSNR vs. frame number for the synthesised views

The MGM models were built with either two or three levels, with respectively $M_0 = 50$, $M_1 = 5$ and $M_0 = 250$, $M_1 = 50$, $M_2 = 5$ components, an arrangement that was chosen empirically. It was found that the sampler converged after 200 iterations and this was chosen for the estimation. The prior weights were set to $\alpha = M_{l-1}/M_l$, $r = 8$, $\tau = 1$ and W_i was diagonal, with variances based on the spatial

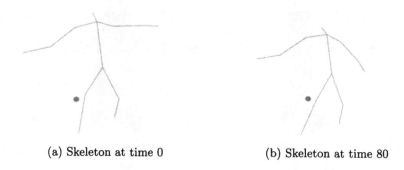

(a) Skeleton at time 0   (b) Skeleton at time 80

Fig. 3. Skeleton, animated using motion field from 'Kate'

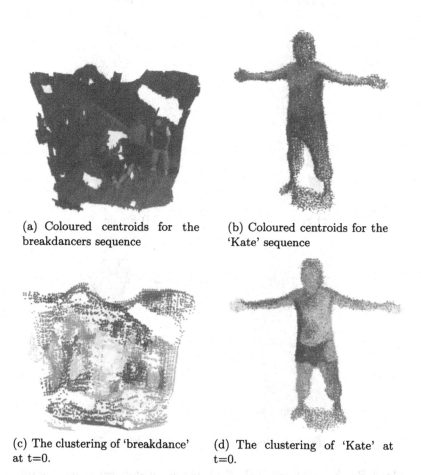

(a) Coloured centroids for the
breakdancers sequence

(b) Coloured centroids for the
'Kate' sequence

(c) The clustering of 'breakdance'
at t=0.

(d) The clustering of 'Kate' at
t=0.

Fig. 4. Clustering the 'Breakdancers' and 'Kate' data sets using uniform and seeded
priors

(a) Frame 0   (b) Frame 15

(c) Frame 30   (d) Frame 45

(e) Frame 60   (f) Frame 75

Fig. 5. Synthesised views of the 'Kate' sequence at different time instants

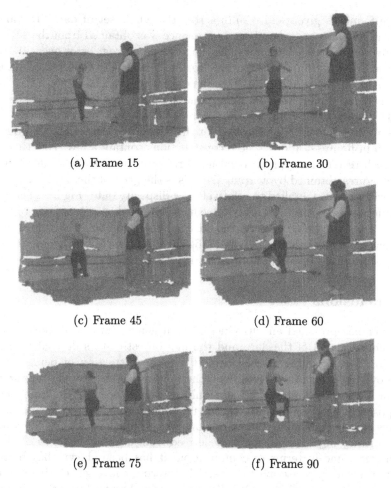

(a) Frame 15   (b) Frame 30

(c) Frame 45   (d) Frame 60

(e) Frame 75   (f) Frame 90

Fig. 6. Synthesised views of the 'Ballet' sequence at different time instants

and colour variances, after extensive experimentation [6]. The MGM approach was compared to publicly available K-means and hierarchical clustering algorithms, both in terms of model fit, measured by squared error and computation times on different data sets. The results are summarised in Tables 1 and 2, which show that MGM significantly outperforms both the other methods in terms of error and is faster, surprisingly, than this implementation of K-means. The appearance of the induced clusters is illustrated in figure 3, which shows the cluster centres in colour for two sequences.

Motion estimation was only practicable for the Warwick sequences: the Microsoft data do not provide sufficient coverage to obtain reliable estimates, The multiresolution Gaussian particle filter used 10000 particles and the likelihoods were calculated using a set of at most 2000 patches for each component. The MGM model and motion estimator were reinitialised every 25-30 frames, to prevent error accumulation. These choices were arrived at after experimentation and were found to give good results across the whole set of data. To validate the algorithms, a short 'ground truth' sequence was obtained from the sequence 'Kate', by manually tracking her index finger. The average error over 30 frames was of the order of 15mm, comparable to the best results reported to date, as can be seen from figure 1. To illustrate the estimator's ability to produce a dense motion field, we used it to animate a manually initialised skeleton, as shown in figure 3. Despite having no constraints on joint angles, the results were quite compelling. Finally, views synthesised for the 'Kate' and 'Breakdance' sequences are shown in figures 4 and 5. The reconstructions contain a few rendering arte-facts, which result in a typical signal-noise ratio of the order of 25-30dB, worse than the figures obtained by warping [2]; this is the price of the much less restric-tive algorithms when applied to relatively low disparity data. Figure 2 shows the reconstruction peak-rms SNR for both sequences, based on a 'leave-one-out' test, in which a known view is reconstructed from the remaining data. Full details of the rendering algorithm are given in [6]. Overall, the results demonstrate the usefulness of a fully Bayesian approach within a hierarchical model framework.

4   Conclusions

This paper has provided an introduction to a general model of motion, using a hierarchical model of the data and the motion estimators derived from that model, for use in multi-camera video. It has the attraction of being flexible, while providing a set of constraints on the motion via the use of a hierarchical Bayesian motion estimator. This not only prevents the problem from becom-ing ill-posed, it also significantly speeds up computation. The resulting motion estimates can be interpolated in an obvious way using the mixture model to an-imate arbitrary objects with motions derived from a given sequence. Although far from real time in terms of computation, it has been shown that both the model initialisation phase and the particle filtering converge relatively quickly because of the strong priors, so that typically a few hundred iterations are suffi-cient to obtain satisfactory results. Moreover, the methods are designed to allow real time rendering of novel views from the representation and this goal has been achieved. In summary, while particular applications will always benefit from im-posing tighter constraints than the model presented here, our techniques seem sufficiently promising to warrant further investigation.

References

1. Cheung, K.M., Baker, S., Kanade, T.: Shape from silhouette across time part I: theory and algorithms. Int. J. Comput. Vision 62, 221–247 (2005)
2. Zitnick, C.L., Kang, S.B., Uyttendaele, M.: High-quality video view interpolation using a layered representation. ACM Trans. Graphics 23, 600–608 (2004)
3. Mitchelson, J., Hilton, A.: Hierarchical tracking of multiple people. In: Proc. BMVC 2003, Norwich (2003)
4. Bowen, A., Mullins, A., Wilson, R., Rajpoot, N.: Video based Rendering Using Surface Patches. In: Proc. IEEE 3DTV Conf., Kos (2007)

5. Mullins, A.: Stochastic Geometry Estimation for Video based Rendering. PhD Thesis, University of Warwick (2008)
6. Bowen, A.: Video based Rendering and Coding using a Planar Patch Model. PhD Thesis, University of Warwick (2008)
7. Mo, X., Wilson, R.: Video modelling and segmentation using Gaussian mixture models. In: Proc. ICPR 2004, Cambridge (2004)
8. McLachlan, G., Peel, D.: Finite Mixture Models. Wiley, New York (2000)
9. http://research.microsoft.com/vision/InteractiveVisualMediaGroup/
10. Kotecha, J.M., Djuric, P.M.: Gaussian particle filtering. IEEE Trans. Sig. Proc. 51, 2592–2601 (2003)
11. http://www.dcs.warwick.ac.uk/~fade/

Learning to Look at Humans — What Are the Parts of a Moving Body?*

Thomas Walther and Rolf P. Würtz

Institut für Neuroinformatik
Ruhr-Universität
D–44780 Bochum
Germany
thomas.walther@neuroinformatik.rub.de,
rolf.wuertz@neuroinformatik.rub.de

Abstract. We present a system that can segment articulated, non-rigid motion without a priori knowledge of the number of clusters present in the analyzed scenario. We combine existing algorithms for tracking and extend clustering techniques by a self-tuning heuristic. Application to video sequences of humans shows good segmentation into limbs.

1 Introduction

Despite considerable effort creating an artificial system capable of analyzing human body pose and motion is still an open challenge. Such a *pose estimation system* (PE-system) would enable machines to communicate with their users in a more natural way (body language interpretation) or to survey activities of individuals to anticipate their intentions (traffic/security). For a detailed overview of the different approaches, [1] is a useful source. Existing PE-Systems are by far no match for the human brain when it comes to the task of motion and pose estimation, let alone behavior interpretation. These systems are narrowly tuned to their field of application and work with relatively inflexible, pre-defined models of human shape and motion. In our project, we attempt to create a PE-System which initially has no idea of its environment and the humans inhabiting it. Instead, it should gather knowledge during its lifetime and build up its own environmental and human model, like the human visual cortex does at some time in its development. For this, we combine state-of-the-art computer vision techniques and biologically inspired principles like (controlled) self-organization and machine learning.

To build an abstract model of a human from a video stream it is necessary to state what type of model is best suited to capture human shape and motion. A human body is, from a technical point of view, an articulated ensemble of non-rigid objects (clothed limbs) performing relatively smooth and coherent movements over time. The first task to be performed in order to extract

* Funding by the Deutsche Forschungsgemeinschaft (MA 697/5-1, WU 314/5-2) is gratefully acknowledged.

F.J. Perales and R.B. Fisher (Eds.): AMDO 2008, LNCS 5098, pp. 22–31, 2008.
© Springer-Verlag Berlin Heidelberg 2008

a human body model from a video sequence will be to find coherently moving objects (limbs) and to store their outer shapes and connections among them as an abstract model.

Coherent motion detection is a basic functionality of the human visual cortex and construction of its artificial counterpart represents a topic of special interest in the computer vision community. Two algorithmic methods are commonly used to tackle this problem: *spectral clustering* (and related matrix factorization techniques) like [2,3,4,5] and *Markov random field*-segmentation [6] of moving image pixels. Probabilistic methods are also applied, for which [7] (clustering) and [8] (motion recognition and analysis) are recent examples.

Due to its simplicity and effectiveness, we decided to use spectral clustering as our basic method for coherent motion segmentation. When taking a look at existing approaches to coherent motion detection from video, two main challenges are apparent: to segment a scene without knowing the number of moving objects a priori and to handle non-rigid (cloth) motion. There are approaches to non-rigid motion segmentation, e.g., [5], but finding the correct number of clusters from input data alone is still an unsolved problem. In this paper, we concentrate on the problem of segmenting a simple video scene containing articulated, non-rigid motion into coherently moving clusters without a priori knowledge.

2   Feature Tracking

There are two main approaches to finding coherently moving objects in a video sequence: tracking optical flow from image I_t of the sequence to image I_{t+1} (e.g., [5,2]), or tracking a (sparse) set of salient features from one image to the next [9,10]. When using full optical flow, motion of each pixel in the image sequence is computed. In our situation, we have relatively simple scenes with a (mostly) static background and only some dedicated moving objects, so such a technique would waste computation time. Using the sparse tracking technique described in [10] together with the feature initialization techniques of [11] we are able to produce acceptable tracking of features through all frames of our image sequences. It has to be stated that the tracking quality of all state-of-the-art tracking algorithms, to our knowledge, is strongly dependent on the degree of saliency of the tracked features. For this reason, we used easily trackable clothing in all of our training experiments with real data. This seems to be common practice, see e. g. [4] and [12]. Clearly, sparse features, even if tracked and clustered correctly, don't give a convincing impression of the coherently moving objects (limbs) they represent. Complete limb segmentation on the basis of feature segmentation could be performed by MRF-techniques as proposed in [12], or, as we intend to do, by using more biologically inspired approaches.

3   Spectral Clustering

We will shortly glance over the basic terms and working principles of spectral clustering methods following the very comprehensive course in [13]. A data collection $\mathbf{E}$ of N arbitrary data objects $e_1, ..., e_N$ and some similarity function w_{ij} defining their pairwise similarity yields a similarity matrix $\mathbf{W}$. Each data element is assigned a degree d_i, the total *amount of similarity* e_i has with all data elements in $\mathbf{E}$:

$$d_i = \sum_{j=1}^{N} w_{ij} , \tag{1}$$

and the degree matrix $\mathbf{D}$ is the diagonal matrix with $\mathbf{D}_{ii} = d_i$. The Laplacian matrix $\mathbf{L}$ is the difference $\mathbf{L} = \mathbf{D} - \mathbf{W}$. By analyzing the spectrum and eigenvectors of $\mathbf{L}$ or of some normalized form of $\mathbf{L}$, it is possible to detect clusters in the original data $\mathbf{E}$.

The main advantages of spectral clustering methods are simplicity of implementation and their ability to cope with arbitrary input data (clusters need not adhere to some a priori known distribution like Gaussian). Furthermore, spectral clustering methods need no heuristic initialization step like *k-means*. The aforementioned items outline the working principle of almost all spectral clustering methods. Nevertheless, differences between the specific realizations of spectral clustering for data segmentation arise from the choice of the similarity function, from the matrix used for analysis (Laplace-, Similarity-Matrix, normalized, unnormalized) and the handling of multiple clusters (sequentially/simultaneously).

We decided to use a relatively recent method for spectral clustering, the so called *self-tuning* spectral clustering and to adapt it to suit our needs.

3.1   Self-tuning Spectral Clustering

The idea of self-tuning spectral clustering as proposed in [14] tries to alleviate two main problems of standard spectral clustering methods (like in [15]): the global definition of the similarity function w_{ij} and the k-means postprocessing step.

Generally, the similarity function within $\mathbf{E}$ is derived from a distance function a_{ij} by means of a Gaussian:

$$w_{ij} = e^{-\frac{a_{ij}^2}{\sigma^2}} . \tag{2}$$

According to [14] this function works well, if all clusters hidden in the data are of the same *scale*, meaning the analyzed data collection consists of some dedicated clusters having a high constant intra- and a low constant inter-cluster similarity, so that a global σ can correctly separate those clusters. As soon as this assumption fails to hold, a similarity function like (2) causes the spectral clustering algorithm to fail. The correct choice of σ is highly critical — the authors of [14] try to overcome the σ-difficulty by introducing a locally adaptive similarity function w^L:

$$w_{ij}^L = e^{-\frac{a_{ij}^2}{\sigma_i \sigma_j}} , \tag{3}$$

where σ_i and σ_j are separately defined for each data element of $\mathbf{E}$ and allow for graceful handling of clusters of different scales hidden within the data. [14] uses spectral clustering to cluster point data in $\mathbf{R}^2$, using the Euclidean distance between two data elements (points) in $\mathbf{E}$ as a_{ij}.

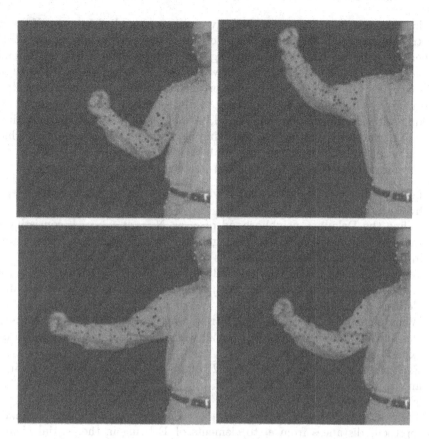

Fig. 1. A simple sequence, which is correctly segmented into body, forearm and upper arm

3.2　Clustering of Point Trajectories

In our case, a_{ij} means a measure of distance between two motion trajectories, which were acquired by tracking. Such trajectory distance measures can be defined in several ways [16], with trajectory sampling density and allowed trajectory lengths being the most important parameters. For simplicity, we assume equidistant temporal sampling at the frame rate and equal length, meaning that all trajectories extend through all frames of a video sequence.

Our choice of the trajectory distance measure a_{ij} between two trajectories e_i and e_j is inspired by [17]:

$$a_{ij} = \alpha \sum_{t=A}^{B} (\Delta_{ij}^t - \overline{\Delta_{ij}})^2 + \beta \sum_{t=A}^{B-1} \left\| \mathbf{v}_i^t - \mathbf{v}_j^t \right\|^2 \tag{4}$$

with $\Delta_{ij}^t = \left\| \mathbf{x}_i^t - \mathbf{x}_j^t \right\|$, $\mathbf{v}_i^t = \mathbf{x}_i{}^t - \mathbf{x}_i{}^{t-1}$, and $\overline{\Delta_{ij}}$ is the mean of Δ_{ij} over frames $[A \ldots B]$. α and β are two parameters that will be discussed below.

This distance function is not the only change we applied to use self-tuning spectral clustering for our purpose. The choice of the local σ_i-parameters in [14] turned out to be inadequate for clustering motion data. Their clustering depends on the proper choice of a parameter u, which guides the selection of the kernel radii of σ_i — too small a value causes erroneous splitting of coherent clusters, and a large value can lead to merging of clusters that should stay separate. Lacking relevant information beforehand, we were not able to assign an optimal value of u, and we developed the following heuristic for choosing our σ_i, which yielded acceptable clustering results in all of our experiments.

Our assumptions for defining this heuristic are the following:

1. Let $\mathbf{E}$ be a trajectory data source with N elements, consider element e_i in frame t.
2. Define the Delaunay-neighborhood of e_i as $N_i = [n_1 \ldots n_{k_i}]$, consisting of those k_i data elements which are neighbors of e_i in a Delaunay-Triangulation in $\mathbf{R}^2$ constructed over the positions of all elements in $\mathbf{E}$ at time t.
3. For each element e_i build up a sorted list $L_i = [v_1, \ldots v_{k_i}]$ with $a_{iv_1} \leq a_{iv_2} \leq \ldots a_{iv_{k_i}}$ and $v_1 \ldots v_{k_i} \in N_i$, where a_{ij} is the Euclidean distance between data element e_i and e_j at time t.
4. When element e_i moves in an arbitrary way, it is highly likely that its M closest Delaunay-neighbors $L_i[1 \ldots M]$ will move coherently with e_i. In our experiments, we used $M = 3$.
5. Each element e_i owns a sorted list T_i of trajectory distances between itself and all other elements of $\mathbf{E}$: $T_i = [a_{i1}, \ldots, a_{iN}]$ with $a_{i1} \leq a_{i2} \ldots \leq a_{in}$. a_{ij} is identical to (4).
6. The first P entries of T_k with $k \in L_i[1 \ldots M] \cup \{i\}$ will, with high likelihood, represent distances from e_i to elements of $\mathbf{E}$ being in the spatial vicinity of e_i and simultaneously moving coherently with e_i. Let $\tilde{\sigma}_k$ be the mean of those P distances for each data element e_k. $P = 3$ in all our experiments.
7. For each data element e_i sum up all $\tilde{\sigma}_k$ with $k \in L_i[1 \ldots M] \cup \{i\}$. Let this sum be σ_i.
8. Experimentally, this σ_i-value turned out to be too small, so we decided to artificially enlarge it by coupling it to the total number of Delaunay-neighbors of i: $\sigma_i = \sigma_i \cdot \frac{K}{M}$.

This heuristic approach can surely be rendered into producing wrong results by using strongly corrupted input data or constructing pathological situations. Nevertheless, it yields very good results in practice, as can be seen in figures 1 and 2.

3.3 The Eigenspace Approach

Another principal feature of self-tuning spectral clustering [14] is the reliance on eigenspace perturbation methods instead on k-means techniques for final clustering, which is briefly explained in the following.

Assume that $\mathbf{E}$ is a data source with N elements and symmetric, real Laplacian $\mathbf{L}$, and contains K distinct clusters. Then, the spectrum of $\mathbf{L}$ has a 0 eigenvalue with multiplicity K and the orthonormal eigenvectors $\mathbf{y}_1 \ldots \mathbf{y}_K$ determine the position of the image of data element e_i in the eigenspace of $\mathbf{L}$ by their ith components $y_{1i} \ldots y_{Ki}$ [14,15,13]. Due to the K-multiplicity the eigenvectors of $\mathbf{L}$ are only determined up to some rotation matrix $\mathbf{R}$ [15]. The eigenvector components are normalized,

$$y_{ji} = \frac{y_{ji}}{\sqrt{\sum_{p=1}^{K} y_{pi}^2}} ,$$

(5)

which projects the images of the elements of $\mathbf{E}$ onto a unit K-sphere in the 0-eigenspace of $\mathbf{L}$. By rotating the eigenspace of $\mathbf{L}$ in such a way that only one normalized eigenvector component y_{ji} for $j \in [1 \ldots K]$ takes on values close to 1 whereas all other components approach zero, cluster membership of each e_i can easily be found. Additionally, the eigenspace rotation technique of [14] yields an alignment score Θ, which measures the clustering quality. In our implementation we defined Θ as:

$$\Theta = 1 - \frac{1}{K} \left(\frac{\sum_{j=1}^{K} \sum_{i=1}^{N} \frac{y_{ji}^2}{\max_p y_{pi}^2}}{N} - 1 \right) .$$

(6)

3.4   Treating Multiple Clusters

More than two clusters can be detected by either *parallel* or *iterative* spectral clustering[2]. Parallel clustering tries to find all clusters at once, while iterative clustering splits the data into two parts and then recursively splits those parts until some termination criterion is reached. Parallel clustering is usually more stable but requires the number of clusters to be known beforehand. Thus, for our task iterative spectral clustering is the method of choice. It has the additional advantage that purely data-based decisions can be made whether to split an already found cluster or not.

3.5   Implementation Issues

Our actual implementation combines iterative spectral clustering from [2] with the methods presented in [14]. Furthermore, we use the normalized Laplacian matrix constructed from video trajectory data in our clustering algorithm:

$$\mathbf{L}_n = \mathbf{D}^{-\frac{1}{2}} \mathbf{L} \mathbf{D}^{-\frac{1}{2}} .$$

(7)

This matrix definition is taken from [2]. [14] instead directly works with the normalized version of the affinity matrix $\mathbf{W}$. This is feasible, since the spectral properties of Laplacian and Affinity matrices are closely related. Luxburg [13] argues that using the normalized Laplacian matrix gives better clustering results than using the unnormalized version. Additionally, the normalized Laplacian is always positive semi-definite, while the normalized affinity matrix not necessarily is+[13]. If SVD should be used to do matrix decomposition, positive semi-definiteness of the dissected matrix is mandatory.

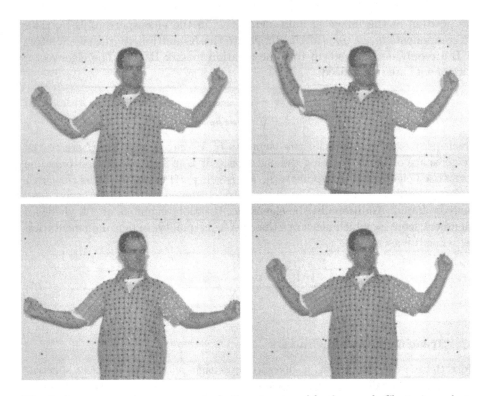

Fig. 2. A more complex sequence including structured background. Clustering selects both forearms and upper arms, body, head, and background.

From [14] the idea of self-tuning spectral clustering has been adopted, with the modifications described above. The eigenspace rotation of [14] has been integrated into our system. Clustering starts with the data set **E** and an empty list of limb clusters. The Θ-score, as given in (6) is a good measure for clustering quality in every iteration. We could identify three different types of outcomes for subdividing a cluster **C** into subclusters $\mathbf{C}_1$ and $\mathbf{C}_2$ during iterative clustering:

Case 1: $\Theta < 0.975$: invalid clustering, **C** is added to the list of limb clusters.

Case 2: $\Theta \in [0.975 \ldots 0.995[$: imperfect clustering, try to boost clustering quality by identifying one outlier in $\mathbf{C}_1$ and $\mathbf{C}_2$. Those are temporarily removed from **C**, subdivision is again attempted, and the outliers are then reassigned to the subclusters they were in before if the new subdivision is successful.

Case 3: $\Theta > 0.995$: valid clustering, continue recursive splitting on both $\mathbf{C}_1$ and $\mathbf{C}_2$.

The α- and β-values used in (4) still have to be discussed. When clustering motion data produced by relatively rigid objects, it turned out that $\alpha > \beta$ gives acceptable results. When clustering non-rigid motion data, making $\beta > \alpha$ produces good results. Since the type of motion data is not known beforehand, we use both methods concurrently and let the system choose the optimal method at runtime. We used $\alpha = 5, \beta = 1$ in the first method and $\alpha = 1, \beta = 5$ in the second. This additional complexity is required for handling real world motion data — for synthetic examples $\alpha = 1, \beta = 0$ produce optimal results.

Since we use short video sequences for analysis, due to time constraints, we have to be sure that each separate object we try to detect shows significant motion within this short timespan. Our system is not allowed to forget any motion it has already seen, i. e., for a motion analysis in frame I_t it uses trajectory data from frame I_0 to frame I_{t-1}. Motion analysis is performed in each frame.

3.6 Results and Discussion

In first experiments with synthetic sequences generated by computer graphics our method solves the task of segmenting an unknown number of clusters with high precision, there are no wrong cluster assignments for any of the input trajectories. More interesting is the question in how far our system is able to deal with real world trajectory input data, produced by moving limbs covered with cloth. The results for these highly non-rigid motion examples are shown in figure 1, where three clusters were identified, and in figure 2, where the motion is more complex and led to the identification of seven clusters. The results are quite precise, nearly all generated segmentations are very close to the actual limb structure. Errors in the segmentation, shown in figure 3, are due to the fact that sometimes motion of the limbs to be segmented was not strong enough or that the tracking algorithm produced unstable trajectory data. It can be stated that in the case of well-behaved input data (separate limbs showing strong motion, tracker data smooth and continuous) our system finds correct segmentations of the complete articulated body structure.

Our approach is not the first one to segment human motion data for limb detection, see, e.g., [4,17,6,18]. Nevertheless, it is one of the very few dealing with articulated, non-rigid motion and simultaneously using no a priori knowledge of the number of clusters present in the analyzed scenario. We tested our algorithm with several types of synthetic and clothed motion input data, and found a quite stable behavior at least for short sequences with vivid limb motion. Clothed, articulated motion segmentation has been quite neglected so far in present literature, and in the rare cases where it is treated, no thorough stress testing results were shown. We tried to analyze sequences with nasty tracking behavior (bare forearms in combination with clothed body, see figure 2) and different types of clothing under varying lighting conditions and monitored acceptable behavior of our system.

The convincing quality of the produced segmentations seems to be mainly due to our new, heuristic definition of the adaptive, local σ's and the termination criteria we use. The behavior of our system depends only on one variable: Θ. By manipulating the Θ-interval values for detecting a valid, imperfect or invalid cluster, one can easily adapt the overall system behavior to suit one's needs, if this should be necessary. Since we plan to utilize our spectral clustering method as an input stage for a more sophisticated fine segmentation stage based on biological principles, our next step will be to identify potential approaches to this

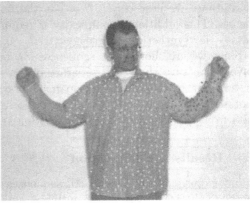

Fig. 3. Examples of failed segmentation. The body is clustered together with the background, because of a lack of relative movement. One point in each armpit is erroneously assigned to the cluster of the opposite upper arm.

problem. From the generated fine segmentation an abstract human model should be derived by evaluating spatial and motion constraints between the segmented limbs. Using this model we plan to analyze more complicated scenarios in order to see in how far an autonomously generated, abstract model can improve human pose and motion estimation.

References

1. Moeslund, T.B., Hilton, A., Krüger, V.: A survey of advances in vision-based human motion capture and analysis. Computer Vision and Image Understanding 104, 90–126 (2006)
2. Shi, J., Malik, J.: Normalized cuts and image segmentation. IEEE Trans. PAMI 22, 888–905 (2000)
3. Brand, M., Huang, K.: A unifying theorem for spectral embedding and clustering. In: Bishop, C.M., Frey, B.J. (eds.) Proceedings of the Ninth International Workshop on Artificial Intelligence and Statistics (2003)
4. Yan, J., Pollefeys, M.: Automatic kinematic chain building from feature trajectories of articulated objects. In: Proceedings of CVPR 2006, pp. 712–719 (2006)
5. Zelnik-Manor, L., Machline, M., Irani, M.: Multi-body factorization with uncertainty: Revisiting motion consistency. International Journal of Computer Vision 68, 27–41 (2006)
6. Kumar, M.P., Torr, P., Zisserman, A.: Learning layered motion segmentation of video. International Journal of Computer Vision 76(3), 301–319 (2008)
7. Brostow, G.J., Cipolla, R.: Unsupervised bayesian detection of independent motion in crowds. In: Proceedings of CVPR 2006, pp. 594–601 (2006)
8. Song, Y.: A probabilistic Approach to Human Motion Detection and Labeling. PhD thesis, California Institute of Technology (2003)
9. Lucas, B., Kanade, T.: An iterative image registration technique with an application to stereo vision. In: Proceedings of IJCAI 1981, pp. 674–679 (1981)

10. Tomasi, C., Kanade, T.: Detection and tracking of point features. Technical Report CMU-CS-91-132, Carnegie Mellon University (April 1991)
11. Shi, J., Tomasi, C.: Good features to track. In: Proceedings of CVPR 1994, Seattle (June 1994)
12. Krahnstoever, N., Yeasin, M., Sharma, R.: Automatic acquisition and initialization of articulated models. Machine Vision and Applications 14(4), 218–228 (2003)
13. von Luxburg, U.: A tutorial on spectral clustering. Statistics and Computing 17, 395–416 (2007)
14. Zelnik-Manor, L., Perona, P.: Self-tuning spectral clustering. In: Advances in Neural Information Processing Systems, NIPS, vol. 17 (2004)
15. Ng, A., Jordan, M., Weiss, Y.: On spectral clustering: Analysis and an algorithm. In: Advances in Neural Information Processing Systems, NIPS, vol. 14 (2002)
16. Porikli, F.: Trajectory distance metric using hidden markov model based representation. Technical report, Mitsubishi Electric Research Labs (2004)
17. Krahnstoever, N.: Articulated Models from Video. PhD thesis, Pennsylvania State University (2003)
18. Ross, D., Tarlow, D., Zemel, R.: Learning articulated skeletons from motion. In: Proceedings of Workshop on Dynamical Vision at ICCV 2007 (2007)

Continuous Hand Gesture Recognition in the Learned Hierarchical Latent Variable Space

Lei Han and Wei Liang

Department of Computer Science, Beijing Institute of Technology, Beijing, China
{hanlei,liangwei}@bit.edu.cn

Abstract. We describe a hierarchical approach for recognizing continuous hand gestures. It consists of hierarchical nonlinear dimensionality reduction based feature extraction and Hierarchical Conditional Random Field (Hierarchical CRF) based motion modeling. Articulated hands can be decomposed into several hand parts and we explore the underlying structures of articulated action spaces for both the hand and hand parts using Hierarchical Gaussian Process Latent Variable Model (HGPLVM). In this hierarchical latent variable space, we propose a Hierarchical CRF, which can simultaneously capture the extrinsic class dynamics and learn the relationship between motions of hand parts and class labels, to model the hand motions. Approving recognition performance is obtained on our user-defined hand gesture dataset.

Keywords: gesture recognition, dimensionality reduction, crf, hierarchical.

1 Introduction

With the potential for many interactive applications, continuous hand gestures recognition has recently attracted increasing interest from computer vision and pattern recognition community [1]. Generally, how to extract effective features to represent kinetic objects and how to model motions are two crucial problems involved in this recognition task.

Various cues have been used recently, e.g., key poses [2], optical flow [3], temporal templates [4], joint angles from tracking [5, 8], etc. However, key poses lack motion information. The optical flow of motions may be impracticable in cases of smooth surface and motion singularities. Temporal templates could be unauthentic for occlusion and intense varieties of appearances. However, dynamic hand gestures can be regard as trajectories of joint angles. These joint angles could be captured by tracking articulated human hands. With the hand model of joint angels, we could take no account of occlusions, variational views and illumination. So our approach uses angle joints obtained by the tracking method presented in [14] for hands motion representation. Moreover, since human hands can be decomposed into several hand parts with corresponding hierarchy according to human biology prior, a hierarchical latent variable space analysis is also introduced.

On the other hand, human gestures evolve dynamically over time. Dynamic gestures are often subtle, can happen at various timescales and may exhibit long-range dependencies. Furthermore, the transition between simple gestures naturally has

F.J. Perales and R.B. Fisher (Eds.): AMDO 2008, LNCS 5098, pp. 32–41, 2008.

temporal segments of ambiguity and overlap. These issues make continuous hand gesture recognition a challenging problem.

One of the most common approaches for dynamic gesture recognition is using HMM (Hidden Markov Model) or its variants [5]. However, a strong assumption that observations are conditionally independent is usually made in such generative models in order to ensure computational tractability. This restriction makes it difficult or impossible to accommodate long-range dependencies among observations or multiple overlapping features of the observations at multiple time steps.

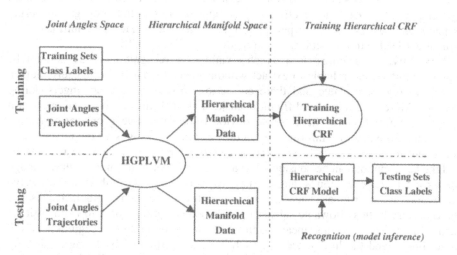

Fig. 1. Flowchart of the proposed approach for continuous hand gestures recognition

Conditional random fields (CRF) and its variants use an exponential distribution to model the entire sequence given the observation sequence [7, 8] which avoids the independence assumption between observations and makes it possible to incorporate both overlapping features and long-range dependencies into the model. Most CRFs can estimate a label for each observation, so they are competent for the task of recognizing continuous hand gestures from unsegmented gesture sequences. To the best of our knowledge, only one relevant work has used CRF or its varieties for motion or gesture recognition in latent variable space [10] and there was no relevant work has ever introduced hierarchy idea for this recognition task. Moreover, we explore a novel discriminative model, hierarchical CRF, for continuous hand gesture recognition in the learned hierarchical latent variable space. As shown in Fig. 1, we use Hierarchical Gaussian Process Latent Variable Model (HGPLVM) to discover the intrinsic hierarchical structure of the articulated hand motion space and propose hierarchical CRF for continuous dynamic gestures modeling and recognition.

2 Related Work

Since many literatures have demonstrated that discriminative models compare favorably to generative models like HMMs, we would not list any generative models.

CRF is first introduced by Lafferty et al. [6] and has been widely used in natural language processing community for tasks such as noun coreference resolution, name entity recognition and information extraction. Here we only review the methods using CRF or its varieties for vision action/gesture recognition.

Sminchisescu et al. [8] first applied discriminative models to classify human motion activities (i.e. walking, jumping, etc). They used a linear-chain CRF based on motion capture data or image descriptors. HCRF has been used for arm and head gesture recognition from segmented sequences [9]. Morency et al. [11] improved the above HCRF by associating a disjoint set of hidden states to each class label. Then inference on LDCRF can be efficiently computed using belief propagation during training and testing. Since capturing both extrinsic dynamics and intrinsic substructure, LDCRF thus combines the strengths of CRF and HCRF.

Obviously, the features used as observations in recognition model should be simple, intuitive and reliable to extract without manual labor. Unfortunately, human hands are high articulated and there are serious occlusions among fingers during motions. Moreover, it is also difficult to make a clear distinction between every two different fingers because there are no obviously discriminable geometry or texture characters. So extracting informative features of human hands is a complicated task. As stated in section one, we use joints angles from tracking for gesture recognition and the hand motion can be considered as a set of trajectories of joints angles. Though the original space of joints angles may be very high, the subset of allowable configurations in original space is generally restricted by human biomechanics and the trajectory in this allowable subspace can be expected to lie on a low-dimensional manifold. Research on nonlinear manifold learning for gesture recognition is still quite limited and the little close approach to ours is proposed by Wang et al. [10]. They use KPCA to discover the intrinsic structure of the articulated action space, and exploit factorial CRF [7] for activity modeling and recognition.

During learning the low-dimensional representation of hand motions, we decompose human hands into five fingers based hands skeleton model and obtain the hierarchical latent variable space of hands motion using HGPLVM, rather than learn a single manifold. Since the manifolds on the lower level have determinate meaning and the manifolds on the highest level may model both the dynamic of hand motion and the motion constraint among manifolds on lower levels, the hierarchical latent variable spaces are more reasonable and skillful for representing the intrinsic of hand motion. In particular, we proposes a novel Hierarchical CRF for modeling and recognizing hand gestures on both finger level and hand level. Since our discriminative model can estimate a label for each observation, it can deal with continuous dynamic hand gesture sequences.

3 Hierarchical Latent Variable Space

The informative observation features are crucial for the performance of recognition model. We use joints angles as the basic input and perform hierarchical dimensionality reduction technology that can learn more effective representation for hand motion.

3.1 GPLVM

Gaussian process latent variable model (GPLVM) [12] is a fully probabilistic, non-linear, latent variable model that generalizes principal component analysis.

Given high-dimensional data space Y with the dimensionality D, the purpose is to estimate the latent variable $x_i \in X$ for each training data $y_i \in Y$. The kernel matrix K is the core of the GPLVM model. There uses the Radial Basis Function (RBF) kernel function because it smoothly interpolates the latent space. The RBF kernel function takes the form:

$$k(x_i, x_j) = \alpha_{rbf} \exp(-\frac{\gamma}{2}(x_i - x_j)^T (x_i - x_j)) + \alpha_{bias} + \beta^{-1}\delta_{ij} \tag{1}$$

where $k(x_i, x_j)$ is the element in i-th row and j-th column of the kernel matrix K, α_{rbf} controls the scale of the output functions, γ is the inverse width parameter, α_{bias} is the variance of the kernel bias, δ_{ij} denotes the Kronecker delta. The scale $k(x_i, x_j)$ models the proximity between two points x_i and x_j. GPLVM learning is the process of learning the kernel parameters $\theta = (\alpha_{rbf}, \beta, \alpha_{bias}, \gamma)$ and latent variables x_i. Then we maximize the posterior $P(\{x_i\}, \theta) | \{y_i\}$, which corresponds to minimizing the following objective function:

$$L = \frac{D}{2}\ln|K| + \frac{1}{2}tr(K^{-1}YY^T) + \frac{1}{2}\sum_i^N \|x_i\|^2 \tag{2}$$

with respect to the kernel parameter and latent variables. The optimization process is realized through the Scaled Conjugate Gradient (SCG) method.

3.2 Hierarchical Manifold Space of Hand Motion

Motions of the hands can be divided into several motions of different hand parts. We use HGPLVM [13], a hierarchical tree based model, to learn the hierarchical latent variables space of hand motion.

As shown in Fig. 2, we decompose the whole hand into five fingers and learn the hierarchical latent variable space of hand motion. The joint probability distribution represented by Fig 2 is given by

$$p(Y_1, Y_2, Y_3, Y_4, Y_5) = \int p(Y_1 | X_1) \times \int p(Y_2 | X_2) \times \int p(Y_3 | X_3) \times \int p(Y_4 | X_4) \times \int p(Y_5 | X_5)...$$
$$\times \int p(X_1, X_2, X_3, X_4, X_5 | X_6)dX_6 X_5 X_4 dX_3 dX_2 dX_1 \tag{3}$$

where each conditional distribution is given by a Gaussian process. However, the required marginalisations are not tractable. Therefore we turn to MAP solutions for finding the values of the latent variables. It means maximization of

$$\log p(X_1, X_2, X_3, X_4, X_5, X_6 | Y_1, Y_2, Y_3, Y_4, Y_5) = \log p(Y_1 | X_1) + \log p(Y_2 | X_2)$$
$$+ \log p(Y_3 | X_3) + \log p(Y_4 | X_4) + \log p(Y_5 | X_5) + \log p(X_1, X_2, X_3, X_4, X_5 | X_6) \tag{4}$$

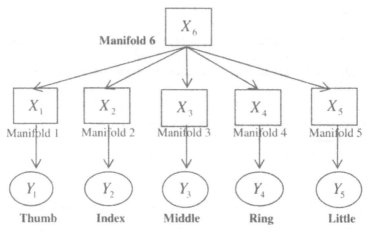

Fig. 2. A simple hierarchy for capturing interaction among five fingers

which is the sum of six Gaussian process log likelihoods. The first five terms are associated with five fingers and the sixth term provides co-ordination between all the fingers.

The algorithm for optimization of the latent variables proceeded as follows:

1. Initialize each leaf node's latent variable set $(X_1, X_2, X_3, X_4, X_5)$ using principal component analysis (PCA) of the corresponding dataset $(Y_1, Y_2, Y_3, Y_4, Y_5)$.
2. Initialize the root node's latent variable set (X_6) using PCA of the concatenated latent variables of its dependents $[X_1, X_2, X_3, X_4, X_5]$.
3. Optimize jointly the parameters of the kernel matrices for each Gaussian process model and the latent variable positions $(X_1, X_2, X_3, X_4, X_5, X_6)$.

Fig. 3 shows the result of mapping hand motions into the hierarchical model.

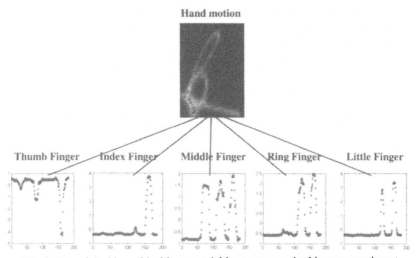

Fig. 3. One of the hierarchical latent variable spaces acquired in our experiment

4 Hierarchical CRF

Continuous gesture recognition can be regard as the prediction of a class label for each frame in an unsegmented sequence. Based the learned hierarchical latent variable space, we proposed a tree-based hierarchical CRF model for the task of continuous gesture recognition. The topology of this tree model depends on the hand decomposition and every node has its own observation sequence. Since every finger's motion can be simply regard as several specific movements (i.e. bending, expanding, etc), we also assume the same vector of hidden states for each finger and these hidden states are not observed in the training examples.

4.1 Model Description

Consider a Hierarchical CRF with L levels, our task is to learn the mapping between a hierarchical observation sequence set $X = \{X_l\}_{l=1}^{L}$ ($X_l = \{x_{l,1}, x_{l,2}, ..., x_{l,T}\}$) and a sequence of labels $Y = \{y_1, y_2, ..., y_T\}$ with sequence length of T . For the nodes except the root nodes, we define the number of its hidden states is N and define the number of hidden states in level l is M_l (i.e. In our experiments, $M_1 = 5 \times N$, which equals to N times of the finger number.). $H_{l,t} = \{h_{i,t}^{i}\}_{i=1}^{M_l}$ represents the hidden state set in level l at time t . The hierarchical CRF model is defined as

$$P(Y \mid X, \theta) = \frac{1}{Z(X,\theta)} \left(\prod_{t=1}^{T-1} \Phi_L(y_t, y_{t+1}, X_L, t) \right)$$
$$\left(\prod_{t=1}^{T} \prod_{i=1}^{M_{L-1}} \Psi_{L-1}(h_{L-1,t}^{i}, y_t, X_{L-1}, t) \right) \tag{5}$$
$$\left(\prod_{t=1}^{T} \prod_{l=1}^{L-2} \prod_{i}^{M_l} \prod_{j}^{M_{l+1}} \Psi_l(h_{l,t}^{i}, h_{l+1,t}^{j}, X_1, X_2, ..., X_{L-2}, t) \right)$$

where Φ_L is the potentials over class labels edges , Ψ_{L-1} and Ψ_l are the potentials over the between-level edges, exactly the edge between every parent node and its children node. And these potentials factorize according to the features $\{f_k\}$ and the weights $\{\theta_k\}$, with the form of

$$\Phi_L = \exp\left(\sum_k \theta_k f_k(y_t, y_{t+1}, X_L, t) \right);$$

$$\Psi_{L-1} = \exp\left(\sum_k \theta_k f_k(h_{L-1,t}^{i}, y_t, X_{L-1}, t) \right) \tag{6}$$

$$\Psi_l = \exp\left(\sum_k \theta_k f_k(h_{l,t}^{i}, h_{l+1,t}^{j}, X_1, X_2, ..., X_{L-2}, t) \right).$$

4.2 Learning and Inference

Given n labeled training sequences $(x_{1,i}, x_{2,i},..., x_{L,i}, y_i)$ for $i = 1...n$. Following [6, 11], we use the following objective function to learn the parameter θ:

$$L(\theta) = \sum_{i=1}^{n} \log P(y_i \mid x_{1,i}, x_{2,i},..., x_{L,i}, \theta) - \frac{1}{2\sigma^2} \|\theta\|^2 \tag{7}$$

where the first term is the conditional log-likelihood of the training data, and the second term is the log of a Gaussian prior with variance σ^2, i.e., $P(\theta) \sim \exp(\frac{1}{2\sigma^2} \|\theta\|^2)$. Gradient ascent technology is used to search for the optimal parameter values, $\theta = \arg\max_\theta L(\theta)$.

For continuous gesture recognition, given a new test sequence $x*$, the goal is to estimate the most probable label sequence $y*$ that maximized our conditional model:

$$y* = \arg\max_y P(y \mid x*, \theta*) \tag{8}$$

where the model parameter $\theta*$ are learned from training samples. For our experiments, we use a two-level discriminative model in the learned hierarchical latent variable space of hand motion and each finger is considered as a hand part, the previous equation can be rewritten as:

$$y* = \arg\max_y \left(P(y \mid x*, \theta*) + \sum_{l=1}^{L-1} \sum_{i=1}^{M_l} P(h_l^i \mid x*, \theta*) \right) \tag{9}$$

To estimate the label y_j* of the sample j, the marginal probabilities are computed for all the levels from the lower level to the highest one and the label associated with the optimal set is chosen. In our model, the edge potentials are defined one for each parent node and its children node pair (h', h'') or (h', y') and every two neighboring class labels (y', y''). We define $H_{h''}$ and $H_{y'}$ are the hidden set of the children node of h' and y'. Then edge potentials are expressed as

$$f_k(y_t, y_{t+1}, X_L, t) = \begin{cases} 1 & if \ y_t = y' \ and \ y_{t+1} = y'' \\ 0 & otherwise \end{cases}$$

$$f_k(h_{L-1,t}^i, y_t, X_{L-1}, t) = \begin{cases} 1 & if \ h_{L-1,t}^i \in H_{y'} \ and \ y_t = y' \\ 0 & otherwise \end{cases} \tag{10}$$

$$f_k(h_{i,t}^i, h_{i+1,t}^j, X_1, X_2,..., X_{L-2}, t) = \begin{cases} 1 & if \ h_{i,t}^i \in H_{h''} \ and \ h_{i+1,t}^j = h'' \\ 0 & otherwise \end{cases}$$

5   Experiments

We compare the performance of our hierarchical CRF model with CRF and LDCRF and the features used in our experiments are joints angles derived from the previous 3D hand tracking algorithm [14].

5.1   Hand Gesture Dataset

There is no common evaluation database in the domain of hand gesture recognition. Here we design a continuous hand gesture dataset which consists of 9 common hand gestures. In the Hand Waiting (HW) gesture, all the fingers expand and it means there are no significative gestures or the waiting state. In the Pinch (PH) gesture, the thumb finger and index finger osculate to a close loop and the Reverse Pinch (RP) gesture is the reverse process of PH. In the Prepare Flip (PF) gesture, the thumb finger and middle finger osculate to a close loop and the Flip (FL) gesture is the reverse process of PF. In the Shooting (SH) gesture, all the fingers except the thumb finger close with each other and then they fold to the palm of the hand. Similarly, the Reverse Shooting (RS) gesture is the reverse process of SH. In the Grasp (GA) gesture all the five fingers fold to the palm of the hand and the reverse process of GA gesture is Reverse Grasp (RG) gesture. Typically, Fig. 4 shows four hand activities (i.e. PH, FL, SH and GA) and another four hand activities RP, PF, RS and RG are respective the reverse process of them. HW gesture can be considered as a middle state and we suppose it has no sharp change.

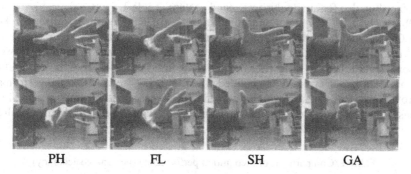

| PH | FL | SH | GA |

Fig. 4. Illustrations of the four typical hand gesture class for the experiments. Below each image column is the abbreviation for the gesture class. The first image in each column is approximate the start of the corresponding dynamic gesture and the second one is approximate the end of the gesture.

The user is asked to perform these gestures in front of a common camera. Only one user is asked to perform the all nine gestures and an average of 5 gestures per class are collected. From each image frame, a 14 dimensionality hand joint angle model is estimated using a 3D hand tracking algorithm [14]. The latent variables are used as observations for our recognition experiments.

5.2 Models

In our experiments, the Hierarchical CRF model is compared with two models: CRF and LDCRF and all these discriminative models can be trained and applied to unsegmented sequences.

CRF Model: We train a single CRF chain model where every gesture class has a corresponding state. The optimal label for a specific frame is selected to be the label with the highest marginal probability. Note that the observations of this model are latent variables in the lowest level gained by the hierarchical manifold learning algorithm (i.e. 5-dimensionality in our experiments).

LDCRF Model: We train a LDCRF model and the number of hidden state for each class label is set to be 3. The label with the highest marginal probability is chosen to be the optimal label for a given specific frame. The observations of LDCRF model is the same with the above CRF model.

Hierarchical CRF Model: In our gesture recognition experiment, this model has two levels and we train it over the hand gesture dataset. The whole hand is decomposed into five fingers and a 1D latent variable are learned for each finger. Then we impose a higher latent variable space with 2 dimensionalities over the lower space. The label with the highest probability is chosen.

5.3 Results and Analysis

In this section, we test the three discriminative models on our hand activity dataset and compare their recognition performance not only for the entire continuous gesture sequence but also for single dynamic hand gesture. Table 1.

Obviously, LDCRF model and our Hierarchical CRF model perform much better than CRF model at both window size zero and window size one. Our Hierarchical CRF model performs the best among all the three discriminative models. However, without regard to the difference of the recognition model, the most significant improvement in performance is obtained when w=1, but we note that the performance improvement does not always along with the increase of the window size. In our extensive experiments, we find that the competent recognition performance is already achieved by setting window size with one.

Table 1. Comparisons of recognition performance (percentage accuracy)

	HW	PH	RP	PF	FL	SH	RS	GA	RG	Sequence
CRF w=0	91.1	33.3	0.50	95.8	64.3	88.9	64.3	0.50	85.7	75.5
LDCRF w=0	100	94.4	0.00	79.2	100	88.9	92.9	100	92.9	87.0
Hierarchical CRF w=0	96.4	100	0.00	92.9	100	94.4	100	100	100	90.2
CRF w=1	92.7	100	85.7	95.8	92.9	100	100	100	100	95.7
LDCRF w=1	100	94.4	91.1	100	100	100	100	100	100	96.7
Hierarchical CRF w=1	100	100	92.9	100	100	100	100	100	100	99.5

6 Conclusion

In this paper we presented a hierarchical recognition method for continuous hand gesture recognition task which includes a hierarchical dimensionality reduction technology based feature extraction and a hierarchical discriminative model based gesture modeling and recognition. With the prior of hand biologic decomposition, the learned hierarchical latent variables space can represent more intrinsic motions of human hands than original joint angle space or other single embedded manifold space. Our Hierarchical CRF model makes use of the tree-based structure which model the dynamics between class labels and the inherent relationship between the motion of every hand part and each class label. We performed comparative experiments on the task of recognizing continuous hand gestures from unsegmented joint angles sequences and our model outperforms CRF model and the most up-to-date discriminative model (LDCRF). In future work, some observed middle states may be defined for every hand part (or hand finger) and edge potentials between the middle states at different time steps should be considered.

References

1. Wu, Y., Huang, T.S.: Vision-based gesture recognition: A review. In: Braffort, A., Gibet, S., Teil, D., Gherbi, R., Richardson, J. (eds.) GW 1999. LNCS (LNAI), vol. 1739, p. 103. Springer, Heidelberg (2000)
2. Lv, F., Nevatia, R.: Single View Human Action Recognition using Key Pose Matching and Viterbi Path Searching. In: CVPR (2007)
3. Efros, A., Berg, A., Mori, G., Malik, J.: Recognizing action at a distance. In: ICCV (2003)
4. Bobick, A., Davis, J.: The recognition of human movement using temporal templates. PAMI 23(3), 257–267 (2001)
5. Nguyen, N., Phung, D., Venkatesh, S., Bui, H.: Learning and detecting activities from movement trajectories using the hierarchical hidden Markov models. In: CVPR (2005)
6. Lafferty, J., McCallum, A., Pereira, F.: Conditional random fields: probabilistic models for segmenting and labeling sequence data. In: ICML (2001)
7. Sutton, C., Rohanimanesh, K., McCallum, A.: Dynamic conditional random fields: Factorized probabilistic models for labeling and segmenting sequence data. In: ICML (2004)
8. Sminchisescu, C., Kanaujia, A., Li, Z., Metaxas, D.: Conditional models for contextual human motion recognition. In: ICCV (2005)
9. Wang, S., Quattoni, A., Morency, L., Demirdjian, D., Darrell, T.: Hidden conditional random fields for gesture recognition. In: CVPR (2006)
10. Wang, L., Suter, D.: Recognizing Human Activities from Silhouettes: Motion Subspace and Factorial Discriminative Graphical Model. In: CVPR (2007)
11. Morency, L., Quattoni, A., Darrell, T.: Latent-Dynamic Discriminative Models for Continuous Gesture Recognition. In: CVPR (2007)
12. Lawrence, N.D.: Gaussian Process Latent Variable Models for Visualization of High dimensional Data. In: NIPS (2004)
13. Lawrence, N.D.: Hierarchical Gaussian Process Latent Variable Models. In: Proceedings of the 23rd International Conference on Machine Learning (ICML 2007), Corvallis, USA (2007)
14. Han, L., Wu, X., Liang, W., Jia, D.: Tracking 3D Hand on a learned Smooth Space. In: CNCC (2007)

Real-Time 3D Body Pose Tracking from Multiple 2D Images

Chi-Wei Chu and Ramakant Nevatia

Institute for Robotics and Intelligent System
University of Southern California
Los Angeles, CA 90089-0273
chuc@usc.edu, nevatia@usc.edu

Abstract. We present a human body motion tracking system for an interactive virtual simulation training environment. This system captures images using IR illumination and near-IR cameras to overcome limitations of a dimly lit environment. Features, such as silhouettes and medial axis of blobs are extracted from the images which lack much internal texture. We use a combination of a 2D ICP and particle filtering method to estimate the articulated body configuration of a trainee from image features. The method allows articulation of the arms at elbows and shoulders and of the body at the waist; this is a considerable improvement over previous such methods. Our system works in real-time and is robust to temporary errors in image acquisition or tracking. The system serves as part of a multi-modal user-input device for interactive simulation.

1 Introduction

Communication by visual gestures can be an important component of a natural Human-Computer Interaction (HCI) system. The gestures may be deictic or natural (beat) gestures. In either case, good estimation of human body articulations is necessary to recognize the gestures. We address this task in this paper.

In particular, we focus on operations in a virtual training environment, though the issues and approach apply to other applications as well. In our environment, a large screen is placed in front of user where a scenario of interest, that includes virtual humans unfolds. The goal is to train a human in interacting with the virtual humans for cognitive decision making. Much of the interaction is verbal but visual gestures are natural enhancements that can greatly enhance the immersive experience.

Our environment places certain difficult challenges. First, the environment is dimly lit to maintain immersion. There are further design decisions made that the trainees should not be required to wear special clothing or require preparation by putting markers on their body or face. The trainee is not stationary but free to walk around in a limited working area. Visual processing must also be real-time to be useful in an interactive system.

We illuminate the scene with IR lights and use normal CCD cameras to capture images. These images are rather featureless with little texture or interior detail visible. We use multiple cameras to partially compensate for these deficiencies and to make acquisition of 3-D position and pose easier. We extract features such as motion blobs,

F.J. Perales and R.B. Fisher (Eds.): AMDO 2008, LNCS 5098, pp. 42–52, 2008.

silhouettes and their medial axes. Features are then used to estimate the positions of body joints. We ignore the lower body as it is less important for gestural communication. Our method is limited to having only one human trainee in the field of view at one time. This paper also does not address facial processing though it is part of our larger plan to include facial gestures.

Our method recovers several articulations of the upper body including movements of the arm at the shoulder and elbow joints and bending at the waist. This is a substantial enhancement over previous capabilities [5] which focused on upright body tracking and rigid arm movements. The increased degrees of freedom pose severe difficulties, both in achieving robust and accurate tracking and in maintaining real-time operation. We present a novel combination of a 2D-3D iterative closest point (ICP) and particle filtering algorithms to overcome these difficulties. Our system operates in real-time (at about 12frames per second, which is adequate for many interaction tasks) and is robust to occasional errors in image capture or loss of tracks.

1.1 Related Work

Various methods have been proposed for the estimation and tracking of of human body postures. Many approaches recognize the postures directly from 2D images, as single camera image sequences are easier to acquire. Some of them try to fit body models (3D or 2D) into single-view images [14,16] or classify postures by image features [10,17]. There are two main difficulties those methods must overcome. One is the loss of depth information. Thus it's difficult to tell if the body parts are orienting toward to or away from the camera. These system must either maintain both hypotheses or regulate the estimate with human body kinetic constraints. The other problem comes from self-occlusion: body parts that are not seen from the image cannot be estimated. Roughly one third of the degrees of freedom of the human model are unobservable due to motion ambiguities and self-occlusions.

To compensate for these ambiguities due to 2D acquisition, several approaches rely on using multiple cameras. These approaches use an array of two or more cameras or 3D body scanners to capture the human shape and motion from different views. Some of these approaches extract 2D image features from each camera and use these features to search for, or update the configuration of, a 3D body model [12,8]

Others introduce an intermediate step of reconstructing the 3D shape of human body. The characterization of the human pose is then done by fitting a kinematics model into the 3D shape information [13,6]. However, those approach usually use 3D data that is relatively stable and accurate. These methods also have difficulty to recover from tracking errors caused by ambiguity or faulty shape data. To compensate the shortcoming, recent works combine iterative algorithm with example-based approach [7] or Particle Filtering that maintains multiple hypothesis.

Particle Filtering (PF) has become increasingly popular for tracking body poses in recent work. Bernier et al. [2] combine Particle Filtering and Markov Network belief propagation to track 3D articulated pose in real-time, using stereo depth images. In [18], Schmidt et al. use Kernel Particle Filter and mean-shift methods to avoid large number of particles using intensity and color images cues, while also achieving near real-time performance.

Many of the methods above make an implicit assumption that the image quality is stable and high enough to extract useful image features. They utilize features such as motion flow, color and texture of skin and clothing to improve the classification or model-fitting accuracy. Such features are not available in our environment.

1.2   Outline of Our Approach

To overcome limitations of very limited natural light, to illuminate the room with diffused IR light; we use 4 to 5 normal CCD cameras to capture the images. The resulting images are without much texture and the only useful features are the silhouettes extracted by a background subtraction method. 2D symmetry axis points are then extracted from the silhouettes; 3-D axis points are then estimated form multiple cameras. The body of the user is modeled as an articulated model with 21 degrees of freedom (DOF); ellipsoids are used to model each body part.

We propose a 2D-3D Iterative Closest Points (ICP) method that converges the projected 2D model to 2D contour, then updates the 3D model based on 2D tracking results. The 2D tracking does not work well when arms are near the body, we use a Support Vector Machine (SVM) classifier to recognize the "rest state" of the arms. A particle filter is utilized to provide automatic ICP initialization and multiple hypotheses. This system can run in real-time and provide reliable pose estimation. The flow chart of our approach is shown in Fig.1.

Fig. 1. Approach Outline

2   Image Feature Extraction

As explained above, we capture images of the environment illuminated by IR lights from normal CCD cameras with an IR filter in front of the lens. We use an array of four or five synchronized, calibrated cameras. The images are rather noisy and feature-less as can be seen in Fig.2(a). Hence, we rely on the silhouettes for further processing. The silhouettes are extracted by a usual background subtraction approach as the environment is static. Shadows can be removed as the illumination is diffused.

We then extract the skeleton axis points from the silhouettes. Several techniques exist for this task [15,20]. We scan the silhouettes with arrays of scan lines and intersect the scan-lines with the silhouettes. The middle point of each segment is extracted as an axis point. The arm and torso axis points are selected by the point location and scan line segment length information. An example is shown in Fig.2(b).

Given 2D body axis points from multiple cameras, the 3D axis points can be constructed by multiple view geometry (Fig.2(c)). Both 2D silhouette information and 3D shape information are used to estimate 3D body pose configurations. We skip further details of the early image feature extraction due to limitations of space.

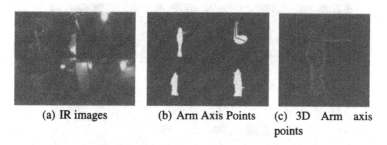

(a) IR images   (b) Arm Axis Points   (c) 3D Arm axis points

Fig. 2. Axis points

3   2D-3D Pose Tracking

For our body tracking task, we define a body model as show in Fig. 3. The degrees of freedom (DOF) of the model include the free rotation and translation of the body and waist, shoulders, elbows joints. Each joint rotation is represented as ZXY Euler angles. This gives a total of 21 degrees of freedom (DOF) for the model. The shapes of body segments are modeled as 3D ellipsoids.

In [6], Demirdjian et al. used Iterated Closest Points (ICP) method to match body model to 3D shape data created from stereo vision. However, since the background in the images can be cluttered and the IR image is featureless , the silhouettes, and subsequently the 3D visual hull constructed from them, can be very noisy. It is not uncommon that an arm is missing from the visual hull for some frames, due to segmentation error. An ICP tracking method using the faulty 3D data may converge to an arbitrary configuration and has no way to correct itself. We propose a new tracking method which applies ICP to the 2D data instead, and then integrates the 2D tracking results to 3D model. The method is outlined below.

Fig. 3. Articulated Body Model

At each time frame t:

1. the 3D body model is projected into each image to form a 2D rigid articulated model. Fig.4(a), 4(b) is an example of this projection.
2. The 2D model in each image is then fit to the corresponding silhouette contour using 2D ICP. See Fig.4(c).
3. The 2D rigid transformation that fits the 2D model to the contour is then back-projected to 3D space. A 3D rotation and translation of each body segment is inferred from the back-projection.
4. 3D rigid transformations inferred from multiple camera images are then averaged. The 3D body model is updated by the average transformation. See Fig.4(d).
5. Repeat to step 1. Terminate if the error computed by 2D ICP is below a threshold ϵ, or a fixed number of iterations have been performed.

Each step in the method is described in more detail below.

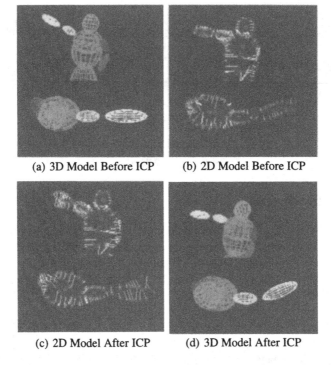

(a) 3D Model Before ICP   (b) 2D Model Before ICP

(c) 2D Model After ICP   (d) 3D Model After ICP

Fig. 4. ICP Process, white lines in 2D models indicate closest point pairs

3.1 3D Model Projection

An advantage of using ellipsoids for body segments is that the perspective projection from an ellipsoid forms an ellipse and this mapping can be represented in analytical form. Assume that we have a 3D ellipsoid body segment S_k. An arbitrarily rotated and translated ellipsoid in 3D space can be represented as $X^T A' X = 1$, where $X = [x, y, z, 1]^T$ is the homogeneous coordinate of a point on the surface. We want to project S_k into camera c, which has a 3×4 projection matrix P. P^+ is the 4×3 pseudo inverse matrix of P. Let the $4d$ row vectors $P_1^+ \ldots P_4^+$ be the 4 rows of P^+. Then, the projected ellipse s_k takes the form

$$U^T \left[P^{*T} A' \overrightarrow{e} \overrightarrow{e}^T A' P^* - \left(\overrightarrow{e}^T A' \overrightarrow{e} - 1 \right) P^{*T} A' P^* \right] U = 0 \qquad (1)$$

where $U = [u, v, 1]$ is the 2D point on the ellipse. $\overrightarrow{e} = [x_e, y_e, z_e, 1]^T$ is the focal point of the camera c. and the 4×3 matrix P^* is

$$P^* = \left[P_1^{+T}, P_2^{+T}, P_3^{+T}, 0 \right]^T - diag\left(x_e, y_e, z_e, 0 \right) \left[P_4^{+T}, P_4^{+T}, P_4^{+T}, 0 \right]^T \qquad (2)$$

3.2 2D Iterative Closest Points

Iterative Closest Points (ICP) is a standard 3D registration algorithm [3]. Given a set of 3D data and a 3D model, ICP estimates the rigid motion between the data and model. A 2D variation of ICP is proposed here.

Assume we have a 2D rigid model consisting of K ellipses. First we uniformly select N points $Q = \{q^i | i = 1 \ldots N\}$ on the curve of ellipse $s_k, k = 1 \ldots K$. Let $\bar{q} = avg_i(Q)$ is the average point of Q.

Second, for each point q^i, we find the nearest point p^i on the silhouette contour. Let $P = \{p^i | i = 1 \ldots N\}$ and $\bar{p} = avg(P)$ to be the mean coordinate of all p^i. To simplify computation, we approximate the silhouette contour by a polygon. Instead of computing and comparing the distance between q^i and all contour pixels, the nearest point can now be found by computing the shortest distance between q^i and each polygon edge segment. A human body silhouette contour in our images 320×240 usually has 800-1000 pixels, which is reasonably accurately approximated by 20-30 polygon edges.

When searching for nearest points, the normals of the ellipse and the polygonal contour are also taken into consideration. For each edge, if the angle between its normal and the normal of p^i is larger than a certain threshold, the edge is omitted in searching for q^i. We set the threshold to be $\pi/2$ in our implementation.

After finding the nearest point pairs, we want to estimate the 2D rigid transformation M that minimize the sum of square error $E = \sum_i |p^i - Mq^i|^2$. The transformation consists of a 2D rotation angle θ and translation T.

θ is estimated by $\theta = \arctan\left(\sum_i w^i \left(p^i_y q^i_x - p^i_x q^i_y\right) / \sum_i w^i \left(p^i_x q^i_x + p^i_y q^i_y\right)\right)$

Where w^i is the exponential weight. $w^i \cong e^{\left(-|p^i - q^i|^2\right)}$. With the weighting, outlier points will less interference in computing the transformation. T is estimated by $T = \bar{p} - R_\theta \bar{q}$ where R_θ is the 2D rotation matrix of θ.

3.3 Convert 2D Transformation to 3D

For each camera c, and for each body segment S_k, a 2D rotation θ and translation T are found in previous step. The 2D transformation is now converted to 3D as follows:

Let the 3D point J_k be the joint of S_k, let L_k the line connecting J_k and the focal point $\vec{e}$. L_k is also the projection ray of J_k. The 2D rotation can be converted to 3D as a rotation of S_k around L_k by angle θ. An example is shown in Fig.5. T is converted to a 3D displacement on a plane parallel to the image plane. For each body segment, the 2-D ICP tracking applied to multiple camera images may produce different 3D transfor-

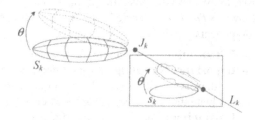

Fig. 5. Back-project 2D rotation to 3D

mations. Body model updates are inferred from a combination of these transformations.

We integrate the 3D rigid transformations together by averaging them. Averaging the translations is straightforward: $\bar{T} = avg_c(T_c)$ where c is camera index. For rotations, there are several ways to compute the average [11]. Since our 3D model segments rotate around an axis, the rotation can be conveniently represented by an unit quaternion $q_c = \{a + bi + cj + dk | a, b, c, d \in \mathbb{R}, a^2 + b^2 + c^2 + d^2 = 1\}$. The average of a rotation is then given by:

$$\bar{q} = \sum_c q_c \Big/ \left| \sum_c q_c \right| \tag{3}$$

Quaternions in eq.(3) must also satisfy $\langle q_i, q_j \rangle \geq 0$ for any two quaternions. This can be achieved by flipping the signs of the quaternion, since $-q_c$ and q_c represent the same rotation. The averaged rotation is applied to each 3D body joint. The translation is only applied to full body and not the individual segments.

Since the shapes of 2D models change with every iteration due to re-projection, this process is not guaranteed to converge. However, empirically we find that 2-3 iterations are sufficient to provide good seeds to the subsequent particle filter process. The 2D-3D ICP is less prone to segmentation errors than by using the 3-D visual hull. For example, a lost limb in one silhouette removes the limb in the visual hull, formed by intersection of the silhouette data. A tracking method using the 3D shape will likely fail in such a case. On the contrary, the 2D-3D ICP uses the union of all silhouettes. The effect of one faulty segmentation is reduced by the averaging step.

4   Particle Filtering

The ICP method, like other iterative convergence methods, relies heavily on the initial configuration of the model. An initial body model configuration that differs too much from the correct one may converge to a pose far from the correct one. Also, if the tracking fails at one time instance, it is unlikely to correct itself in the ICP process. To automate the track initialization process and improve robustness, we integrate a Particle Filtering method with the 2D-3D ICP.

Assume x_t represents the joint angles of the body model and y_t is the captured image information at time t. We want to estimate the posterior probabilities $p(x_t \mid y_{1:t})$ given the sequence of images $y_{1:t}$, to find the most likely x_t. One way that is often used to estimate the posterior probability is the *Sequential Monte Carlo method*, also known as *Particle Filtering* [1,9]. The standard generic Particle Filter has the following components:

- **Initialization:** at beginning, N data samples α_0^i are drawn from a prior distribution.
- **Importance Sampling:** at each time step t, new sample are spawned according to the density distribution of the proposal function: $\widetilde{\alpha}_t^i = q\left(\alpha_t^i \mid y_t, \alpha_{t-1}^i\right)$. Evaluate the weight w_t^i of each particle α_t^i
- **Resampling:** sample N new particles α_t, from the set $\left\{\widetilde{\alpha}_t^1 ... \widetilde{\alpha}_t^N\right\}$ with replacements, with probability according to w_t^i.

Some hybrid approaches add an additional *Refine-Prediction* step after the importance sampling [19]. These methods adjust the sample set either to increase the sample diversity or increase sample importance. In our approach, the 2D-3D ICP is utilized as the Refine-Prediction step, which improves sample importance by moving samples toward nearby local optima. Each step of the Particle Filter in our implementation is described below.

Observation Probability: The observation probability $p\left(y_t \mid \alpha_t^i\right)$ is estimated as the ratio of pixel areas: $p\left(y_t \mid \alpha_t^i\right) = \prod_c \left(\left\|P_c^i \cap S_c\right\| \Big/ \left\|P_c^i \cup S_c\right\|\right)$, where P_c^i is the projected image of α_t^i into camera c, and S_c is the silhouette. $\| \cdot \|$ is the area of image region.

Proposal Functions: We define a set of different proposal functions, $Q = \{q_i\}$. A function is randomly selected in the importance sampling step and used as the proposal function. The selection probabilities are set empirically. The proposal functions we uses are:

Random Walk function: We model the displacement of each DOF as a 1-D Gaussian distribution. New DOF values are drawn from this distribution.

Body Position Function: This function randomly samples points from 3D torso axis points as new body position on the stage.

Arm Fitting Function: The 3D arm axis points are used to estimate the shoulder and elbow joint angles in the new samples. For each arm, one of the 3D axis line strip at the same side of the body is randomly selected. And the shoulder and elbow joint angles are alter to make body model aligns with the axis lines.

4.1 Particle Refinement

After importance sampling step, a set of particles is randomly selected for further Prediction-Refinement. 2D-3D ICP method is applied to converge those particle to match the body silhouettes. The advantage of the additional refinement step, compared the generic Particle Filter, is the reduction of particles. Instead of relying on a large swarm of particles trying to hit the best guess, a small number of particles can be guided towards the local optima. During both importance sampling and particle refinement, if the resulting model configuration violates the joint constraints, the new model configuration is discarded and the old one is kept.

The tracking system detects the presence of the user in the scene by thresholding the summed observation weights of the particles. When the user first enters the scene, the tracking system scales the body model proportionally to the height of the torso axis.

During both importance sampling and particle refinement, if the resulting model configuration violates the joint constraints, the new model configuration is discarded and the old one is kept.

In each time frame, the particle with the highest weight in the the sampling step is selected and the articulated body configuration represented by this particle is used to estimate the pointing direction.

Our tracking method is robust and is able to keep tracking user pose in the absence of usable image features, and quickly recovers from erroneous states when good data is available. The system does not need manual initialization. When a user enters the stage from any location, the proposal functions quickly converge the particles around the user and start tracking automatically.

5 Rest State

The tracking system uses the silhouettes as the basis of visual information. When the arms of user are wrapped near the body, the silhouettes are visually nearly undistinguishable. The 2D-3D ICP might converge the arms arbitrarily around or even into the torso. The tracking result is meaningless in such situation. To address this problem, we use a Support Vector Machine (SVM) [4] to classify the pose into "rest" and "non-rest" states for each arm. The $6d$ feature vector used by the SVM consists of 3D positions of elbow and wrist joints, in the upper body coordinate system. One SVM is trained for the right arm; the coordinates of the joints of left arm are mirrored before applying the SVM classification. An arm classified as being in rest state is forced to a resting down state regardless of the tracking result.

6   Experiment Results

We have set up the system in two different environments One is used in a virtual-reality theater with a curved surrounding screen, the other is in a set simulating a war-torn town with projection screens as walls and doors.

We use four to five synchronized IR firewire cameras connected to a 2.8 GHZ Dual-Core Dual-Xeon workstation.The system is able to run in 12 frame per second on average with 50 particles; this speed is acceptable for simple interactions with the environment. More particles provide better estimation robustness and accuracy but slow down the performance. Some frames from a tracking sequence are shown in Fig.6. An example tracking error occurred in the second frame, but the method recovered quickly.

The rest-state SVM uses a radial basis function. The SVM parameters are trained using 5-fold cross-validation method on 2000 manually labeled frames. The classification has 98.95% accuracy.

To test quantitative accuracy, we collected video sequences of users interacting in the system performing various gestures. We recorded videos of 5 different people, each of length 200-300 frames. We manually marked the 2D pixel coordinates of body joints, including waist, head, shoulders, elbows and wrists, in each image; 3D coordinates of the joints were then computed to provide the "ground truth". This approach is time-consuming and hence the amount of data on which we could evaluate is limited. a We compute tracking errors as the Euclidean distance between joints in the estimated body model and the estimated ground truth. We find the average error to be about 8 cms. Distance criterion can be somewhat misleading as the errors of the hand position accumulate the errors from other joints. Hence, we also computed average angular error between estimated and annotated arm segments (upper and lower arm); this average error in angles is about 8.9 degrees. If an arm is labeled as in rest state in target data, the corresponding joints and segments are not included to compute the average error. We think that these error numbers are acceptable in an interactive environment where feedback is available to the user from the reactions of the agents in the environment; however, we have not yet performed the integrated experiments.

Jitter, representing rapid fluctuations of the estimated pose, can occur because our proposal functions do not take motion smoothness into account when spawning new particles. We could gain some smoothness by backward filtering but this would introduce additional latency into the system; we have not explored the trade-off between the two. Currently our system works with a single user only. Segmentation of multiple users is made more difficult in IR images due to lack of color or texture. We intend to explore this in our future work.

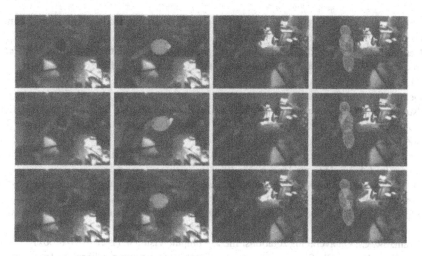

Fig. 6. Example Tracking Sequences, One frame per Row

7 Conclusion and Future Work

We described a near real-time body pose estimation and tracking system for a user in a poorly illuminated environment by use of IR lights. Use of axis finding methods provides a rough part segmentation and hypotheses for part orientations; use of particle filtering provides robust estimation of the pose from noisy sequences. The 2D-3D ICP particle refinement method reduces the particle number while offering higher accuracy.

In the future, we plan to integrate the visual modality into a larger system and evaluate its effectiveness in the training task.

Acknowledgment

The research in this paper was sponsored, in part, by the U.S. Army Research, Development and Engineering Command (RDECOM). The content of the information does not necessarily reflect the position or the policy of the Government and no official endorsement should be inferred

References

1. Arulampalam, S., Maskell, S., Gordon, N., Clapp, T.: A tutorial on particle filters for on-line non-linear/non-gaussian bayesian tracking. IEEE Transactions on Signal Processing 50(2), 174–188 (2002)
2. Bernier, O., Chan, P.C.M.: Real-time 3d articulated pose tracking using particle filtering and belief propagation on factor graphs. In: BMVC 2006, vol. 2, p. I:7 (2006)
3. Besl, P.J., McKay, N.D.: A method for registration of 3-d shapes. IEEE Trans. Pattern Anal. Mach. Intell. 14(2), 239–256 (1992)
4. Chang, C.-C., Lin, C.-J.: LIBSVM: a library for support vector machines (2001), http://www.csie.ntu.edu.tw/~cjlin/libsvm

5. Chu, C., Nevatia, R.: Real time body pose tracking in an immersive training environment, pp. 146–156 (2007)
6. Demirdjian, D., Darrell, T.: 3-d articulated pose tracking for untethered diectic reference. In: Proceedings of ICMI 2002, Washington, DC, USA, p. 267. IEEE Computer Society, Los Alamitos (2002)
7. Demirdjian, D., Taycher, L., Shakhnarovich, G., Grauman, K., Darrell, T.: Avoiding the "streetlight effect": tracking by exploring likelihood modes. In: Tenth IEEE International Conference on Computer Vision, 2005. ICCV 2005, October 17-21, 2005, vol. 1, pp. 357–364 (2005)
8. Deutscher, J., Blake, A., Reid, I.: Articulated body motion capture by annealed particle filtering. In: CVPR 2000, pp. II: 126–133 (2000)
9. Doucet, A., de Freitas, N., Gordon, N.: Sequential Monte Carlo Methods in Practice. Springer, Heidelberg
10. Elgammal, A., Lee, C.-S.: Inferring 3d body pose from silhouettes using activity manifold learning (2004)
11. Gramkow, C.: On averaging rotations. Int. J. Comput. Vision 42(1-2), 7–16 (2001)
12. Izo, T., Grimson, W.: Simultaneous pose estimation and camera calibration from multiple views. In: Non-Rigid 2004, p. 14 (2004)
13. Kehl, R., Bray, M., Van Gool, L.: Full body tracking from multiple views using stochastic sampling. In: IEEE Computer Society Conference on CVPR 2005, vol. 2, pp. 129–136 (2005)
14. Lee, M., Nevatia, R.: Dynamic human pose estimation using markov chain monte carlo approach. In: Motion 2005, pp. II: 168–175 (2005)
15. Leymarie, F.F., Kimia, B.B.: Medial Representations: Mathematics, Algorithms and Applications, ch. 11. Kluwer, Dordrecht (to be published, 2006)
16. Parameswaran, V., Chellappa, R.: View independent human body pose estimation from a single perspective image. In: CVPR 2004, pp. II: 16–22 (2004)
17. Rahman, M., Ishikawa, S.: Appearance-based representation and recognition of human motions. In: Proceedings. ICRA 2003. IEEE International Conference on Robotics and Automation, 2003, vol. 1, pp. 1410–1415 (2003)
18. Schmidt, J., Fritsch, J., Kwolek, B.: Kernel particle filter for real-time 3d body tracking in monocular color images. In: FGR 2006, pp. 567–572 (2006)
19. Wang, P., Rehg, J.: A modular approach to the analysis and evaluation of particle filters for figure tracking. In: IEEE Computer Society Conference on Computer Vision and Pattern Recognition, 2006, June 17-22, 2006, vol. 1, pp. 790–797 (2006)
20. Zerroug, M., Nevatia, R.: Segmentation and 3-d recovery of curved-axis generalized cylinders from an intensity image. In: Proceedings of the 12th IAPR International Conference on Computer Vision and Image Processing, October 1994, vol. 1, pp. 678–681 (1994)

Applying Space State Models in Human Action Recognition: A Comparative Study

M. Ángeles Mendoza and Nicolás Pérez de la Blanca

University of Granada,
ETSI Informática y e Telecomunicación
18071 Granada, Spain
{nines,nicolas}@decsai.ugr.es

Abstract. This paper presents comparative results of applying different architectures of generative classifiers (HMM, FHMM, CHMM, Multi-Stream HMM, Parallel HMM) and discriminative classifier as Conditional Random Fields (CRFs) in human action sequence recognition. The models are fed with histogram of very informative features such as contours evolution and optical-flow. Motion orientation discrimination has been obtained tiling the bounding box of the subject and extracting features from each tile. We run our experiments on two well-know databases, KTH´s database and Weizmann´s. The results show that both type of models reach similar score, being the generative model better when used with optical flow features and being the discriminative one better when uses with shape-context features.

1 Introduction

HMMs have been applied in action recognition for more of a decade [1,4,5,6,10,25], because that they encode very properly the human motion nature from sample data. Extensions, like Factorial HMM (FHMM) [7] and Coupled HMM (CHMM) [5], Parallel HMM [23] or Multi-Stream HMM [2] have been proposed, for overcoming the deficiencies of traditional HMMs. All these models are particular cases of Dynamic Bayesian Networks (DBN). Recently, a different approach to the classification task based on Conditional Random Fields (CRF) models ([13]) has been proposed, [8,16,21,24]. In [21] a linear-chain CRF to model human motion from 2d shape is used. In [8] subject position, velocity and pose is used for recognizing events from a vending machine. In [24] hidden states are added to the CRF model in order to code the underlying structure of gestures, Hidden CRFs (HCRF). In [16] each disjoint set of hidden states is associated to each class label for recognizing human gestures from unsegmented sequences, Latent-Dynamic CRFs (LD-CRF). Comparative experiments between the generative and the discriminative approaches are usually given using only the linear models, HMM and CRF respectively. In this paper we extend the comparative study including the extensions of the HMMs.

CRFs model directly the conditional distribution over hidden states given the observations, so they do not need make independence assumptions between

F.J. Perales and R.B. Fisher (Eds.): AMDO 2008, LNCS 5098, pp. 53–62, 2008.

observations, therefore observations at different time instants can be jointly considered. So they can handle large contextual dependences and complex and overlapped observations. Human activity often exhibits long-term dependences, in this case to remove ambiguities and to improve the recognition rate the context needs be considered.

Extracting appropriate features with meaningful information to be used with the model is also an important issue. We trained the models with two different types of features. One is based on shape context histograms, and the other is based on optical flow histograms. Both type of features are shown to be very discriminating when used in object or action recognition tasks [9] [3]. In [21] a 50-dimensional histogram based on shape context and pair-wise edge features at different scales is used. In our study we only use shape-context features calculated at one scale showing that simpler features give good results too.

The paper is organized as follows: Section 2 outlines the models that we used in our system. Section 3 describes our feature vectors. Section 4 gives an overview of our experimentation and results. Finally, conclusions are drawn in Section 5.

2   Probabilistic Graphical Models for Action Recognition

In this section we outline the models that we used for recognizing human actions: HMMs and its extensions, representing the generative models, and the CRF model representing the discriminative ones.

2.1   HMMs and Extensions

Hidden Markov Models are a very well type of state models in which two basic assumptions are made: the probability of a state in a time instance depends only on state in previous instance and the generated observation depends only on current state, so successive observations are independent. See [19] for more information. HMMs can be represented as a Markov chain where each node represents the discrete hidden state variable at each time instant, in our case, at each frame of the sequence.

All information about the time series history is contained in the state variable. When the amount of information to remember can be codified in few states this model works properly, but unfortunately the number of states increase exponentially with the number of bits to remember. In order to solve this problem more complex architectures with lower number of states are been proposed. In [11] a distributed HMM denominated FHMM was introduced. Several independent models with different dynamics are composed where the observation vector depends upon the current state in each of the chain. FHMMs allow us to decouple the dynamics of different body parts, for example, upper body part and lower body part. Due to the factorization of the state variable into multiple state variables, FHMMs allows large state spaces to be represented with a small number of parameters. In this model the features choice is essential due to the weak coupling between chains.

In CHMMs each HMM generates a different observation from a state-variable chain, but these chains are coupled each other, see [5]. CHMMs can model asynchronous observation vectors while keeping their correlation over time. The influence between the HMM-component depends on the state structures between the chains. We use CHMMs with coupling of length one, that is, the state variable of each chain in time t depends only on the state variables of the other chains in time t-1. This model allows us to code coordination between movements, as for example, when people walk, they swing their arms for keeping equilibrium. So the state of the arms on each instant depends on the arms and legs states in previous instants.

In Parallel HMMs, the chains are not coupled, but each HMM models its own observation vector, the resulting probabilities being the product of the probabilities from each HMM [2]. In Multi-Stream HHM models, only one chain models all observation vectors, it is very useful when all features have the same dynamic.

In all the above models, we use a continuous observation distribution defined by one single Gaussian. We also use linear left-right structure where each node represents a frame of action sequence. Left-right models fit better those signals whose properties change over time [19]. In particular, these models relate in a straightforward way the model states with partial motions defining the full motion. In multi-chain models, CHMMs, FHMMs and parallel HMMs we use two chains of state variables. For simplicity it is assumed that the number of possible states in each chain is equal, the square root of the number of states in the linear-chain models.

2.2 Conditional Random Fields

These model are especially suitable for recognition problems with rich and interrelated observations. Actions are composed by a combination of primitive motions, many of them common to different actions, so context and long-term dependences are necessary for removing ambiguities.

A detailed study about CRF can be found in [22]. Basically, a CRF is an undirected graphical model, G, that factorizes the conditional distribution into a product of real-valued functions, which are called potentials.

$$p(y|x) = \frac{1}{Z(x)} \prod_A \Psi_A(y_A, x_A) \ . \tag{1}$$

where $\{\Psi_A\}$ is the set of factors in G. $Z(x)$ is the normalizing partition function. Potentials are usually described by log-linear combinations of feature functions f. These feature functions can be designed for extracting the better possible information from data. Here, we also use a linear-chain, where each state depends only on previous one, but in contrast to HMMs and extensions we use observations from any time. The conditional probability is:

$$p(y|x) = \frac{1}{Z(x)} exp \Big\{ \sum_{t=1}^{T} \sum_{i,j} \lambda_{ij} f_{ij}(y_t, y_{t-1}) + \sum_{t=1}^{T} \sum_{i} \lambda_i f_i(y_t, x_t) \Big\} \tag{2}$$

where λ are the associated weights to each feature function giving the importance of each particular function in the potential function. We use the following feature functions: a) A function, $f_i = I(y_t = i) * x$ associated to the label action and whose value is the observation vector x if y is in the state i and 0 in the remainder, b) A transition function, $f_{ij} = I(y_{t-1} = i, y_t = j)$, which depends on the consecutive label in the sequence, 1 if i y_{t-1} and y_t y have labels i and j respectively and 0 otherwise. This function measures the transition between labels, so that captures the dynamic among activities. This model do not try to learn the hidden structure underling the human action, but to learn a function assigning each observation to its most probable class.

Figure 1 shows the graphical models of these models.

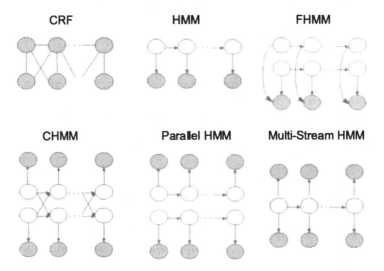

Fig. 1. Graphical models. Empty circles represent hidden states nodes, shaded circles represent observed data.

3   Observables for CRF and HMMs Training

We trained the anterior models with two feature vectors, a vector based on contours and the other one based on optical flow.

3.1   Shape-Contexts-Based Feature Vector

Shape contexts [3] has shown to be a very robust feature in matching object by shape. Basically, the shape-context feature associated with a point in a contour is a 2D histogram measuring distances and angles from such point to the remaining points in the contour. One approach to characterize a human action is using the temporal sequence of locations of each part of the body. Therefore, we do not calculate the shape-context feature over the full shape of subject, but we split the subject 's bounding box into uniform no-overlapped meaningful tiles and calculate the shape-context in each tile, see [15]. This strategy increases the discriminate power of the feature vector, compare for instance *walking* and *waving*, and will show that it also allows us to distinguish orientation in the action.

We use eight tiles with the main motion areas: two horizontal sections, in order to exploit human symmetry; and four vertical sections corresponding approximately to head-shoulders, trunk-arms, hips-thighs and knees-feet. Smaller tiles do not permit to capture sufficient information from the human outline. We use 4 distance bins and 8 angle bins (from $0°$ to $360°$ in steps of $45°$). We obtain a $256D$ feature vector (4 *distance bins* × 8 *angle bins* × 8 tiles).

3.2   Optical Flow-Based Feature Vector

The main drawback of the contours-based features is the presence of noise due to cluttered environments, shadows and bad segmentation. In addition, it is often hard to distinguish among actions with similar poses but with different velocities, for example walking and jogging. Due to this, we have also used an observation vector based on optical flow. We estimated optical flow using the Lucas-Kanade's method [14]. We calculated a two-dimensional histogram of direction angle and magnitude of optical flow on each one of the tiles described in previous section. In total, we obtain a $256D$ feature vector (4 *magnitude bins* × 8 *angle bins* × 8 tiles).

3.3   Dimension Reduction: Principal Component Analysis (PCA)

The dimension of the space where of the feature vectors live is much less than the length of the vector. So in order to reduce the dimensionality of the feature vector we compute the principal components of the training samples in each tile. Training and testing samples are projected over these axes. We select only the first axes to represent the feature vectors.

4   Experiments

We trained a model per class (one-vs.-all). During testing, samples were passed through each of these models, the model with highest probability assign the action to the data. Results were validated on multi-subject open tests by cross validation. We use the toolbox BNT for Matlab [18] for HMMs and extensions. For CRFS, we use hCRF library [17].

4.1   Data

We run our experiments using the KTH's database [20] and the Weizmann's database [12]. The KTH's sequences are made up of grey images with a resolution of $160 × 120$ pixels to 25 fps. 25 different people of both genders carry out 10 different actions: *walking, jogging, running* and *boxing*, parallel to the camera in both directions; and *clapping* and *waving*, facing to the camera. Actions were performed outdoors and indoors, with different lighting conditions and in the images appeared shadows and compression artifices. The Weizmann´s database consists of colour images with resolution 144×180 to 25 fps. The actions were performed by 9 different people of both genders outdoors. In this work we only take the actions common to KTH: *walking, running* and *clapping*. Figure 2 shows the outline images from the database, which we extract the features from. The images are contaminated by realistic noise conditions, shadows, people's own clothes, background elements, and bad segmentation. In some sequences of *boxing* there is a continuous zoom during the recording, therefore the subject appears with different size. In order to obtain the person bounding box, we learn the background distribution using only one frame on each scenario and we assign weights to the pixels depending on its probability of being background. The subject is not always centered in the bounding box, the same that in real applications.

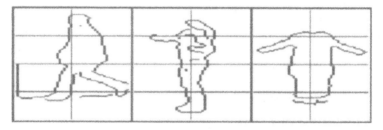

Fig. 2. Outline images obtained from the database

4.2 First Experiment: CRFs vs Simple HMMs Fed with Shape Contexts

We run experiments on the KTH´s database [20] and Weizmann´s database [12] jointly. Each video was segmented into activity cycles. We defined the activity cycle for *walking* and *jogging* as a step with both legs (as in most of the pedestrian

Table 1. Confusion matrix for CRF with $W = 1$

	Walk L	Walk R	Jog L	Jog R	Run L	Run R	Box L	Box R	Clap	Wav	
Walk_L	15	0	0	0	0	0	0	0	0	0	100%
Walk_R	0	21	0	0	0	0	0	0	0	0	100%
Jog_L	0	2	10	0	0	0	0	0	0	0	83.3%
Jog_R	0	0	0	10	0	1	0	0	0	0	90.9%
Run_L	0	0	0	0	18	0	0	0	0	0	100%
Run_R	0	1	1	5	0	21	0	0	0	0	75%
Box_L	0	0	0	0	0	0	37	0	0	0	100%
Box_R	0	2	0	0	0	0	0	32	0	0	94.1%
Clap	0	0	0	0	0	0	0	0	52	1	98.1%
Wav	0	0	0	0	0	0	0	0	0	45	100%

Table 2. Confusion matrix for HMM with 8 states

	Walk L	Walk R	Jog L	Jog R	Run L	Run R	Box L	Box R	Clap	Wav	
Walk_L	12	0	2	1	0	0	0	0	0	0	80.0%
Walk_R	0	19	0	2	0	0	0	0	0	0	90.5%
Jog_L	2	0	8	0	2	0	0	0	0	0	66.7%
Jog_R	0	2	0	5	0	4	0	0	0	0	45.5%
Run_L	0	0	3	0	15	0	0	0	0	0	83.3%
Run_R	0	0	0	3	0	25	0	0	0	0	89.3%
Box_L	0	0	0	0	0	0	37	0	0	0	100%
Box_R	0	0	0	0	1	0	0	33	0	0	97.1%
Clap	0	0	0	1	0	0	0	0	51	1	96.2%
Wav	0	0	0	0	0	0	0	0	1	44	97.8%

Table 3. Average recognition rate (%) of second experiment. Q is number of hidden states per chain and W context window.

	$Q = 2$	$Q = 3$	$Q = 4$	$Q = 5$	$Q = 6$	$Q = 7$	$Q = 8$	$Q = 9$	$Q = 10$
HMM	89.1	88.6	88.7	89.6	89.7	90.9	88.2	91.4	90.2
FHMM	87.9	90.2							
CHMM	81.5	83.7							
paral HMM	84.3	87.2							
mstr HMM	81.8	78.5	79.8	80.3	82.5	75.6	79.5	79.6	77.44

	$W = 0$	$W = 1$	$W = 2$
CRF	82.8	83.8	80.8

recognition approaches); for *running* cycle we only consider one step with either leg; one *boxing* cycle is defined as a punch with both fists; *clapping* a single clap; and *waving* to raising the arms and returning to the initial position. In total, 837 samples, 280 samples for testing and 560 for training. In CRFs estimation, we consider an observation context with window size $W = 1$, that is, 3 frames $(2 * W + 1)$ centered at the current observation. For HMMs, we set the number of states to 8, which corresponds to the number of frames of the shortest sequence (*running*). The new feature vectors have dimension 64 (8 *components* × 8 *tiles*).

The average recognition is 90.2% for 8-state single Gaussian HMM and 92.5% for CRF with a context $W = 1$. CRF performs 2% better than HMM. In [21] the total recognition rate of CRF over real images was 79% ($W = 0$), 81% ($W = 1$) and 82% ($W = 2$) for 7 actions , they used histograms of shape-context and edges features at different scales. We obtained higher rate with simpler features. Table 1 and table 2 shows the confusion matrix for the test with highest score using CRF and HMM respectively. We observed from table 1 that the action with smallest recognition rate is *running to the right*, which is confused with *jogging* and *walking*. We explain this by the very short recorded sequences for this action. It is worth mentioning that the two *boxing* actions, which are erroneously classified as *walking*, were recorded indoors appearing the shadow of the subject projected on the floor. The two *jogging to the left* that confuse with *walking to right*, correspond to the same person (the 15th person in KTHs database), but wearing loose clothes. Apart from these cases, the confusion matrix has a high recognition percentage for almost all the actions. It is worth to note the good score obtained on the *boxing* sequences despite the strong zoom changes. In addition, thanks to the locality introduced in the features, it is possible to distinguish oriented motions. As table 2 shows, there is more confusion for similar motions using HMMs that using CRFs. This was expected due to the higher discriminative power of the CRF models.

4.3   CRFs vs HMMs and Extensions Fed with Optical Flow

In this second experiment we compute our observation vectors from optical flow. Two observation vectors from the upper body part and/or lower body part respectively are considered. For the models with only a observation vector, HMM and FHMM, we linked both vectors into only a augmented vector.

We run experiments for all sequences of KTH´s except for scenario 2, where a viewpoint change respect to the camera is present. Videos were not segmented in activity cycles, so no-aligned sequences contains different number of cycles, depending on the person velocity, which is much more realistic. Although there exist automatic segmentation techniques based on periodicity, it imply additional computational cost and a possible error source. In total, 1987 samples are considered, 595 samples for testing and 1190 for training. For models with only a hidden state chain (HMM and Multi-Stream HMM), The number of hidden states Q was varied from 2 to 10 hidden states , and for multi-chain models (FHMM, CHMM and Parallel HMM), from 2 to 3 per chain ($Q \times Q$). For CRFs, we considered three observation context windows, $W = 0$, $W = 1$, $W = 2$, that is, $(2 * W + 1)$ frames centered at the current observation. In this case only the PCA first four components, representing about 90% of information, as considered. The vector size is 32 (4 *components* $\times$ 8 *tiles*). Table 3 shows average results.

In this case, CRF performs worse than HMM and extensions. Multi-Stream HMM. Linear HMM and FHMM are the models with the best and the next better score, 91.4% with 9 states and 90.2% with 3×3 states respectively. But to calculate two matrices $Q \times Q$ (FHMM) is more efficient than one matrix $Q^2 \times Q^2$ (HMM) [11]. CHMM performs slight worse than parallel HMM, therefore, the assumption of coupling among the dynamics of upper and lower body is not too relevant. In this case, CRF performs worse than HMM and extensions except for multi-stream HMM. It is no possible to model both observation vectors, with different dynamics, by using an only chain of hidden states. The results shows that there exist processes with different dynamics, which are independents.

5   Conclusions

We have presented a comparative study between different discriminative and generative space state classifier models, on the human action recognition task.

We have used to two well-known database of sequences to run our experiments. We conclude that CRF model performs slightly better than HMM with feature extracted from shape-contexts. HMM fails mainly because of actions with similar poses (walking, jogging and running). Using optical-flow as alternative feature, the results show a improvement using HMMs, since this model learns the hidden underlying structure in the action. We have also compared extensions of the HMMs, assuming independence between the dynamics of the upper and lower body part respectively. Here we do not exploit the flexibility of CRFs for designing new feature functions that permit to add news features and extract more meaningful information. For example, we can use to capacity of CRFs to working with complex observations and utilize overlapped tiles of different sizes, rather than uniformly sized tiles, in order to use our knowledge of human body. One possible improvement to our work would be to combine contour and optical-flow features and to weight them depending on its relevance in the specific action.

References

1. Ahmad, M., Lee, S.: Human Action Recognition Using Multi-View Image Sequence Features. In: Proc. of the 7th International Conference on Automatic Face and Gesture Recognition, pp. 523–528 (2006)
2. Bach, N.H., Shinoda, K., Furui, S.: Robust Scene Extraction Using Multi-Stream HMMs for Baseball Broadcast. IEEE Trans. on Information and Systems E89-D(9), 2553–2561 (2006)
3. Belongie, S., Malik, J.: Matching with Shape Contexts. In: IEEE Workshop on Content-Based Access of Image and Video Libraries, pp. 20–26 (2000)
4. Bobick, A.F., Ivanov, Y.A.: Action recognition using probabilistic parsing. In: Proc. of the IEEE Conf. on Computer Vision and Pattern Recognition, pp. 196–202 (1998)
5. Brand, M., Oliver, N., Pentland, A.: Coupled hidden Markov models for complex action recognition. In: Proc. of the IEEE Conf. on Computer Vision and Pattern Recognition, pp. 994–999 (1997)
6. Bregler, C.: Learning and Recognizing Human Dynamics in Video Sequences. In: Proc. of the IEEE Conf. on Computer Vision and Pattern Recognition, pp. 568–574 (1997)
7. Chen, C.H., Liang, J.M., Hu, H.H., Jiao, L.C., Yang, X.: Factorial Hidden Markov Models for Gait Recognition. In: Proc. of The 2nd International Conf. on Biometrics, pp. 124–133 (2007)
8. Connolly, C.I.: Learning to Recognize Complex Actions Using Conditional Random Fields. In: Interntional Symposium on Visual Computing, vol. 2, pp. 340–348 (2007)
9. Efros, A.A., Berg, A.C., Mori, G., Malik, J.: Recognizing Action at a Distance. In: International Conf. on Computer Vision, pp. 726–733 (2003)
10. Feng, X., Perona, P.: Human action recognition by sequence of movelet codewords. In: Proc. of 1st International Symposium on 3D Data Processing Visualization and Transmission, pp. 717–721 (2002)
11. Ghahramani, Z., Jordan, M.I.: Factorial Hidden Markov Models. Machine Learning 29(2-3), 245–273 (1997)
12. Gorelick, L., Blank, M., Shechtman, E., Irani, M., Basri, R.: Actions as Space-Time Shapes. IEEE Trans. on Pattern Analysis and Machine Intelligence 9(12), 2247–2253 (2007)

13. Lafferty, J., McCallum, A., Pereira, F.: Conditional random fields: Probabilistic models for segmenting and labeling sequence data. In: Proc. of the 18th International Conf. on Machine Learning, pp. 282–289 (2001)
14. Lucas, B.D., Kanade, T.: An Iterative Image Registration Technique with an Application to Stereo Vision. In: Proc. of Imaging Understanding Workshop, pp. 121–130 (1981)
15. Mendoza, M.A., de la Blanca, N.P.: HMM-Based Action Recognition Using Contour Histograms. In: Proc. of the 3th Iberian Conf. on Pattern Recognition and Image Analysis, pp. 394–401 (2007)
16. Morency, L.P., Quattoni, A., Darrell, T.: Latent-Dynamic Discriminative Models for Continuous Gesture Recognition. Massachussetts Institute of Technology, Computer Science and Artificial Intelligence Laboratory (CSAIL) Technical Reports (2007)
17. Morency, L.P., Quattoni, A., Christoudias, C.M., Wang, S.: Hidden-state Conditional Random Field Library. User Guide (2007)
18. Murphy, K.P.: The Bayes Net Toolbox for MATLAB. Computing Science and Statis (2001)
19. Rabiner, L.: A Tutorial on Hidden Markov Models and Selected Applications in Speech Recognition. Proceedings of the IEEE 77(2), 257–286 (1989)
20. Schuldt, C., Laptev, I., Caputo, B.: Recognizing Human Actions: a Local SVM Approach. In: Proc. of the 17th International Conf. on Pattern Recognition, vol. 3(1), pp. 32–36 (2004)
21. Sminchisescu, C., Kanaujia, A., Li, Z., Metaxas, D.: Conditional models for contextual human motion recognition. In: IEEE International Conf. on Computer Vision, vol. 2(1), pp. 1805–1808 (2005)
22. Sutton, C., McCallum, A.: An Introduction to Conditional Random Fields for Relational Learning. In: Introduction to Statistical Relational Learning. MIT Press, Cambridge (2006)
23. Vogler, C., Metaxas, D.: Parallel Hidden Markov Models for American Sign Language Recognition. In: International Conf. on Computer Vision, pp. 116–122 (1999)
24. Wang, S., Quattoni, A., Morency, L.P., Demirdjian, D., Darrel, T.: Hidden Conditional Random Fields for Gesture Recognition. In: IEEE Conf. on Computer Vision and Pattern Recognition, vol. 2(1), pp. 1521–1527 (2006)
25. Yamato, J., Ohya, J., Ishii, K.: Recognizing human action in time-sequential images using hidden Markov model. In: Proc. of the IEEE Conf. on Computer Vision and Pattern Recognition, pp. 379–385 (1992)

Bone Glow: An Improved Method for the Assignment of Weights for Mesh Deformation

Rich Wareham and Joan Lasenby

Department of Engineering, University of Cambridge,
Trumpington Street, Cambridge, CB2 1PZ, UK
{rjw57,jl221}@cam.ac.uk

Abstract. Many real-time algorithms for mesh deformation driven by animation of an underlying skeleton make use of a set of per-bone weights associated with each vertex. There are few unguided algorithms for the assignment of these weights with a recent proposed solution being *bone heat* [1]. In this paper, we briefly discuss bone heat and provide examples where it performs poorly. We then develop a refinement of bone heat, termed bone glow, which, in our validation, performed as well as bone heat in simple cases while not suffering from bone heat's observed weaknesses.

Keywords: mesh deformation, skeletal animation, bone heat, bone glow, vertex weighting, skinning, realtime, animation.

1 Introduction

The requirement to animate, in real time, on-screen characters for the computer video game industries places a number of restrictions on the mesh deformation scheme used. It must be quick to run, both in its computational requirements and its suitability for implementing on modern graphics accelerators, and quick to use. Most existing methods used in this area rely on associating a meshed surface description of a character with an armatured skeleton. This skeleton is then animated and the mesh is deformed accordingly.

In this paper we concentrate on these *skinning* schemes and, in particular, those which represent the association between skeleton and mesh as a series of weights. Each vertex has a per-bone weight giving a measure, in the range $[0, 1]$, of the influence of the particular bone on that vertex. These weights are normalised so that the sum of all per-bone weights for a particular vertex is 1.

Once assigned, these weights can be used by a number of deformation algorithms. Systems in use in the game industry include Linear Blend or Skeleton Subspace deformation [2], rotor-based deformation [3] and spherical and dual-quaternion interpolation schemes [4,5].

The actual assignment of weights, however, has traditionally been a somewhat manual affair. Existing 3D modelling applications expose the task to artists in the form of 'weight painting' operations whereby the artists 'paint' the weights for one bone onto the mesh with a virtual airbrush.

F.J. Perales and R.B. Fisher (Eds.): AMDO 2008, LNCS 5098, pp. 63–71, 2008.

Automated weight assignment techniques fall into two camps; those that require the artist to specify some parameters, such as bone size or a region of influence for a joint, and those that proceed using only the mesh surface and bone positions. The former methods are best suited to the animation and game industries which have artistic resource to use on a problem. In some cases the latter approach must be taken. A prime example of a use-case in which minimal artist input is required is the emerging field of 'user generated content' in which relatively unsophisticated users of an online service author a three-dimensional avatar representation of themselves which they expect to be animated. A method to animate such a character is given only the avatar model and user-authored skeleton and cannot rely on the user to provide sophisticated parameters about the bones.

A recent technique proposed as a suitable algorithm for this unguided skeleton-mesh association is *bone heat* [1]. This method aims to model weight assignment as a heat diffusion system on the surface of the mesh; for each bone, the vertices which have that bone as their nearest visible bone are initialised to have a surface temperature inversely proportional to the square of their closest distance to the bone. A diffusion equation is then solved to 'smear' this nearest neighbour weight assignment. This approach has a number of disadvantages, primarily that the technique aims to 'blur' an undesirable solution in the hope that it will become more acceptable.

Figure 1 illustrates the effect of incorrect bone heat weight assignment on skinning. Here, the relatively sophisticated real time dual quaternion skinning algorithm built into the Blender 3D animation software [6] was applied to weights calculated from Blender's internal implementation of bone heat. The bone heat algorithm incorrectly assigned strong weights between the arm bone and chest area leading to unacceptable distortion.

In section 2, we construct a technique which performs at least as well as bone heat in the simple cases and gives a more natural weight assignment where bone heat fails. Our technique uses a different conceptual model to that of bone heat yet generates similar results.

2   Weight Assignment

The method of bone heat solves a diffusion equation over the surface of the mesh. Specifically, for bone i, the diffusion equation solved is

$$- \Delta \mathbf{w}^i + \mathbf{H}(\mathbf{p}^i - \mathbf{w}^i) = 0 \qquad (1)$$

where Δ is the discrete surface Laplacian [7], $\mathbf{H}$ is a diagonal matrix with element H_{jj} being the heat contribution of the nearest bone to vertex j, and $\mathbf{p}^i$ is a vector where element $p^i_j = 1$ if bone i is the closest bone to vertex j and $p^i_j = 0$ otherwise. The above equation is solved for $\mathbf{w}^i$ which is a vector in which element j gives the final weight of bone i for vertex j. In [1], $\mathbf{H}$ was constructed in the following manner; if the shortest line segment joining vertex j to the nearest bone was entirely within the mesh volume, the element $H_{jj} = 1/d(j)^2$ with $d(j)$

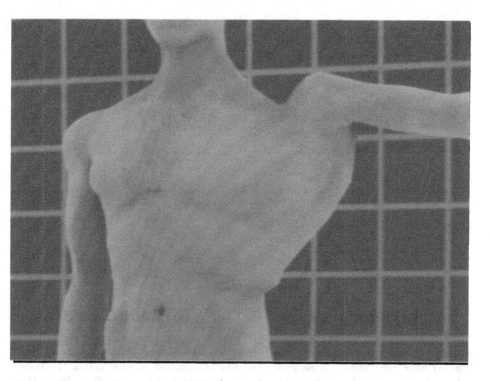

Fig. 1. An example of bone heat failing to correctly assign weights to an arm bone causing obvious distortion in the chest even when a more sophisticated skinning scheme (dual quaternions) is used

being the shortest distance from vertex j to the closest bone. If the shortest line segment was not within the mesh volume, $H_{jj} = 0$.

The bone heat algorithm in effect calculated two sets of weights; an initial set, $\mathbf{p}^i$, is calculated based upon a nearest visible bone solution. This initial set is then refined, or 'blurred' via the diffusion equation above. Such a scheme has merits in terms of the 'natural' results the blurring gives but suffers from artifacts arising from this implicit initial solution step. An item of note, shown in fig. 2, is the over-weighting of the arm bone in the chest area. The tip of the arm bone is visible to many of the vertices which make up much of the side of the chest. It is also closer than the upper back bone which, arguably, should be the bone exerting the greatest influence. Using just this nearest-bone initial solution leads to highly displeasing results which the diffusion step must attempt to mitigate.

The nature of bone heat's initial solution leads to its poor performance in certain cases, especially in the common arm/chest joint case. We aim to modify bone heat so that this initial solution is closer to an acceptable solution thereby relying on the diffusion step only as a post processing operation to increase the smoothness of the final result.

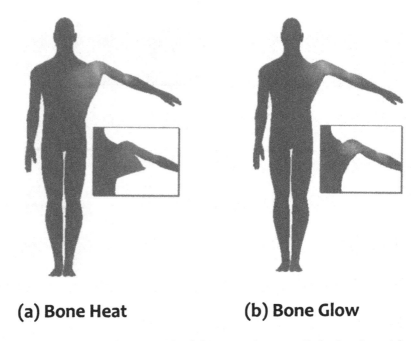

(a) Bone Heat   **(b) Bone Glow**

Fig. 2. A comparison of a simple linear blend skinning scheme applied using the weights from a) bone heat and b) bone glow. The weight assigned to each vertex has been indicated using a gradation from blue to red to indicate the range $[0, 1]$. Inset: the solutions without applying a diffusion step.

Our approach will be to define an initial weighting which is not binary for each bone/vertex pair but is instead smooth over the boundaries between the regions of influence of each bone. We then feed this result into the diffusion solver in place of the vector $\mathbf{p}^i$ in eqn. 1.

We calculate a per-vertex influence for each bone by computing the amount of incident light which each vertex receives from the bone under consideration. For this we use an adaptation of the classic lighting integral. To calculate the incident illumination on vertex j from bone i we integrate along the length of the bone calculating the contribution of each point along the bone. Specifically, the illumination, L_j^i, received by vertex j from bone i is given by

$$L_j^i = l^i \int_0^1 l^i V_j^i(\lambda)\, R_j^i(\lambda)\, T_j^i(\lambda)\, d\lambda \qquad (2)$$

where l^i is the length of bone i and λ is a normalised co-ordinate along the bone with $\lambda = 0$ being the root of the bone and $\lambda = 1$ being the tip. Each of the terms within the integral represents a different factor in the lighting equation. The $V_j^i(\lambda)$ term is a simple binary function representing the visibility of the bone; if the point at λ on bone i is visible from vertex j then $V_j^i(\lambda) = 1$ and $V_j^i(\lambda) = 0$ otherwise. The $R_j^i(\lambda)$ term gives the proportion of illumination received by vertex

j from the point λ along bone i assuming that the bone is visible. The $T_j^i(\lambda)$ term gives the proportion of illumination transmitted from the point λ along bone i in the direction of vertex j.

There exist well known models for the $R_j^i(\lambda)$ and $T_j^i(\lambda)$ terms which we shall cover below, but first we shall explain the notation used. The location of vertex j, relative to a fixed world frame, is given by the vector $\mathbf{v}_j$. Similarly the normal to the surface at vertex j is parallel to the unit vector $\hat{\mathbf{n}}_j$. The point on the bone i at normalised co-ordinate λ is represented by the vector $\mathbf{b}_\lambda^i$ and the axis of bone i is parallel to the unit vector $\hat{\mathbf{a}}_i$. Finally, we define $\mathbf{d}_j^i(\lambda) \equiv \mathbf{v}_j - \mathbf{b}_\lambda^i$. Using the notation $||\cdot||$ to mean 'length of', we also define the unit vector $\hat{\mathbf{d}}_j^i(\lambda) \equiv ||\mathbf{d}_j^i(\lambda)||^{-1}\mathbf{d}_j^i(\lambda)$.

To model the received illumination we use a Lambertian falloff; the proportion of incident illumination received is the cosine of the incident angle. We can compute this via the dot product between the incident illumination direction and the vertex normal:

$$R_j^i(\lambda) = \frac{\max\left(\hat{\mathbf{d}}_\lambda^i \cdot \hat{\mathbf{n}}_j, 0\right)}{||\mathbf{d}_j^i(\lambda)||^2} \tag{3}$$

where we have suppressed, via the max() function, all light which is received along a path which does not come from within the mesh. In addition we have imposed a quadratic falloff of incident illumination consistent with a local source of light.

The proportion of illumination transmitted from the bone is modelled as falling off as the sine of transmission angle. That is to say that we assume no light is transmitted parallel to the bone and the maximum transmission is perpendicular to the bone axis. We choose the sine function since it may easily be calculated via a cross product:

$$T_j^i(\lambda) = ||\hat{\mathbf{d}}_\lambda^i \times \hat{\mathbf{a}}^i|| \tag{4}$$

Substituting these relations into (2) gives the final illumination integral:

$$L_j^i = l^i \int_0^1 V_j^i(\lambda) \, \frac{\max\left(\hat{\mathbf{d}}_\lambda^i \cdot \hat{\mathbf{n}}_j, 0\right)}{||\mathbf{d}_\lambda||^2} \, ||\hat{\mathbf{d}}_\lambda^i \times \hat{\mathbf{a}}^i|| \, d\lambda \ . \tag{5}$$

Once the lighting calculation has been performed, an initial set of weights are calculated for each bone. These are used in place of the binary vector $\mathbf{p}^i$ in the diffusion equation above. To ensure a normalised set of initial weights, the j-th element of this initialisation vector is computed as $p_j^i = L_j^i / \sum_i L_j^i$.

Figure 2 shows, as an inset figure, the result of using these initial weights directly. These initial weights, although crude, are already suitable for use in skinning as opposed to the bone heat initial weights which lead to unacceptable levels of mesh distortion.

Bone Heat   **Bone Glow**

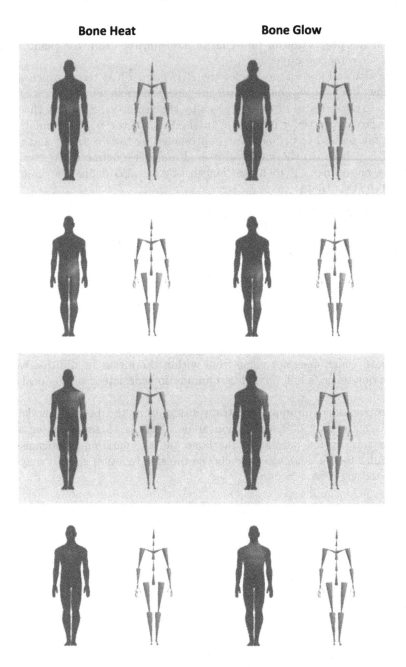

Fig. 3. A side-by-side comparison of bone heat and bone glow applied to a human mesh. In each sub figure, a particular bone has been highlighted and the weight assigned to each vertex has been indicated as in Fig. 2.

Bone Heat   **Bone Glow**

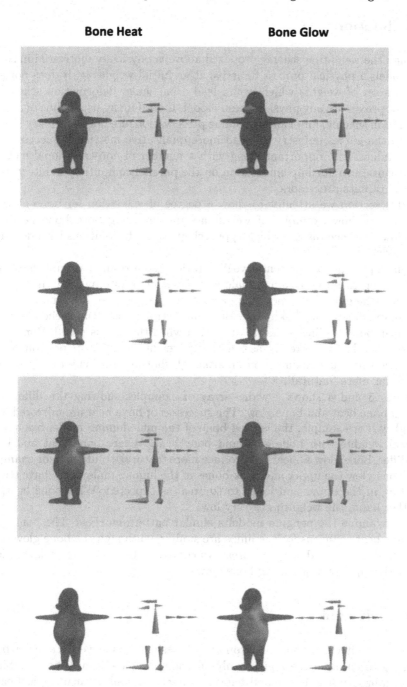

Fig. 4. A side-by-side comparison of bone heat and bone glow applied to a penguin mesh. In each sub figure, a particular bone has been highlighted and the weight assigned to each vertex has been indicated as in Fig. 2.

3   Validation

Although the weighting scheme proposed above is physically motivated in so far
as it models a physical process to arrive at an initial weighting, it does not aim
to form a set of weights which would lead a particular deformation scheme to
closely approximate any physical mesh model. Indeed many usual aims of a mesh
deformation scheme, for example volume preservation, are not of primary importance to the games industry. Instead more qualitative metrics of success, such
as 'naturalness' are important along with a number of non-traditional metrics,
such as suitability for implementation on the parallel computing architecture of
modern graphics processors.

In this section we attempt to show a degree of validation for bone glow by
example; we show examples of weight assignment using both bone heat and
bone glow. We then discuss which approach gives rise to solutions with desirable
characteristics.

Figure 2 provides a representative illustration of our results; a simple mesh and
armature representing a human male were associated automatically using bone
heat and bone glow. The underlying armature was posed and the mesh skinned
using simple linear blend skinning. Bone heat strongly associates the chest and
upper arm bone leading to severe distortion when the arm is posed. Bone glow,
on the other hand, correctly assigns most weight to the arm portion of the
mesh. The subsequent skinned mesh, although showing some chest deformation,
appears far more 'natural'.

Figures 3 and 4 shows a wider array of examples showing the differences
between bone heat and bone glow. The successes of bone heat are mirrored with
bone glow. For example, the left leg bone of the male human model has almost
identical weights with bone glow and bone heat. Where bone heat and bone
glow differ, bone glow appears to produce more 'natural' solutions. For example,
using bone glow the upper and back bones of the human male figure have strong
weighting in the upper and lower torso area, as expected. With bone heat, on
the other hand, the weighting is very low.

If we examine the penguin model a similar pattern emerges. The bone glow
and bone heat solutions for the limbs are similar—although the bone glow solution is 'tighter' around the joint areas. In contrast, the back and beak solutions
are clearly superior when using bone glow.

4   Conclusions

We have presented a method for automatically assigning a per-vertex and per-bone
weighting to an input mesh given only an underlying skeleton. When combined
with an appropriate weight-based deformation scheme it allows an unsophisticated
user to rapidly go from a self-authored model and skeleton to animating that model
in a natural manner.

In the current implementation, the lighting integral is calculated numerically
by stepping along the bone calculating the integrand at each point and summing

the results. Given a suitable approximation for the visibility function this integral could be approximated with an analytic result speeding up the computation considerably.

Acknowledgements. This research was supported by funding from Geomerics Ltd and the UK Department of Trade and Industry. We thank Andrew Kator and Jennifer Legaz for licensing the male human and tux meshes used within this paper under a Creative Commons Attribution 3.0 United States License.

References

1. Baran, I., Popović, J.: Automatic rigging and animation of 3D characters. ACM Transactions on Graphics 26(3) (2007)
2. Lewis, J.P., Cordner, M., Fong, N.: Pose space deformation: a unified approach to shape interpolation and skeleton-driven deformation. In: SIGGRAPH 2000: Proceedings of the 27th annual conference on Computer graphics and interactive techniques, New York, NY, USA, pp. 165–172. ACM Press/Addison-Wesley Publishing Co. (2000)
3. Wareham, R.: Computer Graphics Using Conformal Geometric Algebra. PhD thesis, University of Cambridge (January 2007)
4. Kavan, L., Collins, S., Žára, J., O'Sullivan, C.: Skinning with dual quaternions. In: I3D 2007: Proceedings of the 2007 symposium on Interactive 3D graphics and games, pp. 39–46. ACM, New York (2007)
5. Kavan, L., Žára, J.: Spherical blend skinning: a real-time deformation of articulated models. In: I3D 2005: Proceedings of the 2005 symposium on Interactive 3D graphics and games, pp. 9–16. ACM, New York (2005)
6. The Blender project, http://www.blender.org/
7. Meyer, M., Desbrun, M., Schröder, P., Baar, A.H.: Discrete differential-geometry operators for triangulated 2-manifolds. In: Hege, H.C., Polthier, K. (eds.) Visualization and Mathematics III, pp. 35–57. Springer, Heidelberg (2003)

Analysis of Human Motion, Based on the Reduction of Multidimensional Captured Data – Application to Hand Gesture Compression, Segmentation and Synthesis

Sylvie Gibet[1] and Pierre-François Marteau[2]

[1] IRISA/Bunraku, Campus of Beaulieu, F-35042 Rennes Cedex
[2] VALORIA, University of Bretagne Sud, Campus de Tohannic, BP 573,
F-56017 Vannes Cedex
sylvie.gibet@irisa.fr, pierre-francois.marteau@univ-ubs.fr

Abstract. This paper describes a method to analyze human motion, based on the reduction of multidimensional captured motion data. A Dynamic Programming Piecewise Linear Approximation model is used to automatically extract in an optimal way key-postures distributed along the motion data. This non uniform sub-sampling can be exploited for motion compression, segmentation, or re-synthesis. It has been applied on arm end-point motion for 3D or 6D trajectories. The analysis method is then evaluated, using an approximation of the curvature and the tangential velocity, which turns out to be robust to noise and can be calculated on multidimensional data.

1 Introduction

The representation and the thorough understanding of human motion is a crucial and challenging problem which has been raised in many scientific areas, including animation of virtual characters, analysis of motor performances in sport motion and for disabled people. In recent years, the huge development of new technologies for motion capture has made the analysis of human motion feasible, and yielded data-based methods for gesture analysis, retrieval, and computer-generated animation.

One major problem in representing gesture from recorded data is that these data are multidimensional and direct use of them is rather expensive and fastidious. Another problem is the lack of flexibility. Computing motion from real motion chunks necessitates indeed the elaboration of large data sets, and the development of data-driven methods for tracking, adapting or generating new motion. Finally, finding the best motion representation is a central problem, depending on the application. As these processes operate on multidimensional data, one way to characterize gesture is to compress the original information into relevant samples and to use this data reduction to efficiently retrieve or reconstruct the motion, or to identify meaningful motion units. The automatic extraction of key frames (postures or key points) is also an efficient way to synthesize new gestures, which takes into account the spatial variability of gestures and the co-articulation effects.

In this paper we consider motion captured data consisting of sampled trajectories that characterize the evolution with time of the position and orientation of the human joints.

F.J. Perales and R.B. Fisher (Eds.): AMDO 2008, LNCS 5098, pp. 72–81, 2008.

For human gestures, these joint trajectories present specific profiles that can be readable through the analysis of shape (curvature) and kinematics (velocity). In particular variations in velocity are responsible for the aggregation of samples in some areas of the trajectories. We propose here to study both these spatial and cinematic characteristics in a reduced representation space. We use an adaptive sub-sampling algorithm, called DPPLA (Dynamic Programming Piecewise Linear Approximation), which identifies in an optimal manner a set of targets located on the trajectories. This target-based representation of trajectories is applied to automatic segmentation of 3D arm end-point trajectories and to motion reconstruction using inverse kinematics. An evaluation process is defined, using an approximation of the curvature and velocity along the motion sequences. We show that these approximations are strongly correlated to curvature and tangential velocity, not only in the 3D space, but in multi dimensional space. These measures provide a way to automatically analyse gestures. Furthermore, the method can then be extended to multidimensional motion trajectories.

The paper is mainly composed of six sections. Section 2 gives an overview of the related works. After describing in section 3 the adaptive non uniform sampling algorithm (DPPLA) used for data reduction, section 4 proposes an analysis method using an approximation of curvature and velocity. Section 5 presents some results related to segmentation of 3D arm end-point trajectories and the way the obtained segments may be used for synthesis. The paper concludes and gives some perspectives in section 6.

2 Related Works

Numerous techniques have been developed for the analysis of human motion captured data. These studies differ considerably, whether the emphasis is placed on data reduction for retrieval, segmentation, recognition, or synthesis purposes.

There are many different mathematical approaches for curves and surfaces approximations, which tend to reduce the dimensionality of the motion data. Few works concern motion trajectories. Polygonal approximation provides characteristics points to represent the shape of the trajectory. These points, which correspond to local curvature extrema, can be connected by line segments. This method has been used by [1] for non-uniform sub-sampling of motion time-series. Another method proposes curve approximation using active contours [2]. These methods are developed for dance gesture recognition.

Other methods have been proposed to the problem of approximating multidimensional curves using piecewise linear simplification and dynamic programming in $O(kn^2)$ complexity [3]. Some efficient algorithms [3-4] (in $O(nlog(n))$ complexity) have been proposed.

The objective in this paper is not so much to find out the best data reduction method, but to define an adaptive method with a pre-defined compression rate that can be applied to multidimensional data. Moreover, we propose an analysis tool, expressed in the reduced space by measures that approximate the curvature and the velocity of motion trajectories.

3   Non Uniform Sampling Algorithm (DPPLA)

The motion consists of raw data composed of 3D Cartesian trajectories, each trajectory representing the evolution with time of one coordinate x, y, or z expressing the position of a specific joint. For our study, we consider $X(t)$ as constituted of time-series in $3.p$ dimensions, represented by spatial vectors $X(t) = [x_1(t), y_1(t), z_1(t)\ x_2(t), y_2(t), z_2(t)... x_p(t), y_p(t), z_p(t)]$. In practice, we deal with sampled trajectories at a constant frequency of 120 Hz: $X(n)$ where n is the time-stamp index.

The approach consists in seeking an approximation $x_{\hat\theta}$ of $X(n)$, θ being the set of discrete time location $\{n_i\}$ of the segments endpoints. The selection of the optimal set of parameters $\hat\theta = \{\hat n_i\}$ is performed using the adaptive dynamic programming presented below.

Let us define $\theta(k)$ as the parameters of a piece wise approximation containing k segments, and $\delta(k,i)$ as the minimal error between the best piecewise linear approximation containing k segments and covering the discrete time window $\{1,..,i\}$:

$$\delta(k,i) = \underset{\theta(k)}{Min}\left\{\sum_{n=1}^{i}\left\|X_{\theta(k)}(n) - X(n)\right\|^2\right\}$$

$\delta(k,i)$ can be decomposed as follows:

$$\delta(k,i) = \underset{n_k \le i}{Min}\left\{d(n_k,i) + \delta(k-1,n_k)\right\}$$

$$where \quad d(n_k,i) = \sum_{n=n_k}^{i}\left\|Y_{k,i}(n) - X(n)\right\|^2$$

$$and \quad Y_{k,i} = (X(i) - X(n_k)).\frac{n-n_k}{i-n_k} + X(n_k)$$

The end of the recursion gives the optimal piecewise linear approximation, e.g. the set of discrete time locations of the extremity of the linear segments:

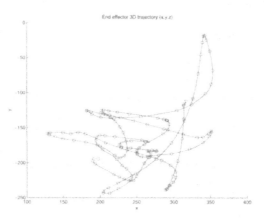

Fig. 1. Approximation of the end-point trajectory using the non uniform sampling algorithm

The result of this method is the optimal identification of discrete X_{Ti} key-points – we call them spatial targets – delimitating the segments, for a given compression rate. The complexity of the algorithm is $O(n^2/k)$ where n is the number of samples, and k the number of segments, but can be decreased down to $O(n)$ if optimality is somehow relaxed [6].

An example of the application of the algorithm on 3D arm end-point data is illustrated in figure 1.

4 Approximation of Curvature and Velocity Using DPPLA Model

First of all we worked on 3D end point trajectories $X(t) = [x(t), y(t), z(t)]$, the coordinates being calculated in the shoulder frame. For any smooth trajectory parameterized with t, we expressed the instantaneous velocity $v(t)$ and the absolute value of the instantaneous curvature $\kappa(t)$:

$$v(t) = \left\| \dot{X}(t) \right\| = \sqrt{\dot{x}^2 + \dot{y}^2 + \dot{z}^2} \tag{1}$$

$$\kappa = \frac{\left\| \dot{X}(t) \times \ddot{X}(t) \right\|}{\left\| \dot{X}(t) \right\|^3} \quad and \quad R(t) = \frac{1}{|\kappa|} \tag{2}$$

where R is the radius of curvature. The curvature measures how fast a curve is changing direction at a given point.

These variables have been extensively studied for a variety of goal-directed experimental tasks. In particular, a number of regularities have been empirically observed for end-point trajectories of the human upper-limb, during 2D drawing movements.

However, for 3D movements with great spatial and temporal variations, it can be difficult to directly extract significant features from these signals. Moreover, computing the radius of curvature raises a problem, when the velocity is too high, or when there are inflexion points in the trajectories. In particular for noisy data the radius of curvature may be difficult to compute. Finally, for higher dimensions, the curvature is not defined, prohibiting its use in the angular space in particular.

We propose to approximate these velocity and curvature by empirical measures calculated from the adaptive samples identified through the *DPPLA* algorithm. We define the target-based velocity by the expression:

$$V_{T_{gi}}(n_i) = \frac{\left\| X(n_{i+1}) - X(n_{i-1}) \right\|}{n_{i+1} - n_{i-1}} \tag{3}$$

where n_{i+1} and n_{i-1} are temporal indices of the associated targets Tg_{i+1} and Tg_{i-1}.

As the targets are not regularly located, the addition effect of this measure, homogeneous to a velocity, is to filter the raw data. The filtering depends on the compression rate.

We define also the inverse distance between adjacent targets as:

$$\kappa_{T_{gi}}(n_i) = \frac{1}{\left\| X(n_i) - X(n_{i-1}) \right\|} \tag{4}$$

With this formulation, we assume that this last quantity might be linked to a measure of aggregation points on the trajectory: when the movement velocity decreases, the distance between original samples decreases and the curvature appears to be important. Therefore, $\kappa_{Td}(n_i)$ expresses a spatial quantity which might be correlated to curvature at time-index n_i.

This approximation has been experimented on arm end-point motion. Raw data are first filtered by a low pass Butterworth filter with a cutoff frequency of 10.0 Hz. We consider sequences of about 10000 frames.

The analysis of correlation is achieved, on the one hand between the log of target-based velocity and the log of its instantaneous value, and on the other hand between the inverse of the distance between targets and the instantaneous curvature. The results concerning the velocity are shown in figure 2 (left). They illustrate an excellent correlation between the two variables, thus allowing us to use target-based velocity as a good approximation of instantaneous velocity. We may also compute the acceleration of arm end-point trajectories on the basis of this target-based velocity.

The correlation between the log of the inverse target distances and the log of its instantaneous curvature is also very good, as illustrated in figure 2 (right). The points with abrupt changes are located at the same place, but the target-based signal seems less noisy than the original one. This makes possible to approximate curvature as the inverse of target density.

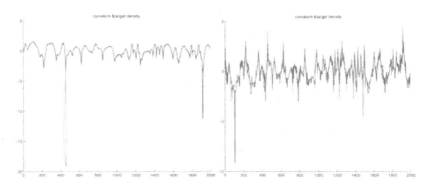

Fig. 2. Correlation for 3D end-point trajectories of arm movements; left: correlation between target-based velocity (black) and instantaneous tangential velocity (red); right: correlation between target density (black) and instantaneous curvature (red);

For each signal x, we computed: $(\log(x) - \text{mean}(\log(x)))/\text{std}(\log(x))$

The influence of the compression factor characterizing the adaptive sampling algorithm is analyzed at the light of the correlation coefficient. The results can be seen in figure 3. It shows that for the target-based velocity, the correlation coefficient remains very close to 1, independently of the compression rate (from 50% to 95%). For the target-based acceleration, the correlation coefficient is very good (0.9), for a compression rate varying until 70%. Beyond this limit, the correlation coefficient abruptly falls. The correlation coefficient is lower for the inverse distance, but still high (.85), even for a high compression rate (until 80%). These results support the assumption that target-based variables can be used without a significant loss of data for the analysis of 3D end-point trajectories.

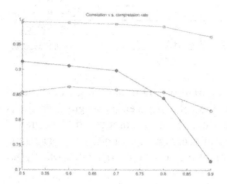

Fig. 3. Correlation coefficient versus compression rate of the adaptive sampling algorithm; (circle): curvature vs. inverse target distance; (star): acceleration vs. target based acceleration; (square): tangential velocity vs. target based velocity

5   Gesture Segmentation and Data-Driven Synthesis

In this section, we explain how the non uniform sampling algorithm as well as the derived target-based cinematic measures (curvature and velocity) can be applied to both the automatic segmentation of gestures and the data-driven synthesis of gestures.

5.1   Segmentation

Studies on gesture [7] showed that human gestures can be segmented into distinct phases. Some researches assumed that objective measures can be used to segment hand movement. In particular, Kita et al. showed that abrupt changes of direction, accompanied by a velocity discontinuity indicate phase boundaries in hand trajectories. These observations have been exploited by [8], who proposed a new distance metric to detect phase boundaries, based on the sign of the first and second derivatives of endpoint trajectories. The analysis method described above can be used for automatically segmenting the 3D arm motion. Moreover, it can be used for a compact gesture representation and for data-driven synthesis.

Our segmentation is based on the observation that phase boundaries might occur when the radius of curvature becomes very small, and the velocity decreases at the same time, indicating a change of direction. The segmentation algorithm is based on the product variable $v(t).\kappa(t)$, and on its approximation, based on the approximated target-based variables : $v_{Tgi}(n_i).\kappa_{Tgi}(n_i)$.

A color-coding method allows us to quantify the variations of the variable, according to an equally distribution of its values. The meaning of this coding is presented in table 1.

Table 1. Coding values for the color coding

coding	Variable values	Interpretation
black	---	lowest values
blue	--	very low values
cyan	-	low values
green	0	average values
yellow	+	high values
magenta	++	very high values
red	+++	highest values

The color-coding is reported on 3D trajectories, as can be seen in figure 4. When the velocity is very low, the color is green (clear gray). In the contrary, when the velocity is high and the curvature low, the color is red (dark gray). The level of quantification indicates the size of the segmental units. A great similarity can be observed between the segmentation of the curve $v(t).\kappa(t)$ and $v_{Tgi}(n_i).\kappa_{Tgi}(n_i)$ (see figure 4 left and right).

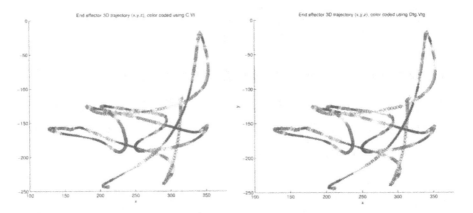

Fig. 4. Example of end-point trajectories segmentation (in the xy plane) using a color-coding of quantified variables (different gray levels); left: segmentation using the product $\kappa(t).v(t)$; right: segmentation using the product $\kappa_{Tgi}(t).v_{Tgi}(t)$; A great similarity between the two sequences can be observed.

5.2 Gesture Synthesis by Inverse Kinematics

When applied to 3D end-point trajectories (hand motion), the discrete representation which is provided by the *DPPLA* algorithm gives a non uniform flow of 3D targets. Figure 5 shows the distribution of targets along the gesture sequence (top). The reconstruction error between the sub-sampled trajectory and the original one is shown on figure 5 (bottom).

These targets can be directly used as input of an animation engine which automatically computes the angular parameters of the articulated chain, given the end-extremity position. This kinematics inversion process can be achieved in two ways, as illustrated in Figure 6.

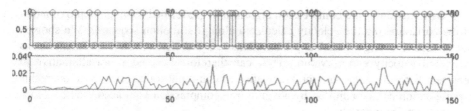

Fig. 5. (top) Motion separation points assigned by the DPPLA algorithm. The x-axis corresponds to the frame number, and the vertical bars specify the target points assigned by the algorithm; (bottom) Reconstruction error between target-based and simulated trajectory.

The first method consists in reconstructing the trajectory from the non uniform target flow, and then using a classical inverse kinematics (IK) [9, 10] model through a tracking process (Fig. 6 (left)). The reconstruction can be simply achieved by linear or cubic interpolation.

The second method directly uses discrete time-stamped targets, which are fed into a GSMM controller [12, 13]. These controllers provide a means of dealing with co-articulation. In the near future we intend to evaluate the quality of the produced movements according to specific compression rates and to compare the two methods.

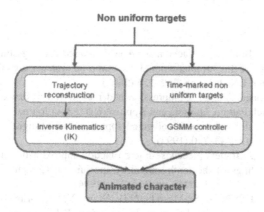

Fig. 6. Synthesis from non uniform targets, using a classical IK algorithm (left), or an adaptive GSMM controller (right)

6 Conclusion and Future Work

This paper presented a method for analyzing human motion based on an adaptive sub-sampling technique that leads to reduce multidimensional data. This technique extracts discrete target patterns from raw data, for a given compression rate. From a 3D trajectory, we showed that the target-based trajectory can be reconstructed while keeping the main spatial and cinematic characteristics of the original trajectory.

The evaluation of the compression algorithm is performed using an approximation of the curvature and the velocity calculated along the motion sequence. We showed indeed that the target-based approximations are correlated with the instantaneous tangential velocity and curvature. They can therefore be used as an alternative to represent both the shape and the kinematics of end-point trajectories. Moreover, this representation can be adjusted by adapting the compression rate, according to its influence on the correlation.

This method has proved to be efficient for 3D or 6D arm-trajectories. It is therefore an interesting method for the analysis of multidimensional data. These empirical approximations provide a significant way to automatically segment gestures. The measure that we propose, characterized by the product of the target-based velocity by the target-based curvature, gives us an original means of delimitating segments which depends on our algorithm parameterization (compression rate). A study in progress intends to determine how this automatic segmentation might help a manual segmentation process for communication gestures.

The sub-sampling of the end-point trajectory also provides a way to reduce the information flow entering an inverse kinematics process. In the near future, we will show how to exploit this sub-sampling to deal with spatial variability and co-articulation inherent to motion.

References

1. Chenevière, F., Boukir, S., Vachon, B.: A HMM-based dance gesture recognition system. In: Proceedings of the 9th international workshop on systems, signals and image processing, Manchester, UK, June, pp. 322–326 (2002)
2. Boukir, S., Chenevière, F.: Compression and recognition of dance gestures using a deformable model. Pattern Analysis and Applications (PAA) Journal 7(3), 308–316 (2004)
3. Perez, J.C., Vidal, E.: Optimum polygonal approximation of digitized curves. Pattern Recognition Letters 15, 743–750 (1994)
4. Goodrich, M.T.: Efficient piecewise-linear function approximation using the uniform metric. In: Proceedings of the tenth annual symposium on Computational geometry Stony Brook, New York, United States, pp. 322–331 (1994)
5. Agarwal, P.K., Har-Peled, S., Mustafa, N.H., Wang, Y.: Near-Linear Time Approximation Algorithms for Curve Simplification. In: Möhring, R.H., Raman, R. (eds.) ESA 2002. LNCS, vol. 2461, pp. 29–41. Springer, Heidelberg (2002)
6. Marteau, P.F., Ménier, G.: Adaptive multiresolution and dedicated elastic matching in linear time complexity for time series data mining. In: Sixth International Conference on Intelligent Systems Design and Applications, IEEE ISDA 2006, Jinan Shandong, China, October 16-18, 2006, vol. 1, pp. 700–706 (2006)
7. Kita, S., van Gijn, I., van der Hulst, H.: Movement phase in signs and co-speech gestures, and their transcriptions by human coders. In: Wachsmuth, I., Fröhlich, M. (eds.) GW 1997. LNCS (LNAI), vol. 1371, pp. 23–35. Springer, Heidelberg (1998)
8. Majkowska, A., Zordan, V., Faloutsos, P.: Automatic slicing for hand and body animations. In: Cani, M.P., O'Brien, J. (eds.) Eurographics/ ACM SIGGRAPH Symposium on Computer Animation, pp. 1–8 (2006)

9. Chi, D., Costa, M., Zhao, L., Badler, N.: The EMOTE model for Effort and Shape. In: ACM SIGGRAPH 2000, New Orleans, LA, pp. 173–182 (2000)
10. Carvalho, S., Boulic, R., Thalmann: Interactive Low-Dimensional Human Motion Synthesis by Combining Motion Models and PIK. Journal of Computer Animation and Virtual Worlds 18, 493–503 (2007)
11. Gibet, S., Marteau, P.F.: A self-organised model for the control, planning and learning of nonlinear multivariable systems using a sensori- feedback. Journal of Applied Intelligence 4, 337–349 (1994)
12. Gibet, S., Marteau, P.F.: Expressive Gesture Animation Based on Non Parametric Learning of Sensory-Motor Models. In: CASA 2003, IEEE Computer Animation and Social Agents, pp. 79–85 (2003)

Exploiting Structural Hierarchy in Articulated Objects Towards Robust Motion Capture

C. Canton-Ferrer, J.R. Casas, and M. Pardàs

Technical University of Catalonia, Barcelona, Spain
{ccanton,josep,montse}@gps.tsc.upc.es

Abstract. This paper presents a general analysis framework towards exploiting the underlying hierarchical and scalable structure of an articulated object for pose estimation and tracking. The Scalable Human Body Model (SHBM) is presented as a set of human body models ordered following a hierarchy criteria. The concept of annealing is applied to derive a generic particle filtering scheme able to perform a sequential filtering over the models contained in the SHBM leading to a *structural annealing* process. This scheme is applied to perform human motion capture in a multi-camera environment. Finally, the effectiveness of the proposed system is addressed by comparing its performance with the standard and annealed particle filtering approaches over an annotated database.

1 Introduction

Automatic capture and analysis of human motion is a highly active research area due both to the number of potential applications and its inherent complexity. This research area contains a number of hard and often ill-posed problems such as inferring the pose and motion of a highly articulated and self-occluding non-rigid 3D object from a set of images. Applications of motion analysis range from gesture recognition or gait analysis to medical applications and human-computer interfaces.

Recovering the pose of an articulated structure such as the human body involves estimating highly dimensional and multi-modal statistic distributions. Monte Carlo based techniques [1] have been thoroughly applied due to its ability to perform this task with an affordable computational complexity. Particle filtering [5] has been the seminal idea to develop specific systems aiming at recovering human body pose such as the annealed particle filter [3], the hierarchical sampling [8] or the partitioned sampling [6] among others. A main characteristic of these approaches is a human body model that is selected beforehand and fitted to the input data. This paper presents a general analysis framework that exploits the underlying hierarchical and scalable structure of an articulated object by using a scalable human body model together with an annealed particle filtering strategy. A sequential fitting is performed over a set of human body models with increasing level of detail by applying the concept of *structural annealing*. Indeed, some of the aforementioned tracking schemes may be considered as particular cases of our general framework.

F.J. Perales and R.B. Fisher (Eds.): AMDO 2008, LNCS 5098, pp. 82–91, 2008.

The proposed scheme is applied to recover and track human body pose in a multi-camera scenario. However, instead of performing our measures on each input image, our system first generates a 3D voxel-based representation of the person, and then performs the matching of the kinematic models directly in this 3D space. Finally, the efficiency of the proposed system is addressed by analyzing a set of sequences from the HumanEva-I database [4] and comparing the results with the standard and annealed particle filtering approaches.

2   Monte Carlo Based Tracking

The evolution of a physical articulated structure can be better captured with model-based tracking techniques. The articulated structure can be fully described by a state vector $\mathcal{X} \in \mathbb{R}^D$ that we wish to estimate. From a Bayesian perspective, the articulated motion estimation and tracking problem is to recursively estimate a certain degree of belief in the state vector $\mathcal{X}_t$ at time t, given the data $\mathcal{Z}_{1:t}$ up to time t. Thus, it is required to calculate the *pdf* $p(\mathcal{X}_t|\mathcal{Z}_{1:t})$.

Particle Filtering (PF) [1] algorithms are sequential Monte Carlo methods based on point mass (or "particle") representations of probability densities. These techniques are employed to tackle estimation and tracking problems where the variables involved do not hold Gaussianity uncertainty models and linear dynamics. PF expresses the belief about the system at time t by approximating the posterior distribution $p(x_t|\mathcal{Z}_{1:t})$, $x_t \in \mathcal{X}$, and representing it by a *weighted particle set* $\{(x, \pi)_j\}_t$, $1 \le j \le N_p$. In this paper, a Sample Importance Re-sampling (SIR) based strategy is adopted to drive particles along time.

PF is an appropriate technique to deal with problems where the posterior distribution is multimodal. To maintain a fair representation of $p(x_t|\mathcal{Z}_{1:t})$, a certain number of particles are required in order to find its global maxima instead of a local one. It has been proved in [6] that the amount of particles required by a standard PF algorithm [5] to achieve a successful tracking follows an exponential law with the number of dimensions. Articulated motion tracking typically employs state spaces with dimension $D \sim 25$ thus normal PF turns out to be computationally unfeasible.

There exist several possible strategies to reduce the complexity of the problem based on refinements and variations of the seminal PF idea. MacCormick et al. [6] presented partitioned sampling as a highly efficient solution to this problem. However, this technique imposes a linear hierarchy of sampling which may not be related to the true body structure assuming certain statistical independence among state variables. Hierarchical sampling presented by Mitchelson et al. [8] tackles the dimension problem by exploiting the human body structure and hierarchically explore the state space. Finally, annealed PF presented by Deutscher et al. [3] is one of the most general solutions to the problem of dimensionality. This technique employs a simulated annealing strategy to concentrate the particles around the peaks of the likelihood function.

(a)   (b)

Fig. 1. Examples of inclusive Scalable Human Body Models. In (a), the refinement hierarchy model and, in (b), the construction model.

3 Scalable Human Body Model

A Human Body Model (HBM) $\mathcal{H}$ is employed to define a meaningful relation among the parameters contained in $\mathcal{X}$. This HBM mimics the structure of the skeleton representing it by a chain of rigid bodies (links) interconnected to one other by joints. The number of independent parameters will define the *degrees of freedom* (DoF) associated to a given HBM. HBMs employed in the literature range from simple configurations involving few DoF [2] to highly detailed models with up to 25 DoF [3]. A Scalable Human Body Model (SHBM) can be defined as a set of HBM:

$$\mathcal{M} = \{\mathcal{H}_0, \cdots, \mathcal{H}_i, \cdots, \mathcal{H}_{M-1}\}, \qquad (1)$$

where the sub-index denotes an order within $\mathcal{M}$. To achieve scalability, a hierarchy among the elements of $\mathcal{M}$ must be defined. A criteria that grants hierarchy to the elements $\mathcal{H}_i$ in $\mathcal{M}$ is the inclusion condition:

$$\mathcal{H}_i \subset \mathcal{H}_j, \qquad i < j, \qquad (2)$$

where the inclusion operation can be understood in terms of the detail or information provided by each model. This information measure is a design parameter and can be defined, for instance, as the number of joints/links, DoF, etc. Two examples of the inclusion operation are the refinement and constructive model. In the first one, depicted in Fig.1a, a model in a higher hierarchy level refines the one in the lower level by adding new limbs to it. In the constructive model, depicted in Fig.1b, segments are progressively added to all limbs until reaching the most detailed HBM.

4 Hierarchical Structure Based Annealed Particle Filtering (HS-APF)

4.1 Theory

This papers presents a general analysis framework towards exploiting the underlying hierarchical structure of an articulated object for pose estimation and

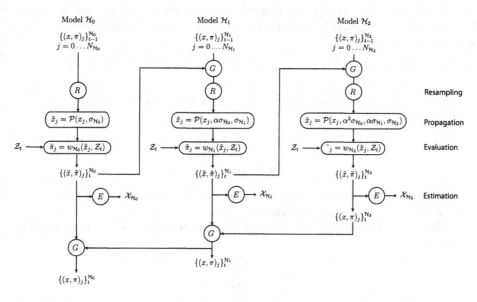

Fig. 2. Hierarchical Structure Annealed Particle Filter scheme for $M = 3$ models in the SHBM

tracking. Assuming that a SHBM $\mathcal{M}$ with a given hierarchy has been defined, a sequential fitting process is conducted over the several HBM $\mathcal{H}_i \in \mathcal{M}$. In order to carry out this task, we borrow the idea of annealing [3] where the particles are placed around the peaks of the likelihood function by means of a recursive search over a set of decreasingly smoothed versions of this function. Our proposal is to use the set of progressively refined HBMs constained in $\mathcal{M}$ instead of a set of smoothed versions of the likelihood function. This process mimics the annealing idea of the coarse-to-fine analysis of the likelihood function thus leading to a *structural annealing* process.

The overall operation of the proposed scheme is to filter the initial distribution associated to the simplest HBM $\mathcal{H}_0$ and then combine the resulting particle set with the initial particle set of the following model, $\mathcal{H}_1$. This process is performed for all the models in the SHBM until reaching the last one. Information contained by the particle set of the last model is back-propagated to the models with lower hierarchy rank thus refining their associated particle sets and closing the information filtering loop. The scheme of the proposed technique is depicted in Fig.2 for $M = 3$

Given a SHBM $\mathcal{M}$ containing M HBMs $\mathcal{H}_i$, a set of $N_{\mathcal{H}_i}$ particles, $\{(x, \pi)_j\}_t^{\mathcal{H}_i}$, associated to every $\mathcal{H}_i$ is defined at a given time t. It must be noted that, due to the hierarchy established in the SHBM, a mapping between the defining parameters of two consecutive HBMs can be always derived. Typically, this can be achieved by a linear or direct mapping between the involved variables. A fitness function $w_{\mathcal{H}_i}(x, \mathcal{Z}_t)$ measuring the likelihood between a particle and the incoming data $\mathcal{Z}_t$ is also constructed.

When a new measurement $\mathcal{Z}_t$ is available, an structural annealing iteration is performed. The hierarchical structure based annealed particle filtering can be summarized as follows:

– Starting from model $\mathcal{H}_0$, its associated particle set $\{(x, \pi)_j\}_{t-1}^{\mathcal{H}_i}$ is resampled with replacement. Then the filtered state $\{(\tilde{x}, \tilde{\pi})_j\}_t^{\mathcal{H}_i}$ is constructed by applying a propagation model $\mathcal{P}(\cdot, \cdot)$ and a weighting function $w_{\mathcal{H}_0}(\cdot, \cdot)$ to every particle as:

$$\tilde{x}_{j,t} = \mathcal{P}(x_{j,t}, \sigma_{\mathcal{H}_0}) = x_{j,t} + \mathbf{N}, \qquad (3)$$
$$\tilde{\pi}_{j,t} = w_{\mathcal{H}_0}(\tilde{x}_{j,t}, \mathcal{Z}_t), \qquad (4)$$

where $\mathbf{N}$ is a multivariate Gaussian noise with mean $\mathbf{0}$ and a covariance matrix $\Sigma = \text{diag}\{\sigma_{\mathcal{H}_0}\}$. Weights are normalized such that $\sum_j \tilde{\pi}_j = 1$. At this point, the output estimation of this model $\mathcal{X}_{\mathcal{H}_0,t}$ can be computed by applying

$$\mathcal{X}_{\mathcal{H}_0,t} = \sum_{j=1}^{N_{\mathcal{H}_0}} \tilde{\pi}_{j,t}\tilde{x}_{j,t}. \qquad (5)$$

– For the following HBMs, $i > 0$, the filtered particle set of the previous model in the hierarchy, $\{(\tilde{x}, \tilde{\pi})_j\}_t^{\mathcal{H}_{i-1}}$, is combined through the operator G with the particle set associated to model $\mathcal{H}_i$, $\{(x, \pi)_j\}_{t-1}^{\mathcal{H}_i}$. State space variables associated to $\mathcal{H}_i$ contain information from model $\mathcal{H}_{i-1}$ due to the imposed hierarchy relation. Since these variables have been already filtered, this updated information can be transferred to particles of model $\mathcal{H}_i$ in order to generate an improved initial particle set. Operator G has been inspired in the genetic algorithms theory and performs a crossover operation combining the common state variables of the two HBMs. Particles with a high weight in HBM $\mathcal{H}_{i-1}$ are combined with particles with a high weight in HBM $\mathcal{H}_i$. Common variables in $\mathcal{H}_i$ particles are replaced by the already filtered variables in $\mathcal{H}_{i-1}$ thus generating a new particle set that contains some information from the previous layer. However, it is also allowed some combination between particles with high weights from $\mathcal{H}_{i-1}$ with particles with low weights in $\mathcal{H}_i$ and viceversa. In this way, some variability is introduced thus being more robust to rapid motion and sudden pose changes.
Then, the filtered state $\{(\tilde{x}, \tilde{\pi})_j\}_t^{\mathcal{H}_i}$ is constructed as:

$$\tilde{x}_{j,t} = \mathcal{P}(x_{j,t}, \alpha^i \sigma_{\mathcal{H}_0}, \alpha^{i-1}\sigma_{\mathcal{H}_1}, \ldots, \sigma_{\mathcal{H}_i}) = x_{j,t} + \mathbf{N}, \qquad (6)$$
$$\tilde{\pi}_{j,t} = w_{\mathcal{H}_i}(\tilde{x}_{j,t}, \mathcal{Z}_t), \qquad (7)$$

where $\mathbf{N}$ is a multivariate Gaussian noise with mean $\mathbf{0}$ and a covariance matrix $\Sigma = \text{diag}\{\alpha^i \sigma_{\mathcal{H}_0}, \alpha^{i-1}\sigma_{\mathcal{H}_1}, \ldots, \sigma_{\mathcal{H}_i}\}$ with $\alpha < 1$. This propagation function assigns a higher drift to the newly added variables of model $\mathcal{H}_i$ while assigning a lower drift to those that have been more recently filtered in the previous models. At this point, the output estimation of this model $\mathcal{X}_{\mathcal{H}_i,t}$ can be computed.

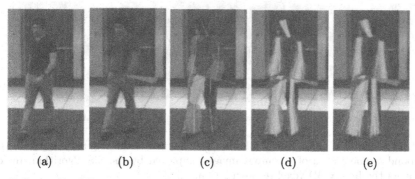

(a)   (b)   (c)   (d)   (e)

Fig. 3. Example of the execution of the HS-APF using a SHBM based on a refinement hierarchy. In (a), the original image is depicted and in (b)-(d) the sequential fitting of the models contained in the SBHM is shown (where the superimposed yellow lines are the particles associated to this HBM). In (e), the final pose estimation.

– Once reaching the highest hierarchy level, that is the most detailed HBM, the information contained in the particle set $\{(\tilde{x}, \tilde{\pi})_j\}_t^{\mathcal{H}_M}$ is back-propagated to the other models in the hierarchy by means of the aforementioned crossover operator G (but in a backwards sense). In this way, the particle sets will be refined thus closing the filtering loop.

An example of the execution of this scheme is depicted in Fig.3.

4.2 Implementation

For a given frame in the video sequence, a set of N images are obtained from the N cameras (see a sample in Fig.4a). Each camera is modeled using a pinhole camera model based on perspective projection with camera calibration information available. Foreground regions from input images are obtained using a segmentation algorithm based on Stauffer-Grimson's background learning and substraction technique [9] as shown in Fig.4b. Redundancy among cameras is exploited by means of a Shape-from-Silhouette (SfS) technique [7]. This process generates a discrete occupancy representation of the 3D space (voxels). A voxel is labelled as foreground or background by checking the spatial consistency of its projection on the N segmented silhouettes (see a sample in Fig.4c). These data will be the input information fed to our HS-APF scheme, that is $\mathcal{Z}_t$. However, this 3D reconstruction is corrupted by spurious voxels, holes, etc. introduced due to wrong segmentation and camera calibration inaccuracies.

Every particle defines an instance of the pose of a given HBM $\mathcal{H}_i$. In order to relate this pose with the input 3D data, this model is fleshed out with super-ellipsoids associated to every limb part (see an example in Fig.3e). Let us denote this 3D HBM representation of the particle state as $\mathcal{D}_{x_j}$. The weighting function $w_{\mathcal{H}_i}(x_j, \mathcal{Z}_t)$ relating the state of a particle x_j with the input data $\mathcal{Z}_t$ is defined as:

$$w_{\mathcal{H}_i}(x_j, \mathcal{Z}_t) = \exp\left\{-\left(1 - \frac{\#\left(\mathcal{D}_{x_j} \cap \mathcal{Z}_t\right)}{\#\mathcal{D}_{x_j}}\right)\right\}, \tag{8}$$

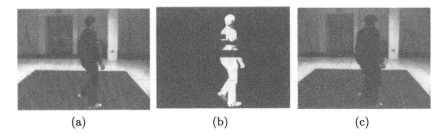

(a)   (b)   (c)

Fig. 4. Input data generation example. In (a), a sample of the original images. In (b), foreground segmentation of the input images employed by the SfS algorithm. In (c), example of the binary 3D voxel reconstruction.

where $\#(\cdot)$ indicates the cardinality of the set, that is the number of foreground voxels in enclosed volume. This likelihood function may be seen as a measure of the overlap between the $\mathcal{D}_{x_j}$ and $\mathcal{Z}_t$.

5   Evaluation and Results

In order to prove the effectiveness of the proposed pose estimation and tracking scheme, a series of experiments have been conducted over a part of the HumanEva-I database [4], thus allowing fair comparison with other algorithms. The original data contained approximately 2000 frames at 25 fps recorded with 3 color and 4 greyscale calibrated cameras at a resolution of 640x480 pixels (however, only the 4 cameras were used to generate the 3D reconstruction of the scene). The 3D position of the most relevant joints in the body is provided in this database captured by means of a professional MOCAP system. This information will allow computing quantitative metrics in order to compare the body pose estimation with respect to the groundtruth.

Several metrics are employed to quantify the performance of the employed algorithm. HumanEva-I project proposes two point-based metrics based on the error measured at the position of the joints, namely the mean of the error μ and its associated standard deviation σ. Since the most natural way to encode a pose is by using the angles associated to every joint, we also provide two angle-based metrics: the mean of the angular error μ_θ and its associated standard deviation σ_θ.

Table 1. Quantitative results for the walking action of the subjects $S2$ and $S3$ of the HumanEva-I dataset. Results are shown in millimeters and degrees.

	μ	σ	μ_θ	σ_θ
SPF	172.87	28.43	14.75	07.86
APF	143.16	23.01	10.79	05.77
HS-APF	115.21	20.32	07.21	03.14

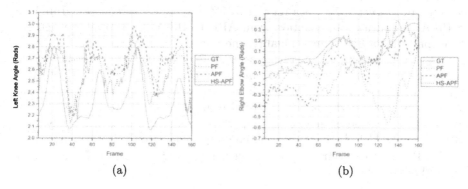

Fig. 5. Evolution of the estimation of the compared tracking systems for the elbow and the knee angles during a walking cycle

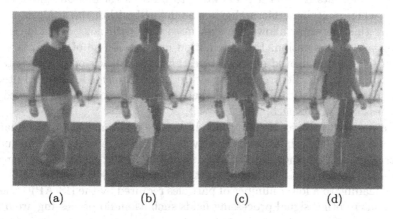

Fig. 6. Example of pose estimation with several filtering schemes. Legend: (a) original image, (b) PF, (c) APF, (d) HS-APF.

The proposed system was compared to the Standard PF (SPF) [5] and the Annealed PF (APF) [3] approaches. The HS-APF scheme employed a SHBM based on a refinement hierarchy as depicted in Fig.1a. In order to provide a fair comparison, the input data and the initial variance parameters employed by the propagation function were the same for all the filters. These variance parameters were set to be the half of the maximum expected movement associated to each joint. The overall number of particles employed by every filter was the same: $N_{\text{SPF}} = 1000$, $N_{\text{APF}} = 250$ (with 4 annealing layers) and $N_{\mathcal{H}_i} = \{250, 500, 250\}$.

Quantitative results of these experiments have been reported in Table 1 and Fig.5 showing the effectiveness of the HS-APF in comparison with the PF and APF approaches. Metrics μ and σ quantize the error when estimating the position of the body joints and there is a relative 33% error reduction from the SPF to the HS-APF, and a 19.5% reduction from APF to HS-APF. Metrics μ_θ and σ_θ quantize the error in terms of angles, being perhaps a more informative measure. In this case, there is a relative 51.5% angular error reduction from SPF to HS-APF and a 33% reduction from APF to HS-APF. Typically, when the state space has a high dimensionality, the number of particles required by the SPF is very high thus not operating accurately with 1000 particles. This problem is efficiently addressed by APF and a noticeable improvement is achieved. Finally, HS-APF exploits the underlying structure of the articulated model thus achieving a better performance. A visual example is depicted in Fig.6. In this example, PF scheme is unable to properly estimate the pose with only 1000 particles while APF does not recover the pose of some limbs (in this case a leg). Finally, HS-APF can retrieve the correct pose taking advantage of the scalable human body model.

6   Conclusions and Future Work

This paper presents a general framework to address estimation and tracking problems where a scalable hierarchy can be defined within the analysis model. Exploiting this hierarchy allows the system to deal with noisy input data thus providing a robust solution. Human motion capture is one of such cases and the proposed scheme proved effective to estimate and track pose. Quantitative results comparing the Hierarchical Structure based Annealed Particle Filtering with the Standard Particle Filter and the Annealed Particle Filter showed the effectiveness of our approach.

Future research involves defining new hierarchy relations within the analysis models and a further validation of this system with larger databases including unconstrained motion and more than one subject in the scene. Including surface and color information will allow constructing more discriminative likelihood functions leading to a lower number of particles required by the HS-APF scheme. Applications in other signal processing fields such as audio processing are under study.

References

1. Arulampalam, M.S., Maskell, S., Gordon, N., Clapp, T.: A tutorial on particle filters for online nonlinear/non-Gaussian Bayesian tracking. IEEE Trans. on Signal Processing, 50(2), 174–188 (2002)
2. Canton-Ferrer, C., Casas, J.R., Pardàs, M.: Human Model and Motion Based 3D Action Recognition in Multiple View Scenarios. In: Proc. European Signal Processing Conf. (2006)
3. Deutscher, J., Reid, I.: Articulated body motion capture by stochastic search. Int. Journal of Computer Vision 61(2), 185–205 (2005)
4. HumanEva - Synchronized video and motion capture dataset for evaluation of articulated human motion, http://vision.cs.brown.edu/humaneva
5. Isard, M., Blake, A.: Condensation–Conditional density propagation for visual tracking. Int. Journal of Computer Vision 29(1), 5–28 (1998)
6. MacCormick, J., Isard, M.: Partitioned sampling, articulated objects and interface-quality hand tracking. In: Proc. European Conference on Computer Vision, vol. 2, pp. 3–19 (2000)

7. Mikič, I.: Human body model acquisition and tracking using multi-camera voxel Data. PhD Thesis, University of California, San Diego (2003)
8. Mitchelson, J., Hilton, A.: Simultaneous pose estimation of multiple people using multiple-view cues with hierarchical sampling. In: Proc. British Machine Vision Conference (2003)
9. Stauffer, C., Grimson, W.: Adaptive background mixture models for real-time tracking. In: Proc. IEEE Int. on Computer Vision and Pattern Recognition, pp. 252–259 (1999)

Estimating Human Skeleton Parameters and Configuration in Real-Time from Markered Optical Motion Capture

Jonathan Cameron* and Joan Lasenby

Signal Processing and Communications Laboratory,
Department of Engineering, Cambridge University
{jic23,jl}@eng.cam.ac.uk

Abstract. This paper is concerned with real-time approaches to using marker-based optical motion capture to identify, parametrize, and estimate the frame by frame configuration of the human skeleton. An overview of the stages of a system is provided with the main emphasis devoted to two new methods for refining the rotation estimates used within the transformational algorithm class of joint parameter estimation methods. Virtual Marker Insertion uses additional markers inserted at the current estimates of joint location to partially enforce the concurrency of available joint location estimates. This simple algorithm is shown to outperform the methods presented in the literature. A conjugate gradient optimization on a minimal parameterization of the standard transformational algorithm cost function gives superior results, but at considerable computational cost, limiting its probable application to those frames which are actually rendered in a feedback system.

Keywords: Motion Capture, Skeletal, Orientation Estimation.

1 Introduction and Motivation

Recent advances in active marker-based optical motion capture have overcome the problem of marker identification whilst remaining unobtrusive enough to use during natural human motion [1,2]. Whilst the primary motivation for such systems was to reduce the manual intervention required to correct marker tracking problems, they also provide real-time labeled data. This allows many of the interaction / real-time feedback systems previously presented (e.g. [3]) to harness far larger data sets and makes many new applications possible.

Real-time skeletal animation systems driven live from motion capture are commonly used within the film industry for previsualization [4]. However, most approaches require time consuming manual model adjustment to match the dimensions of the user and, being based on inverse kinematics, utilize limited motion models to make the real-time computation possible. These models often lead to overly constrained or unrealistic resulting motion [5].

---

* Research partly funding by SESAME project EPSRC (EP/D076943).

F.J. Perales and R.B. Fisher (Eds.): AMDO 2008, LNCS 5098, pp. 92–101, 2008.

Within the biomechanics literature, the automated parameterization of skeletal joints has been the subject of considerable research [6,7,8,9,10,11,12]. Attempting to use such methods to generate and update a skeletal model in a real-time feedback situation brings a unique set of challenges. Such a real-time skeletal system forms a component of an offset perception real-time feedback environment that is proving successful within a number of research projects directed towards the areas of stroke and prosthetic limb rehabilitation.

This paper describes the system structure, with particular emphasis on the algorithms used to estimate the locations of the skeletal joints. New methods are presented to improve the estimation of the limb rotations using available estimated joint parameters.

2   Anatomy of a Real-Time Sequentially Updated Skeleton Algorithm

Figure 1 shows the stages of the skeleton parameterization system. The first utilizes the relative marker positions to identify clusters of markers attached to a common limb segment. This stage is described briefly in Sect. 3. Human intervention is only required to confirm a correct clustering of markers.

The second stage, described in Sect. 4, estimates the parameters required to establish the locations of all possible joints between the identified clusters.

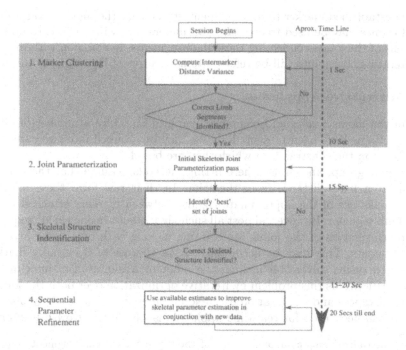

Fig. 1. Program flow for a real-time sequential skeleton estimation program

The question of which joints actually make up the skeleton may be addressed by using the estimated joint parameters. This stage is described in Sect. 5. Human intervention is required to confirm the correct nature of the skeletal structure reducing the number of joints needing subsequent updating.

Once the true skeletal structure has been established, a much restricted set of true joints may be updated as and when new data becomes available.

The algorithms in Fig. 1 must run alongside suitable rendering, data capture and data analysis algorithms and form part of a much larger mulithreaded real-time application. A more complete description may be found in [13].

3   Marker Clustering

No a priori information is supplied about limb-marker attachment. For the overall skeleton building system to succeed at least 3 markers must be attached to each segment. This step establishes clusters of markers attached to common segments. Many different clustering algorithms could be used. Here a hierarchical agglomerative clustering algorithm, with an inter-marker distance variance cost function, is sufficient. Other cost functions such as maximal variation in inter-marker distance and transformational consistency have been evaluated [13] and found to be computationally infeasible or exhibit worse performance.

4   Finding Skeletal Parameters

Having established marker to limb segment attachment the motion over a number of frames may be used to estimate parameters that will allow us to find the locations of the joints connecting these limb segments. In common with much of the literature, the joints will be referred to as Centres of Rotation (CoRs).

4.1   Alternative Approaches

Within the biomechanics and computer graphics literature a number of different algorithms have been presented. These may be grouped into two categories depending on the constraint on which they are based.

The first group, known as sphere fitting methods, assume that the markers remain at a fixed distance from the joint. In their raw form these methods do not make use of the approximate rigidity between markers attached to the same limb segment. However, almost all such algorithms are one sided[1] requiring the transformation of the joint into a frame moving with one of the attached limb segments. This may be accomplished via the use of 3 or more markers and a Procrustes solver [14] making the inherent assumption of inter-marker rigidity. [10] avoids this problem by iterative optimization over both the joint to marker distances and the location of the joints in every frame used. Whilst this method has been used for real-time applications, the linear growth in number

---

[1] One sided algorithms assume that one of the two attached limb segments remains stationary throughout the motion.

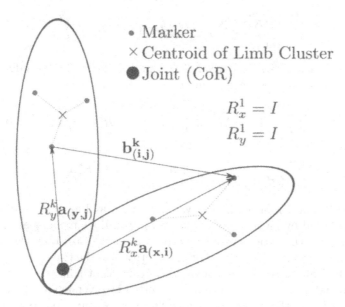

• Marker
× Centroid of Limb Cluster
● Joint (CoR)

$$R_x^1 = I$$
$$R_y^1 = I$$

Fig. 2. A single joint in frame k

of parameters with the number of frames makes it unsuitable where large data sets are to be processed. An alternative symmetric sphere fitting algorithm is presented in [13] but this is unstable in the presence of noise.

The algorithm presented here falls into the class known as transformational methods. These assume inter-marker rigidity on a given limb segment allowing the rotation in each frame to be estimated separately from the vectors needed to parametrize the joint. [8] presented this approach in a one sided situation. The two sided formulation was described in [11] where orientation estimates are directly available from a magnetic motion capture system. [12] applies this approach to optical marker data, obtaining rotation estimates from a Procrustes solver.

4.2 Sequentially Updated Transformational Algorithm

In [15] a sequential variant of the algorithms of [12,11] was presented, in which an alternative approach to solving for the minimum of the cost function is used. In [15] the derivation uses Geometric Algebra [16]. Here rotation matrices are used to aid accessibility.

Consider Fig. 2. As, in an occlusion-free frame k, each segment has 3 or more known marker locations, the rotation matrices, R_x^k and R_y^k from frame 1 to frame k may be estimated by using a Procrustes solver. Define $\mathbf{a}_{(x,i)}$ and $\mathbf{a}_{(y,j)}$ to be the currently unknown vectors from the CoR to the marker of index i, j on the x, y segment. In the noise free case, the vector $\mathbf{b}_{(i,j)}^k$, from the ith marker on the x segment to the jth marker on the y segment, may be expressed as $R_x^k \mathbf{a}_{(x,i)} - R_y^k \mathbf{a}_{(y,j)}$. In the presence of noise, a least squares approach may be used, leading to the cost function S where $n_{\{x,y\}}$ is the number of markers on the x, y limb segment and m gives the number of occlusion-free frames used.

$$S = \sum_{k=1}^{m}\sum_{i=1}^{n_x}\sum_{j=1}^{n_y}\left(\mathbf{b^k_{(i,j)}} - \left(R^k_x\mathbf{a_{(x,i)}} - R^k_y\mathbf{a_{(y,j)}}\right)\right)^2. \tag{1}$$

The solution to such a least squares system may be found by considering the partial differentials with respect to the unknown parameters

$$\partial_{a_{(x,i)}}S = 2\sum_{k=1}^{m}\sum_{j=1}^{n_y}\left[-\left[R^k_x\right]^T\mathbf{b^k_{(i,j)}} + \mathbf{a_{(x,i)}} - \left[R^k_x\right]^T R^k_y\mathbf{a_{(y,j)}}\right] = 0 \tag{2}$$

$$\partial_{a_{(y,j)}}S = 2\sum_{k=1}^{m}\sum_{i=1}^{n_x}\left[\left[R^k_y\right]^T\mathbf{b^k_{(i,j)}} + \mathbf{a_{(y,j)}} - \left[R^k_y\right]^T R^k_x\mathbf{a_{(x,i)}}\right] = 0. \tag{3}$$

Equations (2) and (3) form a linear system in $\mathbf{a_{(x,i)}}$ and $\mathbf{a_{(y,j)}}$, the solution of which may be found by inversion of a 18×18 matrix. If a simple mean [12] is to be used to combine the various resulting estimates of the CoR then the solution for the equivalent cost function based on the centroids of the two clusters instead of the individual markers may be shown to be equivalent [13]. The form of the resulting 6×6 matrix is such that it may be inverted by inversion of a 3×3 matrix using non-iterative methods. The somewhat simpler cost function corresponding to this approach has not been presented here as the individual estimates of the $\mathbf{a_{(x,i)}}$ and $\mathbf{a_{(y,j)}}$ can be used to provide an estimate of a noise free key frame during CoR reconstruction (see Sect. 6.)

The crucial observation to make about this cost function is that the matrix to be inverted consists of sums of separable terms dependent only on individual frames of data. Thus the matrix may be sequentially updated as new data becomes available and more accurate estimates of the skeletal parameter vectors computed throughout the capture session. In [11,12] a non-sequential SVD (Singular Value Decomposition) based method is used to find the optimum. Both approaches will give the same result.

4.3   Estimating the CoR Location in Frame k

Having established estimates for $\mathbf{a_{(x,i)}}$, $\mathbf{a_{(y,j)}}$ and $R^k_{\{x,y\}}$ the simplest method to reconstruct the CoR in a given frame is to take each marker in turn then subtract the relevant vector rotated into the current frame. This will result in at least 6 estimates of the CoR. The simplest means of combining these estimates is to use their mean.

5   Identifying the Skeletal Structure

Without prior knowledge of the skeletal structure, there has until now been no information available to suggest which limb segments may actually be joined. For a typical full body motion capture data set with 15 limb segments, 210 separate CoRs must be initially estimated[2]. Once estimates of the CoR locations are

---

[2] On a P4 3.2Ghz machine this may be accomplished in real-time on 480Hz data from [1].

available, it is possible to establish the true skeletal structure, reducing the number of CoRs to be updated in later stages to a mere 15. This frees computational time for other elements of the system such as rendering virtual environments.

The simplest method applies a minimal spanning tree algorithm using the cost function given in (1). This works well in many situations. However, it may fail if the motion does not fully exercise all degrees of freedom. As this can be readily seen by the user, it is easy to ensure that any incorrect limb segments generated are 'broken' on the next pass of the algorithm (see Fig. 1). More sophisticated model-based methods may be applied if loops exist within the desired skeletal structure (e.g. a golfer) but these are considerably more computationally expensive [13].

6 Improving Rotation Estimates

Having established estimates of $\mathbf{a}_{(x,i)}$ and $\mathbf{a}_{(y,j)}$ the rotation matrices $R^k_{\{x,y\}}$ may be estimated more accurately in a given frame. Two approaches to accomplishing this will be investigated here.

The first, less computationally expensive method, uses a virtual marker inserted into each limb segment at the current estimate of the CoR location in this frame. A Procrustes solver is used to estimate the rotation based on the real markers and this virtual one. This acts to 'drag' the two rotors towards each other. Assuming the mean of the 6 or more CoR location estimates is on average better than the separate estimates from the two sides this should result in a more accurate estimate of the rotation matrices.

The second approach relies on the conjugate gradient algorithm [17] to optimize w.r.t. a minimal parameterization of the rotations using the cost function given in (1). The derivation of the relevant partial differentials is presented in Appendix A. Unfortunately, this approach is extremely sensitive to the noise level on the key frame (here the first frame). One approach to overcoming this uses the vectors from the CoR to the markers as previously estimated. As the algorithm is translation independent, a frame with CoR at the origin and the markers at the positions given by these vectors may be used in place of the original key frame. Both variants of this algorithm are presented in Sect. 7.

If the relationship of this single frame cost function to the centroid-based version is considered, it can be seen that they both exhibit an ambiguity corresponding to the CoR lying on a circle in space. Initializing the optimization from a good estimate of the rotations ensures that a close to optimal point is found in the rotation parameterization subspace.

7 Results and Discussion

As has been observed within the literature [7], it is extremely difficult to obtain accurate ground truth for human joint locations, thus numerical analysis will be carried out using simulated data. No comparison of the base algorithm (Sect. 4.2) with the other major algorithms in the literature is presented as it will

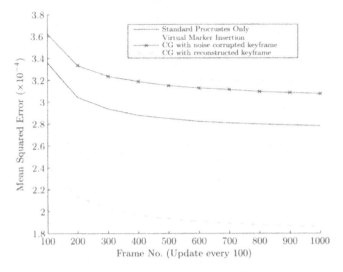

Fig. 3. Error in CoR location estimation over a 100 frame test set, rotation angle limited to 22.5°, noise s.d. 0.01, mean of 1000 runs

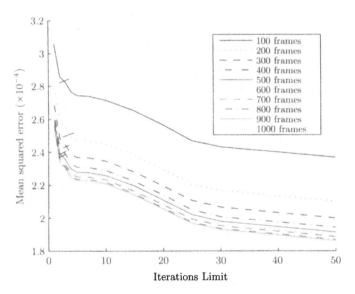

Fig. 4. Effect of truncating the number of iterations of the Conjugate Gradient based rotor refinement. Black markers show the point at which the performance of VMI is exceeded. 100 frame test set, rotation angle limited to 22.5°, noise s.d. 0.01, 100 runs.

give identical results to those of [12]. This section will investigate the relative performance of the variants of the base algorithm described in previous sections.

All simulations are for a single joint with 3 markers on each of the two limb segments. As the algorithms do not make use of inter-frame information, the simulated motion is simply random rotations, from a key frame[3] of the two sides of the joint. As the joints in many motion capture data sets do not exercise full 360° rotation the experiments shown have the rotation limited (via rejection sampling) to 22.5°. The noise is additive Gaussian. Although this is an overly simplistic model covering the affects of several different processes, it allows a comparative evaluation of different methods. The level selected (s.d. 0.01) is consistent with that seen in many real motion capture setups. All comparisons are conducted over a 100 frame test set. This simulates using the current parameter estimates to find the CoR locations in the next 100 frames to be rendered.

Figure 3 illustrates the relative performance of the algorithms described. Clearly, under these typical conditions the conjugate gradient (CG) algorithm, with reconstructed key frame, gives the lowest error over the test set. Without first frame replacement the CG method actually reduces the accuracy of the CoR estimation. Figure 4 shows the effect of truncating the number of iterations allowed for the conjugate gradient algorithm. Whilst ideally tests would be presented of the effect of truncation in time, the small timescales involved make this extremely difficult to achieve and so the number of iterations is considered instead. If sufficient computational time is available to carry out more than 4 iterations, then the error will be lower than with Virtual Marker Insertion (VMI). Four iterations typically take c. 0.0125 secs per frame per joint or 0.1875 seconds per frame. With the simple assumption of half of the total processor time available for this software element and a refresh rate of 30 fps required for the rendering thread, then even if the algorithm is only used on frames rendered, the available time would be c. 0.017 secs. Thus for the current implementation this algorithm is approximately an order of magnitude too slow to be used to improve the accuracy of rendered frames, and several orders of magnitude too slow to be applied to every new data frame. The increase in computational load for VMI is negligible (mainly a single 4×4 SVD) compared to the standard reconstruction method.

8   Conclusions and Future Work

This paper has intentionally focused on one aspect of a real-time skeleton parameterization pose estimation algorithm with only minimal details of the other steps provided. It has introduced two new approaches to refining the rotation estimates needed to establish the locations of the joints. The first of these, Virtual Marker Insertion (VMI) has considerably lower computational cost, merely requiring an additional run of a Procrustes solver. Whilst the second algorithm, a conjugate gradient based optimizer using the same cost function as was used to estimate the skeleton parameters (CG), outperforms VMI when using a reconstructed key frame, this comes at considerable additional computation cost.

Future work will consider more sophisticated optimization methods to solve what may be termed the articulated Procrustes problem, fast and accurately

---

[3] Key frame noise free marker locations are $(1, 2, 0)$, $(-0.25, 3.1, 0)$, $(3, 4, 0)$ and $(0.707, 0.707, 0)$, $(01.871, 1.414)$, $(0, -3, 1)$.

enough to be suitable to use within the real-time framework presented. Particularly important will be considering how to overcome the inherent ambiguity in the cost function used within this paper. It is also worth noting that the improved rotation estimates given by the methods presented here, could be used to drive the main parameter optimization algorithm.

The noise model used within this paper is simplistic and the effects of more complex noise models should be investigated. Another interesting direction would be to investigate higher order models, simultaneously estimating the parameters of several interconnected limb segments.

References

1. PhaseSpace: IMPULSE Motion Capture System, http://www.phasespace.com
2. Codamotion: cx1, http://www.codamotion.com
3. Lee, J., Chai, J., Reitsma, P., Hodgins, J., Pollard, N.: Interactive control of avatars animated with human motion data. In: Proc. GRAPHITE, pp. 491–500 (2002)
4. Autodesk MotionBuilder, http://www.autodesk.com/motionbuilder
5. Peinado, M., Herbelin, B., Wanderley, M., Callennec, B.L., Boulic, R., Thalmann, D., Méiat, D.: Towards configurable motion capture with prioritized inverse kinematics. In: Proc. IVWR, pp. 85–97 (2004)
6. Silaghi, M., Plänkers, R., Boulic, R., Fua, P., Thalmann, D.: Local and global skeleton fitting techniques for optical motion capture. In: Magnenat-Thalmann, N., Thalmann, D. (eds.) CAPTECH 1998. LNCS (LNAI), vol. 1537, pp. 26–40. Springer, Heidelberg (1998)
7. Gamage, S.S.H.U., Lasenby, J.: New least squares solutions for estimating the average centre of rotation and the axis of rotation. J. Biomech 35(1), 87–93 (2002)
8. Holzreiter, S.: Calculation of the instantaneous centre of rotation for a rigid body. J. Biomech 24, 643–647 (1991)
9. Chang, L., Pollard, N.: Constrained least-squares optimization for robust estimation of center of rotation. J. Biomech 40(6), 1392–1400 (2007)
10. Kirk, A., O'Brien, J., Forsyth, D.: Skeletal parameter estimation from optical motion capture data. In: Proc. CVPR, pp. 782–788. IEEE, Los Alamitos (2005)
11. O'Brien, J., Bodenheimer, R., Brostow, G., Hodgins, J.: Automatic joint parameter estimation from magnetic motion capture data. In: Proc. GI., pp. 53–60 (2000)
12. Ehrig, R., Taylor, W., Duda, G., Heller, M.: A survey of formal methods for determining the centre of rotation of ball joints. J. Biomech. 39(15), 2798–2809 (2006)
13. Cameron, J.: Aspects of Conformal Geometric Algebra with Applications in Motion Capture. PhD thesis, Engineering Department, University of Cambridge (2007)
14. Horn, B.: Closed-form solution of absolute orientation using unit quaternions. JOSA A 4, 629–642 (1987)
15. Cameron, J., Lasenby, J.: A real-time sequential algorithm for human joint localization. In: Posters SIGGRAPH (2005)
16. Hestenes, D., Sobczyk, G.: Clifford Algebra to Geometric Calculus. D. Reidel (1984)
17. Press, W., Teukolsky, S., Vetterling, W., Flannery, B.: Numerical Recipes in C++. CUP (2002)
18. Doran, C., Lasenby, A.: Geometric Algebra for Physicists. CUP (2003)

A   Cost Function Partial Differentials

The mathematical framework of geometric algebra (GA) and the associated calculus [16] greatly simplify this derivation. Due to a lack of space, no introduction to GA is provided here and the reader is referred to [18] for a good introduction. Note that as vectors enjoy no special place in this algebra they will not be written differently from other elements.

In this framework the element of the cost function given in (1) due to a single frame of data may be expressed as

$$S^k = \sum_{i=1}^{n_x} \sum_{j=1}^{n_y} \left(b_{(i,j)} - R_x a_{(x,i)} \tilde{R}_x + R_y a_{(y,j)} \tilde{R}_y \right)^2 \tag{4}$$

where $R_{\{x,y\}} = \exp(B_{\{x,y\}})$ and all frame indices have been suppressed.

The partial differentials of the cost function w.r.t. $B_{\{x,y\}}$ are

$$\partial_{B_x} S^k = -2 \sum_{i=1}^{n_x} \sum_{j=1}^{n_y} \partial_{B_x} \left[\left(R_x a_{(x,i)} \tilde{R}_x \right) \cdot b_{(i,j)} + \left(R_x a_{(x,i)} \tilde{R}_x \right) \cdot \left(R_y a_{(y,j)} \tilde{R}_y \right) \right]$$

$$\partial_{B_y} S^k = 2 \sum_{i=1}^{n_x} \sum_{j=1}^{n_y} \partial_{B_y} \left[\left(R_y a_{(y,j)} \tilde{R}_y \right) \cdot b_{(i,j)} - \left(R_y a_{(y,j)} \tilde{R}_y \right) \cdot \left(R_x a_{(x,i)} \tilde{R}_x \right) \right].$$

These may be evaluated using the identity

$$\partial_B (Ra\tilde{R}) \cdot b = 2 \left\{ \mathrm{sinc}(2|B|)(a \cdot b) + \left(\frac{\mathrm{sinc}(2|B|) - \cos(2|B|)}{|B|^2} \right) (B \cdot (a \wedge b)) \right.$$

$$+ \left(\frac{\mathrm{sinc}(2|B|) - \mathrm{sinc}^2(|B|)}{|B|^2} \right) \left. ((BaB) \cdot b) \right\} B$$

$$+ 2\mathrm{sinc}(2|B|)\, (a \cdot b) - 2\mathrm{sinc}^2(|B|) \langle aBb \rangle_2 \tag{5}$$

where a and b are vectors, R is a rotor of the form given above and $\langle aBb \rangle_2$ is simply the bivector component of aBb.

Dealing with Self-occlusion in Region Based Motion Capture by Means of Internal Regions*

Christian Schmaltz[1], Bodo Rosenhahn[2], Thomas Brox[3], Joachim Weickert[1], Lennart Wietzke[4], and Gerald Sommer[4]

[1] Mathematical Image Analysis Group, Faculty of Mathematics and Computer Science, Building E1.1, Saarland University, 66041 Saarbrücken, Germany
{schmaltz,weickert}@mia.uni-saarland.de
[2] Max-Planck Institute for Informatics, 66123 Saarbrücken, Germany
rosenhahn@mpi-sb.mpg.de
[3] Faculty of Computer Science, Dresden University of Technology, 01187 Dresden, Germany
brox@inf.tu-dresden.de
[4] Institute of Computer Science, Christian-Albrecht-University, 24098 Kiel, Germany
{lw,gs}@ks.informatik.uni-kiel.de

Abstract. Self-occlusion is a common problem in silhouette based motion capture, which often results in ambiguous pose configurations. In most works this is compensated by a priori knowledge about the motion or the scene, or by the use of multiple cameras. Here we suggest to overcome this problem by splitting the surface model of the object and tracking the silhouette of each part rather than the whole object. The splitting can be done automatically by comparing the appearance of the different parts with the Jensen-Shannon divergence. Tracking is then achieved by maximizing the appearance differences of all involved parts and the background simultaneously via gradient descent. We demonstrate the improvements with tracking results from simulated and real world scenes.

Keywords: Pose estimation, tracking, kinematic chain, computer vision, human motion analysis.

1 Introduction

Capturing the motion of articulated objects, particularly humans, has been a popular research field for many years. Hundreds of papers have addressed this problem and we refer to [3], [6] and [7] for surveys on this topic.

Generally, pose tracking algorithms can be divided into 2-D approaches, which only track objects in the image plane, and 3-D approaches, which determine the object's pose, i.e., its 3-D position and orientation. Moreover, tracking methods can be classified by means of the tracked features. Two popular features are the object silhouette and local descriptors centered around feature points.

A major drawback of silhouette based 3-D pose tracking, particularly in case of articulated objects, is the problem of self-occlusion. This is, only the silhouette of parts of

---

* We acknowledge funding by the German Research Foundation under the projects We 2602/5-1 and SO 320/4-2, and by the Max-Planck Center for Visual Computing and Communication.

F.J. Perales and R.B. Fisher (Eds.): AMDO 2008, LNCS 5098, pp. 102–111, 2008.

the model is seen, leaving ambiguities in the pose of the remaining parts. For instance, if a person is seen from the front with a hand in front of its body, the contour of the hand and forearm is inside the object region and, hence, not part of the person's silhouette (see left image in Figure 4). As a consequence, there is no information to estimate the joint angles of the hand.

Approaches based on local patches do not suffer from these problems. They have other drawbacks, though. For example, feature detection might fail or produce too few features if there is not enough texture. Furthermore, as long as there is no matching to a reference frame, these features tend to introduce a drift. If such a matching is used, handling large rotations becomes difficult. Since neither method is clearly better than the other, both feature-based and silhouette-based approaches are still topics of open research. Here we focus on a silhouette-based approach that simultaneously computes the 3-D pose and the 2-D object contours seen in the images [8,9].

A common way to deal with ambiguities is by means of learned angle priors [12,15,1]. Based on the correlation of angles in the training samples, unresolved degrees of freedom are set to the most likely solution given the other, non-ambiguous angles. While this approach is reasonable and a last resort in case of body parts that are indeed occluded, the prior also has the tendency to introduce a bias towards the training motions, which is undesirable, e.g., in medical applications. Hence, it is beneficial to fully exploit the information provided by the images.

In this paper, we show how the information of internal silhouettes can be exploited. The main idea is to find components of the object model whose appearance differs from the surrounding model parts. Due to the difference in their appearance, the contours of these components can be extracted in the image and used as additional information for tracking. As a consequence, the tracking algorithm becomes more stable and can successfully track scenes that cannot be tracked with a conventional silhouette based method.

Related work. There are other human tracking approaches that decompose the model into several parts. Bottom-up approaches that learn the appearance of different parts from a training set are very common. The algorithm in [14] learns the appearance of each part modeled by a Gibbs distribution. Results are only given for multi-camera sequences, though. In [5] the appearance of each part is learned using AdaBoost. Another learning approach that considers different appearances of different object regions is explained in [17]. However, there is only 2-D tracking in these two approaches. In [2], average pixel intensities are computed inside parts of the object to estimate their appearance. This can be regarded as a parametric special case of the more general probability density functions we use for modeling the appearance of body parts. The tracking of multiple object parts also comprises similar ideas as the tracking of multiple objects in a scene, as proposed in [10].

Paper organization. In Section 2 we review a basic region based pose estimation algorithms. A new energy function for tracking with internal regions is introduced in Section 3, followed by an explanation how the internal regions used in this new approach can be found automatically. After showing and discussing some experiments in Section 4, we conclude with a summary in Section 5.

2   Pose Estimation from 2-D–3-D Point Correspondences

In this paper, we model humans as free-form surfaces embedded with kinematic chains, i.e., as a number of rigid body parts connected by joints and represented in a tree structure [6]. The n rotation axes ξ_i are part of the model. The joint angles $\Theta := (\theta_1, \ldots \theta_n)$ are unknown and must be determined by the pose estimation algorithm. In total, the sought pose vector $\chi := (\xi, \Theta)$ consists of a 6-D vector $\xi \in se(3)$ corresponding to the rigid body motion of the whole model and the above-mentioned joint angle vector Θ.

We pursue a region-based tracking approach that is based on the work in [9]. It splits the image into two regions in such a way that the features in the foreground and background region are maximally different. In this sense, the approach has a lot in common with segmentation. However, instead of using a segmentation method as an intermediate step, we directly manipulate the pose parameters in order to optimize the partitioning. To this end, we consider the partitioning function $P : \mathbb{R}^{6+n} \times \Omega \ni (\chi, q) \mapsto \{0, 1\}$. It projects the body model with its current pose χ to the image plane Ω in order to determine if an image point q currently belongs to the object region $\{q \in \Omega | P(\chi, q) = 1\}$. The partitioning, and simultaneously the pose, are improved by minimizing the energy function

$$E(\chi) = - \int_\Omega \left(P(\chi, q) \log p_{in} + (1 - P(\chi, q)) \log p_{out} \right) dq \tag{1}$$

with a modified gradient descent. Here, p_{in} and p_{out} denote two probability density functions (pdfs) that represent the feature distribution in the object and background region, respectively. We use the three channels of the CIELAB color space but, in principle, any dense feature set can be used. The densities p_{in} and p_{out} are modeled by independent channel densities. We estimate each channel density either by a kernel density estimator or by a local Gaussian distribution [8]. It is worth noting that the estimated pdfs depend on the partitioning. Thus, they have to be recomputed when χ varies.

For approximating the gradient of E, we assume that $\nabla_\chi p_{in} \approx 0, \nabla_\chi p_{out} \approx 0$. These are reasonable assumptions, since the estimated pdfs only change slowly with varying χ. Furthermore, we assume that P was smoothed, e.g., by convolving it with a small Gaussian kernel. We obtain

$$\nabla E(\chi) = - \int_\Omega \left(\nabla P(\chi, q)(\log p_{in} - \log p_{out}) \right) dq . \tag{2}$$

Thus, a modified gradient descent can be employed for minimizing (1). More precisely, each point on the contour of the projected model is moved either towards the interior or exterior of the object region depending on whether p_{in} or p_{out} is larger, respectively. This is illustrated in Figure 1. The displacement of contour points is transferred to the corresponding 3-D points on the surface model by using a point-based pose estimation algorithm [8]. In this way, a new rigid body motion and the joint angles are estimated and projecting the model with the new pose yields a refined partitioning. These steps are iterated until convergence.

Fig. 1. This figure illustrates the movement applied to contour points by the tracking algorithm used. **Left:** Example input image of a scene. **Middle:** Object model projected in an inaccurate pose into the image plane (magnified). **Right:** Silhouette of the projected model and an example how some contour points might be adapted by the tracking algorithm (magnified). Cyan arrows indicate points that are moved towards the outside and red arrows indicates a movements towards the inside of the object.

3   Tracking Using a Split Model

The tracking algorithm explained so far works very well for rigid objects. However, in case of articulated objects, ambiguities may occur if the projection of a body part lies completely inside the object region and, consequently, yields not silhouette points. In such a situation, there is no cue for the pose of that part.

In this section, we explain how to overcome this problem by using internal silhouettes. To this end, the object model is split into different components and each of these components is projected separately to the image plane. We assume that there are some body parts that look different from other parts. This is reasonable since tracking cannot work if the structure to be tracked looks like the surrounding background. Even a human cannot follow an object that looks like the background after all.

3.1   Extending the Energy Function to Multiple Regions

Assume there are l model components $M_i, i = 1, \ldots, l$ to track the body model M. These components can be chosen arbitrarily, e.g., some points of the model might be part of several components M_i, or of no component at all. This can be useful if a part of the object looks similar to the background, e.g., someone wearing a black T-shirt in front of a black wall. A component does not need to be connected, e.g., both arms may be handled as a single component.

Before introducing an energy function that can deal with such a multiple component model, we need to define some symbols: let $O_i(\chi, q)$ be the set of all 3-D points of the model component M_i with pose χ that are projected to the image point q. Furthermore, for the usual Euclidean metric d, let $d_i(\chi, q) := d(O_i(\chi, q), C) = \min_{x \in O_i(\chi, q)} \{d(x, C)\}$ be the minimal distance of the camera origin C to a 3-D point in the set $O_i(\chi, q)$. Finally, we define visibility functions $v_i : \chi \times \omega \mapsto \{0,1\}$ which are 1 if and only if the i-th object is visible in the image point q, given the current pose, i.e.,

$$v_i(\chi,q) := \begin{cases} 1 & \text{if } d_i(\chi,q) = \min_{j \in \{1,\dots,l\}} \{d_j(\chi,q)\}, \\ 0 & \text{else} \end{cases} \tag{3}$$

These visibility functions are similar to those used in [10] for tracking multiple objects. However, that approach used different pdfs for the inside and outside region of each object, resulting in a total of $2k$ pdfs when tracking k objects. Here, we model each region M_i with a single pdf and one common pdf p_0 representing the background region. This yields a total of only $l+1$ pdfs. After defining the necessary functions for the background as $v_0(\chi,q) := \prod_{i=1}^{l} (1 - v_i(\chi,q))$ (the background is visible if no other object can be seen) and $P_0(\chi,q) := 1$ (ignoring visibility, the background covers the whole image), we can write the new energy function in a compact way:

$$E(\chi) = - \int_{\Omega} \sum_{i=0}^{l} [v_i(\chi,q) P_i(\chi,q) \log p_i] dq. \tag{4}$$

Note the difference between the energies (1) and (4): In (1) the pdfs came in pairs, i.e., only the distributions of foreground and background have been distinguished. Although that model can handle multiple colors (or other features) per region, the spatial content in each region is not available.

In contrast, a separate pdf per region is employed in (4). Since the proposed algorithm partitions the image into more regions, the generated pdfs are more accurate. Moreover, the distributions are separated spatially. This allows to track body parts that lie completely inside the object region.

3.2 Minimization

The minimization of (4) works in a similar way to earlier approaches. However, there are two important differences. Firstly, it is necessary to distinguish the different components M_i. Secondly, it is no longer possible to directly compare the pdfs of the interior and the exterior, since there is no pdf of the exterior of an object anymore.

The first step of the minimization is to project all object components M_i into the image plane to determine the image regions they occupy. To this end, occlusions have to be handled correctly. The visibility of points given the current pose can be computed with openGL [11]. Once it is clear in which image regions the object components M_i are visible, probability density functions for the interior of each component are estimated. Moreover, a single probability density function for the background is estimated from the remainder of the image domain.

After projecting the object components M_i, the 3-D points projected onto the 2-D silhouettes of each component M_i are used as new 2-D–3-D point correspondences. Similar to the basic algorithm, the 2-D parts of those points will be moved toward the interior or the exterior of the projected object component. To decide which of these two directions is appropriate, we evaluate the two pdfs next to that point.

That is, if the pdfs indicate that a 2-D point fits better to the neighboring component, the point is shifted in contour normal direction. These new correspondences are processed in the same way as the points from the original algorithm.

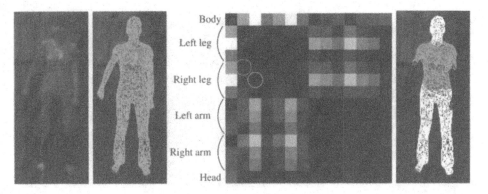

Fig. 2. This figure shows a result for the automatic splitting explained in Section 3.3. **Leftmost:** Input image (cropped). See Figure 4 to see the size of the whole image. **Left:** Object projected into the image in the initial pose. **Right:** Visualization of the similarity matrix computed for the first step of the automatic splitting algorithm. The green circle indicate the first two regions merged (the upper legs) and the blue circle the second pair of regions merged (the lower legs). **Rightmost:** Splitting suggested by the algorithm for a splitting threshold α in the interval $[0.18, 0.4]$.

3.3 Automatic Object Splitting

In order to perform an automatic splitting of kinematic chains, we assume that those parts with similar appearance should be in the same component M_i. Thus, we start by setting each M_i to a single segment of the kinematic chain. For the human model shown in Figure 2, this results in 14 different components, i.e., head, torso, three for each arm (upper, lower, and hand) and three for each leg (upper, lower, foot) (see the left image in Figure 3). Then, pdfs are estimated for every component.

Next, we search the two pdfs with minimal distance. However, there are numerous distances for probability density functions defined in the literature. We tested several of those distances, e.g., minimizing the sum of the squared differences, or the Kullback-Leibler difference [4], and found the Jensen-Shannon divergence [16] to give the best results for our problem.

Given two pdfs p and q, the Jensen-Shannon divergence, which is a smoothed and symmetrized version of the Kullback-Leibler divergence, is defined as

$$JSD(p,q) := \frac{J(p,M) + J(q,M)}{2}, \tag{5}$$

where $M = \frac{p+q}{2}$ and where J is the Kullback-Leibler divergence

$$J(p,q) := \sum_i p(i) \log \frac{p(i)}{q(i)}. \tag{6}$$

The components M_a and M_b whose pdfs a and b have the smallest distance $JSD(a,b)$ are merged to a new component. This merging step is repeated until the Jensen-Shannon divergence of all pairs of regions is bigger than a splitting threshold α. For the example

Fig. 3. Simulation of a human that moves an arm in front of its body. Here, every part of the object model was assigned a unique color and projected onto an image of a street in Palma de Mallorca. The only exception are the upper legs, which are transparent to simulate parts on the object that cannot be distinguished from the background. **From left to right**: (a) Frame 20 of the input sequence. (b) Splitting used in the initial pose in the first frame (magnified). The two components are shown in blue and magenta, respectively. (c), (d) Pose estimation results for frame 20 and 30 (magnified).

shown in Figure 2, this results in the three components also shown in that figure. Furthermore, we show an image which encodes the similarities between the different parts of the model (see left image in Figure 3). The brighter the dot, the large the divergence.

It is also possible to include the background as an additional part M_0 in the initial splitting. Every part of the model that is merged with M_0 is considered as similar to the background, and is therefore not assigned to any model part.

An interesting result of the proposed automatic splitting is that it does not include the upper arms into the same region as the lower arms. This differs from a manual splitting we have tested previously. Since both the torso and the upper parts of the arms are partly orange and partly have the color of the skin, the splitting computed automatically is to be preferred.

4   Experiments

We have tested the proposed algorithm in one synthetic environment and two real-world scenes. Figure 3 shows a synthetic image in which every joint of a human model – except the upper legs, which have intentionally been omitted – was drawn in a different color onto a cluttered background. Additionally, uncorrelated Gaussian noise with standard-deviation 15 was added after projecting to prevent the sequence from being too easy. In this monocular scene, the model moves one arm in front of its body. Consequently, we used two components M_i: One with the moving arm – shown in dark blue in the second image in Figure 3 – and the other with the remainder of the body except the upper legs, which are shown in magenta in that image. The model has 30 degrees of freedom.

Despite the above-mentioned challenges (cluttered background, only one view available, upper legs indistinguishable from the background), all thirty frames are easily tracked with the proposed approach. This is because most of the body is clearly distinguishable from the background and the surrounding body parts. The region of the upper legs, on the other hand, are simply ignored by the tracking algorithm since the upper legs do not belong to any component M_i. Tracking results are shown in Figure 3.

The challenges we created synthetically in the simulation can also appear in real world scenes, as shown in Figure 4. Again, we used one camera view and have to deal with a cluttered background. Also the appearance of the legs is close to that of the background region. As in the simulation, the right lower arm and the hand are completely inside the object region in some frames. Therefore, it is impossible to track this sequence with the basic algorithm explained in Section 2. In contrast, the tracking with multiple components works well.

In another scenario, we tested our algorithm using a sequence from the HumanEva-II database [13]. This database consists of several calibrated videos of humans performing different movements and provides background images and a surface model. These image sequences can be used for benchmarking since it is possible to automatically evaluate tracking results. This is done by using an online interface provided at Brown University which returns the tracking error in millimeter for every frame.

The automatic splitting computed with our algorithm when using a splitting threshold α between 0.12 and 0.31 is nearly identical to the splitting proposed for the sequence with the arm movement presented above. The only difference is that the head was assigned to a different component. The splitting, sample images, and tracking results are shown in Figure 5. A comparison of the proposed model to the basic one, in which the body consists of a single component, reveals that the left arm is tracked much more accurately due to the splitting introduced. This is also reflected by the results of the quantitative comparison. It is worth noting that the good quantitative results have been obtained without exploiting learned a-priori knowledge of probable motion patterns.

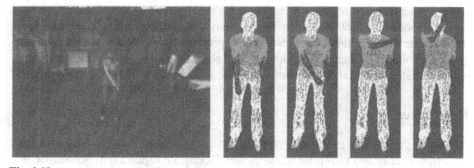

Fig. 4. Here, we tested our algorithm on a monocular real-world sequence of a woman that moves one of her arms in front of her body. The input image (left) was brightened for this paper (but not for pose tracking) in order to improve its visibility. See the left image in Figure 2 to get a feeling about the brightness of the unmodified images. **From left to right:** Input image of frame 38, and pose estimation results for frames 30,38,50, and 70 for the only view used (magnified). The different colors of the model indicate the internal regions used.

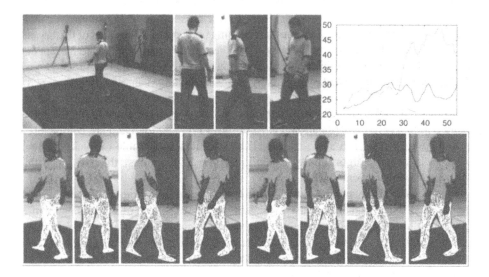

Fig. 5. This comparison shows tracking results with and without the improvements proposed when tracking a sequence from the HumanEva-II database [13]. **Top row, from left to right:** The four views available in frame 50 (three have been magnified) and the tracking error in millimeter plotted against the frame number with (blue) and without (green) using internal regions. **Bottom row:** Pose estimation result for frame 50, projected to the input images with (left) and without (right) using multiple regions. It can be seen that the left arm was only tracked correctly when using internal regions.

5   Summary

In this paper we dealt with a silhouette-based pose tracking technique. In particular, we showed how typical ambiguities of silhouette-based methods caused by self-occlusion can be avoided by splitting the model into multiple components. We presented an energy minimization formulation of the problem, where the appearance of the separate components is modeled by probability density functions and the components interact in order to determine the optimum pose. Moreover, we presented a way to automatically split a given body model by means of the Jensen-Shannon divergence. The experimental evaluation revealed significantly improved results in synthetic as well as real world scenes.

References

1. Brox, T., Rosenhahn, B., Cremers, D., Seidel, H.-P.: Nonparametric density estimation with adaptive anisotropic kernels for human motion tracking. In: Elgammal, A., Rosenhahn, B., Klette, R. (eds.) Human Motion 2007. LNCS, vol. 4814, pp. 152–165. Springer, Heidelberg (2007)
2. Fossati, A., Dimitrijevic, M., Lepetit, V., Fua, P.: Bridging the gap between detection and tracking for 3D monocular video-based motion capture. In: Proc. 2007 IEEE Computer Society Conference on Computer Vision and Pattern Recognition, Minneapolis, MI, June 2007, pp. 1–8. IEEE Computer Society Press, Los Alamitos (2007)

3. Gavrila, D.M.: The visual analysis of human movement: a survey. Computer Vision and Image Understanding 73(1), 82–98 (1999)
4. Kullback, S., Leibler, R.A.: On information and sufficiency. Annals of Mathematical Statistics 22, 79–86 (1951)
5. Micilotta, A., Ong, E., Bowden, R.: Detection and tracking of humans by probabilistic body part assembly. In: Proceedings of the British Machine Vision Conference (BMVC 2005), Oxford, UK, September 2005, pp. 429–438 (2005)
6. Moeslund, T.B., Hilton, A., Krüger, V.: A survey of advances in vision-based human motion capture and analysis. International Journal of Computer Vision 104(2), 90–126 (2006)
7. Poppe, R.: Vision-based human motion analysis: An overview. Computer Vision and Image Understanding 108(1-2), 4–18 (2007)
8. Rosenhahn, B., Brox, T., Weickert, J.: Three-dimensional shape knowledge for joint image segmentation and pose tracking. International Journal of Computer Vision 73(3), 243–262 (2007)
9. Schmaltz, C., Rosenhahn, B., Brox, T., Cremers, D., Weickert, J., Wietzke, L., Sommer, G.: Region-based pose tracking. In: Martí, J., Benedí, J.M., Mendonça, A.M., Serrat, J. (eds.) IbPRIA 2007. LNCS, vol. 4478, pp. 56–63. Springer, Heidelberg (2007)
10. Schmaltz, C., Rosenhahn, B., Brox, T., Weickert, J., Cremers, D., Wietzke, L., Sommer, G.: Occlusion modeling by tracking multiple objects. In: Hambrecht, F., Schnörr, C., Jähne, B. (eds.) DAGM 2007. LNCS, vol. 4713, pp. 173–183. Springer, Heidelberg (2007)
11. Shreiner, D., Woo, M., Neider, J., Davis, T.: OpenGL programming guide, 5th edn. Addison-Wesley, Upper Saddle River (2006)
12. Sidenbladh, H., Black, M.J., Sigal, L.: Implicit probabilistic models of human motion for synthesis and tracking. In: Heyden, A., Sparr, G., Nielsen, M., Johansen, P. (eds.) ECCV 2002. LNCS, vol. 2350, pp. 784–800. Springer, Heidelberg (2002)
13. Sigal, L., Black, M.J.: Humaneva: Synchronized video and motion capture dataset for evaluation of articulated motion. Technical Report CS-06-08, Department of Computer Science, Brown University (September 2006)
14. Sigal, L., Sidharth, B., Roth, S., Black, M., Isard, M.: Tracking loose-limbed people. In: Proc. 2004 IEEE Computer Society Conference on Computer Vision and Pattern Recognition, June 2004, vol. 1, pp. 421–428. IEEE Computer Society Press, Los Alamitos (2004)
15. Urtasun, R., Fleet, D., Fua, P.: 3D people tracking with gaussian process dynamical models. In: Proc. 2006 IEEE Computer Society Conference on Computer Vision and Pattern Recognition, New York, September 2006, pp. 238–245. IEEE Computer Society Press, Los Alamitos (2006)
16. Wong, A.K.C., You, M.: Entropy and distance of random graphs with application of structural pattern recognition. IEEE Transactions on Pattern Analysis and Machine Intelligence 7(5), 599–609 (1985)
17. Zhang, J., Collins, R., Liu, Y.: Bayesian body localization using mixture of nonlinear shape models. In: Proc. Tenth International Conference on Computer Vision, Beijing, China, October 2005, pp. 725–732. IEEE Computer Society Press, Los Alamitos (2005)

Model-Based Analysis and Synthesis
of Time-Varying Mesh

Takashi Maeda[1], Toshihiko Yamasaki[2], and Kiyoharu Aizawa[2]

[1] Department of Frontier Informatics, The University of Tokyo
[2] Department of Information and Communication Engineering, The University of Tokyo
7-3-1 Hongo, Bunkyo-ku, Tokyo 113-8656, Japan
{takashi_maeda,yamasaki,aizawa}@hal.t.u-tokyo.ac.jp

Abstract. Time-varying mesh (TVM) is a technique that describes full shape and motion of a real-world moving object. Thus, TVM is used to capture and reproduce human behavior and natural movements precisely, such as the expression of the face or small changes in cloths. But on the other hand, TVM requires large storage space and computational cost. To solve this problem, we propose a framework of motion editing and synthesis. In our approach, a skeleton model is extracted from each frame and motion tracking and analysis are conducted using the skeleton models. Then, a representative frame is deformed based on the extracted motion information. As a result, 3D scene representation with much smaller data size is made possible.

Keywords: Time-varying mesh, synthesis, compression.

1 Introduction

Recently, with the progress of computers, 3D imaging has been attracting attention. One of the latest developments is called Time-Varying Meshes (TVM) [1–3]. TVM is a sequence of 3D mesh models with high-fidelity surface texture. To generate 3D mesh models, volume intersection is employed to estimate the 3D shape along with mesh refinement techniques such as deformable mesh [1] or stereo matching [2]. One of the main features of TVM is that it can capture and reproduce human behavior and natural movements precisely, such as the expression of the face or small changes in cloths. Thus, TVM could be applied to various scenes, such as sports, movies, games, medical rehabilitations, on-site clothes fitting, and etc. But on the other hand, TVM requires large storage space and computational cost because all the frames are generated independently due to the non-rigid nature of human body and cloths. In addition, there is no explicit correspondence between neighboring frames and this makes very it difficult to process the TVM data efficiently. Therefore, efficient compression and editing method is required for TVM.

Hoppe et al. [4] proposed a progressive mesh algorithm to simplify 3D meshes. This method simplifies the model without losing the approximate shape of the model. This corresponds to a intra-frame compression. Han et al. [5] extended a block matching algorithm for 2D video compression to TVM for inter-frame compression and compressed the data to 9 -19% of the original size. Xu et al. [6] proposed a

F.J. Perales and R.B. Fisher (Eds.): AMDO 2008, LNCS 5098, pp. 112–121, 2008.

method to segment 3D mesh models and deform each segment to interpolate mid-frames of each neighboring frame to have smooth sequence. However, these techniques are not feasible for drastic data reduction of TVM.

In this paper, we propose a method to make a motion similar to TVM using only a single frame. Although there is no explicit correspondence between neighboring frames, the basic shape and color of the model are almost the same throughout the sequence. Therefore, we could still keep the moderate quality of TVM without refreshing the 3D model every frame. Also, our method contributes to reducing the data size and computational cost.

Our method first extracts skeleton data from each frame of TVM, which consists of nine bones connected to the center of the model. After extracting skeletons from each frame, we find a rotation matrix for each bones of the respective frames from the first frame. Next step is to split the first frame of the TVM into 10 segments. At last, we move each segment of the first frame according to the rotation matrices from the skeleton. As a result, we are able to reduce the data size of each frame to 300 bytes, except for the first frame. The proposed motion segmentation and synthesis also makes it possible to apply human motion obtained by motion capture systems to real 3D human models such as our TVM.

Similar approach can be found in [7], in which Reeb-graph-matching-based mesh deformation is proposed for compression. However, in [7], the deformation was applied only to a few frames whose motion is not so large. In our approach, we have developed skeleton extraction, topology matching, segmentation, and deformation methods feasible for longer sequences. In addition, in this paper, we reveal a problem in such a skeleton-based motion extraction and deformation approach, and propose a method to solve the problem.

2 Time-Varying Meshes

The TVM data in this work were obtained employing the system in [2]. They were generated from multiple-view images taken with 22 synchronous cameras in a dedicated studio of 8 m in diameter and 2.5 m in height. Different from 2D video, TVM is composed of a sequence of 3D models. An example of our TVM data seen from a certain view point is shown in Fig. 1. Needless to say, the view point can be changed arbitrary according to the users' taste. Each frame of TVM is represented as a polygon mesh model. Namely, each frame is expressed by three kinds of data: coordinates of vertices, their connection, and color.

3 Skeleton Extraction and Model Segmentation

Although there is no explicit correspondence between frames, the appearance of neighboring frames is quite similar. Furthermore, the basic composition of the model, such as the size or color of the model is almost constant throughout the sequence. For this reason, we propose a method to use only a single frame of the TVM and deform each segment of the frame along with the extracted skeleton from TVM sequence. In this section, we discuss skeleton extraction and model segmentation.

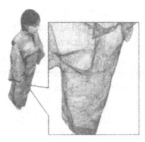

Fig. 1. Detail of 3D mesh model. It consists of coordinates of vertices, their connection, and color for each vertex.

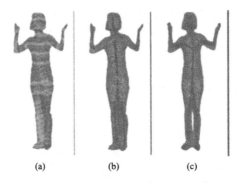

(a)   (b)   (c)

Fig. 2. Skeleton extraction. (a) shows mesh segmentation result using [8]. Each mass of band shows it has the similar geodesic distance from the central cross section of the model. (b) shows the center of each band. Few joints and bones will be added by the proportion of human at (c).

3.1 Skeleton Extraction

To extract a skeleton from each frame, we used Reeb-graph [8–10] and proportion of the human body by Vitruvian Man of Leonardo da Vinci as shown in Fig. 2. Reeb-graph is a method to find a skeleton of the 3D Model based on geodesic distance from the central cross section of the model. Fig. 2(a) shows each mass of band with the similar geodesic distance and Fig. 2(b) shows the center of each band, which some of these centers will be joints. As shown in these two figures, this method cannot divide the shoulder and body.

In order to divide shoulder and body, and to define each bones, we used the proportion of the Vituruvian Man by Leonardo da Vinci. Ratios that we used are as follows.

- human head is about 1/8 of his/her height
- the pelvis is midway between neck and feet
- the length from the finger tip to tip approximates to full height

With this method, a stable and accurate skeleton is extracted as shown in Fig. 2(c).

Fig. 3. Model segmentation results. To divide the model into 10 segments, we find the minimum distance from each vertex to all the bones to find out where each vertex belongs to.

3.2 Model Segmentation

As mentioned, we propose a method to deform the first frame of the TVM along with the extracted skeleton. In order to do so, we need to segment the entire 3D model to rigid parts so that each segment moves with respective bone. As shown in Fig. 3, for each vertex of the model, we calculated the distance from the vertex to all the bones to find the shortest distance which that vertex belongs to. In this paper, we have segmented the model into 10 segments: torso, head, upper legs and arms, lower legs and arms. Please refer to [10] for more details of the segmentation process.

4 Motion Data Extraction from Skeleton

In this section, we discuss how to move each segment of the model along with the extracted skeleton. For this purpose, we need to find the rotation matrix of each bones of the skeleton from the corresponding bones in the first frame. Each bones are defined as (x, y, z) vector from the joints.

4.1 Model Segmentation

Our goal is to find the rotation matrix R from vector $\mathbf{V} = (x, y, z)$ to $\mathbf{U} = (x', y', z')$ as shown in Eq. (1).

$$(x', y', z')^t = R(x, y, z)^t . \tag{1}$$

Generally, there are numerous combinations of rotation matrix R when using X, Y, Z axes. But not all the combinations are valid for our approach. For example, in Fig. 4, both left legs' bones are parallel to Z axis. These two are exactly the same in terms of the direction of the vectors, but segments are facing different ways.

This means that some rotation matrix R could twist the segment to unnatural ways even though the bone is rotated correctly, as shown in Fig. 4. Thus, we need to give some restriction when finding the rotation matrix R.

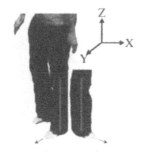

Fig. 4. Problem when rotating segments. Even though both bones have the same vector direction, two segments are not facing the same direction.

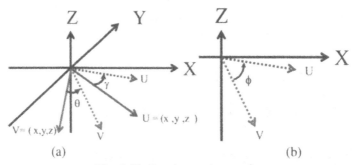

Fig. 5. Finding the rotation matrix

4.2 Finding the Rotation Matrix

As described above, there needs to be some restriction when searching for the rotation matrix R. The major problem is that some combination of matrix could twist segments to unnatural ways. We assume that "unnatural twist" occurs when trying to rotate around the axis of the largest absolute value of the vector. For example, in Fig. 4, this will be the Z axis. Thus, we propose a method to find a rotation matrix with using only the other two axes. This could decrease the accuracy of deformation of respective segment, but we still prefer preventing "unnatural twist".

The procedure to find the rotation matrix R from vector V to U is as follows. Fig. 5 shows the example of finding the rotation matrix R with using only X and Y axes.

- Find X rotation angle θ of V from the inner product of V and the Z axis $(0, 0, z)$
- Find X rotation angle γ of U from the inner product of U and the Z axis $(0, 0, z)$
- Rotate both vector by θ and γ respectively (V to V', U to U').
- Find Y rotation angle ϕ between V' and U' from inner product.
- Rotate V' by ϕ around Y axis.
- Rotate V' by $-\gamma$ around X axis.

Thus, rotation matrix R can be written as Eq. (2).

$$R = X_{-\gamma} Y_{\phi} X_{\theta} .$$

(2)

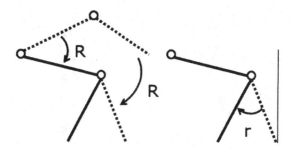

Fig. 6. Hierarchical structure of the skeleton. Lower arms and legs must be rotated only after rotating the upper segment.

4.3 Hierarchical Structure of Skeleton

When finding the rotation matrix, we need to take the hierarchical structure of the skeleton into consideration. For example, when rotating the upper arm, then the lower arm should follow that rotation. Thus, when rotating the lower arm and the lower leg, we need to consider the effect of the upper segment of the model. As shown in Fig. 6, we will find the rotation angles of the lower segment of the model as follows.

- Rotate both the upper and lower segments by upper segments' rotation matrix R.
- After rotating the lower segment by R, find the rotation matrix r.

5 Experimental Results and Discussion

In this section, we discuss our experimental results. In the experiment, we used TVM consisting of 45 frames with the frame rate of 10 fps.

Fig. 7(a) shows the original TVM frames, (b) shows the extracted skeleton, and (c) shows the deformed mesh model from the skeleton. As can be seen, our method has similar motion compared to the original TVM although cloths and face does not change. Also, there is no unnatural twist in joints.

To evaluate the computational cost, we compare the proposed method with the original TVM sequence by the data size throughout the sequence in Fig. 8, memory cost in Fig. 9, time for the initialization in Fig. 10, and time to display each frame in Fig. 11. There are two possible approaches for displaying TVM in conventional browsers [2]. One is reading the whole sequence in the memory in advance (type-A), and the other is reading and displaying one frame after another (type-B). These two approaches have pros and cons. Reading the whole sequence (type-A) takes quite long time for initialization while rendering is very fast. Reading and displaying one by one (type-B) is memory-efficient but the disk access is a bottleneck.

The machine we used in experiment was as follows.

- OS: Windows XP Professional
- CPU: Pentium (R) D 3.40GHz
- Memory: 3GB
- Coding Environment: C and OpenGL with Visual Studio 2005 Professional.

(a)   (b)   (c)

Fig. 7. Motion from extracted skeleton. (a) is the original TVM sequence. (b) is the extracted skeleton from each frame. (c) is the reconstructed TVM frames using the proposed method. Frame numbers in the figure are 1, 5, 15, 30, 36, and 43 from the top.

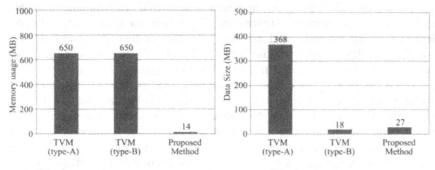

Fig. 8. Data size.   **Fig. 9.** Memory cost.

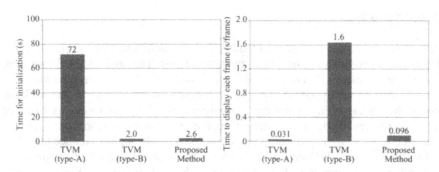

Fig. 10. Initialization time   **Fig. 11.** Time to display each frame.

As shown in Fig. 8, our method requires approximately 1/*TotalFrameNumber* of data size compared to original TVM, because our method uses only a single frame throughout the sequence. The data for rotation information consumes only 300 bytes per frame. This also helps in terms of memory consumption as shown in Fig. 9. It is much better than TVM (type-B) where we have to read all of the frames before running the sequence. Our method requires a little bit more memory than TVN (type-A) because we need data for the original vertices and also for the vertices for rotation.

Our method is also valid in terms of initialization time and display time as shown in Figs. 10 and 11. Type-A takes only 0.031 second to display each frame (32 frames per second), but it takes more than 70 seconds to display the first frame because of reading all the 45 frames of data before displaying. Type-B has the fastest for the initialization, but the display time is desperate as it takes more than 1.5 seconds to display each frame after the initialization. On the other hand, our method takes only a few seconds to initialize and has the display time of about 0.1 second (10 frames per second). Thus, our method is better in terms of data size and computational cost.

Also, our motion extraction and synthesis has high compatibility with the conventional motion capture systems. Since the bone structure and feature points are made clear by our method, it can be made possible to apply motion capture data to TVM to control its motion. In other words, motion capture data can control 3D mesh model of a real human, not a CG model.

But on the other hand, there are some challenges remaining. First of all, we have to sacrifice the main feature of TVM, such as the expression of the faces or small changes in cloths. Therefore, our approach would find applications in mobile terminals where computational resources and display size are quite limited. Another problem is that our method could not deal with the rotation of the model itself, because we calculated each rotation angle by using only two axes to avoid the unnatural twist of joints. Thus, our method could only apply to the sequence without body rotation because if body rotates 90 degrees, we might have to change the rotation axis to find the rotation matrix of each bone. To solve this problem, we need to have some other features other than bones (which is three dimensional vector) when calculating the rotation matrix so that we can find the rotation matrix with using three axis. For this purpose, we have already been developing a more robust motion parameter extraction algorithm using the surface gradient of the 3D meshes [11].

6 Conclusions

In this paper, we have proposed a method to make a motion similar to original TVM with much smaller data size and less computational cost. The original TVM data were segmented and skeleton structure was extracted from the TVM. Then, the rotation of joints was calculated by taking the correspondence of each bone in the skeleton model. Although extracting the rotation parameters using skeleton models is a kind of ill-defined problem, moderate accuracy of motion parameter extraction was achieved by sacrificing one degree of freedom in motion. As a result, we have reduced the data size to approximately $1/TotalFrameNumber$, the memory consumption to about 30MB, the initialization time to about 3 seconds, and display time of about 0.1 second.

Acknowledgments

This work is supported by Ministry of Education, Culture, Sports, Science and Technology, Japan within the research project "Development of fundamental software technologies for digital archives". The generation studio is provided by NHK, Japan.

References

1. Matsuyama, T., Wu, X., Takai, T., Wada, T.: Real-Time Dynamic 3-D Object Shape Reconstruction and High-Fidelity Texture Mapping for 3-D Video. IEEE Trans. CSVT 14(3), 357–369 (2004)
2. Tomiyama, K., Orihara, Y., Katayama, M., Iwadate, Y.: Algorithm for dynamic 3D object generation from multi-viewpoint images. In: Proc. SPIE, vol. 5599, pp. 153–161 (2004)
3. Kanade, T., Rander, P., Narayanan, P.: Virtualized reality: Construction Virtual Worlds from Real Scenes. IEEE Multimedia 4(1), 34–47 (1997)
4. Hoppe, H.: Progressive Meshes. In: Proc. SIGGRAPH, pp. 99–108 (1996)
5. Han, S., Yamasaki, T., Aizawa, K.: Time-varying Mesh Compression Using Extended Block Matching Algorithm. IEEE Transactions on Circuit and Systems for Video Technology 17(11), 1506–1518 (2007)

6. Xu, J., Yamasaki, T., Aizawa, K.: Deformation of time-varying-mesh based on semantic human model. In: Proc. IEEE ICME 2007, pp. 1700–1703 (2007)
7. Tung, T., Schmitt, F., Matsuyama, T.: Topology Matching for 3D Video Compression. In: IEEE Computer Society Conference on Computer Vision and Pattern Recognition (CVPR 2007), Minneapolis, MN, USA, pp. 1–8 (2007)
8. Hilaga, M., Shinagawa, Y., Kohmura, T., Kunii, T.L.: Topology matching for fullyautomatic similarity estimation of 3d shapes. In: Proc. SIGGRAPH 2001, pp. 203–212 (2001)
9. Tadano, R., Yamasaki, T., Aizawa, K.: Fast and robust motion tracking for time-varying mesh featuring Reeb-graph-based skeleton fitting and its application to motion retrieval. In: Proceedings of 2007 IEEE International Conference on Multimedia and Expo (ICME 2007), Beijing, China, July 2-5, pp. 2010–2013 (2007)
10. Lee, N.S., Yamasaki, T., Aizawa, K.: Hierarchical mesh decomposition and motion tracking for time-varying-meshes. In: Proc. 2008 IEEE International Conference on Multimedia & Expo (ICME 2008), Hannover, Germany, July 23-26 (2008)
11. Lee, N.S., Yamasaki, T., Aizawa, K.: Motion Tracking Through Surface Gradient Matching for Time-Varying Mesh. In: Meeting on Image Understanding 2008 (MIRU 2008), Nagano, Japan, July 29-31 (to be presented, 2008)

Mesh Vertex Pose and Position Interpolation Using Geometric Algebra

Rich Wareham and Joan Lasenby

Department of Engineering, University of Cambridge,
Trumpington Street, Cambridge, CB2 1PZ, UK
{rjw57,jl221}@cam.ac.uk

Abstract. This paper presents a method of interpolating between two or more general displacements (rotation and translation). The resulting interpolated path is smooth and possesses a number of desirable properties. It differs from existing algorithms which require factorising the pose into separate rotation and translation components and is derived from an intuitively appealing framework–i.e. a natural extension of the standard interpolation scheme for pure rotations. While this paper presents the theory behind the interpolation and its description as a tool, we also outline the possible advantages of using this technique for vision and graphics applications.

Keywords: Geometric Algebra, keyframes, non-Euclidean geometry, pose interpolation, SLERP.

1 Introduction

Geometric Algebra, the application of Clifford algebras to geometric problems [1], has recently been found to have useful applications in many areas of Physics and Engineering [1,2,3], often resulting in a more compact and clear description of a problem whilst also providing significant geometric insight. In this paper we assume a basic familiarity with Clifford algebras and good introductions are available [4,5].

In this paper we will consider the use of *Conformal Geometric Algebra* [1,6,4] which maps n-dimensional vectors into an $(n + 2)$-dimensional subspace of null-vectors. The extended space these null-vectors occupy is obtained by adding two more orthogonal basis vectors, e and $\bar{e}$ such that $e^2 = 1$, $\bar{e}^2 = -1$. The null-vectors themselves are mapped from the original vectors via an adaptation [6] of the so-called *Hestenes mapping* [1]:

$$x \mapsto \frac{1}{2\lambda^2} \left(x^2 n + 2\lambda x - \lambda^2 \bar{n}\right)$$

where $n = e + \bar{e}$ and $\bar{n} = e - \bar{e}$. The constant λ is an arbitrary length which is present to keep dimensional consistency. For Euclidean geometries its value is usually kept at unity to simplify further calculation. We often express this

F.J. Perales and R.B. Fisher (Eds.): AMDO 2008, LNCS 5098, pp. 122–131, 2008.
© Springer-Verlag Berlin Heidelberg 2008

mapping via the function $F(\cdot)$ such that the n-dimensional vector x is represented by the $(n+2)$-dimensional null-vector $F(x)$.

We shall use the term *general displacement*, or simply *displacement*, to denote an arbitrary rigid-body transformation, combination of pure-rotation and translation, within a particular geometry. We shall also use, unless stated otherwise, Euclidean three-dimensional geometry although the techniques presented here readily generalise into higher-dimensions and even non-Euclidean geometries.

2   Bivector Exponentiation

In [4] it was shown how general displacements can be represented in Conformal Geometric Algebra via an element termed a *rotor*. Such elements are formed by exponentiating another class of elements known as *bivectors*. Rotations are generated by bivectors with no component parallel to n and translations by a bivector with no components perpendicular to n.

We now suppose that we may interpolate rotors by defining some function $\ell(R)$ which acts upon rotors to give the generating bivector element. We then perform direct interpolation of these generators. We postulate that direct interpolation of these bivectors, as in the reformulation of quaternionic interpolation above, will give some smooth interpolation between the displacements. It is therefore a defining property of $\ell(R)$ that

$$R \equiv \exp(\ell(R)) \tag{1}$$

and so $\ell(R)$ may be considered as to act as a logarithm-like function in this context. It is worth noting that $\ell(R)$ does not possess all the properties usually associated with logarithms, notably that, since $\exp(A)\exp(B)$ is not generally equal to $\exp(B)\exp(A)$ in non-commuting algebras, $\ell(\exp(A)\exp(B))$ cannot be equal to $A + B$ except in special cases.

2.1   Form of $\exp(B)$ in Euclidean Space

Lemma 1. *If B is of the form $B = \phi P + tn$ where $t \in \mathbb{R}^n$, ϕ is some scalar and P is a 2-blade where $P^2 = -1$ then, for any $k \in \mathbb{Z}^+$,*

$$B^k = \phi^k P^k + \alpha_k^{(1)} \phi Ptn + \alpha_k^{(2)} \phi^2 PtnP + \alpha_k^{(3)} \phi tnP + \alpha_k^{(4)} tn$$

with the following recurrence relations for $\alpha_k^{(\cdot)}$, $k > 0$

$$\alpha_k^{(1)} = -\phi^2 \alpha_{k-1}^{(2)}, \; \alpha_k^{(2)} = \alpha_{k-1}^{(1)}$$
$$\alpha_k^{(3)} = \alpha_{k-1}^{(4)}, \quad \alpha_k^{(4)} = \phi^{k-1} P^{k-1} - \phi^2 \alpha_{k-1}^{(3)}$$

with $\alpha_0^{(1)} = \alpha_0^{(2)} = \alpha_0^{(3)} = \alpha_0^{(4)} = 0$.

Proof. Firstly note that the theorem is trivially provable by direct substitution for the cases $k = 0$ and $k = 1$. We thereafter seek a proof by induction.

Assuming the expression for B^{k-1} is correct, we post-multiply by $\phi P + tn$ to obtain

$$B^k = \phi^k P^k + \alpha_{k-1}^{(1)} \phi^2 PtnP + \alpha_{k-1}^{(2)} \phi^3 PtnP^2 + \alpha_{k-1}^{(3)} \phi^2 tnP^2 +$$
$$\alpha_{k-1}^{(4)} \phi tnP + \phi^{k-1} P^{k-1} tn + \alpha_{k-1}^{(1)} \phi P(tn)^2 + \alpha_{k-1}^{(2)} \phi^2 PtnPtn +$$
$$\alpha_{k-1}^{(3)} \phi tnPtn + \alpha_{k-1}^{(4)} (tn)^2$$

Substituting $P^2 = -1$, $(tn)^2 = -tn^2 t = 0$ and noting that $nPt = -Ptn$ leading to $tnPtn = -tPtn^2 = 0$

$$B^k = \phi^k P^k - (\alpha_{k-1}^{(2)} \phi^2)\phi Ptn + \alpha_{k-1}^{(1)} \phi^2 PtnP +$$
$$\alpha_{k-1}^{(4)} \phi tnP + (\phi^{k-1} P^{k-1} - \alpha_{k-1}^{(3)} \phi^2)tn$$

Equating like coefficients we obtain the required recurrence relations.

Lemma 2. *Assuming the form of B given in lemma 1, for $k \in \mathbb{Z}^+$,*

$$B^{2k} = (-1)^k \phi^{2k} - k(-1)^k \phi^{2k-1}[tnP + Ptn]$$

and

$$B^{2k+1} = (-1)^k \phi^{2k+1} P + k\phi^{2k}(-1)^k[tn - PtnP] + (-1)^k \phi^{2k} tn$$

Proof. Starting from $\alpha_0^{(\cdot)} = 0$ it is clear that the recurrence relations above imply that $\alpha_k^{(1)} = \alpha_k^{(2)} = 0 \ \forall \ k \geq 0$. Substituting $\alpha_k^{(3)} = \alpha_{k-1}^{(4)}$ it is trivial to show that the relation for $\alpha_k^{(4)}$ is satisfied by

$$\alpha_k^{(4)} = \begin{cases} \frac{k}{2}(\phi P)^{k-1} & k \text{ even,} \\ \frac{k+1}{2}(\phi P)^{k-1} & k \text{ odd.} \end{cases}$$

When substituted into the expression for B^k, we obtain the result stated above.

Theorem 1. *If B is a bivector of the form given in theorem 1 then, defining $t_\parallel$ as the component of t lying in the plane of P and $t_\perp = t - t_\parallel$,*

$$\exp(B) = [\cos(\phi) + \sin(\phi)P][1 + t_\perp n] + \text{sinc}(\phi)t_\parallel n$$

Proof. Consider the power series expansion of $\exp(B)$,

$$\exp(B) = \sum_{k=0}^{\infty} \frac{B^k}{k!} = \sum_{k=0}^{\infty} \left[\frac{B^{2k}}{(2k)!} + \frac{B^{2k+1}}{(2k+1)!}\right]$$

Substituting the expansion for B^{2k} and B^{2k+1} from lemma 2

$$\exp(B) = \sum_{k=0}^{\infty} \left[\frac{(-1)^k \phi^{2k}}{(2k)!} - k\frac{(-1)^k \phi^{2k-1}}{(2k)!}(tnP + Ptn)\right]$$
$$+ \sum_{k=0}^{\infty} \left[\frac{(-1)^k \phi^{2k}}{(2k+1)!}(\phi P + tn) + k\frac{(-1)^k \phi^{2k}}{(2k+1)!}(tn - PtnP)\right]$$

We now substitute the following power-series representations

$$\cos(z) = \sum_{k=0}^{\infty} \frac{(-1)^k z^{2k}}{(2k)!} \qquad\qquad \mathrm{sinc}(z) = \sum_{k=0}^{\infty} \frac{(-1)^k z^{2k}}{(2k+1)!}$$

$$-z\sin(z) = \sum_{k=0}^{\infty} 2k\frac{(-1)^k z^{2k}}{(2k)!} \qquad \cos(z) - \mathrm{sinc}(z) = \sum_{k=0}^{\infty} 2k\frac{(-1)^k z^{2k}}{(2k+1)!}$$

to obtain

$$\exp(B) = \cos\phi + \sin(\phi)\frac{1}{2}(tnP + Ptn) + \mathrm{sinc}(\phi)(\phi P + tn)$$
$$+ \frac{1}{2}\left[\cos(\phi) - \mathrm{sinc}(\phi)\right](tn - PtnP)$$

By considering parallel and perpendicular components of t with respect to the plane of P is easy to verify that $tnP + Ptn = 2Pt_\perp n$ and $PtnP = (t_\parallel - t_\perp)n$ hence

$$\exp(B) = \cos\phi + \sin(\phi)Pt_\perp n + \mathrm{sinc}(\phi)(\phi P + tn) + \left[\cos(\phi) - \mathrm{sinc}(\phi)\right]t_\perp n$$
$$= \left[\cos(\phi) + \sin(\phi)P\right]\left[1 + t_\perp n\right] + \mathrm{sinc}(\phi)t_\parallel n$$

as required.

Definition 1. *A* twist *is a rotor whose action is to rotate by ψ in the plane of P whilst translating along a vector a perpendicular to the plane of P. It may therefore be defined by the rotor*

$$\tau(\psi, P, a) = \left[\cos\left(\frac{\psi}{2}\right) + \sin\left(\frac{\psi}{2}\right)P\right]\left[1 + \frac{na}{2}\right]$$

where ψ is a scalar, P is a 2-blade normalised such that $P^2 = -1$ and a is some vector satisfying $a \cdot n = a \cdot P = 0$.

Lemma 3. *The exponentiation function may be re-expressed using a twist*

$$\exp\left(\frac{\psi}{2}P + \frac{tn}{2}\right) = \left[1 + \mathrm{sinc}\left(\frac{\psi}{2}\right)\frac{t_\parallel n}{2}\tilde{\tau}(\psi, P, -t_\perp)\right]\tau(\psi, P, -t_\perp)$$

Proof. We firstly substitute our definition of a twist into our form for the exponential

$$\exp\left(\frac{\psi}{2}P + \frac{tn}{2}\right) = \tau(\psi, P, -t_\perp) + \mathrm{sinc}\left(\frac{\psi}{2}\right)\frac{t_\parallel n}{2} \qquad\qquad (2)$$

noting that, since twists are rotors, $\tau(\cdot)\tilde{\tau}(\cdot) = 1$, it is trivial to verify that the required expression is equivalent to this form of the exponential.

Lemma 4. *The expression*

$$1 + \mathrm{sinc}\left(\frac{\psi}{2}\right)\frac{t_\parallel n}{2}\tilde{\tau}(\psi, P, -t_\perp)$$

is a rotor which acts to translate along a vector $t'_\parallel$ given by

$$t'_\parallel = -\mathrm{sinc}\left(\frac{\psi}{2}\right) t_\parallel \left(\cos\left(\frac{\psi}{2}\right) - \sin\left(\frac{\psi}{2}\right) P\right)$$

Proof. The expression above may be obtained by substituting for the twist in the initial expression and simplifying. It is clearly a vector since multiplying $t_\parallel$ on the left by P is just a rotation by $\pi/2$ in the plane of P.

We have now developed the required theorems and tools to discuss the action of the rotor

$$R = \exp\left(\frac{\psi}{2}P + \frac{tn}{2}\right)$$

It translates along a vector $t_\perp$ which is the component of t which does not lie in the plane of P, rotates by ψ in the plane of P and finally translates along $t'_\parallel$ which is given by

$$t'_\parallel = -\mathrm{sinc}\left(\frac{\psi}{2}\right) t_\parallel \left(\cos\left(\frac{\psi}{2}\right) - \sin\left(\frac{\psi}{2}\right) P\right)$$

which is the component of t lying in the plane of P, rotated by $\psi/2$ in that plane. We have not yet verified that $\exp(B)$ is indeed a rotor and such a verification is beyond the scope of this paper. Interested readers may find such a verification in [4].

2.2   Method for Evaluating $\ell(R)$

We have found a form for $\exp(B)$ given that B is in a particular form. Now we seek a method to take an arbitrary displacement rotor, $R = \exp(B)$ and reconstruct the original B. Should there exist a B for all possible R, we will show that our initial assumption that all displacement rotors can be formed from a single exponentiated bivector of special form is valid. We shall term this initial bivector the *generator* rotor (to draw a parallel with Lie algebras).

We can obtain the following identities for $B = (\psi/2)P + tn/2$ by simply considering the grade of each component of the exponential:

$$\langle R\rangle_0 = \cos\left(\frac{\psi}{2}\right), \quad \langle R\rangle_2 = \sin\left(\frac{\psi}{2}\right)P + \cos\left(\frac{\psi}{2}\right)t_\perp n + \mathrm{sinc}\left(\frac{\psi}{2}\right)t_\parallel n$$

$$\langle R\rangle_4 = \sin\left(\frac{\psi}{2}\right)Pt_\perp n$$

It is somewhat straightforward to reconstruct $\psi, t_\perp$ and $t_\parallel$ from these components by partitioning a rotor as above. Once we have a method which gives the generator B for any displacement rotor R we have validated our assumption.

In [4] it was shown that the inverse-exponential function $\ell(R)$ is given by

$$\ell(R) = ab + c_\perp n + c_\parallel n$$

where

$$\|ab\| = \sqrt{|(ab)^2|} = \cos^{-1}(\langle R \rangle_0), \quad ab = \frac{(\langle R \rangle_2 \, n) \cdot e}{\operatorname{sinc}(\|ab\|)}$$

$$c_\perp n = -\frac{ab \, \langle R \rangle_4}{\|ab\|^2 \operatorname{sinc}(\|ab\|)}, \quad c_\| n = -\frac{ab \, \langle ab \, \langle R \rangle_2 \rangle_2}{\|ab\|^2 \operatorname{sinc}(\|ab\|)}.$$

3   Interpolation Via Logarithms

We have shown that any displacement of Euclidean geometry[1] may be mapped smoothly onto a linear sub-space of the bivectors. This immediately suggests applications to smooth interpolation of displacements. Consider a set of poses we wish to interpolate, $\{P_1, P_2, ..., P_n\}$ and a set of rotors which transform some origin pose to these target poses, $\{R_1, R_2, ..., R_n\}$. We may map these rotors onto the set of bivectors $\{\ell(R_1), \ell(R_2), ..., \ell(R_n)\}$ which are simply points in some linear subspace. We may now choose any interpolation of these bivectors which lies in this space and for any bivector on the interpolant, B'_λ, we can compute a pose, $\exp(B'_\lambda)$.

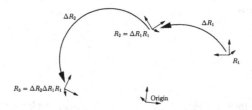

Fig. 1. Rotors used to piece-wise linearly interpolate between key-rotors

Another interpolation scheme is to have the poses defined by a set of chained rotors so that $\{P_1, P_2, ..., P_n\}$ is represented by

$$\{R_1, \Delta R_1 R_1, \Delta R_2 R_2, ..., \Delta R_n R_n\}$$

where $R_i = \Delta R_{i-1} R_{i-1}$ as in figure 1. Using this scheme the interpolation between pose R_i and R_{i+1} involves forming the rotor $R_{i,\lambda} = \exp(B_{i,\lambda}) R_{i-1}$ where $B_{i,\lambda} = \lambda \ell(\Delta R_{i-1})$ and λ varies between 0 and 1 giving $R_{i,0} = R_{i-1}$ and $R_{i,1} = R_i$.

We now investigate two interpolation schemes which interpolate through target poses, ensuring that each pose is passed through. This kind of interpolation is often required for key-frame animation techniques. The first form of interpolation is piece-wise linear interpolation of the relative rotors (the latter case above). The second is direct quadratic interpolation of the bivectors representing the final poses (the former case).

---

[1] Other geometries may be considered with appropriate modification of the rotors [6].

3.1   Piece-Wise Linear Interpolation

Direct piece-wise linear interpolation of the set of bivectors is one of the simplest interpolation schemes we can consider. Consider the example shown in figure 1. Here there are three rotors to be interpolated. We firstly find a rotor, ΔR_n which takes us from rotor R_n to the next in the interpolation sequence, R_{n+1}.

$$R_{n+1} = (\Delta R_n)R_n, \quad \Delta R_n = R_{n+1}\tilde{R}_n.$$

We then find the bivector, ΔB_n which generates $\Delta R_n = \exp(\Delta B_n)$. Finally we form a rotor interpolating between R_n and R_{n+1}:

$$R_{n,\lambda} = \exp(\lambda \Delta B_n)R_n$$

where λ is in the range $[0,1]$ and $R_{n,0} = R_n$ and $R_{n,1} = R_{n+1}$. Clearly this interpolation scheme changes abruptly at interpolation points, something which is reflected in the resulting interpolation as shown in figure 2.

3.2   Quadratic Interpolation

Another simple form for interpolation is the quadratic interpolation where a quadratic is fitted through three interpolation points, $\{B_1, B_2, B_3\}$ with an interpolation parameter varying in the range $(-1, +1)$:

$$B'_\lambda = \left(\frac{B_3 + B_1}{2} - B_2\right)\lambda^2 + \frac{B_3 - B_1}{2}\lambda + B_2$$

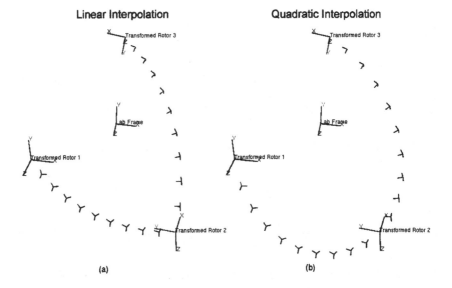

Fig. 2. Examples of a) piece-wise linear and b) quadratic interpolation for three representative poses

giving
$$B'_{-1} = B_1, \quad B'_0 = B_2 \text{ and } B'_{+1} = B_3$$

This interpolation varies smoothly through B_2 and is reflected in the final interpolation, as shown in figure 2. Extensions to the quadratic interpolation for more than three interpolation points, such as smoothed quadratic interpolation [7] are readily available.

3.3   Alternate Methods

It is worth noting that each of the methods described above may be performed using either direct interpolation of the bivector $\ell(R)$ corresponding to a rotor R or by interpolating the relative rotors which take one frame to another. It is not yet clear which will give the best results and indeed it is probably application dependent.

4   Form of the Interpolation

In this section we derive a clearer picture of the precise form of a simple linear interpolation between two frames in order to relate the interpolation to existing methods used in mechanics and robotics. We will consider the method used above whereby the rotor being interpolated takes one pose to another.

4.1   Path of the Linear Interpolation

Since we have shown that $\exp(B)$ is indeed a rotor, it follows that any Euclidean pure-translation rotor will commute with it. Thus we only need consider the interpolant path when interpolating from the origin to some other point since any other interpolation can be obtained by simply translating the origin to the start point. This location independence of the interpolation is a desirable property in itself but also provides a powerful analysis mechanism.

We have identified in section 2.1 the action of the $\exp(B)$ rotor in terms of $\psi, P, t_{\parallel}$ and $t_{\perp}$. We now investigate the resulting interpolant path when interpolating from the origin. We shall consider the interpolant $R_\lambda = \exp(\lambda B)$ where λ is the interpolation co-ordinate and varies from 0 to 1. For any values of $\psi, P, t_{\parallel}$ and $t_{\perp}$,

$$\lambda B = \frac{\lambda \psi}{2} P + \frac{\lambda(t_{\perp} + t_{\parallel})n}{2}$$

from which we see that the action of $\exp(\lambda B)$ is a translation along $\lambda t_{\perp}$, a rotation by $\lambda \psi$ in the plane of P and finally a translation along

$$t'_{\parallel} = -\mathrm{sinc}\left(\frac{\lambda \psi}{2}\right) \lambda t_{\parallel} \left(\cos\left(\frac{\lambda \psi}{2}\right) - \sin\left(\frac{\lambda \psi}{2}\right) P\right).$$

We firstly resolve a three dimensional, orthonormal, basis relative to P where vectors a and b are orthonormal vectors in the plane of P and hence $P = ab$ and

$t_\perp$ is the normal to plane P. We may now express $t_\parallel$ as $t_\parallel = t^a a + t^b b$ where $t^{\{a,b\}}$ are suitably valued scalars.

The initial action of $\exp(B)$ upon a frame centred at the origin is therefore to translate it to $\lambda t_\perp$ followed by a rotation in the plane of P. Due to our choice of starting point, this has no effect on the frame's location (but will have an effect on the pose, see the next section).

Finally there is a translation along $t_\parallel'$ which, using $c = \cos\left(\frac{\lambda\psi}{2}\right)$ and $s = \sin\left(\frac{\lambda\psi}{2}\right)$, can be expressed in terms of a and b as

$$t_\parallel' = -\frac{2s}{\lambda\psi}\lambda(t^a a + t^b b)(c - sab)$$

$$\equiv -\frac{2s}{\psi}a(t^a c + t^b s) + b(t^b c - t^a s).$$

The position, r_λ, of the frame at λ along the interpolation is therefore

$$r_\lambda = -\frac{2s}{\psi}(a(t^a c + t^b s) + b(t^b c - t^a s)) + \lambda t_\perp$$

which can easily be transformed via the harmonic addition theorem to

$$r_\lambda = -\frac{2s}{\psi}\alpha\left[a\cos\left(\frac{\lambda\psi}{2} + \beta_1\right) + b\cos\left(\frac{\lambda\psi}{2} + \beta_2\right)\right] + \lambda t_\perp$$

where $\alpha^2 = (t^a)^2 + (t^b)^2$, $\tan\beta_1 = -\frac{t^b}{t^a}$ and $\tan\beta_2 = -\frac{-t^a}{t^b}$. It is easy, via geometric construction or otherwise, to verify that this implies that $\beta_2 = \beta_1 + \frac{\pi}{2}$. Hence $\cos(\theta + \beta_2) = -\sin(\theta + \beta_1)$. We can now express the frame's position as

$$r_\lambda = -\frac{2\alpha}{\psi}\left[a\sin\left(\frac{\lambda\psi}{2}\right)\cos\left(\frac{\lambda\psi}{2} + \beta_1\right) - b\sin\left(\frac{\lambda\psi}{2}\right)\sin\left(\frac{\lambda\psi}{2} + \beta_1\right)\right] + \lambda t_\perp$$

which can be re-arranged to give

$$r_\lambda = -\frac{\alpha}{\psi}\left[a\left(\sin\left(\lambda\psi + \beta_1\right) - \sin\beta_1\right) + b\left(\cos\left(\lambda\psi + \beta_1\right) - \cos\beta_1\right)\right] + \lambda t_\perp$$

$$= -\frac{\alpha}{\psi}\left[a\sin\left(\lambda\psi + \beta_1\right) + b\cos\left(\lambda\psi + \beta_1\right)\right] + \frac{\alpha}{\psi}\left[a\sin\beta_1 + b\cos\beta_1\right] + \lambda t_\perp$$

noting that in the case $\psi \to 0$, the expression becomes $r_\lambda = \lambda t_\perp$ as one would expect. Since a and b are defined to be orthonormal, the path is clearly some cylindrical helix with the axis of rotation passing through $\alpha/\psi\,[a\sin\beta_1 + b\cos\beta_1]$.

It is worth noting a related result in screw theory, Chasles' theorem, which states that a general displacement may be represented using a screw motion such as we have derived. The fact that the naïve linear interpolation generated by this method is indeed a screw motion suggests that applications of this interpolation method may be wide-ranging, especially since this method allows many other forms of interpolation, such as Bézier curves or three-point quadratic to be performed with equal ease. The pure rotation interpolation given by this method reduces exactly to the quaternionic or Lie group interpolation result allowing this method to easily extend existing ones based upon these interpolations.

4.2   Pose of the Linear Interpolation

The pose of the transformed frame is unaffected by pure translation and hence the initial translation by $\lambda t_\perp$ has no effect. The rotation by $\lambda \psi$ in the plane, however, now becomes important. The subsequent translation along $t'_\parallel$ also has no effect on the pose. We find, therefore, that the pose change λ along the interpolant is just the rotation rotor $R_{\lambda \psi, P}$.

5   Conclusions

This paper has shown how Conformal Geometric Algebra to the problem of provides a natural, intuitive method of extending traditional interpolation schemes to encompass rotation *and* translation simultaneously.

A general method for evaluating rotor logarithms and bivector exponentiations has been developed and an analytical investigation of piece-wise linear interpolation of displacements has been performed. This investigation reveals that this simple scheme gives rise to cylindrical spiral shaped interpolants which have a pleasing, natural appearance. Additionally, this approach is not limited to three dimensions and may readily be extended to form some interpolation within a higher parameter space when solving problems in engineering.

References

1. Hestenes, D., Sobczyk, G.: Clifford Algebra to Geometric Calculus: A unified language for mathematics and physics. Reidel (1984)
2. Lasenby, J., Bayro-Corrochano, E.: Computing Invariants in Computer Vision using Geometric Algebra. Technical Report CUED/F-INFENG/TR-244, Cambridge University Engineering Department (1998)
3. Lasenby, A.: Modeling the Cosmos: The Shape of the Universe, Keynote Address. SIGGRAPH, San Diego (2003)
4. Wareham, R.J.: Computer graphics using Conformal Geometric Algebra. PhD thesis, University of Cambridge (January 2007)
5. Rockwood, A., Hestenes, D., Doran, C., Lasenby, J., Dorst, L., Mann, S.: Geometric Algebra, Course Notes. Course 31. SIGGRAPH, Los Angeles (2001)
6. Lasenby, J., Lasenby, A.N., Wareham, R.J.: A Covariant Approach to Geometry using Geometric Algebra. Technical Report CUED/F-INFENG/TR-483, Cambridge University Engineering Department (2004)
7. Cendes, Z.J., Wong, S.H.: C1 quadratic interpolation over arbitrary point sets. IEEE Computer Graphics and Applications, 8–16 (November 1987)

An Audiovisual Talking Head for Augmented Speech Generation: Models and Animations Based on a Real Speaker's Articulatory Data

Pierre Badin, Frédéric Elisei, Gérard Bailly, and Yuliya Tarabalka

GIPSA-lab / DPC, UMR 5216 CNRS – INPG – UJF – Université Stendhal, Grenoble, 961 rue
de la Houille Blanche, BP 46, F-38402 Saint Martin d'Hères Cedex, France
{Pierre.Badin,Frederic.Elisei,Gerard.Bailly,Yuliya Tarabalka}
@gipsa-lab.inpg.fr

Abstract. We present a methodology developed to derive three-dimensional
models of speech articulators from volume MRI and multiple view video images acquired on one speaker. Linear component analysis is used to model these
highly deformable articulators as the weighted sum of a small number of basic
shapes corresponding to the articulators' degrees of freedom for speech. These
models are assembled into an audiovisual talking head that can produce augmented audiovisual speech, i.e. can display usually non visible articulators such
as tongue or velum. The talking head is then animated by recovering its control
parameters by inversion from the coordinates of a small number of points of the
articulators of the same speaker tracked by Electro-Magnetic Articulography.
The augmented speech produced points the way to promising applications in the
domain of speech therapy for speech retarded children, perception and production rehabilitation of hearing impaired children, and pronunciation training for
second language learners.

1 Introduction

The importance of the visual speech input in language acquisition has been well docu-
mented by [1] in a review on language acquisition in blind children, with data showing
that blind children have difficulty in learning an easy-to-see and hard-to-hear contrast
such as [m] vs. [n]. This importance is also demonstrated by data showing the predominance of bilabials at the first stage of language acquisition ([2]), predominance
which is reinforced in hearing impaired children ([3]), but less clear in blind ones ([4]).
More generally, the importance of vision in speech perception has been demonstrated
in a large number of studies: [5], and more recently [6], among others, have quantified
the gain in speech intelligibility provided by the vision of lips and face in comparison
with the sole acoustic signal (e.g. up to 35% for a signal to noise ratio of –9 dB). In
addition, it is known that human beings possess, up to a certain level, a general *articulatory awareness* skill, i.e. the ability to know the shape and position of one's own
articulators (as measured e.g. by [7] for internal speech articulators such as tongue).

F.J. Perales and R.B. Fisher (Eds.): AMDO 2008, LNCS 5098, pp. 132–143, 2008.
© Springer-Verlag Berlin Heidelberg 2008

Virtual audiovisual talking heads can produce *augmented* audiovisual speech, i.e. can display not only usually visible articulators such as lips but also usually *non* visible articulators such as tongue or velum. These capabilities of augmented display present thus a potentially high interest for applications such as therapy for speech retarded children, rehabilitation of perception and production for hearing impaired children ([8]), or pronunciation training for second language learners ([9]).

In the framework of speech production studies, we develop models of speech articulators ([10], [11], [12], [13]). The present article describes the methods used to build these models from data acquired from a real speaker, how these models are integrated in a virtual audiovisual talking head, and how this talking head can be animated from recordings of the speaker by motion capture.

2   Articulatory Data and Models for Speech Articulators

The speech apparatus is made of a number of articulators, some of them rigid, such as the jaw or the hyoid bone, some of them highly deformable, such as the tongue or the lips. These articulators, in conjunction with other less deformable structures such as the pharyngeal wall or the cheek walls, shape a highly deformable tube – the vocal tract – that extends from the vocal folds to the lips. As mentioned by [14], each articulator may be made of large number of neuromuscular components which offer a potentially huge dimensionality and which must be functionally coupled in order to produce the relatively simple gestures associated with speech production tasks. Modelling these articulators consists thus in extracting their necessarily small number of *degrees of freedom* (henceforth DoF) – or *components* – from appropriate articulatory data acquired from a human subject.

2.1   Modelling Principles

We have developed the articulators' models according to a *speaker-oriented data-driven linear* modelling approach that we summarise in the present section (see details in [10]). Each component is specified by the limited set of movements that it can execute independently of the other components. Rather than defining these components for each articulator *a priori*, and attempting to fit them to real speakers' movements *a posteriori*, we extract them from a corpus of articulations (corresponding to phonemes) representative of the speech production capabilities of a given speaker. This *speaker-oriented* approach allows a rigorous evaluation of the models, by direct comparison with ground-truth data. Besides, using a single speaker avoids merging the anatomical characteristics and the control strategies that can vary fairly much among speakers.

In the framework of our *linear* modelling approach, the geometry of the various non-rigid articulators is modelled as the weighted sum of a small number of basic shapes, associated with the DoFs, which constitutes a minimal basis for the space of articulations. Whereas data-driven models are classically built using *Principal Component Analysis (PCA)*, our models are built using a so-called *guided PCA* where *a priori* knowledge is introduced during the linear decomposition. The weights constitute the *articulatory control parameters* associated with the components: a given set of values of these parameters produces a given shape of the articulators. We ensure that each component is *linearly* uncorrelated with the other components over the set of tasks considered. Our approach aims at finding a compromise between two possibly conflicting criteria: (1) reducing the number of DoFs of the articulators as much as possible by exploiting correlations in the articulatory data; (2) maintaining *biomechanical likelihood*, i.e. making sure that the DoFs are not related to the control strategies actually used by the speaker during the task but are really associated with movements that are plausible from the viewpoint of biomechanics.

Each linear DoF is *iteratively* determined by means of a mixture of PCA applied to carefully chosen data subsets of the articulators' shapes and of multiple regression of the data against control parameters either arbitrarily imposed such as jaw height or determined by the preceding PCA. Note that the solution of this type of linear decomposition is not unique in general: while PCA delivers optimal factors explaining the maximum of data variance with a minimum number of components, our approach allows some freedom to decide the nature and distribution of the variance explained by the components (for instance to make them more interpretable in terms of control), at the cost of a sub-optimal variance explanation and of weak correlation between components.

2.2 Determination of the Articulators' Shapes from Various Type of Data

The complex geometry of the various speech articulators / cavities, e.g. tongue tip, velopharyngeal port, is determined as three-dimensional surfaces from data obtained using different setups. Computed Tomography (CT) and Magnetic Resonance Imaging (MRI) are used for internal articulators, while multiple view video recordings are used for the lips and face. A corpus has been designed to cover the maximal range of French articulations that the speaker can utter: it consists of the oral and nasal vowels [a ɛ e i y u o ø ɔ œ ɑ̃ ɛ̃ œ̃ ɔ̃], of the consonants [p t k f s ʃ m n ʁ l] in three symmetrical contexts [a i u], and of a rest and a pre-phonatory articulations.

Internal articulators. The complete three-dimensional surface representations of the internal articulators that are needed to build the three-dimensional articulators models can only be obtained from images provided by medical imaging systems such as CT and MRI systems. A stack of axial images of the head of the speaker at rest was made by CT, to serve as a reference. These CT images, that provide a good contrast between bones, soft tissues and air, are used to locate bony structures and to determine accurately their shapes. Stacks of sagittal MR images were recorded for the speaker sustaining artificially each of the articulations of the corpus during about 35 sec. A set of 25 sagittal images was obtained for each articulation. These images provide a good contrast between soft tissues and air, and also within soft tissues, but do not image clearly the bones. Due to the complexity of the contours of the various articulators, to the relatively low resolution of the images (about 1 pixel / mm), and to the need of an accurate reconstruction of the articulators, the extraction of contours has been performed manually, plane by plane (see e.g. Fig. 1). In order to improve the determination of the articulator outline in some regions, transverse images were created by re-slicing the initial stack of images in appropriate planes (see e.g. Fig. 2).

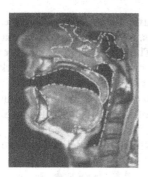

Fig. 1. Example of edited contours in the midsagittal plane on top of an MRI image

Fig. 2. Idem in a transverse plane

The contours of the rigid bony structures involved in the vocal tract (jaw, hard palate, nasal passages, nostrils and various paranasal sinuses) have been manually registered as planar B-spline curves controlled by a limited number of points from CT images in planes with appropriate orientations. The set of all points forming these 2D contours was then expanded into a common reference 3D coordinate system attached to the skull of the speaker. These 3D points were finally processed through a 3D meshing software (Geometrica Research Group at INRIA, http://cgal.inria.fr/Reconstruction) to form a 3D surface meshing based on triangles (see e.g. Fig. 4 for an illustration of the jaw surface).

In order to compensate for possible slight position changes of the speaker's head between the recordings of the various articulations, each stack is aligned with a common reference 3D coordinate system using an appropriate 3D transformation. This transformation, which corresponds to the six degrees of freedom of a solid object, henceforth *3D rototranslation*, is obtained by aligning the rigid structures extracted from CT images (hard palate, nasal passages, paranasal sinuses) with the corresponding ones in the MR images stack. The same procedure is also applied to the jaw for each articulation, to determine its relative position in relation to the fixed rigid structures.

The determination of the deformable structures (tongue, velum, nasopharyngeal wall) is achieved in much the same way as for the rigid structures, but from the MR images of each articulation. The sets of all 2D planar contours edited from the MRI images are expanded into the 3D coordinate system to form the primary 3D description of the deformable articulators' shape. As linear analysis methods such as PCA require each observation to bear on the same number of variables, it is needed to represent the shape of each articulator with the same number of points for all the articulations of the corpus. Such a suitable geometric representation was obtained in the following way each deformable articulator: a unique generic 3D surface mesh, made of triangles, was defined for the articulator, and was fitted by elastic deformation to each of the articulator's 3D primary shapes for all articulations of the corpus.

We finally obtained, the shapes of each articulator as 3D surfaces defined in terms of triangular meshes having the same number of vertices for each of the 46 articulations of the corpus: the tongue is made of 1640 vertices (the RMS reconstruction error over the corpus is 0.06 cm); the velum has 5239 vertices (RMS = 0.06 cm). This forms the basis for the articulatory modelling, as illustrated further.

Visible articulators. Measurements of visible articulators, essentially face and lips surfaces, can be obtained from video recordings. About 250 coloured markers are attached to the speaker's face (cf. [10] or [12]). The use of multiple synchronous and calibrated cameras allows determining the 3D coordinates of these markers with accuracy better than one millimetre. The surface of the face is represented by a mesh of about 450 triangles of which vertices are hooked to these points, as illustrated in Fig. 3. Besides, the lips are described by means of a generic mesh. This mesh, which is speaker-independent, is deformed and fitted to the images by an expert, using the multiple views to capture the lips external contours and to model their visible surface.

Fig. 3. Example of view of a subject's head produced by three synchronous and calibrated cameras, with superimposed lips and face meshes

2.3 Articulatory Models of Jaw, Tongue, Velum, Lips, and Face

The modelling principles described in section 2.1 have been applied to the 3D surface meshes of the various speech articulators. Details can be found in [11] for the tongue, in [13] for the velum, and in [12] for the lips and face.

Jaw displacement model. The six parameters of the 3D rototranslation of the jaw rigid body are very much correlated with the vertical and horizontal coordinates of the upper edge of the lower incisor, called *jaw height*, and *jaw advance*. The centred and normalised versions of these two parameters, *JH* and *JA*, are therefore used as control parameters of the jaw 3D rototranslation (see Fig. 4 for an illustration of the movements of the jaw associated to variations of *JH*).

Tongue model. As the jaw is one of the major tongue carriers, the parameter *JH*, was used as the first control parameter of the tongue model. Its main effect is a tongue rotation around a point in the back of the tongue. The next two parameters, *tongue body TB*, and *tongue dorsum TD*, control respectively the *front-back* and *flattening-bunching* movements of the tongue. The next two parameters, *tongue tip vertical TTV* and *horizontal TTH* parameters, are essentially associated with movements of the tip of the tongue. An extra parameter, related to the hyoid bone height, called *HY*, was used as the sixth control parameter for the tongue model. Altogether, the 3D tongue model is controlled by the six articulatory control parameters. The effects of some of these parameters are demonstrated in Fig. 4 which displays tongue shapes for two extreme values (–2 and +2) of the parameter considered, all other parameters being set to zero. Table 1 displays the variance, relative to the total variance of the full 3D coordinates, explained by each component. It appears that an amount of 87 % is explained by our controlled analysis, which is only 6 % below the optimal result from a raw PCA with the same number of components.

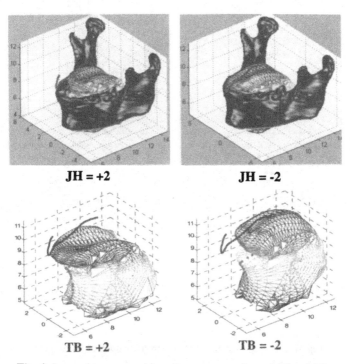

Fig. 4. Jaw and tongue positions for extreme values of JH and TD

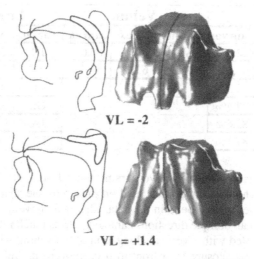

Fig. 5. Velum shape for two extreme values of VL

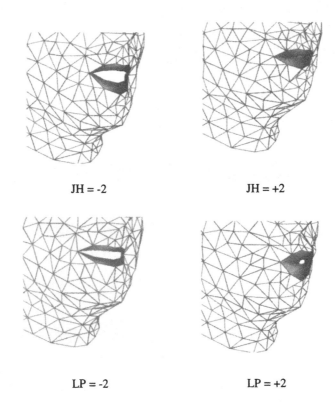

JH = -2   JH = +2

LP = -2   LP = +2

Fig. 6. Lips and face shapes for extreme values of JH and LP

Table 1. Relative data variance explained by each component: *varex* is the explained relative data variance, *cum var* its cumulated value

Tongue			Velum			Lips / face		
Param.	varex	cum var	Param.	varex	cum var	Param.	varex	cum var
JH	22,2%	22,2%	VL	83,0%	83,0%	JH	58,5%	58,5%
TB	41,4%	63,6%	VS	6,0%	89,0%	LP	11,0%	69,5%
TD	11,7%	75,3%				LL	16,7%	86,2%
TTV	3,0%	78,4%				UL	3,1%	89,2%
TTH	4,3%	82,6%				JA	2,0%	91,2%
HY	4,5%	87,1%				LY	0,7%	91,9%

Velum. The velum is controlled by two parameters: VL and VS. The effect of parameter VL on the whole velum is illustrated on Fig. 5 by the shape associated with the two extreme values of VL found in the data. The main movement associated with VL is a movement in an oblique direction. Parameter VS is much related to a horizontal displacement coupled with a vertical elongation of the velum, which complements the velopharyngeal port closure by a front to back movement and may significantly modify the velopharyngeal port constriction. These two components explain almost 90 % of the total variance of the data (cf. Table 1 for complete information).

Face and lips model. The face and lips model is controlled by six parameters for neutral speech (cf. [15], or [12] for an extension to more expressive speech). The first one, *JH*, common with the tongue model, controls the opening / closing movement of the jaw and its large influence on lips and face shape (see Fig. 6 for an illustration). Three other parameters are essential for the lips: *LP* controls the protrusion / spreading movement common to both lips that characterises the /i/ vs. /y/ opposition; *UL* controls the upper lip raising / lowering movement, useful to realise the labio-dental consonant /f/ for instance; *LL* controls the lower lip lowering / raising movement found in consonant /ʃ/ for which both lips are maximally open while jaw is in a high position. The second jaw parameter, *JA*, is associated with a horizontal forward / backward movement of the jaw that is used in labio-dental articulations such as /f/ for instance. Note finally a parameter *LX* related to a movement of larynx lowering. Altogether, more than 90% of the data variance in the corpus is taken into account by these components (cf. Table 1 for more detailed information).

3 The Audiovisual Talking Head

Our audiovisual talking head is made of the assemblage of the individual articulators three-dimensional surface models described above. By construction, all models are properly aligned with the common reference coordinate system related to the skull. Fig. 7 illustrates various possible displays of this talking head. The face and lips can be textured to achieve video-realist rendering. Any part of any articulator can be cut away to provide direct visual access to other articulators that may be located more internally in the head. Alternatively, the skin of the face can be made semi-transparent to allow the vision of the inner articulators while keeping a visual reference to the ordinarily visible face and lips. Altogether, these characteristics allow the possibility to produce *augmented* audiovisual speech, i.e. audiovisual speech complemented with displays that cannot be possible in the real life.

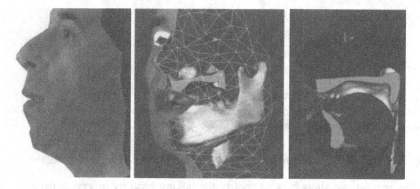

Fig. 7. Examples of displays of the talking head. The face, the jaw, the tongue and the vocal tract walls including the hard and soft palates can be distinguished when needed.

4 Animation of the Talking Head by Motion Capture

4.1 Motion Capture by Means of Electro-magnetic Articulography

Various systems possess some of the motion capture abilities needed to track speech articulators as needed to control and animate a talking head such as that described above: marker-based methods using multiple standard or infrared video cameras to track passive or active light emitting markers attached to the speaker's skin; Electro-Magnetic Articulography (EMA) that allows inferring the coordinates of small electromagnetic receptor coils from the magnetic fields received by these coils from electromagnetic transmitters; medical imaging techniques such as ultrasonic echography, cineradiography or dynamic MRI. However none is perfect: the marker-based techniques allow tracking points only outside the vocal tract; ultrasonic echography is limited mainly to the tongue; cineradiography is too hazardous to allow recording long corpuses; dynamic MRI is still too slow. At present, EMA (cf. [16] or [17]) presents a good compromise: it can track simultaneously up to about 15 points inside and outside the vocal tract, with a typical sampling frequency of 1 kHz, and accuracy better than 0.1 cm; the coils that can be glued to the maxillary, the jaw, the tongue, the velum or the lips (see e.g. Fig. 8) allow tracking *flesh points* i.e. physical locations of the articulators, contrary to medical imaging techniques that provide only contours. A drawback is the poor spatial resolution related to the limited number of points: this can however be dealt with through the high definition articulators models of the talking head, as will be explained in the next section. Finally, note that another important drawback of EMA is its partially invasive nature: the receiver coils have a diameter of about 0.3 cm and must be connected to the device by thin wires that can interfere slightly with the articulation (see illustration in Fig. 8).

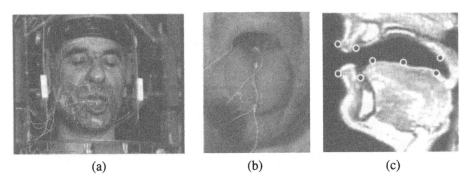

Fig. 8. Illustration of the EMA device: (a) photo of the subject in the EMA device; (b) photo of EMA receptor coils attached to the subject's tongue; (c) possible locations of eight coils (white disks with black centers) in the midsagittal plane

4.2 Control of the Talking Head by Inversion from EMA Recordings

In this section, we show how to control the talking head by inversion from the EMA recordings made on the speaker used for the development of this talking head. We have shown that the various articulators' models can be controlled by a limited number of control parameters: this means that measuring the coordinates of a limited number of carefully chosen points can provide the information necessary to define the complete 3D shape of these articulators. More precisely, as our articulators' models are linear, the 3D coordinates of each vertex are linear combinations of the control parameters. These coordinates can thus be simply obtained by multiplying the vector of control parameters by the matrix of the models' coefficients. Recovering, by inversion, the control parameters of these models can therefore be done from a sufficient number of independent geometric measurements using the (pseudo-) inverse of the model coefficient matrix.

We have thus used the vertical and horizontal coordinates in the midsagittal plane of a set of six coils of an EMA system: a *jaw coil* was attached to the lower incisors, while a *tip coil*, a *mid coil* and a *back coil* were respectively attached at approximately 1.2 cm, 4.2 cm and 7.3 cm from the tongue extremity; an *upper lip coil* a *lower lip coil* were attached to the boundaries between the vermilion and the skin in the midsagittal plane. Extra coils attached to the upper incisors and to the nose served as references. After appropriate scaling and alignment, the coordinates of the coils were obtained in the same coordinate system as the models. No inter speaker normalisation was necessary, since the same speaker is used both for the models and the EMA measurements.

A specific vertex of the 3D tongue mesh was then chosen and associated to each tongue coil in such a way as to minimise the maximum of the distance between the vertex and the coil for a set of articulations representative of the articulatory space of the speaker. The vertices of the lips / face model surface mesh located at the boundary between the vermilion and the skin for each lip in the midsagittal plane were naturally associated with the lips coils. As a first approximation, the left-right coordinates of all the vertices in the midsagittal plane were assumed to be zero, which turned out to be a valid assumption. The three tongue vertices and the two lip vertices associated with the EMA coils have respectively six and four independent coordinates controlled by five parameters each. These control parameters can finally be obtained from the (pseudo-) inverse matrices of the sub-models that predict the coordinates of these specific vertices.

As the *JH* and *JA* parameters are directly proportional to the vertical and horizontal coordinates of the jaw coil, they were computed first in practice, and their linear contributions were removed from the measured EMA coordinates. Parameter *HY* was set to zero, as it was impossible to recover it accurately. The four remaining tongue parameters (*TB, TD, TTV, TTH*) were next obtained by the pseudo-inverse of the matrix for the three tongue coils, and the three remaining lips / face parameters were obtained by the pseudo-inverse of the matrix for the two lips coils. The pseudo-inverse matrices give only sub-optimal solution to the inversion problem, since the number of control parameters is lower than the number of measured coordinates. The mean estimation error, defined as the RMS of the distance between the EMA coils and their associated tongue vertices over a set of 44 articulations was 0.17 cm.

Although in most cases this inversion procedure yields satisfactory results, the resulting tongue contours sometimes cross the hard palate contours, as a consequence of the not modelled nonlinear effect of tongue tip compression when in contact with the palate. In such case, the four tongue parameters are slightly adjusted, using a constrained optimisation procedure that minimises the distance between the coils and the three specific tongue model vertices, with the constraint of preventing the tongue contour from crossing the palate contour.

The video clip PB_phrm6.avi contains an animation obtained by inversion for a sentence in French.

Note finally, that for practical reasons, no coil was attached to the velum in this experiment, and thus no nasal sounds were involved in the study, though we showed in another study that velum could be accurately reconstructed from one EMA coil attached about half way between the hard palate-velum junction and the tip of the uvula ([13]).

5 Example of Application and Perspectives

We have shown that we can control and animate the talking head in a very natural manner from dynamic measurement on a real subject, following a classical paradigm of motion capture, based on EMA recordings. Using this method, we have made a first audiovisual perception experiment aiming at assessing the human tongue reading abilities ([18]), that we briefly present below. We have attempted to determine if direct and full vision of the tongue can be used, based on the augmented speech capabilities of our talking head (in this study, a cutaway profile view). Using the motion capture paradigm based on EMA, we have elaborated a set of audiovisual Vowel-Consonant-Vowel stimuli. These stimuli have been presented to a group of listeners in a series of audiovisual perception experiments using various presentation conditions (audio signal + cutaway view along the sagittal plane *without* tongue, audio signal + cutaway view *with* tongue, audio signal + complete face with skin texture). Each condition was played at four different Signal to Noise Ratios (SNRs) of white noise added to the sound. The analysis of the results has shown some implicit learning effects of *tongue reading*, a preference for a more ecological rendering of the complete face compared to a cutaway presentation, a predominance of lip reading over tongue reading (except for cases where – the audio signal being so much degraded or absent – tongue reading is taking over). These preliminary results need to be complemented by more systematic tests implying notably visual attention measurements.

The talking head appears to possess flexible and various capabilities of augmented audiovisual speech generation: this points the way to a number of promising applications in the domain of speech therapy for speech retarded children, perception and production rehabilitation of hearing impaired children, and pronunciation training for second language learners.

References

1. Mills, A.E.: The development of phonology in the blind child. In: Dodd, B., Campbell, R. (eds.) Hearing by eye: the psychology of lipreading, pp. 145–161. Lawrence Erlbaum Associates, London (1987)
2. Vihman, M.M., Macken, M.A., Miller, R., Simmons, H., Miller, J.: From babbling to speech: A re-assessment of the continuity issue, Language, vol. 61, pp. 397–445 (1985)

3. Stoel-Gammon, C.: Prelinguistic vocalizations of Hearing-Impaired and Normally Hearing subjects. A comparison of consonantal inventories. Journal of Speech and Hearing Disorders 53, 302–315 (1988)
4. Mulford, R.: First words of the blind child. In: Smith, M.D., Locke, J.L. (eds.) The emergent lexicon: The child's development of a linguistic vocabulary, pp. 293–338. Academic Press, New-York (1988)
5. Sumby, W.H., Pollack, I.: Visual contribution to speech intelligibility in noise. Journal of the Acoustical Society of America 26, 212–215 (1954)
6. Benoît, C., Le Goff, B.: Audio-visual speech synthesis from French text: Eight years of models, designs and evaluation at the ICP. Speech Communication 26, 117–129 (1998)
7. Montgomery, D.: Do dyslexics have difficulty accessing articulatory information? Psychological Research 43 (1981)
8. Massaro, D.W., Light, J.: Using visible speech to train perception and production of speech for individuals with hearing loss. Journal of Speech, Language, and Hearing Research 47, 304–320 (2004)
9. Bälter, O., Engwall, O., Öster, A.-M., Kjellström, H.: Wizard-of-Oz Test of ARTUR - a Computer-Based Speech Training System with Articulation Correction. In: Proceedings of the Seventh International ACM SIGACCESS Conference on Computers and Accessibility, Baltimore (2005)
10. Badin, P., Bailly, G., Revéret, L., Baciu, M., Segebarth, C., Savariaux, C.: Three-dimensional linear articulatory modeling of tongue, lips and face, based on MRI and video images. Journal of Phonetics 30, 533–553 (2002)
11. Badin, P., Serrurier, A.: Three-dimensional linear modeling of tongue: Articulatory data and models. In: Proceedings of the 7th International Seminar on Speech Production, ISSP7, Ubatuba, SP, Brazil (2006)
12. Bailly, G., Elisei, F., Badin, P., Savariaux, C.: Degrees of freedom of facial movements in face-to-face conversational speech. In: Proceedings of the International Workshop on Multimodal Corpora., Genoa, Italy (2006)
13. Serrurier, A., Badin, P.: A three-dimensional articulatory model of nasals based on MRI and CT data. Journal of the Acoustical Society of America 123, 2335–2355 (2008)
14. Kelso, J.A.S., Saltzman, E.L., Tuller, B.: The dynamical theory of speech production: Data and theory. Journal of Phonetics 14, 29–60 (1986)
15. Bailly, G., Bérar, M., Elisei, F., Odisio, M.: Audiovisual speech synthesis. International Journal of Speech Technology 6, 331–346 (2003)
16. Perkell, J.S., Cohen, M.M., Svirsky, M.A., Matthies, M.L., Garabieta, I., Jackson, M.T.T.: Electromagnetic midsagittal articulometer systems for transducing speech articulatory movements. Journal of the Acoustical Society of America 92, 3078–3096 (1992)
17. Hoole, P., Nguyen, N.: Electromagnetic Articulography in coarticulation research. Forschungsberichte des Instituts für Phonetik und Spachliche Kommunikation der Universität München, vol. 35, pp. 177–184. FIPKM (1997)
18. Tarabalka, Y., Badin, P., Elisei, F., Bailly, G.: Can you read tongue movements? Evaluation of the contribution of tongue display to speech understanding. In: 1ère Conférence internationale sur l'accessibilité et les systèmes de suppléance aux personnes en situation de handicaps (ASSISTH 2007), Toulouse, France (2007)

Towards Efficiency in Cloth Simulation

Fernando Birra and Manuel Santos

CITI/Departamento de Informática
Faculdade de Ciências e Tecnologia (FCT)
Universidade Nova de Lisboa, Quinta da Torre
2829-516 Caparica, Portugal
{fpb,ps}@di.fct.unl.pt

Abstract. Cloth simulation is an extremely expensive task. Realistic cloth models coupled with stable numerical integration demand all the processing power we can spend. Although implicit integration schemes allow us to use large time steps, the exponential time complexity limits the number of particles that are reasonable to use in any simulation. In this paper, we present a technique that simulates cloth surfaces with adaptive level of detail without degrading the surface physical properties or the stability of the simulation. The underlying mesh operations are derived from subdivision surfaces, but rules are adapted to prevent the numerical simulation from diverging. We also demonstrate how the model constants can be specified in a resolution independent way.

1 Introduction

Although the use of implicit integration on the simulation of deformable modes has been proposed by pioneering work of Terzopoulos *et al.* [11], the approach suffered from the lack of CPU power at the time. A decade later, Barraf and Witkin [1] were able to capitalize on the benefts of implicit integration. Their contribuitions to the field included a modified version of the conjugate gradient linear solver that was able to maintain a set of restrictions on the particles trajectories, without any performance penalty. The authors also proposed an elegant and continuous formulation of a cloth surface model that could easily be applied to irregular triangular meshes.

Desbrun *et al.* [3] took the road of simplification to attain real time performance, but the method cannot be applied to meshes with varying topology and the the simulated surface exhibits a super elastic behavior, requiring post processing measures to make the cloth look good.

Ideally, a simulation should only use as much particles as it needs to capture the realistic behavior of the cloth surface. At any given time, some areas of the surface may be mostly flat and thus a small discretization can be used. Others, may present complex folds and wrinkles and a high resolution polygonal model is required. This paper starts by analyzing related work in cloth simulation with dynamic detail. Next, we identify the major problems, largely emanating from careless manipulations of the topology, and provide a set of viable solutions. We conclude by discussing the results.

F.J. Perales and R.B. Fisher (Eds.): AMDO 2008, LNCS 5098, pp. 144–155, 2008.
© Springer-Verlag Berlin Heidelberg 2008

2 Related Work

First attempts to use adaptive refinement on rectilinear meshes were made by Hutchinson et al. [7] and Zhang et al. [16]. The cloth model proposed by Provot [10] was used. These first approaches didn't contemplate simplification and weren't suitable for animation. Later, Villard et al. [14] also worked with rectilinear meshes that were refined during the simulation as a result of a process of curvature estimation at each vertex. New vertices were classified into two different sets: active and inactive, depending on weather they were directly involved in the simulation or not. Forces computed on inactive nodes were distributed to the surrounding active vertices and only these were really simulated with an explicit integration technique, thus requiring very small time steps. The mesh simplification was not considered and it was left for future work.

Other authors [6,4] also used nodes that do not participate in the simulation and thus do not contribute the realist formation of folds, so characteristic in cloth. The additional virtual nodes are generally computed in a geometrical way, often with the main intention of removing some visual artifacts [4].

Volkov and Ling [15] used $\sqrt{3}$–subdivision [8] on a cloth simulator based on Baraff and Witkin's cloth model. The surface is a set of connected triangles and its curvature is estimated along edges shared by two triangles. Whenever the polygonal mesh is distant enough from an idealized surface passing through that place, the two triangles are subdivided according to $\sqrt{3}$–subdivision. Simplification works the opposite way, when the detail is considered exaggerated.

The authors make no effort explaining the benefits of the particular subdivision scheme adopted in the context of cloth simulation. Topological operations on a mesh, like edge swaps or vertex filtering, may introduce abrupt changes on the orientation of mesh polygons. They also abruptly change the direction and modulus of forces applied on particles, causing instability in the numerical integration process. Ultimately, the system will diverge or, at best, unwanted oscillations will be present. Another missing point in their work is the description of how the physical properties of the material are preserved during mesh refinement and simplification.

Other refinement strategies are presented in [2,5], where subdivision is totally decoupled from simulation and executed as a post-processing step, with the sole purpose of generating artificial detail. We also use a similar technique with the advantage that it is executed almost entirely on the GPU.

3 Dynamic Level of Detail in Cloth Simulation

If the change in detail is only driven by visualization needs, for instance when a very large polygonal model changes its distance to the viewer, there is a greater variety of subdivision schemes that can be used. But, varying the detail of a polygonal mesh that is also being used to run a physical simulation creates additional problems. In cloth simulation, the polygonal mesh usually defines a particle system where mesh vertices are, in fact, particles. The physical model of the surface is evaluated and, as a result, forces are computed and applied to particles which will, in turn, be used to integrate their trajectories through time.

Abruptly changing either the force magnitudes or their orientations, during topological mesh operations, can spoil the entire simulation by voiding the results of the numerical integration technique. In our preliminary tests, we found that explicit integration could hardly cope with these changes and was easily affected by instability and divergence. Implicit integration, on the other hand, was sometimes able to recover from instability in a few steps. While this was not satisfactory, since it created jumpiness and oscillation in the mesh, the revealed increased robustness indicated that implicit methods could probably be used, if the mesh operations were chosen more carefully.

3.1   Subdivision Surfaces and Adaptive Subdivision

Subdivision surfaces can easily provide local variation of detail in both directions. Simply put, starting with a coarse polygonal mesh and, by successively applying a set of subdivision rules, a more refined surface is obtained at each step. After an infinite number of applications of the rules, over the whole surface, we obtain a smooth limit surface. The rules are classified in two different types. Face rules are responsible for inserting new vertices while vertex rules pickup the vertices from the previous steps and filter them.

We are only interested in considering subdivision schemes that will work on triangle meshes since they are the less restrictive and the cloth model we use is almost entirely based on the one proposed by Baraff and Witkin, thus defined over an irregular triangle mesh.

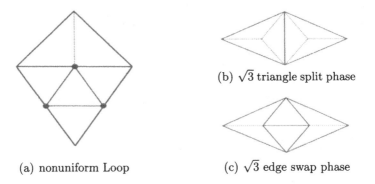

(a) nonuniform Loop   (b) $\sqrt{3}$ triangle split phase

(c) $\sqrt{3}$ edge swap phase

Fig. 1. $\sqrt{3}$ and Loop subdivision schemes

When thinking of subdivision schemes for general triangle meshes, there are two schemes that immediately come to mind. The Loop scheme [9] is probably the most famous and it works by splitting each triangle into four new ones. The new vertices are inserted at the midpoint of the original edges and connected to each other (see lower triangle of figure 1(a)). The other well known scheme for triangles is $\sqrt{3}$–subdivision, already referred here. This later scheme works in two distinct steps. First it inserts a vertex at the middle of each triangle to be divided and connects it to the original vertices, creating three new triangles (see figure 1(b)). In the second stage it performs an edge swap operation between adjacent triangles not contained in the same original triangle (figure 1(c)).

Since our motivation is geared towards efficient simulation, using uniform subdivision over the whole surface is not considered. Instead, we focus on selectively performing local refinement and simplification. Fortunately, subdivision schemes can be made adaptive. For instance, some triangles can be subdivided while neighboring ones are left unchanged, with $\sqrt{3}$–subdivision. In this case, the edge swap phase is delayed until adjacent triangles are at the same subdivision level. In Loop subdivision, triangles adjacent to the subdivided ones still need to be subdivided, although in a different (irregular) way, to avoid generating holes, as can be seen in the upper part of figure 1(a).

3.2   Choice of Subdivision Method

In figure 2, we show the geometric discontinuities that can be introduced during topological changes, if we do not carefully choose the subdivision scheme. On the left, we show a potential initial arrangement of two triangles. In the middle image, we see what can happen to the orientation of the triangles using the Loop subdivision scheme. The arrangement corresponds to the situation when two irregular triangles (those used to avoid cracks) are later transformed into 4 normal triangles. The right part illustrate the discontinuity problem arising from the edge swap phase in $\sqrt{3}$–subdivision.

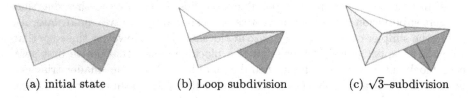

(a) initial state   (b) Loop subdivision   (c) $\sqrt{3}$–subdivision

Fig. 2. Geometric discontinuity in $\sqrt{3}$ and Loop subdivision

Theses changes, in the orientation of the triangles, will stress the numerical integrator without any necessity, since the forces applied on neighboring particles will instantly change their directions, leaving the system in a inconsistent state. For instance, force derivatives will have no knowledge of these modifications. For the same reason, we advocate that, when using a subdivision scheme to vary the detail in cloth simulation, we should not use the rules that filter vertices, since they will also produce the same type of geometric discontinuities. This leaves us with only the face rules that are used to insert new vertices.

From various subdivision schemes studied, we found one that works on triangle meshes, while leaving their orientations unchanged during subdivision. The scheme is called 4–8 subdivision [13] and it operates on 4–k meshes [12].

3.3   Adaptive 4–8 Subdivision

4–k meshes are also called tri-quad meshes, since they can be described as a mesh of triangles grouped in pairs, forming a quad. The only restriction is that a triangle can only belong to a quad. The shared edge between grouped triangles is the block's inner edge, or diagonal. On the boundaries, we can also observe incomplete blocks, since one of the triangles is missing.

The elementary refinement operation is described as the block's inner edge bisection. The shared edge is split in two by placing a vertex in the middle point and connecting it to the opposite vertices of the block. Note that this operation is consistent, regarding the orientation of the new and the old triangles. Another advantage of this rule is that there is no need to irregularly divide neighboring triangles to avoid holes in the mesh and a single simple rule can be used throughout the entire procedure.

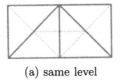   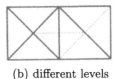

(a) same level   (b) different levels

Fig. 3. Adaptive 4–8 subdivision

Adaptive subdivision, also known as hierarchical subdivision, needs to handle situations when the blocks to be refined do not belong to the same subdivision level. In figure 3, we depict two possible scenarios. In both cases the edge that triggers subdivision is the middle vertical one, shared by the two quadrilaterals.

On the simpler case, both quads are at the same level. However, the edge that we want to split isn't the inner edge of a block. In this situation we first split each block, as shown with the dashed diagonal lines. Now, the smaller triangles around the vertical edge form a block, rotated 45 degrees from the original ones. So, the vertical edge is now an inner edge of a block and another subdivision will split it. On the right side, the triangles to each side of the edge do not belong to the same level of the hierarchy and the first step consists of dividing the bigger block, from the a less refined level. Fortunately, the variance in hierarchy levels between adjacent blocks can be, at most, one unit. For the details of hierarchical 4–8 subdivision we refer the reader to [12].

Although 4–k meshes are not really general triangular meshes it is relatively easy to convert an irregular mesh of triangles to this format. To convert an irregular mesh of triangles we have at least two different methods at our disposal. One such method was proposed in [13] but can generate meshes where triangles have very different sizes. To tackle this problem we propose an alternative method based in $\sqrt{3}$–subdivision. On the first step we split every triangle in the original mesh by placing a vertex in the center of the face and connect it to the original vertices. Next, we group the new triangles that share edges of the original mesh in blocks of two. Finally, we proceed with the edge swap phase. The resultant mesh is more regular with respect to the size of the triangles.

4 Refinement and Simplification

At each simulation step we inspect every shared edge and compute an error estimator similar to the one described in [15]. This estimator lets us know when we need more resolution or when the detail can be sacrified. A numerical value describes the error of the polygonal mesh to an idealized surface. If the value is too big we subdivide, if it is too small we simplify. The particular estimator used is not very important and other alternatives could be used. We prefer to concentrate on the numerical conditions that can make DLOD a reality in cloth simulation. For subdivision, edges are processed by decreasing value of the estimator. In any case, each block can only be divided one level in each time step, to improve stability and keep the local density of changes small. Simplification is also processed according to priority, starting with the more flat arrangements.

4.1 Numerical Conditions

While subdivision, as we saw before, preserve the orientation of the triangles, the same cannot be said about simplification. Unless we are thinking about a totally flat arrangement of two triangles. Note that we can only join triangles that belonged to the same block in the upper subdivision level.

In our experiments, simply trying to join triangles based on the value of the estimator or their flatness proved to be catastrophic. The impact on the numerical integrator caused the system to diverge with ease. We ensure additional stability conditions to be able to simplify the mesh. A more strict condition to perform simplification should consider the variation of the orientation of the two triangles. Not only we need them to be relatively co-planar, as we also want the arrangement to be stable in time, and not merely a transitory state.

Recalling that the condition vector $\mathbf{C}(\mathbf{x})$, used model curvature in Baraff and Witkin's model, is simply the angle θ formed by the normals of the two adjacent triangles (Δ_{ijk} and Δ_{jkl}), we measure its time derivative and only simplify if it is near zero. Fortunately, the time derivative can be obtained from the gradients in the formula below, already needed to evaluate the surface model. The extra effort is thus negligible since velocities (for particles i, j, k and l) are also already available.

$$\frac{\partial \mathbf{C}(\mathbf{x})}{\partial t} = \frac{\partial \mathbf{C}(\mathbf{x})}{\partial \mathbf{x}_i}\mathbf{v}_i + \frac{\partial \mathbf{C}(\mathbf{x})}{\partial \mathbf{x}_j}\mathbf{v}_j + \frac{\partial \mathbf{C}(\mathbf{x})}{\partial \mathbf{x}_k}\mathbf{v}_k + \frac{\partial \mathbf{C}(\mathbf{x})}{\partial \mathbf{x}_l}\mathbf{v}_l$$

To avoid tight loops of subdivision and simplification operations locally we impose a time to die value on newly created triangles. They can only be simplified back if they have lived long enough. However, to quickly adapt to curvature we allow subdivision to occur at rate of one level per block and per step.

4.2 Invariance of Physical Properties

Changing the cloth mesh resolution shouldn't be reflected in the dynamic behavior of the surface. This means that physical quantities such as total mass, linear momentum and internal deformation energies should be invariant with respect to resolution, as much as possible.

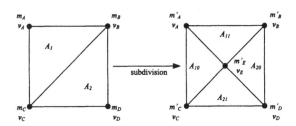

Fig. 4. Mass and linear momentum conservation

In figure 4 we represent the elementary refinement step. To keep the total mass constant we release the load of triangles A_1 and A_2 from their supporting particles. The weight of the newly created triangles is then equally distributed through each of their 3 vertices. The cloth density, ρ, is considered constant throughout the entire surface but it could trivially be made different on each triangle of the initial mesh. The result, after aplying the mass conservation law, is summarized below and we note that particles A and D see their masses unchanged:

$$m'_B = m_B + \frac{\rho}{3}(A_{11} + A_{20} - A_1 - A_2), m'_E = \frac{\rho}{3}(A_1 + A_2),$$
$$m'_C = m_C + \frac{\rho}{3}(A_{10} + A_{21} - A_1 - A_2). \tag{1}$$

From the conservation of linear momentum law, we extract the following velocity formula for the newly created particle:

$$\mathbf{v}_E = \frac{\mathbf{v}_C(A_{11} + A_{20}) + \mathbf{v}_B(A_{10} + A_{21})}{A_1 + A_2}.$$

We also tested the mean velocity between particles B and C and found no visual artifacts with this simpler approach. We note that, in the case of having 4 triangles with the same area, both formulas give the same result.

To preserve elasticity, bending and shearing behavior we force the internal energy associated with the surface deformations to remain invariant during mesh resolution changes. According to Baraff and Witkin's model, stretching energy of a given triangle, t, is directly proportional to the square of its area in the rest state (uv area):

$$e_{st} \propto Area(t)^2,$$

and the same applies to shearing as well. The subdivision rule splits each of the initial 2 triangles of a block in two similar ones, thus halving the area of the resulting triangles. Summing the energies of the new triangles totals half of the initial value. To keep the total energy constant we simply double the associated stiffness constants k_{st} and k_{sh} of the new triangles to compensate.

For bending, the total energy is directly proportional to the square of the angle between two adjacent triangles:

$$e_{be} \propto \theta^2.$$

This angle remains constant during edge bissection and so, at first, we could be tempted to halve the bending constant, k_{be}, to compensate for the fact that, instead of the initial pair, we now have two pairs of triangles with the same hinge angle, both equally contributing to the total bending energy. However this apparent increase in stiffness of the surface is not seen through experimentation. The explanation lies in the fact that, by performing the edge bissection, we are also making the surface more amenable to curve in the orthogonal direction (in the cloth plane), thus also lowering its stiffness. This result is in line with the observation of Baraff and Witkin in [1] where they advocate that bending constant is independent of mesh resolution.

To have a set of normalized rigidity constants for the cloth model – invariant with respect to the level of discretization used for the surface – we only need to discover what should happen to stretching and shearing constants, since bending is already invariant with respect to resolution. For a given triangle, t, we already found that the following relation will always hold for stretching and shearing:

$$k_t.Area(t) = K,$$

with constant K. Thus we only need to use K as the cloth rigidity constant as it will be invariant with the resolution used. This result is very important, since it allows us to assign behavior to the surface without worrying about the discretization level that will be used.

5   Results and Conclusions

To prove that our technique maintains the dynamic behavior of the materials, independently of the resolution used, we did a comprehensive set of experiments. One of those tests is represented in figure 5. A rectangular piece of cloth is hanged by 3 of its 4 corners. We have repeated the same simulation with different mesh resolutions, both with fixed and varying detail. For each run we also traced the energy curves of the different internal deformation modes: elasticity, shearing and bending. Not only the curves were similar enough, both in progression and magnitude of the associated function, as the visual perception of the surface behavior was found to be concordant on the different tests.

As an example, we present the variation of bending energy in figure 6. We start by pointing the instantaneous violations to the conservation of bending

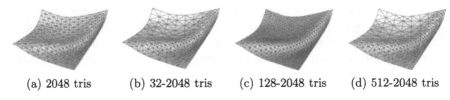

(a) 2048 tris   (b) 32-2048 tris   (c) 128-2048 tris   (d) 512-2048 tris

Fig. 5. Visual concordance with different resolution meshes

energy as we discussed above, visible in the high frequency peaks. But, the similarity of the different curves also show that the analysis that took us to this apparent violation is correct. This, as well as the concordance in final values reached for each simulation, serve to prove that our DLOD technique doesn't change the bending properties of the material. With a set of thinner lines we can also see the number of particles used in each of the 3 simulations analyzed. We make notice of the fact that the bending stiffness used in the simulations was higher than the values applicable to common cloth, with the purpose of making potential differences in behavior more noticeable. The curves for the other internal energies are even more similar.

Figure 7 shows a series of snapshots of a piece of cloth interacting with a solid object. Note that we do not use collision information to steer subdivision. The resolution will simply change as a consequence of the cloth folds created during cloth-solid interaction.

In figure 8 we present the accumulated simulation times for several mesh configurations. The first two cases correspond to fixed resolution meshes and they are used to bound the results from the DLOD cases. Both dynamic resolution meshes are allowed to reach the number of triangles of the more refined fixed resolution mesh. We start by observing that in terms of performance they are

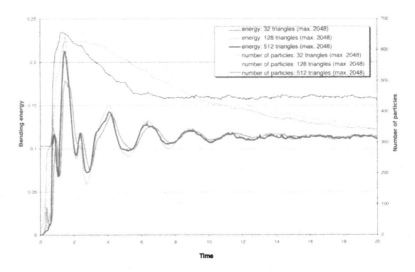

Fig. 6. Variation of bending energy

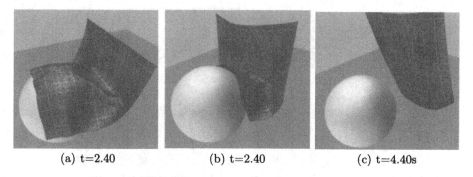

(a) t=2.40   (b) t=2.40   (c) t=4.40s

Fig. 7. Cloth interacting with an object

very identical and follow a similar trend, dictated by the needs of the simulation. We can clearly identify sections where the number of particles has surely increased, noticeable by the increase in steepness. The justification to the fact that the DLOD curves are above the fixed resolution mesh with 1089 particles shows that this particular simulation required a greater number of particles, reaching peek values around 2000 particles. Although the chart doesn't show it, if a mesh with around 2000 particles would be used, the time required would be more than doubled. The results show that we can simulate folds with fine detail in a very small fraction of time that would be needed if we used a fixed resolution mesh.

One important observation that isn't present in the chart is the impact of collision and variation of detail in the time needed for the solver to compute a numerical solution. By carefully profiling the execution time associated with the several parts of the technique, we discovered that, in a significant number of times, whenever there was a very big number of refinement and simplification operations, the integrator needed to reduce the simulation step in order to find a reasonable and stable solution. We intend to explore the position alteration mechanism described in [1] to try to minimize this negative impact. The idea is that, before doing the simplification operations, we instruct the numerical

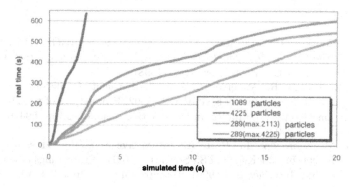

Fig. 8. Accumulated simulation time

(a) DLOD 4-k mesh (constant shading)   (b) GPU refined mesh (phong shading)

Fig. 9. Example of post-processing on the GPU

solver to find a solution where the particle that is about to be removed lied in a perfectly flat and steady arrangement in the plane formed by the block. To conclude the performance analysis we would like to say that the overall weight of the variation of detail in the whole simulation is systematically below the time needed to find the solution from the ODE solver by one order of magnitude. When we add to the total simulation time the costs of evaluating the surface model and collision detection then we are talking about two orders of magnitude smaller times.

Finally, in figure 9 we present the result of applying a post-processing step to increase the detail inside a common low-end GPU, since we only require pixel shader performance. The DLOD mesh is sent to the GPU where it is further subdivided several times until the final detail is reached. No ping pong of data is required and, up to the final rendering (here illustrated with Phong shading), there is no additional CPU intervention, apart from sending the orders to execute the necessary shaders. Although the technique is out of the scope of this paper, we just want to emphasize that the result of our dynamic level of detail simulations can be further improved without stressing the CPU, and all its power is used to run the physical simulation.

References

1. Baraff, D., Witkin, A.: Large steps in cloth simulation. In: SIGGRAPH 1998: Proceedings of the 25th annual conference on Computer graphics and interactive techniques, pp. 43–54. ACM Press, New York (1998)
2. Bridson, R., Fedkiw, R., Anderson, J.: Robust treatment of collisions, contact and friction for cloth animation. In: SIGGRAPH 2002: Proceedings of the 29th annual conference on Computer graphics and interactive techniques, pp. 594–603. ACM Press, New York (2002)
3. Desbrun, M., Schroeder, P., Barr, A.: Interactive animation of structured deformable objects. In: MacKenzie, I.S., Stewart, J. (eds.) Proceedings of the Conference on Graphics Interface (GI 1999), Toronto, Ontario, June 2-4, 1999, pp. 1–8. CIPS (1999)

4. Etzmuß, O., Eberhardt, B., Hauth, M., Straßer, W.: Collision adaptive particle systems. In: Proceedings of the 8th Pacific Graphics Conference on Computer Graphics and Application (PACIFIC GRAPHICS 2000), Los Alamitos, CA, October 3-5, 2000, pp. 338–347. IEEE, Los Alamitos (2000)
5. Hadap, S., Bangarter, E., Volino, P., Magnenat-Thalmann, N.: Animating wrinkles on clothes. In: Ebert, D., Gross, M., Hamann, B. (eds.) IEEE Visualization 1999, San Francisco, pp. 175–182. IEEE, Los Alamitos (1999)
6. Howlett, P., Hewitt, W.T.: Mass-spring simulation using adaptive non-active points. Computer Graphics Forum. 17(3), 345–354 (1998)
7. Hutchinson, D., Preston, M., Hewitt, T.: Adaptive refinement for mass/spring simulations. In: Boulic, R., Hegron, G. (eds.) Computer Animation and Simulation 1996, SpringerComputerScience, pp. 31–45. Springer, New York (1996)
8. Kobbelt, L.: $\sqrt{3}$-subdivision. In: SIGGRAPH 2000: Proceedings of the 27th annual conference on Computer graphics and interactive techniques, New York, NY, USA, pp. 103–112. ACM Press/Addison-Wesley Publishing Co. (2000)
9. Loop, C.T.: Smooth subdivision surfaces based on triangles. Master's thesis, Department of Mathematics, The University of Utah (August 1987)
10. Provot, X.: Deformation constraints in a mass-spring model to describe rigid cloth behavior. In: Davis, W.A., Prusinkiewicz, P. (eds.) Graphics Interface 1995, Canadian Information Processing Society, Canadian Human-Computer Communications Society, May 1995, pp. 147–154 (1995)
11. Terzopoulos, D., Platt, J., Barr, A., Fleisher, K.: Elastically deformable models. Computer Graphics (Proc. Siggraph) 21(4), 205–214 (1987)
12. Velho, L., Gomes, J.: Variable resolution 4-k meshes: Concepts and applications. Computer Graphics Forum 19(4), 195–212 (2000)
13. Velho, L., Zorin, D.: 4-8 subdivision. Computer Aided Geometric Design 18(5), 397–427 (2001)
14. Villard, J., Borouchaki, H.: Adaptive meshing for cloth animation. In: IMR, pp. 243–252 (2002)
15. Volkov, V., Li, L.: Real-time refinement and simplification of adaptive triangular meshes. In: van Wijk, G.T.J.J., Moorhead, R.J. (eds.) Proceedings of the IEEE Visualization 2003, October 2003, pp. 155–162. IEEE Computer Society, Los Alamitos (2003)
16. Zhang, D., Yuen, M.M.F.: Cloth simulation using multilevel meshes. Computers and Graphics 25(3), 383–389 (2001)

2D Articulated Body Tracking with Self-occultations Handling

Eric Para[1], Olivier Bernier[1] and Catherine Achard[2]

[1] Orange Labs, France Telecom R&D,
Technopole Anticipa, 2 Avenue Pierre Marzin
22307 Lannion, France
{eric.para,olivier.bernier}@orange-ftgroup.com
[2] Université Pierre et Marie Curie, 4 Place Jussieu
75005 Paris, France
catherine.achard@upmc.fr

Abstract. Recently many methods for human articulated body tracking were proposed in the literature. These techniques are often computationally intensive and cannot be used for Human-Computer Interface. We propose in this article a real-time algorithm for upper body tracking with occultation handling. The tracking is based on an articulated body model, also used to automatically initialize the target. After an independent search of the most likely positions of each limb, a dynamic programming algorithm is used to find the best configuration according to the links between limbs. The self-occultations between the limbs are directly taken into account by the tracking algorithm and results show the interest of the proposed approach.

Keywords: Tracking, humanoid articulated model, occultations handling, dynamic programming, real-time processing, computer vision.

1 Introduction

Articulated pose tracking raises many problems mainly due to the human body deformability. Many solutions are proposed in the literature [1], global tracking approaches [2] with rigid models, as well as more flexible multiple parts tracking approaches [3,4]. More elaborated geometric models can be used to increase tracking robustness [5,6,7]. However, the computational cost is often too important to allow real time tracking applications. Another problem is the possibility of occultations between limbs. Some authors propose to extend their algorithms to take into account such occultations but with a high computation cost [7]. We propose in this article a real-time articulated body tracking which manage occultations (fig. 1.).

In the following section, the principle of the multiple parts search algorithm and the strategy adopted to enforce the global pose coherence are explained. The third section describes the automatic initialization of an appearance model used to track the limbs. In the fourth section, we present the multiple parts search algorithm employed to track the whole body with occultation handling. Finally, some results are shown

F.J. Perales and R.B. Fisher (Eds.): AMDO 2008, LNCS 5098, pp. 156–165, 2008.
© Springer-Verlag Berlin Heidelberg 2008

Fig. 1. Example of tracking result: even with occultations, each part is correctly tracked

General Principle

his section describes the global principle of the method, based on a geometric model
ed to enforce a global coherence to the structure. Many human models are used in
e literature. The Ju et al. "cardboard people" approach [5] is based on a 2D
ticulated model, whereas Demirdjian et al. [6] use a more precise volumetric
construction. As 3D models are in practice difficult to manipulate and to initialize
e to kinematics minimum problems, we choose to use a 2D model where parts
rrespond to the human limbs (head, torso, arm, forearm and hand). These parts are
nnected with flexible spring joints, as proposed by Sigal et al. [7] (fig. 2.). The
per body is then fully represented by a tree with the torso as the central node.

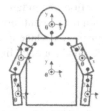

Fig. 2. Model used with 2D connected parts

Each part is limited to three degrees of freedom in the camera plane: the
ordinates of its centre (x_i, y_i) and rotation angle θ_i around the axis perpendicular to
e image plane. The global zoom factor is supposed to be known and rotations
ound other axes are not considered. Therefore, users have to move within the 2D
mera plane to be tracked. This algorithm model can however easily be extend to a
) model to deal with all possible human motions. The method proposed to manage
cultations can be transposed without difficulty to 3D models.

Several methods exist to find the best configuration of an articulated model.
manan et al. [4] opt for example for several deformations of the geometric model.

In order to obtain a less expensive computational method, we based our method on the *"Pictorial Structures"* introduced by Fischler et all. [8]. Felzenszwalb et al. [3] adapt it to the body initialization problem with the use of a particular Mahalanobis distance transform. The indicated processing time for an image is more than a minute. To obtain a real-time framework, we propose a three steps procedure:

- The first step consists of computing a part matching score $c(i,e_i)$ for all potential positions e_i of each objet i. Only the h best positions with their corresponding score are considered.
- In the second step, a link interaction score $\lambda_{\{j,k\}}(e_j,e_k)$ is computed for all selected couple of hypothesis (e_j,e_k) for each pairs of connected limbs $\{j,k\}$.
- The last step finds the configuration C^* corresponding to an hypothesis for each part which maximises the sum of all parts and links scores:

$$C^* = \arg\max\left(\sum_{i=1}^{n} c(i,e_i) + \sum_{\{j,k\}\in L}\lambda_{\{j,k\}}(e_j,e_k)\right). \tag{1}$$

3   Automatic Initialization

This section details the automatic initialization of the model which is essential for a Human-Computer Interface. Several methods such as the features observed in the image, the definition of the parts matching and links scores, and the way to obtain the best configuration of the articulated model will be re-used in the tracking part.

3.1   Features Choice and Parts Scores

In the first step, several positions are tested for each object and a score is assigned to each of them. Several authors use only a generic skin color model to find hands and head but this method is strongly illumination dependant. We therefore prefer to use a fusion of information such as background segmentation [1,3], edge detection [1,4] and head detection [1,2] to initialize our model. Once the initial position of each limb is obtained, a specific colour model is learned for each limb (see section 4).

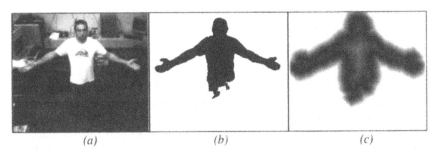

(a)   *(b)*   *(c)*

Fig. 3. *(a)* original camera frame *I*, *(b)* background subtraction *b*, *(c)* distance transform *d*

Using a fixed camera allows us to use the difference between the observed frame and a reference image to detect interesting areas. We use an automatic threshold selection and track global lighting changes to reduce the effect of illuminations changes and to improve the detection (fig. 3(b)). The initialization proposed by Felzenszwalb et al. [3] is based directly on the extracted binary image and is time consuming. Other authors [1,4] only use the edges of the extracted silhouette. This technique needs a precise background subtraction that cannot always be obtained. To deal with false detection errors, a distance transform is computed from the extracted binary image. Two Chamfer distance transforms are respectively applied to the background and foreground pixels to obtain a smoothed silhouette edge picture (fig. 3(c)). The distance of foreground pixels is multiplied by 3 in order to favour inner edge pixels. Moreover, all the distances are normalised in the interval [0,1]. The score $c(i,e_i)$ of the hypothesis of position e_i for a limb i is the sum of the distance transform along the rectangular shape defining the limb model:

$$c(i,e_i) = 1 - \frac{1}{nb(\ell)} \sum_{\{x,y\} \in \ell} d_{(x,y)}$$

(2)

where ℓ represents the pixels of the edges of the rectangle used to model the limb. The choice of the limb model implies the visibility of the chosen edges of the rectangle, for example to avoid loose clothes problems. As an illustration, fig. 4(a) shows the three edges of a rectangle employed to model a forearm. At last, to take into account the particular shape of the head, gradient orientations are used. An oval template g is matched with the picture and the score is computed with angular subtraction:

$$c(head, e_{head}) = \sum \left(\Phi_{I(x,y)} - \alpha_{g(x,y)} \right)$$

(3)

where $\Phi_{I(x,y)}$ corresponds to the gradient orientation of the pixel (x,y) and $\alpha_{g(x,y)}$ to the gradient of the oval template g. This methods is more robust than simple edge pixels for face detection. The weighting of the scores obtained from the different features could be a problem but we observe in practice a similar behaviour with the use of background subtraction and gradient orientation features. An initial pose with the person facing the camera and where the forearms are outspread from the torso is required.

3.2 Best Parts Scores Selection

A score is computed for all hypotheses of part positions defined by the variation of the 3 parameters (x_i, y_i, θ_i) in the 2D model plan. The algorithmic complexity is directly proportional to the number of these potential positions. Felzenszwalb et al. [3] compute for each part all possible configurations with a $11°$ θ_i angle precision and a 4 pixels pitch for x_i and y_i. For a 320×240 pixels image, the reported computation time is more than one minute to test the corresponding 1.5 million hypotheses. To limit the numbers of observations and obtain a better precision, a head detector is used on the upper area of the binary image obtained after background subtraction. This detection allows us to limit the search area for each limb to the neighbourhood of the best head position and to consider all possible poses. The orientation of each part is also limited (for example, $\theta_{forearm}$ $\in [10°;90°]$ from the vertical). A multi-resolution and pyramidal search is employed to decrease computational time by preserving only interesting areas across resolutions. Finally, to limit the final number of hypotheses, a subsampling is done and the h_{MAX} best local hypotheses are kept for further process (fig. 4(b),(c)).

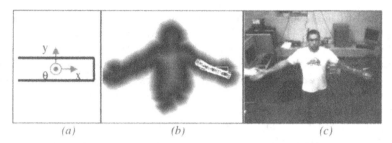

Fig. 4. *(a)* 3 edges forearm model to be search, *(b)* *h* selected hypothesis with the distance transform, *(c)* possible *h* forearm positions

3.3 Links Scores

As introduced in equation *(1)*, two different scores are used for the estimation of the best configuration, the parts matching scores and the links scores. Different solutions exist in the literature to compute the linked interaction scores $\lambda_{\{j,k\}}(e_j,e_k)$ between a pose hypothesis e_j of limb j and a pose hypothesis e_k of limb k (j and k being connected). Demirdjian et al. [6] use a rigid model that imitates human joints with a point centred ball joint. Sigal et al. [7] propose the "Loose-Limbed Model" with springs joints to allow more flexibility. These joints absorb position errors without propagating them to the whole structure. We choose a similar method and model the link scores with a Gaussian function:

$$\lambda_{\{j,k\}}\left(e_j,e_k\right)= e^{-\frac{d^2(e_j,e_k)}{2\sigma^2}} \tag{4}$$

where $d(e_j,e_k)$ is the Euclidian distance between the two joints points for pose hypotheses e_j and e_k respectively (fig. 5.). A score $\lambda_{\{j,k\}}(e_j,e_k)$ of 1 represents an ideal positioning of the connected parts. In practice, the standard deviation σ which controls the links tolerance is experimentally fixed to 1. This score is computed for each couple of selected hypotheses related to the connected parts (see subsection 3.2).

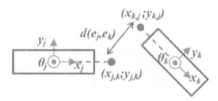

Fig. 5. e_j and e_k hypotheses illustration with their respective joint points

3.4 Best Configuration Choice

As discussed in subsection 2.2, the last step consists in finding the best configuration from the previous computed scores, as defined by equation *(1)*. The exhaustive computation needs h^n operations with h selected hypothesis for each of the n limbs. To decrease computation times, Bernier et al. [9] use the belief propagation which is similar to a relaxation method. We choose here to take advantage of the tree structure to employ a dynamic programming approach [10] and compute the best match of the model to the image in polynomial time (complexity of $O(h^2n)$). The tree graph is cut into as many iterations as the number of links, i.e. $n-1$ with our acyclic tree model (fig. 6). The algorithm propagates the scores from the graph extremities to the torso. At each step, the next part score is updated with the best sum of the previous part score and the link score between them. For example, if part $i-1$ is an extremity part, the score of part i is estimated using equation (5). Part i becomes an extremity part for part $i+1$ and so on. At each step, the final scores contain the accumulated scores of the previous best branch of the tree. The previously explored paths must be memorized in order to select the best one and find the global configuration.

for all hypotheses $e_j \in [1,h]$ of part $i-1$ and $e_k \in [1,h]$ of part i:

$$\hat{c}(i,e_k) = \arg \max_j \left(\hat{c}(i-1,e_j) + \lambda_{\{i-1,i\}}(e_j,e_k) \right) + c(i,e_k) \tag{5}$$

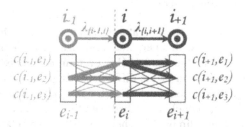

Fig. 6. Two steps of our dynamic programming algorithm with the best solutions in bold line

The multiple parts matching approach with a limited number of selected hypothesis allows a fast computation with good results. Felzenszwalb et al. [3] succeeded in reducing their algorithm to an $O(hn)$ complexity but their method requires that the relationships between connected pairs of parts be expressed in a particular Mahalanobis distance transform form. They keep many of hypotheses and report a computational time of more than a minute per frame. Our solution tests more than 100 complete initialization possible in the same time on a 3,2 GHz simple core processor. This can be used to search the global zoom factor (fig. 7.) or to improve the initialization precision. The N best configurations can also easily be obtained using the same approach with a $O(Nh^2n)$ complexity, by retaining the N best paths at each iteration.

Fig. 7. Automatic initialization results with two different zoom factors

4   Tracking

We present in this section the tracking part of the algorithm. Several authors [3,4] compute a global initialization for each new frame. In spite of using an imprecise grid, this method is computationally intensive because of a too large space to be explorated. The method proposed in this article uses a tracking process to decrease the dimension of the space to explore. It is then less expensive but requires an initialization phase. For each frame, the searched part is limited to the neighbourhood position of the limb in the previous frame. The same framework as for the initialization is used with the computation of limbs and links scores to find the best global configuration. Generic features are however substituted for a more precise and less expensive computational model: a color appearance model learned from the automatic initialization step. The tracking methods also takes into account the occultations between limbs.

4.1   Features Choice and Parts Scores

During tracking, the use of the generic features remains possible. Felzenszwalb et al. [3] for example track a person with a perpetual initialization while Ramanan et al. [4] add a progressive learning to the model. However, more precise features, can be learned for a better discrimination of the different body parts, especially in presence of multiple people. An appearance model of each body part is thus extracted from the automatic initialization. This model is matched with the new frames with a correlation technique to find the different limbs. We choose the SAD correlation often used for disparity computation or MPEG video compression due to its inexpensive computation time. The score $c(i,e_i)$ is thus the Sum of the Absolute Difference in the RGB color space between the part projection pixels in the image $I(x,y)$ and the model pixels $M(x,y)$:

$$c(i,e_i) = 1 - \frac{1}{nb(\ell)} \sum_{\{x,y\} \in \ell} (|I(x,y) - M(x,y)|) \qquad (6)$$

The use of the previous frame allows to limit the search of each limb to an area around the previous position. The search depth corresponds to the maximum speed of a part. We choose a 20 pixels square width window with a full precision. This size is sufficient to follow natural body movements at 25 frames per second. A search limitation of 90° around the previous position is also used for the parameter θ_i with a 1° angle precision. Finally, the appearance model of each part is updated using a global lighting observed change of each limb. Thus, after the final localisation of each part the global intensity of the part model is updated.

4.2   Occultations

One of the most difficult problem for articulated body tracking is the presence of self occultations, and tracking losses are thus often observed [1,2,5,6]. To limit the occultation problem between the head and hands, Bernier et al. [8] add non intersection constraints for these limbs. Sigal et al. [7] introduce an local "occlusion-sensitive" likelihood with binary masks taking into account limbs occultations. These two solutions add non physical links between non contiguous limbs which create more complex graphs with loops. Similarly to Sigal et al. [7], we introduce a binary occultation mask for each limb. An initialization pose within occultation is necessary to have a correct model of each limb. We also suppose the visibility orders of all limbs known and separate the tree in sub-trees corresponding to connected part with the same visibility. The best configuration of a sub-tree can be obtained using the dynamic programming technique. The sub-trees are searched in their visibility orders, once the best configurations of preceding sub-trees are used as constraints and to generate the occultation mask of hidden limbs.

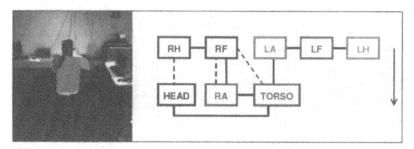

Fig. 8. The continuous lines correspond to physical links and discontinuous lines represent occultations between some limbs. When the hidden limbs are under the non hidden ones, a specific search order is required.

To approach a real time computing, we propose to use our framework again. The equation *(5)* is still used to compute the part hypothesis score, but only for pixels witch are not hidden. To another ones, a neutral score corresponding to the image noise is attributed to it. That allows potential position parts which are mainly hidden to be selected. The independent part search methods must however be updated. The non occluded parts must be searched first to create the mask hypotheses for hidden parts.

The figure 8 illustrates this principle. The right hand *(RH)* which occludes the head must be searched first. The same work must be done with the right arm *(RA)* witch hides the right forearm *(RF)* and the torso. Two graph levels are thus necessary. First, the five non occluded parts (the right hand *(RH)*, the right forearm *(RF)*, the left arm *(LA)*, the left forearm *(LF)* and the left hand *(LH)*) can be searched independently. The right arm *(RA)*, the Head and the Torso can be searched once their respective occultation masks are found (i.e. when the non hidden parts hypotheses are selected). Several hypotheses can be selected for a part which occludes another and multiple masks can be created for the same hidden part and must be consider as much as hypotheses.

4.3 Results

We present in this section the result of a 14 seconds sequence with 350 frames (25fps) computed offline by our algorithm at a 15 fps mean frame rate. Natural body movements of a person in front of the camera are shot and have been successfully deal into lightening variations on the limbs and important self-occultations. Because of an important orientation modification, the 2D projection of the left forearm at frame 293 doesn't match with his real size. Despite this error, the multiple part algorithm search and the flexibility in the links interaction management allow to find a solution that keeps the coherence of the global structure for the remaining frames. The best configuration solution is selected and the limbs continue to be tracked. The algorithm finally loses the left hand at frame 316 where it is confused with the right one. A multiple hypotheses algorithm which keep many configurations would allow to solve that problem.

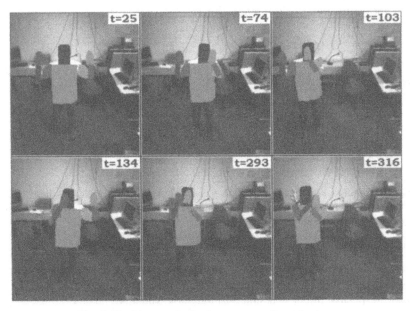

Fig. 9. Tracking results in the presence of occultations

5 Conclusion

One of the challenges of limb tracking algorithms lies in their computational times. Few real time algorithms are proposed in the literature. An exemple is Demirdjian et al. [6] who claim to reach real time with their determinist approach. Bernier et al. [9] come close with a 12 fps algorithm whereas Ramanan et al. [4] announce between 7 and 10 seconds per frame. More computational expensive methods have been proposed by Felzenszwalb et al. [3] -more than a minute with their "Pictorial Structures" implementation- or by Sigal et al. [7] -several minutes for the algorithm with occultations management-. The algorithm proposed in this article runs in 15-20 fps depending on the scene complexity and takes into account occultations to track the limbs. The need to know the visibility order of all parts simillary to [7] currently limits our results. Our proposed approach could be extended by preserving the N best configurations at each frame. This should allow to take into account full self occultation and to improve the tracking results. Moreover, we want to consider the multiple persons tracking problem. The appearance model extracted with the automatic initialization is not only more precise than generic features but should also be able to handle interactions between several persons. Finally, the model could be extended to its third dimension which should improve the tracking results [6,9].

References

1. Moeslund, T.B., Hilton, A., Krüger, V.: A survey of advances in vision-based human motion capture and analysis. Comput. Vis. Image Underst. 104(2), 90–126 (2006)
2. Haritaoglu, I., Harwood, D., Davis, L.S.: W4: Real-time surveillance of people and their actions. IEEE Trans. Pattern Anal. Mach. Intell. 22, 809–830 (2000)
3. Felzenszwalb, P.F., Huttenlocher, D.P.: Pictorial Structures for Object Recognition. Int. J. Comput. Vision 61(1), 55–79 (2005)
4. Ramanan, D., Forsyth, D.A., Zisserman, A.: Tracking People by Learning Their Appearance. IEEE Trans. Pattern Anal. Mach. Intell. 29(1), 65–81 (2007)
5. Ju, S.X., Black, M.J., Yacoob, Y.: Cardboard People: A Parameterized Model of Articulated Image Motion. In: Int. Conf. on Auto. Face and Gesture Recognition, pp. 38–44 (1996)
6. Demirdjian, D., Taycher, L., Shakhnarovich, G., Grauman, K., Darrell, T.: Avoiding the Streetlight Effect: Tracking by Exploring Likelihood Modes. In: IEEE Int. Conf. on Comput. Vis., vol. 1, pp. 357–364 (2005)
7. Sigal, L., Black, M.J.: Measure Locally, Reason Globally: Occlusion-sensitive Articulated Pose Estimation. IEEE Comput. Society Conf. on Comput. Vis. and Pattern Recognition 2, 2041–2048 (2006)
8. Fischler, M.A., Elschlager, R.A.: The representation and matching of pictorial structures. IEEE Transactions on Computer 22, 67–92 (1973)
9. Bernier, O., Cheung-Mon-Chan, P.: Real-Time 3D Articulated Pose Tracking using Particle Filtering and Belief Propagation on Factor Graphs. In: British Machine Vision Conf. (2006)
10. Felzenszwalb, P.F., Huttenlocher, D.P.: Efficient matching of pictorial structures. Comput. Vis. and Pattern Recognition 2, 66–73 (2000)

A Two-Step Approach for
Detecting Individuals within Dense Crowds

Chern-Horng Sim, Ekambaram Rajmadhan, and Surendra Ranganath

Department of Electrical and Computer Engineering
National University of Singapore, Singapore 117576

Abstract. This paper proposes a two-step approach for detecting individuals within dense crowds. First step uses an offline-trained Viola-type head detector in still color images of dense crowds in a cluttered background. In the second step, which aims to reduce false alarm rates at same detection rates, color bin images are constructed from normalized rg color histograms of the detected windows in the first step. Haar-like features from these color bin images are input to a trained cascade of boosted classifiers to separate correct detections from false alarms. Experimental results of both steps are presented as Receiver Operating Characteristics (ROC) curves, in comparison with recent related work. Our proposed two-step approach is able to attain a high detection rate of 90.0%, while maintaining false alarm rate below 40.0%, as compared to other work which attains a high 70.0% false alarm rate when detection rate is still below 90.0%.

1 Introduction

Recent security concerns in crowded places have motivated the detection of individuals in crowds in the vision community. Many works have considered detecting pedestrians in a sparsely crowded scene, using full-body appearance models [1,2,3] or using body part detectors [4,5,6]. Besides using spatial information from still images, Viola et al. [7] also used temporal information in their detection algorithm. Despite yielding high detection rates, these methods do not extend to densely crowded scenes due to severe occlusions which are very common in dense crowds.

On the other hand, Casas et al. in [8], Brostow and Cipolla in [9], and Rabaud and Belongie in [10] have attempted to detect individuals in dense crowds. In [8], skin color is used mainly to detect faces in the dense crowd. This method requires faces in the crowd to be facing the camera, and will miss detecting individuals who are moving away from the camera. In [9] and [10], individuals in dense crowds are detected by clustering detected features over time. They used feature-based approach that makes segmenting out individuals as they appear in the images impossible for further processing such as identification, behavior analysis etc. Nevertheless, Seemann et al. in [11] are able to segment out individuals on a cluttered background even in still images. However, they worked with less dense crowds, with at most 10 people in the scene.

F.J. Perales and R.B. Fisher (Eds.): AMDO 2008, LNCS 5098, pp. 166–174, 2008.
© Springer-Verlag Berlin Heidelberg 2008

This paper proposes a two-step method for detecting individuals in dense crowds against a cluttered background, using still color images. In the first step, a local detector is trained and used to provide initial detection windows. The second step, which is independent of the first step, aims to provide a framework to increase the detection rate of the local detector while maintaining its false alarm rate, or alternatively to reduce the false alarm rate while maintaining the detection rate. This second step relies only on color information in the detected windows obtained in the first step. For every detection window, we first estimate its 2D normalized rg histogram and map it to an image as described in Section 4. Each such color bin image is then classified as a correct detection or a false alarm using a trained cascade of boosted classifiers working with Haar-like features.

The paper is organized as follows: Section 2 briefly describes the problem scenario and Section 3 describes training of the local detector used in the first step. The second step of our approach which uses color bin images is described in Section 4, and the complete detection system is presented in Section 5. Section 6 reports the results and the paper is concluded in Section 7.

2   Problem Description

Figure 1 shows example images of the dense crowds that we are dealing with. We seek to detect as many individuals as possible in such crowds with a local detector and then reduce the false alarm rate with the use of our proposed color bin images. As mentioned, only Casas et al. in [8] has segmented out individuals, within crowds of similar density. However, because they used skin color-based face detection technique for segmenting individuals, their method will not be suitable in our scenario where many individuals may be facing away from the camera.

3   Step One: Building Local Detector

To our knowledge, most available human detectors such as those mentioned in Section 1 did not consider dense crowds. Though [9] and [10] consider dense crowds, they are based on finding and counting the number of distinct motions rather than detecting individuals. Thus in these methods, a distinct motion pattern suggests the presence of an individual, but does not segment out the individual from the image, for possible further processing, e.g. face recognition. Hence, we use a state-of-the-art object detector in still images, proposed by Viola and Jones [12].

To train this local detector, a total of 8032 images of human heads captured at arbitrary visual angles against complex backgrounds were used as positive training samples and 6816 images which do not contain any people were used as negative training samples. See Figure 2. We used the implementation found in Open Source Computer Vision Library [13], setting the target performance for each stage to a minimum detection rate of 0.999 at a maximum false alarm rate

Fig. 1. Example images of dense crowds: (a) People exiting a common area through a doorway; (b) People entering the common area through the doorway

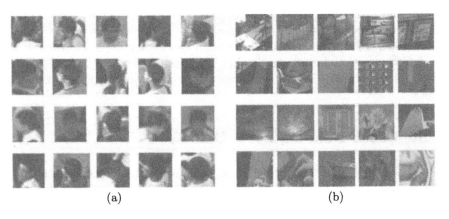

Fig. 2. Training image examples for the Viola-type local detector: (a) Positive samples; (b) Negative samples

of 0.5. The training process took a few days using a PC with 3.4GHz CPU and 3GB memory.

Figure 3 shows the results from this detector. Note that the individuals in our testing images are different from the training samples. A total of 30 images of crowds with an average density of 34 persons per image yielded a 82.3% detection accuracy with a 32.1% false alarm rate. Though the results of the frontal face detector in [12] which uses the same approach yields better results, the results in our scenario seem reasonable because of occlusions and arbitrary orientations of the individuals. Closer to our problem but using less dense crowds is the work of Seemann et al. [11], where detection rate is about 82.0% at a false alarm rate of 30.0%

(a)   (b)

Fig. 3. Example images of dense crowds showing detections: (a) Detections on Figure 1(a); (b) Detections on Figure 1(b)

4   Step Two: Improving Performance of Local Detector

Figures 4(a) and 4(b) show mean rgb histograms of all the positive and negative training samples, respectively. It can be seen that conventional thresholding or maximum likelihood classification will not effectively separate these two classes because the rgb histograms of the negative samples are very broadly distributed and overlap significantly with the left-skewed cone-shaped rgb histograms of the positive samples. Hence, in our approach we use an alternative representation - the color bin image.

4.1   Creating Color Bin Images

First, we obtain all the normalized rgb pixel values of an image where $r = \frac{R}{R+G+B}$, $g = \frac{G}{R+G+B}$, and $b = 1 - r - g$. Then, a 2D rg histogram of the image is estimated. A 20 x 20 color bin image is then formed from the 2D histogram where the mode of the histogram corresponds to the highest pixel intensity in the image and the r and g axes represent the height and width of the image, respectively. See Figure 5.

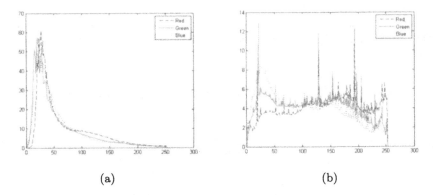

(a)   (b)

Fig. 4. Mean *rgb* histograms: (a) Positive samples; (b) Negative samples

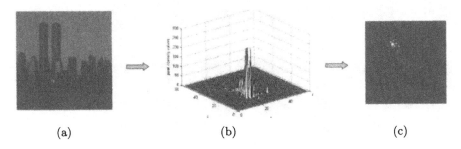

(a)   (b)   (c)

Fig. 5. Creating its color bin image: (a) Original image; (b) 2D r-g histogram; (c) Color bin image

4.2   Training Color Bin Image Classifier

From the histograms in Figure 4, it appears that the color bin images of positive examples have a general pattern which differs from that of negative samples. Since both patterns cannot be separated effectively by conventional threshold-ing or maximum likelihood classification, we use an over-complete set of simple appearance filters, similar to Haar wavelets (i.e. Figure 6), as weak classifiers, which are then combined to form a complex classifier to distinguish between the two classes of color bin images. The training process is similar to the training of the Viola-type local detector mentioned in Section 3. The difference is that the positive and negative samples shown in Figure 2 have been replaced by their respective color bin images, as shown in Figure 7.

5   Complete Detection System

After both the detector and the classifier as depicted in Figure 7 have been trained, they are used in our system to detect individuals in crowds. Our scheme

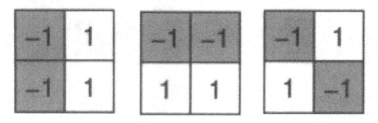

Fig. 6. Examples of Haar-like wavelets

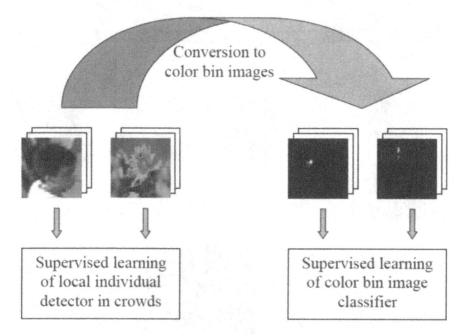

Fig. 7. Off line training process

focusses on reducing the false alarm rate of the Viola-type head detector, while taking advantage of its high detection rate. We rely only on spatial information, and hence any still color image that contains dense crowd, is a suitable candidate for individual detection by our system.

The first step of detections on still color images, uses the trained local head detector set for high detection rates (and concomitantly high false alarm rates). The detected windows in the image are cropped out and each of them is transformed to its color bin image. The color bin images of the detected windows are further classified in a second step as true detections or false alarms with the trained color bin image classifier. This process is depicted in Figure 8.

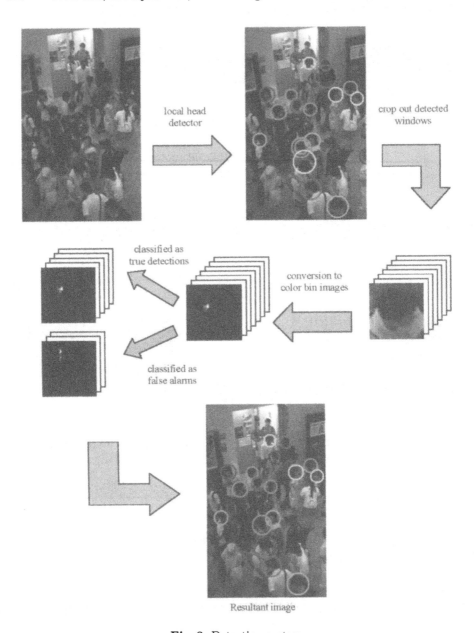

Fig. 8. Detection system

6   Results

As mentioned, we tested 30 different still images of crowds with an average density of 34 persons per image as in Figure 1. The test was repeated with the same set of images at different thresholds to obtain the ROC curves as in Figure 9.

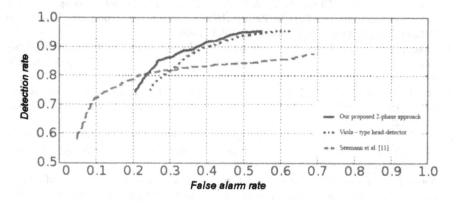

Fig. 9. Receiver Operating Characteristics curves

From Figure 9, it can be observed that our two-step approach improves the performance of the Viola-type head detector used in the first step. For example, at a false alarm rate of 30.0%, our proposed two-step approach has a 5.0% higher detection rate than the Viola-type head detector.

In comparison with the recent work [11], also plotted in Figure 9, our detection rate is significantly higher, especially after the 25% false alarm rate. Moreover, detection rates of both our step one detector and our complete system are able to attain above 90.0% easily, although our crowd density is more than three times that of [11], whose performance saturates below 90%.

7   Conclusion

In this paper, we proposed a two-step approach for detecting individuals within static color images of dense crowds. We first evaluated the use of a Viola-type local detector for this task. We then proposed a second step to improve results: This uses color bin images, constructed from detected windows in the first step and a trained cascade of boosted classifiers using Haar-like features. In comparison with recent related work, the combination of the Viola-type local detector coupled with our color bin image approach gives very promising results for detecting individuals within dense crowds.

References

1. Leibe, B., Seemann, E., Schiele, B.: Pedestrian detection in crowded scenes. In: IEEE Conference on Computer Vision and Pattern Recognition, vol. 1, pp. 878–885 (2005)
2. Rittscher, J., Tu, P.H., Krahnstoever, N.: Simultaneous estimation of segmentation and shape. In: IEEE Conference on Computer Vision and Pattern Recognition, vol. 2, pp. 486–493 (2005)

3. Zhu, Q., Yeh, M.C., Cheng, K.T., Avidan, S.: Fast human detection using a cascade of histograms of oriented gradients. In: IEEE Conference on Computer Vision and Pattern Recognition, vol. 2, pp. 1491–1498 (2006)
4. Mikolajczyk, K., Schmid, C., Zisserman, A.: Human detection based on a probabilistic assembly of robust part detectors. In: Pajdla, T., Matas, J(G.) (eds.) ECCV 2004. LNCS, vol. 3021, pp. 69–82. Springer, Heidelberg (2004)
5. Tuzel, O., Porikli, F.M., Meer, P.: Human detection via classification on riemannian manifolds. In: IEEE Conference on Computer Vision and Pattern Recognition, vol. 1 (2007)
6. Wu, B., Nevatia, R.: Detection and tracking of multiple, partially occluded humans by bayesian combination of edgelet based part detectors. International Journal of Computer Vision 75(2), 247–266 (2007)
7. Viola, P.A., Jones, M.J., Snow, D.: Detecting pedestrians using patterns of motion and appearance. International Journal of Computer Vision 63(2), 153–161 (2005)
8. Casas, J.R., Sitjes, A.P., Folch, P.P.: Mutual feedback scheme for face detection and tracking aimed at density estimation in demonstrations. Vision, Image and Signal Processing 152(3), 334–346 (2005)
9. Brostow, G.J., Cipolla, R.: Unsupervised bayesian detection of independent motion in crowds. In: IEEE Conference on Computer Vision and Pattern Recognition, vol. 1, pp. 594–601 (2006)
10. Rabaud, V., Belongie, S.: Counting crowded moving objects. In: IEEE Conference on Computer Vision and Pattern Recognition, vol. 1, pp. 705–711 (2006)
11. Seemann, E., Fritz, M., Schiele, B.: Towards robust pedestrian detection in crowded image sequences. In: IEEE Conference on Computer Vision and Pattern Recognition, vol. 1 (2007)
12. Viola, P.A., Jones, M.J.: Robust real-time face detection. International Journal of Computer Vision 57(2), 137–154 (2004)
13. Bradski, G., Kaehler, A., Pisarevsky, V.: Learning-based computer vision with intel's open source computer vision library. Intel Technology Journal 9(2), 118–131 (2005)

3D Modeling for Deformable Objects

Yi Song[1] and Li Bai[2]

[1] School of Computing, University of Leeds, LS2 9JT, UK
`yisong@comp.leeds.ac.uk`
[2] School of Computer Science, University of Nottingham, NG8 1BB, UK
`bai@cs.nott.ac.uk`

Abstract. This paper presents an efficient BSpline surface reconstruction technique for modelling deformable objects. The differences of our methods from previous BSpline fitting approaches are: 1) the reconstructed BSpline patch does not need to be square shaped. This significantly reduces the required number of BSpline patches for reconstruction; 2) the dataset to be reconstructed does not have to be grid data. This is important, especially for 3D scan data, which is unstructured dense point cloud, normally with holes. A compact 3D shape description can be obtained using our approach. This shape representation allows 3D metamorphosis, direct manipulation of free-form deformation, and level of detail control (real time multi-resolution rendering). The demonstrated results are reconstructed directly from the dense point clouds collected from our 3D scanner (based on stereo photogrammetry technique) and example datasets provided by Cyberware.

1 Introduction

Recent advances in three-dimensional acquisition techniques have offered alternatives to the traditional 2D applications, e.g. 3D metamorphosis, 3D object rendering etc. Although some difficulties in the 2D context, such as viewing and lighting, could be overcome, others issues have been raised due to the complexity of the 3D shape representation. For example, in computer graphics and the closely related fields of virtual reality, computer aided geometric design, and scientific visualization, compact storage and fast display of shape information are vital. For interactive applications such as video games and computer-aided design, real time performance and the ease of shape editing are of great concern. In fact, the key answer to those concerns is closely related to the 3D shape representation.

In order to address the problems mentioned above, we propose a novel 3D modelling technique using B-Splines. The approach allows one-to-one mapping between the object space and a parameter space, and therefore automatic correspondence between any pair of objects. In addition, being a spline-based shape representation, it has the advantages of easy shape editing and compact storage: compared to the original data collected from the 3D scanner, a compression rate of over 90% can be achieved. Furthermore, a continues family of resolution approximations can be quickly and easily constructed.

F.J. Perales and R.B. Fisher (Eds.): AMDO 2008, LNCS 5098, pp. 175–187, 2008.

B-Spline surface-fitting techniques give smooth, compact and reproducible parametric representations and are commonly supported by current modeling systems. There has been considerable work on fitting B-Spline surfaces to 3D point clouds [FB95] [KL96] and [EH96] [MBV*95] [WW92] [SBW06] [SB06].

For 3D metamorphosis, how to establish the correspondences between source and target objects efficiently is still an open research problem. A common approach is generating a common connectivity for both the source and target objects. This is generally accomplished by decomposing the objects into several corresponding patches, embedding them onto a 2D parametric domain, and finally merging the corresponding embeddings to form a common mesh [Hut04] [KSK00] [LDS*99] [LH03] [LL04] [Ale00]. To achieve high quality rendering, a sequence of approximations to the original model at various levels of detail is required. Previous work in this area can be classified into two categories. One is the classical multi-resolution analysis to arbitrary topology surfaces [Lou94] [LDW97] [EDD*95] [CPD*96]. The other is based on sequential mesh simplification to build up a hierarchical representation of meshes [CCM*97] [HDD*93] [Hop96].

Our modelling approach offers an alternative solution to 3D metamorphosis, direct manipulation of free-form deformation, level of detail control (real time multi-resolution rendering), etc. Three characteristics distinguish our approach from previous work. First, the dataset to be reconstructed does not have to be grid data. Second, the reconstructed BSpline patch does not need to be square shaped. Third, a very compact 3D object representation is obtained. This shape representation provides solutions to 3D metamorphosis, direct manipulation of free-form deformation, level of detail control (real time multi-resolution rendering).

This paper is an extension of the work described in [SBW06] [SB06]. Emphases in this paper lie in the application of the 3D shape representation method. The demonstrated results are reconstructed directly from the dense point clouds collected from our 3D scanner (based on stereo photogrammetry technique) and example datasets provided by Cyberware. The original datasets are in good quality. Some outliers could be automatically excluded from the dataset during the reconstruction. However, no further test has been done on the dataset deteriorated by artificial noise. The rest paper is organised as follows. In section 3, we briefly introduce our surface reconstruction approach. Then its applications on 3D metamorphosis, direct manipulation of free-form deformation, level of detail control (real time multi-resolution rendering), are demonstrated in section 4.

2   Methodology

2.1   Theory

A point on a B-Spline curve of degree k is calculated by the sum of a set of weighted control points c_i, $0 \leq i \leq n$, i.e. C=$\{c_0, c_1, ..., c_n\}$,

$$f(t) = \sum_{i=0}^{n} B_i^k(t)c_i \tag{1}$$

The weight $B_i^k(t)$ is a polynomial function defined over a knot vector $U=\{u_0, u_1, ..., u_n\}$, and is recursively calculated as following:

$$B_i^0(t) = \begin{cases} 1 & if \quad u_i \le t \le u_{i+1} \\ 0 & otherwise \end{cases}$$

$$B_i^k(t) = \frac{t - u_i}{u_{i+k} - u_i} B_i^{k-1}(t) + \frac{u_{i+k+1} - t}{u_{i+k+1} - u_{i+1}} B_{i+1}^{k-1}(t) \qquad (2)$$

Analogically, the BSpline surface is defined over a pair of knot vector $U=\{u_0, u_1, ..., u_n\}$ and $V=\{v_0, v_1, ..., v_m\}$ by:

$$\Gamma(s,t) = \sum_{i=0}^{m} \sum_{j=0}^{n} N_i^k(s) B_j^r(t) c_{i,j} \qquad (3)$$

Therefore, the task of BSpline surface fitting is to find a set of control points, which defines a surface Γ giving the best approximation to a given dataset D. This can be expressed as following:

$$\Gamma(s,t) = D(s,t) = \sum \sum NBc = \sum N(\sum Bc) \qquad (4)$$

This can be further decomposed into two series of BSpline curve-fitting processes:

$$D(s,t) = \sum NP \qquad (5)$$

$$P = \sum Bc \qquad (6)$$

Similarly, weights B and N are polynomial functions calculated from a pair of the knot vectors U and V respectively. From the definition of the BSpline curve/surface, it is clear that the shape of reconstructed BSpline curve is affected by both the distribution of the knots in the knot vector and the value of the control points. Since previous approaches have been mainly done on grid dataset or converted one from the unstructured dataset, the pair of knot vector can be both constructed by a set of evenly spaced knots. For unstructured datasets, the evenly spaced knots could lead to overfitting or even make the equation singular (see Fig. 1 right). So far the chord length method is a widely accepted method, by which the knots are distributed following the distribution of the scattered points to be approximated. Consequently, for m sets BSpline curve-fitting process, m varied knot vectors will be constructed. Therefore, we need to develop a knot vector standardization algorithm to uniform those knot vectors. More detailed implementation can be found in [Song07]. The figurative example of applying knot vector standardization algorithm on one of the unevenly spaced knot vectors is shown in Fig. 2 (right). Note the position of control points is modified accordingly. So after applying the knot vector standardization algorithm, the equation 5 becomes:

$$D = \sum N'P' \qquad (7)$$

Then the BSpline fitting process described in equation 6 will be:

$$P' = \sum Bc \tag{8}$$

The knot vector standardization process can be repeated on the initial results of n BSpline curve-fitting processes. The equation is then modified as:

$$P' = \sum B'c' \tag{9}$$

Now, the set of control points c' and the uniform pair of the knot vectors U and V are sufficient to describe the shape of the reconstructed BSpline surface from the original dataset D.

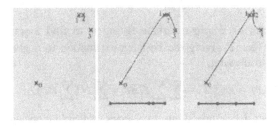

Fig. 1. The relationship between the distributions of knots in knot vector and the shape of the reconstructed curve. Left: original data points (red crosses). Middle: knot vector formed by applying chord length method and the reconstructed curve defined upon it. Right: evenly distributed knots and its corresponding reconstructed curve. Knots are depicted as red dots at the bottom of the middle and right figures.

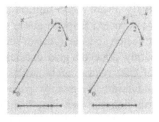

Fig. 2. Applying knot vector standardization on a reconstructed BSpline curve. Left: reconstructed BSpline curve defined on the unevenly space knot vector. Right: reconstructed BSpline curve defined on an evenly spaced knot vector by applying the knot vector standardization algorithm. Knots are depicted as red dots. Control points are represented as red crosses.

2.2 Properties

The ability of reconstructing the BSpline surface on the unstructured dataset directly gives our approach some advantages over other methods. For example, it can fill small holes automatically during the reconstruction process, which exist in almost every 3D scanned data. Without the constraint of reconstruction on the grid dataset, the reconstructed BSpline surface does not have to be square-shaped. This can significantly reduce the required number of BSpline patches for fitting the surface. Consequently, the complexity of enforcing G^1 continuity between adjacent patches has also been minimized. Establishing the correspondences between different objects can also be simplified. The shortcoming of our approach is over smoothing. In this section, we demonstrate the properties of our approach by comparing our results with those of other approaches.

2.2.1 Hole Filling

We compare our approach with an existing BSpline surface fitting method described in [KL96] and the Power Crust approach using the same dataset. All reconstruction processes are automatic. However, the existing BSpline fitting method needs to apply the gridding algorithm on the original dataset, which requires human intervention. The results in Fig. 3 show that:

1) Existing BSpline surface reconstruction method: fine geometric details have been well kept. But for highly curvature areas, e.g. the nose area, some spurious fine details are generated (Fig. 3a). The reconstructed surface has 179 patches. We omit the patches delineation on (a) to prevent clutter.

2) Power crust: it is sensitive to holes and noise in the dataset. Moreover, the reconstruction time increases rapidly with the size of the data set (Fig. 3c).

3) Our approach: is the fastest. Most geometric details have also been kept (Fig. 3b). Holes on the dataset are automatically filled. The reconstructed surface has only one patch.

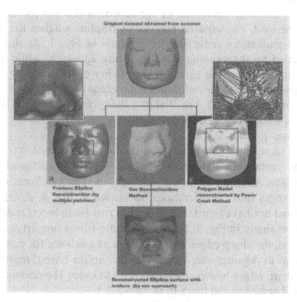

Fig. 3. Comparisons among different surface reconstruction approaches on the same dataset

Table 1. Performance comparisons

Method	Vertices	Triangles	Modelling time	Status
Our approach	10,490	----	0.77 sec.	Automatic
Previous BSpline reconstructure	10,490	20,370	37.05 sec.	Semi-automatic
Power Crust	10,490	----	36 sec.	Automatic

The hole filling property can be used to maintain surface integrity. An example is show in Fig. 4, where the data points belong to the hair on the back of the female model[1] has been ignored at the reconstruction stage.

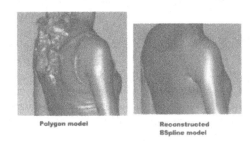

Fig. 4. Alternative application of the hole filling property

2.2.2 Simplicity

Since there is no constraint enforced in our approach that the reconstructed BSpline patch is square-shaped, the required number of BSpline patches for fitting an object surface can be significantly reduced. The example in Fig. 3 has illustrated that 179 patches are needed by the existing BSpline fitting approach, while one patch is required by our approach, for the same dataset. Other examples are given in Fig. 5, 6 and 7. The female upper body is reconstructed by four patches, i.e. left and right arms, front and back of body (Fig. 5). Fig. 7 shows the reconstruction of the left leg of the Armadillo model using one patch by our approach.

Currently, those patches layout are done manually. It is worth pointing out that there is nothing sacrosanct on patches partition and the reconstructed BSpline patch does not to be rectangular. However, as our currently automatic reconstruction scheme has not accommodated topology change, the patch-delineations need to take the topology changes into considerations, as shown in Fig. 5. Another constraint is that the patch must not have holes. Fig. 6 depicts two-patch reconstruction of a human face against the example in Fig. 3, to avoid the hole-filling property taking advantage. On the other hand, the sharp edges also could act as guidance for patch segmentation. This could help to against the nature of the spline-based representation over-smoothing the sharp edges which animators want to keep. The continuity among adjacent patches has been explored more in section 2.2.3.

---

[1] The dataset of female body is provided by Cyberware. http://www.cyberware.com/products/scanners/wbxSamples.html

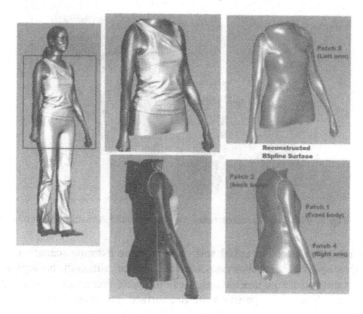

Fig. 5. Female upper body reconstruction

2.2.3 Continuity

The considerations on the continuity among adjacent patches could fall into two categories. First, for shape edge guided patch partitions, keeping G^0 continuity is sufficient. In
such cases, one patch boundary could be interpolated by its adjacent patch boundary. Second, when patch partition is done under the topology constraint, G^1 continuity should be
enforced. Fig. 6 (c) shows the seamless stitch of two reconstructed BSpline patches in (b).
For compassion, the original dataset is displayed as polygon model in (a). The gaps between the two patches are bridged by curvature-based filling process.

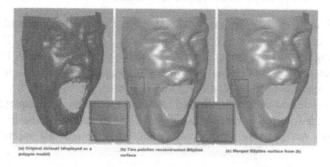

Fig. 6. Enforcing G^1 continuity between patches

2.2.4 Shortcoming

Automatic hole-filling and noise smoothing properties can also be a shortcoming of
our approach. The same example in Fig. 7 has shown that some features on the reconstructed surface (left leg) are over smoothed.

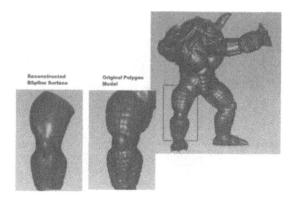

Fig. 7. Right leg reconstruction (one patch) on the Armadillo model[2]

The overshooting problem could still exist in some extreme scenarios, e.g. a flat surface with a series of steep bumps across the surface, although the applying of the chord length method for parameterization can alleviate this problem to great extend. Currently, our solution is to partition the flat surface into several patches. Each contains less bumps.

Briefly, although our approach provides a smooth and compact B-Spline representation for surfaces, it may not be the best for preserving fine geometric details of objects. To overcome this problem, a displacement map [KL96] may be computed for each pixel in which an offset from a point on a reconstructed surface to a point in the original raw data is recorded. Texture mapping is another economical solution to make up for the loss of fine surface details.

3   Applications

3.1   Multi-resolution Representation in Real Time

From the definition of the BSpline surface, it is clear that for each pair of parameters (u,v), there is one and only one corresponding surface point, i.e. $\Gamma(u,v)$. Thus, instead of triangulating the surface, one could triangulate the parameter domain. For example, the u-direction can be subdivided into m segments, i.e. $u_0=0$, u_1, ..., u_i, ..., $u_m=1$; similarly, the v-direction is subdivided into n segments, i.e. $v_0=0$, v_1, ..., v_j, ..., $v_n=1$. Then the parameter domain is subdivided into $m{\times}n$ rectangles. Consequently, the surface is subdivided into $m{\times}n$ rectangles as well. The simplicity of the triangulate the parameter space makes the real-time multi-resolution representation possible.

3.2   3D Metamorphosis

Since there exists one-to-one mapping from the object space to the parameter space, we can easily establish correspondences across objects via a common parameter

---

[2] The Armadillo model is provided by Stanford 3D scanning repository. http://graphics.stanford.edu/data/3Dscanrep/

space. From the discussion in section 3, it can also be known that for each reconstructed surface, its parameter space is made of a pair of knot vectors U and V. Since the knot vectors can be uniformed by applying our knot vector standardization algorithm, we can have any reconstructed surface defined over the parameter space.

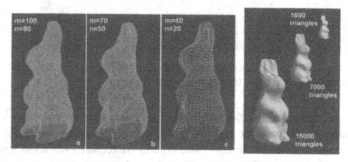

Fig. 8. Three meshes extracted at different resolution by applying different resample scheme on the parameter space. The right figure is an example of 3D object rendering at different levels of detail.

In summary, since a one-to-one mapping between the common parameter space and the object space, there exists

$$(s,t) \mapsto \overset{(i)}{\Gamma}(s,t) \tag{10}$$

$$(s,t) \mapsto \overset{(j)}{\Gamma}(s,t) \tag{11}$$

Consequently, through the pair of parameter (s,t), one-to-one mapping across objects is obtained:

$$\overset{(i)}{\Gamma}(s,t) \mapsto \overset{(j)}{\Gamma}(s,t) \tag{12}$$

By sampling the common parameter space, a set of corresponding B-Spline surface points can be established. More detailed discussion can be found in [Song07].

Recall that the surface-based 3D metamorphosis consists of two steps: 1) establishing a dense correspondence from object Γ^1 to Γ^2 and 2) creating a series of intermediate objects by interpolating corresponding points from their original positions on Γ^1 to the target positions on Γ^2. To create a series of intermediate objects between Γ^1 and Γ^2, one simply applies linear interpolation between corresponding points. Supposing n intermediate objects Γ_i $(1 \leq i \leq n)$ are wanted, they are created by

$$\Gamma_i(s,t) = \Gamma^1(s,t) + \frac{i}{n+1}(\Gamma^2(s,t) - \Gamma^1(s,t)) \tag{13}$$

Smooth morphing result from one face to another is shown in Fig. 9. Four intermediate faces were displayed between the start face (left end) and the destination face (right end).

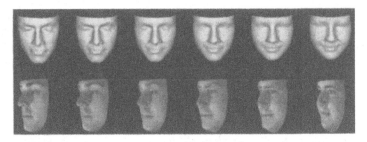

Fig. 9. Smooth 3D metamorphosis sequences between similar objects. Top row: un-textured morphing sequence. Bottom row: textured morphing sequence.

When either the source or the target object is changed, only equation 13 needs to be re-calculated to obtain the morphing sequence. Supposing the target object is changed from Γ^2 to Γ^3 and m intermediate objects are required while the source object is still Γ^1, then the intermediate objects Γ_j $(1 \leq j \leq m)$ are computed as:

$$\Gamma_j(s,t) = \Gamma^1(s,t) + \frac{j}{m+1}(\Gamma^3(s,t) - \Gamma^1(s,t)) \tag{14}$$

Fig. 10 demonstrates the morphing sequence where we change the target object but keep the source object the same as the one in Fig. 9. Another example is shown in Fig. 11, where the source and target objects have very different sizes, scales and topologies.

Fig. 10. Smooth 3D metamorphosis sequences. The source and target have different sizes, scales and topologies.

Fig. 11. 3D Metamorphosis between two objects of very different sizes, scales and topologies

3.3 Freeform Deformation

Moving the control points is the most obvious way of changing the shape of a B-Spline curve, since the shape change is translational in the direction of the control point being moved. The proof is given in the following. Suppose $f(t)$ is a given B-Spline curve of degree k defined as follows:

$$f(t) = \sum_{i=0}^{n} B_i^k(t)c_i \tag{15}$$

Suppose the control point C_i is moved to a new position $Q_i = C_i + v$. Then the new B-Spline curve $f'(t)$ of degree k is:

$$
\begin{aligned}
f'(t) &= \sum_{j=0}^{i-1} B_j^k(t)c_j + B_i^k(t)(c_i + v) + \sum_{j=i+1}^{n} B_j^k(t)c_j \\
&= \sum_{j=0}^{n} B_j^k(t)c_j + B_i^k(t)v \\
&= f(t) + B_i^k(t)v
\end{aligned}
\tag{16}
$$

Therefore, the new curve $f'(t)$ is simply the sum of the original curve $f(t)$ and a translation vector $B_i^k(t)v$. Since $B_i^k(t)$ is non-zero on the interval $[u_i, u_{i+k+1})$, and if t is not in this interval, this translation term is zero. Hence, moving a control point only affects the shape of a section of the curve. This local property is desirable in application of 3D free-form deformation. Similar proof can be given for BSpline surfaces.

Thus the set of control points which describes our reconstructed surface can be used for free-form deformation. Moreover, unlike statistic models, e.g. principal component analysis (PCA), which describes an object as a weighted sum of principal components which often bear little resemblance to the underlying interdependent structure of biological forms, shape descriptors have clear physical information attached to them. Therefore, it is straightforward to change a face shape by modifying the shape descriptors. The underlying surface is modified in a predictable way, as shown in Fig. 12 and 13.

Fig. 12. Changing facial attributes. (a) Thin (b) Normal (c) Fat.

Fig. 13. Changing facial attributes (nose). (a) Before. (b) After.

4 Conclusion and Future Works

A novel 3D modelling technique is presented offering an alternative solution to 3D metamorphosis, free-form 3D deformation and real time multi-resolution display. In contrast to previous works using vertices and polygons, our approach provides compact representations for 3D objects. Despite the high compression rate, rendering result using our reconstructed surface is still similar to that using the original polygon representation. Moreover, one-to-one mapping from the object space to a common parameter space can be established. Through the common parameter space, any pair of objects can automatically have dense correspondences established, which is independent to the 3D modelling process. Therefore, shape descriptors of each object only needs to be computed once in advance. Consequently, whenever the source or the target object is changed, only a linear equation needs to be re-calculated to obtain a new morphing sequence. This is advantageous over the common connectivity generation process, with which the the correspondences must be re-calculated.

The system has been tested on a personal computer (Pentium 4/512M RAM). For a typical dataset, i.e. a dataset consisting of 10,000 vertices, our approach takes 0.77 seconds to reconstruct the surface. We also examine the performance when the dataset is large - it takes 1.55 seconds to reconstruct the surface on a dataset of 75,232 points.

To overcome the shortcoming of not being able to preserving fine geometric details (i.e. as discussed in section 2.2.4), a displacement map in our future work could be implemented. Displacement maps are usually applied during rendering and are available in a number of commercial renderers.. Texture mapping is another economical solution to make up for the loss of fine surface details.

References

[Ale00]   Alexa, M.: Merging Polyhedral Shapes with Scattered Features. The Visual Computer 16(1), 26–37 (2000)

[CCM*97]   Ciampalini, A., Cignoni, P., Montani, C., Scopigno, R.: Multi-resolution Decimation Based on Global Error. The Visual Computer 13, 228–246 (1997)

[CPD*96]   Certain, A., Popović, J., DeRose, T., Duchamp, T., Salesin, D., Stuetzle, W.: Interactive Multi-resolution Surface Viewing. In: Computer Graphics (SIGGRAPH 1996 proceedings), pp. 91–98 (1996)

[EDD*95]   Eck, M., DeRose, T., Duchamp, T., Hoppe, H., Lounsbery, M., Stuetzle, W.: Multi-resolution Analysis of Arbitrary Meshes. In: Proceedings of 22nd International Conference on Computer Graphics and Interactive Techniques, August, pp. 173–182 (1995)

[EH96]   Eck, M., Hoppe, H.: Automatic Reconstruction of B-Spine Surfaces of Arbitrary Topological Type. In: Proceedings of 23rd International Conference on Computer Graphics and Interactive Techniques, pp. 325–334 (1996)

[FB95]   Forsey, D., Bartels, R.: Surface Fitting with Hierarchical splines. ACM Transactions on Graphics 14(2), 134–161 (1995)

[HDD*93]   Hoppe, H., DeRose, T., Duchamp, T., McDonald, J., Stuetzle, W.: Mesh Optimization. In: Proceedings of SIGGRAPH 1993, August, pp. 19–26 (1993)

[Hop96]   Hoppe, H.: Progressive Meshes. In: Proceedings of the 23rd annual conference on Computer graphics and interactive techniques, pp. 99–108 (1996)

[Hut04]   Hutton, T.: Dense Surface Models of the Human Face, PhD thesis (2004)

[KL96]   Krishnamurthy, V., Levoy, M.: Fitting Smooth Surfaces to Dense Polygon Meshes. ACM-0-89791-746-4/96/008 (1996)

[KSK00]   Kanai, T., Suzuki, H., Kimura, F.: Metamorphosis of Arbitrary Triangular Meshes. IEEE Computer Graphics and Applications, 62–75 (2000)

[LDS*99]   Lee, A., Dobkin, D., Sweldens, W., Schroder, P.: Multi-resolution Mesh Morphing. In: Proceedings of SIGGRAPH 1999, pp. 343–350 (1999)

[LDW97]   Lounsbery, M., Derose, T., Warren, J.: Multi-resolution Analysis for Surfaces of Arbitrary Topological Type. Transactions on Graphics 16(1), 34–73 (1997)

[LH03]   Lee, T., Huang, P.: Fast and Intuitive Metamorphosis of 3D Polyhedral Models Using SMCC Mesh Merging Scheme. IEEE Transactions on Visualization and Computer Graphics 9(1) (2003)

[LL04]   Lin, C., Lee, T.: Metamorphosis of 3D Polyhedral Models Using Progressive Connectivity Transformations. IEEE Transactions on Visualization and Computer Graphics 10(6) (2004)

[Lou94]   Lounsbery, M.: Multi-resolution Analysis for Surfaces of Arbitrary Topological Type, PhD thesis, Department of Computer Science, University of Washington (1994)

[MBV*95]   Milroy, M., Bradley, C., Vickers, G., Weir, D.: G1 Continuity of B-spline Surface Patches in Reverse Engineering. CAD 27, 471–478 (1995)

[SB06]   Song, Y., Bai, L.: Single B-Spline Patch 3D Modelling for Facial Analysis. In: Proceedings of 6th International Conference on Recent Advances in Soft Computing (RASC 2006), Canterbury, United Kingdom (July 2006)

[SBW06]   Song, Y., Bai, L., Wang, Y.: 3D Object Modelling for Entertainment Applications. In: International Conference on Advances in Computer Entertainment Technology, Hollywood, USA (June 2006)

[Song07]   Song, Y.: 3D Free-form Surface Representation and Its Applications. PhD thesis (2007)

[WW92]   Welch, W., Witkin, A.: Variational Surface Modelling. In: Proceedings of the 19th annual conference on Computer graphics and interactive techniques, pp. 157–166 (1992)

Active-Vision System Reconfiguration for Form Recognition in the Presence of Dynamic Obstacles

Matthew Mackay and Beno Benhabib

Department of Mechanical & Industrial Engineering,
University of Toronto, 5 King's College Road
Toronto, ON, Canada, M5S 3G1
mackay@mie.utoronto.ca,
benhabi@mie.utoronto.ca

Abstract. This paper presents a novel, agent-based sensing-system reconfiguration methodology for the recognition of time-varying geometry objects or subjects (*targets*). A multi-camera active-vision system is used to improve form-recognition performance by selecting near-optimal viewpoints along a prediction horizon. The proposed method seeks to maximize the visibility of such a time-varying geometry in a cluttered, dynamic environment. Simulated experiments clearly show a tangible potential performance gain.

Keywords: Sensing System Reconfiguration, Active Vision, Human Form Recognition, Human Action Recognition.

1 Introduction

A common tactic in surveillance is sensing-system planning (also known as *sensor planning* or *sensing-system reconfiguration*), which is defined as selecting (using a formal method) the number, types, locations, and internal parameters of the sensors employed in the surveillance of an object or subject [1], [2]. By improving data quality, and thus reducing the uncertainty inherent in the sensing process, one seeks to improve the performance of the surveillance task. The focus of this paper is sensing-system reconfiguration, restricted to the on-line modification of camera poses (position and orientation) in a multi-camera active-vision system, for the real-time surveillance of time-varying geometry targets (such as humans), in dynamic, cluttered environments. Due to the potential real-world applications, and for comparison to other research, this paper focuses primarily on human subjects.

A real-time surveillance system must be able to cope with the presence of multiple static or dynamic (maneuvering) obstacles as part of its sensing solution, in order to be effective [3]. As such, viewpoints are often ranked in terms of the useful target data that can be extracted, with a given amount of effort. Time-varying geometry targets introduce some complications into the recognition process, such as: non-uniform importance, partial occlusions, and self-occlusions, as well as the need for continuous surveillance [4], [5].

To date, there have been few surveillance methodologies that utilize reconfiguration for time-varying geometry objects. A rare example is [6], where an off-line planning

F.J. Perales and R.B. Fisher (Eds.): AMDO 2008, LNCS 5098, pp. 188–207, 2008.

method is used to track the motion of an articulated human form. Using eight static cameras, obstacles and self-occlusions are addressed through data fusion and a robust recognition method, rather than on-line system reconfiguration. The majority of other reported methods propose the application of principles developed for fixed-geometry objects to the problem of time-varying geometry objects. A typical example is [7], where human identification is performed using multiple active cameras, tracking only a relatively time-invariant portion of the overall human, the face. Other research papers simply acknowledge that reconfiguration of the sensing system could improve recognition quality for time-varying geometry objects (e.g., [8]), but present no specific framework.

1.1 Sensing-System Planning

Earlier works in sensor planning have typically focused on determining the configuration of a given set of sensors for a static environment containing only fixed (time-invariant) geometry objects. In the survey paper [1], such planning methods are characterized as *generate-and-test* or *synthesis*. A generate-and-test method evaluates possible sensor configurations with respect to task constraints, discretizing the domain to limit the number of options that must be considered. An established example of such a method is the HEAVEN system [9], which uses a discretized virtual sphere around the Object of Interest (OoI) to determine achievable, un-occluded poses for a single sensor.

Synthesis methods, on the other hand, characterize task requirements analytically, and determine sensor poses by finding a solution to the set of constraints presented. These systems are often application-specific, as in [10], where the planner synthesizes a region of viewpoints by imposing 3D position bounds from task constraints. In [11], points on the outer edge of the OoI form a virtual box, which the camera must be positioned to view while minimizing the local distortion in the image. In [2], sensing-system reconfiguration is used as part of an overall determination of sensing strategy (including number and type of sensors, as well as placement). In another, more recent example [12], sensor planning is used for mapping a static environment. Solid models from an incremental modeler are used to compute future positions for sensors to better explore the environment. In [13], an agent-based system is proposed to allow intelligent feedback between multiple sensors, reducing data redundancy and improving surface coverage of the OoI. The scene is static and individual sensors use a generate-and-test method to evaluate potential viewing positions.

A natural extension to the static environment sensing problem is the continuous reconfiguration of sensor poses with moving OoIs, and multiple obstacles and sensors – *active sensing*. For example, in [8], an 11-camera system was used to examine the effects of viewpoint on recognition rates for human gait. It was determined that the traditional static, off-line single-camera placement methods may lead to poor performance for multi-camera systems [14]. Recently, agent-based planning methods were also applied to the on-line sensing-system reconfiguration problem (e.g., [3], [15], [16]).

In fully dynamic environments, the obstacles themselves may also be moving. In [17], for example, a method to optimize data quality, by controlling a team of mobile robots equipped with cameras, was presented. The goal was addressed as an optimization problem with consideration to the *Next-Best-View* (NBV).

Attention-based behavior ([18]-[20]), where the attention of the system is focused on a single target until the vision task is performed, can also be used to reduce a multi-target problem to single-target observation.

1.2 Form and Action Recognition

Recognition of time-varying geometry objects (such as humans) includes the identification of both (static) form and motion. The logical starting point in any time-varying geometry recognition algorithm would be the identification of a single static form. However, since this would require an existing database of characteristic data for known poses, past work merely focused on reconstructing the model of an unknown object [21]. The concept of NBV is critical to such reconstruction, in that one may seek to optimize the amount of unknown information about an object uncovered by each subsequent reconfiguration. However, most existing works in time-varying geometry object recognition consider sensor poses as an unchangeable constraint – no formal planning, either off-line or on-line, is applied.

Many objects also exhibit specific, repeatable sequences of form (motions or actions) that one might wish to recognize. In template matching, for example, input images are compared directly to stored templates, and multiple pose matches over time form a sequence template (e.g., [22]). Here, template matching is performed using a database of views captured from multiple cameras.

Semantic approaches are analogous to template matching, except the data used in the templates is high-level object configuration data. These are model-based approaches, in that a high-level representation of the OoI may be constructed. In [23], the geometry of a human body (specifically, the leg joints involved in walking) is recovered over several frames in the presence of occlusions.

Statistical approaches attempt to reduce the dimensionality of matching through statistical operations on the template database. For instance, in [24], the authors seek to identify what particular information is most important in identifying a positive match to a template. Analysis of Variance (ANOVA) is used to identify features that highlight differences between subjects. Then, Principal Component Analysis (PCA) is used to reduce the data set to a lower dimensionality for matching.

In these works, sensing-system reconfiguration was not considered as part of the methodology – input data was taken to be fixed, with no opportunity for quality improvement.

1.3 Time-Varying Geometry Objects

Sensing-system reconfiguration for time-varying geometry objects introduces additional complications to the process, such as non-uniform importance, partial occlusions, and self-occlusions, as well as the need for continuous surveillance. While these issues do not invalidate the use of past work, they do necessitate a novel framework designed specifically to cope with these constraints. The goal of this paper is, thus, to demonstrate that (1) sensing-system reconfiguration techniques can tangibly benefit recognition performance for time-varying geometry objects, and that (2) factors not addressed by majority of past works must be addressed for improved recognition. From this, the focus of this paper shifts to quantifying the effect of real-world pose estimation noise and pose prediction uncertainty on the proposed methodology, given that one can show that the proposed method is applicable and useful in the chosen application.

2 Problem Formulation

From the literature review above, one can conclude that an active-vision system using multiple, mobile cameras may provide autonomous surveillance of a single, dynamic Object of Interest (OoI), as it moves within the confines of a workspace on an initially unknown path (e.g., [20]). The workspace may also be cluttered with multiple, dynamic obstacles (each with unknown movement paths) that can generate. Herein, surveillance is defined as the collection and analysis of sensor data to estimate the object parameters of pose (position and orientation) and form, uniquely identifying the object and categorizing its current action. As such, a system that can perform the following tasks is necessary:

- *Detection*: All objects in the scene must be detected and categorized as either the OoI or obstacle
- *Tracking*: Each object must be tracked, and an estimate of its future pose maintained.
- *Reconfiguration*: Given historical, current, and predicted data about the OoI and obstacles, an achievable set of poses for all sensors that minimizes uncertainty for the surveillance task at hand must be determined.
- *Recognition*: Data from all sensors must be fused into a single estimate of the object's current geometry. A further estimate must reconcile this geometry data with historical data to determine the current action of the target.

The system must also posses the following properties, in order to be effective in any real-world application:

- *Real-time operation*: All operations must be limited in computational complexity and depth, such that real-time operation of the system is not compromised.
- *Robustness*: The system must be robust to faults and the likelihood of false object identification or action classification must be minimized.

The performance of a surveillance system can be characterized by the success of the vision task in recognizing the target's form and its current action. This task depends primarily on the quantity and quality of the sensor data that is collected, characterized herein by a visibility metric, V. This metric in turn depends on the current form of the OoI, the poses of any obstacles, the poses of the sensors, and the pose of the OoI. However, the only variables that the sensing system has direct control over are the poses of the cameras. The visibility metric for the ith camera at the jth demand instant, t_j, is expressed herein as a function of $p_{S_i}^j$. This is the pose of the ith sensor, S_i, at the jth instant where pose is defined as a 6D vector representing position (x, y, z) and orientation (φ, ψ, θ):

$$V_i^j = f_i^j(p_{S_i}^j), \quad \text{and} \tag{1}$$

$$p = \begin{bmatrix} x & y & z & \varphi & \Theta & \theta \end{bmatrix} \tag{2}$$

This paper proposes a global formulation of the reconfiguration problem for a sensing-system with n_{sens} sensors, n_{obs} obstacles, and with prediction over the time horizon ending at the mth demand instant:

For each demand instant, t_j, j=1..m, perform the following:

    For each sensor, S_i, i=1..n_{sens}, solve the following:

        Given:

$$p^0_{S_i}, \; p^0_{OoI}, \; u^0, \; p^0_{obs_k}; k = 1 \text{ to } n_{obs}$$

        Maximize:

$$Pr = g\left(V_i^l\right); l = 1 \text{ to } j \tag{3}$$

        Subject to:

$$p^1_{S_i} \in P_i$$

$$p^1_{S_i} \in A^1_i$$

$$V_i^l \geq V_{min}; l = 1 \text{ to } j$$

End of loop.

Continue while: t_{proc} < t_{max},

where p^j_{OoI} is the OoI pose at the jth demand instant, $p^j_{obs_i}$ is the pose of the ith obstacle at the jth demand instant, u^j is the feature vector of the OoI at the jth demand instant, P_i is the discretized set of feasible sensor poses for the ith sensor, A_i^j is the discretized set of achievable sensor poses for the ith sensor at the jth demand instant, V_{min} refers to a user-defined threshold of minimum visibility, t_{proc} is the time spent processing data, and t_{max} is the maximum time before a final pose set must be chosen. The two sets, P_i and A_i^j, are governed by:

$$A_i^j \subseteq P_i \tag{4}$$

$$p \in P \text{ if and only if } P_{low} \leq p \leq P_{upp} \tag{5}$$

where P_{low} and P_{upp} are the lower and upper movement limits of the sensor motion. The determination of the subset $A_i^j \subseteq P_i$ depends on the model of motion used, and is not specified.

The proposed objective function, *performance*, or Pr, depends on the visibility metric of each sensor at all demand instants in the horizon. It is a measure of success in achieving the sensing objective [20]. The proposed formulation first seeks to maximize visibility of the OoI at the immediate future demand instant, t_1, for all sensors. If sufficient time remains, the system seeks to maximize expected visibility at t_1 and t_2, then, t_1, t_2, and t_3, and so on. As such, a higher overall metric value may be achieved at later demand instants, at the expense of near-future visibility. This trade-off can be controlled externally by adjusting the minimum desired visibility and the sensor assignment at each demand instant. More weight can be assigned to nearer demand instants in order to minimize exposure to future uncertainties in estimated poses. Computational complexity is bounded, though the determination of poses at each future instant does depend on the poses determined for each previous instant, back to the current time, t_0.

3 Proposed Methodology

An agent-based approach for sensing-system reconfiguration, shown in Fig. 1, is proposed for the surveillance of time-varying geometry objects:

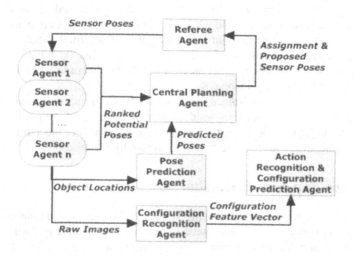

Fig. 1. Overview of the proposed sensing-system reconfiguration methodology for human surveillance

At the lowest level, each sensor agent is associated with a single sensor. The exact configuration (in terms of number and composition of the sensor set) can be determined through a number of established methods (e.g., [1], [9], [10]). For our system, it is assumed that each sensor is reconfigurable in terms of pose, (position and orientation) and that each is limited in capability by positional and rotational velocity and acceleration:

$$t_d = t_1 - t_0 \tag{6}$$

$$L_{min} < x_1 < L_{max} \tag{7}$$

$$x_{L-} < x_1 < x_{L+} \tag{8}$$

$$x_{L-} = f(x_0, t_d), \ x_{L+} = f(x_0, t_d), \tag{9}$$

where x_0 is the initial position, x_1 is the final position, t_0 is the initial time, t_1 is the final time, t_d is the total time between the demand instants, and $L_{min/max}$ are the outer limits of the motion axis, respectively. A similar set of equations can be used to determine the rotational limits in terms of angular velocity and acceleration. This position space is discretized into n_{pos} possible final positions, where $n_{pos} \propto (t_1 - t_0)$, to bound computational complexity. The visibility metric is evaluated at each discretized sensor pose.

All known obstacles and the OoI are modeled as elliptical cylinders. A clipped projection plan is established, and all objects projected onto this plane. The visibility metric is thus defined as:

$$V \propto \sum_{i=1}^{n_{area}} (A_i) \tag{10}$$

where n_{area} is the number of distinct un-occluded regions and A_i is i^{th} distinct subsection of the projection of the OoI, visible on the projection plane. This is effectively measuring visible amount of surface area of a virtual cylinder bounding the OoI. The effect of foreshortening is not removed; this is intentional, as the effective surface area visible decreases as the angle from camera focal direction to the cylinder tangent-plane normal increases.

Such a system tends to *look-ahead* and assign sensors to improve future visibility whenever necessary. This metric is used as part of a weighted sum, which further ranks poses according to the largest object surface area visible, the largest possible view of this same area, and the least distance traveled by the sensor.

4   Simulated Experiment Results

In order to validate the proposed sensing-system reconfiguration methodology in a single-target, dynamic environment with a time-varying geometry OoI, a set of controlled, simulation-based experiments were carried out.

The purpose of these experiments is to quantify the effect of the previously mentioned real-world difficulties on form recognition, and to determine to what extent our system is able to address these issues. As seen in Section 3, the system is specifically designed to select un-occluded camera poses whenever possible. In this section, we seek to quantify the ability of the system to do so. However, all vision algorithms used are robust, and are tolerant of partial occlusions, image noise, etc. In addition, the methodology itself is designed to be robust to uncertainty introduced at various points, such as during pose and form recovery. As such, the experiments have been carefully designed to highlight only a single factor at a time for comparison, otherwise any quantitative measure would be meaningless. However, as in any vision-based system, any determinations are still highly dependent on the target application and experimental environment.

4.1   Simulated Experimental Set-Up

A total of four sensor agents were implemented – each sensor is responsible for solving the proposed local optimization problem directly. The central planner accepts the highest ranked solutions, and utilizes a simple set of rules to select a subset of the sensors to service the OoI at the current demand instant, and to select the final sensor poses:

1. Sensors with a visibility metric less than the minimum, V_{min}, at all poses, are unassigned.
2. The three highest-visibility sensors are assigned to this instant.
3. The sensor with the lowest metric is asked to re-evaluate the visibility metric for an additional demand instant and is assigned to the next instant.
4. For assigned sensors, a weighted sum of metrics is evaluated.

These rules are valid for the simulated experiments that follow only; generalized rules usable in any (non-simulated) application cannot easily be constructed, and this particular set has not been rigorously derived.

In order to provide synthetic images under carefully controlled conditions, a simulation environment was designed. This environment can produce images from any of the virtual cameras, and includes a segmented model that approximates the human form. A simple walking action was used in all the simulated experiments.

Form recognition is provided by a model-based algorithm using color segmentation. First, the location of a reference point in the world-coordinate system is found through robust estimation of the head center in 2D images. Contiguous regions of the OoI are then identified, and key-points determined. For the synthetic images, these points can be uniquely identified using color cues, so robust estimation is subsequently used to find the 3D world coordinates of as many points as possible. A moving camera calibration method, similar to that presented in previous works [3], would be necessary at this stage if real-world cameras were used. Such work is outside the scope of this paper, and is not necessary for the experiments that follow (the simulator was written to provide the calibration matrices). A fitting method is used to form the feature vector via four form-invariant reference points on the OoI:

1. Subtract the reference from each interest point location to remove dependence on world position.
2. Remove the effects of rotation and scaling from the object data using a change of basis utilizing vectors formed by three other points around the reference point.
3. Merge all points with distance $|x_1\text{-}x_0|<K_1$ into a single point, where x_0 and x_1 are the two points.
4. Start with an empty feature vector. For each point, x, and each model location, x_m, if $\|x\text{-}x_m\| < K_2$, place x in the blank feature vector at the position corresponding to x_m. For all remaining points, place them in the feature vector location corresponding to $\min(\|x\text{-}x_m\|)$, subject to $\|x\text{-}x_m\| < K_3$, where $K_3 \gg K_2$.

A measure of the uncertainty of the fit is defined as:

$$E \propto C_1 \sum \left(\|\mathbf{x} - \mathbf{x}_m\| \right) + C_2 n_{ua} + C_3 n_{ms}, \qquad (11)$$

where C_1, C_2, and C_3 are proportionality constants, n_{ua} is the number of unassigned points, n_{em} is the number of missing points, and the sum is over all assigned points. This method of fitting is performed on each model in the database and a minimum uncertainty fit determined (subject to some upper limit for recognition, application and algorithm dependent).

In order to recognize the current OoI action, a post-process method is used. Using *time normalized* input data, a metric of distance from the library data is formulated for each database set that contains both two distinct *start* and *end* forms.

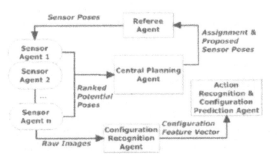

Fig. 2. Overview of sensing-system reconfiguration methodology used for the simulations

An overall block diagram of the system used for these trials is presented in Fig. 2. One can note the simplifications from the proposed methodology. The function of the prediction agent is replaced with perfect prediction given by the simulator (not shown on the diagram). Similarly, the current positions of all obstacles and the subject are given exactly (no uncertainty) by the simulator for this ideal case.

4.2 Comparison of System Reconfiguration Capability

An initial simulated test, consisting of three runs, each showing 100 frames of a subject walking was performed to determine how the 'level' of sensing-system reconfiguration affects recognition performance. Static sensor poses were used for the first trial. The remaining two runs were conducted using a velocity-constrained and ideal (unconstrained) reconfiguration system, respectively.

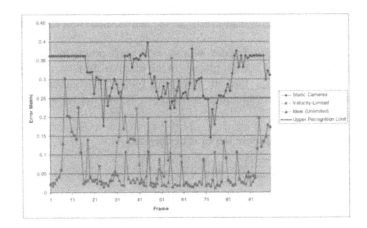

Fig. 3. Comparison of error metric over three trials of 100 frames each, with walking action performed by the target

The results for each of the three runs are shown in Fig. 3. For each frame, the error metric is calculated from the recovered feature vector. In each trial, the target maintained a constant velocity of 10 mm/frame on a straight-line path through the center of the workspace (Fig. 4). A virtual frame-rate of 10 frames-per-second was assumed for the quasi-static simulations. For the velocity limited system, the maximum velocity is given as 45 mm/frame, with a maximum acceleration of 90 mm/frame^2. The ideal system is considered to have unlimited maximum velocity and acceleration (instantaneous repositioning of cameras). The static-camera system uses a standard off-line sensor placement common in many other works, such as [24]. The four cameras are placed in a square configuration, each with its focal line on a normal to the path of the OoI. For the two final trials, the initial camera poses were the same as the static-camera poses, but two of the cameras were given a linear-translation axis, and all cameras could pan up to ±90° from their initial pose.

An upper limit for the error metric (given by Formula 11) of 0.25 was selected for these simulations. Any frame with an error value above this limit is not considered to have a positive match from the form-recognition process. This value was determined through statistical analysis of multiple previous runs, resulting in at least 95% true positive matches for un-rejected frames. The choice of this metric is somewhat arbitrary; it is application and vision-algorithm dependent. The key point is to establish some limit on the error metric, past which the system is considered to have completely failed to recognize the subject's form. In this example, this is done purely as a mnemonic device, for comparison.

The results showed a clear overall reduction in error values with the use of sensing-system reconfiguration over static camera placement.

1st Run: For the case of static cameras, performance was poor in Frames 1 to 20 and 80 to 100, since the object is near the limits of the workspace. Frames 32 to 45 showed that an obstacle would also make most of the object's form unrecoverable.

2nd Run: The use of constrained sensing-system reconfiguration lowered overall error, as the majority of frames are now considered to be positively recognized. Significant error still remained, for example in Frames 31 to 41, where the system was unable to move to its 'best' sensor positions due to movement-time constraints. One can also note that the use of reconfiguration is not guaranteed to produce improved results if movement is constrained – Frames 56 to 59. For these frames, the system chooses the best pose from those achievable, but the previous reconfiguration choices have resulted in a poor set of choices. Here the current sensor poses are too far from the ideal set for the system – it cannot achieve them before several demand instants have passed. As a result, the algorithm cannot recover some portions of the model for these frames.

3rd Run: The 'ideal' run showed strong correlation to the velocity-limited case, but only when the best pose for a given frame was achievable by the velocity-limited system. For frames where previous reconfiguration choices or motion time constraints limited the achievable poses to a poor set of alternatives, there is a definite improvement – Frames 30 to 41 and 56 to 59. However, there were still some frames where sub-sections of the object could not be recognized due to missing data (e.g., Frames 34, 44, 54, and 59), resulting in a higher than average error metric.

4.3 An Example Frame

Consider Frame 85, where a positive form match was determined by the ideal algorithm, but significant error in the recovered model still exists. This is the result of the system rejecting incomplete data on one or more model sub-sections and, thus, not recovering that portion of the model. Specifically, as shown in Fig. 4, the left arm of the subject is not visible. Note that the images are shown without noise for clarity. However, all simulated images have Gaussian noise added, with distribution parameters determined from the measurement of real-world cameras. Also note the cluttered backgrounds, used to improve realism.

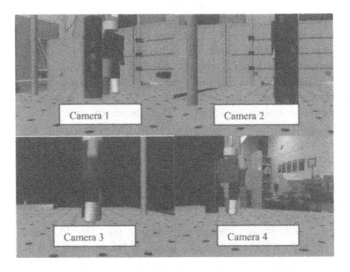

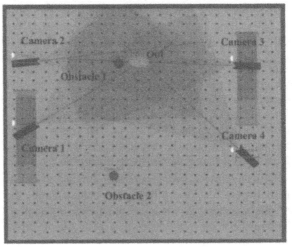

Fig. 4. A motion example, showing the OoI view from each camera (top), and current system configuration (bottom)

Using the proposed algorithm, each sensor uses a weighted combination of three metrics to rank its desired poses: the area of the target bounding cylinder that is visible, the angle to the target, and the distance to the target. For Camera 1, a plot of these metrics, plus the weighted combination metric, is shown in Fig. 5.

One can note that if Camera 1 (and Camera 3, as well) were to select a non-optimal pose under the current rules, the left arm of the subject would be visible and, thus, it would be recovered. This pose would likely have a translational d value closer to the maximum of 1.6. However, such poses cannot be distinguished from other, less informative, poses using any of the current metrics (Fig. 5). In this specific case, the current target distance metric would act against such poses. The addition of a fourth metric, which can differentiate viewpoints that contain unique information from those that do not, could potentially solve this problem. The only way to determine (without *a priori* knowledge of the target's actions) which views are likely to contain unique data is to predict the form of the object at a future instant. As such, feedback from the form-prediction process could be used to improve this sensing-system reconfiguration algorithm for time-varying geometry object/action recognition.

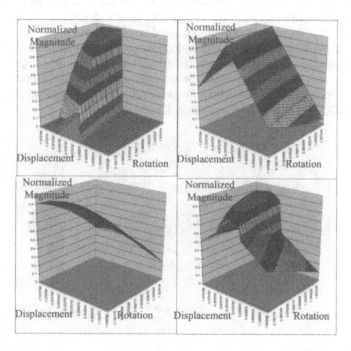

Fig. 5. (Upper Left) Visibility Metric (Upper Right) Angle Metric (Lower Left) Distance Metric (Lower Right) Combined Metric

4.4 Addition of Pose Prediction

From the results presented in Section C, one can conclude that the addition of reconfiguration to the problem has reduced the average error-metric values and improved recognition performance over using only traditional static camera placement. A need for a system specific to time-varying geometry objects over traditional methods has also been identified. However, additional simulated experiments are necessary to validate the performance of the system under non-ideal prediction and pose estimation, which is inherent in any real-world application.

For these simulated experiments, the proposed methodology for real-world prediction shown in Fig. 1 was implemented. The prediction agent implementation was that of a Kalman Filter (KF), with second-order (position, velocity, and acceleration) state variables. The KF itself is not novel, and has been studied in detail in the past – in fact, the actual implementation of the prediction agent is not critical to the work, rather the uncertainty that any real prediction method introduces is. The input observations to the KF are taken from the form recognition agent, which tracks the position of the head of the subject as a reference center-point. Only 2D tracking will be considered, as it is assumed for these trials that the subject does not change elevation significantly. Input images to the system still come from the simulation environment developed for the previous trials.

A total of four trials were performed for this section. As before, an error metric upper limit of 0.25 was been selected, and real-world velocity- and acceleration-limited reconfiguration has been used (with parameters identical to the second run in the previous set of experiments) to mimic a real-world system.

The initial positions of all obstacles and the subject are similar to the previous trial, except the initial locations of the obstacles, which have been moved slightly. The four trials consist of: (1) Ideal prediction, Static Obstacles (Similar to Trial 2 from the previous section), (2) Ideal Prediction, Dynamic Obstacles, (3) Real-world prediction, Static Obstacles, (4) Real-world prediction, Dynamic Obstacles.

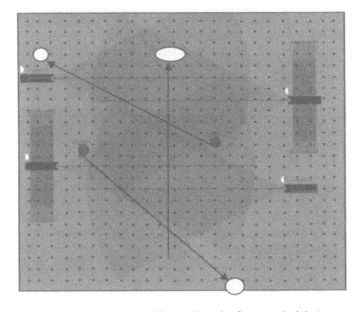

Fig. 6. Initial Positions and obstacle/subject trajectories for second trials (not to scale)

For the two cases where the obstacles are moving, prediction will be performed by the simulator (ideal), and the prediction agent (real-world), respectively. Fig. 6 shows the trajectories of the obstacles and subject for these trials. The same 100 walking frames will be used for the articulated model. However the demand instant spacing will now be 4 frames of separation, to highlight the effects of prediction on the system. Thus, a total of 25 data points will be presented for each run, where the equivalent frame in the previous trial is simply $frame_{old} = frame_{new} \times 4$.

Trial 1

The first trial presents results which are very similar to those found in the previous section. All obstacles in the system are static, and the subject follows the same trajectory and action sequence as before, with ideal prediction. As expected, the frames which are correctly recognized correspond closely to those from the previous results, as does the average value of the error metric, and its standard deviation.

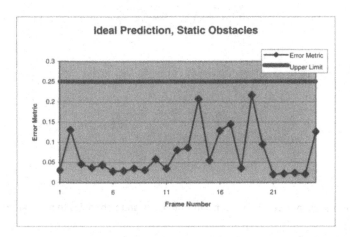

Fig. 7. Resulting error metric plot for ideal prediction with static obstacles

As before, there are some frames (Fig. 7 – Points 2, 13, 19) where the form was positively recognized, but significant error remains. These are cases where some portion (an arm or leg, for example) of the model data was rejected by the form-recognition agent due to a poor estimate from the input images. The solution identified in the previous section can address this issue, where feedback from the recognition agent can be used to improve the input data for these unknown regions. All frames in this trial, however, were considered positively recognized, regardless of any missing data. The principal use of this trial is to provide a basis for comparison with the remaining trials.

Trial 2

For this trial, the obstacles have been given a linear trajectory with a constant velocity of $v = \begin{bmatrix} 10 & 0 & 10 \end{bmatrix}$ mm/frame and $v = \begin{bmatrix} -10 & 0 & -5 \end{bmatrix}$ mm/frame for obstacles one and two, respectively. Again, prediction is assumed to be ideal for this trial, and thus a plot of the predicted locations has not been added to the graph.

From Fig. 8, one can see that the overall error metric has been reduced in some regions, notably the points previously highlighted in Trial 1 as containing an unrecognized section of the model. This is most likely due to fortuitous locations of the obstacles and subject at these frames, since as will be explained for Trials 3 and 4, the paths chosen for the obstacles are designed to exhibit fewer occlusions in the second half of the sequence. Regardless of this, all frames are still considered positively recognized, and the average error metric is not significantly different from the previous trial. Also, other regions, such as frames 6-11 and 21-24 show close correlation to the previous trial. This indicates that the reconfiguration is able to effectively handle the changing locations of the obstacles in selecting sensor poses.

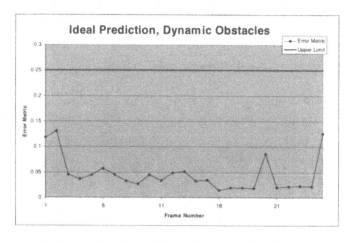

Fig. 8. Error metric plot resulting from addition of dynamic obstacles to previous experiment

Trial 3

This is the first trial that introduces non-ideal prediction using the KF. Input to the filter (for subject location prediction) is taken from the form recognition agent, and from the ideal positions given by the simulation environment (for obstacle pose prediction).

It is assumed that a method is readily available to track the obstacles with low overall error in world coordinate position; this is not the focus of the trial, as many established methods exist. The tracking results for the trial are shown in Fig. 9, overlaid on the initial obstacle and subject positions. It is clear from the plot that tracking is lost near the end of the trial, as the estimated points show significant deviation from the straight-line path.

Examining the error metric plot in Fig. 10, one can see that for this trial, the overall error metric and sequence of recognized frames closely corresponds to that of the first trial, (static obstacles under ideal prediction) at least for the first few frames. However, near the second half of the sequence (Fig. 10), we can again see that the prediction agent loses its track of the subject, and now overall system lock on the

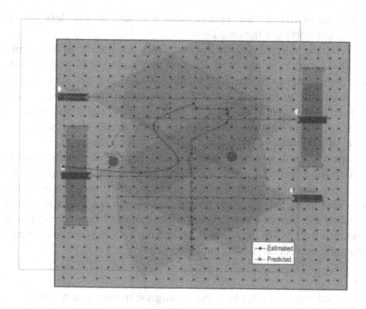

Fig. 9. Plot showing estimated (from form recognition) and predicted (from prediction agent) positions of the subject for Trial 3

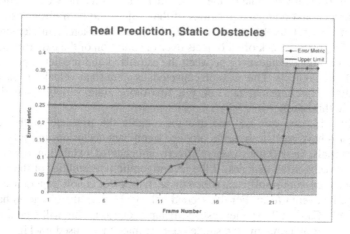

Fig. 10. Error metric plot for the addition of the prediction agent to the case with static obstacles only

subject is also lost (since the form recognition agent now provides the estimated OoI position).

From the paths, one can notice that this is the result of a temporary occlusion around Frame 17, possibly caused by poor sensor pose alternatives presented to the system. However, this uncovers a potentially incorrect assumption in the methodology. The work assumed that as long as the target is positively tracked, it is within the workspace and vice versa – that is, if the system were to lose track of the target during surveillance, the system assumes that it has left the workspace. However, this is clearly not the case here.

Furthermore, the method assumed a relatively accurate *a priori* estimate of the subject's initial position, which in reality one may not have (it may be inaccurate, or even unavailable). As such, one can identify a need for two key changes: (1) the system must be able to initially search for a subject if no estimate is provided, and search to verify any initial estimates of pose given. (2) If a subject is lost during surveillance, provisions must be added to both detect this case and terminate surveillance, or to re-acquire the subject.

For this specific case, a weakness in the prediction agent implementation itself has also been identified, in that a highly erroneous observation for Frame 17 has affected the state of the predictor such that the subsequent estimates it produces are not reasonable. This feeds back through the system, as without reasonable predictions of future positions, the system chooses poses for sensors that may not contain the subject at all. In essence the control loop is broken, and the system is out of control. Detection (and, potentially, correction) of this state is critical.

Trial 4

For the final trial, the obstacles have been assigned dynamic paths identical to that of Trial 2. Now, however, prediction of the obstacle poses is not ideal, but instead is performed by the prediction agent. The path for this trial (and by extension, Trial 2) was chosen to highlight some of the issues identified in the previous sections. A plot of the estimated and predicted positions of the subject and both obstacles is shown in Fig. 11. In contrast to the previous trial, the prediction agent implementation has maintained a positive track of all objects over the duration of the experiment.

In addition, the average error between the estimated and predicted position is very low for all three objects. This is to be expected, as a constant velocity is easily tracked by the KF in this case (in fact, only a first-order state variable would really be necessary in this case).

From Fig. 11, one can also see that for roughly the first half of the frames, the obstacle paths have been designed to produce significant occlusions in Cameras 1 and 3. In previous trials, these frames were relatively un-occluded, exhibiting low error metrics and positive recognition matches. If the reconfiguration capabilities of the system were not beneficial (or were insufficient), then these frames would now experience significant error in the recovered form. For the second half of the trial, the obstacles have moved such that only Camera 2 experiences significant occlusion. This will examine the issue shown in Trial 3 by removing the single poor estimate that caused tracking to be lost in that case. The graph of the error metric is shown in Fig. 12.

From this figure, there is a very close correlation to Trial 2, where ideal prediction was used in the presence of dynamic obstacles. Thus, there are several important observations to make here.

First, there is, on the average, a slight increase in the error metric for the early frames, 1-8, which has been identified as expected due to the increased occlusion present for these frames. Most importantly, however, is that all frames in this region are still considered positively recognized, and there is not a significant increase in the overall error. This indicates that the reconfiguration of the system has effectively dealt with the occlusions presented by the mobile obstacles, indicating that performance has

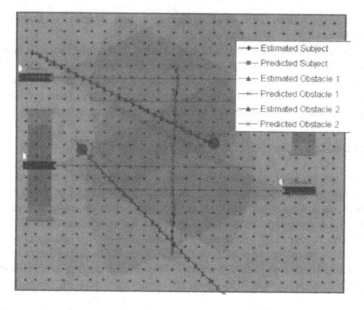

Fig. 11. Plot showing estimated (form prediction) and predicted (prediction agent) positions of the subject and both obstacles for Trial 4

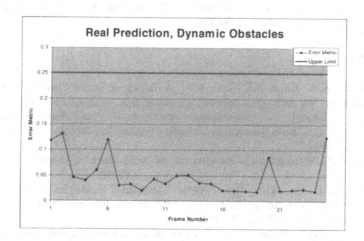

Fig. 12. Error metric plot for real prediction with dynamic obstacles

indeed been increased over the worst case scenario of 'no reconfiguration and dynamic obstacles.' Thus, it is valid (and useful) to apply reconfiguration here.

Secondly, the close correlation seen in the overall error metric graph to the previous trials indicates that the uncertainty introduced by the real-world prediction method (the Kalman filter) has not significantly influenced our algorithm. This uncertainty, is certainly present, however, as one can clearly see from Fig. 11 that neither the recovered (estimated) nor predicted positions of any object in the workspace exactly follow their ideal straight-line path. Indeed, all frames are still recognized, with a low error metric value.

Finally, the case where tracking was lost in Trial 3 around Frame 17 is no longer present in this trial. This shows that the tracking loss was the result of a singularity that introduced significant error into the predicted poses, and not a fundamental problem in the methodology. However, a method for detecting (and correcting) such tracking losses must still be addressed and included to guarantee reliability.

5 Conclusions

In this paper, sensing-system reconfiguration is proposed for the surveillance of time-varying geometry objects. Overall, a tangible improvement in form-recognition performance has been shown, through controlled simulation experiments, over the static case. A proportionate relationship between the reconfiguration ability of the system and the recognition performance is also shown. The addition of dynamic obstacles to the system was also addressed through careful simulated experimentation. The proposed methodology was shown to be capable of dealing with uncertainty in pose estimation and prediction in the presence of multiple, dynamic obstacles.

Acknowledgements

We acknowledge the financial support of the Natural Science and Engineering Research Council of Canada (NSERCC).

References

[1] Tarabanis, K.A., Allen, P.K., Tsai, R.Y.: A Survey of Sensor Planning in Computer Vision. IEEE Transactions on Robotics and Automation 11(1), 86–104 (1995)

[2] Miura, J., Ikeuchi, K.: Task-Oriented Generation of Visual Sensing Strategies in Assembly Tasks. IEEE Transactions on Pattern Analysis and Machine Intelligence 20(2), 126–138 (1998)

[3] Naish, M.D.: Sensing-System Planning for the Surveillance of Moving Objects. Ph.D. Thesis, University of Toronto, Toronto, ON., Canada (2004)

[4] Zhang, Y., Ji, Q.: Active and Dynamic Information Fusion for Facial Expression Understanding from Image Sequences. IEEE Transactions on Pattern Analysis and Machine Intelligence 27(5), 699–714 (2005)

[5] Derpanis, K.G.: A Review of Vision-Based Hand Gestures. Internal report, Centre for Vision Research, York University, Canada (2004)

[6] Sundaresan, A., Chellappa, R.: Multi-Camera Tracking of Articulated Human Motion Using Motion and Shape Cues. In: Narayanan, P.J., Nayar, S.K., Shum, H.-Y. (eds.) ACCV 2006. LNCS, vol. 3852, pp. 131–140. Springer, Heidelberg (2006)

[7] Stillman, S., Tanawongsuwan, R., Essa, I.: A System for Tracking and Recognizing Multiple People with Multiple Cameras. In: Audio and Video-Based Biometric Person Authentication, Washington, D.C, pp. 560–566 (1999)

[8] Yu, S., Tan, D., Tan, T.: A Framework for Evaluating the Effect of View Angle, Clothing, and Carrying Condition on Gait Recognition. In: Proc. of 18th Int. Conf. on Pattern Recognition (ICPR 2006), Hong Kong (2006)

 [9] Sakane, S., Sato, T., Kakikura, M.: Model-Based Planning of Visual Sensors Using a Hand-Eye Action Simulator: HEAVEN. In: Proc. of Conf. on Advanced Robotics, Versailles, France, pp. 163–174 (1987)

[10] Cowan, C.K., Kovesik, P.D.: Automated Sensor Placement for Vision Task Requirements. IEEE Transactions on Pattern Analysis and Machine Intelligence 10(3), 407–416 (1988)

[11] Anderson, D.P.: Efficient Algorithms for Automatic Viewer Orientation. Comp. & Graphics 9(4), 407–413 (1985)

[12] Reed, M.K., Allen, P.K.: Constraint-Based Sensor Planning for Scene Modeling. IEEE Transactions on Pattern Analysis and Machine Intelligence 22(12), 1460–1467 (2000)

[13] Hodge, L., Kamel, M.: An Agent-Based Approach to Multi-sensor Coordination. IEEE Transactions on Systems, Man, and Cybernetics – Part A: Systems and Humans 33(5), 648–662 (2003)

[14] Urano, T., Matsui, T., Nakata, T., Mizoguchi, H.: Human Pose Recognition by Memory-Based Hierarchical Feature Matching. In: Proc. of IEEE International Conference on Systems, Man, and Cybernetics, The Hague, Netherlands, pp. 6412–6416 (2004)

[15] Spletzer, J.R., Taylor, C.J.: Dynamic Sensor Planning and Control for Optimally Tracking Targets. Int. Journal of Robotic Research 22(1), 7–20 (2003)

[16] Kamel, M., Hodge, L.: A Coordination Mechanism for Model-Based Multi-Sensor Planning. In: Proc. of the IEEE International Symposium on Intelligent Control, Vancouver, pp. 709–714 (2002)

[17] Spletzer, J., Taylor, C.J.: Sensor Planning and Control in a Dynamic Environment. In: Proc. of IEEE Int. Conf. Robotics and Automation, Washington, D.C, pp. 676–681 (2002)

[18] Goodridge, S.G., Luo, R.C., Kay, M.G.: Multi-Layered Fuzzy Behavior Fusion for Real-Time Control of Systems with Many Sensors. IEEE Transactions on Industrial Electronics 43(3), 387–394 (1996)

[19] Goodridge, S.G., Kay, M.G.: Multimedia Sensor Fusion for Intelligent Camera Control. In: Proc of IEEE/SICE/RSJ Multi-sensor Fusion and integration for intelligent systems, Washington, D.C, pp. 655–662 (1996)

[20] Bakhtari, A.: Multi-Target Surveillance in Dynamic Environments: Sensing-System Reconfiguration. Ph.D. Thesis, University of Toronto, Canada (2006)

[21] Marchand, E., Chaumette, F.: Active Vision for Complete Scene Reconstruction and Exploration. IEEE Transactions on Pattern Analysis and Machine Intelligence 21(1), 65–72 (1999)

[22] Dimitrijevic, M., Lepetit, V., Fua, P.: Human Body Pose Recognition Using Spatio-Temporal Templates. In: ICCV workshop on Modeling People and Human Interaction, Beijing, China, pp. 127–139 (2005)

[23] Cunado, D., Nixon, M.S., Carter, J.: Automatic Extraction and Description of Human Gait Models for Recognition Purposes. Computer Vision and Image Understanding 90, 1–41 (2003)

[24] Veres, G.V., Gordon, L., Carter, J.N., Nixon, M.S.: What Image Information is Important in Silhouette-Based Gait Recognition? In: Proc. of IEEE Computer Society Conf. on Computer Vision and Pattern Recognition (CVPR 2004), Washington, D.C., pp. 776–782 (2004)

View-Invariant Human Action Detection
Using Component-Wise HMM of Body Parts

Bhaskar Chakraborty[1], Marco Pedersoli[1], and Jordi Gonzàlez[2]

[1] Computer Vision Center & Dept. de Ciències de la Computació, Edifici O, Campus UAB,
08193 Bellaterra, Spain
[2] Institut de Robòtica i Informàtica Industrial (UPC – CSIC), Llorens i Artigas 4-6, 08028,
Barcelona, Spain

Abstract. This paper presents a framework for view-invariant action recognition in image sequences. Feature-based human detection becomes extremely challenging when the agent is being observed from different viewpoints. Besides, similar actions, such as walking and jogging, are hardly distinguishable by considering the human body as a whole. In this work, we have developed a system which detects human body parts under different views and recognize similar actions by learning temporal changes of detected body part components. Firstly, human body part detection is achieved to find separately three components of the human body, namely the head, legs and arms. We incorporate a number of sub-classifiers, each for a specific range of view-point, to detect those body parts. Subsequently, we have extended this approach to distinguish and recognise actions like walking and jogging based on component-wise HMM learning.

1 Introduction

View-invariant action recognition is a constantly expanding research area due to number of applications for surveillance (behaviour analysis), security (pedestrian detection), control (human-computer interfaces), content-based video retrieval, etc. It is, however, a complex and difficult-to-resolve problem because of the enormous differences that exist between individuals, both in the way they move and their physical appearance, view-point and the environment where the action is carried out. Fig. 1 shows some images from the HumanEva database[1], demonstrating the variation of the human poses w.r.t. different camera views and for different actions.

Toward this end, several approaches can be found in the literature [5]. Some approaches are based on holistic body information where no attempt is made to identify individual body parts. However, there are actions which can be better recognized by only considering body parts, such as the dynamics of the legs for walking, running and jogging [2]. Consequently, action recognition can be based on a prior detection of the human body parts [7].

In this context, human body parts should be first detected in the image: authors like [4,8] describe human detection algorithms by probabilistic body part assembly. However, these approaches either use motion information, explicit models, a static camera,

---

[1] http://vision.cs.brown.edu/humaneva/

F.J. Perales and R.B. Fisher (Eds.): AMDO 2008, LNCS 5098, pp. 208–217, 2008.

Fig. 1. Images from the HumanEva database demonstrate some of the challenges involved with detecting people in still images where the positions of their body parts changes with great variety while performing some actions like walking, jogging and boxing etc

assume a single person in the image, or implement tracking rather than pure detection. Mohan et al. [6] used Haar-Like features and SVM for component-wise object detection. However, Haar-Like features cannot obtain certain special structural features that can be useful to design a view invariant human detection. Moreover, there is no method to select the best features for the SVM so that the performance can be improved by minimizing the feature vector size. Lastly, these works do not cope well for the detection of profile poses.

Due to these difficulties in the view-invariant detection of the human body parts , action recognition has been restricted by analysing the human body as a whole from multiple views. For example, Mendoza and Pérez de la Blanca [3] detect human actions using Hidden Markov Models (HMM) by using the contour-based histogram of the full body. Also, authors in [1] combine shape information and optical flow based on the silhouette to achieve this goal. Likewise, [11] uses the sum of silhouette pixels.

Our approach solves these issues by introducing a framework for view-invariant human detection and subsequently learning the stochastic changes of the body part components to recognize actions like walking and jogging. On the one hand, we use a hierarchy of multiple example-based classifiers for each of different body part-components and view-invariant human detection is achieved by combining the result of those detectors in a meaningful way. Since human action is viewed as a combination of the motion of different body parts, action detection can be analysed as a stochastic process by learning the changes of such components. A HMM based approach is used to learn those changes. In this way we can only consider features from those body part-components which actually taking part into the action e.g. the legs for walking and jogging. We observe that this component-wise stochastic behaviour is good enough to distinguish between similar displacement actions. Our result has been compared with [9]. Lastly, our method for action recognition is also able to detect the direction of motion from the likelihood map obtained from HMM.

This paper is organised as follows. In Section 2 we have presented view-invariant human detection method in detail. Section 3 describes the component wise HMM method towards the detection of human actions. Section 4 reports on the performance of our system. Finally conclusions are drawn in Section 5.

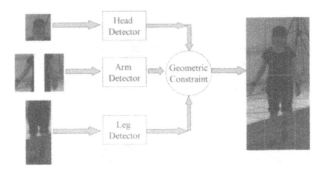

Fig. 2. The overall system architecture of view-invariant human detection. There are three component detectors head, arms and leg. These detectors are combined using geometric constraint for full human detection.

2   View-Invariant Human Detection

The overall structure of the present system is to detect the human action independent of view-point. To achieve this goal our system first detects human body part-components and then combining those body parts to detect the full human. The body parts are combined based on the proper geometric configuration. To ensure the view invariant human detection for each body part more than one detector has been designed and the knowledge of each of those body part detectors are combined finally to increase the robustness of the whole system see Fig. 2.

The component-based human detection has some inherent advantages over existing techniques. A full-body person detector relies solely on visual information and does not take full advantage of the known geometric properties of the human body. The other problem in full human detection is that the system fails to detect the human where body parts are partially occluded. This partial occlusion is accomplished by designing the system, using an appropriate geometric combination algorithm, so that it detects people even if all of their components are not detected.

2.1   Detection of Human Body Parts

The system starts detecting people in images by selecting a 72 x 48 pixels window from the top left corner of the image as an input for head, 184 x 108 pixels window for leg and 124 x 64 for arms. These inputs are then independently classified as either a respective body parts or a non-body part and finally those are combined into a proper geometrical configuration in a 264 x 124 pixels window as a person. All of these candidate regions are processed by the respective component detectors to find the strongest candidate components. Those component-wise window sizes and full human window size comes from HumanEva Database [10], since it is used for training sample creation.

The component detectors process the candidate regions by applying the modified Histogram of Oriented Gradient (HOG) features and then these features become resultant data vector for respective quadratic Support Vector Machine (SVM). Then a standard deviation based feature selection method is applied to take those features where the standard deviations of oriented gradients are less than one predefined threshold. This threshold has been computed after running the test several times. The strongest candidate component is the one that produces the highest positive raw output, as the component score, when classified by the component classifiers. If the highest component score for a particular component is negative, i.e. the component detector in question did not find a component in the geometrically permissible area, then it is discarded as false positive.

The raw output of an SVM is a rough measure of how well a classified data point fits in with its designated class. The each component where the component score is highest is taken to check whether they are in proper geometrical configuration with the 264 x 124 pixel window. The image itself is processed at several sizes. This allows the system to detect various sizes of people at any location in an image.

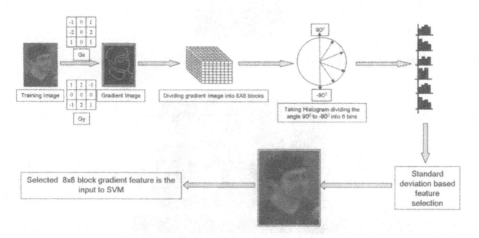

Fig. 3. Feature extraction and selection method from a training image. The training image is divided into several blocks and then HOG features are extracted. Finally standard deviation based feature selection method is applied to obtain feature vector for SVM.

2.2 Feature Extraction and Selection

In our approach for the body part detectors modified HOG feature is used. HOG features are extracted from a 8x8 pixel window from top left hand corner of the training image dividing gradients into 6 bins from $-90°$ to $+90°$. In this way that 8 x 8 pixels window slides over the total area reserved for head (72 x 48), leg (184 x 108) or arms (124 x 64). From each of this 8x8 pixel window 6 feature vectors has obtained.

Next step is to select the best 6 feature packs obtained from the method described above. This feature selection method is based on standard deviation (σ). For each position of that 8x8 pixel window the σ is calculated for each of the gradient of that 6 bin taking into account the total training image. Now the σ value has been sorted and those 6 feature packets are taken where the σ is less than a predefined threshold value. In this way the feature size is minimized and those features are fed into the corresponding detector. Fig. 3 shows the general scheme for feature extraction and selection.

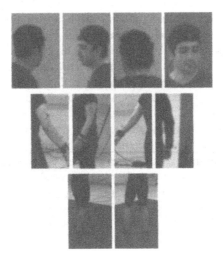

Fig. 4. Training samples for each body part detectors e.g. head, arm and leg

Fig. 5. Results of head, arm and leg detector as a validation process. Images with detection of heads with different views, detection of arms and legs are shown.

2.3   Training Body-Part Detectors

To identify human into one particular scale of image each of the individual body part detector has been applied simultaneously. In the present system there are four head detector one leg detector and four arm detector. The four head detectors are for the view angle 45° to 135°, 135° to 225°, 225° to 315° and 315° to 45°. For arm, there are four classifiers corresponding different position of arms. Detecting arms is a difficult task since arms have more degree of freedom than the other components. We have used major four poses of the arm with the pose symmetry the detection of other pose

Fig. 6. Validation process of full human detection. Detection of human with all the visible body parts and with profile pose are shown.

possibilities can be achieved. To detect the legs two sub-classifiers have been added to the leg detector, one for open legs and other for profile legs. In the training of component wise detectors 10,000 true positive and 20,000 false positive samples are used.

Fig. 4 shows few training samples of our body part component training database.

The results of those component detectors have combined based on geometrical configuration. Since the head is the most stable part of the body, the geometric combination has been done by first considering the head. Subsequently, the leg component is taken into account and, after that, both arms are combined. We include the Leg Bounding Box (LBB) (of size 184 x 108) after the Head Bounding Box (HBB) is computed (of size 72 x 48) from the head detector. This is done by checking that the x component of the center of the LBB must be within the width of HBB and the y component must be greater than the y component of the centre of the Full Human Bounding Box (FHBB) (of size 264 x 124). We then include arms in a similar way.

We have chosen the result from that sub classifiers which gives the best score result. When a person is moving in a circular path in some cases we can have best score for two sub classifier for arms and other cases provide us only one best score since the arms can be occluded behind the body. We have used some sequences of HumanEva Database [10] to train each body part component and after training we use those detector on the other sequences of such a Database. Fig. 5 shows the result of this validation process. Full detection has been in Fig.6.

3   View-Invariant Human Action Recognition

The aforementioned component wise view invariant human detection is next extended to human action recognition. Toward this end, we learn the stochastic changes of detected body parts using HMM to recognize human actions like walking and jogging. In our system we use HMM for each body part component which has major contribution on the action. From the HMM likely-hood we can recognise and distinguish very similar actions. From the HMM likelihood map we can detect the direction of motion by which we can infer the view point of the person with respect to camera.

3.1   HMM Learning

The feature set used to learn HMM is almost same as that used for SVM of each body part detector. Instead of selecting features here we take mean of each 6 bin angle

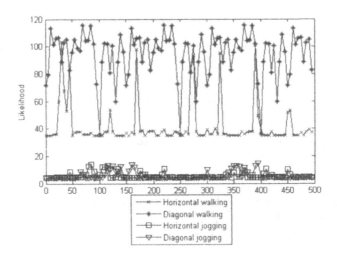

Fig. 7. Likelihood map of walking and jogging actions tested on a walking HMM

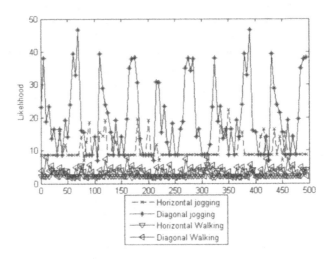

Fig. 8. Likeliihood map of jogging and walking actions tested on a jogging HMM

histogram vector. The significance of taking mean is to get general orientation of body parts which intern signify one pose or series of similar poses in a action e.g. walking. We fit Gaussian Mixture model in to those feature value to obtain different states and key pose of particular action, the pose alphabet of our HMM. To detect actions like walking and jogging we only use legs for HMM and we have found that this HMM is quite good enough to distinguish the similar action like walking and jogging.

Fig. 9. Frames corresponding to maximum likelihood values of walking

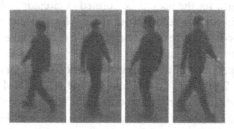

Fig. 10. Performance of full human detection in KTH's database

We have used same training set as of the body part detectors to train component wise HMM. We have chosen a sequence of frames to define one cycle for walking and jogging. After that we map those frame sequence into pose alphabet to obtain one state sequence for HMM learning. We use HumanEval Database as our validation database. This database contains several action sequences like walking, jogging and boxing which are performed by 4 different agents of both sex. We have trained our component HMM using some sequence of that database and tested the same with other similar sequences to validate the HMM learning.

The likelihood map has been computed using the probability values obtained from the HMM for each frame of the test sequence. The maximum values of likelihood map actually describe the end of each walking cycle. We here use two steps starting with right leg as one walking and jogging action cycle. Fig. 9 demonstrates frames corresponding to first 6 maximum likelihood values which clearly shows the end of each walking cycle and also detects the direction of motion.

4   Experimental Results

We have used KTH's [9] Database[2] to test the performance of our system architecture. In that database we have found different types of actions: walking to the right, walking to the left, jogging to the right, jogging to the left etc. These actions were performed outdoors by 25 different people of both sexes with different lighting conditions and shadows. Fig. 10 shows some examples of the performance of our component wise

---

[2] http://www.nada.kth.se/cvap/actions/

Table 1. Comparison of detection action detection with other two approaches. Column (a) is Local feature and SVM based detection [9], and (b) is our approach.

	Approach (a)	Approach (b)
Walking	83.8	**100.0**
Jogging	60.4	**60.0**

human detection. In this figure we have shown one example of profile pose detection and one example of frontal pose detection. We have tested our component HMMs, which have been learned for the actions performed in circular path, on KTH's database where agents are not in circular path and our approach can detect those actions robustly which justify the view-invariance action detection. We have taken all sequences of the walking and jogging for testing of HMM.

Fig. 7 shows the likelihood of the walking sequence and jogging sequence when applied to walking HMM. Fig. 8 is just the same but for jogging HMM. In both the figures we can observe that a difference in likelihood values. When the walking action sequence is tested in the walking HMM we have found the higher likelihood values and when jogging action sequence is tested on the same the likelihood value decreases and this is same for jogging HMM. The two actions presented in the figure are horizontal and diagonal walking and jogging for two different agents. Table 1 shows detection rates of action recognition using local feature and SVM from [9] and using our approach. We have achieved higher detection rate in walking and similar result in jogging. Since our method considers the stochastic change of body parts having major contribution in action so if there is some similarity in movement of those components then recognition using HMM becomes difficult. We have found some of jogging sequences are misclassified as walking.

5   Conclusions

This paper presents one approach to detect view point invariant human action detection. Human detection in a view-invariant framework is achieved by example-based classifiers for each body part components. Our work performs really well in profile poses. The performance can be improved by adding more training samples and introducing more angular views. One difficultly is that there is not good database for different body part components so building component database is an important task.

In the action detection phase focus is given to distinguish similar actions by considering only the major contributing body parts. This approach is computationally efficient since we have used the same kind of features for the body part detectors and results show that it is enough to consider leg to distinguish those similar actions. We can use this approach to learn HMM for hands and to apply that to detect and distinguish actions like boxing, different gestures e.g. waving.

Acknowledgements

This work is supported by EC grants IST-027110 for the HERMES project and IST-045547 for the VIDI-video project, and by the Spanish MEC under projects TIN2006-14606 and CONSOLIDER-INGENIO 2010 MIPRCV CSD2007-00018. Jordi Gonzàlez also acknowledges the support of a Juan de la Cierva Postdoctoral fellowship from the Spanish MEC.

References

1. Ahmad, M., Lee, S.: Human action recognition using multi-view image sequence features. In: FGR, pp. 10–12 (2006)
2. Davis, J., Taylor, S.: Analysis and recognition of walking movements. In: Analysis and recognition of walking movements, Quebec, Canada, pp. 11–15 (2002)
3. Mendoza, M., Pérez de la Blanca, N.: Hmm-based action recognition using contour histograms. In: Martí, J., Benedí, J.M., Mendonça, A.M., Serrat, J. (eds.) IbPRIA 2007. LNCS, vol. 4477, pp. 394–401. Springer, Heidelberg (2007)
4. Micilotta, A., Ong, E., Bowden, R.: Detection and tracking of humans by probabilistic body part assembly. In: British Machine Vision Conference, pp. 429–438 (2005)
5. Moeslund, T., Hilton, A., Krüger, V.: A survey of advances in vision-based human motion capture and analysis. In: CVIU 104, pp. 90–126 (2006)
6. Mohan, A., Papageorgiou, C., Poggio, T.: Example-based object detection in images by components. IEEE Transaction on Pattern Analysis and Machine Intelligence 23(4), 349–361 (2001)
7. Park, S., Aggarwal, J.: Semantic-level understanding of human actions and interactions using event hierarchy, 2004. In: CVPR Workshop on Articulated and Non-Rigid Motion, Washington DC, USA (2004)
8. Ramanan, D., Forsyth, D., Zisserman, A.: Tracking people by learning their appearance. IEEE Transaction on PAMI 29(1), 65–81 (2007)
9. Schuldt, C., Laptev, I., Caputo, B.: Recognizing human actions: a local svm approach. In: ICPR III, pp. 32–36 (2004)
10. Sigal, L., Black, M.: Humaneva: Synchronized video and motion capture dataset for evaluation of articulated human motion. Technical Report CS-06-08, Brown University (2006)
11. Sundaresan, A., RoyChowdhury, A., Chellappa, R.: A hidden markov model based framework for recognition of humans from gait sequences. In: ICIP, pp. 93–96 (2003)

A Generative Model for Motion Synthesis and Blending Using Probability Density Estimation

Dumebi Okwechime and Richard Bowden

University of Surrey, Guildford, Surrey, GU2 7XH, UK
{d.okwechime,r.bowden}@Surrey.ac.uk

Abstract. The main focus of this paper is to present a method of reusing motion captured data by learning a generative model of motion. The model allows synthesis and blending of cyclic motion, whilst providing it with the style and realism present in the original data. This is achieved by projecting the data into a lower dimensional space and learning a multivariate probability distribution of the motion sequences. Functioning as a generative model, the probability density estimation is used to produce novel motions from the model and gradient based optimisation used to generate the final animation. Results show plausible motion generation and lifelike blends between different actions.

Keywords: Animation, Motion capture, Probability Distribution Function, Principal Component Analysis, Least Square Curve Fitting, Linear Interpolation.

1   Introduction

The purpose of this work is to develop a generative model of motion that allows motion synthesis and blending of different cyclic movements such as walking or running. The model is capable of generating novel motion whilst preserving the same style and realism of the original motion capture data. This allows animators to edit, extend and blend between different cyclic movements providing the ability to reuse motion captured data. This paper builds upon previous work into synthesising motion using probability density estimation and proposes a multivariate probability distribution for use in synthesis and blending.

The human visual system has the ability to efficiently and easily recognise characteristic human movement. As a consequence, in order to generate character animations that look realistic, it is necessary to develop methods to capture, maintain and synthesis intrinsic style to give authentic realism to animated characters. The aim of this work is to provide the general framework that addresses this issue. The framework is based on transforming biological motion into a representation that allows analysis using statistical techniques. Additionally, this model will also be used to synthesise and blend realistic motion patterns.

In this paper, we present two approaches to motion synthesis and blending. One approach uses a sine function to model a cyclic motion sequence and utilises linear interpolation to blend between different motions. The second, more flexible

F.J. Perales and R.B. Fisher (Eds.): AMDO 2008, LNCS 5098, pp. 218–227, 2008.

approach, models motion as a probability density function (PDF). This model can synthesise novel motion whilst retaining the natural variances inherent in the original data. Blending is a result of linearly interpolating between different PDF's.

This paper is divided into the following sections. Section 2, briefly details current techniques of modelling and editing motion capture data. Section 3 and Section 4 present the techniques used for learning models that capture the statistics and dynamics of a set of motion capture sequences. The remainder of the paper describes the results and ends with a brief conclusion.

2   Related Work

Character animation using interpolation was one of the earliest techniques used in computer animation and is still used by many animators today [1]. The traditional technique uses interpolation to generate intermediate frames from manually defined key-frames [2]. This method offers high controllability to the animator, but it is very time consuming and requires a highly skilled animator to produce the animation.

Motion capture provides a cost effective solution to realism as life-like motion is easily acquired and large libraries of motion are available for use. However, to provide realistic results, multiple sequences need to be blended together resulting in a seamless and life-like animation. Furthermore, recorded animation lacks the variability of natural motion and repeating a motion can look false due to its lack of natural variance.

One solution is to develop a generative model of motion using motion capture data. With the ability to blend between motions, one can create a sequence of realistic actions which would otherwise be difficult to achieve using keyframing. This approach is made possible by fitting a parametric function to the joint coordinates of the character and interpolating between discrete points in this parametric space. An early approach was presented by Rose et al. [3]. They defined each degree of freedom of a character as a uniform cubic B-spline curve in time. With this representation, they use radial basis functions (RBF) to interpolate between sample motions in this space. Kovar et al. [4] improved on this approach by introducing motion graphs which automatically construct novel motion from a mass of motion capture data. By representing frames in terms of point clouds, they calculate the weighted sum of squared distance between corresponding points in the clouds. If the distance is below a user-specified threshold, the relative motions are considered similar. Similar motions can then be blended by linearly interpolating the corresponding root positions and spherically linearly interpolating their corresponding joint rotations.

Carvalho et al. [5] follows a simlar approach to this paper using Principal Component Analysis (PCA) to learn motion models from motion captured data. However, they use a Prioritised Inverse Kinematics strategy to apply constraints with different levels of importance to synthesis the motion. As opposed to using PCA, Grochow et al. [6] learns a PDF over character poses represented by a

Scaled Gaussian Process Latent Variable Model. This model represents the data in a low-dimensional latent space, and motion synthesis occurs by optimising the likelihood of new poses given the original poses.

Unuma et al. [7] create a functional model of motion using Fourier series expansion. The model is used to make variations of human behaviour via the interpolation and extrapolation of their Fourier coefficients. In related work, Troje [8] uses sine functions instead of Fourier expansion to model walks. Using PCA, they extract relevant information from the data, representing them as discrete components. The temporal behaviour of these components is modelled using a sine function, and sinusoidal curve fitting is used to parameterise them based on their respective frequency, amplitude and phase. A limitation to this approach is that it produces identical motion cycles which are not natural, and the sine assumption limits the type of motion that can be modelled.

Pullen and Bregler [9] introduce the idea of synthesising motion by extracting the 'motion texture' i.e. the personality and realism, from the motion and using it to drive hard constraints such as foot positions on the floor. They comprise their motion of three important features, frequency band, phase, and correlation. These features are represented with a kernel-based probability distribution. This distribution is used to synthesis the walk and a gradient based method used to optimise the data. Part of this approach is adopted in the paper whereby we use a multivariate probability distribution to model the data and synthesis a walk, however, we are also able to blend between different distributions to create novel motion.

3   Methods

3.1   Walking Data

The motion captured data used in this work are in a format which details the 3D Cartesian coordinates (x,y,z)[10] for all the markers corresponding to the frames for the full body motion capture data, although similar approaches can be applied in polar spaces. Given a motion sequence $\mathbf{X}$, each frame is formally represented as a vector $\mathbf{x}_i$ where $\mathbf{X} = [\mathbf{x}_1, ..., \mathbf{x}_F]$ and F is the number of frames containing R markers. Each frame/posture is represented as a high dimensional vector $\mathbf{x}_i = [x_{i1}, y_{i1}, z_{i1}, ..., x_{iR}, y_{iR}, z_{iR}] \in \Re^{D=3R}$.

3.2   Dimensional Reduction and Statistical Modelling

Working with full-body, motion capture data produces a high dimensional dataset. However, the dimensionality of the resulting space does not necessarily reflect the true dimensionality of the subspace that the data occupies. Principal Component Analysis (PCA) [11] is therefore used to perform dimensional reduction.

For a given D-dimensional data set $\mathbf{X}$ as defined in Section 3.1, the D principal axes $\mathbf{T}_1, \mathbf{T}_2, ..., \mathbf{T}_D$ can be given by the D leading eigenvectors of the sample covariance matrix:

$$S = \frac{1}{N} \sum_{i=1}^{F} (x_i - \mu)(x_i - \mu)^T \qquad (1)$$

where μ is the sample mean $\mu = \frac{1}{F}\sum_{i=1}^{F} x_i$. An eigen decomposition gives $S = \sum \lambda_i T_i$, $i \in \{1, ..., D\}$, where λ_i is the ith largest eigenvalue of S.

The dimension of the data can be reduced by projecting into the eigenspace

$$y_i = V^T(x_i - \mu) \qquad (2)$$

where V are the feature vectors $V = [T_1, ..., T_d]$ and d is the chosen lower dimension $d \leq D$. This results in a d-dimensional representation of each motion sequence in eigenspace. We will refer to each dimension as modes of variation within the data. d is chosen such that $\sum_{i=1}^{d} \frac{\lambda_i}{\sum \forall \lambda} \geq .95$ or 95% of the energy is retained.

Figure 1 shows a plot of the first mode against the second mode for a male and female walk sequence. It produces a geometric shape characteristic of a cyclic motion, showing that the projection retains the non-linearity of cyclic movement.

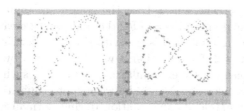

Fig. 1. Plot of PCA projection of the first mode against the second mode

3.3   Time Alignment

Using the PCA space data representation detailed in Section 3.2, the first mode of each motion sequence can be represented as discrete sine waves, a technique developed by Troje [8]. This is possible since walks are cyclic movements that repeat sinusoidally. Using least square curve fitting, the first mode of each motion sequence is parameterised as:

$$\sin(\omega t + \varphi) \qquad (3)$$

where ω is the fundamental frequency and φ is the phase.

It can be seen in Figure 2 that the first mode is almost a perfect sine wave and is closely approximated by the sine function, the parameters of which can be used to normalise the data.

$$t' = ((t * \omega) + \varphi) \qquad (4)$$

where t' is the new time.

Since the first mode contains most of the motion's variance, it is not necessary to fit a sine function to the subsequent modes. The first mode is sufficient to normalised the time domain of the sequence.

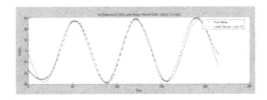

Fig. 2. Least square curve fitting of first mode wave representation for a male walker

Blending using Time Aligned Sine Waves. With two or more walking sequences time aligned as above, it is possible to blend between them using linear interpolation. For two sequences, male walk (mw) and female walk (fw), blending can be achieved using linear interpolation, where a weight w indicates the contribution of each sequence to the resulting motion.

$$\mathbf{y}'(t) = \frac{\mathbf{y}_{mw}(t) + \mathbf{y}_{fw}(t)}{2} + w\frac{\mathbf{y}_{mw}(t) - \mathbf{y}_{fw}(t)}{2} \tag{5}$$

where $\mathbf{y}$ is the respective posture at a given time t, and w is the weighting variable $(1 < w < -1)$ where $w = 1$ for the male walk animation, $w = -1$ for the female walk animation and $w = 0$ for the mid-point between them.

However, there are a number of issues with this approach. Firstly, time alignment will only work well if the motion is well represented by a sine wave. Secondly, it can only blend between similar cyclic motions such as walks or runs and cannot provide successful blends between more sophisticated motions. It also destroys the time/velocity information during normalisation. Finally, the synthesised motions have no variability, unless the original data is retained and resampled. In the next section we overcome these problems by representing the original data as a PDF in the eigenspace.

4 Generative Model of Motion Using a Probability Distribution Function

A statistical model of the constraints and dynamics present within the data can be created using a probability distribution. This model is created using kernel estimation. Each kernel $p(\mathbf{y}_i)$ is effectively a Gaussian centred on a data example. Since we want our probability distribution to represent the dimensionally reduced data set Y of d dimensions, where $Y = \{y_i\}_{i=1}^{F}$ as noted in Section 3.2, the likelihood of a pose in eigenspace is modelled as a mixture of Gaussians using multivariate normal distributions.

$$P(\mathbf{y}) = \frac{1}{F}\sum_{i=1}^{F} p(\mathbf{y}_i) \tag{6}$$

Figure 3 shows a plot of such a distribution for the case of a male and female walker with the first mode plotted against the second mode. The width of the Gaussian in the ith dimension is set to $\alpha\sqrt{\lambda_i}$. For these experiments $\alpha = 0.25$.

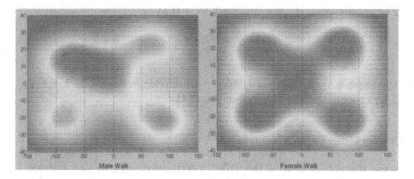

Fig. 3. PDF of a male walk sequence vs female walk sequence

4.1 Motion Synthesis

To generate novel motion the procedure is:

(1) $P(\mathbf{y})$ is constructed as PDF in the pose space that gives the likelihood of any particular pose configuration.

(2) As we are particularly interested in motion, a second PDF is constructed that encodes the likelihood of motion in the pose space for a given configuration $P(\mathbf{y}, \frac{d\mathbf{y}}{dt})$ where

$$\frac{d\mathbf{y}_i}{dt} = \mathbf{y}_{i+1} - \mathbf{y}_i \tag{7}$$

assuming regular sampling over the motion capture data. $P(\mathbf{y}, \frac{d\mathbf{y}}{dt})$ is constructed similarly to Equation 6 using F Gaussian kernels in $\Re^{2d}$. Similarly to Equation 6, the covariance is set to

$$\alpha \begin{pmatrix} \sqrt{\lambda_1} \cdots & \cdots & \cdots & \cdots & \cdots & 0 \\ \vdots & \ddots & \cdots & \cdots & \cdots & \vdots \\ \vdots & \cdots & \sqrt{\lambda_d} \cdots & \cdots & \cdots & \vdots \\ \vdots & \cdots & \cdots & \sigma_1 \cdots & \cdots & \vdots \\ \vdots & \cdots & \cdots & \cdots & \ddots & \vdots \\ 0 & \cdots & \cdots & \cdots & \cdots & \sigma_d \end{pmatrix} \tag{8}$$

where σ_i is the standard deviation of the derivatives.

(3) To locate a suitable starting configuration, the kernel that generates the highest likelihood is found.

$$max = \underset{i=1}{\overset{F}{\arg\max}}(P(\mathbf{y}_i)) \tag{9}$$

(4) From this configuration $\mathbf{y}_t = \mathbf{y}_{max}$ the highest likelihood movement is selected

$$max\Delta = \underset{\forall \frac{d\mathbf{y}}{dt}}{\arg\max}(P(\mathbf{y}_t, \frac{d\mathbf{y}}{dt})) \tag{10}$$

(5) The model pose is then updated such that

$$\mathbf{y}_{t+1} = \mathbf{y}_t + \frac{d\mathbf{y}_{max\Delta}}{dt} \qquad (11)$$

and the pose is then reconstructed for rendering as $\mathbf{x}_{t+1} = \mu + \mathbf{V}\mathbf{y}_{t+1}$
(6) The process then repeats from step (4).

4.2   Correction Term Constraint

To increase the robustness of the PDF distribution and to account for the increasing probability estimation error, a correction term is added to the optimisation process. The correction term constrains the estimated posture to remain within the PDF. This is brought about by adding a weighting to all estimated postures. Each estimation is multiplied by the likelihood of that posture being a valid posture, discouraging movement outside the pose PDF. Step (4) therefore becomes

$$max\Delta = \underset{\forall \frac{d\mathbf{y}}{dt}}{\arg\max}(P(\mathbf{y}_t, \frac{d\mathbf{y}}{dt})P(\mathbf{y}_t + \frac{d\mathbf{y}}{dt})) \qquad (12)$$

This improves the optimisation in step (4), reducing drift, resulting in plausible poses.

4.3   Gradient Based Optimisation

Gradient based optimisation works well with the assumption that the optimisation in stage (4) finds a good global maximum. Since the surface is smooth (due to the use of Gaussian kernels) and the space contiguous (in that the positions of two adjacent frames are spatially close in the eigenspace), a simple gradient ascent method can be used. A Mean Shift approach works well since it is only necessary to asses the likelihood at the corners of the search region (again assuming the surface is smooth). However, such a search is $O(D^2k)$where k is the number of iterations to convergence and D, the dimensionality of the space. It is worth noting that in the case of $P(\mathbf{y}, \frac{d\mathbf{y}}{dt})$ this dimensionality is twice the number of eigenvectors retained in the projection. Line optimisation methods such as Powells Method work well as the surface is smooth and the search become linear in the number of dimensions $O(Dk)$. Newton type methods requiring Jacobian and Hessians are more problematic due to the large number of kernels in the PDF. We therefore optimise along the direction of each eigenvector in turn, using the previous location as the starting point of the search.

4.4   Blending Using a PDF

Blending between different sequences using the PDF follows a very similar procedure to motion synthesis. The different walk sequences are firstly projected

Fig. 4. Plot of four synthesised cyclic motion sequences superimposed over their respective distributions

into the same eigenspace by performing PCA on their combined data (as explained in Section 3.2). After projection down into the combined eigenspace, separate PDF's are constructed for each of the sequences. The PDF used in synthesis is the weighted average of all distributions. By changing the weighting, the influence of each sequence on the final animation can be changed and transitions between the sequences made. If $P(\mathbf{y}_a) = \frac{1}{F_a}\sum_{i=1}^{F_a} P(\mathbf{y}_i^a)$ for walk a and $P(\mathbf{y}_b) = \frac{1}{F_b}\sum_{i=1}^{F_b} P(\mathbf{y}_i^b)$ for walk b, then step (3) is replaced with:

$$max = \arg\max_{i=1}^{F}(\frac{1}{2}(P_a(\mathbf{y}_t) + P_b(\mathbf{y}_t)) + w\frac{1}{2}(P_a(\mathbf{y}_t) - P_b(\mathbf{y}_t))) \tag{13}$$

and similarly, step (4) is replaced with:

$$max\Delta = \arg\max_{\forall \frac{d\mathbf{y}}{dt}}(\frac{1}{2}(P_a(\mathbf{y}_t, \frac{d\mathbf{y}}{dt}) + P_b(\mathbf{y}_t, \frac{d\mathbf{y}}{dt})) + w\frac{1}{2}(P_a(\mathbf{y}_t, \frac{d\mathbf{y}}{dt}) - P_b(\mathbf{y}_t, \frac{d\mathbf{y}}{dt})))$$
$$\tag{14}$$

However, with slight rearranging, these equations can be re-written to reduce the number of access to the kernel functions.

5   Results

To illustrate the approach, 4 motion capture sequences were projected down into their combined eigenspace and 4 models constructed each consisting of two PDF's, one for pose and one for motion. The datasets were 'male walk', 'female walk', 'female running', and 'female skipping'. Figure 4 shows a visualisation of the PDFs of 4 sequences projected onto the two primary eigenvectors. It can be seen that these distributions vary considerably but occupy the same space. Using the outlined procedure, a maximum likelihood path was generated from each of the PDF's. The result of which are superimposed on top of their respective distributions. As can be seen, the data points, corresponding to a sequence of postures, remain within the distributions and follow the characteristic shapes of their original data. Also note that small errors in the optimisation procedure produce natural variation in the trajectory. An additional noise term could be added to the estimation procedure, however, in practice these inherent errors are sufficient to produce natural variation 'novelty'.

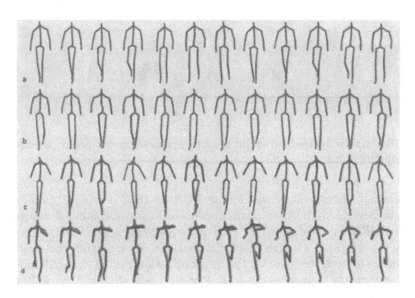

Fig. 5. Image showing animations of synthesised walks using PDF. (a) Male walk, (b) Female walk, (c) Female skipping, (d) Female running.

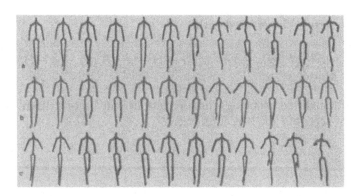

Fig. 6. Image showing animations of blended walks using PDF. (a) Blend from a female walk to a female run, (b) Blend from a male walk to female skipping, (c) Blend from a female skipping to female run.

When animated (as shown in Figure 5), they resemble their original data and produce plausible animations.

Figure 6 shows the effect of blending between motions by changing the weighting attributed to the contribution of any one PDF to the overall density estimate. Again it can be seen that smooth and natural transition are achieved, even when moving between less usual motions such as 'male walk' to 'female skip'.

6 Conclusion

It has been shown that a generative model of motion can be used to synthesis and blend novel motion, whilst retaining the important characteristic motion features from the original data. As the results show, it is possible to learn from motion captured data and provide unlimited novel animation that blends between motions automatically. Style is chosen by selecting the relative contribution of different styles and motions using simple weights. In addition, as no time alignment is required for the process, the temporal information in the animation is preserved. This approach can be extended to blend between different types of non-cyclic movement. The success of this is dependent upon the quantity of motion sequences used, since a larger more disparate eigenspace would require more samples to provide sufficient connectivity between the distributions. Further work will investigate this possibility.

References

1. Tanco, L.M.: Human Motion Synthesis from Captured Data. PhD in Computer vision, University of Surrey, University of Surrey, Guildford, Surrey, GU2 7XH, UK (2002)
2. Ahmed, A.: Parametric Synthesis of Human Motion. PhD in Computer vision, University of Surrey, University of Surrey, Guildford, Surrey, GU2 7XH, UK (2003)
3. Rose, C., Cohen, M., Bodenheimer, B.: Verbs and adverbs: Multidimensional motion interpolation. In: IEEE Computer Graphics and Applications, September/October, pp. 32–40. IEEE Computer Society Press, Los Alamitos (1998)
4. Kovar, L., Gleicher, M., Pighin, F.: Motion graphs. In: Proceedings of ACM SIGGRAPH, July, vol. 21(3), pp. 473–482 (2002)
5. Carvalho, S.R., Boulic, R., Thalmann, D.: Interactive low-dimensional human motion synthesis by combining motion models and pik. Computer Animation and Virtual Worlds (in press, 2007)
6. Grochow, K., Martin, S.L., Hertzmann, A., Popovic, Z.: Style-based inverse kinematics. In: Proceedings of the 2004 SIGGRAPH Conference, pp. 522–531 (2004)
7. Unuma, M., Anjyo, K., Takeuchi, R.: Fourier principles for emotion-based human figure animation. In: Proceedings of the 22nd annual ACM conference on Computer graphics, Los Angeles, California, August 06-11, pp. 91–96. Addison Wesley, Reading (1995)
8. Troje, N.F.: Decomposing biological motion: A framework for analysis and synthesis of human gait patterns. J. Vis. 2(5), 371–387 (2002)
9. Pullen, K., Bregler, C.: Synthesis of cyclic motions with texture (2002)
10. Chung, H.S., Lee, Y.: Mcml: motion capture markup language for integration of heterogeneous motion capture data. Computer Standards and Interfaces 26, 113–130 (2004)
11. Alexa, M., Muller, W.: Representing animations by principal components. Computer Graphics Forum. 19(3), 411–418 (2000)

Gestural Interaction Using Feature Classification

Cornelius Malerczyk

ZGDV Computer Graphics Center
Rundeturmstrasse 10
64283, Darmstadt, Germany
cmalerc@zgdv.de

Abstract. This paper describes our ongoing research work on deviceless interaction using hand gesture recognition with a calibrated stereo system. Video-based interaction is one of the most intuitive kinds of Human-Computer-Interaction with Virtual-Reality applications due to the fact that users are not wired to a computer. If interaction with three-dimensional environments is considered, pointing, grabbing and releasing are the most intuitive gestures used by humans. This paper describes our video-based gesture recognition system that observes the user in front of a large displaying screen, identifying three different hand gestures in real time using 2D feature classification and determines 3D information like the 3D position of the user's hand or the pointing direction if performed. Different scenario applications like a virtual chess game against the computer or an industrial scenario have been developed and tested. To estimate the possible count of distinguishable gestures a sign language recognition application has been developed and tested using a single uncalibrated camera only.

1 Introduction

Hand gesture recognition in computer vision is an extensive area of research that encompasses anything from static pose estimation of the human hand to dynamic movements such as the recognition of sign languages. This paper describes our ongoing research work on deviceless interaction using hand gesture recognition with a calibrated stereo system. Video-based interaction is one of the most intuitive kinds of Human-Computer-Interaction with Virtual-Reality applications due to the fact that users are not wired to a computer. People frequently use gestures to communicate. Gestures are used for everything from pointing at an object or at a person to get their attention or to conveying information about space and temporal characteristics. Gesture recognition used for human computer interaction (HCI) comprehends both advantages and disadvantages depending on the technical constraints of the recognition system. One of the most important advantages is that no menu structure for an application is needed. Gesture recognition systems can be very powerful, for example in combination with speech recognition and speech synthesis systems. This multi-modal type of interaction with a computer is one of the most intuitive way for a human to communicate with a technical system. But there are also disadvantages using gesture recognition systems: Calibration inaccuracies of data gloves for example can destroy the performance of a system, this is often caused by a hand size problem. Further on, the user often needs to learn gestures,

F.J. Perales and R.B. Fisher (Eds.): AMDO 2008, LNCS 5098, pp. 228–237, 2008.

Fig. 1. Three different gestures seen by one of the cameras of the stereo system: Pointing (top), grab/closed hand (middle) and release/opened hand (bottom)

while there is no self-explanatory interaction. Users are easily cognitively overloaded. Last but not least device driven recognition systems need a direct cable connection to the computer, which decreases the freedom of action of the user and leads to an uncomfortable feeling of the user. Therefore, we propose an easy and as far as possible self explanatory interaction with virtual environments using the three different static gestures: pointing, grabbing (closed hand) and releasing (opened hand) that are intuitive enough to be used by all kinds of different and even technically unversed users (see figure 1). The demands on the gesture recognition and tracking system proposed in this paper arise from the scenarios of interacting with virtual 3D environments itself. It is necessary to have a tracking system at hand that is able to handle the interaction of different users, no matter if they are left- or right-handed, if they use just the index finger for pointing or even the opened hand. In order to avoid new users are loosing patience, the training phase that has to be performed before the application starts has to be as simple and short as possible.

2   Related Work

Hand gesture recognition in computer vision is an extensive area of research that encompasses anything from static pose estimation of the human hand to dynamic movements such as the recognition of sign languages. A primary goal of gesture recognition research for Human-Computer-Interaction is to create a system, which can identify specific human hand gestures and use them to convey information or for device control. Therefore, hand gesture recognition systems can be divided into different tasks: Hand tracking, dynamic gesture recognition, static gesture recognition, sign language recognition and pointing. Elaborate reviews on vision-based hand pose estimation can be found in [Ero07] and [Coh07]. Due to the high amount of different approaches and methods for hand pose estimation, we only consider approaches, that are capable of tracking the human hand in real-time and differentiating static hand postures. Exemplarily, [Sch07] presented an approach for tracking the position and the orientation of four different postures of two hands in real-time by calculating the visual hulls of the hands on the GPU directly. Therefore, the results necessarily depend on the correct reconstruction of the 3D pose of the hand using at least three cameras. [Oha00] uses a calibrated stereo system with two colour cameras to estimate the position and orientation of different hand postures in 3D. The approach is based on 2D feature extraction using various techniques based on geometric properties and template matching. Therefore, it is necessary to identify corresponding feature in image pairs and to derive 3D features that are afterwards fitted to an underlying 3D hand model to classify different gestures. Due to the fact that no orientation of the hand is determined in our approach, we are able to reduce the classification problem to pure 2D feature extraction and to calculate the 3D position of the hand for interaction purposes using the center of gravity of the segmented hand only.

3   System Calibration

The equipment for the gesture recognition system consists of one single standard PC, which is used for both rendering of the scenario applications and gesture recognition and tracking. A standard video beamer or a large plasma display is connected to the PC, displaying the application scenario in front of the interacting user. Two Firewire (IEEE1394) cameras are connected to the computer feeding the system with grey-scaled images of the interaction volume in real time. Lenses with additional infrared light diodes (without infrared light filters) are used to ensure a bright reflection of the human skin (see figure 2), which is necessary for the segmentation task described in section 4.

The purpose of the tracking system is to recognize and to track three different static gestures of the user (pointing, opened hand and closed hand) to enable intuitive interaction with the scenario applications. The approach is based on the recognition of the position of the human hand in 3D space within a self-calibrated stereo system [Aza95]. Therefore, position and orientation of the cameras are determined with respect to each other by swaying a small torch light for a few seconds in the designated interaction volume [SM02]. Afterwards only the world coordinate system has to be defined by marking the origin and the end of two axes of the world coordinate system. Within this coordinate system the corners of the displaying screen have to be declared to ensure a correct interpretation of especially the pointing gesture and its pointing direction. This calibration procedure has to be performed only once after setting up the cameras. During runtime of the system, difference images are used to detect moving objects, which then are analyzed and the 2D probabilities of a posture and its relevant parameters in 3D space is calculated. Smoothing of the tracking results like e.g. the 3D position of the hand using smoothing splines is used to reduce jittering effects [SE00], which leads to an immersing experience during the interaction without the need of any technical device.

4   Gesture Extraction

The segmentation of the user's hand is performed on 2D image basis. At the startup of the tracking system reference images of the empty interaction volume are taken from both cameras, smoothed using a 3*3 Gaussian filter mask and afterwards edge images are calculated using a standard 3*3 Sobel kernel. During runtime of the tracking system images captured by the stereo system are again smoothed and edge images are calculated. These edge images are then compared with the edge reference images by calculating difference images. The resulting pair of images is afterwards segmented at a predefined threshold. Due to the camera setup at the left and right hand side of the user and due to the fact that the user is always interacting with a screen in front of him/her, it can be easily assumed that the lowest extracted segment larger then an adequate segment size can be chosen as the user's hand. Nevertheless, often not only the user's hand but also his/her forearm is extracted into one segment. Therefore, an approximately square rectangle at the bottom of the segment is chosen containing the final hand segment (see figure 2). This segment is used afterwards for feature extraction. For example the centers of gravity in both images are projected into 3D space to define the position of the user's hand in the world coordinate system. Accordingly, the lowest points of the segments are identified to be the finger tip if a pointing gesture is recognized.

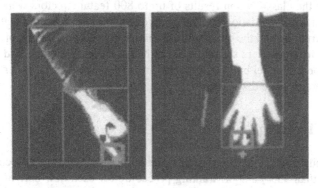

Fig. 2. Segmentation: Moving arm, hand extraction and index finger (left) and open hand (right) indicated by superimposed boxes

5   Gesture Classification

For each frame pair of the stereo camera system several two-dimensional features of the segmented human hand (as described in the previous section) are extracted using standard image processing methods. Important examples of these parameters are:

- Boundary length of the segmented hand
- Ratio between boundary length and area of the segment
- Eccentricity of the segment
- Elongatedness of the segment
- Direction of the segment, if elongated
- Compactness of the segment
- Curvature of the segment boundary

Using two-dimensional feature extraction only has the advantage of a robust and fast parameter determination. However, parameters of one single object may differ in both camera images. Therefore, all parameter pairs are sorted by their size and stored as a feature vector for classification of the gestures. Feature classification is a well known task for image understanding and object recognition. Often used classification methods are Hidden Markov Models (HMM) as e.g. described in [Sta96] and Artificial Neural Networks (ANN) as e.g. described in [Kje97] for the visual interpretation of hand gestures. For our system algorithms for machine learning for data mining tasks described in [Wit05] like the Naïve Bayes Classifier are used for gesture identification as e.g. described in [Gun05] for the analysis of expressive face and upper-body gestures. We tested the following four algorithms with respect to time of model calculation, classification rate and feature separation:

- Naïve Bayes Classifier
- Bayesian Network with K2-Hill-Climbing
- Sequential Minimal Optimization and
- Random Tree Classifier

A validation of the classification results of up to 800 feature vectors were performed using a standard cross-validation method using one half of the captured feature vectors for model construction and the other half to examine the recognition rate of the system. Our tests with different users showed that the Naïve Bayes Classifier leads to a sufficient balance for the model building process time of less then 5 seconds and an online classification rate of more than 50 Hz.

6   Gesture Training

To ensure a robust and stable recognition of the different gestures (with a classification result of more than 95%) a short training procedure for each new user of the system is necessary. Basically, this training procedure can be skipped using a large predefined training data set consisting of the training data of several users, whereas the recognition result decreases by up to 10% and therefore sporadic misinterpretations of the system may occur. For the training procedure the user is asked to perform the different gestures for approximately ten seconds each at the startup of the system. This procedure is easy and short enough so that the user does not lose interest in starting to interact with the application itself. If desired the training result may be individually saved for a later personalized usage of the tracking system.

7   Pointing Gesture

Using the hand-as-a-tool metaphor, hand gestures are used for mode changes. One should make a division between postures (static movement) or gestures (posture with change of position and/or orientation hand, or moving fingers). The term gesture is often used for both postures and dynamic gestures. Gesture recognition systems used for human-computer interaction require thorough feedback to reduce user's cognitive load. Interaction always needs a visual feedback directly and without delay on the output device. Since the human pointing posture is naturally not as precise as a technical device like e.g. a laser pointer, it is important to permanently provide the user of the system with a visual feedback for comprehensible perception of his/her interaction instead of calculating the pointing direction as precise as possible. In opposite to both other used gestures the pointing posture demands on an extra parameter in 3D space: The pointing direction and therefore the intersection point of a pointing ray with the displaying screen is calculated by the definition of a target point. Due to the fact that the position

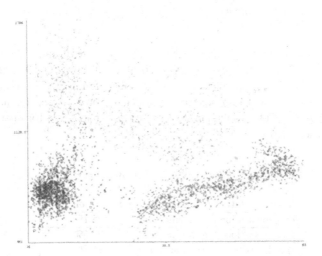

Fig. 3. Scatterplot of two selected features used for classification of pointing (blue), grabbing (red) and releasing (green)

of the user is predefined (indicated by footstep markers on the floor), a 3D target point can easily be defined behind the user. The intersection of a ray starting at the target point and the direction defined by the currently reconstructed 3D position of the fingertip with the displaying screen is used to determine the position on the screen the user is pointing at.

8 Results

Using the hardware setup described in section 2 the system provides interaction feedback in real-time. After the calibration procedure performed only once at the system setup that needs approximately three minutes and after an initial training phase of three minutes (to perform the three different postures for ten seconds each and to build the classification model), the runtime recognition rates are at twenty frames per second and higher. The cameras deliver up to 30 frames per second with a delay shorter then 1/5 of a second. Even all image processing and computer vision tasks like segmentation, edge calculation and 3D reconstruction of corresponding image points last less then 50ms. Overall a recognition rate of up to 25 Hz is achieved. Nevertheless, as important is the classification rate of the system. Figure 3 shows the classification results of one single user for three different gestures (pointing, grab/closed hand and release/open hand). The user performed each gesture 10 seconds during the training procedure, which leads

Table 1. Classification matrix for three different gestures using a Naïve Bayes probabilistic model

Gesture performed vs. classified			
	Pointing	**Grab**	**Release**
Pointing	449	6	33
Grab	3	426	1
Release	24	2	379

to approximately 250 feature vectors for each gesture. Tables 1 and 2 show the recognition and classification results for 60 seconds of interaction with a recognition rate of approximately 95% for new single feature vectors. Due to the fact that outliers (single incorrect classified gestures) can be eliminated using a post-processing queue a completely correct visualization of the performed gestures is achieved for interaction with the application scenario.

Table 2. Recognition rates for three different gestures

Training data	Test data	Recognition rates
Training session	Cross validation	95.1%
Testing session	Cross validation	97.6%
Training session	Testing session	94.7%

9   Applications

As a proof of concept two different scenario applications using virtual 3D environments for interaction have been developed. For a Virtual Chess application the user is standing in front of a large scaled screen rendering a three-dimensional chess board (see figure 4). Using the 3D position of the recognized gestures for grabbing and releasing the user is able to move chess pieces and therefore to play a game of chess against the computer. In the second scenario application the user is asked to place color labeled filters to virtual 3D industrial air pump system. An additional object snapping method is used to ensure a precise assembly of the three-dimensional objects, even if the user releases a filter object only roughly at the outlet of the air pump (see figure 4).

10   Sign Language Recognition

To estimate how may different gesture can be recognized and separated using the proposed methods a further application for the recognition and understanding of the American Manual Alphabet (AMA, American Sign Language Alphabet) has been developed. AMA is a manual alphabet that augments the vocabulary of American Sign Language (ASL) when spelling individual letters of a word is the preferred or only option. This application task is an obviously more complex scenario due to the fact that overall 26 different alphabetic characters have to be recognized and classified by the system. Due to the fact that all letters should be signed with the palm facing the viewer the usage of a

Fig. 4. Playing virtual chess against the computer (left) and Learning assistance scenario: Placing filters to an industrial air pump (right)

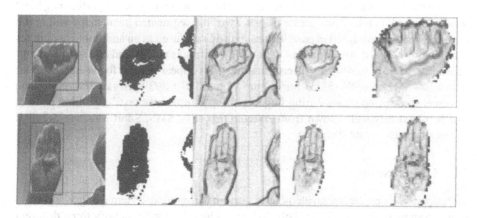

Fig. 5. Image processing pipeline for letters A (top row) and B (bottom): From left to right: Original camera image with augmentations, skin color segmentation, Sobel edge image, hand shape extraction, normalization of hand shape to 50*50 pixels

single camera system like a standard webcam is sufficient. Without the special needs of a camera calibration procedure within a stereo setup as described in the scenarios above the most simple way to extract the hand shape is to use a simple color based webcam and a standard skin color segmentation of the captured image. In a first pre-processing step the captured image is smoothed using a 3*3 Gaussian kernel. Afterwards, the image is converted from RGB color space to YCbCr[1] color space and a skin color segmentation within the intervalsand is performed. Assuming that the largest extracted segment seen

---

[1] Defined in the ITU-R BT.601 (formerly CCIR 601) standard for use with digital component video.

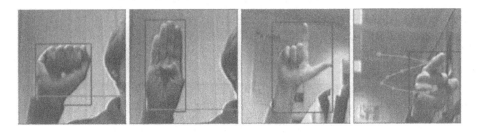

Fig. 6. ASL letters A, B, L, Z (from left to right), blue motion paths superimposed

in the image is the letter performing hand shape, the Sobel edge image of this segment is calculated. Finally, the extracted image is normalized to a given size of 50*50 pixels (see figure 5). For the classification procedure the normalized edge image of the hand shape (see figure 5, right) is used as the feature vector. Therefore, feature vectors for each frame are 2500-dimensional (50*50 luminance values). For classification a Bayesian Network with K2-Hill-Climbing is used, which leads to a model generation time of approximately one minute and an classification rate of up to 15 Hz. Due to the fact that the American Sign Language Alphabet uses the motion of the performing hand for the letters 'J' and 'Z' the center of gravity of the segmented hand shape within the captured image is analyzed in parallel (see figure 6) and used as an additional feature for classification. The system operates with up to 10 frames per second and with a recognition rate of 90% (±4%). Incorrect classifications appear mainly for visually similar letters like 'M' and 'N' (32/37 errors) or 'V' and 'K' (48/39 errors). To compensate incorrect recognized letters during finger spelling a "predicted text"-algorithm is used, which is basically well known from entering text (like SMS, Short Message Service) on the keypad of a mobile phone.

11   Conclusion

In this paper we presented a video-based gesture recognition system using a calibrated stereo system with two off-the-shelf cameras, which is able to identify three different hand gestures (pointing, grabbing and releasing) and determine the relevant parameters like 3D position of the hand and the pointing direction to enable an easy to learn and intuitive interaction with 3D virtual environments. Only a short training phase is needed to ensure high recognition rated of more than 95% in real-time. Two different scenario applications have been developed and tested addressing the application domains of entertainment and learning assistance. Furthermore, an application for sign language recognition has been developed to estimate the limit of distinguishable gestures using the proposed classification methods. Using one uncalibrated camera only, the recognition rate is up to 90% at a frame rate of up to 10 frames per second.

Acknowledgments

Parts of the work presented here were accomplished with support of the European Commission through the SIMILAR (www.similar.cc) Network of Excellence (FP6-507609).

References

Azarbayejani, A., Pentland, A.: Camera self-calibration from one point correspondence. Media Lab Technical Report 341 (1995)

Cohen, C.: The Gesture Recognition Home Page - A brief overview of gesture recognition, Website (retrieved, October 2007), http://www.cybernet.com/~ccohen/

Erol, A., et al.: Vision-based hand pose estimation: A review. Computer Vision and Image Understanding 108(1-2), 52–73 (2007); Special Issue on Vision for Human-Computer Interaction

Gavrila, D.: The Visual Analysis of Human Movement: A Survey. Computer Vision and Image Understanding 73(1), 82–98 (1999)

Gunes, H., Piccardi, M.: Bi-modal affect recognition from expressive face and upper-body gesture by single frame analysis and multi-frame post integration. In: National ICT Australia HCSNet Multimodal User Interaction Workshop, Sydney, September 13-14 (2005)

Kjeldsen, F.: Visual Interpretation of Hand Gestures as a Practical Interface Modality, Dissertation. Columbia University, New York (1997)

Kohler, M.: Vision based hand gesture recognition systems. University of Dortmund (Retrieved, October 2007), http://ls7-www.cs.uni-dortmund.de/research/gesture/

Malerczyk, C.: Interactive Museum Exhibit Using Pointing Gesture Recognition. In: Skala, V. (ed.) u.a.; European Association for Computer Graphics (Eurographics): WSCG 2004. Short Communications, vol. II, pp. 165–171. University of West Bohemia, Plzen (2004)

Malerczyk, C., Daehne, P., Schnaider, M.: Exploring Digitized Artworks by Pointing Posture Recognition. In: 6th International Symposium on Virtual Reality, Archaeology and Cultural Heritage, Pisa, Italy, November 8 – 11 (2005)

O'Hagen, R., Zelinsky, A.: Visual Gesture Interfaces to Virtual Environments. In: Proceedings if AUIC 2000, Canberra, Australia (2000)

Sun, S., Egerstedt, M.: Control theoretic smoothing splines. IEEE Transactions on automatic control 45, 12 (2000)

Schlattman, M., Klein, R.: Simultaneous 4 gestures 6 DOF real-time two-hand tracking without any markers. In: Proceedings of the 2007 ACM symposium on Virtual reality software and technology, Newport Beach, California, USA, pp. 39–42 (2007)

Schwald, B., Malerczyk, C.: Controlling virtual worlds using interaction spheres. In: Vidal, C.A. (ed.) Proceedings of 5th Symposium on Virtual Reality (SVR), pp. 3–14 (2002)

Starner, T., Pentland, A.: Real-Time American Sign Language Recognition from Video Using Hidden Markov Models, Technical Report 375, Massachusetts Institute of Technology Media Laboratory, Cambridge (1996)

Witten, I., Frank, E.: Data Mining Practical machine learning tools and techniques, 2nd edn. Morgan Kaufmann, San Francisco (2005)

Predicting Missing Markers to Drive Real-Time Centre of Rotation Estimation

Andreas Aristidou, Jonathan Cameron, and Joan Lasenby

Department of Engineering
University of Cambridge
Cambridge, UK, CB2 1PZ
{aa462,jic23,jl221}@cam.ac.uk

Abstract. This paper addresses the problem of real-time location of the joints or centres of rotation (CoR) of human skeletons in the presence of missing data. The data is assumed to be $3d$ marker positions from a motion capture system. We present an integrated framework which predicts the occluded marker positions using a Kalman filter in combination with inferred information from neighbouring markers and thereby maintains a continuous data-flow. The CoR positions can be calculated with high accuracy even in cases where markers are occluded for a long period of time.

Keywords: Kalman Filter, Missing Markers, Joint Localisation, Motion Capture.

1   Introduction

Estimating the location of centres of rotations (CoRs) using markered optical motion capture data is useful within technique analysis for sports training [1]; observation of asymmetries and abnormalities in rehabilitation medicine [2]; and generation of virtual characters for films and computer games [3]. However, even with many cameras, there are instances where occlusion of markers by elements of the scene leads to missing data. In order to unambiguously establish its position, each marker must be visible to at least two cameras in each frame. Although many methods have been developed to handle the missing marker problem, most of them are not applicable in real-time and often require manual intervention.

This paper proposes a real-time approach for estimating the position of occluded markers using previous positions and information inferred from an approximate rigid body assumption. The predicted marker positions are then used to locate the human joints. Without assuming any skeleton model, we take advantage of the fact that for markers on a given limb segment, the inter-marker distance is approximately constant. Thus, the neighbouring markers[1] provide us with useful information about the current positions of any non-visible markers. With a continuous stream of accurate $3d$ data, we can perform real-time CoR estimation, thereby producing skeletal information for use in visual performance

---

[1] Neighbouring markers are considered as markers belonging to the same limb segment.

F.J. Perales and R.B. Fisher (Eds.): AMDO 2008, LNCS 5098, pp. 238–247, 2008.

feedback. Experiments demonstrate that the method presented effectively recovers good estimates of the true positions of the missing markers, even if all the markers on a limb are occluded for a long period of time.

2 Related Work

Recent papers have focused on real-time localisation of the CoR. [4] uses the assumption of inter-marker rigidity between neighbouring markers. This allows a closed form sequential algorithm. In this respect it differs from [5,6,7,8]. However, this algorithm neglects frames containing missing markers.

Whilst several methods to estimate the location of missing markers have been proposed, the performance of most is unsatisfactory in the presence of unusual motions or of many contiguous occlusion-effected frames. Methods may interpolate the data using linear or non-linear approaches [9,10,11]; this can produce accurate results, but is useful only in post-processing.

[12] proposes a model-based system for composite interaction devices (CID). The system automatically constructs the geometric skeleton structure and degrees of freedom relations and constraints between segments. The system supports segments with only a single marker, allowing CIDs to be very small. Unfortunately, this is an off-line procedure unsuitable for real-time applications.

[13,14] use an extended Kalman filter to predict the missing marker locations using previous marker positions and a skeletal model. These methods become ineffective when markers are missing for an extended period of time.

[15,16] use post-processing to increase the robustness of motion capture using a sophisticated human model. They predict the $3d$ location and visibility of markers under the assumption of fixed segment inter-marker distances. However, the skeleton information must be known a priori.

Recently, [17] presented a piecewise linear approach to estimating human motions from pre-selected markers. A pre-trained classifier identifies an appropriate local linear model for each frame. Missing markers are then recovered using available marker positions and the principal components of the associated model. The pre-training session and the classifier limit the approach to off-line applications.

[18] presented a reliable system that could predict the missing markers in real-time under large occlusions. However, this system did not consider the useful information available when the markers are visible by a single camera. The missing markers are usually not entirely occluded and this additional information is used in this paper to produce a more reliable system.

3 Estimating CoR

Locating the CoRs is a crucial step in acquiring a skeleton from raw motion capture data. The data discussed here is from an active marker system, hence no tracking is necessary. To calculate the joints between two sets of markers it is helpful to have the rotation of a limb at any given time. We can estimate the orientation of a limb at time k relative to a reference frame using the *Procrustes* formulation [19].

The location of the joints can be calculated using [4]. This approach takes advantage of the approximation that all markers on a segment are attached to a rigid body. Suppose the markers are placed on two segments (x and y) joined by a CoR. Let the CoR location in frame k be $\mathbf{C}_k$. The vectors from the CoR to markers in the reference frame are denoted by $\mathbf{a}_x^i$ and $\mathbf{a}_y^j$ for limb x and y respectively, where i and j are marker labels. The position of the markers in frame k is given by:

$$\mathbf{x}_i^k = \mathbf{C}^k + R_x^k \mathbf{a}_x^i \tilde{R}_x^k \qquad\qquad \mathbf{y}_j^k = \mathbf{C}^k + R_y^k \mathbf{a}_y^j \tilde{R}_y^k \qquad (1)$$

where R_x and R_y are the rotors (quaternions) expressing the rotation of the joint limbs x and y respectively. $\tilde{R}$ is the quaternion conjugate of R. Let $\mathbf{b}_{ij}^k$ be the vector from $\mathbf{x}_i^k$ to $\mathbf{y}_j^k$, that is:

$$\mathbf{b}_{ij}^k = \mathbf{x}_i^k - \mathbf{y}_j^k = R_x^k \mathbf{a}_x^i \tilde{R}_x^k - R_y^k \mathbf{a}_y^j \tilde{R}_y^k \qquad (2)$$

Now a cost function S can be constructed that has a global minimum at the correct values of $\mathbf{a}_x^i$ and $\mathbf{a}_y^j$ if the data is noise free, and returns a good estimate in the presence of moderate noise.

$$S = \sum_{k=1}^{m} \sum_{i=1}^{n_x} \sum_{j=1}^{n_y} \left[\mathbf{b}_{ij}^k - \left(R_x^k \mathbf{a}_x^i \tilde{R}_x^k - R_y^k \mathbf{a}_y^j \tilde{R}_y^k \right) \right]^2 \qquad (3)$$

where n_x, n_y are the number of markers on limbs x and y respectively, and m is the number of frames used for the calculations. The minimum is given by the solution of the simultaneous linear equations, obtainable by differentiation:

$$\mathbf{a}_x^i = \frac{1}{m} \sum_{k=1}^{m} \tilde{R}_x^k \bar{\mathbf{b}}^k R_x^k + \frac{1}{m} \sum_{k=1}^{m} \tilde{R}_x^k R_y^k \bar{\mathbf{a}}_y \tilde{R}_y^k R_x^k \qquad (4)$$

$$\mathbf{a}_y^j = \frac{1}{m} \sum_{k=1}^{m} \tilde{R}_y^k \bar{\mathbf{b}}^k R_y^k + \frac{1}{m} \sum_{k=1}^{m} \tilde{R}_y^k R_x^k \bar{\mathbf{a}}_x \tilde{R}_x^k R_y^k \qquad (5)$$

where

$$\bar{\mathbf{b}}^k = \frac{1}{n_x n_y} \sum_{i=1}^{n_x} \sum_{j=1}^{n_y} \mathbf{b}_{ij}^k \qquad\qquad \bar{\mathbf{a}}_w = \frac{1}{n_w} \sum_{i=1}^{n_w} \mathbf{a}_w^i \qquad\qquad w = \{x, y\} \qquad (6)$$

Having calculated the R_w^k and $\bar{\mathbf{a}}_w$, we can locate the CoR. However, due to occlusions, there are instances where not all marker positions are available. If and only if all markers are available on one limb segment, w, the CoR may be estimated using only R_w^k in the current frame and $\bar{\mathbf{a}}_w$ as estimated in the previous frame, via (1). If markers are occluded on both segments a method such as that in the next section is needed.

4 Missing Marker Position Estimation

The marker position estimates can by predicted using a Kalman filter [20], where constraints from the neighbouring markers are applied for a more reliable system.

4.1 Framework

The process model to update the *state* of the Kalman filter is given by (7), where the state $\mathbf{x}_k$ at frame k is obtained from the state at frame $k - 1$;

$$\mathbf{x}_k = A\mathbf{x}_{k-1} + B\mathbf{u}_{k-1} + \mathbf{w}_{k-1} \tag{7}$$

where A is the state transition model, B is the control input model, $\mathbf{u}_{k-1}$ is the control vector and $\mathbf{w}_{k-1}$ is the process noise. The measured data $\mathbf{Z}_k$ is

$$\mathbf{Z}_k = H\mathbf{x}_k + \mathbf{v}_k \tag{8}$$

where H is the *observation model* and $\mathbf{v}_k$ is the observation noise. $\mathbf{w}$ and $\mathbf{v}$ are assumed to be zero mean multivariate normal with covariance Q and R.

The predicted state $\mathbf{y}_k$ and its error E_k can be written as

$$\mathbf{y}_k = A\hat{\mathbf{x}}_{k-1} + B\mathbf{u}_{k-1} \qquad\qquad E_k = AP_{k-1}A^T + Q \tag{9}$$

where $\hat{\mathbf{x}}$ refers to the *estimate* and P is the covariance of the state estimate.

The *Kalman gain* between actual and predicted observations is:

$$K_k = E_k H^T \left(H E_k H^T + R \right)^{-1} \tag{10}$$

Thus given an estimate $\hat{\mathbf{x}}_{k-1}$ at $k - 1$, the time update predicts the state value at frame k. The measurement update then adjusts this prediction based on the new $\mathbf{y}_k$. The estimate of the new state is

$$\hat{\mathbf{x}}_k = \mathbf{y}_k + K_k \left(\mathbf{Z}_k - H\mathbf{y}_k \right) \tag{11}$$

K_k is chosen to minimise the steady-state covariance of the estimation error. Finally, the error covariance matrix of the updated estimate is;

$$P_k = \left(I - K_k H \right) E_k \tag{12}$$

In this work, a constant velocity model is used. Hence,

$$\mathbf{y}_k = \mathbf{x}_{k-1} + \dot{\mathbf{x}}_{k-1} dk \tag{13}$$

where $\mathbf{x}_i$ and $\dot{\mathbf{x}}_i$ are the position and velocity in frame i, and dk is the time step.

4.2 Applying Constraints

The observation vector, $\mathbf{Z}_k$, gives the observed position of the tracked marker when available, otherwise it represents estimated position. The state vector represents true position and velocity as given above. To cope with cases where markers are missing for long periods of time, we implement a tracker that uses information from both the previous frames and the current positions of neighbouring visible markers. We assume three markers on each limb. In the presence of noise the observation vector is updated as given below for 4 different scenarios;

All markers are visible on a given limb

$$\mathbf{Z}_k = H\mathbf{x}_k + \mathbf{v}_k \tag{14}$$

where $\mathbf{x}_k$ is the current state of a tracked marker on the limb. In this case H is the identity and R is determined empirically. Many factors contribute to marker noise, and hence R, including optical measurement noise miscalibration of the optical systems, reflection, motion of markers relative to the skin and motion of the skin relative to the rigid body (underlying bone).

One missing marker on a limb segment

$$\mathbf{Z}_k = H\hat{\mathbf{x}}_1^k + \mathbf{v}_k \tag{15}$$

where $\hat{\mathbf{x}}_1^k$ is the estimated position of the occluded marker m_1 in frame k. $\hat{\mathbf{x}}_1^k$ can be calculated as given below. Firstly we calculate $\mathbf{D}_{1,2}^{k-1}$ and $\mathbf{D}_{1,3}^{k-1}$ which correspond to the vectors between marker m_1 and markers m_2, m_3 in frame $k-1$ respectively. These vectors are given by $\mathbf{D}_{i,j}^{k-1} = \mathbf{x}_j^{k-1} - \mathbf{x}_i^{k-1}$. Thereafter, these vectors are rotated as $\hat{\mathbf{D}}_{i,j}^k = R^{k-2,k-1}\mathbf{D}_{i,j}^{k-1}\tilde{R}^{k-2,k-1}$ where $R^{p,q}$ is the rotor expressing the rotation between frames p to q, assuming that the rotation of the markers between two consecutive frames remains constant. One obvious way to proceed is to calculate the point $\tilde{\mathbf{x}}_1^k$ which is an average of the estimated positions in frame k using the $\hat{\mathbf{D}}$ vectors;

$$\tilde{\mathbf{x}}_1^k = \frac{\left(\mathbf{x}_2^k - \hat{\mathbf{D}}_{1,2}^k\right) + \left(\mathbf{x}_3^k - \hat{\mathbf{D}}_{1,3}^k\right)}{2} \tag{16}$$

where $\mathbf{x}_i^k$ is the position of marker i in frame k. We now improve on this estimate by finding the solution of the intersection of the two spheres in frame k with centres $\mathbf{x}_2^k$, $\mathbf{x}_3^k$ and radii $|\hat{\mathbf{D}}_{1,2}^k|$ and $|\hat{\mathbf{D}}_{1,3}^k|$ respectively. $\hat{\mathbf{x}}_1^k$ is assigned as the closest point on the circle of intersection to $\tilde{\mathbf{x}}_1^k$. Figure 1 illustrates this process.

Two missing markers on a limb segment

$$\mathbf{Z}_k = H\hat{\mathbf{x}}_j^k + \mathbf{v}_k \tag{17}$$

where $\hat{\mathbf{x}}_j^k$ is the estimated position of the occluded marker m_j ($j = 1, 3$) in frame k. $\hat{\mathbf{x}}_j^k$ is given by:

$$\hat{\mathbf{x}}_j^k = \mathbf{x}_2^k - \hat{\mathbf{D}}_{j,2}^k \tag{18}$$

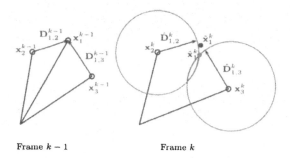

Frame $k-1$ Frame k

Fig. 1. The observation vector in the case of 2 visible markers. The red dot, $\tilde{\mathbf{x}}_1^k$, represents the average value as given in equation 16. The green dot, $\hat{\mathbf{x}}_1^k$, is the point on the intersection of the 2 spheres which is closest to $\tilde{\mathbf{x}}_1^k$.

where $\mathbf{x}_2^k$ is the position of the visible marker m_2 on the limb in the current frame and $\hat{\mathbf{D}}_{j,2}^k$ is as described above. In this case, we are using the constant velocity assumption as we cannot estimate the rotation.

All markers on a limb segment are missing: Here we consider two possible subcases; the case where the other limb segment has some markers visible and the case where both limb segments have all of their markers occluded. If some markers on the other limb segment are visible, the missing marker positions can be calculated using the CoR estimate, $\hat{\mathbf{C}}_k$ as calculated in Sect. 3. In that case the observation vector of the Kalman filter is updated as:

$$\mathbf{Z}_k = H\hat{\mathbf{x}}_j^k + \mathbf{v}_k \tag{19}$$

where $\hat{\mathbf{x}}_j^k$ is the estimated position of the occluded marker m_j $(j = 1, 2, 3)$ in frame k. $\hat{\mathbf{x}}_j^k$ is given by;

$$\hat{\mathbf{x}}_j^k = \hat{\mathbf{C}}_k + \hat{\mathbf{D}}_{j,c}^k \tag{20}$$

where $\hat{\mathbf{D}}_{j,c}^k$ is an estimate of the distance between marker m_i and the CoR. This approach takes advantage of the fact that the distance between markers and the CoR is constant. This distance is equal to $\hat{\mathbf{D}}_{j,c}^k = R^{k-2,k-1}\mathbf{D}_{j,c}^{k-1}\tilde{R}^{k-2,k-1}$ where $\mathbf{D}_{j,c}^{k-1} = \mathbf{x}_j^{k-1} - \mathbf{C}_{k-1}$. This assumes that the rotation of the markers between two consecutive frames remains constant.

If both limb segments have all markers occluded, only information from previous frames is used. The observation vector, $\mathbf{Z}_k$, in this instance is calculated using a quaternion based method. This method also assumes that the segment rotation between two consecutive frames is constant. The observation vector is now equal to

$$\mathbf{Z}_k = H\hat{\mathbf{x}}^k + \mathbf{v}_k \tag{21}$$

where $\hat{\mathbf{x}}^k$ is equal to $\hat{\mathbf{x}}^k = R^{k-2,k-1}\mathbf{x}^{k-1}\tilde{R}^{k-2,k-1}$.

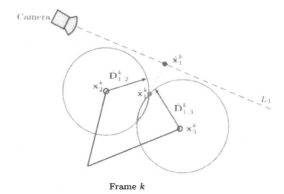

Frame k

Fig. 2. The observation vector in the case of 2 visible markers and one marker visible only by one camera. The magenta dot, $\acute{\mathbf{x}}_1^k$, is now used for the calculation of the observation vector, $\mathbf{Z}_k = H\acute{\mathbf{x}}^k + \mathbf{v}_k$.

However, the motion capture system also provides us with additional information which could be used for prediction of missing marker locations. Each marker can be reconstructed by the motion capture system if it is visible in at least two cameras. It is often the case that some markers are visible in only one camera. This information identifies a line, L_1, starting from the camera and passing through the position of the missing marker. By relaxing the constraints that the inter-marker distance is constant and accepting that the real position of the marker is on the line L_1, we can obtain a more accurate estimate of the position of the relevant marker. This position, $\acute{\mathbf{x}}_1^k$, corresponds to the projection from the point $\hat{\mathbf{x}}_1^k$ onto the line L_1, as in Fig. 2. This is applicable for the cases in which the motion capture system fully reconstructs one or two markers locations and another marker is visible in one camera. If a limb segment has only one known and one partially visible marker, the system is more reliable when it first predicts the partially visible marker and then the entirely occluded marker.

5   Results and Discussion

Experiments were carried out using a 16 camera Phasespace motion capture system capable of capturing data at $480Hz$ [21]. The algorithm was implemented

Table 1. Average results on real data with occlusions generated by deletions. Case of one missing marker on each limb segment for more than 1500 frames.

The error when the missing markers are entirely occluded		The error when the missing markers are visible by one camera	
	Error (mm)		Error (mm)
Marker position	3.348151	Marker position	0.585351
CoR (when $\bar{\mathbf{a}}_w$ is updated using the predicted data.)	5.905546	CoR (using the predicted markers positions)	1.281958

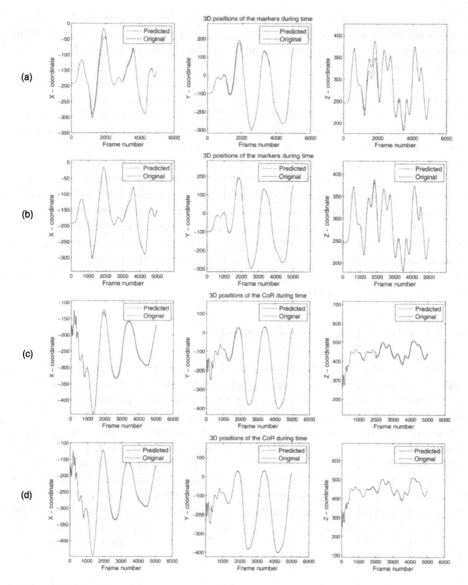

Fig. 3. An example of the 3D positions of predicted and the true coordinates of the *Markers* (a), (b) in the case of one missing marker on a limb segment and a missing marker visible by one camera respectively, and the *CoR* (c), (d) under the same conditions. The occlusion periods are between frames 1000-2000 and 3000-3600.

in MATLAB and run on a Pentium IV PC. The system can process up to 350 *frames per second* (using MATLAB). Our datasets comprise both simulated and real data (i.e. captured data with natural occlusions or occlusions generated by artificial deletion) with more than 5000 *frames* in each. There are two categories: one with 7 segment leg datasets and the other with 5 segment arm datasets. The

3d location of the markers can be reliably reconstructed even when we have single marker occlusion for more than 1000 *frames* at a time, returning mean position errors of less than 3.5mm from the true value. The position of the CoR using the predicted marker positions can be calculated with a mean error of approximately 6.35mm in cases where one marker on each limb segment is entirely occluded, this increases to 11.8mm in cases where 2 out of 3 markers on a limb are not visible. However, in the case where one of the limb segments has all its markers available, the CoR can be calculated with higher accuracy using information only from that limb segment, as in Sect. 3, where $\bar{a}_w$ is now updated using the predicted positions of the markers. The error between the true and the CoR estimate for that instance is 5.9mm when one marker is occluded and 9.5mm when two markers are missing. This error is significantly decreased to 0.6mm for marker position estimations and 1.3mm for the CoR positions estimation in the case where the missing markers are visible by one camera. Table 1 presents the average results (over 30 runs) in the case of one missing marker on each limb segment. Figure 3 shows an example of the 3D position variation over time between the true and the predicted position of the markers and the CoR for two particular cases of occlusion.

6   Conclusion and Future Work

This paper describes an algorithm related to the problem of using marker-based optical motion capture data to automatically establish a skeleton model to which the markers are attached. It presents a prediction method that estimates the missing markers and reconstructs the skeletal motion. These positions are calculated in real-time using a Kalman filter updated via information from neighbouring visible markers. Also, the system takes advantage of the information returned by each single camera regarding the position of the missing markers. The predicted data is then used for real-time joint localisation. This approach works reliably even if large sequences with occluded data exist, in which more than 1 marker is occluded on each limb, and also when the limb rapidly changes direction. Future work will introduce biomechanical constraints to restrict motions to those from a feasible set and a reliable model for predicting the rotors expressing the rotation of each limb segment.

References

1. Hashiguchi, J., Nivomiya, H., Tanaka, H., Nakamura, M., Nobuhara, K.: Biomechanical analysis of a golf swing using motion capture system. In: Proc. of the Japanese Society for Orthopaedic Biomechanics, vol. 27, pp. 325–330 (2006)
2. Broeren, J., Sunnerhagen, K.S., Rydmark, M.: A kinematic analysis of a haptic handheld stylus in a virtual environment: a study in healthy subjects. Journal of NeuroEngineering and Rehabilitation 4,13 (2007)
3. Menache, A.: Understanding Motion Capture for Computer Animation and Video Games. Morgan Kaufmann Publishers Inc, USA (1999)

4. Cameron, J., Lasenby, J.: A real-time sequential algorithm for human joint localization. In: ACM SIGGRAPH Posters, USA, p. 107 (2005)
5. Gamage, S., Lasenby, J.: New least squares solutions for estimating the average centre of rotation and the axis of rotation. J. of Biomechanics 35(1), 87–93 (2002)
6. Kirk, A.G., O'Brien, J.F., Forsyth, D.A.: Skeletal parameter estimation from optical motion capture data. In: Proc. of the IEEE CVPR, pp. 782–788 (2005)
7. O'Brien, J.F., Bodenheimer, R.E., Brostow, G.J., Hodgins, J.K.: Automatic joint parameter estimation from magnetic motion capture data. In: Proceedings of Graphic Interface, pp. 53–60 (2000)
8. Ehrig, R.M., Taylor, W.R., Duda, G.N., Heller, M.O.: A survey of formal methods for determining the centre of rotation of ball joints. Journal of Biomechanics 39(15), 2798–2809 (2006)
9. Wiley, D.J., Hahn, J.K.: Interpolation synthesis of articulated figure motion. IEEE Comp. Graphics and Applications 17(6), 39–45 (1997)
10. Rose, C., Cohen, M., Bodenheimer, B.: Verbs and adverbs: Multidimensional motion interpolation. IEEE Comp. Graphics and Applications 18(5), 32–40 (1998)
11. Nebel, J.: Keyframe interpolation with self-collision avoidance. In: Proc. of the Workshop on Comp. Animation and Simulation, pp. 77–86. Springer, Heidelberg (2006)
12. Van Rhijn, A., Mulder, J.D.: Optical tracking and automatic model estimation of composite interaction devices. In: IEEE VR Conference, pp. 135–142 (2006)
13. Dorfmüller-Ulhaas, K.: Robust optical user motion tracking using a kalman filter. Technical Report TR-2003-6, Institut fuer Informatik 2, 86159 Augsburg (2003)
14. Welch, G., Bishop, G., Vicci, L., Brumback, S., Keller, K., Colucci, D.: The HiBall tracker: High-performance wide-area tracking for virtual and augmented environments. In: VRST, December 20-22, 1999, pp. 1–10. ACM, New York (1999)
15. Herda, L., Fua, P., Plänkers, R., Boulic, R., Thalmann, D.: Using skeleton-based tracking to increase the reliability of optical motion capture. Human Movement Science Journal 20(3), 313–341 (2001)
16. Hornung, A., Sar-Dessai, S.: Self-calibrating optical motion tracking for articulated bodies. In: Proceedings of the IEEE Conference on VR, Washington, DC, USA, pp. 75–82 (2005)
17. Liu, G., McMillan, L.: Estimation of missing markers in human motion capture. The Visual Computer 22(9-11), 721–728 (2006)
18. Aristidou, A., Cameron, J., Lasenby, J.: Real-time estimation of missing markers in human motion capture. In: Proceedings of the iCBBE 2008 (2008)
19. Horn, B.: Closed-form solution of absolute orientation using unit quaternions. Journal of the Opt. Society of America 4, 629–642 (1987)
20. Kalman, R.E.: A new approach to linear filtering and prediction problems. Journal of Basic Engineering, 35–45 (1960)
21. PhaseSpace Inc.: Optical motion capture systems, http://www.phasespace.com

Accurate Human Motion Capture Using an Ergonomics-Based Anthropometric Human Model

Jan Bandouch[1], Florian Engstler[2], and Michael Beetz[1]

[1] Intelligent Autonomous Systems Group, Department of Informatics,
Technische Universität München, Munich, Germany
{bandouch,beetz}@cs.tum.edu
[2] Ergonomics Department, Faculty of Mechanical Engineering,
Technische Universität München, Munich, Germany
engstler@lfe.mw.tum.de

Abstract. In this paper we present our work on markerless model-based 3D human motion capture using multiple cameras. We use an industry proven anthropometric human model that was modeled taking ergonomic considerations into account. The outer surface consists of a precise yet compact 3D surface mesh that is mostly rigid on body part level apart from some small but important torsion deformations. Benefits are the ability to capture a great amount of possible human appearances with high accuracy while still having a simple to use and computationally efficient model. We have introduced special optimizations such as caching into the model to improve its performance in tracking applications. Available force and comfort measures within the model provide further opportunities for future research.

3D articulated pose estimation is performed in a Bayesian framework, using a set of hierarchically coupled local particle filters for tracking. This makes it possible to sample efficiently from the high dimensional space of articulated human poses without constraining the allowed movements. Sequences of tracked upper-body as well as full-body motions captured by three cameras show promising results. Despite the high dimensionality of our model (51 DOF) we succeed at tracking using only silhouette overlap as weighting function due to the precise outer appearance of our model and the hierarchical decomposition.

1 Introduction

The problem of understanding human action is one of the main challenges towards robot interaction with humans and also towards natural computer interfaces for humans. As an example, service robots interoperating in human environments must be able to predict human behavior and intentions or else they will be more of a burden then a relief to humans. A first important step in understanding human action is to observe human actions or more general to observe human motions. Such observations can provide the basis for further analysis and true understanding of actions and intentions.

Human motion analysis can also be of value in the area of industrial design. Ergonomic studies aim at analyzing comfort and user-friendliness of new products. Providing high precision motion data coupled with a human model based on anthropometric and ergonomic considerations yields valuable data for these kinds of studies,

F.J. Perales and R.B. Fisher (Eds.): AMDO 2008, LNCS 5098, pp. 248–258, 2008.
© Springer-Verlag Berlin Heidelberg 2008

that are currently mostly relying on static pose analyses. Motion analysis is also becoming increasingly popular in the area of high performance sports, for the optimization of motion sequences of athletes.

In this paper we present our approach at markerless human motion capture. Our setup is a multiple camera setup with 3 cameras capturing the human subject from different sides. The industry proven ergonomics-based digital human model *RAMSIS* is used for tracking. It is capable of capturing different anthropometries, i.e. human appearances, while being computationally efficient and relatively easy to use. A wide range of existing applications and available domain knowledge such as force and comfort measures within the model further motivate its use. The tracking of the 3D articulated pose of the model is done in a Bayesian *Sampling Importance Resampling* (SIR) framework, more generally referred to as *Particle Filtering*. To succeed despite the high dimensionality of the model, a hierarchical decomposition of the pose space based on the hierarchical structures in the human model is performed. Therefore it is possible to sample efficiently from the high dimensional space of articulated human poses without constraining the allowed movements.

The remainder of this paper is organized as follows. In the next section we give an introduction of related work and show where to classify our work. We present the ergonomics-based digital human model *RAMSIS* and the optimizations integrated for its use in motion tracking in section 3. Section 4 gives an insight into the Bayesian tracking framework and the hierarchical decomposition of the pose space for successful tracking. Results on sequences of upper- and full-body motions are presented in section 5. We finish the paper in section 6 with our conclusions.

2   Related Work

Human Motion Analysis is one of the most active topics in Computer Vision research. Several surveys give a good overview of recent work and taxonomies [11,12,13]. In contrast to commercial applications that usually rely on professional marker-based systems, most of the research done in the field is targeting at markerless tracking. While it has been shown that it is possible to extract 3D motion information from single views [8] given initial training of corresponding silhouette appearances, accurate and reliable 3D tracking is more likely to be performed in multiple camera settings. Usually a search of the optimal pose given an initial estimate is performed. Modified particle filters have been applied to successfully deal with the high dimensionality of the pose space. While standard particle filtering is unsuitable for higher dimensions (> 8) as computational costs grow exponentially, Deutscher and Reid [6] use a so-called *Annealed Particle Filter* to escape the local minima inherent in the pose space. *Partitioned Sampling* [10] is another method suitable for articulated models to reduce the number of particles needed for tracking. Apart from particle filtering, many approaches use optimization methods to find the best pose [9,14]. Usually a good initial guess is needed to avoid getting trapped in local minima, which makes optimization based methods harder to apply when tracking with low frame rates. An interesting combination of an optimization scheme with particle filters is presented by Bray et al. [3], although applied to hand tracking, which has a hierarchical structure very similar to the human body. One option to reduce the dimensionality is to project the space of articulated poses to a lower-dimensional manifold by learning the manifold for specific activities [17,16]. These approaches work well for the specified motions, but also constrain the amount of detectable motions.

The objective function (or weight function) used is often based on observed silhouette or contour overlap between image observations and model projections [6,14]. Another option is to calculate the point to surface errors given the visual hull of the human [9,1,5]. These approaches require the human to be surrounded by several cameras for a precise estimate of the visual hull and are usually computationally more expensive.

In this context, our approach can be classified among the particle filter based approaches for unconstrained motions. We are using plain silhouettes instead of the visual hull to be able to get along with a minimal camera setting and fast evaluations of the weight function. Three cameras seem to be the minimum necessary to overcome ambiguities in the silhouette projections [2].

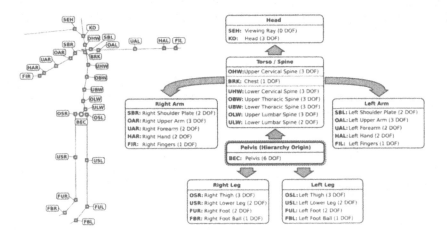

Fig. 1. Inner model of the digital human model *RAMSIS*. The joint locations with abbreviations are shown on the left, the hierarchical structure of the model including the degrees of freedom per body part are shown on the right. The hierarchical origin is the pelvis. The pose for the shown inner model is the same as in Figure 2.

3   Anthropometric Human Model

In our work we take the new approach to integrate the digital human model *RAMSIS* for tracking of human motions. *RAMSIS* is an industry-proven and far-developed model from the ergonomics community, that is widely-used especially in the automotive community [4]. It was initially developed to ease CAD-based design of car interior and human workspaces, as well as for use in ergonomic studies. The following advantages for motion analysis tasks come along with the use of this model:

1. The model is capable of capturing different body types according to anthropometric considerations, i.e. the different appearance of a wide range of humans. Its design has been guided by ergonomic considerations from leading experts in the field.

2. The locations of the inner joints correspond precisely to the real human joint locations. This makes the model ideal for analyzing the detected motions e.g. in sport analytics or ergonomic studies.
3. It is capable to capture most of the movements humans can perform while retaining a correct outer appearance. Absolute motion limits as well as inter-frame motion limits are integrated and help to reduce the search space when tracking. Motion limits can be queried for different percentiles of the population using anthropometric knowledge. Furthermore, existing motion knowledge (e.g. links in the degrees of freedom of the spine) is integrated to guarantee physiologically realistic postures.

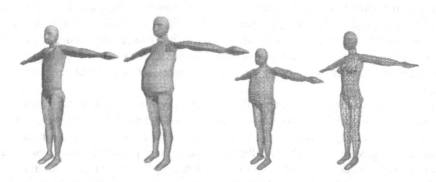

Fig. 2. Outer model of the digital human model *RAMSIS* for different anthropometries and gender. The surface is modeled as a 3D triangle mesh with some posture dependant deformations.

Apart from these advantages, several extensions to the model have been developed that provide space for promising future improvements of our motion tracking algorithm. To name one, Seitz et al. presented an approach for posture prediction using internal and external forces as well as discomfort [15]. We plan to integrate such cues in future work.

We will now discuss the digital human model *RAMSIS* in more detail. It consists of an inner model (Figure 1) that is modeled very closely after a real human skeleton (e.g. with an accurately approximated spine), and an outer model (Figure 2) for the surface representation of the human skin. Both inner and outer model are adaptable to different anthropometries (height, figure, body mass, etc.). This is usually done by hand in an initialization step. We are currently working on reducing the parameters needed for the anthropometric adjustment using *Principal Component Analysis*, so that the initialization is simplified.

The outer surface model is a simple triangle mesh, with absolute vertex coordinates being calculated from the pose dependant underlying part coordinate system and the anthropometric length parameters for a given model instance. It is rigid with respect to the individual body parts, except for rotations around tangential body part directions, where an additional torsion deformation is applied to the vertices. The surface connections between body parts provide for some pose dependant deformations and have been carefully modeled in the initial design step. This becomes particularly apparent in the shoulder region that can be naturally shifted and rotated as it is modeled as a self-contained body part. The model resolution used is a good compromise between accurate outer appearance and fast computations. Using a higher surface resolution doesn't improve the appearance very much, and using a lower resolution would result in unrealistic torsion deformations and body-part connection surfaces. Silhouettes and contours of the outer surface are easily calculated for each camera view using projective geometry given the calibrated camera parameters.

Figure 1 shows the hierarchical structure of the body parts along with the number of degrees of freedom. Without the optional hand model, the human model has 65 degrees of freedom (note the accurate modeling of the spine). For the model to be usable for tracking tasks, we reduced the complexity in the spine by only considering the OLW joint (upper lumbar spine) and the UHW joint (lower cervical spine). The joints inbetween are interpolated relatively to their maximal ergonomic motion limits, which is perfectly sound with the real movements produceable in the spine. A similar optimization was made with the OHW joint (upper cervical spine), which is interpolated from movements of the head (KO joint). The reduced model we use for tracking features 51 degrees of freedom when considering hand and feet, and 39 degrees of freedom without hands and feet considered.

Another optimization tailored towards tracking tasks that we have incorporated into the model is a cache for the body part transformations and the surface meshes, so that only the changed body parts need to be recalculated. This is an important optimization resulting in a huge speedup when dealing with hierarchical particle filters, as there are a lot of repeated local pose variations during each resampling step in each hierarchy.

Having shown the intentions behind our model selection, we will now focus on the tracking algorithm for the remainder of this paper.

4   Hierarchical Particle Filtering

Tracking of articulated human motions in 3D is a very complex task due to the high dimensionality of human poses and the highly non-linear observation models with many local maxima. Particle filters cope well with non-linear observation models, but quickly become unfeasible with growing dimensionality of the state space (see [7] for a detailed introduction of particle filters). Several variations of particle filters have been proposed that have been shown to successfully track in the high dimensionality of the human pose space. Deutscher and Reid [6] proposed *annealed particle filters* to overcome local maxima and to concentrate the particle spread near the global maximum. Although they integrated a sort of hierarchical decomposition by adapting particle motion to the variance of each body joint, they are still estimating all joint angles at once. The downside to this is that in each iteration joint angles are estimated that are only valid in the context of their hierarchical predecessors. As these predecessors are not yet reliably estimated in the early annealing stages of each iteration, some computational effort is wasted here. *Partitioned sampling* is an approach at hierarchical decomposition of the pose space that has been introduced by MacCormick and Isard [10] in the context of hand tracking, where subparts of the pose space are estimated independently of each other. Partitioned sampling can be seen as the statistical analogue to a hierarchical search, and is especially suited to cope with the high dimensionality of articulated objects. Applied to a human articulated pose, it means to first estimate the torso of a person, before focusing the search to the joints in the arms, legs and head hierarchies. We have chosen to adopt this approach for our tracking algorithm. The prerequisites for using partitioned sampling [10] are fulfilled in the case of human motion tracking: The pose space can be partitioned as a Cartesian product of joint angles, the dynamics of joint angles do not influence the dynamics of hierarchically preceding joint angles, and the weight function can be evaluated locally for each body part.

As already hinted, our tracking algorithm is a particle filter approach using partitioned sampling, which can also be seen or implemented as a hierarchically coupled series of local particle filters for individual body parts. We have split the pose space in a way that no subspace needs to evaluate more than 8 DOF at once. Therefore we divided the estimation of the torso in a lower torso including the initial 3D pose and an upper torso. We will now describe our choice for the *motion model* $P(x_t \mid x_{t-1})$ and the *observation model* $P(y_t \mid x_t)$.

As we want to track unconstrained human motions, we do not use a specific motion model except for Gaussian distributed diffusion ($x_{t+1} = x_t + \mathcal{N}(0, \sigma^2)$). The amount of diffusion for each joint angle j is controlled via the inter-frame standard deviations σ_j of the Gaussian distribution. They are dependent on the number of image frames per second (fps) and have been estimated with the help of experts from the ergonomics community. For a sequence captured with 25 fps, they range from 0.5 deg for some degrees of freedom in the spine up to 38 deg for torsion of the forearms. In our experiments, we have limited the maximal joint angle standard deviations to 12.5 degrees, or else the tracking would become inaccurate. For tracking very fast motions we recommend a higher framerate. Furthermore, minimal and maximal joint angles are restricted for each joint taking ergonomic and anthropometric considerations into account.

For the observation model and the calculation of the weighting function, we have decided to select the silhouette overlap between the projected outer model and the silhouettes observed in the video frames. This choice has been guided by the consideration that silhouette shapes from multiple cameras provide rich and almost unambiguous information about a human pose. Although no depth or luminance information is considered, we believe that given the detailed outer appearance of our model, silhouette information is sufficient for simple tracking tasks (constrained environments, no occlusions with other objects). Silhouette shapes are relatively easy to extract from images using standard background subtraction techniques. Furthermore, they fulfill the requirement of being locally evaluable for each body part, as requested for partitioned sampling approaches. The weight $\pi^{(i)}$ for each of the N particles with index i is computed as follows:

$$e^{(i)} = \sum_{x,y} I_e^{(i)}(x,y) ; \qquad I_e^{(i)} = I_p^{(i)} \, XOR \, I_s ; \qquad i = 0 \ldots N ; \qquad (1)$$

$$\tilde{\pi}^{(i)} = 1 - \frac{e^{(i)} - \min_i(e^{(i)})}{\max_i(e^{(i)}) - \min_i(e^{(i)})} \qquad (2)$$

$$\pi^{(i)} = 1 - \left(1 - \tilde{\pi}^{(i)a}\right)^b \qquad (3)$$

Here, $e^{(i)}$ is the absolute error between the silhouette mask I_s from the background subtraction and the projection $I_p^{(i)}$ of the outer model. It is calculated by applying a pixelwise XOR between the two image masks and counting the non-zero pixels (Equation 1). We then normalize all particles according to Equation 2 by scaling particle weights between 0 (highest error) and 1 (lowest error). Equation 3 calculates the final particle weights by further suppressing low and reinforcing high weights. We have set $a = 16$ and $b = 8$ in our approach. Using the normalizations as in Equations 2 and 3, we are able to influence the survival diagnostic $\mathcal{D}$ as introduced by MacCormick and Isard [10]. The survival diagnostic gives an estimate of the number of particles that will survive a resampling step, and is an important tool for controlling the particle spread. A survival diagnostic of about $\mathcal{D} = \frac{1}{3}N$ has provided the best results in our experiments, and proved to be a good trade-off between focusing particles in the most likely areas and tracking multiple hypotheses.

After all weights have been updated for every hierarchy, the particle with the highest weight is selected as the Maximum Likelihood Estimate of the human pose in that timestep. We apply a Gaussian weighted mean filter on the estimated poses in a final post-processing step to smooth the tracked motions that tend to be trembling a bit due to the characteristics of particle filtering.

5   Results

We have evaluated our approach on several videos captured in a setup with three cameras. To ensure that the extracted silhouettes carry enough information for unambiguous tracking, the cameras were placed in a way to capture the subject from different sides. Our experience has shown that the angle between each two cameras should differ by at least 45 degrees. It should also be avoided that two cameras are placed exactly opposite of each other, as this results in mirrored silhouettes that do not provide additional information. Using less than three cameras substantially reduces reliability due to ambiguities, as has been shown by Balan et al. [2].

Due to missing ground truth data, we are not able to give a qualitative evaluation in terms of pose errors. We therefore rely on a manual visual inspection of the results, that is easy to do due to the precision of our outer model. A high overlap of the model projection with the silhouettes extracted from the background subtraction in all images indicates good tracking results. Furthermore, projections of only the inner joints onto the original videos shows the precise estimation of true articulated joint positions in the human skeleton. Figure 3 shows in detail a single tracked frame from a sequence with only upper-body motion. The sequence shows a human grabbing and throwing dart arrows and features fast motions of the arm and both stretching and rotating movements of the upper torso. The sequence is captured with 3 cameras at 25 fps and was tracked correctly without interruptions for about 1000 frames. Successful tracking of upper-body motions is possible with as little as 250 particles, but the screenshots are taken from a sequence that has been tracked with 5000 particles for higher accuracy.

We have also run tests on full-body motion sequences as shown in Figure 4. This is an extended sequence captured by 3 cameras at 25 fps that lasts for more than 9000 frames. We have tracked most of the sequence in chunks starting at different initialization

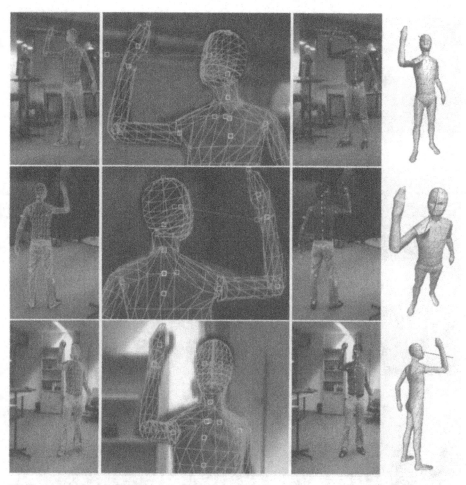

Fig. 3. A single tracked frame from the upper-body dart sequence with human model as seen from three cameras. The first column shows the outer model overlaid on the original images. The second column shows a zoomed in view of the same images. The third column shows the inner model. The last column features the 3D human model rendered from arbitrary virtual viewpoints.

points. Successful tracking has been observed for up to 1500 frames at once, using 5000 particles. We recommend to use at least 2000 particles for full-body tracking.

A critical part of the tracking when using only silhouette information is the head, as it is not well distinguishable from different perspectives. This results in shaky motions of the head. We propose to fix this problem in the future by considering color appearance at least on the head part, as this would provide a more informed estimate of the head position due to the distinct appearance from different sides (skin, eyes, hair). Other tracking problems occur when tracking in natural environments with occlusions caused by tables or other furniture. Such situations could be improved by using more cameras, however this comes at a higher computational cost. Inaccuracies in the silhouette extraction due to problems in the background subtraction step (changing lighting,

Fig. 4. Screenshots of the first camera from full-body tracking sequence

shadows, bad color contrast) can be dealt with to a certain amount, but become a problem when whole body parts, e.g. arms, disappear. We plan to increase the robustness of our tracking by extending the silhouette based approach with an appearance model and by integrating optical flow predictions into the motion model of the particle filters.

6   Conclusion

We have presented our take on human motion capture and introduced the human model *RAMSIS* in this context. The following advantages come with the use of this model: First, *RAMSIS* has been specifically designed under ergonomic and anthropometric considerations, making it especially valuable in the context of human motion analysis.

Second, a realistic and detailed outer model and a flexible parameterization with respect to different human appearances make it a powerful model in many possible scenarios. Third, our introduced optimizations such as caching and ergonomically sound dimensionality reduction make it easy to use and computationally competitive for particle filter based tracking applications. We have shown successful and accurate markerless tracking for upper-body (35 DOF) and full-body (51 DOF) sequences captured by three cameras, using only silhouette information extracted with standard background subtraction techniques and an intelligent hierarchical decomposition of the human pose space.

References

1. Anguelov, D., Koller, D., Pang, H.-C., Srinivasan, P., Thrun, S.: Recovering articulated object models from 3d range data. In: AUAI 2004: Proceedings of the 20th conference on Uncertainty in artificial intelligence, Arlington, Virginia, United States, pp. 18–26. AUAI Press (2004)
2. Balan, A.O., Sigal, L., Black, M.J.: A quantitative evaluation of video-based 3d person tracking. In: ICCCN 2005: Proceedings of the 14th International Conference on Computer Communications and Networks, Washington, DC, USA, pp. 349–356. IEEE Computer Society, Los Alamitos (2005)
3. Bray, M., Koller-Meier, E., Gool, L.V.: Smart particle filtering for high-dimensional tracking. Computer Vision and Image Understanding (CVIU) 106(1), 116–129 (2007)
4. Bubb, H., Engstler, F., Fritzsche, F., Mergl, C., Sabbah, O., Schaefer, P., Zacher, I.: The development of RAMSIS in past and future as an example for the cooperation between industry and university. International Journal of Human Factors Modelling and Simulation 1(1), 140–157 (2006)
5. Cheung, K.M., Baker, S., Kanade, T.: Shape-from-silhouette of articulated objects and its use for human body kinematics estimation and motion capture. In: Proceedings of the IEEE Conference on Computer Vision and Pattern Recognition (June 2003)
6. Deutscher, J., Reid, I.: Articulated body motion capture by stochastic search. International Journal of Computer Vision (IJCV) 61(2), 185–205 (2005)
7. Doucet, A., Godsill, S., Andrieu, C.: On sequential monte carlo sampling methods for bayesian filtering. Statistics and Computing 10(3), 197–208 (2000)
8. Grauman, K., Shakhnarovich, G., Darrell, T.: Inferring 3d structure with a statistical image-based shape model. In: ICCV 2003: Proceedings of the Ninth IEEE International Conference on Computer Vision, Washington, DC, USA, p. 641. IEEE Computer Society, Los Alamitos (2003)
9. Kehl, R., Gool, L.V.: Markerless tracking of complex human motions from multiple views. Computer Vision and Image Understanding (CVIU) 104(2), 190–209 (2006)
10. MacCormick, J., Isard, M.: Partitioned sampling, articulated objects, and interface-quality hand tracking. In: Vernon, D. (ed.) ECCV 2000. LNCS, vol. 1843, pp. 3–19. Springer, Heidelberg (2000)
11. Moeslund, T.B., Granum, E.: A survey of computer vision-based human motion capture. Computer Vision and Image Understanding (CVIU) 81(3), 231–268 (2001)
12. Moeslund, T.B., Hilton, A., Krüger, V.: A survey of advances in vision-based human motion capture and analysis. Computer Vision and Image Understanding (CVIU) 104(2), 90–126 (2006)
13. Poppe, R.: Vision-based human motion analysis: An overview. Computer Vision and Image Understanding (CVIU) 108(1-2), 4–18 (2007)

14. Rosenhahn, B., Brox, T., Kersting, U., Smith, A., Gurney, J., Klette, R.: A system for marker-less motion capture. Künstliche Intelligenz 20(1), 45–51 (2006)
15. Seitz, T., Recluta, D., Zimmermann, D.: An approach for a human posture prediction model using internal/external forces and discomfort. In: Proceedings of the SAE 2005 World Congress (2005)
16. Taylor, G.W., Hinton, G.E., Roweis, S.T.: Modeling human motion using binary latent variables. In: Proc. of the 20th Annual Conference on Neural Information Processing Systems (NIPS), pp. 1345–1352. MIT Press, Cambridge (2006)
17. Urtasun, R., Fleet, D., Fua, P.: 3D People Tracking with Gaussian Process Dynamical Models. In: Conference on Computer Vision and Pattern Recognition, pp. 238–245 (2006)

A Deformable Surface Model with Volume Preserving Springs

Sylvester Arnab and Vinesh Raja

University of Warwick
CV4 7AL, Coventry, UK
s.arnab@warwick.ac.uk

Abstract. This paper discusses the possibility of employing a surface model to emulate volume behaviour. This is inspired by a significant interest in employing the surface data due to its simplicity. However, there are issues in properties estimation and volume preservation. Therefore, the aim of the ongoing research includes exploring the potential of a surface mass spring model with shape-preserving springs for volume simulation. Initial evaluations illustrate the feasibility of employing a mass spring model with volume preserving springs to simulate the dynamic behaviour of a soft volume. The proposed framework can be further explored to address other material properties.

Keywords: Deformable Model, Mass Spring Systems, Volume Preservation.

1 Introduction

The dynamic behaviour of human organs can be replicated using the soft solid simulation techniques. These organs are initially modelled into 3 dimensional volumes based on medical data such as CT/MRI scans. This volume data can then be rendered in a virtual environment based on the organ's material and mechanical properties. The haptic devices provide the tactile interaction with the model in the virtual environment, which makes it more useful in areas such as the medical training.

However, due to the benefit of having a less complex mesh network, surface data is increasingly being utilised to emulate volumetric solid behaviour. The main issue is constant volume preservation as well as correct volume behaviour during simulation. Generally, a surface model would collapse under gravity and without the internal volume, determining the correct deformation effect would be a challenge.

2 Related Works

Commonly, surface data is re-meshed in order to create internal volume. However, this creates computational overhead during simulation imposed by a more complex volume network. The addition of new artificial springs [1] to the existing volume mesh produces a stiffer object [2]. [3] [4] addressed shape preservation and [2] introduced weighted constraints that control the deformation distribution of the muscle

F.J. Perales and R.B. Fisher (Eds.): AMDO 2008, LNCS 5098, pp. 259–268, 2008.

instead of using additional springs. However, this method is fundamentally focusing on the local radius of influence of the interaction and is not influenced by the orientation of the interaction force.

A more effective shape preserving method has been embedded into the Mass Spring Systems (MSS) where springs are placed at the nodes. They are also known as the Local Shape Memory [5]. These springs have been employed to simulate non-linear skin behaviour of a virtual thigh [6] [7]. [8] administered these springs to preserve object shape during simulation. However, the stiffness of the springs was either statistically fine-tuned based on predefined properties [9] or regularly distributed. [10] extended this method by extracting the properties of the springs based on radial links [11][12].

Volume behaviour is influenced by the properties estimated for the model. Regular properties distribution is very common where the regular node concentration is assumed [1] [13] [14] [15]. In the case of irregular node concentrations, the mesh topology is modified to be as regular as possible [16] [17]. However, when a portion of the surface model is refined, the regular topology becomes irregular. Consequently, the properties require re-estimation within the refined area. [8] attempted properties re-estimation after surface refinement but the behaviour patterns between the coarse and the refined area do not coincide. The behaviour has been improved by our method discussed in [10] where these patterns achieve a higher level of co-incidence.

3 The Proposed Deformable Model

The scope of dynamic behaviour in this research is within a constrained space such as a human breast fixed on a static body (Fig. 1). The model is constructed from the surface mesh and the dynamic behaviour is achieved by employing the surface MSS with volume preserving springs.

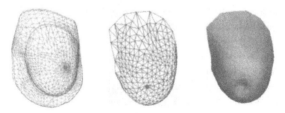

Fig. 1. A breast model (geometrical mesh and rendered model)

To address the issue of properties estimation as well as the non-existence of inner volume for the proposed surface model, the object's internal volume represented by the surface elements has to be considered. This framework extended the scheme described in [10], where a surface mass spring systems with additional shape preserving springs are employed.

3.1 Surface Mass Spring Systems (SMSS)

The SMSS is based on the surface mesh topology where the springs are represented by the edges of the triangular elements (Fig. 2). For instance, the edge that connects the nodes with mass m_i and m_j is the spring with stiffness k_{ij}.

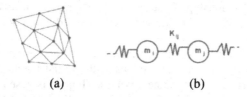

(a)   (b)

Fig. 2. a) Nodes connected by edges (b) A pair of nodes connected by a spring

For the spring link ij, the internal force F_{ij} is

$$F_{ij} = K_{ij}\left(\|p_j - p_i\| - l_{ij}\right)\frac{p_j - p_i}{\|p_j - p_i\|}, \tag{1}$$

where $\|p_j - p_i\|$ is the magnitude of the displacement of the current state of the spring link ij, l_{ij} is the rest length of the spring link, and K_{ij} is the stiffness (spring) coefficient of the node pair. The spring stiffness is estimated based on a distribution algorithm described in [10] [13] [18] [19].

3.2 Volume Preserving Springs

The proposed volume springs (Fig. 3) are commonly utilised to preserve the shape of the model at equilibrium. They behave in a similar way as the surface spring but the rest length of each spring is zero.

Fig. 3. The inner spring that provides a volumetric support to the mass at i

Based on Equation (1), the reaction force imposed on the mass at node i,

$$F_i = K_i\left(\|p'_i - p_i\|\right)\frac{p'_i - p_i}{\|p'_i - p_i\|}, \tag{2}$$

where K_i is the stiffness of the inner spring at node i, p'_i is the new position of node i at runtime and p_i is the anchored position of node i. In order to not only preserve the object shape but also maintain a constant volume during simulation, the concept of these shape preserving springs has been extended.

3.3 Volume Discretisation for Properties Estimation

The relationship between the deformable model and the real material is important. The elasticity modulus of a material is extracted from the stress and strain relationship, where a constant magnitude of force is imposed along the axis parallel to the normal of the surface. The initial volume discretisation supported by each node should support this relationship. In a MSS, force directly influences the dynamic behaviour of the nodes. Therefore, the volume supported by a node should be discretised along its normal.

The radial link method in [10] is extended, where the new distance vector with length L'_i, relative to the object centre of mass, the initial length L_i and the surface normal at the node, are derived. The new volume (Fig. 4) is based on node i relative to the new centre point c_i and the other nodes or vertices of the triangular element. The new L'_i is the scalar projection of L_i along the normal unit vector of point i. This explicit method guides the estimation of mass and spring stiffness for all nodes relative to their respective normals and neighbouring triangles.

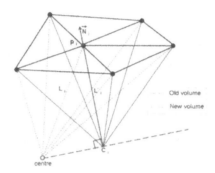

Fig. 4. Volume discretisation relative to the normal at node i

3.4 Properties Estimation

Based on the discretisation (Fig. 4), mass at node i is estimated as

$$m_i = \frac{\sum_{i \in t} V_i}{\sum_{j=0}^{n} V_j} M \; ,$$

where the estimation ratio for each node is the total volume under the neighbouring triangular elements t (of which node i is a member) divided by the total volume for all n nodes, and M is the object mass.

The stiffness of the volume preserving springs describes the level of elasticity of the virtual space or volume represented by the node. Therefore, the value of the stiffness is influenced by the stress and strain relationship along the axis parallel to the normal at the node. The stiffness dimension based on Young's Modulus and shear modulus is initialised before the simulation. The dimension is defined as

$$\begin{bmatrix} K_E \\ K_G \end{bmatrix}_i = E \sum_{i \in I} \frac{V_i}{L'^2_i} \begin{bmatrix} 1 \\ 1/2(1-v) \end{bmatrix},$$

where, K_E and K_G are the spring stiffness based on linear elasticity modulus and shear (rigidity) modulus respectively, E is the Young's Modulus and v is the Poisson Ratio of the material.

The behaviour of the spring stiffness at runtime depends on the orientation of the acting force along each spring. The stiffness K_i of the spring at each node i can be determined at runtime:

$$K_i = \left[\left\| \vec{N}_i \cdot \vec{F}_i \right\| \quad 1 - \left\| \vec{N}_i \cdot \vec{F}_i \right\| \right] \begin{bmatrix} K_E \\ K_G \end{bmatrix}_i,$$

where N and F are the normal and force at node i.

3.5 Volume Preservation

In order to preserve volume during simulation, the spring dimension can be extended to address other properties such as bulk elasticity as a factor against volume variation during simulation. Bulk stiffness K_B at node i is

$$K_{Bi} = \frac{E}{3(1-2v)} \sum_{i \in I} \frac{V_i}{L'^2_i}$$

Volume displacement during simulation can be derived based on the volume calculation employed in [2]. This calculation will be correct even when the surface becomes concave during simulation. Therefore, force at node i along its normal unit vector at a time step without any external force interaction on the surface is

$$F_i = K_{Bi} \Delta V w_i \vec{N}_i , \tag{3}$$

where ΔV is the volume displacement, and w_i is the constraint that controls the distribution of the volume penalty force. The constraint is set to 1, which means volume change affects all nodes equally but constrained by their respective bulk stiffness. Therefore, in order to correctly distribute the interaction force effect to the object surface, the constraint is estimated based on the interaction radius of influence where, the sum of the constraints is equal to the number of nodes. The radius of influence [2] has been modified and the interaction force orientation is introduced as the correction factor. If the surface nodes are within the radius of influence r, weight at node i is

$$w_i = \left(\frac{P_i - P_f}{\left\| P_i - P_f \right\|} \cdot \vec{F}_f \right) \left(\cos \left(\frac{\left\| P_i - P_f \right\|}{r * 2} * \pi \right) \right) . \tag{4}$$

where p_i and p_f are the position vector of node i and the position of where force is imposed respectively. Since the sum of weighted constraints is equal to the number of nodes [2], the constraint values have to be normalised. Therefore, based on Equation (3) and (4), the penalty force at node i is

$$F_i = K_B \Delta V w_i \frac{P_i - P_f}{\left\| P_i - P_f \right\|} .$$

4   Empirical Experiments

The framework for the experiments has been implemented on top of Microsoft Visual C++, OpenGL and OpenHaptics platforms. Phantom Desktop haptic device enables interaction and the desktop PC has the specification of Intel Pentium 4, 2.40 GHz and 1 G RAM. Each time step denotes 0.01 s. To evaluate the estimation method and the feasibility of having a 3 dimensional stiffness, 2 schemes have been compared:

- **Scheme A:** Irregular mass and inner stiffness (single stiffness dimension)
- **Scheme B:** The Proposed Estimation

Further comparisons are carried out against the Finite Element Model (FEM) and volume MSS (VMSS). The elasticity modulus is re-extracted from the model to evaluate if the proposed model emulates the same material behaviour.

4.1   Properties Estimation

To evaluate properties estimation, a local area is refined and the properties are then re-estimated. A constant force is imposed on a node and the displacement data is collected. The displacement patterns within the coarse and the refined area are compared. If the patterns are identical, the deformation behaviour is preserved despite the change in the mesh topology. The displacement behaviours are studied where 2 values are analysed:

- i)   The standard deviation between the 2 patterns determines their level of co-incidence. The smaller the standard deviation, the more identical the patterns are
- ii)   The mean deviation of the 2 patterns represents the error in behaviour after refinement. The least value indicates the least deviation from the original behaviour

Fig. 5 describes the findings based on a sphere model with irregular mesh topology to illustrate the concept. The standard deviations comparison in 5(a) shows that B produces high level of co-incidence between the patterns. Furthermore, it maintains a minimal displacement deviation for any magnitude of force compared to A which deviation increases with force (5(b)). Hence, the analysis concludes that B preserves the properties and behaviour with minimal standard deviation when a local area is refined. Tests have been carried out on models with various mesh complexities and they also draw similar conclusions.

The stiffness of the springs is based on the real elasticity properties of the material. Therefore, to evaluate scheme B, the Young's modulus (E) can be derived from the strain and stress relationship of the deformable model and compared to the original E. The values (Table 1) demonstrate that the deformable surface model can closely emulate the volume material behaviour.

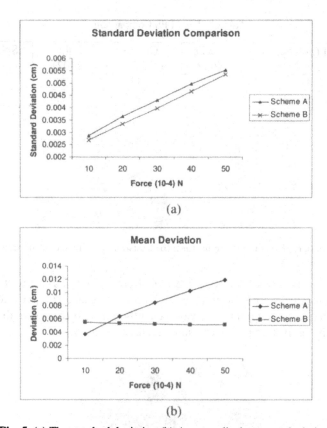

Fig. 5. (a) The standard deviation (b) Average displacement deviation

Table 1. The Young's Modulus (E) extracted from the model when a constant stretching force is imposed on the surface of a cube

Model (nodes)	Cube (602)	Cube (1352)	Cube (2402)
E (67 Pascal)	67.80	66.80	67.00
E (100 Pascal)	100.07	98.70	98.70
E (3.25 Kpa)	3.30	3.17	3.11

4.2 Performance

A simple performance test has been carried out to illustrate that the surface data reduces the computational cost. Table 2 shows that the average frame per second (FPS) achieved by the VMSS and the proposed surface model.

4.3 Volume Behaviour

To produce a more realistic global deformation based on the interaction force radius and orientation of influence, the weighted constraint is manipulated at runtime.

Table 2. Total FPS Comparison

Model (number of surface nodes)	Cube (602)	Cube (1352)	Cube (2402)	Sphere (1000)
VMSS	77	37	20	47
Scheme B	80	44	25	77

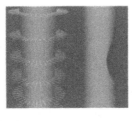
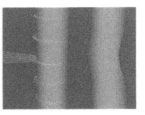

Fig. 6. (a) Constraints are uniform (b) Constraints extracted at runtime

When the constraints are set to 1, the global deformation as in Fig. 6 (a) is produced. Upon interaction, the constraint at each node is updated in regards to the radius and the interaction force orientation. Consequently, figure 6 (b) shows that the automatic constraint derivation produces a more realistic behaviour.

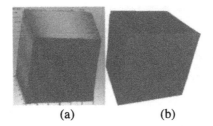

(a)   (b)

Fig. 7. Shape comparison (a) FEM (b) Scheme B

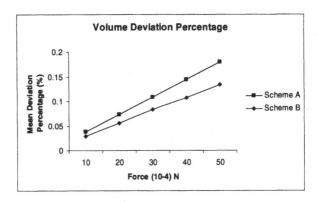

Fig. 8. The percentage of the average volume deviation

Other models such as cubes with different surface mesh complexities have been compared with the FEM model as analysed by SolidWorks/Cosmos. A shear force is imposed on the top surface while the opposite surface is fixed. When compared with FEM, the shape produced is similar with minor deviation (Fig. 7).

When a constant force is imposed on the surface, the object shape changes and deforms. The analysis concludes that scheme B preserves the object volume with the least volume deviation as illustrated in Fig. 8.

5 Conclusions

This paper has illustrated the feasibility of employing a surface mesh to simulate soft volume. The proposed framework introduces volumetric discretisation based on the node normal, the anisotropic extraction of inner spring relative to force orientation as well as weighted constraints to control global deformation effect. Local deformation behaviour is preserved regardless of the mesh resolutions and global deformation effect is achieved despite the non-existence of internal volume. It displays similar behaviour with the FEM model and produces minimal deviation from the original elasticity modulus. Furthermore, the computational performance is better than the volume counterpart. Even though the proposed method is based on materials that are linearly elastic, homogeneous and incompressible, it can also be extended to address other properties.

The framework is currently explored in the ongoing research in breast simulation. Further evaluations such as the perception test with the users will be carried out to verify the visual and haptic feedback experienced by the users.

References

1. Bourguignon, D., Cani, M.P.: Controlling Anisotropy in Mass-Spring Systems. Computer Animation and Simulation, 113–123 (2000)
2. Hong, M., Jung, S., Choi, M., Welch, S.: Fast Volume Preservation for a Mass-Spring System. IEEE Computer Graphics and Applications, 83–91 (September/October 2006)
3. Nedel, L.P., Thalmann, D.: Real-Time Muscle Deformations Using Mass Spring Systems. In: Proc. Computer Graphics Int'l, pp. 156–165. IEEE Press, Los Alamitos (1998)
4. Aubel, A., Thalmann, D.: Realistic Deformation of Human Body Shapes. In: Proc. Computer Animation and Simulation 2000, Interlaken, August 2000, pp. 125–135 (2000)
5. Marchal, M., Promayon, E., Troccaz, J.: Simulating Complex Organ Interactions: Evaluation of a Soft Tissue Discrete Model. In: Bebis, G., Boyle, R., Koracin, D., Parvin, B. (eds.) ISVC 2005. LNCS, vol. 3804, pp. 175–182. Springer, Heidelberg (2005)
6. Mendoza, C., Sundaraj, K., Laugier, C.: Issues in Deformable Virtual Objects Simulation with Force Feedback. In: International Advanced Robotics Program (IARP): International Workshop on Human Robot Interfaces, Rome, Italy (2002)
7. Laugier, C., Mendoza, C., Sundaraj, K.: Towards a Realistic Medical Simulator using Virtual Environments and Haptic Interaction. In: Robotics Research: The Tenth International Symposium, Springer Tracts in Advanced Robotics, vol. 6. Springer, Heidelberg (2003)
8. Choi, Y., Hong, M., Choi, M., Kim, M.: Adaptive Surface-deformable Model with Shape-preserving Spring. Journals of Computer Animation and Virtual Worlds 16, 69–83 (2005)

9. Zhang, J., Payandeh, S., Dill, J.: Haptic Subdivision: an Approach to Defining Level-of-Detail in Haptic Rendering. In: Proceedings of the 10 Symposium on Haptic Interfaces for Virtual Environment and Teleoperator Systems, Orlando, FL, March, pp. 201–208 (2002)

10. Arnab, S., Raja, V.: Irregular Surface Mesh Topology for Volumetric Deformable Model. In: The 4th INTUITION International Conference and Workshop, Athens, Greece, October 4-5 (2007)

11. Vassilev, T., Spanlang, B.: A Mass-Spring Model for Real Time Deformable Solids. In: Proceedings of East-West Vision 2002, Graz, Austria, September 12-13, pp. 149–154 (2002)

12. Balaniuk, R., Salisbury, K.: Soft Tissue Simulation using the Radial Element Method. In: IS4TM-International Symposium on Surgery Simulation and Soft Tissue Modelling, France, June 12-13 (2003)

13. Gelder, A.V.: Approximate Simulation of Elastic Membranes by Triangulated Spring Meshes. Journal of Graphics Tools 3(2), 21–41 (1998)

14. Delingette, H.: Towards Realistic Soft Tissue Modeling in Medical Simulation. In: Proceedings of the IEEE: Special Issue on Surgery Simulation, April 1998, pp. 512–523 (1998)

15. Brown, J., Sorkin, S., Bruyns, C.: Real Time Simulation of Deformable Objects: Tools and Application. In: Comp. Animation (2001)

16. Deussen, O., Kobbelt, T.P.: Using Simulated Annealing to Obtain Good Nodal Approximations of Deformable Objects. In: Computer Animation and Simulation 1995. Springer, Heidelberg (1995)

17. Bielser, D.: A Framework for Open Surgery Simulation, Doctor of Technical Sciences Thesis, Swiss Federal Institute of Technology, ETH, Zurich (2003)

18. Maciel, A., Boulic, R., Thalmann, D.: Towards a Parameterization Method for Virtual Soft Tissues Based on Properties of Biological Tissue. In: International Symposium on Surgery Simulation and Soft Tissue Modeling (2003)

19. Lloyd, B.A., Szekely, G., Harders, M.: Identification of Spring parameters for Deformable Object Simulation. IEEE Transactions on Visualisation and Computer Graphics 13(5) (September/October 2007)

Temporal Nearest End-Effectors for Real-Time Full-Body Human Actions Recognition

Oscar Mena[1], Luis Unzueta[1], Basilio Sierra[2], and Luis Matey[1]

[1] CEIT and Tecnun, University of Navarra. Manuel de Lardizabal 15, 20018
Donostia-San Sebastián, Spain
{omena,lunzueta,lmatey}@ceit.es
http://www.ceit.es/mechanics/index.htm
[2] Computer Engineering Faculty, University of the Basque Country. Manuel de
Lardizabal 1, 20018 Donostia-San Sebastián, Spain
b.sierra@ehu.es
http://www.sc.ehu.es/ccwrobot/index.html

Abstract. In this paper we present a novel method called Temporal Nearest End-Effectors (TNEE) to automatically classify full-body human actions captured in real-time. This method uses a simple representation for modeling actions based exclusively on the recent positions of the user's end-effectors, i.e. hands, head and feet, relative to the pelvis. With this method, the essential information of full-body movements is retained in a reduced form. The recognition procedure combines the evaluation of the performed poses and the temporal coherence. The performance of TNEE is tested with real motion capture data obtaining satisfactory results for real-time applications.

Keywords: Human Action Recognition, Human Tracking, Articulated Motion, End-Effectors.

1 Introduction

One of the biggest issues that an action recognition system has to overcome is to define a representation of actions, i.e. to establish the features that allow the classification of movements. These features are data extracted from the information provided by the motion capture (mocap) system and they are directly dependent on the way it works. If movement is captured using image analysis, the features are extracted from changes that appear in video frames through time. On the other hand, if movement is captured using physical markers located on the user's body, features are extracted from the positions, angles, angle velocities, etc. of these markers.

As stated by Liu et al. [1] data that comes from most mocap systems exhibit considerable redundancy and demonstrate that there can be a reduced set of information, the principal markers, which retain the essential information of movement. In their work they reconstruct full-body postures using as input data only the positions of some markers situated in the areas around the hands,

F.J. Perales and R.B. Fisher (Eds.): AMDO 2008, LNCS 5098, pp. 269–278, 2008.
© Springer-Verlag Berlin Heidelberg 2008

feet, head and the middle of the torso and with this information they search their database using the Random Forest classifier [2]. This way they can obtain postures of which the principal markers are the nearest possible to the current values and from these they can obtain a posture adjusted to the features. Besides, Boulic et al. [3] demonstrate that it is possible to reconstruct upper body postures in real-time with no markers and no human postures database to back it up, having as input data only the positions of the hands, head and a point in the middle of the torso obtained by computer vision algorithms.

Having these results in mind, we present a novel approach, called Temporal Nearest End-Effectors (TNEE), that extends the principal markers philosophy for real-time full-body action recognition instead of motion reconstruction. Therefore we model poses for action labeling following this idea in order to reduce the data to be stored and compared, but maintaining the essence of the semantic movements for a wide range of full-body actions. Apart from the proximity to the learned action poses, the presented recognition procedure also considers their temporal coherence.

In the following section, the reduced form full-body pose model used for action recognition is described. Next, the action recognition procedure is explained in detail. Section 4 comprises a set of tests with real full-body motion capture data, that evaluate the performance of this approach for real-time applications. And finally, we analyze the obtained results and establish the conclusions and the future work derived from them.

2   Full-Body Pose Model for Action Recognition

Classically, in computer graphics, a human pose is determined with the relative rotation angles of the joints and the position of the root joint of the multi-body mechanism that defines the subject. Thus, a high number of degrees of freedom (DOF) is used, in the order of 40, but it may occur that most of them do not really contribute significantly in the performance of a meaningful movement.

On the other hand, we propose to define poses for action recognition with only 15 DOF: the 3D positions of hands, feet and head relative to a coordinate system attached to the pelvis (Fig. 1). This way we extend the philosophy of the work of Liu et al. [1] for action recognition instead of motion reconstruction. The advantages of this representation are multiple:

- The essential information about movement is retained in a significantly reduced form without the need of applying statistical techniques such as PCA.
- Actions can be represented in the same way independently of the position and orientation of the person with respect to the 3D absolute coordinate system.
- These data are easy to be tracked by most mocap systems, even by the computer vision based markerless strategies such as [4], [5], [6] and [7]
- No motion reconstruction is required for action recognition.
- Unlike rotations positions are Euclidean so true distances between positions are much easier to calculate.

– Minor differences in rotations may lead to big differences in posture unlike the cases of minor differences in positions.

On the other hand, its main drawback is that the database necessary to classify actions needs to be rescaled to get the anthropometry of the user. Nevertheless, it can be avoided if we rescale the database in the training phase.

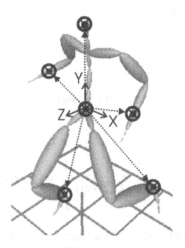

Fig. 1. Full-body pose model for action recognition: relative positions of end-effectors with respect to pelvis

In a marker based mocap system the orientation of the pelvis can be obtained by placing at least three markers on it. On the other hand, in markerless mocap systems the measurement of this orientation is not a straightforward task, but it is possible to estimate it from the detected positions of some body features. Boulic et al. [3] estimate it from the positions of hands, head and pelvis, for the reconstruction of the upper body as in Fig. 2.

The estimation starts from the previous frame's orientation $^{t-1}\mathbf{R}_p$. This initial coordinate system is rotated so as to align its Y axis with the vector that connects the current positions of the pelvis p and head h with Eq. (1).

$$\left.\begin{array}{l} {}^{t-1}\mathbf{y}_p = \frac{{}^{t-1}\mathbf{p}_h - {}^{t-1}\mathbf{p}_p}{|{}^{t-1}\mathbf{p}_h - {}^{t-1}\mathbf{p}_p|} \\ {}^{t}\mathbf{y}_p = \frac{{}^{t}\mathbf{p}_h - {}^{t}\mathbf{p}_p}{|{}^{t}\mathbf{p}_h - {}^{t}\mathbf{p}_p|} \\ \mathbf{u}_{rot1} = \frac{{}^{t-1}\mathbf{y}_p \times {}^{t}\mathbf{y}_p}{|{}^{t-1}\mathbf{y}_p \times {}^{t}\mathbf{y}_p|} \\ \theta_{rot1} = \arccos({}^{t-1}\mathbf{y}_p \cdot {}^{t}\mathbf{y}_p) \end{array}\right\} \quad ({}^{t}\mathbf{R}_p)_{step1} = \mathbf{R}(\mathbf{u}_{rot1}, \theta_{rot1})({}^{t-1}\mathbf{R}_p) \qquad (1)$$

Then the resulting orientation is rotated around the Y axis to align the X axis with the weighted average vector obtained from its previous orientation and the XZ projection of the vector that connects the current positions of right and left hands (rh and lh) with Eq. (2).

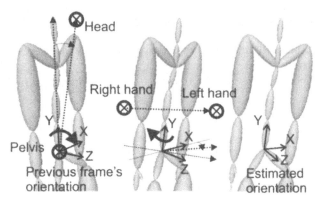

Fig. 2. Estimation of the orientation of the pelvis from the captured positions of hands, pelvis and head

$$
\left.
\begin{aligned}
\mathbf{u}_{rot2} &= \frac{{}^{t-1}\mathbf{x}_p \times ({}^{t}\mathbf{p}_{lh} - {}^{t}\mathbf{p}_{rh})^{XZ}}{|{}^{t-1}\mathbf{x}_p \times ({}^{t}\mathbf{p}_{lh} - {}^{t}\mathbf{p}_{rh})^{XZ}|} \\
\theta_{rot2} &= \frac{w}{2} \arccos\left({}^{t-1}\mathbf{x}_p \cdot \frac{({}^{t}\mathbf{p}_{lh} - {}^{t}\mathbf{p}_{rh})^{XZ}}{|({}^{t}\mathbf{p}_{lh} - {}^{t}\mathbf{p}_{rh})^{XZ}|}\right) \\
w &\in [0, 2]
\end{aligned}
\right\} \quad {}^{t}\mathbf{R}_p = \mathbf{R}(\mathbf{u}_{rot2}, \theta_{rot2})({}^{t}\mathbf{R}_p)_{step1}
$$

$$(2)$$

This way, a pelvis orientation that moves with a certain damping with respect to the movements of hands is obtained. The resulting pelvis movements are satisfactory enough for a wide set of movements such as walking, running or jumping.

This pose model does not include neither the absolute position nor the orientation of the pelvis because actions should be recognized independently from them. The inclusion of the height of the pelvis could be helpful for the recognition of actions such as jumping or falling but it could also be disturbing for actions being performed at different heights so it is not added. In any case, as stated by Gonzàlez i Sabaté [8], actions need the user to adopt some specific postures in order to be recognized.

3   Action Recognition Procedure

Once the user's desired features are tracked, a classifier tries to tag input features with a previously known class. Classification accuracy depends on several factors: training set, classifier adjustment parameters, data origin, etc. The correct choice of them is decisive for obtaining good predictions. The classifiers used the most for action recognition are the following: Hidden Markov Models (HMM), K-Nearest Neighbors (K-NN), Neural Networks, Kernel methods such as Support Vector Machines (SVM) and Relevant Vector Machines (RVM), Bayesian Networks and the Expectation-Maximization algorithm. A review of these methods can be found in the work of Jain et al. [9] and Mitchel [10].

Ibarguren et al. [11] demonstrate the robustness of K-NN (with K=1, i.e. 1-NN) with real data in the recognition of static hand gestures. In their posterior work [12] they use the distance to enhance the classification rates having only one learned posture per class in the database. On the other hand, our purpose is to detect full-body movements while they are being performed instead of static poses distinguished from gesture transition periods. Hence, apart from the proximity to the action poses it is also necessary to quantify the temporal correctness. The TNEE approach makes an evaluation of the movement history making a weighted measure of the performed most recent poses in which weights indicate the movement progression. Thus, the class corresponding to the movement being performed is that with the nearest poses and the most likely temporal advance.

Consider we have n classes in the database $D = (C_1, C_2, ..., C_i, ..., C_n)$ and a movement M_x to be labeled. These consist on animations of full-body poses modeled as expressed in section 2. The animations of the database are resampled to a certain user defined number of frames f to relieve the database from too large animations. The unknown action M_x must be tagged per frame in a real-time application in order to adapt to action changes during the motion capture. To achieve it, we focus on the p most recent postures of the movements. The unknown action M_x will correspond to a class of D if the majority of its p most recent poses are labeled as belonging to that class. This pose labeling is achieved by obtaining two measurements. First, the average nearest proximity to each class calculated from of its $p - 1$ predecessors and itself with Eq. (3). And secondly, a count of votes of the temporal advance with Algorithm 1 for each class ($nVotes_i$), where a pose index refers to the frame position on the class ($poseIndex \in [1, f]$).

$$averageMinDist_{C_i} = \frac{\sum_{j=1}^{p} minDist(pose_j, poses_{C_i})}{p} \tag{3}$$

These two measurements are combined in order to obtain a weighted proximity measure to each class with Eq. (4). Thus, each of the most recent poses is labeled according to its nearest distance. The more proximal are the performed poses and the higher is the temporal advance continuity respect to a class, the most likely it is to label the new input.

$$weightedAverageMinDist_{C_i} \begin{cases} = \frac{averageMinDist_{C_i}}{nVotes_i}, \text{ if } nVotes_i > 0 \\ = averageMinDist_{C_i}, \text{ if } nVotes_i = 0 \end{cases} \tag{4}$$

4 Experimental Results

In order to evaluate the performance of the TNEE approach we have run the following set of tests. The database is composed of 12 sequences obtained from a marker-based mocap system containing one action each labeled as: climb

Algorithm 1. Temporal Advance Counting Algorithm

1: **procedure** TEMPORALADVANCECOUNTING($recentPoses, poses_{C_i}$)
2:     $nVotes_i \Leftarrow 0$
3:     $nearestPoseIndex_i \Leftarrow -1$
4:     $previousIndex_i \Leftarrow -1$
5:     **for** $j = 1$ to p **do**
6:         $nearestPoseIndex_i \Leftarrow$ getNearestPoseIndex($recentPoses_j$)
7:         **if** $nearestPoseIndex_i > previousIndex_i$ **then**
8:             $nVotes_i \Leftarrow nVotes_i + 1$
9:         **end if**
10:         $previousIndex_i \Leftarrow nearestPoseIndex_i$
11:     **end for**
12:     **return** $nVotes_i$
13: **end procedure**

(CLB), jump normal (JNL), jump sideways (JSW), push (PSH), run (RUN), swim breaststroke (SBS), swim butterfly (SBF), swim crollstroke (SCS), walk normal (WNL), walk stiff (WSF), walk zombie (WZB) and washing windows (WWS) (Fig. 3).

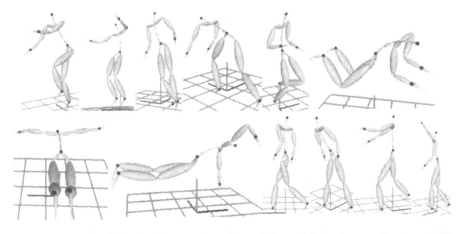

Fig. 3. Snapshots of the database actions. From left to right and top to bottom: CLB, JNL, JSW, PSH, RUN, SBS, SBF, SCS, WNL, WSF, WZB and WWS.

Each action is resampled to 100 frames, therefore there are 1200 poses in the database. Tests consist in running similar sequences performing these actions and computing the frames in which actions are being correctly labeled. The recognition rate is calculated as the relation between the number of correctly labeled frames and the total number of answered frames. The number of frames in the testing sequences are the following: CLB (170), JNL (300), JSW (156), PSH (610), RUN (148), SBS (861), SBF (344), SCS (962), WNL (247), WSF

(463), WZB (214) and WWS (251). In these, pelvis' orientations are estimated as explained in section 2 while in the database animations they are already known. The number of the considered most recent frames is set to 50, so labeling answers occur from that frame on. The testing user's height is of 1.78 m, which differs from those of the database animations, so they have been rescaled accordingly.

In this way, the obtained total recognition rate is of 93.53% and its confusion matrix is shown in Table 1. With the addition of a random noise of 1 cm of amplitude, which is considerable, the result descends slightly to 91.22%. It can be seen that five classes are perfectly recognized (JSW, RUN, SBF, SCS and WZB). While in the rest there are some errors that have to be taken into account. It has to be noticed that the worst case is the WNL class in which 36 frames are classified as RUN and 22 as WSF. Even so, the whole average provides promising expectatives from the presented experiments. Fig. 4 and 5 show four graphics each for the three best classification results in the SBS and WNL test sequences: (1) the distances to nearest frames, (2) the temporal advance, (3) the average minimal distances, and (4) the weighted average minimal distances.

Table 1. Confusion matrix of the labeled frames

Assigned Class	Real Class											
	CLB	JNL	JSW	PSH	RUN	SBS	SBF	SCS	WNL	WSF	WZB	WWS
CLB	101			5								
JNL		219										3
JSW		13	106									
PSH	13			555								
RUN	6				98				36	45		
SBS						785						
SBF					26		294					7
SCS								912				
WNL		18							139			
WSF									22	368		
WZB											164	
WWS												191

In Fig. 4 it can be seen that the action labeling would be incorrect considering only the distance graphics. However, the combination of both the average minimal distance and temporal advance votes results in a more clear differentiation between the SBS label and the rest, leading to a much better classification. On the other hand, in Fig. 5 it can be seen that WNL obtains better results in distances graphics but in temporal advance graph the results are not so clear, which leads to confusion in some frames. Nevertheless, due to the much better results in the postural distances, most of times along the sequence the action is correctly labeled.

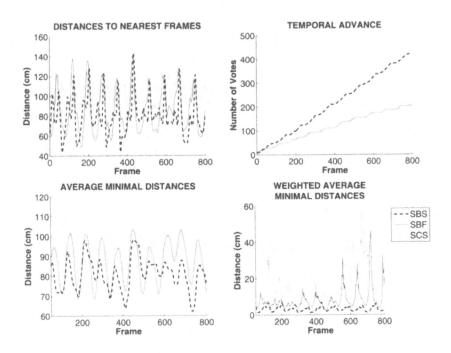

Fig. 4. The three best classification results in the SBS test sequence

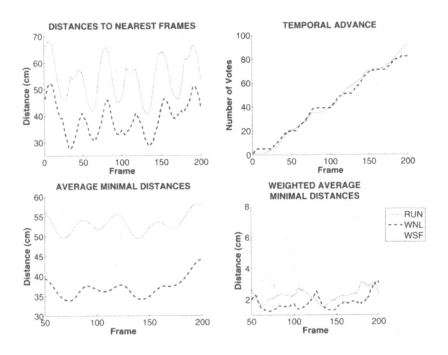

Fig. 5. The three best classification results in the WNL test sequence

5 Conclusions and Future Work

In this paper we have presented a new approach called TNEE, to automatically label full-body human movements in real-time applications. Human poses are modeled in a reduced form following the philosophy of the principal markers of Liu et al. [1]. This way full-body poses are defined with 15 DOF corresponding to the 3D positions of hands, head and feet respect to the pelvis, which retain the essential information of movements for a wide range of full-body actions. The recognition procedure classifies movements taking in consideration both the proximity to the performed poses and the temporal progression respect to the database classes. This way, most plausible actions are those with the nearest poses and the highest temporal advance continuities. Results indicate that this approach is able to distinguish real and proximal human actions, such as different walking styles, with a total recognition rate of 93.53%. Future work will focus in the improvement of the recognition procedure in order to distinguish combined actions being performed at the same time but stored in the database independently. The real-time automatic extraction of the body features that retain the semantic gestures, for the generalization of movements labeling to any kind of action, will also be explored.

Acknowledgments. This work has been supported by AmIGUNE research program promoted by the Basque Government, the Association of Friends of the University of Navarra (Amigos de la Universidad de Navarra), the Ministry of Education of Spain within the framework of the Torres Quevedo Program, and cofunded by the European Social Fund. The motion capture data used in this project was obtained from http://mocap.cs.cmu.edu. This database was created with funding from NSF EIA-0196217.

References

1. Liu, G., Zhang, J., Wang, W., McMillan, L.: Human Motion Estimation from a Reduced Marker Set. In: Proceedings of the 2006 Symposium on Interactive 3D Graphics and Games, Boston, MA, USA (2006)
2. Breiman, L.: Random Forests. Machine Learning 45(1), 5–32 (2001)
3. Boulic, R., Varona, J., Unzueta, L., Peinado, M., Suescun, Á., Perales, F.J.: Evaluation of on-line analytic and numeric inverse kinematics approaches driven by partial vision input. Virtual Reality 10, 48–61 (2006)
4. Wren, C., Azarbayejani, A., Darrell, T., Pentland, A.: Pfinder: Real-time Tracking of the Human Body. IEEE Transactions on Pattern Analysis and Machine Intelligence (1997)
5. Theobalt, C., Magnor, M., Schueler, P., Seidel, H.P.: Combining 2D Feature Tracking and Volume Reconstruction for Online Video-Based Human Motion Capture. In: Proceedings of Pacific Graphics, Beijing, China, pp. 96–103 (2002)
6. Kolsch, M., Turk, M.: Fast Hand Tracking with Flock of Features and Multi-Cue Integration. In: Proceedings of the IEEE Computer Society Conference on Computer Vision and Pattern Recognition Workshops (2004)

7. Varona, J., Buades, J.M., Perales, F.J.: Hands and face tracking for VR applications. International Journal of Systems & Applications in Computer Graphics 29, 179–187 (2005)
8. Gonzàlez i Sabaté, J.: Human Sequence Evaluation: the Key-Frame Approach. PhD Thesis. University of Barcelona. Bellaterra, Spain (2004)
9. Jain, A.K., Duin, R.P.W., Mao, J.: Statistical Pattern Recognition: A Review. IEEE Transactions on Pattern Analysis and Machine Intelligence 22(1), 4–37 (2000)
10. Mitchel, T.: Machine Learning. McGraw-Hill, New York (1997)
11. Ibarguren, A., Maurtua, I., Sierra, B.: Recognition of sign language in real time through Data Gloves. In: Borrajo, D., Castillo, L., Corchado, J.M. (eds.) CAEPIA 2007. LNCS (LNAI), vol. 4788, pp. 307–316. Springer, Heidelberg (2007)
12. Ibarguren, A., Maurtua, I., Sierra, B.: Layered Architecture for Real-Time Sign Recognition (Submitted to The Computer Journal)

Fusing Edge Cues to Handle Colour Problems in Image Segmentation

I. Huerta[1], A. Amato[1], J. Gonzàlez[2], and J.J. Villanueva[1]

[1] Dept. d'Informàtica, Computer Vision Centre, Edifici O. Campus UAB, 08193,
Bellaterra, Spain
[2] Institut de Robòtica i Informàtica Ind. UPC, Llorens i Artigas 4-6,
08028, Barcelona, Spain
Ivan.Huerta@cvc.uab.es

Abstract. This paper presents a new background subtraction algorithm
for mobile objects segmentation from a static background scene. Firstly,
a case analysis of colour-motion segmentation problems is presented.
Secondly, an architecture which fuses colour, intensity and edge cues is
developed to cope the motion segmentation problems presented in the
case analysis. Our approach first combines both colour and intensity
cues in order to solve problems, such as saturation or the lack of the
colour when the background model is built. Nonetheless, some colours
problems presented in the case analysis are not solved yet, such as the
camouflage in chroma. Then, in order to solve this problems a new cue
based on edges is proposed. Finally, our approach which fuses colour,
intensity and edge cues is presented, thereby obtaining accurate motion
segmentation in both indoor and outdoor scenes.

1 Introduction

The evaluation of human motion in image sequences involves different tasks,
such as acquisition, detection (motion segmentation and target classification),
tracking, action recognition, behaviour reasoning, and natural language modelling. However, the basis for high-level interpretation of observed patterns of
human motion still relies on *when* and *where* motion is being detected in the image. Thus, segmentation constitutes the most critical step towards more complex
tasks such as Human Sequence Evaluation (HSE) [2].

Motion segmentation is the extraction of moving objects from a background.
Different techniques have been used for motion segmentation, such as background subtraction, temporal differencing and optical flow [12]. Nevertheless,
motion segmentation is still an open and significant problem due to dynamic
environmental conditions such as illumination changes, shadows, background in
motion (branches in the wind), camouflages, etc.

In order to overcome these difficulties, different techniques can be applied
[9]. The most employed technique is background subtraction which is based on a
background model used to compare the current image with such a model. Among
these background subtraction methods, statistical approaches are very popular:
W[4] use a bimodal distribution; Pfinder [13] uses a single Gaussian to model

F.J. Perales and R.B. Fisher (Eds.): AMDO 2008, LNCS 5098, pp. 279–288, 2008.

the background; Stauffer et al. [3] use a mixture of Gaussians; and Elgammal et al. [1] present a non-parametric background model.

On the other hand, several cues are used in the literature for segmentation process: Horprasert et al. [5] use colour information to classify a pixel as foreground, background, shadow or highlighted background, while Wallflower [11] uses a three-level categorization, namely pixel, region, and frame level. Mckenna et al. [8] and Jabri et al. [7] use colour and edge information, and Shen [10] uses a RGB/HSL colour space plus fuzzy classification.

The information obtained from this step is the base for a wide range of applications such as smart surveillance systems, control applications, advanced user interfaces, motion based diagnosis, identification applications among others.

In this paper an evolved approach based on [6], which handles non-physical changes such as illumination changes, is presented. Huerta et al. [6] cope with those changes based on a casuistry of colour-motion segmentation problems by combining colour and intensity cues. Nevertheless, some problems presented in the casuistry still remain: colour and intensity segmentation cannot differentiate camouflage in chroma (dark and light camouflage) from the local and global illumination changes. In order to solve these problems a new cue based on edges is proposed, and integrated in the previous scheme.

This paper is organized as follows. Next section presents a case analysis of the problems using the different models for motion segmentation. This leads to our approach to confront segmentation. Section 3 explains our approach to solve the above aforementioned problems, such as camouflage in chroma, fusing colour, intensity and edge cues. Experimental results are described in section 4. Lastly, section 5 concludes this contribution and discusses about future work.

2   Problems on Colour Models

Colour information obtained from the recording camera is based on three components which depend on the wavelength λ: the object reflectance R, the illuminant spectral potency distribution E, and the sensor wavelength sensitivity S:

$$S_r = \int_\lambda R(\lambda)E(\lambda)S(\lambda)d\lambda. \tag{1}$$

where S_r is the sensor response.

Unfortunately, the *sensitivity of the sensor* may depend on the luminous intensity which can cause changes in the observed chrominance. In addition, if the *illuminant* changes, the perceived chrominance also changes, so the colour model can be wrongly built.

Fig. 1 shows a case analysis based on a background model which separates the chrominance from the brightness component. The base case is the correct operation of the theoretical colour model, and the anomalies are problems that may appear. The theoretical base case solves some of the segmentation problems, such as sudden or progressive global and local illumination changes (such as shadows and highlights). However, some problems still remain.

Case Analysis (Colour Model Casuistry)					
Cues	Chromatic	Equal			Different
	Brightness	Lower	Equal	Higher	-
Description	Base case	Global shadow Local shadow	Background	Global Highlight Local Highlight	Foreground
	Anomalies	Dark Camouflage Dark Foreground	Camouflage	Light Camouflage Light Foreground	Sensitivity of Sensor Change of illuminant Gleaming surface Saturation Minimum Intensity

Fig. 1. This table analyses the differences between an input image and the background model

First, foreground pixels with the same chrominance component as the background model are not segmented. If the foreground pixel has the same brightness as the background model, then the *Camouflage* problem appears. A *Dark Camouflage* is considered when the pixel has less brightness and it cannot be distinguished from a shadow. Next, *Light Camouflage* happens when the pixel is brighter than the model, therefore the pixel cannot be distinguished from a highlight.

Secondly, *Dark Foreground* denotes pixels which do not have enough intensity to reliably compute the chrominance. Therefore it cannot be compared with the chrominance background model. On the other hand, *Light Foreground* happens when the present pixel is saturated and it cannot be compared with the chrominance background model either.

Further, the observed background chrominance may change due to the *sensitivity of the sensor*, or *illumination changes*. Therefore, for instance background pixels corresponding to shadows can be considered as foregrounds. *Gleaming surfaces*, such as mirrors, cause that the reflect of the object is considered as foreground. On the other hand, due to sensor dynamic range (saturation or minimum intensity problems) the colour model cannot be correctly built. Therefore, a background pixel can be considered foreground erroneously. The *saturation problem* happens when the intensity value of a pixel for at least one channel is saturated or almost saturated. Therefore, the colour model would be wrongly built. The *minimum intensity problem* occurs when there is not enough intensity to build a colour model. This is mainly due to pixels that do not have the minimum intensity value to built the chrominance line.

3   Handling Colour-Based Segmentation Problems

The approach presented in [6] can cope with different colour problems as dark foreground and light foreground. Furthermore, it solves saturation and minimum intensity problems using intensity cue. Nevertheless, some colour segmentation problems still remains, since the intensity and colour model cannot differentiate dark and light camouflage from local and global illumination changes.

This approach is enhanced from [6] by incorporating edges statistics, depending on the casuistry. First, the parameters of the background model are learnt; next, the colour, intensity and edge models are explained; and finally the segmentation procedure is presented.

3.1 Background Modelling

Firstly, the background parameters and the Background Colour and Intensity Model (BCM-BIM) are obtained based on the algorithms presented in [6,5]. The BCM computes the chromatic and brightness distortion components of each pixel. The BIM is built based on the mean and the standard deviation over the training period.

The Background Edge Model (BEM) is built as follows: first gradients are obtained by applying the Sobel edge operator to each colour channel in horizontal (x) and vertical (y) directions. This yields both a horizontal and a vertical gradient image for each frame during the training period. Thus, each background pixel gradient is modelled using the gradient mean $(\mu_{xr}, \mu_{yr}), (\mu_{xg}, \mu_{yg}), (\mu_{xb}, \mu_{yb})$, and gradient standard deviation $(\sigma_{xr}, \sigma_{yr}), (\sigma_{xg}, \sigma_{yg}), (\sigma_{xb}, \sigma_{yb})$ computed from all the training frames for each channel. Then, the gradient magnitude of the mean $\mu_m = (\mu_{mr}, \mu_{mg}, \mu_{mb})$ and the standard deviation $\sigma_m = (\sigma_{mr}, \sigma_{mg}, \sigma_{mb})$ are computed in order to build the background edge model.

3.2 Image Segmentation

The combination of colour and intensity models permits to cope with different problems. The pixel is classified as FI (Foreground Intensity) or BI (Background Intensity) using BIM if the BCM is not feasible. If the BCM is built but the current pixel has saturation or minimum intensity problems, then the pixel is classified using the BCM brightness as DF (Dark Foreground), LF (Light Foreground) or BB (Background Border). Finally, the remaining pixels are classified as F (Foreground), B (Background), S (Shadow) or H (Highlight) using the chrominance and the brightness from BCM. See [6] for more details.

To obtain the foreground edge subtraction, several steps are followed. Firstly, the Sobel operator is used over the new image in horizontal (x) and vertical (y) directions to estimate the gradients for every pixel $(r_x, r_y), (g_x, g_y), (b_x, b_y)$. Then, the magnitude of the current gradient image is calculated $V_m = (V_{mr}, V_{mg}, V_{mb})$. In order to detect the Foreground pixels, the difference between the mean magnitudes of current image and background model is compared with the background model standard deviation magnitude. Therefore, a pixel is considered as foreground if:

$$V_m - \mu_m > k_e * max(\sigma_m, \overline{\sigma}_m) \tag{2}$$

where K_e is a constant value that gives a confidence region, and the average standard deviation $\overline{\sigma}_m = (\overline{\sigma}_{mr}, \overline{\sigma}_{mg}, \overline{\sigma}_{mb})$ is computed over the entire image area to avoid noise.

Subsequently, the pixels classified as foreground are divided into two different types: the first one comprises the foreground edges belonging to the current image —*positive edges*— which were not in the background model, and the second one comprises the edges in the background model which are occluded by foreground objects —*negative edges.*

3.3 Fusing Colour, Intensity and Edge Models (BCM-BIM-BEM)

The edge segmentation used isolatedly is not enough robust approach to segment the foreground objects. It can sometimes handle dark and light camouflage problems and it is less sensitive to global illumination changes than colour and intensity cue. Nevertheless, problems like noise, false negative edges due to local illumination problems, foreground aperture, and camouflage prevents from an accurate segmentation of foreground objects. Furthermore, due to the fact that it is sometimes difficult to segment the foreground object borders, it is not possible to fill the objects and solve the foreground aperture problem.

Since it is not possible to handle dark and light camouflage problems only by using edges due to the foreground aperture drawback, the brightness of colour model is used to solve this problem and help to fill the foreground object. Dark and light intensity mask[1] (DI/LI) gives a lot of information, since it contains not only the dark and light camouflage but also the global and local illumination changes. Therefore, to avoid the false positives due to global and local illumination changes, an edge mask is created by applying several morphological filters to the edge segmentation results. Thus, the edge mask is applied to the dark and light intensity mask, thereby allowing only the foreground objects detected by the edge mask to be filled with the dark and light intensity mask. In this way, the dark and light camouflage problem are solved and global and local illumination problems are avoided. Morphological filtering over the edge segmentation results is needed in order to know whether the interior of the foreground objects are segmented or not, due to the foreground aperture problem.

This edge mask could be applied to the Background Colour Model (BCM) to avoid some of the segmentation problems, such as the false positives due to noise, the changes in chrominance due to local illumination changes, and partially solve the ghost problem (only when the background is homogeneous). Nevertheless, detect all the foreground objects is sometimes difficult because the edge mask is not accurately build. Foreground object borders are not always segmented due to edge segmentation problems.

Since the mask cannot be applied to the BCM and BIM, their segmentation results can be used to solve part of the BEM problems, thereby helping to achieve foreground object detection more accurately than before. Therefore, the BEM

---

[1] This mask comes from the brightness thresholds $T_{\alpha lo}$ and $T_{\alpha Hi}$ used in [6] over the Shadow (S) and Highlights (H) obtained using the BCM.

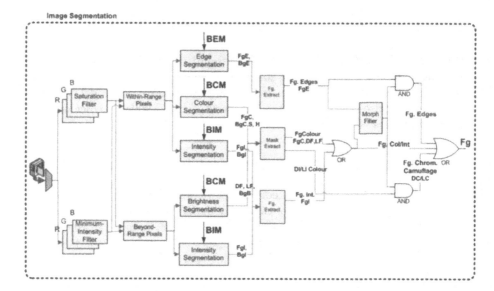

Fig. 2. Image segmentation approach. As a result of applying background model to the current frame, pixels are classified in a first step according to the BCM as foreground (FgC), background (BgC), shadow (S), and highlight (H); using the BCM on pixels beyond the sensor dynamic range, as dark foreground (DF), light foreground(LF), and background (BgB); according to the BEM as foreground (FE) and background (BE); and according to the BIM as foreground(FgI) and background (BgI). In a second step, using morphological filter over the Fg's obtained and dark and light intensity mask (DI/LI) the foreground chromaticy camouflage is solved as dark(DC) and Light(LC) camouflage.

results are combined with the BCM and BIM results to achieve a better edge mask. Thus, this new edge mask will be later applied over the dark and light intensity mask in order to segment the dark and light camouflage problem. A sketch of the system which fuses the three cues can be seen in Fig. 2.

The Edge mask is built using a combination of threshold in order to reduce noise and to avoid the problem with the false negative edges (edges which do not belong to any occluded edge by a foreground object) caused by local illumination changes. A low threshold is applied to segment positive edges, and a high threshold is applied to segment negative edges, thus achieving a better edge mask.

The BEM give us a high number of true positives which were not obtained using the BCM and BIM. Furthermore, negative edges can solve part of the camouflage problem, since these edges are foreground edges which are occluded by foreground objects. Nevertheless, as it has been above mentioned, BEM segmentation results also contain a lot of false positives due to noise, and false negative edges. In order to avoid these problems, the edges incorporated to the segmentation process have a high threshold. Since the BCM and the BIM results are good enough, the BEM results added to the segmentation process will be

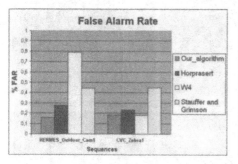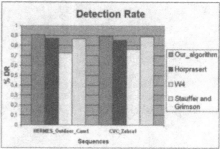

Fig. 3. False Alarm Rate and Detection Rate results. The first sequence is from HER-MES Database and the second one is from own database. Our approach has been compared with different approaches [4,3,5] using a ground-truth manually segmented. Our algorithm obtains the best results in both sequences evaluated.

restricted in order to improve the segmentation results avoiding losing performance. Therefore, the edge segmentation only includes true positives avoiding incorporating false positives.

4   Experimental Results

Our approach has been tested with multiple and different indoor and outdoor sequences under uncontrolled environments, where multiples segmentation problems appear.

In order to evaluate the performance of the proposed approach in a quantitative way ground-truth segmentation masks have been generated by manual segmentation. The sequences hand-segmented are *Hermes_Outdoor_Cam1* sequence (HERMES database, 1612 frames @15 fps, 1392 x 1040 PX), and *CVC_Zebra1* sequence (CVC database, 1343 frames @20 fps, 720 x 576 PX). Furthermore, several approaches from other authors [4,3,5] have been implemented to compare the performance. Fig. 3 shows two well-know quantitative expressions employed to evaluate segmentation process, False Alarm Rate and Detection Rate. Results show that our algorithm obtains the best results in both sequence evaluated.

Fig. 4 shows the comparison between our approach and some well known methods. It can be seen why our approach performs better. The first column of Fig. 4 shows two significant processed frames from *Hermes_Outdoor_Cam1* sequence. In this Fig. 4, agents and vehicles are segmented using different approaches: the approach by Horprasert et al. [5] (second column), and our final approach, which fuses colour, intensity and edge cues (third column). These compare the different motion segmentation problems found in the sequence.

First row from Fig. 4 shows a frame with global illumination and light camouflage problem (the white car is camouflaged with the grey road). The results from [5] (second column) shows that part of the car is not segmented due to light camouflage problem. Furthermore, this approach only differentiates between dark camouflage from global and local illumination problems based on

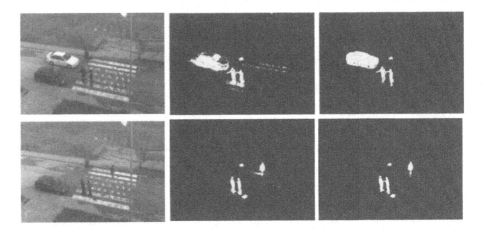

Fig. 4. Foreground segmentation results from HERMES database: First column is the original image; Second column results from [5]. First row shows that part of car is not segmented due to light camouflage problem. Moreover, car and agents shadows are segmented due to dark foreground problem. Second row shows shadows are segmented due to dark foreground and saturation problem; Third column results from our approach. First row shows that the car is segmented and light camouflage problem is solved. Second row shows that the trousers are segmented and shadows are not segmented, thereby coping with the dark camouflage, dark foreground and saturation problem. See text for more details.

Fig. 5. Foreground detection results applying our approach to different datasets: PETS, CAVIAR, VS-PETS and CVC_Zebra1 results. All the agents and vehicles are correctly detected showing robustness to global and local illumination problems, and problems with camouflage in chroma. Image notation: each black ellipse represents each detected object and yellow lines denote their contour.

an intensity threshold. Therefore, shadows from the white car and agents are erroneously segmented as dark foreground. The third column shows that these problems are solved using our approach.

Second row from Fig. 4 shows a frame with an illumination change and dark foreground problem (the trousers of the agent are camouflaged with the crosswalk when he is crossing it). In this case, both approaches are able to cope with this problem. Nevertheless, the approach proposed in [5] segments the shadow of the agent due to the above explained problem with the dark foreground, moreover the saturation problem due to the crosswalk colour. In our approach it is solved as it can be seen in the third column.

By using the combination of cue features, each of them can be used in a more restrictive way without compromising the detection rate. Nevertheless, false positive rate is cut down. Fig. 5 shows how our approach works in different datasets (PETS, CAVIAR, VS-PETS, and CVC_Zebra1).

5   Conclusions

The approach proposed can cope with different colour problems like dark and light camouflage. Furthermore, it can differentiate dark and light camouflage from global and local illumination problems, thereby reducing the number of false negatives, false positives and increasing the detected foreground regions.

The approach using colour, intensity and cue cues is based on a collaborative architecture, in which each model is devoted to specific tasks. These are performed by a particular algorithm, but they can be substituted by enhanced ones without modifying the architecture itself. Hence, this structured framework combines in a principal way the main advantage of each cues. In this way, by taking advantage of several cues, the system is allowed to benefit from all the cues capabilities, thereby simultaneously coping not only with global and local illumination, and dark and light camouflage; but also, handling saturation and lack of colour problems.

Experiments on complex indoor and outdoor scenarios have yielded robust and accurate results, thereby demonstrating the system ability to deal with unconstrained and dynamic scenes.

In the future work updating process should be embedded to the approach in order to solve incorporating objects and ghost problems. Furthermore, the use of a pixel-updating process can reduce the false positive pixels obtained using the dark and light intensity mask due to intense illumination problems. In addition, the detected motionless objects should be part of a multilayer background model.

Furthermore, colour invariant normalisations or colour constancy techniques can be used to improve the colour model, thereby handling illuminant change problem. These techniques can also improve the edge model in order to avoid false edges due to intense illumination changes. Further, edge linking or B-spline techniques can be used to avoid the partial lost of foreground borders due to camouflage, thereby improving the edge mask. Lastly, the discrimination between the agents and the local environments can be enhanced by making use of new cues such as temporal difference technique, and the approach will benefit from high-level information about the context and current situations provided by higher levels in the HSE framework.

Acknowledgements. This work is supported by EC grants IST-027110 for the HERMES project and IST-045547 for the VIDI-video project, and by the Spanish MEC under projects TIN2006-14606 and CONSOLIDER-INGENIO 2010 MIPRCV CSD2007-00018. Jordi Gonzlez also acknowledges the support of a Juan de la Cierva Postdoctoral fellowship from the Spanish MEC.

References

1. Elgammal, A., Harwood, D., Davis, L.S.: Nonparametric background model for background subtraction. In: Vernon, D. (ed.) ECCV 2000. LNCS, vol. 1843, pp. 751–767. Springer, Heidelberg (2000)
2. Gonzàlez, J.: Human Sequence Evaluation: the Key-frame Approach. PhD thesis (May 2004)
3. Grimson, W.E.L., Stauffer, C.: Adaptive background mixture models for real-time tracking, vol. 1, pp. 22–29 (1999)
4. Haritaoglu, I., Harwood, D., Davis, L.S.: W4: Real-time surveillance of people and their activities. IEEE Trans. Pattern Analysis and Machine Intelligence 22(8), 809–830 (2000)
5. Horprasert, T., Harwood, D., Davis, L.S.: A statistical approach for real-time robust background subtraction and shadow detection. In: IEEE Frame-Rate Applications Workshop (1999)
6. Huerta, I., Rowe, D., Mozerov, M., Gonzàlez, J.: Improving background subtraction based on a casuistry of colour-motion segmentation problems. In: Martí, J., Benedí, J.M., Mendonça, A.M., Serrat, J. (eds.) IbPRIA 2007. LNCS, vol. 4478, pp. 475–482. Springer, Heidelberg (2007)
7. Jabri, H.W.S., Duric, Z., Rosenfeld, A.: Detection and location of people in video images using adaptive fusion of color and edge information, September 2000, vol. 4, pp. 627–630 (2000)
8. McKenna, S.J., Jabri, S., Duric, Z., Rosenfeld, A., Wechsler, H.: Tracking groups of people. Computer Vision and Image Understanding: CVIU 80(1), 42–56 (2000)
9. Moeslund, T.B., Hilton, A., Krger, V.: A survey of advances in vision-based human motion capture and analysis. Computer Vision and Image Understanding 104, 90–126 (2006)
10. Shen, J.: Motion detection in color image sequence and shadow elimination. Visual Communications and Image Processing 5308, 731–740 (2004)
11. Toyama, K., Krumm, J., Brumitt, B., Meyers, B.: Wallflower: Principles and practice of background maintenance, vol. 1, pp. 255–261 (1999)
12. Wang, L., Hu, W., Tan, T.: Recent developments in human motion analysis. Pattern Recognition 36(3), 585–601 (2003)
13. Wren, C.R., Azarbayejani, A., Darrell, T., Pentland, A.P.: Pfinder: Real-time tracking of the human body. IEEE Trans. Pattern Analysis and Machine Intelligence 19(7), 780–785 (1997)

Body-Part Templates for Recovery of 2D Human Poses under Occlusion

Ronald Poppe and Mannes Poel*

Human Media Interaction Group, Dept. of Computer Science, University of Twente
P.O. Box 217, 7500 AE, Enschede, The Netherlands
{poppe,mpoel}@ewi.utwente.nl

Abstract. Detection of humans and estimation of their 2D poses from a single image are challenging tasks. This is especially true when part of the observation is occluded. However, given a limited class of movements, poses can be recovered given the visible body-parts. To this end, we propose a novel template representation where the body is divided into five body-parts. Given a match, we not only estimate the joints in the body-part, but all joints in the body. Quantitative evaluation on a HumanEva walking sequence shows mean 2D errors of approximately 27.5 pixels. For simulated occlusion of the head and arms, similar results are obtained while occlusion of the legs increases this error by 6 pixels.

1 Introduction

Detection and analysis of humans in images and video has received much research attention. Much of this work has focussed on improving pose estimation accuracy, while partly ignoring the difficult localization task. Despite increased awareness, the two processes are still researched in relative isolation, inhibiting use in realistic scenarios. Another issue with the current state of the art is the sensitivity to cluttered environments and, in particular, partial occlusions.

In this paper, we aim at simultaneous human detection and 2D pose recovery from monocular images in the presence of occlusions. We do not model the background, thus allowing our algorithm to work in cluttered and dynamical environments. Moreover, we do not rely on motion, which makes this work suitable for estimation from a single image. The output of our approach can be used as input for a more accurate pose estimation algorithm.

Our contribution is a novel template representation that is a compromise between half-limb locators and full-body templates. We observe that, for a limited class of movements, there is a strong dependency of the location of body-parts. For example, given a walking motion, we can accurately predict the location of the left foot while observing only the right leg. To this end, we divide the human body into five body-parts (arms, legs and torso), each of which has associated

* This work was supported by the European IST Programme Project FP6-033812 (publication AMIDA-105), and is part of the ICIS program. ICIS is sponsored by the Dutch government under contract BSIK03024.

F.J. Perales and R.B. Fisher (Eds.): AMDO 2008, LNCS 5098, pp. 289–298, 2008.

edge and appearance templates. Given a match of body-part template and image, we not only vote for the locations of joints within the body-part but for all joint locations. This approach allows us to recover the location of joints that are occluded (see Figure 1). We first apply the templates over different scales and translations, which results in a number of estimations for each 2D joint location. In a second step, we approximate the final joint locations from these estimations. In this paper, we focus on the matching, and keep the estimation part trivial.

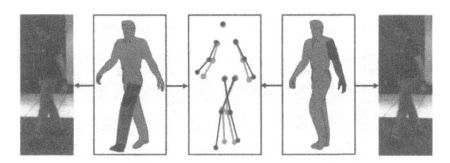

Fig. 1. Conceptual overview of our method. Templates from different exemplars and body-parts match with part of the image. Joint estimates are combined into a pose estimate. Anchor points are omitted for clarity. Occlusion of the right arm is simulated.

We first discuss related work on human pose recovery. The two steps of our approach, template matching and pose estimation, are discussed in Section 3 and 4, respectively. We present quantitative results on the HumanEva data set in Section 5, both on original image sequences and with simulated occlusion.

2   Related Work on Monocular Pose Recovery

Human motion analysis has received much attention [1]. Here, we focus on monocular approaches that can deal with cluttered, dynamic environments and occlusion. In general, we can distinguish two main classes of approach.

Discriminative approaches learn a mapping from image to human pose, where the image's region of interest is conveniently encoded in an image descriptor. Such approaches focus on poses that are probable, which is a subset of all physically feasible ones. Shakhnarovich et al. use histograms of directed edges and an efficient form of hashing to find similar upper-body examples from a database [2]. Agarwal and Triggs learn regression functions from extracted silhouettes to the pose space [3]. These approaches are efficient, but require accurate localization of the human from the image. Also, they are sensitive to noise in the region of interest, due to incorrect localization or segmentation, and occlusions. Some of these drawbacks have been partially overcome. Agarwal and Triggs suppress background edges by learning human-like edges [4], thus alleviating the need for good segmentation. Howe uses boundary fragment matching to match partial shapes [5]. His approach requires that background and foreground are labelled, which limits its applicability to domains where such a segmentation is available.

The second class is that of *generative* approaches. These use a human body model that describes both the visual and kinematic properties of the human body. Pose estimation essentially becomes the process of finding the parameters that minimize the matching error of the visual model with the image observation. The direction of estimation is either top-down or bottom-up.

In top-down estimation, a projection of the human body is matched with the image observation, and usually improved iteratively. The process is hindered when occlusion occurs, since no image observation is present for the occluded part of the body. This can lead to unrealistic poses. A practical problem is the high dimensionality of the parameter space, which makes initialization difficult. A recent trend to overcome this problem is to use dimensionality reduction in the kinematic space, which can be regarded as a strong prior on the poses that can be observed. This reduction is motivated by the observation that there is a strong correlation in the movement of different body-parts, especially within a single movement class such as walking.

In bottom-up estimation, individual body-parts are found first and then assembled into a human body. In general, weak half-limb detectors are used, which results in many false positives. Many of the bottom-up works resemble the pictorial structures idea, which was applied to human pose recovery by Felzenszwalb and Huttenlocher [6]. The key idea is to model the appearance of each body-part individually, and represent the deformable assembly of parts by spring-like connections between pairs of parts. Most of this work relies on inference in a tree-like structure [6,7,8]. Again, there are two major drawbacks with the bottom-up approach. First, the templates are usually at the level of half-limbs (e.g. upper leg) which results in many false positives. Second, the 2D location of a template does not give any information about the rotation in 3D. This makes it difficult to enforce 3D constraints, such as joint limits, on the relative position between two adjacent parts. Such constraints are needed to be able to recover realistic poses when part of the body in the image is occluded.

In this paper, we propose an approach that combines several of the ideas above, while it aims at circumventing the major drawbacks. First, we use body-part templates that encode exactly one body-part (arm, leg or torso). Such a representation is more meaningful than that of half-limbs, and reduces false positives since the templates implicitly encode the view. Second, by voting over all joints, we can cope with occlusions and recover the pose even when only part of the human body is visible. See also Figure 1. Our work resembles that of Demirdjian and Urtasun [9], who vote over the pose space using patches that are similar to those in the image. Patches and their joint location densities are learned from a large annotated database. Our work differs since our few templates can be generated automatically using 3D modelling software. We focus on walking movements only. This effectively puts a strong prior on the poses that we can recover, which is a limitation of our work.

3   Template Matching

We introduce full-body templates that consist of five, possibly overlapping, body-part templates, see Figure 2. We will call a full-body template *exemplar*. For the estimation of articulated poses, we use a collection E of n exemplars $\mathbf{E}_i \in E$ ($1 \leq i \leq n$). Each exemplar consists of a tuple that describes the 2D pose $\mathbf{u}$ and the body parts $\mathbf{p}$, $\mathbf{E}_i = (\mathbf{u}, \mathbf{p})$. Note that we do not include information about the 3D orientation and scaling since this is implicitly encoded in the templates and 2D pose. For clarification of notation, subscripts are omitted where possible.

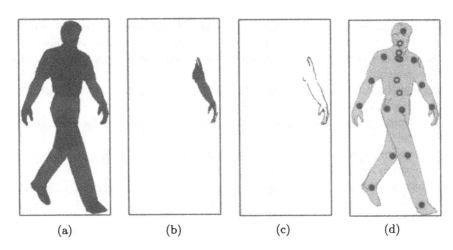

Fig. 2. (a) Exemplar with all color regions, (b) color regions and (c) edge template of left arm, (d) 2D joint locations (body shown for reference). Closed dots are used in the evaluation, see Section 5. The anchor point is the left-upper corner of the box.

Each element in $\mathbf{u}$ is a 2D joint location written as a tuple $\mathbf{u}_i = (x_i, y_i) \in \mathbf{u}$ ($1 \leq i \leq m$). These locations are relative to the anchor point, which is by default the left upper corner of the minimum enclosing box of all templates. In principle, we use $m = 20$ joints, as shown in Figure 2(d).

Each $\mathbf{p}_i \in \mathbf{p}$ ($1 \leq i \leq 5$) represents exactly one body-part (leg, arm or torso). We can write it as a tuple $\mathbf{p}_i = (\mathbf{t}, \mathbf{r})$. Here, $\mathbf{t}$ is an edge template, where each element $\mathbf{t}_i = (x_i, y_i) \in \mathbf{t}$ ($1 \leq i \leq |\mathbf{t}|$) represents an edge pixel at a given location, relative to the anchor point. $|\mathbf{t}|$ is the number of elements in $\mathbf{t}$. Each body-part has several color regions, each of which is assumed to have a constant color. The number of regions per body-part, $|\mathbf{r}|$, is three for each leg and arm, and five for the torso (see also Figure 2(a-b)). Similar to our edge representation, each region $\mathbf{r}_i$ ($1 \leq i \leq |\mathbf{r}|$) consists of a number of relative pixel locations, which can be considered the foreground mask. The total number of foreground pixels in a region is denoted with $|\mathbf{r}_i|$ for the ith region.

In summary, each exemplar consists of five body-parts, each of which represents a limb or the torso. Each body-part has an associated edge template, and a number of color regions. Templates and 2D joint locations are positioned relative to the anchor point.

3.1   Template Distance

For the matching, the notion of an exemplar is not needed, rather that of the body-parts individually. The match of a body-part and an image region is determined by calculating the distance of the edge and color templates individually.

For the edge matching, distance transforms such as the Chamfer distance are common. For such a transform, both image and template need to be converted to a binary edge map. The distance transform gives the (approximate) distance to the nearest edge pixel. The matching score is calculated by summing all distance transform values in the image "under" the edge pixels. One problem that we found while using this technique is that is favors areas that are densely covered with edges. Also, the performance proved to be very sensitive to the value of the edge magnitude threshold. Therefore, we use the edge magnitudes of the image directly, by calculating the derivative I_{edge} of the image in gray scale. Distance score Δ_{edge} for template $\mathbf{t}_j$ with the anchor at location (sx, sy) is given by:

$$\Delta_{edge}(I_{edge}, \mathbf{t}_j, sx, sy) = \frac{\sum\limits_{(x,y)\in \mathbf{t}_j} I_{edge}(sx + x, sy + y)}{|\mathbf{t}_j|} \tag{1}$$

To evaluate the distance of the color template, we determine the color deviation score Δ_{color} for each region $\mathbf{r}_k$ at anchor point (sx, sy):

$$\Delta_{color}(I_{color}, \mathbf{r}_k, \mathbf{c}, sx, sy) = \frac{\sum\limits_{c_i \in \mathbf{c}} \sum\limits_{(x,y)\in \mathbf{r}_k} |I_{color}(sx + x, sy + y, c_i) - \mu|}{|\mathbf{c}||\mathbf{r}_k|} \tag{2}$$

Here, I_{color} is the color image, $\mathbf{c}$ is a vector with $|\mathbf{c}|$ color channels. We make no assumptions about the color space of the image. μ is the shorthand notation for $\mu(I_{color}, \mathbf{r}_k, c_i, sx, sy)$, the mean value of all "region" pixels in the color channel when no appearance assumptions are made. Alternatively, if the region colors are set beforehand, μ corresponds to $a(j, k, i)$ the specified value for body-part j, region k and channel i. Alternatively, we could have used color histograms, as in [8] but it seems unrealistic that these can be determined beforehand.

The distance for all color regions together is the sum of the means of each region, weighted on the size of the regions $|\mathbf{r}_k|$. We have distances rather than probabilities, so we need to determine when a match occurs. Therefore, we introduce thresholds η and θ for the minimum edge distance and maximum color deviation distance, respectively. We determine the values of these thresholds empirically.

4   Pose Estimation

To estimate the 2D joint locations of a person in an image, we evaluate the distances of the body-parts of all exemplars in collection E. Each template is matched over multiple scales with the anchor point at different locations. For each match (with the distance scores satisfying the thresholds), a vote is made for the location of all joints in **u**. The body-parts are unrelated to the exemplar, except for the common joint locations.

After processing the image, we have a number of estimates for each joint location. This "density" usually has multiple modes, depending on the number of persons, and the modes of uncertainty. For simplicity, we assume only a single person in the image. Therefore, we simply take the average location of all estimates for a given joint. This presents the risk of averaging over multiple modes. To be able to handle multiple persons, a more advanced density estimation scheme could be used such as the one described in [9].

5   Experimental Results and Discussion

To evaluate the performance of our technique, we evaluate the algorithm on the publicly available HumanEva benchmark set [10]. To our best knowledge, there is no data set that contains partially occluded human figures and 2D annotated joint positions. Therefore, we simulate occlusion on the HumanEva set.

5.1   Training Set

One of the advantages of our approach is that templates can be generated using 3D modelling software. This makes it possible to generate templates that do not require manual labelling of joint positions, edge locations and color regions.

Curious Labs' Poser 5 was used, with the "Poser 2 default guy" as human model. We selected the "P4 Walk" as motion, and sampled 6 key frames within the cycle. The camera was placed at eye height, and was pointed slightly downwards. Each key frame was further viewed from 8 different angles at every 45° around the vertical axis. This yields 48 exemplars. For each exemplar, we used the "Cartoon with line" renderer to generate edge templates and color regions. See Figure 2(b-c) for examples of templates. In a post-processing step, the joint locations and templates are normalized with respect to the left-upper corner of the minimum enclosing bounding box of all templates.

5.2   Test Set

We evaluated our approach on the HumanEva data set [10]. This set contains sequences with synchronized video and pose data. For the test sequences, ground truth is held back and validation is performed online. We present results for Walking and Jog sequence 2, performed by subject 2 and viewed from color camera 1. This sequence shows a man walking or jogging in circles.

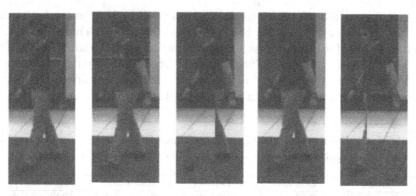

Fig. 3. Simulated occlusion. Left to right: head, left arm, left leg, right arm, right leg.

In order to test the accuracy of our approach against occlusions, we simulate occlusions for different body-parts. Instead of placing black boxes, as in [9], we remove the body-parts by replacing the foreground with background patches. Note that we do not model the background, so we have no knowledge where occlusion occurs. The location and size of the patch is determined by the 2D location of the shoulder and wrist, hip and ankle, and head for an arm, leg and head respectively. These locations were annotated manually. Figure 3 shows example frames with occlusion for different body-parts. The patches often occlude other body-parts, which is especially the case for the legs. Also, due to the location of the selected joints, there are still some parts visible, notably hands and feet. However, it is unlikely that this aids in the matching phase.

5.3   Results

We defined values for the color of the skin, shirt, pants, shoes and hair in HSV color space. Hue values were transformed to be the distance to the center value (180°), to avoid wrap-around errors. To reduce computation time, we assume that the person is entirely within the image. We move the anchor point through the image with steps of 10 pixels. This causes the edge term to function as a rejector of false positives. The human model in our exemplars is approximately 350 pixels high. We evaluate the templates at three scales: 90%, 100% and 110%. The human figure in our test sequence is between 275 and 410 pixels high, so in the range 79-117% of our exemplars. We further reduce computation time by ignoring body-parts with an area smaller than 1500 pixels. This excludes occluded or almost occluded limbs from being evaluated. These templates have a high probability of matching, while providing little information about the pose.

We used Walking sequence 1 of subject 2 to determine the thresholds for the templates. The exemplars and the HumanEva set use different joint sets. We selected the joints corresponding to the wrist, elbow, shoulder, ankle, knee, hip and head. In Figure 2(d), these are the closed dots. The mean 2D error over the Walking test sequence is 27.48 pixels, with a SD of 3.26. This corresponds to an error of approximately 14 cm, if we average over the scales. We evaluated the Jog sequence, frames 100339, which corresponds to a full cycle. The average error is 30.35 pixels, with a SD of 3.90. For the evaluation of the occluded images, we used frames 1400 (one walking cycle) with an increment of 5 frames. We used the same settings as for the unmodified sequence. Specifically, we did not alter the thresholds. Results are presented in Table 1. In addition, we applied the method to some frames of the movie *Lola Rennt* (sample frames in Figure 4(a-b)).

Table 1. Mean 2D error (and SD) in pixels on HumanEva Walking 2 sequence, subject 2, viewed with color camera 1. Results are given for different occlusion conditions.

Head	Left arm	Left leg	Right arm	Right leg
27.32 (3.64)	27.31 (3.49)	32.77 (8.57)	27.65 (3.40)	32.95 (7.52)

5.4 Discussion and Comparison with Related Work

Other works have reported 2D errors on the HumanEva data set [8,11]. While these works are substantially different than ours, comparison may reveal the strong and weak aspects of the respective approaches. Siddiqui and Medioni present results on the Gesture sequence in the training set of subject 2. They report mean errors of approximately 13 pixels, for the upper-body. Templates are used, but for half-limbs, and colors specified as a histogram. In addition, motion information obtained from frame differencing is used. The background is modelled and temporal consistence is enforced through tracking. Their method can deal with a broader range of poses and is considerably faster.

Howe [11] uses a discriminative approach with a database of reference poses with corresponding image representation to retrieve similar observations. Temporal consistency is enforced using Markov chaining. On the Walking sequence in the training set of subject 1, mean errors of approximately 15 pixels are obtained. Howe's approach works in real-time, but requires good foreground segmentation. Also, it remains an open issue whether similar results can be obtained for subjects that are not in the training set.

Unlike both approaches above, our method is able to deal with occlusions, at a cost of higher computational cost and lower flexibility with respect to the range of poses that can be detected. Our larger errors are partly due to our evaluation method, and are partly inherent to our approach. There is a discrepancy between the joint locations in our exemplars and those defined for HumanEva. We selected those joints that have similar locations but differences are still present. The hips are placed more outwards in our exemplars, and the elbow and knee locations are more at the physical location of the joint. Also, the human model used in our exemplars differs in body dimensions, compared to subject in our test data (see Figure 1).

To reduce the computational cost, we used only 6 different key poses, viewed at 45° intervals. Also, the walking style differs substantially from the one observed in the test sequence. A similar observation can be made for the Jog sequence. Our results could be improved by adding exemplars and viewpoints, at the cost

of increased computational complexity. By moving the anchor point with steps
of 10 pixels, our edge template functions as a false positive rejector. Changing
the matching function could improve results.

Closer analysis of our results shows that part of the error is caused by matches
that are the 180° rotation of the real match. This happens especially when the
person is facing the camera, or facing 180° away from it. This happens in frames
50, 250, 450, etc., see Figure 4(c). Consequently, we see lower error values around
frames 150, 350, 550, etc. Here, the subject is either walking to the right or
walking to the left. The number of left-right ambiguities are lower, resulting
in a lower error. The relatively higher errors around frames 350 and 750 are
caused by the subject being close to the camera. Here, matches with a larger
scale are selected, which causes higher errors for ambiguities. Joints closer to the
symmetry axis are much less affected by these errors, but these are not used in
the evaluation. Overall, the estimated joint locations are closer to the symmetry
axis than the real locations. A final observation can be made that the majority
of the matches is from the leg templates, which explains the higher errors when
one of the legs is occluded.

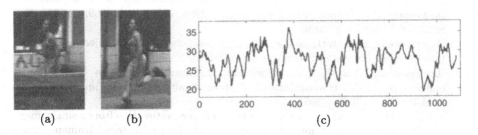

 (a)   (b)   (c)

Fig. 4. Sample frames from *Lola Rennt*. (a) Legs occluded, (b) "out-of-vocabulary"
pose. (c) Errors in pixels for Walking sequence 2, subject 1. See discussion in Section 5.4.

6 Conclusion and Future Work

We presented a novel template representation, where the body is divided into
five body-parts. Each body-part implicitly encodes the viewpoint and is used to
predict the location of other joints in the human body. By matching body-part
templates individually, our approach is able to detect persons, and estimate their
2D poses under occlusions. We match edge and color templates associated with
a body-part at different locations and scales. For a good match, an estimate for
all joints is made. Subsequently, we determine the final pose estimate.

The HumanEva data set was used for evaluation. We simulated occlusion by
replacing limbs with background patches. For the original walking sequence, and
for occlusion of head and arms, we obtained mean 2D errors of approximately
27.5 pixels. Occlusion of the legs resulted in a 6 pixel increase.

These results can be improved by adding exemplars and viewpoints. Also, the
edge matching could be improved to better fit the observations. A better pose

estimation process would allow for multiple persons, and could favor matches close to the actual joint location. To reduce computational cost, we propose a coarse-to-fine matching approach. Other future work is aimed at combining our work with a discriminative or generative approach.

References

1. Poppe, R.: Vision-based human motion analysis: An overview. Computer Vision and Image Understanding (CVIU) 108(1-2), 4–18 (2007)
2. Shakhnarovich, G., Viola, P.A., Darrell, T.: Fast pose estimation with parameter-sensitive hashing. In: Proceedings of the International Conference on Computer Vision (ICCV 2003), Nice, France, October 2003, vol. 2, pp. 750–759 (2003)
3. Agarwal, A., Triggs, B.: Recovering 3D human pose from monocular images. IEEE Transactions on Pattern Analysis and Machine Intelligence (PAMI) 28(1), 44–58 (2006)
4. Agarwal, A., Triggs, B.: A local basis representation for estimating human pose from cluttered images. In: Narayanan, P.J., Nayar, S.K., Shum, H.-Y. (eds.) ACCV 2006. LNCS, vol. 3851, pp. 50–59. Springer, Heidelberg (2006)
5. Howe, N.R.: Boundary fragment matching and articulated pose under occlusion. In: Perales, F.J., Fisher, R.B. (eds.) AMDO 2006. LNCS, vol. 4069, pp. 271–280. Springer, Heidelberg (2006)
6. Felzenszwalb, P.F., Huttenlocher, D.P.: Pictorial structures for object recognition. International Journal of Computer Vision 61(1), 55–79 (2005)
7. Ramanan, D., Forsyth, D.A., Zisserman, A.: Tracking people by learning their appearance. IEEE Transactions on Pattern Analysis and Machine Intelligence (PAMI) 29(1), 65–81 (2007)
8. Siddiqui, M., Medioni, G.: Efficient upper body pose estimation from a single image or a sequence. In: Elgammal, A., Rosenhahn, B., Klette, R. (eds.) Human Motion 2007. LNCS, vol. 4814, pp. 74–87. Springer, Heidelberg (2007)
9. Demirdjian, D., Urtasun, R.: Patch-based pose inference with a mixture of density estimators. In: Zhou, S.K., Zhao, W., Tang, X., Gong, S. (eds.) AMFG 2007. LNCS, vol. 4778, pp. 96–108. Springer, Heidelberg (2007)
10. Sigal, L., Black, M.J.: HumanEva: Synchronized video and motion capture dataset for evaluation of articulated human motion. Technical Report CS-06-08, Brown University, Department of Computer Science, Providence, RI (September 2006)
11. Howe, N.: Recognition-based motion capture and the HumanEva II test data. In: Proceedings of the Workshop on Evaluation of Articulated Human Motion and Pose Estimation (EHuM) at the Conference on Computer Vision and Pattern Recognition (CVPR 2007), Minneapolis, MN (June 2007)

Autonomous Virtual Agents for Performance Evaluation of Tracking Algorithms

Pau Baiget[1], Xavier Roca[1], and Jordi Gonzàlez[2]

[1] Computer Vision Center & Dept. de Ciències de la Computació, Edifici O, Campus UAB, 08193 Bellaterra, Spain
[2] Institut de Robòtica i Informàtica Industrial (UPC – CSIC), Llorens i Artigas 4-6, 08028, Barcelona, Spain

Abstract. This paper describes a framework which exploits the use of computer animation to evaluate the performance of tracking algorithms. This can be achieved in two different, complementary strategies. On the one hand, augmented reality allows to gradually increasing the scene complexity by adding virtual agents into a real image sequence. On the other hand, the simulation of virtual environments involving autonomous agents provides with synthetic image sequences. These are used to evaluate several difficult tracking problems which are under research nowadays, such as performance processing long–time runs and the evaluation of sequences containing crowds of people and numerous occlusions. Finally, a general event–based evaluation metric is defined to measure whether the agents and actions in the scene given by the ground truth were correctly tracked by comparing two event lists. This metric is suitable to evaluate different tracking approaches where the underlying algorithm may be completely different.

1 Introduction

Performance evaluation of multi–objects tracking algorithms for video–surveillance has recently received significant attention [16,14]. Indeed, evaluation metrics for surveillance are almost as numerous as multi–object tracking methods themselves. In this work we focus on the evaluation of tracking systems specialized in open–world image sequences. Within this context, the tracked targets are expected to be the typical elements in urban environments, i.e. pedestrian, animals and vehicles.

Nowadays, research in multi–object tracking algorithms has achieved great results when tracking non–grouped targets in few frames image sequences including soft illumination changes. However, several problems, inherent to computer vision in general, are still unsolved and constitute a big challenge towards an unconstrained multiple–target tracking, namely long occlusions, grouping disambiguation and camouflage.

One typical drawback comes up when testing the tracking algorithm in a different environment or image sequence [3]. As long as difficult frames appear in the new image sequence, some modifications must be done to the algorithm

F.J. Perales and R.B. Fisher (Eds.): AMDO 2008, LNCS 5098, pp. 299–308, 2008.

(parameters, thresholds) in order to achieve good results. However, these modifications could damage the results obtained in former image sequences. Instead of using completely new sequences, it would be useful to have a method to gradually increase the difficulty of a given sequence. However, when recording a new sequence, even in the same scenario, we are exposed to several condition changes due to illumination, weather, or scenario configuration. In addition, it is sometimes hard to record image sequences containing crowds of people in public urban environments for legal or security reasons.

In this paper we solve the aforementioned difficulties by providing a new framework that combines real image data with virtual environments, allowing the user to test a tracking algorithm with augmented reality. This paper is organized as follows. Section 2 reviews the state of the art in tracking evaluation metrics and virtual environments. Section 3 presents our contribution to generate synthetic image sequences within a virtual environment and to compare the tracking results with those obtained with real sequences. Section 4 evaluates the proposed framework in an open–world scenario. Finally, 5 concludes this paper and discusses different alternatives for future research.

2   Related Work

This section reviews recent works in the main topics of this paper, performance evaluation of tracking algorithms and the generation of virtual environments. On the one hand, related work in the field of performance evaluation for object tracking can roughly be classified into different semantic classes as they specifically address one or more of the following semantic levels: pixel-level [1,11], frame-level [3,1], object trajectory level [3,15], and behaviors or higher level events [5]. Bashir and Porikli [3] presented a set of unbiased metrics on the frame and object level which leaves the final evaluation to the community. However, the total number of 48 different metrics makes the interpretation difficult. Aguilera et al. [1] presented an evaluation method for the frame and pixel level, all based on segmentation. The pixel-level metric is currently used for the online service called PETS metrics[16]. Wu et al. [15] evaluate their body part detector-based tracker using five criteria on the trajectory level which cover most of the typical errors they observed. Furthermore, occlusion events were separately evaluated defining short and long scene or object occlusions. The metric then gives the number of successful handled occlusions against all occlusions of a certain category by dataset. Desurmont et al. [5] presented a general performance evaluation metric for frequent high level events where they use dynamic programming to specifically address the problem of automatic realignment between results and ground truth. Their definition of an event is however very much limited to the detection of blobs crossing predefined lines in order to count people passing by.

Regarding virtual environments, previous works on behavior modeling in virtual environments can be summarized into two different approaches: on the one hand, bottom–up approaches make use of machine learning techniques to represent human behaviors from a set of motion patterns. Thus, *behavioral learning*

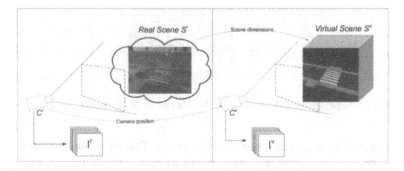

Fig. 1. Overall scheme of the virtual representation of a real scenario. The virtual scenario is modeled using the measurements from the camera calibration. Virtual agents are defined by either ground–truth trajectories or by simple behavior models.

has begun to be exploited using machine learning techniques such as k–Nearest Neighbors [4] or reinforcement learning (RL) [13], to cite few. On the other hand, top–down techniques predefine a set of behavior patterns which represent the set of agent behaviors to be synthesized [2]. Top–down approaches cannot learn, but they represent human behaviors in a consistent manner, and they do not depend on the specific data from the training set.

Consequently, none of the approaches described above has exploited the use of virtual environments and autonomous virtual agents to generate image sequences towards tracking performance evaluation.

3   Evaluation Framework

This section describes two different methods to evaluate the performance of tracking algorithms. Firstly we define the elements involved in our framework. Let $Tracker$ be the tracking algorithm to evaluate and let S^r be a real scenario. An image sequence I^r is recorded using a static camera C^r. Let O^r be the output obtained when processing I^r by $Tracker$. Although this output may vary from different trackers, most of them include either a list of target positions for each frame, *frame–oriented* [14], or a list of targets including their tracked trajectory, *target–oriented* [6]. In this work we assume a target–oriented output, therefore

$$O^r = \{T_1^r, \ldots, T_n^r\} \tag{1}$$

is a list of tracked targets where $T_i^r = \{t_{i_1}, \ldots, t_{i_k}\}$ is the sequence of position coordinates in each frame step for the target i.

Subsequently, a synthetic scenario S^v is modeled by using the real scene dimensions obtained with the calibration of C^r, see Fig. 1. Finally, a virtual camera C^v is located in S^v at the exact location of C^r in S^r.

In order to generate a synthetic sequence with moving targets, a set of virtual agents is added to the created environment. Thus, two types of moving targets

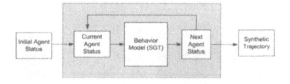

Fig. 2. Synthetic trajectory generation by means of SGT–based behavior models

are considered so far, pedestrians and vehicles. The development of a virtual agent inside the environment is determined by one of the following strategies:

- *Trajectory–based*:a predefined, possibly manually provided trajectory $T = \{t_1, \ldots, t_k\}$ is assigned to the virtual agent, where t_i defines the agent position in the frame i.
- *Behavior–based*: virtual agents are provided with behavior models which automatically generate the trajectories. To this end, we use the deterministic framework proposed in [2]. In essence, the system automatically generates image sequences involving virtual agents which perform a set of precomputed behavior models. Such a model consists of a set of semantic states ordered in a hierarchy named *situation graph tree* (SGT) [8] and uses fuzzy metric temporal logic [10] as a state inference engine. Each node (situation) represents the state of an agent in a given frame step. The node contains the logic predicates to be satisfied by an agent to be in that state. In addition, it specifies the actions to be performed in the future frames enabling thus a trajectory generation loop. Fig. 2 depicts the scheme of generation of synthetic trajectories as a set of *agent status*, that is, position and velocity of the agent at each frame.

3.1   Generation of Synthetic Sequences Using the Ground Truth

A common strategy to evaluate tracking performance is to compare an output with the corresponding ground–truth data. In our case, the ground–truth is defined as a list of targets obtained by means of manual annotation of the trajectories observed in I^r, and it is considered as the ideal output O^{gt} of the tracker:

$$O^{gt} = \{T_1^{gt}, \ldots, T_n^{gt}\} \tag{2}$$

where n corresponds to the number of targets. Given the ground–truth of I^r, a synthetic image sequence is generated by modeling a set of virtual agents performing the trajectories stored in O^{gt}. The resulting sequence, namely I^v, is processed by the tracker and an output O^v is obtained, see Fig. 3.

The evaluation metric is based on the comparison between the ground–truth O^{gt} and the outputs O^r and O^v which are the results obtained by the tracker when processing the real sequence and the virtual sequence, respectively. In order to perform a qualitative evaluation of the results, a list of events is extracted

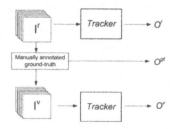

Fig. 3. Comparison of two outputs of the tracker with ground-truth trajectories (O^{gt}). O^r is the output given by a real image sequence I^r and O^v is the output obtained from processing the synthetic image sequence I^v, which has been generated using n virtual agents performing the ground–truth trajectories $O^{gt} = \{T_1^{gt}, \ldots, T_n^{gt}\}$.

by analyzing the trajectories contained in O^{gt}, O^r and O^v. These events can be related either to low or high–level feature events. On the one hand, events like the target interaction with the scene boundaries (*entering* or *leaving* the scene) or occlusions between agents (*start / end* occlusion) require to analyze and compare the trajectory positions over time. On the other hand, higher level events require a semantic evaluation of the trajectories [7]. This implies to deal with semantic knowledge about human behavior in the selected environment, as well as to know the semantic explanation of every part of the scene [2]. For example, if a part of the scenario is labeled as *crosswalk*, a high–level event can be defined as *entering / exiting the crosswalk*.

3.2 Augmenting Scene Complexity by Adding Virtual Agents

In order to permit a gradual increase of complexity of a previously recorded image sequence I^r recorded inside a real scenario S^r, the number of moving targets should be increased. Thus, the more of agents involved in the scenario, the more complex the image sequence will be. However, the initial conditions of the scenario must be kept in order to avoid distortions prompted by e.g. illumination changes or alterations of the background configuration. To this end, a set of m virtual agents $\{A_1, \ldots, A_m\}$ is modeled, either by assigning predefined trajectories or by simulating behavior models, and those are rendered into a synthetic image sequence I^{va}. Finally, I^r and I^{va} are fused into a new image sequence I^{rv}, containing real and virtual agents in the real scenario S^r, see Fig. 4. This resulting image sequence increases complexity in terms of occlusions, camouflages, and events.

The obtained image sequence is processed by the tracker, thus generating an output O^{rv}. The evaluation of the results implies the comparison with a ground–truth O^{gtrv}, which is a combination of the original ground–truth O^{gt} and the trajectories $\{t^{A_1}, \ldots, t^{A_m}\}$ performed by the virtual agents:

$$O^{gtrv} = \{t_1^{gt}, \ldots, t_n^{gt}, t^{A_1}, \ldots, t^{A_m}\} \tag{3}$$

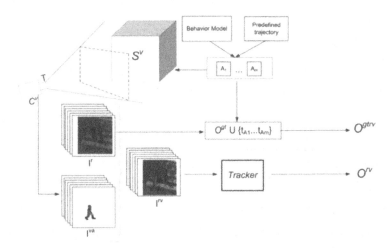

Fig. 4. Generation of an augmented reality image sequence I^{rv}. A set of virtual agents $\{A_1, \ldots, A_m\}$ performing different behaviors is rendered into a synthetic image sequence I^{va}. Finally, I^{va} and the real image sequence I^r are fused to generate I^{rv}.

Finally, given O^{rv} and its corresponding ground–truth O^{gtrv}, the event–based metric explained above is applied to evaluate the tracker performance.

4   Case Study: Evaluation in a Pedestrian Environment

4.1   Tracking Algorithm

The architecture of the analyzed tracking algorithm [12] is based on a modular and hierarchically-organized system. A set of co-operating modules, which work following both bottom-up and top-down paradigms, are distributed through three levels. Each level is devoted to one of the main different tasks to be performed: Target Detection, Low-Level Tracking (LLT), and High-Level Tracking (HLT). Since high-level analysis of motion is a critical issue, a principled management system is embedded to control the switching among different operation modes, namely motion-based tracking and appearance-based tracking. This tracking algorithm has the ability to track numerous targets while they group and split while maximising the discrimination between the targets and potential distracters.

4.2   Virtual Environment

The proposed approach has been applied into a real urban scenario involving a pedestrian crossing, see Fig. 5.(a). Using a camera calibration process [9], the ground–plane representation is generate, as shown in Fig. 5.(b). For this scenario, four semantic labels have been considered, namely *road*, *crosswalk*, *sidewalk*, and *waiting line*(a small area separating sidewalk and crosswalk). The labels are then

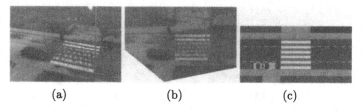

(a)   (b)   (c)

Fig. 5. Creation of the virtual environment. a) Real scenario S^r b) Homography applied to the image to obtain a ground–plane image c) Top view of the resulting virtual scenario S^v.

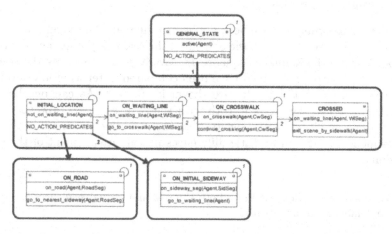

Fig. 6. Example of behavior modeled to generate virtual agents. This SGT describes the behavior *crossing_the_crosswalk*: A virtual agent is located somewhere in the scenario and reaches the crosswalk. When crossed, it leaves the scene walking by the opposite sidewalk.

assigned to different parts of the scenario and are finally rendered into the virtual environment by using different textures, see Fig. 5.(c).

In order obtain augmented reality image sequences on the selected scenario, three simple behavior models related to pedestrian crossings have been defined:

- *Walking on the Sidewalk (WS)*: A virtual human agent is located over the scenario. It reaches the closest sidewalk and exits the scenario walking to the farthest point of the sidewalk.
- *Crossing the Crosswalk (CC)*: A virtual human agent is located over the scenario. It first reaches a sidewalk (if in another region) and then moves to the crosswalk. After crossing it, the agent leaves the scene walking through the opposite sidewalk. Fig. 6 shows the SGT defined to represent this behavior.
- *Driving on the Road (DR)*: A virtual vehicle agent is located over the scenario. It reaches the road (if in another region) and finally leaves the scene driving to the farthers point of the road.

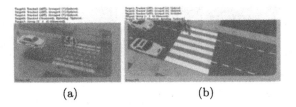

(a)   (b)

Fig. 7. Results of the tracking performed to (a) Real image sequence I^r (b) Synthetic image sequence I^v generated using the ground–truth trajectories from I^r

4.3 Evaluation Results

Two different experiments have been applied to the real scenario and its conversion to virtual environment. On the one hand, the real image sequence I^r and its correspondent synthetic image sequence I^v have been processed by the tracker, see Fig. 7. The outputs obtained have been compared in terms of low–level and high–level events and the results are shown in Table 1. As can be observed, the tracker matched the ground–truth with the real sequence. However, it has detected a false positive for the events *Entering / Exiting crosswalk* in the synthetic sequence, produced by little differences in the measurement of the scene dimensions.

Table 1. Event recognition results in both the real and virtual sequences, compared to the hand–labelled ground–truth

Events	Ground–truth O^{gt}	Output O^r	Output O^v
Entering Scene	6	6	6
Exiting Scene	4	4	4
Starting Occlusion	5	5	5
Ending Occlusion	5	5	5
Entering Crosswalk	6	6	7
Exiting the Crosswalk	5	5	6

On the other hand, a new image sequence I^{rv} has been obtained by fusing the original sequence I^r with a synthetic image sequence I^{va} generated by simulating 30 virtual agents. 15 agents were assigned the CC behavior, 10 were assigned the WS behavior, and 5 were assigned the DR behavior. This sequence has been then input to the tracker and an output O^{rv} has been obtained. In order to balance this result, a new ground–truth has been computed, joining O^{gt} with the trajectories generated after behavior simulation. The results are depicted in Table 2. The *entering / exiting scene* events were successfully recognized given the tracking results. However, due to camouflage, the number of occlusions detected is higher than the annotated ground–truth. Finally, most of the high–level events *entering / exiting crosswalk* have been detected.

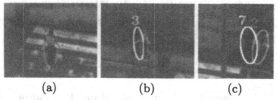

(a)   (b)   (c)

Fig. 8. Tracking results in the augmented reality sequence. Example frames of the obtained image sequence containing both real and virtual agents.

Table 2. Event recognition results for the tracker T processing the augmented reality sequence, compared to the augmented reality ground–truth, which has been obtained by joining the hand–labelled ground–truth of the real sequence with the trajectories generated by the virtual agents

Events	Ground–truth O^{gtrv}	Augmented Reality Tracking O^{rv}
Entering Scene	36	36
Exiting Scene	35	35
Starting Occlusion	17	21
Ending Occlusion	17	21
Entering Crosswalk	20	19
Exiting the Crosswalk	20	19

5   Conclusions

This paper described a framework which exploits the use of computer animation to evaluate the performance of tracking algorithms. This has been achieved in two different, complementary strategies. On the one hand, augmented reality has allowed to gradually increase the scene complexity by adding virtual agents into a real image sequence. On the other hand, the simulation of virtual environments involving autonomous agents has provided with synthetic image sequences, which have been used to evaluate several difficult tracking problems which are under research nowadays, such as performance processing long–time runs and the response capability against sequences containing crowds of people, which generate numerous occlusions. Finally, a general event–based evaluation metric has been defined in order to measure whether the agents and actions in the scene given by the ground truth were correctly tracked. Future work will focus on the two strategies presented in this paper. On the one hand, the integration of virtual agents in a real scenario should be provided with mor realism, in terms of illumination conditions and complex behavior models. On the other hand, virtual environments will be exploited to generate long sequences involving crowds of people and to analyze agent interactions.

Acknowledgements

This work is supported by EC grants IST-027110 for the HERMES project and IST-045547 for the VIDI-video project, and by the Spanish MEC under projects TIN2006-14606 and CONSOLIDER-INGENIO 2010 (CSD2007-00018). Jordi Gonzàlez also acknowledges the support of a Juan de la Cierva Postdoctoral fellowship from the Spanish MEC.

References

1. Aguilera, J., Wildenauer, H., Kampel, M., Borg, M., Thirde, D., Ferryman, J.: Evaluation of motion segmentation quality for aircraft activity surveillance. In: ICCCN 2005, Washington, DC, USA, pp. 293–300 (2005)
2. Baiget, P., Soto, J., Roca, X., Gonzàlez, J.: Automatic generation of computer animated sequences based on human behavior modeling. In: 10th International Conference in Computer Graphics and Artificial Intelligence, Athens, Greece (2007)
3. Bashir, F., Porikli, F.: Performance evaluation of object detection and tracking systems. In: IEEE International Workshop on Performance Evaluation of Tracking and Surveillance (PETS) (2006)
4. Conde, T., Thalmann, D.: Autonomous virtual agents learning a cognitive model and evolving. In: Intelligent Virtual Agents, pp. 88–98 (2005)
5. Desurmont, X., Sebbe, R., Martin, F., Machy, C., Delaigle, J.-F.: Performance evaluation of frequent events detection systems. In: IEEE International Workshop on Performance Evaluation of Tracking and Surveillance (PETS) (2006)
6. Gonzàlez, J., Roca, F.X., Villanueva, J.J.: Hermes: A research project on human sequence evaluation. In: Computational Vision and Medical Image Processing (Vip-IMAGE 2007), Porto, Portugal (2007)
7. Haag, M., Nagel, H.-H.: Incremental recognition of traffic situations from video image sequences. Image and Vision Computing 18(2), 137–153 (2000)
8. Varona-, J., Roca, F.X., Gonzàlez, J., Rowe, D.: Understanding dynamic scenes based on human sequence evaluation. Image and Vision Computing
9. Mozerov, M., Amato, A., Al Haj, M., Gonzàlez, J.: A simple method of multiple camera calibration for the joint top view projection. In: 5th International Conference on Computer Recognition Systems, Wroclaw, Poland (2007)
10. Nagel, H.-H.: From image sequences towards conceptual descriptions. Image and Vision Computing 6(2), 59–74 (1988)
11. Nghiem, A.T., Bremond, F., Thonnat, M., Ma, R.: A new evaluation approach for video processing algorithms. In: Motion 2007, p. 15 (2007)
12. Rowe, D., Huerta, I., Gonzàlez, J., Villanueva, J.J.: Robust multiple-people tracking using colour-based particle filters. In: Martí, J., Benedí, J.M., Mendonça, A.M., Serrat, J. (eds.) IbPRIA 2007. LNCS, vol. 4477, pp. 113–120. Springer, Heidelberg (2007)
13. Tambellini, W., Conde, T., Thalmann, D.: Behavioral animation of autonomous virtual agents helped by reinforcement. In: Rist, T., Aylett, R.S., Ballin, D., Rickel, J. (eds.) IVA 2003. LNCS (LNAI), vol. 2792, pp. 175–180. Springer, Heidelberg (2003)
14. CAVIAR: Context Aware Vision using Image-based Active Recognition. Ec's information society technology, http://homepages.inf.ed.ac.uk/rbf/CAVIAR/
15. Wu, B., Nevatia, R.: Tracking of multiple, partially occluded humans based on static body part detection. In: Proceedings of the 2006 IEEE Computer Society Conference on Computer Vision and Pattern Recognition, Washington, DC, USA, pp. 951–958. IEEE Computer Society, Los Alamitos (2006)
16. Young, D.P., Ferryman, J.M.: Pets metrics: On-line performance evaluation service. In: 2nd Joint IEEE International Workshop on Visual Surveillance and Performance Evaluation of Tracking and Surveillance, 2005, October 15-16, 2005, pp. 317–324 (2005)

A Manipulable Vision-Based 3D Input Device for Space Curves

Vincenzo Caglioti, Alessandro Giusti, Lorenzo Mureddu, and Pierluigi Taddei

Politecnico di Milano, Italy
alessandro.giusti@polimi.it, pierluigi.taddei@polimi.it

Abstract. This paper presents a novel and user friendly input device for 3D curves. The system is based on a piece of flexible wire and a single off-the-shelf photo camera: the user bends the wire to the desired 3D shape; then, an ad-hoc technique for 3D reconstruction is used to recover its 3D shape (a space curve) from a single image.

The result is a simple, unusual input device with many potential applications, ranging from games to 3D modeling. For untrained users, this is a much more intuitive input technique than alternative methods. A disadvantage is that changes to the wire's shape are not reflected in real time on the recovered representation.

We give a detailed description of the system's structure, briefly recall the reconstruction technique, and describe a prototype in which the input device is seamlessly integrated in the popular Blender 3D modeling software. We finally show simple example applications in which the shape of the wire is used to define the trajectory of moving objects, to deform a 3D object, and to animate a 3D character.

1 Introduction

We propose a system for human-computer interaction, for the input of a 3D curve. The goal is to digitize a space curve whose shape is defined by the user. The physical, manipulable support adopted allows the user to define the 3D shape incrementally, unlike what happens with devices requiring the user to draw a trajectory (with some visible marker) in the space.

The system is composed by a piece of flexible, circular-section wire, which the user bends to the desired shape, and a calibrated camera. The image of the bent wire is used to reconstruct its shape, which is the output of our system. Although counter-intuitive, single-image 3D reconstruction of the wire shape is possible by exploiting its tube-like geometry and perspective effects[1], as shown in [2] and summarized in Section 3.

Fig. 1. Manually modeling 3D curves by operating on handles is precise but counter-intuitive

[1] This is the reason why thickening 3D curves to tubes is an often-used expedient for visualization.

F.J. Perales and R.B. Fisher (Eds.): AMDO 2008, LNCS 5098, pp. 309–318, 2008.

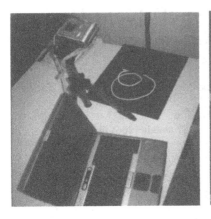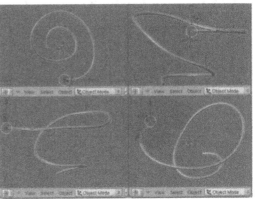

Fig. 2. Our system at work

Unlike most possible alternatives, our system is simple and cheap because it requires only low-profile, generic-purpose hardware (a single off-the-shelf digital camera) and relegates most complexity to software. Moreover, we maintain that the main advantage of our system is user-friendliness: even untrained users should be able to immediately, intuitively master its usage.

The input of 3D shapes is a challenging task, much more difficult than in two dimensions. The problem is both due to visualization difficulty of the shape, and, more importantly, difficulty for a user to express 3D positions.

1.1 Related Works

Due to the wide array of applications, ranging from human computer interaction (HCI), scientific visualization and 3D CAD modeling, many input device concepts have been devised explicitly for 3D input.

The possibilities of tangible user interfaces (TUIs), and in particular the general benefit over standard interaction were first demonstrated in [5]; [10] presents a review of the first few TUIs.

Virtual manipulation and physical manipulation of entities are particularly different since a designer's physical modeling skills do not wholly transfer to virtual modeling. For example, a designer can express a particular shape using a flexible cable by simply bending it. However, current interfaces for manipulating curves typically use a standard point cursor to indirectly adjust curve parameters, thus it may not be clear how to modify such parameters in order to attain the required shape.

Haptic devices such as [7] and [4] are particularly effective for free-form and solid modeling of surfaces. In these cases the user is using a *PHANToM* device to manipulate a dynamic implicit solid by "drawing in the air", without a real visualization of the modeled object in space but sensing the virtual object through the device feedback.

Certain physical objects can also quickly produce curves and surfaces that are hard to create using virtual techniques. For example [9] proposed an user interfaces based on virtual French curves, which are plastic or metal templates composed of many different curves. Those predefined planar templates allow design curves to accurately reflect a personal or corporate style. French curves are carefully crafted to have a minimal curve complexity and desirable curvature properties.

On the other hand [1] and [6] propose a system based on a high degree-of-freedom curve input device, *ShapeTape*, to interactively create curves and surfaces. In particular their tape is represented by a continuous bend and twist sensitive strip; those deformations are measured at regular intervals by two fiber optic bend sensors. This type of input device, being physically manipulable, like in our case, encourages manipulations that use both hands and, at times, all 10 fingers.

These approaches, although very accurate, are usually expensive and require specialized hardware. Our technique, on the contrary, is very simple, can be cheaply implemented and also offers, with respect to pure virtual interfaces, a tangible, physical representation of the modeled entity, at the expense of being less versatile and non-realtime.

In Section 2 we describe the system in its physical part, whereas Section 3 details the geometric aspects and software algorithms we employ. In Section 4 we further elaborate on our specific implementation, also detailing the interface to the user. We finally provide some usage examples in Section 5, and conclude the paper (Section 6) presenting current work to overcome some of the system's limitations.

2   System Description and Hardware

The system is composed by a camera placed on a tripod, pointed at a flexible wire with one end fixed to a weighed base, and one end free. Colored cardboard may be used as a backdrop should the background be similar in color to the wire.

The wire must be flexible and should keep the given shape (e.g. should not spring back to the original position nor collapse under its own weight); moreover, cross sections should be circular and of constant diameter, even when the wire is bent; this ensures that the shape can be modeled as a *canal surface* (see Section 3).

In practice, many objects, such as ropes, power cords and computer cables meet these geometrical constraints, except when tightly bent; however, they rarely have the necessary mechanical properties. Building such an object is straightforward, for example by embedding a thin metal wire which conveys rigidity; in our prototype, instead, we used an electrical wire which has all the desired properties out of the box.

Fig. 3. Hardware components of our system

Length is not a critical factor, and depends on the specific application; on the contrary, the cross section must not be too thin, so that the image of the wire is at least 10-15 pixels wide.

The camera must be positioned as close as possible to the wire, provided that, in any configuration, the wire is fully visible. The volume to be covered can be modeled as an hemisphere with the length of the wire as radius, and the fixed end as center.

The reconstruction is more precise if the camera optics is wide angle; the widest angle possible with ordinary zoom lenses of off-the-shelf digital cameras (35mm equivalent focal length, corresponding to about 90 deg of horizontal field of view) is more than enough for a good reconstruction.

A more critical issue is depth-of-field, which should be maximized by using an aperture as narrow as possible, in such a way that wire apparent contours appear sufficiently sharp along the entire image.

A calibrated camera is required in order to reconstruct the 3D shape of the wire; in practice, precise calibration is not necessary, and assuming the principal point to be at the center of the image and using the focal length written by the camera in the EXIF data is enough.

After the user bends the wire to the desired shape, the camera shoots (either automatically or triggered by the user) and software processing begins, as described in the following section. Although appropriate image processing algorithms may be able to reliably extract the needed information from the image without additional strict requirements, we simplify the following by additionally requiring that the background behind the wire is uniform, that no strong, sharp shadows are present, and that the wire image appears uniform, without sharp highlights or self-shadows. This allows a straightforward and robust extraction of the wire apparent contours.

In practice, obtaining these conditions is often easy especially if the wire surface is dull: some attention is only needed to proper lighting and to providing a uniform background.

In the ideal operating conditions, the wire is imaged against a bright background such as a back-lit fabric; this allows us to get, at once:

- a very narrow aperture, leading to extended depth of field;
- low sensor ISO, leading to reduced noise;
- no shadows or highlights, and a sharp, strong silhouette to be precisely extracted.

However, as we are aiming at a solution as simple as possible, we simply implemented our prototype with a white wire with a black backdrop (which reduces the artifacts due to shadows, while maximizing contrast at the wire silhouette) without any special lighting.

3   Technique and Algorithms

3.1   Contour Extraction

Once the image is acquired, the first step is to accurately extract the apparent contours of the wire; if shooting conditions are good enough, this reduces to applying the Canny [3] edge extraction algorithm followed by edge tracking, in order to create edge-pixel chains. Since contour accuracy is critical, we compute edges in sub-pixel coordinates, and exploit the expected contour smoothness by fitting splines; this also allows us to readily compute tangent directions to the contour, which will be needed in the following.

Once two facing contours are identified, we use the following geometrical reconstruction technique (see [2] for details) in order to reconstruct the shape of the wire, which is modeled as a *canal surface*.

3.2   3D Reconstruction

A canal surface can be defined as the envelope surface of a family of spheres with constant radius R, whose centers lie on a space curve called axis, such that, at any axis point, the axis curvature radius is strictly larger than R.

Equivalently, the canal surface is the union of circumferences with radius R, called cross sections, such that each cross section is centered on the axis. An axis point and the cross section centered on it are said to be associated. A cross section has a supporting plane perpendicular to the tangent to the axis at its associated point.

A core concept in the reconstruction technique for canal surfaces is that of coupled points: two contour points are said to be coupled if and only if they are the image of two points belonging to the same cross-section.

Once a pair of coupled points on facing contours are identified in a calibrated image, the associated cross section in space can be uniquely reconstructed, provided that its radius its known.

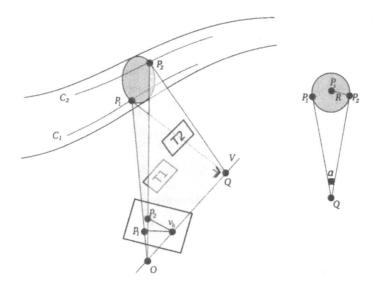

Fig. 4. Cross section reconstruction geometry

In particular, the orientation of the cross section is found as the direction identified by vanishing point v_h (see figure 4): v_h is the intersection of the tangents to the contours (c_1 and c_2) at the coupled points (p_1 and p_2). Likewise, the position of the cross section is uniquely determined as soon as its radius R is known.

Note that a scaled version of the canal surface can be reconstructed by using an arbitrary value for the canal surface radius R.

Since a pair of coupled points allows us to reconstruct the related cross section, we need to detect pairs of coupled points along the canal surface contours. This is possible owing to the following property:

Property 1. Let c_1 and c_2 be two facing contours on the image; let t_1 (t_2) be the tangent to c_1 (c_2) at point p_1 (p_2), and let v_h be the intersection between t_1 and t_2.

The points p_1 and p_2 are coupled only if the angle formed by $\overrightarrow{Op_1}$ and $\overrightarrow{Ov_h}$ coincides with the angle formed by $\overrightarrow{Op_2}$ and $\overrightarrow{Ov_h}$, where O is the camera viewpoint.

This allows us to identify a large number of coupled point pairs on the canal surface lateral contours: from each pair, the related cross section is reconstructed. If a sufficient number of cross sections is available, the shape of the canal surface (and, equivalently, its axis) can be reconstructed as well.

In practice, once many points on the axis are identified, we fit a smooth 3D spline, which represents the reconstructed shape of the wire.

4   Discussion

4.1   Implementation Details

The geometric technique described so far can be efficiently implemented:

- initially, a point p_1^0 is randomly chosen on a contour c_1, and the coupled point p_2^0 is determined on the facing contour c_2 by iterative minimization of

$$J = \text{abs}(\text{angle}(\overrightarrow{Op_1^0}, \overrightarrow{Ov_h}) - \text{angle}(\overrightarrow{Op_2}, \overrightarrow{Ov_h}))$$

  The initial estimate for p_2 is the point on c_2 nearest to p_1^0.
- Once the first pair of coupled points is identified, further pairs of coupled points are found by "crawling" the contours: p_1^{i+1} is chosen next to p_1^i, at a predefined distance $\delta = 1 \div 10$ pixels. p_2^{i+1} is found by iterative minimization of the measure J above, using p_2^i as an initial estimate.

As the contours are internally represented as smooth splines, very precise sub-pixelar localization is possible, and a continuous domain exists for iterative minimization; moreover, tangents are immediately defined. δ can be tuned to higher values for faster but marginally less precise and robust reconstruction.

If some sections of the wire contours are (possibly self-) occluded the related cross-sections can not be reconstructed; in our system, we are not currently handling this case automatically: instead, we assume that the wire contours are completely visible and never occluded. This is also the reason why realtime reconstruction of the curve is unlikely, as the manipulating hands would occlude most of the object.

4.2   Interface

In our prototype, we integrated the reconstruction code (which is implemented in the Matlab environment) in the popular Blender 3D modeling software, by exploiting its Python scriptability. We automate photo shooting by means of the canon SDK for Matlab [8].

Fig. 5. Our simple interface integrated in the Blender UI

The user is presented with a simple interface including photographic options (such as whether the flash should be used while shooting) and format of results. After processing, a spline curve (optionally thickened to an extruded tube) is created in the Blender workspace. From this point on, the user can exploit all of Blender's features (such as game engine, physical engine, transforms, animation capabilities, rendering...) exploiting the new object. Some examples are shown in the following Section.

5   Demo Applications

We provide some examples of our system's functionality implemented using Blender's python interface: after the curve is acquired, it is automatically

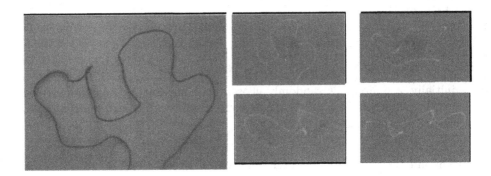

Fig. 6. Digitizing a complex 3D shape

processed in order to obtain a number of different results and applications. All presented experiments are acquired using real images of different types of flexible wires, in varying operating conditions. The most obvious application is importing a 3D shape in the 3D modeling software for further user-driven processing; this is illustrated in figures 2 and 6.

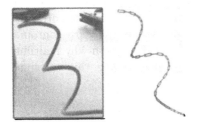

Figures 8 and 7 depict how the imported curve can be automatically used as a guide for deforming a linear 3D model; the implementation trivially maps the curve to a chain of bones which have been used to rig the 3D model. This chain thus is used as a skeleton for guiding the deformation. By repeating the acquisition of different shapes, the different bone configurations can be used as key frames for character animations.

Fig. 7. Our prototype allows using the curve as a guide for object deformation

As curves can only be used for the direct modeling of linear, simple objects, we implemented a nesting feature for easy creation more complex shapes such as trees or stick figures.

Moreover, we are developing other simple applications exploiting the full functionality of the Blender platform, such as its physical engine, game engine or animation capabilities. For example, we are developing a simple roller-coaster construction script, which creates a physically plausible animation depicting a ride on a roller coaster whose shape is given by the user by manipulating the wire.

The results we got so far highlight that the device is extremely easy and intuitive to use; although it does not allow fine control over the resulting shape, nor live adjustments, it results very convenient in many applications where ease of use is an important factor.

Experimental results show that the curve can be imported in few seconds – albeit easy optimizations may significantly reduce this time – and with an acceptable accuracy.

Fig. 8. Expressing 3D deformation of linear objects (and its animation)

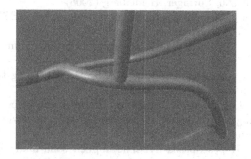

Fig. 9. Our prototype supports nesting curves on other curves for iterative construction of complex objects

6   Conclusions and Future Works

In this work we propose a system for the input of a space curve, composed by a physical wire which the user bends to the desired shape; a camera which images the object after manipulation; and software routines for 3D reconstruction of the shape, which is then imported in a 3D modeling software. The interface is remarkably user-friendly, in that it is based on a stable, manipulable physical device: this allows the user to easily express the 3D curve, while incrementally improving its accuracy.

Our prototype integrates with the Blender 3D modeler, in which most applications can be implemented with minimal effort. We are also planning a standalone library providing image shooting and reconstruction functionality, usable by external software.

As we mentioned in Section 4, our prototype can not currently handle self-occlusion of the wire contours. Since this happens rather often when the wire is given a complex shape, we are exploring ways to handle multiple pieces of contours, and robustly determining whether a point on a contour is "orphan" – i.e. it misses a visible coupled point. A sound technique for implementing this is considering (possibly at a lower resolution) all plausible coupled points in multiple contours visible in the image, then looking for a globally-optimal and consistent association of facing contours, by also exploiting that the sorting of successive coupled points along facing contours must not change. Led to the extreme consequences, this approach may allow single-image 3D reconstruction of complex physical structures described by multiple sections of wire.

References

1. Balakrishnan, R., Fitzmaurice, G., Kurtenbach, G., Singh, K.: Exploring interactive curve and surface manipulation using a bend and twist sensitive input strip. In: SI3D (1999)
2. Caglioti, V., Giusti, A.: Reconstruction of canal surfaces from single images under exact perspective. In: Leonardis, A., Bischof, H., Pinz, A. (eds.) ECCV 2006. LNCS, vol. 3951, pp. 289–300. Springer, Heidelberg (2006)
3. Canny, F.: A computational approach to edge detection. IEEE Transactions on Pattern Analysis and Machine Intelligence 8, 679–698 (1986)
4. Chen, H., Sun, H.: Real-time haptic sculpting in virtual volume space. In: VRST, vol. 220
5. Fitzmaurice, G.W., Ishii, H., Buxton, W.A.S.: Bricks: laying the foundations for graspable user interfaces. In: SIGCHI (1995)
6. Grossman, T., Balakrishnan, R., Singh, K.: An interface for creating and manipulating curves using a high degree-of-freedom curve input device. In: SIGCHI, pp. 185–192. ACM Press, New York (2003)
7. Hua, J., Qin, H.: Haptics-based dynamic implicit solid modeling. IEEE Transactions on Visualization and Computer Graphics 10(5) (2004)
8. O'Malley, S.: Canon camera control toolbox for matlab, http://www2.cs.uh.edu/~somalley/camerabox.html
9. Singh, K.: Interactive curve design using digital french curves. In: SI3D (1999)
10. Srinivasan, M.A., Basdogan, C.: Haptics in virtual environments: Taxonomy, research status, and challenges. Computers & Graphics 21(4), 393–404 (1997)

A Comparative Study on Using Zernike Velocity Moments and Hidden Markov Models for Hand Gesture Recognition

Moaath Al-Rajab, David Hogg, and Kia Ng

Computer Vision Group, School of Computing, University of Leeds
7.27 E.C. Stoner Building, School of Computing, University of Leeds, Leeds, LS2 9JT, UK
{moaath,dch,kia}@comp.leeds.ac.uk

Abstract. Hand-gesture recognition presents a challenging problem for computer vision due to the articulated structure of the human hand and the complexity of the environments in which it is typically applied. Solving such a problem requires a robust tracking mechanism which in turn depends on an effective feature descriptor and classifier. Moment invariants, as discriminative feature descriptors, have been used for shape representation for many years. Zernike moments have been particularly attractive for their scale, translation and rotation invariance. More recently, Zernike moments have been extended to a spatio-temporal descriptor, known as the Zernike velocity moment, through combining with the displacement vector of the centre of mass of the target object between video frames. This descriptor has hitherto been demonstrated successfully in human gait analysis. In this paper, we introduce and evaluate the application of Zernike velocity moments in hand-gesture recognition, and compare with a bank of hidden Markov models with Zernike moments as observations. We demonstrate good performance for both approaches, with a substantial increase in performance for the latter method.

Keywords: Spatio-temporal description, hand gesture recognition, skin-colour segmentation, Zernike velocity moments, HMM.

1 Introduction

Interest in hand gesture recognition has increased in recent years motivated in large part by the range of potential applications for human-machine interaction mediated by hand gestures. More generally, the human hand poses a substantial challenge for tracking and action recognition due to the way in which it deforms and self-occludes and the range of different semantically distinguishable actions it can perform.

Within the wide range of application scenarios, hand gestures can be classified into several categories [1], including conversational gestures, controlling gestures, manipulative gestures, and communicative gestures. For instance, sign language is an important example of a domain involving communicative gestures [2]. Our work is aimed at the use of controlling gestures within multimedia applications similar to [3-5].

F.J. Perales and R.B. Fisher (Eds.): AMDO 2008, LNCS 5098, pp. 319–327, 2008.

Recognizing gestures automatically from visual input is a complex task that typically involves several stages, including signal processing, tracking, shape description, motion analysis, and pattern recognition. Machine learning methods have been used widely, particularly in recent years, and inspiration has come from several quarters including psychology and human behaviour studies.

In selecting a method for shape description, a key requirement is to provide sufficient discriminative information for successful classification of hand gestures. The use of moments for shape description was introduced by Hu [6] in 1962. Hu introduced a set of six functions of standard central moments which provide a description that is invariant to scaling, translation and rotation, and a seventh function invariant to scaling, translation and skew. Another form of moments are the Zernike moments (ZM) where the kernel is a set of orthogonal Zernike polynomials defined over polar co-ordinates inside a unit circle. ZMs are the projection of the image function onto these orthogonal basis functions [14, 16]. This original idea has been extended recently by Shutler and Nixon [7] to produce the so-called Zernike Velocity Moments ZVMs. These are generated from sequences of images depicting objects in motion and were shown in [7] to be effective for human gait analysis. The current paper introduces the use of ZVMs coupled with an appropriate classifier for hand-gesture recognition. We evaluate and compare the performance of this classification method based on ZVM with Zernike Moments coupled with a bank of HMMs.

In Section 2 we review the background that is most relevant to the study. We explain the formulation of Zernike Velocity Moments in Section 3, and the dataset used in both sets of experiments in Section 4. Section 5 and 6 deal with the two experiments, the first on classification using Zernike Velocity Moments and the second on classification using a bank of HMMs over Zernike Moments. Finally, in Section 7 we draw conclusions from the experiments and briefly address further work.

2 Background and Related Work

The literature on hand gesture recognition using computer vision can be categorized into those approaches that use a 3-D model for tracking the hand, and those that use an entirely image-based representation. An early development in the former category used a 3D mesh with vertices embedded in a linear subspace to characterize allowable shape variations [8]. The linear subspace was obtained from a set of examples using principal component analysis, generalising earlier applications of the same technique to sets of point landmarks in the image plane. The model was used to detect the pose of a hand in the visual field and subsequently to track this hand from frame to frame.

Later, Athitsos and Sclaroff [9] used a 3D model to generate projections of a 3D hand in different shapes and from different viewpoints. The projected hands were then matched to hands depicted in the incoming video stream, both through edge matching and through the use of Hu moments. In related research Sudderth et al. [10] introduced probabilistic methods for visual tracking of a three-dimensional geometric hand model from monocular image sequences. Model components are represented by their positions and orientations. A prior model is then defined which enforces the kinematic constraints implied by the joints of model. They enhanced matching between the 3D geometric model and the tracked hand using a redundant representation, that measures Chamfer distance for colour and edge-based likelihood features. They tracked the hand's motion using non-parametric belief propagation (NBP) algorithm.

Tracking methods that depend entirely on an image-plane representation of the hand have been worked on extensively. Typically such systems are computationally less expensive than those methods that use a 3D model. Skin colour segmentation is a common method for locating the hand due to its fast implementation, where usually skin colour is modelled as a Gaussian distribution in a suitable colour space. Static background subtraction and adaptive background models are also commonly used for segmentation. Shadows can be a problem for such algorithms, although the worst effects can be ameliorated to some extent; for example, by using infrared (IR) cameras as in Ahn [11, 12].

For recognizing gestures, Ng and Ranganath [13] divided the process into two stages. The first stage was to find the poses of the gesture in each frame and the second stage was to analyse the motion of the gesture. Zernike moments and Fourier descriptors were used to generate the feature vectors used to train a Radial Basis Function (RBF) neural network combined with an HMM. Park et al. [3] used HMMs for gesture classification on 13 different gestures. They divided the gesture into four distinctive states: start, intermediate, distinctive and the end of the gesture. They assumed that the gestures start and end from the same state. Skin-colour is used for hand segmentation.

3   Zernike Velocity Moments (ZVM)

The concept of moments comes from physics, where it relates to the force required to affect a given angular acceleration on an object of known mass distribution. For the purpose of image analysis, a set of generalized moments is defined for a 'density' distribution $f(x, y)$ derived in some fashion from an image and often a binary function denoting membership of a target region. The discrete centralized moment of order (p, q) is given in equation 1:

$$\mu_{pq} = \sum_x \sum_y (x - \bar{x})^p (y - \bar{y})^q f(x, y) \qquad (1)$$

Different degrees of moments represent different features of the target shape. For example, moments with $p=q=0$ $(0, 0)$ compute the summation of all density values of the image (e.g. the number of 'on' pixels for a binary density function). Moments $(1, 0)$ and $(0, 1)$ represent the pixel distribution along X and Y axis respectively. Moments of degree two represent the variance of the density function, moments of degree three represent skewness, and moments of degree four represent kurtosis of the distribution.

The central moments are invariant to translation in the image plane and can be normalized for variation in scale by forming the so-called normalized central moment η_{pq} derived from the corresponding central moment as follows (for p and q both greater than zero):

$$\eta_{pq} = \frac{\mu_{10}}{\mu_{00}^{\gamma}} \quad \text{and} \quad \gamma = \frac{p+q}{2} + 1 \tag{2}$$

The original definition has been extended and combined with the theory of algebraic invariants to become the mathematical device used today in image analysis.

Zernike moments are a class of orthogonal complex moments, which in contrast to Hu moments can be computed for higher degrees, giving more discriminative potential – for example, higher order moments characterize the detailed shape of an object. The magnitudes of Zernike moments are rotation and reflection invariant [14] and can be easily constructed to an arbitrary order [15]. By projecting the image function onto the basis set, the Zernike moment A_{pq} of order p and repetition q is defined by:

$$A_{pq} = \frac{p+1}{\pi} \sum_{x} \sum_{y} f(x,y)[V_{pq}(x,y)]^{*} \qquad x^2 + y^2 \leq 1 \qquad |q| \leq p \tag{3}$$

$$V_{pq}(\rho,\theta) = R_{pq}(\rho)e^{jq\theta} \quad \text{where } \theta = \tan^{-1}\frac{y}{x} \quad \rho = \sqrt{x^2 + y^2} \tag{4}$$

$$R_{pq}(\rho) = \sum_{s=0}^{(p-|q|)/2} (-1)^s \frac{(p-s)!}{s!\left[\frac{p+|q|}{2}-s\right]!\left[\frac{p-|q|}{2}-s\right]!} \rho^{p-2s} \tag{5}$$

Zernike Velocity Moments (ZVM) [7, 16] are essentially a weighted sum of Zernike moments over a sequence of frames (length T), weighted by a real-valued scalar function of the displacement of the centre of mass (CoM) between consecutive frames:

$$A_{pq\beta\lambda} = \alpha \sum_{i=2}^{T} \sum_{x} \sum_{y} f_i(x,y)U(i,\beta,\lambda)[V_{pq}(x,y)]_i^{*} \quad \text{where } x^2 + y^2 \leq 1 \tag{6}$$

$$U(i,\beta,\lambda) = (\bar{x}_i - \bar{x}_{i-1})^{\beta}(\bar{y}_i - \bar{y}_{i-1})^{\lambda} \tag{7}$$

U is the series of weights derived from the displacements of the CoM, and * donates the complex conjugate. Usually (β,λ) are set to (0, 1) or (1, 0) to avoid zero weights derived from the displacement of the CoM when there is only horizontal or vertical motion of the hands.

Normalized Zernike velocity moments $\overline{A}_{mn\beta\lambda}$ are defined in equation 8:

$$\overline{A}_{pq\beta\lambda} = \frac{A_{pq\beta\lambda}}{A.T} \tag{8}$$

Where A is the average area (in pixels) of the moving object, T is the length of the video segment.

4 Dataset and Experiment Setup

For our comparative study of classification performance, we captured a video stream depicting a series of hand gestures using a normal webcam (30 fps, 320x240 pixels) in an office environment, as illustrated in figure 1. The video consists of 80 instances for each of five distinct gestures (referred to as A-E), performed in total by 10 different people (i.e. 8 instances of each gesture by each person). The five gestures used are shown in figure 2. More information about our dataset is available online[1]. We marked the start and end of each gesture manually for the entire dataset to provide a ground-truth for training and testing, experiments were conducted on a machine of 2.2 GHz dual-core cpu speed, 2 GB RAM.

A Gaussian skin-colour model [17] is used to produce a map of skin likelihood values for each frame, and we then track the hand using a CAMShift tracker [18, 19]. The CAMShift output is cleaned up automatically to remove small isolated regions and finally the result is binarised to give a final segmented hand region. For our hand gesture dataset, the procedure gives a well segmented hand region in each frame.

The start of gesture "A"   *The end of gesture "A"*

Fig. 1. Start and end of gesture "A" (see figure 2) as an example of gesture. It shows the webcam input and the output of the CAMShift tracker in office environment after skin-colour segmentation. First frame is input stream and the second is the projection of HSV colour after weighting.

5 Classification Using CvR and ZVM

In the first experiment, we used a ZVM descriptor to characterise the video segment corresponding to each gesture instance. The speed at which a gesture is performed results in video segments of different lengths within the dataset (between 45 and 150 frames). We did not attempt to interpolate gestures to a fixed number of frames, since the weighted mean computed by the ZVM is invariant to the overall speed of a gesture, although not to non-linear variations in the temporal execution. Computing the ZVM on a typical video segment takes up to 1 sec.

For this experiment, we used a feature vector obtained from three Zernike Velocity Moments, defined by setting the four parameters (p, q, β, λ) to (12,4,0,0), (12,4,0,1), and (12,4,1,0) (see equation 6).

We experimented with a number of standard classifiers and obtained the best overall performance using the 'Classification via Regression' (CvR) classifier reported in [20] and implemented as part of the WEKA package [21]. This builds a decision tree with a

---

[1] http://www.comp.leeds.ac.uk/moaath/gHand/DS/

linear regression function at the leaves. We used ten-fold cross validation on our entire dataset and obtained the results laid out in the confusion matrix shown in Table 1, giving a mean accuracy of 84.22%. It can be seen that the greatest confusion is between gestures "A" and "E" where hand poses in the first part of the gesture and the horizontal displacement are similar.

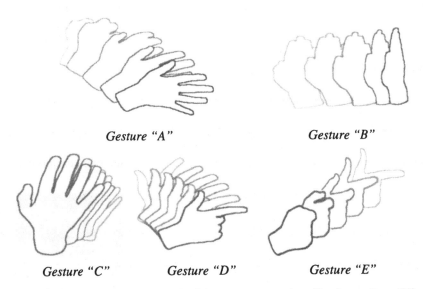

Gesture "A"   Gesture "B"

Gesture "C"   Gesture "D"   Gesture "E"

Fig. 2. Training and testing gestures. Each of these gestures can be utilized to perform different actions. For example, in photo albums application, *Gesture "A"* may be used to change the album; *Gesture "B"* for rotating a photo; *Gesture "C"* for zooming a photo by moving the hand towards/away from the camera; *Gesture "D"* for navigating to the next photo; *Gesture "E"* for switching the application on/off.

A potential problem with the ZVM is that low displacement components of the centre of mass will result in clustering of feature vectors around the origin in feature space. For classifiers, this may impact on the ability to discriminate between gestures that involve little horizontal or vertical motion – for example, gesture B.

Table 1. The confusion matrix using CvR classifier and ZVM descriptor with (p,q,β,λ) set to (12,4,0,0), (12,4,0,1), (12,4,1,0), see equation 6

		Predicted Gesture				
		"A"	"B"	"C"	"D"	"E"
Actual Gesture	"A"	66	2	3	1	8
	"B"	5	64	3	5	3
	"C"	5	2	70	1	2
	"D"	0	1	2	72	5
	"E"	6	2	2	4	66

6   Classification Using HMMs and ZM

In the second experiment, we used hidden Markov models (HMMs) for classification [23], with observations defined by a vector of Zernike moments with parameters (p, q) set to (10, 2), (10, 4), (12, 2) and (12, 4) - see equation 3. We used Matlab HMM code from [22]. Prior to training and testing, we linearly interpolate each gesture sequence to a fixed number of frames. The reported results are for HMMs with four hidden states and a Gaussian observation density.

We train a separate HMM for each of the five gestures. Given an observation sequence O, the likelihood of the observation sequence given the model λ is obtained by summing the likelihood over all possible state sequences S:

$$P(O \mid \lambda) = \sum_{all\_S} P(O \mid S, \lambda) P(S \mid \lambda) \tag{9}$$

We then select the model with maximum likelihood as the chosen gesture:

$$\lambda = \arg \max_{k} (P(O \mid \lambda_k)) \tag{10}$$

The optimal number of hidden states chosen for each of the five HMMs was four- see figure 3(a). In training the HMM (as in gesture A), the increase in observation likelihood with each iteration is shown in figure 3(b). As for the first experiment, we use ten-fold cross validation giving a mean accuracy of 94.45%. Table 2 shows the confusion matrix using Hidden Markov Models which can be compared to table 1. Computing the ZMs on a typical frame of the video segment takes 30 ms.

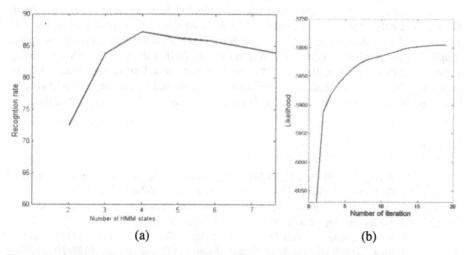

(a)   (b)

Fig. 3. (a) shows that 4 is the optimal number of states for each of the HMM models. (b) shows the increasing likelihood of gesture A against the number of iterations during training.

Table 2. Confusion matrix presents the obtained results using the ZMs as shape descriptor to generate the training and testing sequences that been used to train and test 5 HMM models for the gestures

<table>
<tr><th rowspan="2"></th><th></th><th colspan="5">Predicted Gesture</th></tr>
<tr><th></th><th>"A"</th><th>"B"</th><th>"C"</th><th>"D"</th><th>"E"</th></tr>
<tr><td rowspan="5">Actual Gesture</td><td>"A"</td><td>70</td><td>8</td><td>0</td><td>2</td><td>0</td></tr>
<tr><td>"B"</td><td>0</td><td>78</td><td>0</td><td>2</td><td>0</td></tr>
<tr><td>"C"</td><td>0</td><td>1</td><td>79</td><td>0</td><td>0</td></tr>
<tr><td>"D"</td><td>4</td><td>1</td><td>0</td><td>75</td><td>0</td></tr>
<tr><td>"E"</td><td>0</td><td>0</td><td>0</td><td>0</td><td>80</td></tr>
</table>

7 Discussion and Conclusion

From the confusion matrices and relative accuracies obtained in the two experiments, it is clear that the ZM+HMM combination used in the second experiment has given substantially better results than the ZVM+CvR combination used in the first. However, it seems intuitively plausible that the displacement of the centre of mass between frames carries discriminative information on the set of gestures. To explore this further, we carried out a third experiment in which this displacement is added to the feature vector of Zernike moments used in the HMM. This increased the mean accuracy obtained to 98.3%, although this only represents a small number of additional examples being correctly classified.

In this paper, we have introduced and investigated hand gesture recognition with Zernike Velocity Moments, previously used successfully for human gait analysis. The results yield a potential use for their simplicity, but not as good as Zernike moments coupled with a bank of HMMs. We aim to explore further the use of ZVMs spanning a short time interval to replace the ZMs in the HMM-based classifier. This would in principle provide an alternative way of introducing displacement into the HMM+ZM formation together with the discriminative abilities of an HMM for sequential data.

References

1. Wu, Y., Huang, T.S.: Human Hand Modeling, Analysis and Animation in the Context of HCI. In: IEEE International Conference Image Processing, Kobe, Japan (1999)
2. Yuan, Q., Sclaroff, S., Athitsos, V.: Automatic 2D Hand Tracking in Video Sequences. In: IEEE Workshop on Applications of Computer Vision (2005)
3. Park, H., Kim, E., Jang, S., Kim, H.: An HMM Based Gesture Recognition for Perceptual User Interface. In: Advances in Multimedia Information Processing, pp. 1027–1034 (2004)
4. Carbini, S., Viallet, J.E., Bernier, O.: Pointing Gesture Visual Recognition for Large Display. In: International Conference of Pattern Recognition. IEEE Computer Society Press, Los Alamitos (2004)

5. Sepehri, A., Yacoob, Y., Davis, L.S.: Parametric Hand Tracking for Recognition of Virtual Drawings. In: Proceeding of the fourth IEEE International Conference on Computer Vision Systems. IEEE Computer Society Press, Los Alamitos (2006)
6. Hu, M.: Visual Pattern Recognition by Moment Invariants. IEEE Transactions On Information Theory 8, 179–187 (1962)
7. Shutler, J.D., Nixon, M.S.: Zernike velocity moments for sequence-based description of moving features. Image and Vision Computing 24, 343–356 (2006)
8. Heap, A.: Learning deformable shapes models for object tracking. In: Computing School Leeds, University of Leeds (1998)
9. Athitsos, V., Sclaroff, S.: An Appearance-based Framework for 3D Hand Shape Classification and Camera Viewpoint Estimation. In: Fifth IEEE International Conference Proceedings on Automatic Face and Gesture Recognition, vol. 1, IEEE Computer Society Press, Los Alamitos (2002)
10. Sudderth, E.B., Mandel, M.I., Freeman, W.T., Willsky, A.S.: Visual Hand Tracking Using Nonparametric Belief Propagation. In: Conference on Computer Vision and Pattern Recognition Workshop. IEEE Computer Society Press, Los Alamitos (2004)
11. Ahn, S.C., Lee, T., Kim, I., Kwon, Y., Kim, H.: Large Display Interaction Using Video Avatar and Hand Gesture Recognition. In: Campilho, A.C., Kamel, M. (eds.) ICIAR 2004. LNCS, vol. 3211, pp. 261–268. Springer, Heidelberg (2004)
12. Pham, Q., Gond, L., Begard, J., Allezard, N., Sayd, P.: Real-Time Posture Analysis in a Crowd using Thermal Imaging. In: IEEE Conference on Computer Vision and Pattern Recognition CVPR 2007. IEEE Computer Society Press, Los Alamitos (2007)
13. Ng, C.W., Ranganath, S.: Gesture Recognition via Pose Classification. In: 15th International Conference on Pattern Recognition, vol. 3. IEEE Computer Society Press, Los Alamitos (2000)
14. Bailey, R., Srinath, M.: Orthogonal Moment Features for Use with Parametric and Non-Parametric Classifiers. IEEE Transactions on Pattern Analysis and Machine Intelligence 18, 389–399 (1996)
15. Hse, H., Newton, A.R.: Sketched Symbol Recognition using Zernike Moments. In: 17th International Conference on Pattern Recognition (ICPR 2004), vol. 1. IEEE Computer Society Press, Los Alamitos (2004)
16. Shutler, J.D., Nixon, M.S.: Zernike velocity moments for the description and recognition of moving shapes. In: Proceeding of British Machine Vision Conference BMVC, Manchester, vol. 2 (2001)
17. Jones, M.J., Rehg, J.M.: Statistical Color Models with Application to Skin Detection. International Journal of Computer Vision, 81–96 (2002)
18. Bradski, G.R.: Computer Vision Face Tracking For Use in a Perceptual User Interface. Intel Technology Journal (1998)
19. François, A.R.J.: CAMSHIFT Tracker Design Experiments with Intel OpenCV and SAI. Institute for Robotics and Intelligent Systems IRIS-04-423 (2004)
20. Frank, E., Wang, Y., Inglis, S., Holmes, G., Witten, I.H.: Using Model Trees for Classification, Department of Computer Science. University of Waikato, Hamilton, New Zealand (1998)
21. University of Waikato, Weka 3: Data Mining Software in Java (Accessed April 2008), http://www.cs.waikato.ac.nz/~ml/weka/
22. Murphy, K.: Hidden Markov Model (HMM) Toolbox for Matlab (Accessed April 2008), http://www.cs.ubc.ca/~murphyk/Software/HMM/hmm.html
23. Rabiner, L.R.: A Tutorial on Hidden Markov Models and Selected Applications in Speech Recognition. IEEE Transactions on Information Theory 77, 257–286 (1989)

Deformable Volumetric Simplex Meshes

Luis Cruz[1,2] and Luis Gerardo de la Fraga[1]

[1] Cinvestav, Computer Science Department,
Av. Instituto Politécnico Nacional 2508. 07360 México City, México
lcruz@computacion.cs.cinvestav.mx, fraga@cs.cinvestav.mx
[2] Unidad Profesional Interdisciplinaria en Ingeniería y Tecnologías Avanzadas del IPN
Av. Instituto Politécnico Nacional 2580, 07340 México City, México

Abstract. In this article, two possible ways to build volumetric meshes of simplexes are described. One structure uses the crystalline organization of carbon atoms in diamond and it is used to simulate the deformation under internal pressure of a container. The second structure is in layers and it is used to simulate human body tissues that could be cut. We also describe the cutting process for this layered structure.

Keywords: surface cutting, simplex meshes, surface deformation, non-elastic model, physically based simulation.

1 Introduction

The simplex meshes is one of the forms to represent deformable models. Simplex meshes have been used to model the surface of solids, such as human body tissues; however they had not been used to represent the volume inside a solid. In this work two ways are shown to build an object with volumetric simplex meshes, this is, simplex meshes are used to represent not only the object's surface but also its interior. One way is to build an object like the structure of carbon atoms in the diamond, and this form is used to simulate a container subject to internal pressure. A second way is taking into account that a human organ can be modeled as layers of tissues; and this second structure can be cut easily.

Previous works in simplex meshes have mainly by Dellingette and Ayache in [1,2]. The authors used such meshes to model human livers [3], and more recently, to model lungs and other organs [4,5]. Their models only represent the surfaces of the organs, and they leave aside the modeling of the organs' volume.

The volumetric models that have been used are meshes of tetrahedrons and hexahedrons [6]. To the best of our knowledge, a volumetric simplex mesh has not been used before to build a volumetric model.

One motivation of this work is to solve the problem of cutting a mesh. This problem has been solved by mesh refinement [7], but also this solution has a prohibitive computational cost for a real time application. Cutting a volumetric simplex mesh, in the layer configuration, involves the adaptation of its vertices and edges to keep the constant connectivity of the simplex mesh, and has therefore a better performance for a real time application.

F.J. Perales and R.B. Fisher (Eds.): AMDO 2008, LNCS 5098, pp. 328–337, 2008.
© Springer-Verlag Berlin Heidelberg 2008

This paper is organized as follows: in Sec. 2, the definition of simplex meshes and the two volumetric structures are described; in Sec. 3, examples of applications of objects built with volumetric simplex meshes are presented. Finally, in Sec. 4, conclusions of this work are drawn.

2 Simplex Meshes

The simplest definition of a simplex is a vertex and a constant connectivity with its neighboring vertices, but without to include them. A simplex mesh has a fixed vertex connectivity: if the vertex connectivity is equal to n, it means that each vertex has n adjacent vertices, it is a n-simplex; and the mesh built with this n-simplex is a $(n-1)$-mesh. A 0-simplex is a single vertex. An 1-mesh is built with 2-simplexes, and this mesh represents the perimeter of a 2D object [8]. If 3-simplexes are used, then the resulting mesh is a 2-mesh, and a surface can be represented with them. A volumetric simplex mesh is built with 4-simplexes, therefore it is a 3-mesh. Formally, in this section, two forms to build 3-meshes will be shown, these two forms will be called *diamond structure* and *layered structure*.

2.1 Diamond Structure

The carbon atoms in the diamond form a crystalline structure very compact, with 4 adjacent atoms to every one, this means that the crystalline structure is composed by 4-simplexes, and also it is a natural 3-mesh. The silicon used to produce chips has also this structure.

The basic form of the crystalline structure, in Fig. 1, is not used directly to build the volumetric mesh. Instead, a basic cell, a cube, is used. This basic cell is shown in Fig. 2. Thus, the volumetric mesh is constructed in two steps: 1) the

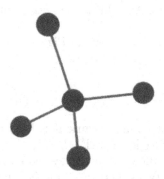

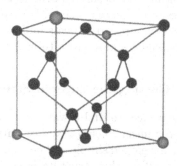

Fig. 1. Structure of carbon atoms in diamond

Fig. 2. Basic cell of diamond structure. Lighter vertexes are not part of the built structure, and also showed cube's edges are not part of the mesh edges.

space is filled with the basic cell, and (2) more vertices and edges are added in the borders to correct the connectivity. One example of a solid cube built with this volumetric simplex mesh is shown in Fig. 3.

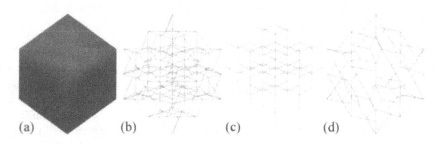

Fig. 3. A solid cube built with diamond structure is shown in (a), the whole mesh is in (b), the internal part is in (c), and the superficial part of the mesh in (d)

To build the cube in Fig. 3, a base cube of size $2 \times 2 \times 2$ basic cells is formed. The cube's surface is formed with a procedure that add, to each external vertex, new vertices in order to keep the constant connectivity of a 3-mesh.

2.2   Layered Structure

When one cuts the diamond structure, this is, when an edge or face is erased, it is very difficult to keep the constant connectivity of the mesh and the crystalline structure at the same time. Therefore, other model was generated, having in mind that cutting the mesh should be an easy task.

Imaging a plane built with a 2-mesh, it looks as a floor filled with hexagonal mosaics. If a copy of this plane it translated above the first one, and the corresponding vertices below and above are joined, a 3-mesh is obtained. It is possible to continue the described process to add new planes. And this is the reason why the resulted form is called a *layered structure*.

Two examples of objects built with this structure are shown in Fig. 5, in (a) a thin plane, and in (b) a tube.

2.3   Cutting the Layered Structure

It is not easy to find a way to cut the diamond structure because it is hard to keep the mesh constant connectivity if a edge of face is deleted.

We developed simple and efficient operations to allow to cut the layered structure. Cutting this structure is equivalent to cut two superficial 2-meshes, but must take into account the edges that joint both 2-meshes. To see the cutting process, one example will be given with the plane shown in Fig. 6.

Cutting the mesh means to delete an edge or a face on the mesh, and then reorganize, or even create new ones, vertices and edges to keep the constant

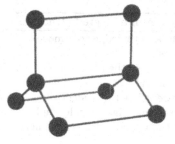

Fig. 4. Layered structure. Two 3-simplexes are joined with new edges to create 4-simplexes.

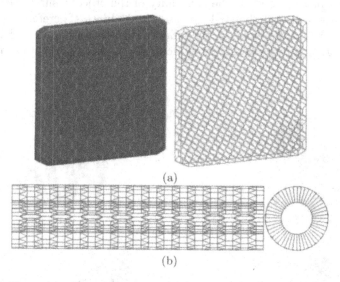

Fig. 5. Examples of layered objects, (a) a thin plane, and (b) a solid tube

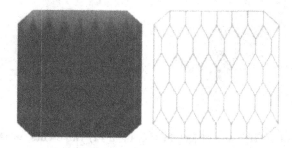

Fig. 6. Layered structure used to explain its cutting process

Algorithm 1. Cut an edge from a layered structure
___
Require: A simplex 3-mesh, and the edge to remove
Ensure: The cut simplex mesh
   1. Find the corresponding edge to the given one, in the opposite 2-mesh
   2. Cut the two 2-meshes, or the two superficial meshes, using those edges. In this
step, one or several faces are deleted (see algorithms 2 to 5)
   3. Find the isolated vertexes and edges, inside the hole produced in step 2.
   4. Create new faces to fill the interior faces of the hole.
___

vertex connectivity. Algorithm 1 describes the necessary steps to remove an edge from the volumetric mesh.

In step 4 of Algorithm 1, the continuity of the object's surface is kept. This means that the model should looks as a real object. Therefore, we add new faces to fill the created holes on the model's surface. Fig. 7 shows the cut of the plane in Fig. 6, and the new created faces, also is showed two steps of cutting a solid tube.

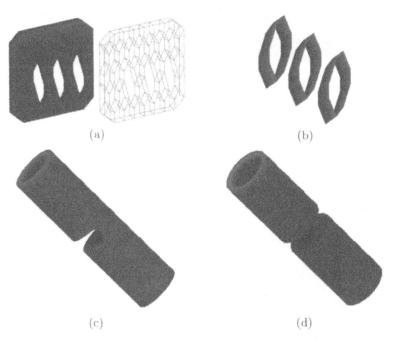

        (a)   (b)

        (c)   (d)

Fig. 7. Example of cutting the object in Fig. 6; in (a) three cuts, in (b) it is shown the new internal faces created in the cutting process, in (c) it is shown an intermediate step in cutting a solid tube and, in (d) the cut is finished

Step 2 involves other four algorithms. These algorithms are:

1. *Remove one mesh's edge*: The algorithm 2 removes vertexes and faces, and creates new edges to preserve the simplex's vertex connectivity, and also keeps the respective adjacent faces. In Fig. 8 we can see the mesh state before to remove the corresponding edge.

Algorithm 2. Edge remove

Require: A simplex mesh (M), and the edge to remove (E)
Ensure: Removed adjacent faces to the removed edge
  1. Find adjacent vertices V_1 and V_2 of E.
  2. Find adjacent vertices V_3, V_4, V_5 and V_6 of V_1 and V_2
  3. Remove adjacent mesh faces, F_1 and F_2, of E using algorithm 4
  4. Verify if it is some special case, if so proceed to normalize edges and there is not a triangle adjacent to edge E
  5. Remove E and add two new edges E_1 and E_2
  6. Modify opposite faces, F_3 and F_4, of E
  7. Remove V_1, V_2, E_3, E_4, E_5 and E_6

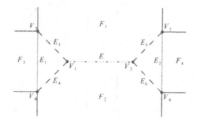

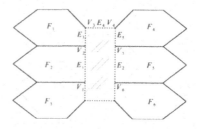

Fig. 8. Mesh state before to remove edge E

Fig. 9. Following edges to know if the mesh is already split

2. *Check if the connectivity is preserved between two mesh edges*: The algorithm 3 verifies if there exists a path between two edges, using one as a starting edge, follow the mesh boundary and trying to reach the second one. If the path does not exist, then we have two new meshes (this is due to the cutting process). This algorithm is used each time one edge is removed from the mesh. Fig. 9 shows how this algorithm works.

3. *Remove one face*: The algorithm 4 is used when there is only one face connecting two parts of a mesh. Fig. 10 shows the original mesh and Fig. 11 shows the mesh after the face has been removed.

4. *Extract one or more meshes*: The algorithm 5 gets the mesh's disjoint parts when, by example, the last face is cut by algorithm 4. It works putting its connected elements in new lists of elements.

Algorithm 3. Verify the connectivity between edges

Require: Simplex mesh (M) and the two edges to test E_1 and E_2
Ensure: Verify if mesh was split in two parts
  1. Set E to edge E_1 and choose a vertex, V_1, from E
repeat
    2. Find opposite vertex to E, V_2
    3. Find adjacent edge to V_2, which does not have a face and is not E
    4. Set this edge to E and set V_2 to vertex V_1
until Reach the edge E_1 or E_2
if Reached the edge E_2 **then**
    5. The mesh was not split
else
    6. The mesh was split

Algorithm 4. Remove jointed face

Require: Simplex mesh (M) and face to remove (F)
Ensure: Removed face, and one or two disjointed meshes
  1. Remove edges E_1 and E_2, which are adjacent to empty faces
  2. Use algorithm 3 to verify if connectivity is preserved
if Connectivity was lost **then**
    3. Use algorithm 5 to get new two meshes

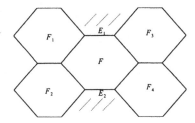

Fig. 10. The mesh with the face to be removed

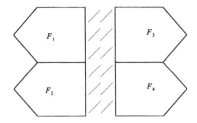

Fig. 11. The mesh without the removed face

Algorithm 5. How to get two disjoint meshes

Require: A simplex mesh (M)
Ensure: Two or more disjoint meshes
  1. Set L_F, L_E and L_V to empty list of faces, edges and vertices, respectively.
  2. Set all faces of M as *non-processed*
  3. $i = 0$
while There are non-processed faces **do**
    4. Take the next face F_j from M
    if There are no more adjacent faces **then**
      5. $i \leftarrow i + 1$
    6. Put face F_j in L_{F_i} list, its edges in L_{E_i} and its vertices in L_{V_i}

3   Simulations

We perform two simulations in order to show how the developed structures can be used. In the first simulation a hollow container built with diamond structure is subject to internal pressures. The second simulation consists of a model of three tissues: tendon-membrane-bone. We are going to describe each simulation and how the model are deformed. For the simulations we have used the deformation model described in detail in [9].

3.1   Hollow Containers

We create a hollow container with the diamond structure, a couple of these containers are shown in Fig. 12.

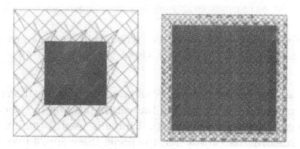

Fig. 12. Hollow containers built using the diamond structure

The containers in Fig. 12 were deformed by an internal pressure. In Fig. 13, two views of the deformed containers are shown. In the case of the second container, the pressure deforms it to a sphere, this is because its thickness is relatively small.

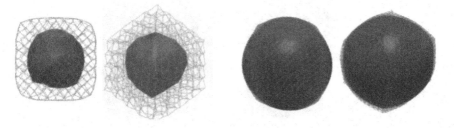

Fig. 13. Deformed containers, in the final steady state

3.2   Tissues Deformation

Using the layered structure, we built three objects that represents three different tissues: tendon, membrane, and bone. The tendon and the bone are two cylinders, and the membrane is a plane. The used cylinders are like the ones shown in Fig. 5; the membrane is a single surface of a 2-mesh. There are 22 common vertices between the tendon and the membrane, and also between the membrane and the bone. The three objects are shown in Fig. 14. The carried simulation apply a force in two points of the membrane in order to separate the tendon from the bone. We believe that this simulation is one of the most common tasks that a student of medicine has to perform.

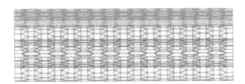

Fig. 14. Tendon-membrane-bone model. The tendon and the bone were built with the layered structure, analogue to the cylinder shown in Fig. 5.

In the deformation model, for the simulated tendon and bone, an internal force that is calculated as the sum of initial vertex position to the current vertex positions has been included. This internal force is used to maintain the whole structure of the deformable object. For the bone, there are 24 fixed vertices over its central axis in order to keep its structure.

Fig. 15 shows the deformation of the simulated tendon-membrane-bone tissues.

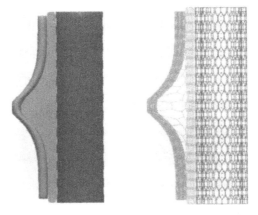

Fig. 15. Deformed tissues. The two cylinders were build using the layered structure and are used to simulate a tendon and a bone (it is the wider one).

4 Conclusions and Future Work

Volumetric simplex meshes offers a relatively simple model to build, to visualize and to deform an virtual object. The main characteristic of that meshes is that their vertex connectivity is constant, and this characteristic allows to use a same deformation engine in all the mesh.

We proposed two structures to build volumetric simplex meshes: a diamond structure, that looks like the carbon atoms configuration in a diamond, and a layered structure, which is used to simulate human tissues. The diamond structure was used to simulate hollow containers, subject to internal pressures. The layered structure was used to simulate a scenario of three tissues: a tendon and a bone jointed by a membrane; in the simulation, the tendon has been separated from the bone. This second structure allows the development of simple cutting operations over the mesh.

Our goal is develop a whole real time virtual scenario to train medicine students. We are developing a deformable model with elastic–plastic and hysteresis (the model does not return to the same initial state) characteristics. In this scenario cutting will be available in any part of the virtual tissues.

References

1. Montagnat, J., Delingette, H.: Volumetric medical image segmentation using shape constrained deformable models. Proceedings of computer vision, virtual reality and robotics in medicine 97, 13–22 (1997)
2. Delingette, H., Montagnat, J.: General deformable model approach for model based reconstruction. In: IEEE international workshop on model-based 3D image analysis, January 1998, vol. 98 (1998)
3. Delingette, H., Ayache, N.: Hepatic surgery simulation. Communications of the ACM 48(2), 31–36 (2005)
4. Delingette, H.: General object reconstruction based on simplex meshes. International Journal of Computer Vision 32(2), 111–146 (1999)
5. Battger, T., Kunert, T., Meinzer, H., Wolf, I.: Application of a new segmentation tool based on interactive simplex meshes to cardiac images and pulmonary mri data. Academic Radiology 14(3), 319–329 (2007)
6. Zhang, Y., Bajaj, C., Sohn, B.S.: Adaptive and quality 3d meshing from imaging data. In: SM 2003: Proceedings of the eighth ACM symposium on Solid modeling and applications, pp. 286–291. ACM, New York (2003)
7. Montagnat, J., Delingette, H., Ayache, N.: A review of deformable surfaces: topology, geometry and deformation. Image and vision computing 19(14), 1023–1040 (2001)
8. Ramírez-Flores, J., de la Fraga, L.: Basic three-dimensional objects constructed with simplex meshes. In: 2004 1st International Conference on Electrical and Electronics Engineering, September 2004, pp. 166–171. IEEE, Los Alamitos (2004)
9. Ramírez-Trejo, C.M., de la Fraga, L.: Animation of deformable objects built with simplex meshes. In: 2005 2nd International Conference on Electrical and Electronics Engineering, September 2005, pp. 36–39. IEEE, Los Alamitos (2005)

Analytical Simulation of B-Spline Surfaces Deformation

Manuel González-Hidalgo, Antoni Jaume Capó, Arnau Mir,
and Gabriel Nicolau-Bestard

Math and Computer Science Dept.
manuel.gonzalez@uib.es, antoni.jaume@uib.es, arnau.mir@uib.es,
gabriel.nicolau@gmail.com
http://dmi.uib.es

Abstract. In this paper an analytic solution of an evolution model is proposed in order to deform B-splines parametric surfaces. The deformation model is based on an associated energy functional to one surface and its variational formulation is introduced. After some simplifications including assumptions regarding the mass and damping matrices and taking into account the properties of B-splines when are used as finite elements, a second order differential equations is obtained which can be solved analytically. The spatial discretization where these finite elements are defined and computed appears as a reduced number of control points and is deformed instead of all the surface points, obtaining an efficient and fast method in order to simulate surface deformations.

Keywords: Computer graphics, surface deformation, B-splines.

1 Introduction

The deformation models include a large number of applications and they have been used in fields such as edge detection, computer animation, geometric modelling etcetera. In this work, a deformation model will be introduced which uses B-splines as finite elements. The model includes a deformation equation, its analytical solution, examples of deformations and the computational cost.

The use of B-splines and their properties as finite elements was introduced by Höllig in [8]. The model of deformation is based on the model used in [1] where the finite elements are classical finite elements (triangles and squares). We choose B-splines as finite elements to solve our deformation equation. The use of classical finite elements makes a mosaic that - fills all space with a large computational cost if we wish to solve our problem because a huge data structure is needed. Otherwise, the B-splines finite elements combine the computational advantage of B-splines and standard mesh-based elements because the obtained data structure is smaller than the data obtained using classical finite elements. Moreover, the B-splines allow us to solve analytically the deformation model taking into account some considerations on mass and damping matrices.

Following [6] and [7], this paper solves analytically the differential equation of the model of deformation which was introduced there. Therefore, we can extend

F.J. Perales and R.B. Fisher (Eds.): AMDO 2008, LNCS 5098, pp. 338–348, 2008.
© Springer-Verlag Berlin Heidelberg 2008

the applied surfaces and thus reduce the computational cost of the method of resolution of the differential equation.

This paper is organized as follows: in section 2, we introduce B-splines finite elements and their properties; in section 3, the static model is presented showing the variational formulation and the space discretization. The dynamic evolution model is the aim of section 4 where we solve analytically the equation associated with the model. In the next section, section 5; we calculate the computational cost related to the equation resolution. In section 6, several examples of deformation simulations are shown applying different forces. Finally, some conclusions are reached and future work to be carried out is proposed.

2 B-Splines

The B-splines are piecewise polynomial functions with good local approximations for smooth functions [12]. We have chosen B-splines as piecewise polynomial approximation because of its local support. This property reduces the computational cost of the model. Uniform B-splines can be defined in several ways [3] [4] [12] [8]. In this work we have taken the definition given by Höllig in [8], which it will be described next.

Definition 1. *An uniform B-spline of degree n, b^n, is defined by*

$$b^n(x) = \int_{x-1}^{x} b^{n-1}(t)dt$$

starting with $b^0(x) = \begin{cases} 1, & x \in [0,1), \\ 0, & \text{otherwise.} \end{cases}$

To evaluate the B-splines in a simple form and fast computationally, we use the following recurrence equation (De Boor [3] and Cox [2]).

$$b^n(x) = \frac{x}{n}b^{n-1}(x) + \frac{(n+1-x)}{n}b^{n-1}(x-1) \tag{1}$$

In order to construct the finite elements bases, we will use a scaled and translated uniform B-spline. They are defined by transforming the standard uniform B-spline, b^n, to the grid $h\mathbb{Z} = \{..., -2h, h, 0, h, 2h, ...\}$, where h is the scaled step.

Definition 2. *The transformation for $h > 0$ and $k \in \mathbb{Z}$ is $b^n_{k,h}(x) = b^n(\frac{x}{h} - k)$. The support of this function is $[k, k+n+1)h$.*

The first order derivative of the transformed B-spline is given by

$$\frac{d}{dx}b^n_{k,h}(x) = h^{-1}(b^{n-1}_{k,h}(x) - b^{n-1}_{k+1,h}(x)) \tag{2}$$

[8]. Higher order derivatives can be computed as a linear combination of lower degree B-splines:

Theorem 1. *The mth derivative of a degree n transformed B-spline following the definition 2 is given by the recurrence relation*

$$\frac{d^m}{dx^m}b^n_{k,h}(x) = h^{-m}\sum_{i=0}^{m}(-1)^i \binom{m}{i} b^{n-m}_{k+i,h}(x) \tag{3}$$

Obviously, this equation has sense if $m \leq n$ since in others cases the derivative is 0.

The generalization of one-dimensional B-splines is described in the following. The N-variate B-spline of degree $\mathbf{n} = (n_1, ..., n_N)$, of index $\mathbf{k} = (k_1, ..., k_N)$ and the space discretization $\mathbf{h} = (h_1, ..., h_N)$ is defined as

$$B^{\mathbf{n}}_{\mathbf{k},\mathbf{h}}(\mathbf{x}) = \prod_{i=1}^{N}b^{n_i}_{k_i,h_i}(x_i). \tag{4}$$

The support of this function is $\prod_{i=1}^{N}[k_i, k_i + n_i + 1)h_i$.

Applying basic properties of differential calculus and applying theorem 1, a compact expression for any partial derivative of multivariate B-spline can be obtained. Using theorem 1, the derivatives can be evaluated and are obtained with a smaller computational cost, since less recurrences are applied.

A B-spline parametric surface is given by $S : \Omega \subset I\!R^2 \rightarrow I\!R^3$ where

$$S(\mathbf{x}) = \sum_{\mathbf{k}\in\mathbb{Z}^2} P_{\mathbf{k}}B^{\mathbf{n}}_{\mathbf{k},\mathbf{h}}(\mathbf{x}) \tag{5}$$

(see [6] and [7]) where $P_{\mathbf{k}}$ are the so-called the *control points* and they are the elements that determine the B-spline surface.

3   Static Model

The static model, also called deformation model, is based on an associated energy towards one surface that checks the shape of it. The energy function is a non convex function with a local minimum. The goal is to achieve this minimum using an evolution model. This minimum depends on the initial surface and the used evolution model.

The associated energy functional, $E : \Phi(S) \rightarrow I\!R$, $S \mapsto E(S)$, is defined as

$$E(S) = \int_{\Omega} \omega_{10}\left|\frac{\partial S}{\partial u}\right|^2 + \omega_{01}\left|\frac{\partial S}{\partial v}\right|^2 + \omega_{11}\left|\frac{\partial S}{\partial u\partial v}\right|^2$$
$$+ \omega_{20}\left|\frac{\partial^2 S}{\partial u^2}\right|^2 + \omega_{02}\left|\frac{\partial^2 S}{\partial v^2}\right|^2 + \mathcal{P}(S(u,v))dudv$$

where $\mathcal{P}$ is a potential of the forces that work on the surface. This energy functional has been used in [15], [1], [11] in order to deform surfaces and compute the contour of images.

Using the equations of Euler-Lagrange, it can be proved [1] that an energy local minimum must satisfy:

$$-\omega_{10}\frac{\partial^2 S}{\partial u^2} - \omega_{01}\frac{\partial^2 S}{\partial v^2} + 2\omega_{11}\frac{\partial^4 S}{\partial u^2 \partial v^2} + \omega_{20}\frac{\partial^4 S}{\partial u^4} \tag{6}$$

$$+ \omega_{02}\frac{\partial^4 S}{\partial v^4} = -\nabla P(S(u,v)) + \text{boundary conditions}$$

The surface domain is $\Omega = [0,1]^2$ and the boundary conditions are: $S(u,0) = (u,0,0)$, $S(u,1) = (u,1,0)$, $S(0,v) = (0,v,0)$, $S(1,v) = (1,v,0)$.

3.1 Variational Formulation

With the purpose of establishing the variational formulation of the boundary value problem done by (6), we recall the definition of a Sobolev Space of order two $H^2(\Omega)$,

$$H^2(\Omega) = \{S \in L^2(\Omega) : \frac{\partial^{(\alpha_1 + \alpha_2)} S}{\partial x_1^{\alpha_1} \partial x_2^{\alpha_2}} \in L^2(\Omega), 0 \le \alpha_1 + \alpha_2 \le 2, \alpha_1, \alpha_2 \in \mathbb{N}\}$$

We will consider the set of functions $(H^2(\Omega))^3$ satisfying the previous boundary conditions. We will denote this set by $\mathcal{H}$. It can be proved [1] [14] that solving equation (6) is equivalent to find an element $S \in \mathcal{H}$, such that $a(S,T) = L(T)$ for all $T \in \mathcal{H}$, where $a(\cdot,\cdot)$ is a bilinear form defined as

$$a(S,T) = \int_{\Omega} \left(\omega_{10}\frac{\partial S}{\partial u}\frac{\partial T}{\partial u} + \omega_{01}\frac{\partial S}{\partial v}\frac{\partial T}{\partial v} + \right.$$
$$\left. 2\omega_{11}\frac{\partial^2 S}{\partial u \partial v}\frac{\partial^2 T}{\partial u \partial v} + \omega_{20}\frac{\partial^2 S}{\partial u^2}\frac{\partial^2 T}{\partial u^2} + \omega_{02}\frac{\partial^2 S}{\partial v^2}\frac{\partial^2 T}{\partial v^2} \right) dudv \tag{7}$$

and $L(\cdot)$ is the following linear form

$$L(T) = -\int_{\Omega} \nabla P(S)T \, dudv.$$

3.2 Discretization

We want to find a function $S \in \mathcal{H}$ such that

$$a(S,T) = L(T), \ \forall T \in \mathcal{H}. \tag{8}$$

In order to do this, the surface domain will be discretized. The spatial discretization is given by $h_1\mathbb{Z} \times h_2\mathbb{Z}$ where $h_1 = \frac{1}{N_1 + n_x - 1}$ and $h_2 = \frac{1}{N_2 + n_y - 1}$, where $N_1 \times N_2$ are the control points of the B-spline surface that we will to evolve (see [6] and [7] for details). This spatial discretization will fix the control points that are not zero. The index $\mathbf{k} = (k_1, k_2)$ belongs to the set

$\{-n_x, ..., N_1 + n_x - 1\} \times \{-n_y, ..., N_2 + n_y - 1\}$. So, the B-spline surface will be determined by the relevant B-splines And are specified by the following equation

$$S(u, v) = \sum_{k_1=-n_x}^{N_1+n_x-1} \sum_{k_2=-n_y}^{N_2+n_y-1} P_{(k_1,k_2)} B^n_{(k_1,k_2)\mathbf{h}}(u, v). \tag{9}$$

The B-spline bases are determined by the following set of finite elements of finite dimension: $V^n_{\mathbf{h}} = < \{(B^n_{\mathbf{k},\mathbf{h}}(u, v), 0, 0) : \mathbf{k} \in \mathcal{I}\} \cup \{(0, B^n_{\mathbf{k},\mathbf{h}}(u, v), 0) : \mathbf{k} \in \mathcal{I}\} \cup \{(0, 0, B^n_{\mathbf{k},\mathbf{h}}(u, v)) : \mathbf{k} \in \mathcal{I}\} >$ where $\mathcal{I} = \{0, ..., N_1 - 1\} \times \{0, ..., N_2 - 1\}$. Thus, taking into account the boundary conditions, the control points $P_{\mathbf{k}}$ associated to B-splines belonging to the set $V^n_{\mathbf{h}}$ are the unique ones that are computed using the equation (10). (see below).

Using equations (8) and (9) we can obtain three linear systems, one for each coordinate:

$$AP_i = L_i, \quad i = 1, 2, 3, \tag{10}$$

where A is a square matrix and their elements are:

$$a((B^n_{k,h}, 0, 0), (B^n_{j,h}, 0, 0))_{(k,j)\in\mathcal{I}\times\mathcal{I}},$$

P_i is a vector of component i of each control point and L_i is a vector with components $L_1 = L((B^n_{k,h}, 0, 0))_{k\in\mathcal{I}}$, $L_2 = L((0, B^n_{k,h}, 0))_{k\in\mathcal{I}}$ and $L_3 = L((0, 0, B^n_{k,h}))_{k\in\mathcal{I}}$. The computational cost of A is constant and the computational cost of L_i, $i = 1, 2, 3$ is $O(N_1 \times N_2)$ (see [6] and [7]).

4   Dynamic Evolution Model

The classical dynamic model of evolution has been applied [1], [13], [11], [5], [9] [10]. In our dynamic model, the surface depends on time. So, we have $S(u, v, t)$. Nevertheless, this dependency only affects the control points, which is an advantage since in each iteration we do not have to calculate all the surface. Therefore, we must only calculate the new control points. Thus, our dynamic model of evolution IS determined by the equations

$$M\frac{d^2 P_i}{dt^2} + C\frac{dP_i}{dt} + AP_i = L_i, \ i = 1, 2, 3. \tag{11}$$

where M is a mass matrix, C is the damping matrix, A is the stiffness matrix and L_i is the applied force on the surface. The stiffness matrix and the applied force are computed as in the previous section.

The mass and damping matrices, M and C respectively, will be diagonals and constants in respect to time. The forces are also considered constant in time, but it depends on the surface domain. That is, it can be applied to different points on the surface.

It can be observed, that the stiffness matrix only depends on the initial grid and the B-splines degree. Thus, we obtain a second order differential equation which can be solved analytically.

The stiffness matrix A is diagonal because it is a symmetrical matrix (as we can see in the previous section, it is obtained from a bilinear form). Therefore, A can be written as $K\Lambda K^{-1}$, where K is the matrix of eigenvectors of A and Λ is a diagonal matrix with the eigenvalues of A in its diagonal.

The evolution equation (11) can be written

$$M\frac{d^2 P_i}{dt^2} + C\frac{dP_i}{dt} + K\Lambda K^{-1}P_i = L_i, \ i = 1, 2, 3, \tag{12}$$

multiplying by K^{-1},

$$K^{-1}M\frac{d^2 P_i}{dt^2} + K^{-1}C\frac{dP_i}{dt} + \Lambda K^{-1}P_i = K^{-1}L_i, \ i = 1, 2, 3. \tag{13}$$

Let $Q_i = K^{-1}P_i$, $i = 1, 2, 3$ be the new variables. Taking into account that M and C are diagonals, the previous equation can be written as:

$$M\frac{d^2 Q_i}{dt^2} + C\frac{dQ_i}{dt} + \Lambda Q_i = K^{-1}L_i, \ i = 1, 2, 3. \tag{14}$$

Let $\mathbf{N} = N_1 \times N_2$ be the cardinal of $\mathcal{I}$. The previous system of differential equations can be written as $\mathbf{N}$ differential equations in one variable q_{ij}, $j = 1, \ldots, \mathbf{N}$, where $Q_i = (q_{i1}, \ldots, q_{i\mathbf{N}})^\top$:

$$m_j q_{ij}'' + c_j q_{ij}' + \lambda_j q_{ij} = \widehat{l_{ij}}, \quad j = 1, \ldots, \mathbf{N}, \ i = 1, 2, 3, \tag{15}$$

where $M = \operatorname{diag}(m_1, \ldots, m_{\mathbf{N}})$, $C = \operatorname{diag}(c_1, \ldots, c_{\mathbf{N}})$ and $\widehat{l_{ij}} = (K^{-1}L_i)_j$.

The solution of the previous differentials equations is:

$$q_{ij}(t) = -\frac{1}{2\lambda_j\sqrt{c_j^2 - 4m_j\lambda_j}}\widehat{l_{ij}} \tag{16}$$

$$\left(e^{t\alpha_j}(-c_j + \sqrt{c_j^2 - 4m_j\lambda_j}) + e^{t\beta_j}(c_j + \sqrt{c_j^2 - 4m_j\lambda_j}) - 2\sqrt{c_j^2 - 4m_j\lambda_j}\right),$$

where $\alpha_j = \frac{-c_j - \sqrt{c_j^2 - 4m_j\lambda_j}}{2m_j}$ and $\beta_j = \frac{-c_j + \sqrt{c_j^2 - 4m_j\lambda_j}}{2m_j}$.

So, the evolution of vector of control points can be computed as:

$$P_i(t) = KQ_i(t) = K(q_{i1}(t), \ldots, q_{i\mathbf{N}}(t))^\top, \ i = 1, 2, 3. \tag{17}$$

recall that P_i is a vector of component i of each control point. Then, we obtain the control points of the evolution surface as a time function.

5   Computational Cost

In this section, we are going to calculate the computational cost in order to obtain $P_i(t)$, for a fixed time t. The computational cost of the computation of $K, \lambda_j, \widehat{l_{ij}}, j = 1, \ldots, \mathbf{N}, i = 1, 2, 3$ are not considered. Moreover, the coefficients

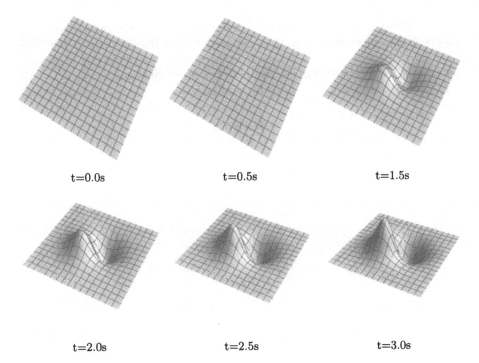

t=0.0s   t=0.5s   t=1.5s

t=2.0s   t=2.5s   t=3.0s

Fig. 1. Several iterations of the obtained deformation applying two forces in opposite sense

of $e^{t\alpha_j}$ and $e^{t\beta_j}$ in (16) can be calculated and stored before the computation of $q_{ij}(t)$, for any value of t.

The number of operations we have to make to calculate $q_{ij}(t)$ is $O(1)$. That is, let c be the computational cost to compute e^z, for $z \in \mathbb{R}$ and we consider 1 the computational cost for the elementary operations $(+, -, \cdot, /)$. So, the number of operations required in order to compute $q_{ij}(t)$ is $4 + 2c$, which is $O(1)$.

The computational cost of $Q_i(t)$ will be $O(\mathbf{N})$ because $Q_i(t)$ has $\mathbf{N}$ components and the computational cost to calculate each component is $O(1)$.

Finally, the computational cost to obtain $P_i = KQ_i(t)$ (made by Eq. 17) will be $O(\mathbf{N}^2)$ because if we multiply a $\mathbf{N} \times \mathbf{N}$ matrix by a $\mathbf{N} \times 1$ vector, the computational cost of the product is $O(\mathbf{N}^2)$.

6   Examples

In this section, we show several examples of deformations using the analytical solution of the dynamic model presented in the previous section. The chosen surface is the plane $[0, 1] \times [0, 1] \times \{0\}$ and bicubic B-splines has been used to obtain all the deformations.

The figure 1 shows the obtained deformation applying two forces using $N_1 \times N_2 = 25$ control points. One of the forces is $(0, 0, 100)$ and the

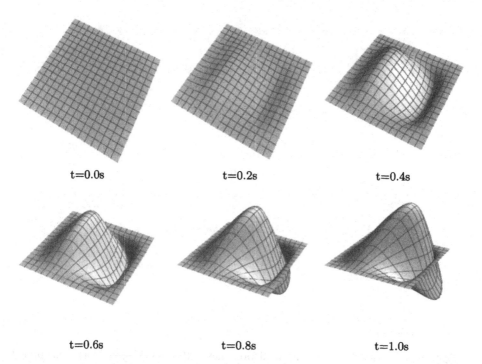

$t=0.0s$ $t=0.2s$ $t=0.4s$

$t=0.6s$ $t=0.8s$ $t=1.0s$

Fig. 2. Several iterations of the obtained deformation applying the sinusoidal force $(50\sin v\pi, 50\sin u\pi, 200\cos u\pi\sin v\pi)$

other one, $(0,0,-100)$. The $(0,0,100)$ force has been applied to the square $(0.4, 0.5) \times (0.4, 0.5)$ and the other one, $(0,0,-100)$, has been applied to the square $(0.5, 0.6) \times (0.5, 0.6)$. The energy functional parameters have been $\omega_{10} = \omega_{01} = 0.1$ and $\omega_{11} = \omega_{20} = \omega_{02} = 0.01$.

Figure 2 shows a deformation applying a sinusoidal force over all the surface. This force is given by $(50\sin v\pi, 50\sin u\pi, 200\cos u\pi\sin v\pi)$, where $(u, v) \in [0, 1] \times [0, 1]$ represents the coordinates of our surface. In this case, $N_1 \times N_2 = 36$ control points are used. The energy functional parameters are the same as in the previous example.

In the deformation of figure 3, a force like $(0, 0, \sin\frac{8\pi u + 8\pi v}{2})$ over all surface has been applied using $N_1 \times N_2 = 36$ control points.

Finally, in figure 4, we show a deformation where 100 control points have been used. We have applied the force $(0, 0, -60)$ to the four corners of the surface. More specifically, the forces have been applied to the next squares $(0.1, 0.2) \times (0.1, 0.2)$, $(0.1, 0.2) \times (0.8, 0.9)$, $(0.8, 0.9) \times (0.1, 0.2)$ and $(0.8, 0.9) \times (0.8, 0.9)$.

The first two examples are used as test examples. In the second one, we obtain a very good surface deformation. The third one simulates a wind force applied to cloth when the boundaries are fixed. The last one simulates how four holes in a flat surface extend down. The two last simulations can be used in some real applications. The third example can be the simulation of the movement of a flag

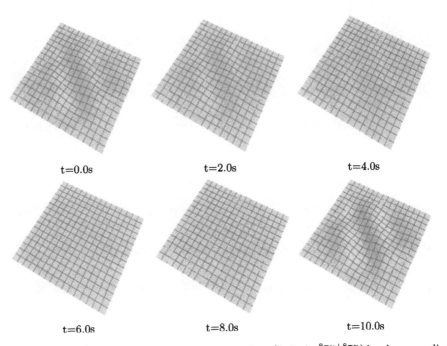

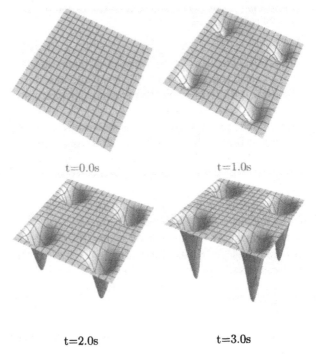

Fig. 3. Deformations where a sinusoidal force such as $(0, 0, \sin \frac{8\pi u + 8\pi v}{2})$ has been applied

Fig. 4. Deformations where four vertical forces has been applied on a plane using Bicubic B-splines

when the wind drives it and in the last one, a natural disaster can be used as a model. This simulation can also be used to model a cloth which is put on a table and is stretched by the force of gravity.

7 Conclusions and Future Work

We have introduced a model which allows us to make deformations of parametric surfaces using B-splines finite elements. The model includes the variational formulation, the analytic solution and the computational cost. To check the model, we have shown several examples with different kinds of applied forces. The examples show us that the model is efficient and provides good deformations. All the examples have been made using C++ and Coin3D libraries.

At present, non-constant forces in time are studied. Moreover, we are working on other kinds of surfaces, such as paraboloids, ellipsoids and so on. Also, more boundary conditions will be considered.

Acknowledgements

This work is supported by the project TIN2007-67993, ITADA, of the Spanish Government. The authors would like to thank to the Department of Mathematics and Computer Science of University of the Balearic Islands.

References

1. Cohen, I.: Modèles Déformables 2-D et 3-D: Application à la Segmentation d'Images Médicales. PhD thesis, Université Paris IX, Dauphine (1992)
2. Cox, M.G.: The numerical evaluation of b-splines. IMA Journal of Applied Mathematic 10(2), 134–149 (1972)
3. de Boor, C.: A practical guide to splines. Springer, New York (1978)
4. Farin, G.: Curves and Surfaces for Computer-Aided Geometric Desing: A Practical Guide. Academic Press, London (1997)
5. González, M., Mascaró, M., Mir, A., Palmer, P., Perales, F.: Modeling and animating deformable objects. In: Proceedings of IX Spanish Symposium on Pattern Recognition and Image Analysis, Benicasim, Castellón, Spain, pp. 279–290. AERFAI Society (2001)
6. González-Hidalgo, M., Mir, A., Nicolau, G.: An evolution model of parametric surface deformation using finite elements based on B-splines. In: Proceedings of CompImage 2006 Conference, Computational Modelling of Objects Represented in Images: Fundamentals, Methods and Applications, Coimbra, Portugal (2006)
7. González-Hidalgo, M., Mir, A., Nicolau, G.: Dynamic parametric surface deformation using finite elements based on B-splines. International Journal of Computer vision and Biometrics 1(1) (to appear, May 2007)
8. Höllig, K.: Finite element methods with B-Splines. Frontiers in Applied Mathematics. SIAM, Philadelphia (2003)
9. Mascaró, M.: Modelo de Simulación de Deformaciones de Objetos Basado en la Teoría de la Elasticidad. PhD thesis, Universitat de les Illes Balears (2002)

10. Mascaro, M., Mir, A., Perales, F.: P³DMA: A physical 3D deformable modelling and animations system. In: Perales, F.J., Hancock, E.R. (eds.) AMDO 2002. LNCS, vol. 2492, pp. 68–79. Springer, Heidelberg (2002)
11. Montagnat, J., Delingette, H., Ayache, N.: A review of deformable surfaces: topology, geometry and deformation. Image and Vision Computing 19(14), 1023–1040 (2001)
12. Piegl, L., Tiller, W. (eds.): The NURBS book. Springer, Berlin (1997)
13. Qin, H., Terzopoulos, D.: Triangular nurbs and their dynamic generalizations. Computer Aided Geometric Design 14, 325–347 (1997)
14. Raviart, P.A., Thomas, J.M.: Introduction à l'analyse numérique des équations aux derivées partielles. Masson, Paris (1992)
15. Terzopoulos, D.: Regularization of inverse visual problems involving discontinuities. IEEE PAMI 8(4), 413–424 (1986)

Apperance-Based Tracking and Face Identification in Video Sequences

José Miguel Buenaposada[1], Juan Bekios[2], and Luis Baumela[3]

[1] Dept. de Ciencias de la Computación, Universidad Rey Juan Carlos
Calle Tulipán s/n, 28933, Móstoles, Spain
josemiguel.buenaposada@urjc.es
[2] Dept. de Ingeniería de Sistemas y Computación, Universidad Católica del Norte
Av. Angamos 0610, Antofagasta, Chile
juan.bekios@ucn.cl
[3] Dept. Inteligencia Artificial, Facultad Informática
Universidad Politécnica de Madrid
lbaumela@fi.upm.es

Abstract. We present a technique for face recognition in videos. We are able to recognise a face in a video sequence, given a single gallery image. By assuming that the face is in an approximately frontal position, we jointly model changes in facial appearance caused by identity and illumination. The identity of a face is described by a vector of appearance parameters. We use an angular distance to measure the similarity of faces and a probabilistic procedure to accumulate evidence for recognition along the sequence. We achieve 93.8% recognition success in a set of 65 sequences of 6 subjects from the LaCascia and Sclaroff database.

1 Introduction

Face recognition (FR) is perhaps one of the oldest challenges of computer vision. Although the first results date back to the early 70s, in the last 15 years research in this field has grown significantly caused by the commercial importance of its applications.

Although it can be solved by humans in an effortless way, FR is a daunting task for a computer since the appearance of a face may change dramatically depending on face orientation, illumination, facial expression, occlusions, etc. Traditionally FR has been solved in a static way, *still-to-still*, e.g. [1,2,3,4], and only more recently the problem of FR in video sequences has attracted attention [5,6,7,8]. This interest may be attributed to the increasing importance of FR in surveillance. The poor quality of video in these type of applications make the problem of recognising faces in video an even more challenging task.

Two main approaches to FR have been introduced in the literature, holistic and feature-based. Holistic approaches use a whole face region as input for recognition [6,7,4]. Feature-based approaches use the location of a certain set of points in the image and local statistics as input data [1]. Some authors report that feature-based techniques are less stable an accurate than holistic approaches

F.J. Perales and R.B. Fisher (Eds.): AMDO 2008, LNCS 5098, pp. 349–358, 2008.

[9]. In this paper we will introduce an appearance-based holistic approach for FR in videos.

Two problems must be considered to recognise faces in videos. First, locating the face image in each frame of the sequence. Appearance-based approaches are usually very sensitive to geometric or photometric face misalignment. So, a fundamental prerequisite for recognition is accurately registering the face in each frame of the sequence. A key element here is the existence of a good model to represent all possible sources of appearance variation. In second place, the face must be recognised by accumulating evidence for recognition over the whole sequence.

In this paper we propose a technique for face recognition in videos. We use an image-based approach to represent the appearance of a frontal face and to model the changes caused by illumination and identity. By jointly modelling the appearance changes of illumination and identity we achieve a tightly integrated face tracking system in which the identity information contributes to tracking and vice-versa. We use a recently introduced subspace-based minimisation procedure [10] to efficiently fit the face model to each frame in the image sequence. Finally, we use an angular distance to measure the similarity of faces and a probabilistic procedure to accumulate evidence for recognition along the sequence.

Our recognition technique is most closely related to two previous results [6,7]. Like in [6] we consider the problem of *still to video* face recognition (the gallery of images is composed of a frontal picture of each individual). They use a particle filter to track the face and recognise identity, whereas we use an efficient Gauss-Newton minimisation procedure. On the other hand, in [7], the problem of *video-to-video* face recognition is considered (both the gallery and the input data are videos). They build a non-linear manifold for each subject in the gallery and compute a probabilistic distance of the input set of images to each stored gallery sequence. Although they consider changes in face orientation and illumination, both sources of appearance change are not separated in the manifold. So the recogniser will probably fail if the combination of orientation and illumination in the input sequence is different from that in the gallery sequence.

2   Face Alignment

In this section we describe the face alignment used in our FR algorithm. The face is initially located using a face detection algorithm, in our case we use the well known Viola-Jones procedure [11]. Face detection algorithms provide a rough estimate of the location and scale of the face (geometrical alignment) which does not suffice for face recognition. We use the a model-based face alignment procedure to accurately locate the face and compensate illumination effects.

2.1   The Face Model

We will assume that faces are in frontal view. In this case the major changes in the appearance of a face are caused by identity and illumination variations. Our model is based on a first order approximation to the gray value of face pixels.

Let $I(\mathbf{x}, t)$ be the image acquired at time t, where $\mathbf{x}$ is a vector representing the co-ordinates of a point in the image, and let $\mathbf{I}(\mathbf{x}, t)$ be a vector storing the brightness values of $I(\mathbf{x}, t)$. The first order approximation to the grey value of pixel $\mathbf{x}$ can be expressed as $\bar{\mathbf{I}}_d(\mathbf{x}) + [\mathbf{B}_i \mathbf{c}_{i,t}](\mathbf{x}) + [\mathbf{B}_d \mathbf{c}_{d,t}](\mathbf{x})$, where $\mathbf{B}_i$ and $\mathbf{B}_d$ are the Jacobian matrices representing the derivative of the grey value of pixel $\mathbf{x}$ w.r.t. changes in illumination and identity respectively. These matrices may also be interpreted as the basis of the illumination and identity subspaces. Vectors $\mathbf{c}_i$ and $\mathbf{c}_d$ are respectively the illumination and identity appearance parameters. $\bar{\mathbf{I}}_d(\mathbf{x})$ is the average image representing the point in illumination and identity space in which the first order expansion is made.

The rigid motion of the face is modelled by $f(\mathbf{x}, \boldsymbol{\mu})$, being $\boldsymbol{\mu}$ the vector of rigid motion parameters. So, the brightness constancy equation is

$$\mathbf{I}(f(\mathbf{x}, \boldsymbol{\mu}_t), t) = \bar{\mathbf{I}}_d(\mathbf{x}) + [\mathbf{B}\mathbf{c}_t](\mathbf{x}) \quad \forall \mathbf{x} \in \mathcal{F}, \tag{1}$$

where $\mathbf{B} = [\mathbf{B}_i | \mathbf{B}_d]$, $\mathbf{c}_t^\top = (\mathbf{c}_{i,t}^\top, \mathbf{c}_{d,t}^\top)^\top$, $k = \dim(\mathbf{c}_t)$, and $\mathcal{F}$ represents the set of pixels of the face used for alignment. This first order approximation implies that illumination and identity subspaces are independent. This assumption will simplify the training of the model. Instead of having to use image sequences in which all combinations of illuminations and identities appear, both models will be trained independently.

We train this generic appearance model with the PIE and FERET databases. Matrix $\mathbf{B}_i$ is estimated by selecting the nine[1] directions with highest variance of the eigenspace spanning the set of frontal images of the PIE database. Here, each illumination is averaged across all identities. The result is an average image for each illumination direction (see Fig. 1).

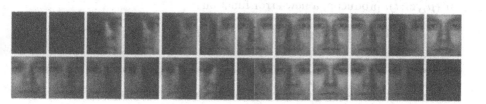

Fig. 1. Aligned images used to build the illumination subspace

We build the basis of the identity subspace, $\mathbf{B}_d$, using frontal images from the FERET database [13]. We have chosen 781 images from the *fa* FERET gallery (see Fig. 2) displaying a neutral facial expression. Again we choose the 66 directions with highest variance as the components of the basis of the identity subspace (see Fig. 3), once removed the illumination component.

---

[1] Nine components suffice to represent 97% of the energy in the image[12].

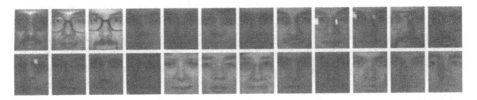

Fig. 2. Some sample aligned images used to build the identity subspace

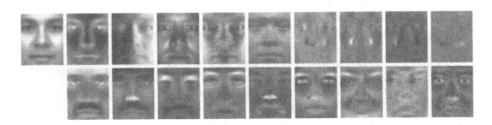

Fig. 3. Mean of illumination and identity training images (first image in first row). Illumination subspace basis vectors (remaining images in first row). Most significative components of the identity subspace basis (second row).

2.2 Model Fitting

We fit the previous model to a target image by estimating the motion, μ, and appearance, c, parameters which minimise $E(\mu, c) = ||I(f(x, \mu_t), t) - \bar{I}_d - [Bc_t](x)||^2$. This is efficiently achieved by making a Taylor series expansion of I at (μ_t, c_t, t), producing a new error function

$$E(\delta\mu, \delta c) = ||M\delta\mu + I(f(x, \mu_t), t + \delta t) - \bar{I}_d - B(c_t + \delta c)||^2, \qquad (2)$$

where $M = \left[\frac{\partial I(f(x, \mu), t)}{\partial\mu} \Big|_{\mu=\mu_t} \right]$ is the $N \times n$ ($n = \dim(\mu)$) Jacobian matrix of I.

An efficient solution for estimating the minimum of (2) is given by

$$\delta\mu = -(\Sigma^\top \Lambda_{M1}\Sigma)^{-1}\Sigma^\top \Lambda_{M2}\mathcal{E}; \qquad \delta c = \Lambda_B[M\delta\mu + \mathcal{E}], \qquad (3)$$

where Λ_B, Λ_{M1} and Λ_{M2} are constant matrices that can be precomputed off-line and Σ is a matrix that depends on μ_t and c_t [10].

3   Face Identification

In this section we introduce a probabilistic procedure for FR by accumulating evidence along the image sequence. The identity of one subject is represented by the vector c_d of appearance parameters in the identity subspace. We use a cosine distance to measure the similarity between the identity parameters of the gallery image and those of input image sequence provided by the alignment algorithm. Finally, we use a probabilistic procedure to accumulate evidence for recognition along the image sequence.

Let $I_1, \ldots, I_t$ be a temporally ordered image sequence of a face and $\mathbf{x}_1, \ldots, \mathbf{x}_t$ be the be the temporally ordered set of co-ordinates of the face in the identity subspace, which we will denote $\mathcal{X}_{1:t}$. Let $G_t = \{g_1, g_2, \ldots, g_c\}$ be a discrete random variable representing the probability of the c gallery images at time t and X_t be a continuous random associated to the co-ordinates in the identity subspace of the image acquired at time t. We will denote by $P(g_i) \equiv P(G_t = g_i)$ the probability that the discrete random variable G_t takes value g_i and by $p(\mathbf{x}) \equiv p(X_t = \mathbf{x})$ the probability density function (p.d.f.) of the continuous variable $\mathbf{x}$ at time t.

The facial identity $g(t)$ at time instant t is obtained as the maximum of the posterior distribution of G_t given the sequence of images up to time t

$$g(t) = \arg\max_i \{P(G_t = g_i | \mathcal{X}_{1:t})\}. \tag{4}$$

We will estimate the posterior distribution using a recursive Bayesian filter. For the first image in the sequence the problem can be immediately solved by

$$P(G_1 | \mathbf{x}_1) = \frac{p(\mathbf{x}_1 | G_1) P(G_1)}{p(\mathbf{x}_1)} \propto p(\mathbf{x}_1 | G_1) P(G_1),$$

where $P(G_1)$ represents our prior knowledge of the probabilities of facial expressions.

Now, if we have a temporal sequence $\mathcal{X}_{1:t}$, we can then update G_t as

$$P(G_t | \mathcal{X}_{1:t}) = \frac{p(\mathbf{x}_t | G_t, \mathcal{X}_{1:t-1}) p(G_t, \mathcal{X}_{1:t-1})}{p(\mathcal{X}_{1:t})}.$$

If we assume that measurements depend only on the current identity, then $p(X_t | G_t, \mathcal{X}_{1:t-1}) = p(X_t | G_t)$ and, hence,

$$P(G_t | \mathcal{X}_{1:t}) \propto p(X_t | G_t) P(G_t | \mathcal{X}_{1:t-1}),$$

where $P(G_t | \mathcal{X}_{1:t-1})$ is the prediction of G_t, given the data up to time instant $t - 1$. This probability can be estimated as

$$P(G_t | \mathcal{X}_{1:t-1}) = \sum_{i=1}^{c} P(G_t, G_{t-1} = g_i | \mathcal{X}_{1:t-1}) = \sum_{i=1}^{c} P(G_t | g_i, \mathcal{X}_{1:t-1}) P(g_i | \mathcal{X}_{1:t-1}).$$

If we assume that our system is Markovian (G_t depends only on G_{t-1}), then

$$P(G_t | \mathcal{X}_{1:t-1}) = \sum_{i=1}^{c} P(G_t | G_{t-1} = g_i) P(G_{t-1} = g_i | \mathcal{X}_{1:t-1}),$$

where $P(G_t | G_{t-1})$ would represent the identity transition probability. Of course, the identity of a subject does not change in a sequence, so $P(G_t | G_{t-1}) = \delta(G_t, G_{t-1})$, where $\delta(a, b)$ is the Kronecker delta function.

$p(\mathbf{x}|g_i)$ represents the p.d.f. of identity parameters for an image of gallery subject g_i. Given that $\cos(\mathbf{x}, \mathbf{y})$ gives a measure of similarity between vectors $\mathbf{x}$ and $\mathbf{y}$, we make the following approximation

$$p(\mathbf{x}|g_i) \approx |\cos(\mathbf{x}, \mathbf{x}_{g_i})|,$$

where $\mathbf{x}_{g_i}$ are the identity parameters associated to gallery subject g_i.

4   Experiments

In this section we describe some results of the test that we have performed with the algorithm described above. We have processed 71 sequences of 6 subjects from the LaCascia and Sclaroff database[2] [14]. The database consists of mug-shots videos of 6 subjects labelled as: *jam, jim, llm, ssm, vam* and *mll*. There are sequences with uniform illumination (8 for *jam*, 9 for *jim*, 9 for *llm*, 9 for *ssm*, 9 for *vam*) and with varying illumination (9 for *jam*, 9 for *ssm* and 9 for *mll*). See Fig. 4 for sample images of the 6 subjects in the database.

Fig. 4. The 6 subjects in the Sclaroff and LaCascia image sequence database, from left to right: *jam, jim, llm, ssm, vam* and *mll*

4.1   Tracking Results

We have used the alignment algorithm described in section 2 to process the 71 sequences in the LaCascia and Sclaroff database. The rigid face motion model is a rotation, translation and scale of the face texture, $f(\mathbf{x}, \boldsymbol{\mu}) = s\mathrm{R}(\theta)\mathbf{x} + \mathbf{t}$, being $\boldsymbol{\mu} = (s, \theta, t_x, t_y)$. With Viola and Jones' face detector [11] we locate the face in the first image of each sequence and track the face motion with the image alignment procedure. In 65 of the 71 sequences the tracking was perfect from the first to the last frame (200 frames per sequence). Only in 6 sequences the face was lost at the end of the sequence. All tracking failures are caused by strong rotations of the face out of the camera plane.

In Fig. 5 we display some results from the *llm5* sequence, in which the *llm* subject moves in front of the camera under uniform illumination. The estimated position of the face is overlayed in red. To the right side of each result image we show four smaller images: the rectified image estimated from the motion parameters $(I(f(\mathbf{x}, \boldsymbol{\mu}_t), t + \delta t))$ on the left-upper side, the image reconstructed with the face model $(I_d(\mathbf{x}) + [\mathrm{B}_i \mathbf{c}_{i,t}](\mathbf{x}) + [\mathrm{B}_d \mathbf{c}_{d,t}](\mathbf{x}))$ on the right-upper side,

---

[2] http://www.cs.bu.edu/groups/ivc/data.php

the illumination reconstructed image $(I_d(\mathbf{x}) + [\mathbf{B}_i\mathbf{c}_{i,t}](\mathbf{x}))$ on the left-lower side and the identity subspace reconstructed image $(I_d(\mathbf{x}) + [\mathbf{B}_d\mathbf{c}_{d,t}](\mathbf{x}))$ on the right-lower side. Note that the reconstruction of the face with the subspace identity parameters is near perfect although the subject was not in the identity subspace training images.

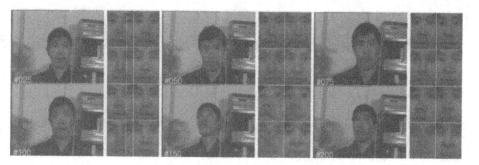

Fig. 5. Alignment results for *llm5* sequence

In Fig. 6 we show some results from the *jal4* sequence corresponding to subject *jam* moving in front of the camera under varying illumination. The tracker can cope with illumination and head motion while estimating the identity parameters with no problem. Here the more out of plane the rotation of the head is, the worst is the identity reconstruction.

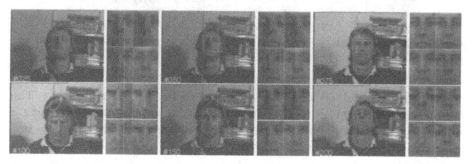

Fig. 6. Alignment result for *jal4* sequence

In Fig. 7 we show the results of the system in a similar situation. In sequence *ssl6* the subject *ssm* also moves with head rotations out of camera plane under varying illumination. In this case, the identity reconstruction is still qualitatively quite good.

4.2 Identity Recognition

Once we have shown the performance of the image alignment algorithm, we test the quality of FR using the identity subspace parameters. First of all, we have

Fig. 7. Alignment result for *ssl6* sequence

chosen one image of each subject as gallery for face identification (See Fig. 8). Gallery images are the result of the image alignment process performed in one image of the sequences *jam1, jim2, llm1, ssm1, vam1* and *mll1*. These sequences images are not used for evaluation. The result of this process is that we have a training video (although we are only using one image from it) and 65 test sequences.

Fig. 8. Probe gallery images. From left to right subjects *jam, jim, llm, ssm, vam* and *mll*.

After processing all 65 sequences we get the confusion matrix in table 1. The overall recognition rate is 93.85% quite remarkable given that we are using a single image as gallery and there are pose and illumination changes in the test sequences.

Table 1. Confusion matrix (expressed in percentage) of the FR experiment

	jam	jim	llm	ssm	vam	mll	total
jam	100.0	12.5	0	0	0	0	
jim	0	75.0	0	0	0	12.5	
llm	0	0	100.0	0	0	0	
ssm	0	0	0	100.0	12.5	0	
vam	0	0	0	0	87.5	0	
mll	0	12.5	0	0	0	87.5	
total							93.85

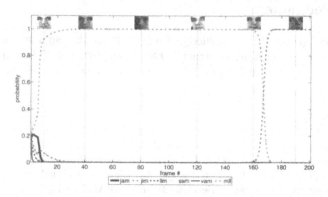

Fig. 9. A successful recognition using *jal4* sequence

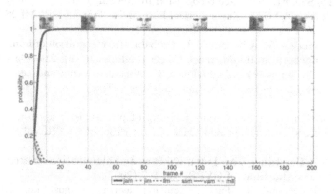

Fig. 10. A partial recognition failure with *mll4*

In Fig. 9 is displayed a successful identification, in spite of important illumination changes in the sequence. The identification is correct from the beginning because the head is not rotating out of plane and therefore the illumination appearance model can cope with the changing conditions. In Fig. 10 we show a partially failed identification. The performance of the FR algorithm is correct until the rotation of the head clearly violates the frontal image assumption.

5   Conclusions

We have introduced a fully automatic algorithm for face detection, tracking and recognition. It uses a single frontal image as probe gallery. It performs remarkably well in presence of illumination changes and translational and/or rotational motion in camera plane. Performance degrades when the frontal image assumption is violated. We are working towards improving the performance of the system for out of camera plane face rotations and to make *video-to-video* FR.

Acknowledgements

The authors gratefully acknowledge funding from the Spanish *Ministerio de Educación y Ciencia* under contract TRA2005-08529-C02-02. They also thank M. LaCascia and S. Sclaroff for providing the image sequences data base.

References

1. Wiskott, L., Fellous, J.M., von der Malsburg, C.: Face recognition by elastic bunch graph matching. Trans. on PAMI 19(7), 775–779 (1997)
2. Belhumeur, P., Hespanha, J., Kriegman, D.: Eigenfaces vs. fisherfaces: Recognition using class specific linear projection. Trans. on PAMI 19(7), 711–720 (1997)
3. Martinez, A.: Recognizing imprecisely located, partially ocluded and expression variant faces from a single sample per class. Trans. on PAMI 24(6), 748–763 (2002)
4. Zhang, L., Samaras, D.: Face recognition from a single training image under arbitrary unknown lighting using spherical harmonics. Trans. on PAMI 28(3), 351–363 (2006)
5. Zhou, S., Krueger, V., Chellappa, R.: Probabilistic recognition of human faces from video. Computer Vision and Image Understanding 91(1-2), 214–245 (2003)
6. Zhou, S., Chellappa, R., Moghaddam, B.: Visual tracking and recognition using appearance-adaptive models in particle filters. Trans. on IP 13(11), 1491–1506 (2004)
7. Lee, K.C., Kriegman, D.: Online learning of probabilistic appearance manifolds for video-based recognition and tracking. In: Proc. of CVPR, vol. I, pp. 852–859 (2005)
8. Xu, Y., Roy Chowdhury, A., Patel, K.: Pose and illumination invariant face recognition in video. In: Proc. of CVPR, pp. 1–7 (2007)
9. Brunelli, T., Poggio, T.: Face recognition: features versus templaes. Trans. on PAMI 15(10), 1042–1052 (1993)
10. Buenaposada, J.M., Muñoz, E., Baumela, L.: Efficiently estimating facial expression and illumination in appearance-based tracking. In: Proc. BMVC, pp. 57–66 (2006)
11. Viola, P., Jones, M.J.: Robust real-time face detection. International Journal of Computer Vision 57(2), 137–154 (2004)
12. Basri, R., Jacobs, D.W.: Lambertian reflectance and linear subspaces. Trans. on PAMI 25(2), 218–233 (2003)
13. Phillips, P., Moon, H., Rauss, P., Rizvi, S.: The feret evaluation methodology for face recognition algorithms. Trans. on PAMI 22(10), 1090–1104 (2000)
14. La Cascia, M., Sclaroff, S., Athitsos, V.: Fast, reliable head tracking under varying illumination: An approach based on robust registration of texture-mapped 3d models. Trans. on PAMI 22(4), 322–336 (2000)

Interactive Constrained Deformations of NURBS Surfaces: N-SCODEF

Marcos Clapés, Manuel González-Hidalgo*, Arnau Mir-Torres,
and Pere A. Palmer-Rodríguez*

Computer Graphics, Vision and Artificial Intelligence Group. Maths. and Computer
Science Dept. University of the Balearic Islands, Spain
marcos@mecanograficaibiza.com, manuel.gonzalez@uib.es, arnau.mir@uib.es,
pere.palmer@uib.es
http://dmi.uib.es/~ugiv/

Abstract. In this paper we propose a generalized SCODEF deformation
method in order to deform NURBS surface. The deformation method
propose a wide class of deformation functions applied to a set of select-
user constraints and a wide range of influence zones, expanding the used
one for the original SCODEF method. Also, we propose the use of several norms and distances in order to define and compute the deformation
function and the constraint influence zone, ensuring a wide range of deformed shapes.

Keywords: Computer graphics, deformation, NURBS.

1 Introduction

Deformations play an important role in Computer Graphics, allowing objects
to assume interesting new shapes, and one of the goal of geometric modelling
is to provide tools that modify the shape of objects in an intuitive way. At
the beginning of the eighties ([4], [12], [22]) the Computer Graphics community has devoted much attention to the problem of modelling and animating of
deformable objects, based not only on the Geometrical/Mathematical intrinsic
characteristics of surfaces and solids, but also on their material properties in
the context of continuum and discrete mechanics. The objects are modeled and
moved following geometrical or physical laws that govern their static and/or
dynamic behavior. Several discretization methods have been proposed, such as,
finite-difference methods, finite-element methods, implicit surfaces, particle systems, and so on (see [11], [2], [9], [16], [14]). The problem is that most of them
have the drawback to use numerous primitives, the complexity and computational cost is very high and the parameters of the model are nonintuitive being
difficult to manipulate.

At the same time, geometrical techniques have been developed, better from
the point of view of the computational cost. Among them is to highlight the

---

* This work is supported by the project TIN2007-67993, ITADA, of the Spanish
Government.

F.J. Perales and R.B. Fisher (Eds.): AMDO 2008, LNCS 5098, pp. 359–369, 2008.
© Springer-Verlag Berlin Heidelberg 2008

Free-From Deformation techniques (FFD). The term FFD was originally given in the literature by Sederberg and Parry [21]. Many variants and extensions has been developed over the years. Around year 1990 a constraint-based deformation model, first presented by Borrel and Bechmann [7] and called Dogme, they replaced the embedded solid for a direct manipulation, requiring less end-user intervention. Many variants has been developed over the years [5], [8], [20], [19], [6], [1] and recently [15]. Borrel and Rappoport in [8] proposed a method based on Dogme associating a radius of influence to each constraint called *simple constrained deformation, SCODEF*.

In this paper we propose a generalized scodef deformation method in order to deform NURBS surface. The deformation method propose a wide class of deformation functions applied to a set of select-user constraints and a wide range of influence zones, expanding the used one for the original scodef method. Also, we propose the use of several norms and distances in order to define and compute the deformation function and the constraint influence zone, ensuring a wide range of deformed shapes. After a brief description in the next section of parametric surfaces, we recall in section 3 the scodef method and we describe the extensions included in it. The role of our work is to demonstrate the usefulness of N-SCODEF curves and surfaces in the scope of the research project ITADA, so a demonstration tool is necessary. Section 4 is devoted to the data representation and the description of the designed tool, providing in section 5 some examples of deformed shapes that can be obtained. Finally some conclusions and future work are exposed.

2   NURBS Surfaces

The parametric surface models are most commonly used today in the world of design and manufacturing computer-aided (CAD / CAM). The way of such a model surface is controlled is by a set of control points that defines its control net. The deformation of a parametric curve or surface implies the handling and positioning of its control points in space. The NURBS surfaces represent the most general definition of parametric surfaces. It contains non-rational B-splines and rational and non-rational Bézier curves as special cases. So, NURBS become the most important geometric entity in design, and represents a key topic in computer graphics. The NURBS surfaces are piecewise rational functions with a local support, providing good local approximations for smooth functions ([17]) and they are defined as a combination of the so-called *B-splines basis functions*. There are a number of ways to define the *B-splines basis functions* and to prove their important properties: by divided differences of truncated power functions, by blossoming, by a recurrence formula an so on, see [10], [13], [14]. Once the notation to define such surfaces has been introduced (following [17]), the technique used in order to deform these models will be addressed in the next section.

Let S be a parametric surface of degree p in the u direction and degree q in the v direction. A point of S, $S(u,v)$ where $(u,v) \in [0,1]^2$, is given by

$$S(u,v) = \frac{\sum_{i=0}^{n} \sum_{j=0}^{m} w_{i,j}\, \mathbf{P}_{i,j}\, N_{i,p}(u)N_{j,q}(v)}{\sum_{i=0}^{n} \sum_{j=0}^{m} w_{i,j}\, N_{i,p}(u)N_{j,q}(v)} = \sum_{i=0}^{n} \sum_{j=0}^{m} \mathbf{P}_{i,j}\, R_{i,j}(u,v), \quad (1)$$

where

$$R_{i,j}(u,v) = \frac{w_{i,j}\, N_{i,p}(u)M_{j,q}(v)}{\sum_{i=0}^{n} \sum_{j=0}^{m} w_{i,j}N_{i,p}(u)N_{j,q}(v)},$$

being $\mathbf{P}_{i,j}$ the bidirectional net of control points, $w_{i,j}$ are the weights, where $w_{i,j} > 0$ for all i,j, and the $N_{i,p}(u)$ and $N_{j,q}(v)$ are the B-spline basis functions, of degree p and q, respectively, defined on the knot vectors $U=\{u_0, u_1, \ldots, u_{k-1}, u_k\}$ ($k = n+p$) where $u_i \le u_{i+1}$ and $V = \{v_0, v_1, \ldots, v_{l-1}, v_l\}$ ($l = m+q$) where $v_j \le v_{j+1}$. The i-th B-spline basis function $N_{i,p}(u)$ of degree p is defined by the following recurrence equation

$$N_{i,1}(u) = \begin{cases} 1 & \text{if } u_i \le u \le u_{i+1}, \\ 0 & \text{otherwise}, \end{cases} \quad (p=1)$$

$$N_{i,p}(u) = \frac{u - u_i}{u_{i+p-1} - u_i} N_{i,p-1}(u) + \frac{u_{i+p} - u}{u_{i+p} - u_{i+1}} N_{i+1,p-1}(u) \quad (p > 1)$$

Also, a NURBS surface can be considered as a four dimensional B-spline surface, so the expression 1 can be obtained by perspective projection [17].

3   Constraint-Based NURBS Deformation

Using the notation and language established in [7] and used in [8] by Borrel and Rappoport in order to define the SCODEF deformations, the deformation of an object is defined by the displacement of points called *constraints*. In particular, a constraint can be applied to a sample point of the object. As we will see, it is easy to achieve the exact placement of sample points. Our goal is to use this general notation in order to deform parametric surfaces, or more exactly NURBS surfaces. Next let's take a look to the scodef model and its relations with the deformations of NURBS surfaces.

Let n be the dimension of the space where the object, S, to be deformed is included. A deformation of S, $\mathcal{D}(S)$, is characterized by the deformation function $\mathcal{D} : \mathbb{R}^n \longrightarrow \mathbb{R}^n$

$$\mathcal{D}(S) = S + d(S) = \tilde{S} \quad (2)$$

where $\tilde{S}$ is the deformed object and $d : \mathbb{R}^n \longrightarrow \mathbb{R}^m$, is the composition of a function $\mathcal{F} : \mathbb{R}^n \longrightarrow \mathbb{R}^m$, which specifies how the deformation is applied to the object points, with a linear transformation $M : \mathbb{R}^m \longrightarrow \mathbb{R}^n$, represented by its matrix and computed in order to satisfies all the constraints and combining, if necessary, the interaction of the nondisjoints constraints. As was pointed by

Borrel and Rappoport (see [8]) the columns of M do not have any special meaning. They are just computed in order to satisfy the m constraints previously imposed to some points of the object S. Then,

$$\tilde{S} = S + (M \circ \mathcal{F})(S) = S + M \cdot \mathcal{F}(S),$$

and

$$d(S) = M \cdot \mathcal{F}(S) \tag{3}$$

This model can be modified in many ways, depending on the chosen function $\mathcal{F}$. Our method is an extension of scodef ([8]) deformation method. In our case, one influence region is defined on the object surface rather than within a 3D volume (of all the euclidean space $\mathbb{R}^n$). The influence region of a constraint point consists on all the points on the reference model whose distance to the constraint point are smaller than a given radius. Several distances and influence regions can be used, as can be seen in the experiments displayed in Section 5.

The constraint-based deformation method can be split into three parts.

a) User selection of the displacements, D_i, of arbitrary user-selected points, C_i (called constraints) and region of influence for each constraint. Choice of the radius of the influence region and the formulation of $\mathcal{F}$.
b) Following Eq. 3, computation of the matrix M, whose elements are obtained in order to satisfy the user-defined constraints. That is, a linear system of equations should be solved, $d(C_i) = M\,\mathcal{F}(C_i)\ 1 \leq i \leq m$, where m is the number of selected constraints. To find the matrix M standard numerical methods can be used (see [18]). The control of the mutual influence of nondisjoint constraints should be took into account following the method described in [8], or the extension method done by Raffin et al. in [19].
c) Once the matrix M has been computed, all the surface points are successively deformed using Eq. 2.

Our goal is to deform NURBS curves and surfaces in an interactive way following a generalization of the scodef method. Borrel and Rappoport ([8]) used this scheme introducing the notion of constraint and adding a radius of influence to each constraint. The user has to define the constraint points, generally on the surface (or near to it) and its displacement. That is, the final position, D_i, to achieve for each of the constraints points, done by a vector (a linear displacement, but it can be curvilinear, as we can see for example in [20], [19], [6]). A deformation function is applied to the surface S representing the contribution of each constraint to the deformation of the surface points . This deformation model is expressed following 3 as follows. Let $d : \mathbb{R}^n \longrightarrow \mathbb{R}^n$ $(n = 2, 3,$ or $4)$ the deformation function. It expresses the displacement $d(S(u,v))$ $(u,v) \in [0,1]^2$. This function is given by

$$\forall (u,v) \in [0,1]^2 \quad d(S(u,v)) = \sum_{i=1}^{m} M_i\, f_i(S(u,v))$$

where

- m is the number of constraints.
- M_i is the ith column of the matrix M.
- Let $\tilde{f}_i : \mathbb{R} \longrightarrow \mathbb{R}$ be a scalar and monotonically decreasing function with $\tilde{f}(0) = 1$ and $\tilde{f}(x) = 0$ for all $|x| \geq 1$; associated to the ith constraint, C_i. It quantifies the influence of that constraint on the surface point $S(u,v)$. Then, the function $f_i : \mathbb{R}^n \longrightarrow \mathbb{R}$, depending on the C_i and R_i, the radius of influence of C_i, is defined as

$$f_i(S(u,v)) = \tilde{f}_i\left(\frac{\|S(u,v) - C_i\|}{R_i}\right) \tag{4}$$

We have

$$f_i(Q) = \begin{cases} 1 & \text{if } \|Q - C_i\| = 0, \\ 0 & \text{if } \|Q - C_i\| \geq R_1, \\ 0 \leq f_i(Q) \leq 1 & \text{otherwise.} \end{cases}$$

If we want to ensure the continuity of the surface deformation, obviously $\tilde{f}_i$ must be continuous. In this case, the deformation function $\mathcal{F} = (f_1, f_2, \ldots, f_m)$ is a composition of continuous functions.

Fig. 1. Elements of the constraint-based deformation method and its action over a NURBS plane

In Figure 1 all the elements of the constraint-based deformation method are shown. On the left, we can see the chosen constraint deformation function in order to deform the NURBS plane. The yellow point on the plane is the constraint point C_i. Around it, the influence zone can be seen. We have used the euclidean distance in order to compute it and the deformation function. If one point lies near to the constraint point location and it is in the influence zone, it is deformed by the deformation constraint vector, displayed by a yellow line from the constraint point (yellow) to the white point which is the deformation end point D_i. Conversely, if one point lies outside the influence zone, it is not deformed. The deformation of the points follows the shape of the selected deformation function, as we can see on the left in Figure 1.

In our application, several end-user constraints deformation functions are defined satisfying the previous conditions, some of then are displayed in Figure 2. The simple form displayed in Fig. 1.a is identical to the other one used in [8], also called *radial deformation* by its isotropic propagation of the deformation in the influence region. Obviously the shape of the ith deformation function, $\tilde{f}_i$, directly influences the shape of the deformed object, as we can see in Figure 3, where we display the effect of the two constraint deformation functions displayed in Fig. 2.a and Fig. 2.c on the same point of a NURBS circle. In order to modify the shape of deformation function, the user can select the desired function in a menu of functions, ensuring a wide range of deformed shapes using predefined deformations functions.

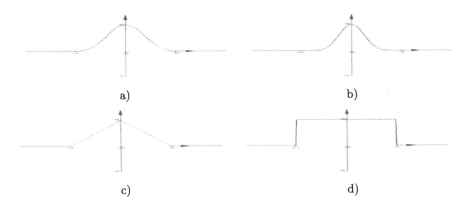

a)   b)

c)   d)

Fig. 2. Several pre-defined constraints deformation functions

Fig. 3. Figure showing the effect of two different deformation functions acting on the same point with the same influence region

But, not only the shape of $\tilde{f}_i$ influences in the deformation of the surface, but also, taking into account Eq. 4, the chosen norm and the radius of influence region plays an important role. The user interactively can change both, the used norm in Eq. 4 and the radius of influence, changing the influence zone, and expanding the range of deformed shapes.

The concept of radius of influence, as was introduced in [8], greatly helps to modelling. As was pointed by Raffin et al. in [19] *it controls the locality of the deformation, limiting the spatial influence of the constraint.* The effect of the

Fig. 4. Figure showing the effect on a NURBS plane of different radius in a spherical influence region deformation on a fixed constraint point

radius of influence can be seen in Fig. 4, where a NURBS plane is deformed using a spherical region of influence, taking successively radius equal to 2, 3 and 4 (from left to right in the figure) with the euclidean distance.

We propose to use a zone of influence that may be not spherical, but without avoiding non-euclidean distances. In Fig. 5 we show different distances proposed in order to compute equation 4. Also, we display different zones of influence. Moreover, we propose to the use of superquadric shaped hulls as defined in Bardinet et al. [3] to get various hulls. The user is able to modify the shape of the NURBS surface by simply interactively varying a little set of parameters. So, we obtain anisotropic influence of a constraint on the deformed shape.

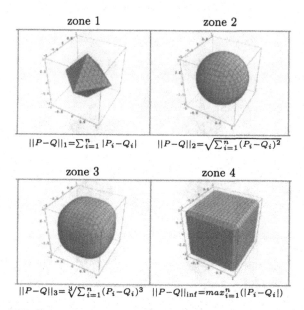

Fig. 5. Figure showing different influence zones and distances in order to compute the deformation function. These zones are the ones used in the examples depicted in figures 7 and 8.

4   Data Representation and Tool Description

The representation of the NURBS shapes and the corresponding deformations requires a visual environment in order to simplify the user interaction. This means that a WYSIWYG environment is needed.

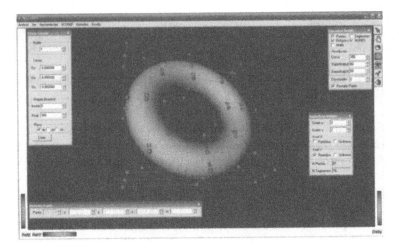

Fig. 6. General aspect of the application showing de Coin/OpenInventor window and some auxiliary windows

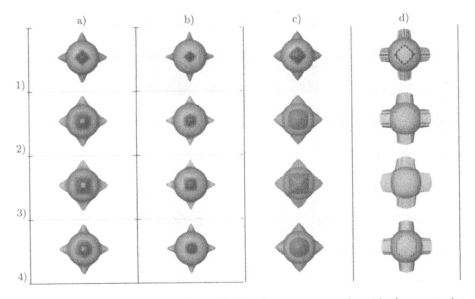

Fig. 7. The deformation of a sphere. Each column corresponds with the constraint function with the same letter depicted in figure 2. Each row represents the influence zone as described in figure 5.

The most extended API used to develop 2D and 3D graphics is OpenGL. With this environment, it is possible to implement interactive graphical applications in a very easy way.

OpenInventor is an OpenGL based API. With OpenInventor the representation of complex scenes and the development of complex visualization applications

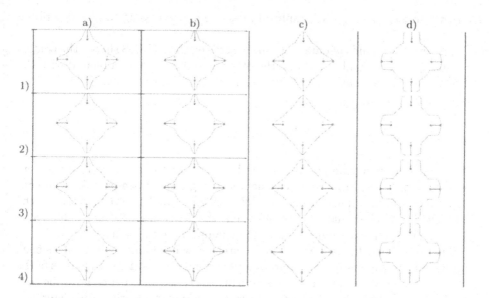

Fig. 8. The same kind of deformations as figure 7 but applied to a circle. In this figure the constraints applied are also shown.

becomes more simple than using only OpenGL. In fact it is the standard *de facto* 3D Computer Graphics API for complex visualization applications [23] [24]. Both API were developed originally by Silicon Graphics Inc. but now an independent consortium, the *OpenGL Architecture Review Board*, guides the OpenGL specification. Unfortunatelly the evolution of OpenInventor didn't had the same way, the only way it was available was under proprietary licensing from TGS (emphTemplate Graphics Software), but finally Silicon Graphics released an open source specification.

In our work, we have used Coin, an OpenInventor derived API fully compatible with the original specification. Coin brings the possibility to integrate a great powerful scene representation engine with a platform-independent interface which can be integrated in a broad range of windows environments (Windows, XWindow System, Aqua, and more), in figure 6 a general view of the application can be seen.

The interaction with the application is based on two topics, the shape to be deformed and the kind of deformation to be applied. The design of the interface reflects this in an easy form. The user can modify all the parameters defining the NURBS shape using a simple window, the same occurs with the deformation data. The general aspect of the application is one window showing the scene with the shape and the other graphical components and where the user can interact directly with these components. Furthermore, some other auxiliary windows can be used to perform a fine tuning of the parameters.

The data needed to implement the model involves the NURBS shape to be deformed, but it also requires the data describing the way in which the deformation has to be done. This can be supplied in two ways: requesting the information directly to the user via the graphical interface and accessing to files describing the data.

There are two kinds of data files, one describing the NURBS shape (the control points, the degree, and so on) and the other describing the data related with the deformation constraints (the type of restriction, and a list of constraints of that type).

5 Examples

Here there are two examples of our method. The first one, figure 7, is a sphere with six constraints applied, each one stretching the surface outside. The constraints has been applied using the different zones and functions showing the different behaviours that can be achieved, the functions used are depicted in figure 2. The influence zones used in the examples are the same as figure 5.

The second one, figure 8, represents a circle on which four constraints has been applied, in the same way as in figure 7, showing more accurately the details of the deformation. The way in which the shape fits the constraints depends on the constraint function and the influence zones can be seen more clearly in this figure.

6 Conclusions and Future Work

In this paper we propose an extension of the scodef method, in order to deform NURBS curves and surfaces, the most important geometric entity in design, improving it and obtaining a fast end-user tool of easy manipulation, and ensuring a wide range of deformed shapes. The end-user can modify a lot of parts independently and interactively: the deformation function, the form and size of the influence zone, its radius, the distance used to compute the others elements and, also the constraints and displacement points. All these features allow us to obtain several 3D deformations that can be stored as images and combining it to produce an animation.

One problem that appears when NURBS are deformed is that the obtained curve or surface is not a NURBS. One way to solve the problem is trying to solve the inverse problem, or applying the subdivision algorithm to get a NURBS within the influence zone and deform the control points that fall within it. At the present we are working in these points. Other future work is the generalization of the constraint point and to use other displacement constraints instead of linear displacement. Also we can use the tool for solid deformation.

References

1. Angelidis, A., Wyvill, G., Cani, M.-P.: Sweepers: Swept user-defined tools for modeling by deformation. SMI 00, 63–73 (2004)
2. Bardinet, E., Cohen, L.D., Ayache, N.: A parametric deformable model to fit unstructured 3D data. Technical Report RR–2617, INRIA Institut National de Recherche en Informatique et en Automatique (1995)

3. Bardinet, E., Cohen, L.D., Ayache, N.: A parametric deformable model to fit unstructured 3D data. Computer Vision and Image Understanding: CVIU 71(1), 39–54 (1998)
4. Barr, A.: Global and local deformations of solid primitives. Computer Graphics 18(3), 21–30 (1984)
5. Bechmann, D., Dubreuil, N.: Animation through space and time based on a space deformation model. Journal of Visualization and Computer Animation 4(3), 165–184 (1993)
6. Bechmann, D., Gerber, D.: Arbitrary shaped deformations with dogme. The Visual Computer 19(2-3), 175–186 (2003)
7. Borrel, P., Bechmann, D.: Deformation of n-dimensional objects. In: SMA 1991: Proceedings of the first ACM symposium on Solid modeling foundations and CAD/CAM applications, pp. 351–369. ACM, New York (1991)
8. Borrel, P., Rappoport, A.: Simple constrained deformations for geometric modeling and interactive design. ACM Trans. Graph. 13(2), 137–155 (1994)
9. Cani–Gascuel, M.-P., Desbrun, M.: Animation of deformable models using implicit surfaces. IEEE/Transactions on visualization and Computer Graphics 3(1) (1997)
10. de Boor, C.: A practical guide to splines. Springer, New York (1978)
11. Delingette, H.: Simplex meshes: a general representation for 3D shape reconstruction. Technical Report 2214, INRIA Institut National de Recherche en Informatique et en Automatique (1994)
12. Feynman, R.: Modeling the appearance of cloth. Master's thesis, Department of Electical Engineering and Computer Science. MIT, Cambridge (1986)
13. Gallier, J.: Curves and surfaces in geometric modeling: theory and algorithms. Morgan Kaufmann Publishers Inc., San Francisco (2000)
14. González-Hidalgo, M., Mir, A., Nicolau, G.: An evolution model of parametric surface deformation using finite elements based on B-splines. In: Proceedings of CompImage 2006 Conference, Computational Modelling of Objects Represented in Images: Fundamentals, Methods and Applications, Coimbra, Portugal (2006)
15. Lanquetin, S., Raffin, R., Neveu, M.: Generalized scodef deformations on subdivision surfaces. In: Perales, F.J., Fisher, R.B. (eds.) AMDO 2006. LNCS, vol. 4069, pp. 132–142. Springer, Heidelberg (2006)
16. Mascaró, M., Mir, A., Perales, F.: P³DMA: A physical 3D deformable modelling and animations system. In: Perales, F.J., Hancock, E.R. (eds.) AMDO 2002. LNCS, vol. 2492, pp. 68–79. Springer, Heidelberg (2002)
17. Piegl, L., Tiller, W.: The NURBS book, 2nd edn. Springer, New York, Inc. (1997)
18. Press, W., Teukolsky, S., Vetterling, W., Flannery, B.: Numerical Recipes in C, 2nd edn. Cambridge University Press, Cambridge (1992)
19. Raffin, R., Neveu, M., Jaar, F.: Curvilinear displacement of free-from based deformation. The Visual Computer 16, 38–46 (2000)
20. Raffin, R., Neveu, M., Jaar, F.: Extended constrained deformations: a new sculpturing tool. In: International Conference on Shape Modeling and Applications, March 1999, pp. 219–224. IEEE Computer Society, Los Alamitos (1999)
21. Sederberg, T.W., Parry, S.R.: Free-form deformation of solid geometric models. SIGGRAPH Comput. Graph. 20(4), 151–160 (1986)
22. Terzopoulos, D., Platt, J., Barr, A., Fleischer, K.: Ellastically deformable models. Computer Graphics (Proceedings SIGGRAPH) 21(4), 205–214 (1987)
23. Wernecke, J.: The Inventor Toolmaker: Extending Open Inventor, release 2. Addison-Wesley, Reading (1994)
24. Wernecke, J.: The Inventor Mentor: Programming Object–oriented 3D graphics with Open Inventor release 2. Addison-Wesley, Reading (1995)

A 3D Shape Descriptor for Human Pose Recovery

Laetitia Gond[1], Patrick Sayd[1], Thierry Chateau[2], and Michel Dhome[2]

[1] CEA, LIST, Laboratoire Systèmes de Vision Embarqués
Boîte Courrier 94, F-91191 Gif-sur-Yvette
[2] LASMEA CNRS, Université Blaise Pascal, Clermont-Ferrand, France

Abstract. This paper deals with human body pose recovery through a multicamera system, which is a key task in monitoring of human activity. The proposed algorithm reconstructs the 3D visual hull of the observed body and characterizes its shape with a new 3D shape descriptor. The body pose is then infered through an original two-stage regression process. As the learning step is independant of the camera configuration, the resulting system is easy to set up. This solution is evaluated on synthetic scenes and promising results on real images are also presented.

1 Introduction

Recovering the 3D posture of a human body from 2D images is a key task in many applications, ranging from visual surveillance to video games and motion capture. A robust solution should cope with variations between people in shape and appearance, occlusions and visual ambiguities caused by the lack of depth information inherent to image projection.

Over the past decade, this problem has received a growing attention and two main approaches have emerged. Model-based (or generative) approaches use a complete 2D [1] or 3D [2] body model and define a likelihood function measuring how well its projection in the image fits with image observations. Maximization of this function is challenging due firstly to its complexity (it has many local maxima) and secondly to the high dimension of state space (i.e. the number of degrees of freedom - DOF - of the underlying kinematic structure). Consequently, these methods are often too computationally expensive for real-time applications. To restrict the search area, resolution is often performed in a tracking framework [1,2], not enabling the system to provide an (re)initialisation in case of lost tracks. Model-free (or discriminative) approaches directly produce a body pose estimate from images data. Among these methods, example-based approaches [3] store a database of image-pose exemples, and given a new input perform a search for similar samples in the database to interpolate a pose estimate. In the more recently proposed learning-based approaches, a compact mapping is learnt from the image space to the pose space. Various works cope with the problem of monocular pose estimation. In [4], the authors recover 2D image positions of reference body points from the silhouettes Hu moments, by clustering the training set and learning specialized mapping functions on each cluster. In [5], the correspondence between images and 3D human pose is learnt by the use of sparse regressors and an image description based on shape context. While monocular approaches have a wider potential application field,

F.J. Perales and R.B. Fisher (Eds.): AMDO 2008, LNCS 5098, pp. 370–379, 2008.

they remain unsuitable for robust pose estimation, due to visual ambiguities that make lots of DOF of the body nearly unobservable.

Multi-camera setup is a way to tackle this problem. Different ways to combine multi-view information can be proposed. The easiest is to concatenate the descriptors from each view to create a big feature vector, as proposed by [6]. As outlined by [7], such a strategy implies that the regressor has to be relearnt every time the camera setup is changed. In our study, we choose to estimate the posture from the 3D voxel visual hull that can be obtained with the extracted silhouettes. This 3D shape synthesizes all the information concerning camera parameters (intrinsic and extrinsic) and background subtraction.

In this paper, we introduce a new learning-based approach to estimate human pose from images acquired by a multicamera system. First, the pose representation is presented in §2. We then introduce in §3 the algorithm used to compute the 3D visual hull of the body. §4 presents a new 3D shape descriptor to characterize this reconstructed shape. Our learning process is described in §5, and experimental results are reported in §6. The workflow of our method is presented in figure 1.

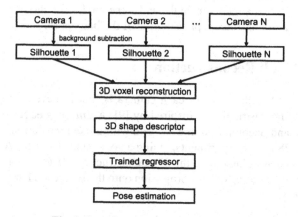

Fig. 1. Overview of the proposed approach

2   Posture Parameterization

We used the software POSER (www.e-frontier.com) to generate and animate realistic human avatars for training and testing. The skeletal structure (shown in fig. 2) employed for animation is a hierarchical system, in which each joint corresponds to a node in a tree. The position and orientation of a joint affect the position and orientation of its child nodes. Each joint has three DOF consisting of the rotation angles around the axes of the local coordinate system (defined by its parent node), except for the root joint, which owns three additional translation degrees. As a consequence, the position and orientation of the root joint of the skeleton (hip in our structure) fix the global position and orientation of the body.

In our study, a human body pose is described by the vector of major body joints angles, including one hip angle to determine global body orientation. To reduce its

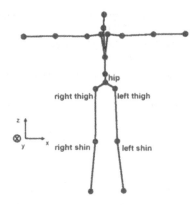

Fig. 2. Skeletal structure of the human body in its default configuration (all joint angles equal 0). The joint "hip" is the root of the kinematic chain.

dimension, we only kept the significant DOF of each body part (one angle for shins, forearms and chest, two angles for thighs and three angles for shoulders and collars). This results in a 22-dimensional representation of the body pose.

3   3D Visual Hull Reconstruction

Recovery of the body silhouette for each camera is first achieved using [8]. Our algorithm for voxel reconstruction is inspired by [9]. A $2meters$ edge cube is centered around the body, and decomposed in a 3D grid with a fixed resolution. The resolution is chosen equal 128 in our experiments, giving a voxel size of $1.6cm$. A voxel v of the 3D grid is classified as belonging to the 3D reconstruction REC or not as follows. Let C_v be the center of v, and $p_i(C_v)$ its projection onto the foreground image of camera i, $i \in \{1, ..., nCam\}$.

1. set $i = 1$
2. if $p_i(C_v) \in foreground_i$
   then set $v \in REC$
      – if $i = nCam$, end
      – else set $i = i + 1$, go to step 2
   else set $v \notin REC$, end

4   3D Shape Descriptor

Our shape descriptor has to be translation invariant to take into account different positions of the body in the scene, but the rotation dependence has to be maintained to enable the estimation of the body global orientation. In the particular case of a human body, real scale invariance is hard to obtain because it has to cope with the height of the body, the corpulence (two people with the same size may have different thickness), the morphology of the body (two people with the same average corpulence may have

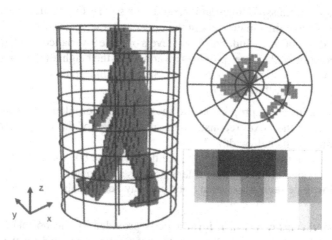

Fig. 3. Left: an example of voxel data with the reference cylinder. Right: a voxel layer with its 2D shape histogram ($n_{rad} = 3$ radial bins and $n_{angles} = 12$ angular sectors).

different limbs proportions, for example thinner legs, bigger belly...), and the width of clothing. All these parameters are relatively independent and can strongly differ from one person to another.

To be robust to noise and segmentation errors, an important requirement for the shape descriptor is locality: a localized error in the shape reconstruction must not affect all the components of the feature vector (e.g. as for global moments). Moreover, to make the learning procedure more efficient, the shape representation must be compact enough and continuous with regard to pose changes.

Given a 3D voxel silhouette, we define a reference cylinder (see fig. 3, left), with main axis being the vertical axis passing through the center of mass of the shape, and with radius being proportional to the height of the body. For each horizontal cross section of the shape, the circle defined by this cylinder is split into a grid consisting of shell-sector bins (see fig. 3, right). A 2D shape histogram is computed by counting the number of voxels falling inside each bin. In our experiments, we used 12 radial sectors, and 3 graduations along the radial direction, giving 36-bins histograms. To avoid the biggest sectors of the grid being over-weighted in the feature vector, we divide each component of the histogram by the maximum number of voxels that could be present in the corresponding sector, so that each bin of the histogram represents the proportion of occupied voxels in a sector. To smooth the effects of spatial quantization, we apply a 2D gaussian convolution mask to the voxels of each layer before computing the histogram. Thus, a voxel localized near sector boundary vote for the neighbour sectors.

The height of the voxel shape is then divided into n_{Slices} equal slices ($n_{Slices} = 10$ in our experiments) and we compute the mean histogram of the sections contained in each slice. The concatenation of these mean histograms gives the 3D feature vector. To ensure continuity with regard to posture changes (for example an arm raised at the interface between two slices), we attribute gaussian weights to the voxel layers before computing the mean histogram. The mean μ of the gaussian function is positioned at the vertical center of the slice, and its standard deviation σ is set to its half height.

The support of the gaussian function is fixed to 4σ so that the feature vector of a slice contains in fact some information about the upper and lower slices.

Our shape description includes different levels of scale invariance. First, the choice of the vertical position of the slices provides invariance to the height of the body (assuming the arms are not raised higher than the head). Secondly, bin-graduations along the radial direction are fixed as follows (see fig. 3):

- the inner radius is set proportional to the estimated corpulence (the ratio between the volume of the voxel reconstruction and the size of the body), and chosen to approximate waist half-width.
- the external radius is proportional to the height of the body in order that all voxels can be contained in the cylinder if legs or arms are spread.
- the intermediate radius is chosen to be halfway between the inner and the external radius.

Finally, another layer of scale invariance is provided by the normalization of the mean 36-bins histograms: each 2D slice feature vector is divided by the sum of the scores of its sectors. Moreover, this normalization can help to smooth the effects of missing or additional voxels (avoiding the scores being too different from those of the database silhouettes) in the case of a noisy reconstruction (see part 6.3).

5 Training and Regression

The body pose is infered from the shape descriptor through an example-based learning step. The examples are generated from synthetic data in order to get ground truth on internal angles of the body. From public motion capture data (www.mocapdata.com), avatars are animated and rendering software generates set of registred 2D silhouette images. For each sample, the 3D visual hull is built and the descriptor is computed.

5.1 Regression

The relationship between a shape descriptor x and a body configuration y is modeled by a linearly-weighted sum of M basis functions:

$$y(x, w) = \sum_{m=1}^{M} w_m \phi_m(x), \tag{1}$$

where w_m are the weights vectors and ϕ_m are the basis functions. We used gaussian kernels for the basis functions: $\phi_m(x) = K(x, x_m) = e^{-\frac{\|x-x_m\|^2}{2\sigma^2}}$. The weights w_m are estimated from training data with a least-squares algorithm, minimizing the error measure:

$$\epsilon = \sum_{n=1}^{N} \|y_n - \sum_{m=1}^{M} w_m \phi_m(x_n)\|^2, \tag{2}$$

where (x_n, y_n) are the N training examples. The optimal weights matrix w_{LS} is obtained in closed-form via the pseudo-inverse $pinv(\Phi)$ of the kernel matrix Φ (defined by $\Phi_{nm} = \phi_m(x_n)$):

$$w_{LS} = pinv(\Phi).Y, \tag{3}$$

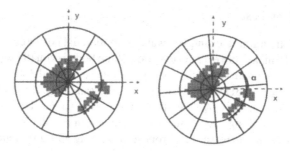

Fig. 4. Alignment of the descriptor fiducial line (in red) with the estimated angle α of the torso

where $Y = [y_1, ..., y_N]$ is the matrix of the output poses. To obtain a sparse regressor that generalizes well on unseen examples, we only retain a subset of the training examples for the basis functions ($M < N$). In our experiments, about 10 % of the training examples from the database were randomly selected as support vectors. Experiments were also conducted using a SVM based regression (learning a single SVM for each output dimension) with similar performance.

5.2 Two Step Estimation

A solution to improve the regression quality is to reduce the complexity of body pose space. To achieve such a reduction, we propose a two-step estimation process. First, only the body orientation is computed, and then, the remaining DOF of the body are processed after a new descriptor computation process. By body orientation we mean orientation of torso, which was found to be the most stable part of the body with regard to global body orientation.

- For the first descriptor, the fiducial line 0° of the shape histogram is aligned with the world coordinate axis x. This descriptor is used to estimate the torso orientation α with respect to world axis z.
- The second descriptor is computed with fiducial line forming the angle α (previously computed) with axis x (see fig. 4). This descriptor is used to estimate all the other joint angles (legs, arms...).

These estimations are based on two mapping functions. The orientation of the descriptor allows the second regressor to concentrate on the limbs configuration and achieve more precision in their estimation. We found empirically a real improvement in estimation with this two-step approach, especially in the case of noisy reconstructions obtained from real data. The main drawback of this process is that the second stage can generally not recover a correct pose if the orientation has been wrongly estimated. However, an aberrant estimate of this orientation on one frame can be easily detected and filtered out with a simple analysis of temporal coherence in sequence processing.

6   Experimental Results

In the following experiments, we used a system of four calibrated cameras similar to the grayscale cameras that were used to generate the HumanEva dataset (vision.cs.brown.edu/).

6.1   Synthetic Database

To generate realistic training examples, walking motion data of three different persons were employed. To make sure every orientation of the body is equally represented in the database, hip orientation around z axis was randomly set around 360°. The coordinates (x, y) of the avatar in the 3D world system were also randomly chosen in the common field of view of the cameras. As the shape description cannot be invariant to every morphological and clothing specificities, we included in our database several avatars (shown in 5) to train the regressor to be robust to clothing and corpulence variations.

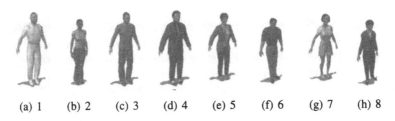

(a) 1   (b) 2   (c) 3   (d) 4   (e) 5   (f) 6   (g) 7   (h) 8

Fig. 5. The 8 avatars employed to generate our synthetic database

6.2   Tests on Synthetic Data

To obtain a quantitative evaluation of the robustness of our system with regard to corpulence and clothing variations, we successively reserved one of the 8 avatars and trained the regressor on the 7 other avatars. We also split our motion data into a training set composed by the motion data of two persons and a test set with the entire sequence of the third person. In this manner, the test set contained unseen motion performed by an unseen avatar. The graphs of fig. 6 show the estimation of few angles over 300 frames of the test sequence, compared with ground truth. The avatars used for testing were respectively 2 and 4. The corresponding mean errors are given in table 1. As can be seen on fig. 5 the second avatar wears clothes that are more loose than the other avatars, so this experiment gives an idea on how well scale invariance is achieved by the combination of the shape description and the learning stage. The difference between estimation and ground truth can be in part explained by the fact that motion is performed by different people in training and test sets, and that the angle intervals covered by their motion are not exactly the same. However, as can be seen on fig. 7, the rendered poses obtained by animating an avatar with these estimated angles are quite correct.

6.3   Real Images

For the tests on real images, the whole motion set was used (i.e. the motion of three persons), and all the avatars shown in fig. 5 were employed. About 15000 training pairs were synthetised. Experiments were conducted on a sequence of the HumanEva dataset (only the four grayscale cameras were used), fully independent of training set. Fig. 8 illustrates some results of our method on real data. In this sequence, the subject performs

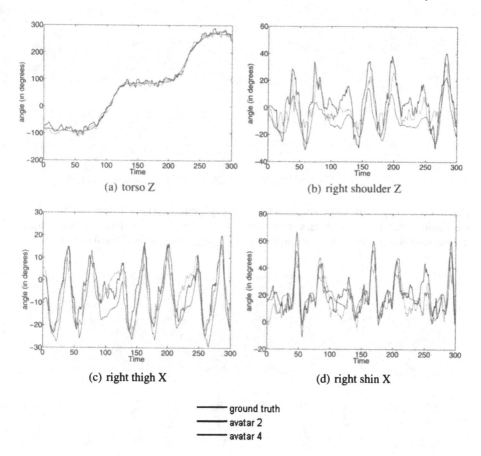

(a) torso Z

(b) right shoulder Z

(c) right thigh X

(d) right shin X

———— ground truth
———— avatar 2
———— avatar 4

Fig. 6. Estimation of some body angles on a synthetic test sequence, compared with ground truth

Table 1. Average errors (in degrees) of the estimated angles for the 2 avatars

avatar	torso Z	right shoulder Z	right thigh X	right shin X
2	7.62	13.56	6.87	6.54
4	7.57	8.64	6.47	6.67

a circular walk in the capture space. Fig. 8 shows some pose estimates for positions regularly spaced on his trajectory. As can been seen on the voxel reconstructions, the use of black and white cameras does not allow an optimal foreground extraction, making difficult, in particular, shadow removal. As a consequence, holes and noise appear in various 3D silhouettes, and the reconstruction sometimes misses an important part of the body. However, the pose was correctly estimated in most frames. The last two columns show the influence of a noisy reconstrution on pose estimates. Estimation can be robust to a certain amount of noise (9th column) but results degrade with too noisy voxel data (last column). With such a reconstruction, some voxel layers are nearly empty, and the descriptor of the 3D shape becomes too different from those of the training examples.

Fig. 7. Some sample pose reconstructions for a walking sequence on two avatars (not included in the training data). First row: images of the test sequence with avatar 2 (left) and avatar 4 (right). Second row: pose reconstructions (from the same viewpoint) with the estimated angles.

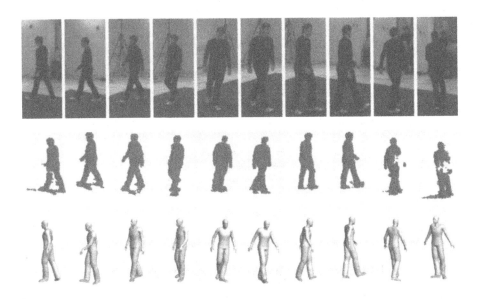

Fig. 8. A few results for a walking sequence of the HumanEva database. Top row: test images from one of the 4 cameras. Middle row: voxel reconstructions obtained from the extracted silhouettes. Lower row: estimated poses from the same viewpoint.

7   Conclusion

In this article, we introduced a new 3D human-shape descriptor. We also proposed an original regression process which infers the body posture from the descriptor of its 3D visual hull. While tests on real images show promising results, results on synthetic data underline the process efficiency to estimate internal angles of the body when the silhouettes are correctly extracted. We have also presented a two step estimation process (global orientation and internal angle) which improves quality results. Concerning the system setup, the use of 3D visual hull reduces the dependency between the camera configuration and the learning step. Moreover, weak computation complexity makes possible the real-time human activity monitoring.

We are currently adding information on the previous state estimate in the learning procedure to introduce temporal coherence. Another perspective is to extend the estimation to a wider variety of postures by coupling the regression with a classification into several posture groups (such as standing, laying down, sitting...).

References

1. Cham, T.J., Rehg, J.M.: A multiple hypothesis approach to figure tracking. In: CVPR (1999)
2. Sminchisescu, C., Triggs, B.: Estimating articulated human motion with covariance scaled sampling. I. J. Robotic Res (2003)
3. Shakhnarovich, G., Viola, P., Darrell, T.: Fast pose estimation with parameter-sensitive hashing. In: ICCV (2003)
4. Rosales, R., Sclaroff, S.: Specialized mappings and the estimation of human body pose from a single image. In: HUMO 2000 (2000)
5. Agarwal, A., Triggs, B.: Recovering 3d human pose from monocular images. PAMI (2006)
6. Grauman, K., Shakhnarovich, G., Darrell, T.: Inferring 3d structure with a statistical image-based shape model. In: ICCV (2003)
7. Sun, Y., Bray, M., Thayananthan, A., Yuan, B., Torr, P.: Regression-based human motion capture from voxel data. In: BMVC (2006)
8. Tuzel, O., Porikli, F., Meer, P.: A bayesian approach to background modeling. In: CVPR (2005)
9. Cheung, G.K.M., Kanade, T., Bouguet, J.Y., Holler, M.: A real time system for robust 3d voxel reconstruction of human motions. In: ICCV (2000)

Fast Detection and Modeling of Human-Body Parts from Monocular Video

Weilun Lao[1], Jungong Han[1], and Peter H.N. de With[1,2]

[1] Eindhoven University of Technology
P.O. Box 513, 5600MB Eindhoven, The Netherlands
[2] CycloMedia Technology B.V
P.O. Box 68, 4180BB Waardenburg, The Netherlands
{w.lao,jg.han,P.H.N.de.With}@tue.nl

Abstract. This paper presents a novel and fast scheme to detect different body parts in human motion. Using monocular video sequences, trajectory estimation and body modeling of moving humans are combined in a co-operating processing architecture. More specifically, for every individual person, features of body ratio, silhouette and appearance are integrated into a hybrid model to detect body parts. The conventional assumption of upright body posture is not required. We also present a new algorithm for accurately finding the center point of the human body. The body configuration is finally described by a skeleton model. The feasibility and accuracy of the proposed scheme are analyzed by evaluating its performance for various sequences with different subjects and motion types (walking, pointing, kicking, leaping and falling). Our detection system achieves nearly real-time performance (around 10 frames/second).

Keywords: motion analysis, trajectory estimation, body modeling, object detection.

1 Introduction

Successful estimation of the pose and modeling of human body facilitates the semantic analysis of human activities in video sequences [1,2]. The detection of human-body parts lays a solid ground to capture the human motion in more detail, which is essential for object/scene analysis and behavior modeling of deformable objects. Such semantic analysis can be explored for specific applications, such as surveillance, human computer interaction, virtual reality, sports analysis and 3-D gaming.

Accurate detection and efficient tracking of various body parts are ongoing research topics. However, the computation complexity needs significant reduction to meet a real-time performance, especially for surveillance applications. Existing fast techniques can be classified into two categories: appearance-based and silhouette-based methods. *Appearance-based* approaches [3,4] utilize the intensity or color configuration within the whole body to infer specific body parts. They can simplify the estimation and collection of training data. However, they

F.J. Perales and R.B. Fisher (Eds.): AMDO 2008, LNCS 5098, pp. 380–389, 2008.

are significantly affected by the variances of body postures and clothing. For the *silhouette-based* approach [5,6,7,8], different body parts are located employing the external points detected along the contour, or internal points estimated from the shape analysis. The geometric configuration of each body part is modeled prior to performing the pose estimation of the whole human body. However, the highly accurate detection of body parts remains a difficult problem, due to the effectiveness of segmentation. Human limbs are often inaccurately detected because of the self-occlusion or occlusion by other objects/persons. Summarizing, both silhouette and appearance-based techniques do not offer a sufficiently high overall accuracy of body-part detection. Also, the assumption of upright posture is generally required.

To address the challenging problem of accurately detecting and modeling human-body parts in a fast way, we contribute in two aspects. First, various differentiating body features (e.g. body ratio, shape, color) are integrated into one framework to detect different body parts without the assumption of the human's posture being upright. Second, we have proposed a novel scheme for capturing human motion, that combines the trajectory-based estimation and body-based modeling. This is effective to improve the detection accuracy. Our approach differs from current state-of-the-art work in the sense that it lacks training, while efficiently preserving the overall quality of the final results. More generally, the presented work aims at the object/scene analysis and behavior modeling of deformable objects. As our system is efficient and achieves nearly real-time performance (around 10 frames/second), we facilitate its application in a surveillance system.

The structure of this paper is as follows. Section 2 briefly presents the scheme. Section 3 introduces every detection component involved. The body-part detection that is based on seamless integration of different observation clues, is explained in detail. Promising experimental results and analysis are presented in Section 4. Finally, Section 5 discusses conclusions and our future work.

2   System Architecture

When combining the trajectory-based estimation and body-based detection, we intend to capture the human motion and locate the body parts using a skeleton model. The block diagram of our proposed scheme is shown in Figure 1. First, each image covering an individual body is segmented to extract the human silhouette after shadow removal. Second, both the trajectory-based and body-based modules are co-operating based on a particular sequence of internal functions. The position of the moving object in every frame is extracted. Occurring situations (behaviors) can be validated along the estimated trajectory for every individual person. Based on the trajectory-based estimation, the system initializes the local body-part detection. In this body-modeling module, various features are applied, such as appearance, body ratio and posture direction. As the fundamental anchor point in our skeleton modeling scheme, the center point of the whole body is also extracted. After different body parts are detected,

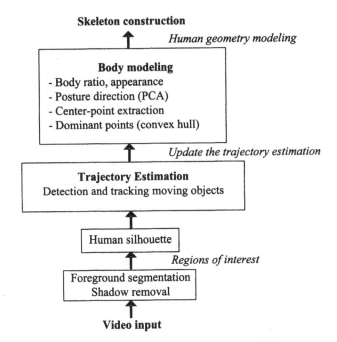

Fig. 1. Block diagram of our body-part modeling system

the human geometry is modeled. Finally, the skeleton model of every person is constructed.

3   Component Algorithms

3.1   Background Substraction

Background modeling is generally the first step of detection and/or analysis of moving objects in a video sequence. We perform an adaptive background subtraction to support person-behavior analysis. The intention is to maintain a statistical background model at every pixel.

In the case of common pixel-level background subtraction, the scene model has a probability density function for each pixel separately. A pixel from a new image is considered to be a background pixel if its new value is well described by its density function. For a static scene the simplest model could be just an image of the scene without the intruding objects. After the background modeling, the next step would be to e.g. estimate appropriate values for the variances of the pixel intensity levels from the image, since the variances can vary from pixel to pixel. Pixel values often have complex distributions and more elaborate models are needed. The Gaussian mixture model (GMM) is generally employed for the background subtraction. We apply the algorithm from reference [9] to produce the foreground objects using a Gaussian-mixture probability density. The parameters for each Gaussian distribution are updated in a recursive way.

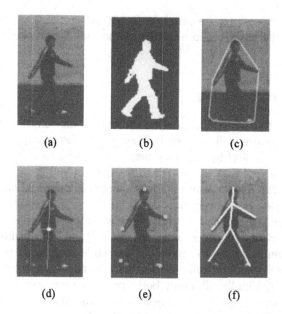

(a)   (b)   (c)

(d)   (e)   (f)

Fig. 2. Procedure of body-based processing: a) original frame, b) foreground segmentation (after shadow removal), c) body modeling based on convex hull, d) center-point estimation, e) body-part location and f) skeleton construction in single-person motion

Furthermore, the method can efficiently select the appropriate number of Gaussian distributions during pixel processing so as to fully adapt to the observed scene.

In the actual segmentation of foreground and background, shadow removal is another important issue. Based on the assumption that shadows decrease the brightness of pixels but do not affect their color, shadows are detected and removed [9]. To consider lighting changes during the process of video acquisition, the pixels labelled as background are used to update in a recursive manner. Finally, the labelled foreground pixels are grouped together to represent potentially moving objects.

3.2   Trajectory Estimation

The trajectory-based module estimates the human position over time, i.e. the movement, which is regarded as a fundamental function of surveillance systems. In our trajectory-based module, we apply blob tracking in two approaches. In a simple setting (e.g. static background, no occlusion), the first approach is based on an object's segmented binary mask. In the second approach, we employ the broadly accepted mean-shift algorithm for tracking persons, based on their individual appearance model represented as a color histogram. When the mean-shift tracker is applied, we detect every new person entering the scene and calculate the corresponding histogram model in the image domain. In subsequent frames for tracking that person, we shift the person object to the location whose histogram is the closest to the previous frame. After the trajectory is located, we can conduct the body-based analysis at the location of the person in every frame.

3.3 Body-Based Modeling

The body-based processing block models the human motion by a skeleton model. The detailed procedure is illustrated in Figure 2. In the example of single-person motion, the input frame (Fig. 2a) is segmented to produce a foreground blob after shadow removal is applied(Fig. 2b). Then the convex hull is implemented for the whole blob (Fig. 2c). The dominant points along the convex hull are strong clues, in the case of single-person body-part detection. They infer the possible locations of body parts, like head, hands and feet. Here we employ a *content-aware* scheme (Section 4.1) to estimate the center point (Fig. 2d), which is fundamentally used to position the human skeleton model. Meanwhile, dominant points along the convex hull are selected and refined (Section 4.2) to locate the the head, hands and feet (Fig. 2e). Finally, different body parts are connected to a predefined skeleton model involving a center point, where the skeleton is adapted to the actual situation of the person in the scene (Fig. 2f).

4   Construction of Skeleton Model

We represent the body by using a skeleton model, which is used to infer the relative orientation of body parts and body posture. The center point is first estimated from the silhouette. Afterwards, it is connected to different body parts to construct the skeleton model.

4.1   Center-Point Extraction

The center point plays an important role in the skeleton model as a reference point. Its estimation accuracy significantly affects the detection of body parts. Here we apply a *content-aware* scheme to detect the center point c_i at the frame with index i. Contents of posture direction, human-body ratio and appearance are taken into account.

The posture direction of a human body can be estimated by the major axis m_i of the body's foreground region at the frame i. The major axis is determined by applying the *Principal Component Analysis* (PCA) to the foreground pixels. Its direction is given by an Eigenvector v associated with the largest Eigenvalue of its covariance matrix. Along the above direction and based on the somatological knowledge, we initially classify the whole body into three segments: head, upper body (including torso and hands) and lower body (two legs). Also, an initial body boundary b_i, dividing upper body and lower body, is produced. Next, within the neighboring area A from body boundary b_i, we perform the Laplacian filter $L_i(x, y)$ to each pixel (x, y) prior to a thresholding function $f(.)$ by value δ.

If $L_i(x, y) > \delta$, $f(.) = 1$. Otherwise, $f(.) = 0$. Then we search the optimal boundary line $\hat{b}'_i$ between the upper body and lower body in Equation (1) by

$$\hat{b}'_i = \arg\max_{b'_i} \sum_{(x,y) \in b'_i} f(L_i(x,y), \delta), \tag{1}$$

where $L_i(x, y)$ indicates the Laplace operation with the 3×3 kernel at point (x, y). Finally, the center point C_i is located by the crossing point of the major axis m_i and the boundary line $\hat{b}'_i$ in Equation (2), hence

$$C_i = m_i \odot \hat{b}'_i, \tag{2}$$

where "$\odot$" denotes returning the intersection position between two lines. During our experiments, we have found that this center-point extraction is effective and accurate, and it is superior to the centroid-of-gravity (CoG) approach of the whole blob, as used in [5]. An example is visualized in Figure 3. Our proposed scheme is simple but effective, even when disturbed by residual noise after shadow removal. If the clothes between the upper body and the lower body are similar in the appearance, only the silhouette feature is employed. The center point is estimated based on the domain knowledge of the human-body ratio.

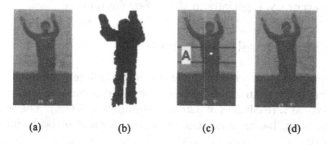

(a)   (b)   (c)   (d)

Fig. 3. Estimation of center point: (a) original frame, (b) silhouette after foreground segmentation, (c) result of CoG approach, (d) result of *content-aware* center point

4.2   Skeleton-Model Extraction

Different body parts are connected to the center point according to a predefined human geometry model, which is similar to the one reported in [8]. Every individual part is estimated according to the Euclidean distance between the center point C_i and every dominant point along the convex hull at the frame i. Based on the body-ratio knowledge, we initially select a set of dominant points P_i with the maximum distance in the three body segments, i.e. head, upper body and lower body. These dominant points are used to infer the locations of potential body parts. As we obtain the body segments (head, upper body, lower body) along the posture direction from Section 4.1, we can refine the points P_i in each individual segment to locate the body parts. Then we use a simple nearest-neighbor filtering scheme to correlate different body parts over time. Afterwards, a Double Exponential Smoothing (DES) filter is added to refine the results. This filter provides good performance for moving object tracking [10].

The DES smoothing operator is defined by

$$\begin{cases} s_i = \alpha \cdot o_i + (1 - \alpha) \cdot (s_{i-1} + d_{i-1}) \,, \\ d_i = \gamma \cdot (s_i - s_{i-1}) + (1 - \gamma) \cdot d_{i-1} \,, \end{cases} \tag{3}$$

where o_i is the observed body-part position value at the frame i. The parameter s_i refers to the position after smoothing the observed position, d_i represents the trend of the change of body-part position, and α and γ are two weighting parameters controlling motion smoothness. Equation (3) applies to every detected body-part position for the individual person. The first smoothing equation adjusts s_i directly for the trend of the previous period with d_{i-1}, by adding it to the last smoothed value s_{i-1}. This helps to eliminate possible position discontinuities. The second smoothing equation updates the trend, which is expressed as the weighted difference between the last two position values.

After the smoothing filter is performed on the observed body parts, another post-processing step is implemented to improve the detection accuracy. If the distance between the detected hands and the center point is below a predefined threshold, we set the location of the hands as a default value, i.e. the position of center point. This additional processing can remove some inaccurate observation and improve the accuracy, especially in the self-occlusion case.

5   Experimental Results and Analysis

In our experiments, we have tested the algorithm for different monocular video sequences covering more than 2,500 frames. The video sequences were recorded at 15-Hz frame rate at a resolution of 320×240 samples (QVGA). The sequences cover different persons, background, clothes and behaviors in both indoor and outdoor situations.

We have evaluated our scheme with different motion types such as walking, pointing, kicking, leaping and falling. We implemented two state-of-the-art contour-based methods [5,8] for performance comparison. Figure 4 summarizes the accuracy comparison when using the different methods. In our experiments, the ground truth of body-part locations were manually obtained. The maximum tolerable errors in the evaluation is set to 15 pixels. Some visual examples of our experimental results are illustrated in Figure 5. After the body-part detection, the skeletons are superimposed on the images. Our system is implemented in C++ on a 3.0-GHz PC. The detection system operates at nearly real-time speed (around 10 frames/second).

From our experiments, we have found that the dominant points (with high curvature) along the contour play an important role in the three presented contour-based methods. If the dominant points are highly observable, e.g. in the motion types of pointing and kicking, all three methods yield similar performance. However, as we integrate the temporal constraints by employing the DES filter, our

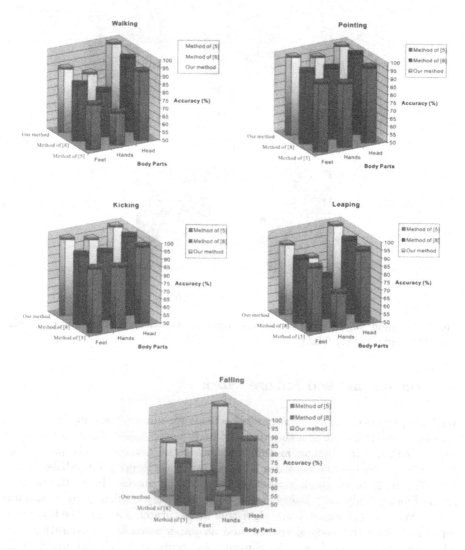

Fig. 4. Comparison of the detection accuracy of three different methods for walking, pointing, kicking, leaping and falling

detection accuracy is higher by around 5%, especially in the case of the self-occlusion when the hands/legs appear within the silhouette. Another interesting point is that our method does not assume that the human posture is upright. Moreover, the posture direction can be estimated in our algorithm. In the falling case, our method clearly outperforms the other two [5,8] by around 20% in the detection of hands.

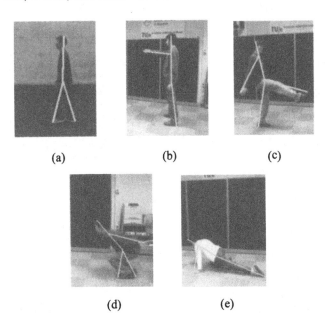

(a)   (b)   (c)

(d)   (e)

Fig. 5. The modeling result of single-person motion: (a) walking, (b) pointing, c) kicking, (d) leaping and (e) falling

6   Conclusions and Future Work

We have proposed a novel dual-module scheme for human-body modeling, that combines trajectory-based estimation and body-based analysis in a co-operating way, to capture the human motion and locate the different body parts. The trajectory-based module provides a platform for performing body-based analysis. The body-based module updates the tracking process, infers the posture of the human body and describes the body geometry efficiently by a skeleton model. We have presented a new algorithm for accurately locating the body center point, using the body silhouette and an upper/lower-body separation line. This algorithm outperforms the conventional center-of-gravity approach from existing literature, addressing the same center-point usage. Body-part detection was performed after estimation of the center point, analysis of body ratio, silhouette and appearance. An advantage is that the conventional assumption of upright body posture is not required. The above scheme has proven to be a fast (nearly real-time speed at 10-Hz frame rate) and effective technique for the automatic detection of different body parts within monocular video sequences in indoor/outdoor areas.

However, the current system has a few limitations. The self-occlusion problem is not completely solved, requiring additional exploration, as the dominant points along the convex hull fail to differentiate and locate the underlying body parts within the silhouette. We have found that the color appearance of the person is important in the case of self-occlusion. The region-based nature of color will be utilized to improve the body-part segmentation. Also, we are going to capture motion sequences from different viewpoints and train the optimal parameters for different motion types, aiming at becoming more view-independent in performance.

References

1. Moeslund, T.B., Hilton, A., Kruger, V.: A Survey of Advances in Vision-Based Human Motion Capture and Analysis. Computer Vision and Image Understanding 104, 90–126 (2006)
2. Lao, W., Han, J., de With, P.H.N.: A Matching-Based Approach for Human Motion Analysis. In: Cham, T.-J., Cai, J., Dorai, C., Rajan, D., Chua, T.-S., Chia, L.-T. (eds.) MMM 2007. LNCS, vol. 4352, pp. 405–414. Springer, Heidelberg (2006)
3. Viola, P., Jones, M., Snow, D.: Detecting Pedestrians Using Patterns of Motion and Appearance. In: Proc. Int. Conf. Computer Vision, pp. 734–741 (2003)
4. Aggarwal, K.: Simultaneous Tracking of Multiple Body Parts of Interacting Persons. Computer Vision and Image Understanding 102, 1–21 (2006)
5. Fujiyoshi, H., Lipton, A., Kanade, T.: Real-time Human Motion Analysis by Image Skeletonization. IEICE Trans. Information and System 87, 113–120 (2004)
6. Haritaoglu, I., Harwood, D., Davis, L.: W4: Real-Time Surveillance of People and Their Activities. IEEE Trans. Pattern Analysis and Machine Intelligence 22, 809–830 (2000)
7. Yu, C., Hwang, J., Ho, G., Hsieh, C.: Automatic Human body Tracking and Modeling from Monocular Video Sequences. In: IEEE Proc. Int. Conf. Acoustics, Speech and Signal Processing, Hawaii, vol. 1, pp. 917–920 (2007)
8. Peursum, P., Bui, H., Venkatesh, S., West, G.: Robust Recognition and Segmentation of Human Actions Using HMMs with Missing Observations. EURASIP Journal on Applied Signal Processing 13, 2110–2126 (2005)
9. Zivkovic, Z., van der Heijden, F.: Efficient Adaptive Density Estimation per Image Pixel for the Task of Background Subtraction. Pattern Recognition Letters 27, 773–780 (2006)
10. Han, J., Farin, D., de With, P.H.N., Lao, W.: Real-Time Video Content Analysis Tool for Consumer Media Storage System. IEEE Trans. Consumer Electronics 52, 870–878 (2006)

Kinetic Pseudo-energy History for Human Dynamic Gestures Recognition

Luis Unzueta[1], Oscar Mena[1], Basilio Sierra[2], and Ángel Suescun[1]

[1] CEIT and Tecnun, University of Navarra, Manuel de Lardizabal 15, 20018
Donostia-San Sebastián, Spain
{lunzueta,omena,asuescun}@ceit.es
http://www.ceit.es/mechanics/index.htm

[2] Computer Engineering Faculty, University of the Basque Country, Manuel de
Lardizabal 1, 20018 Donostia-San Sebastián, Spain
b.sierra@ehu.es
http://www.sc.ehu.es/ccwrobot/index.html

Abstract. In this paper we present a new approach, based on the kinetic status history, to automatically determine the starting and ending instants of human dynamic gestures. This method opens up the possibility to distinguish static or quasi-static poses from dynamic actions, during a real-time human motion capture. This way a more complex Human-Computer Interaction (HCI) can be attained. Along with this procedure, we also present a novel method to recognize dynamic gestures independently from the velocity with which they have been performed. The efficiency of this approach is tested with gestures captured with a triple axis accelerometer, and recognized with different statistical classifiers, obtaining satisfactory results for real-time applications.

Keywords: Human Action Recognition, Human Tracking, Kinetic Pseudo-Energy.

1 Introduction

At present, marker-based systems are the most popular human motion capture (mocap) systems. We can distinguish mainly among optical, magnetic, mechanical and inertial mocap systems. Depending on the system, the data provided can be the marker positions, orientations, accelerations, etc. Users need to wear these markers all over the body in specific configurations and the system must be calibrated properly which, along with their high cost, makes this method cost prohibitive for home-users. Nevertheless, more recently, new devices that have embedded accelerometers have appeared in order to obtain the user's movements at an affordable cost, such as the Nintendo Wii [6] video game console remote, and the Apple iPhone [5] and Sony Ericsson W910i [7] mobile phones. On the other hand, in recent years, optical markerless mocap systems have been developed. Cameras are capable of detecting pixel colors and intensities and from

F.J. Perales and R.B. Fisher (Eds.): AMDO 2008, LNCS 5098, pp. 390–399, 2008.

these computer vision algorithms can be applied to distinguish the user's silhouette, the positions of the end-effectors, the centroid, etc. [8,9,10].

Both marker-based and markerless strategies can get human postures and movements usable to communicate with the computer. Gestures can be static (the user adopts a certain pose) or dynamic. Recognizing static poses can be interesting for many applications such as sign language [1,2] and facial expression [3,4] interpretation, while recognizing also movements can lead to broader and more complex applications such as locomotive skills analysis and transferring. During a real-time motion capture both circumstances may occur: (1) the user may attempt to perform certain poses and (2) may attempt to perform specific movements. It is not a trivial task to discern looking only at measured data when do meaningful static and dynamic gestures happen, because users do not perform poses perfectly static, and they also may trace non-relevant movements.

Hence, in next section we present a method that, thresholding the historic kinetic status of the features used for recognition, determines when static or quasi-static gestures happen, and also when the starting and ending instants of dynamic gestures occur. Along with this, in section 3 we present a procedure to recognize dynamic gestures independently from the velocity of the performances, that also discriminates meaningful gestures from those which are not. In section 4 we provide the experimental results of both the dynamic gestures determination and recognition. Finally, we discuss the obtained results, which are satisfactory for Human-Computer Interaction (HCI), and conclude with the future work derived from this study.

2   Kinetic Pseudo-energy History

The determination of the starting and the ending instants of dynamic gestures is a challenging task due to non-relevant movements can be performed. Lee and Kim [11] call this task *gesture spotting*, derived from *pattern spotting*, that refers to the location of meaningful patterns from a data stream [12]. Their approach consists in thresholding the probability of performed movements to be a gesture of the database using Hidden Markov Models [13]. They obtain a 93.14 percent reliability, but its main drawback is that the response is given when next gesture is performed and not immediately, which preserves the interface from naturalness.

On the other hand, in our approach we make use of the data-flow's most recent kinetic status to determine when a potentially meaningful dynamic gesture happens. This strategy combined with the gestures recognition method presented in next section, is able to distinguish really meaningful static or quasi-static and dynamic gestures from those which are not.

The kinetic status of a solid of mass m moving with a velocity v can be depicted with the kinetic energy $E_k = \frac{1}{2}m\,|v|^2$. This energy provides a positive (or zero) scalar quantity that reflects the motion of the solid, which can correspond to a body part of the user being tracked. In the case of detecting gestures we are only interested on the velocity scalar magnitude $|v|$. The mass m keeps constant and does not affect for our purpose. Therefore we define kinetic pseudo-energy as $psE_k = |v|$.

A simple way of detecting when a dynamic gesture may happen can be to threshold psE_k. But it may occur during the performance of the gesture, that the body part changes its direction from one side to another getting at a certain time $psE_k = 0$. This situation arises, for example, in *hand waving* or *shaking* gestures. Therefore this approach is not sufficient to detect gestures involving direction changes. On the other hand, we can consider the n most recent frames of a body part's kinetic pseudo-energy at frame t, or in other words, the kinetic pseudo-energy history:

$$psE_k^{history} = [psE_k^{(t-(n-1))}, psE_k^{(t-(n-2))}, ..., psE_k^{(i)}, ..., psE_k^{(t-1)}, psE_k^{(t)}] \quad (1)$$

We propose to threshold the mean value of $psE_k^{history}$ in order to handle with direction changes. This magnitude evolves with a higher inertia than the instantaneous psE_k and therefore it is more robust to sudden changes. On the other hand, it moves with a certain delay respect to the real movements, that must be determined in order to get properly the starting and ending instants of gestures. This delay can be estimated with Algorithm 1.

Algorithm 1 Mean Kinetic Ps-Energy History Delay Determination Algorithm

---

1: **procedure** DELAYDETERMINATIONALGORITHM($psE_k^{history}$, $meanPsE_k^{threshold}$)
2:     $startingPoint \Leftarrow t$
3:     **for** $i = t - (n - 1)$ to t **do**
4:         **if** $psE_k^{history}(i) < meanPsE_k^{threshold}$ **then**
5:             $startingPoint \Leftarrow i$
6:         **end if**
7:     **end for**
8:     $delay \Leftarrow t - startingPoint$
9:     **return** $delay$
10: **end procedure**

---

3   Quasi-static and Dynamic Gestures Recognition Method

Once the potential dynamic gesture is determined with the kinetic pseudo-energy history, it is necessary to determine whether it is a gesture of the database or not. The tracked m features $[f_1, f_2, ..., f_j, ..., f_m]$ of the body part can represent its position coordinates and/or orientation angles, and evolve in a continuous stream along time. At frame t the feature values represent a pose that can be expressed as a vector of m elements $pose^{(t)} = [f_1^{(t)}, f_2^{(t)}, ..., f_j^{(t)}, ..., f_m^{(t)}]$. Static or quasi-static gestures can be easily classified using the K-Nearest Neighbor (K-NN) procedure [14] with K=1 between the current pose, $pose^{(t)}$, and those of the database. Ibarguren et al. [15] showed the robustness of this procedure to noisy measures respect to other statistical classifiers. Another important feature of K-NN is that the distance allows to determine the *correctness* of a pose. If the current pose is too distant from its nearest neighbor it may be considered as *unknown*.

Meanwhile, a movement, which is a set of poses ordered in time, can also be expressed as a vector of $m \times n$ elements:

$$mov = [f_1^{(t-(n-1))}, ..., f_m^{(t-(n-1))}, f_1^{(t-(n-2))}, ..., f_m^{(t-(n-2))}, f_1^{(t)}, ..., f_m^{(t)}] \qquad (2)$$

In order to recognize dynamic gestures it would also be interesting to measure the distance between the performed gesture and those of the database, but the frames number may vary both from gesture to gesture and also from performance to performance. Therefore, to be able to recognize dynamic actions using K-NN we propose to resample the performed actions to the same number of frames with a cubic spline. The first derivatives of both the starting and ending points should be the same as in the original which can be easily calculated this way (bearing in mind that t is the current frame):

$$\frac{\partial f_j^{(t-(n-1))}}{\partial t} = f_j^{(t-(n-2))} - f_j^{(t-(n-1))}, \text{ and } \frac{\partial f_j^{(t)}}{\partial t} = f_j^{(t)} - f_j^{(t-1)} \qquad (3)$$

This way we can have a database of different dynamic gesture performances expressed as single vectors, making the recognition procedure is independent from the velocity with which dynamic gestures are traced. This allows to measure the distance and therefore evaluate the *correctness* of a new performance. This distance determines the disparity in the posture evolution along time. Again too distant performances can be labeled as *unknown*, which can be used to distinguished meaningful gestures from those which are not. Moreover we can analyze which of the features and in which time instants are further from its reference performance. This can be helpful in applications for skills acquisition and transferring.

4   Experimental Results

We have tested the efficiency of the presented approach with:

- An analysis of the capture of relevant hand movements with a triple axis accelerometer iMEMS®ADXL330 [16] embedded in the Wii™[6] remote.
- A comparison of dynamic gestures recognition with different classifiers: K-NN, Support Vector Machines (SVM) [17] and Random Forest [18]. The database dynamic gestures are numbers from 0 to 9 traced as shown in Fig. 1. It is composed of 200 sequences, containing 20 performances for each class. Furthermore, the recognition of a set of static poses (Fig. 2) is also presented. This static gestures database has 6 performances, 1 per class composed of a set of poses around its intended configuration.

The triple axis accelerometer provides three numbers, that represent the accelerations in three orthogonal axes over a range of at least +/- 3g with a 10%

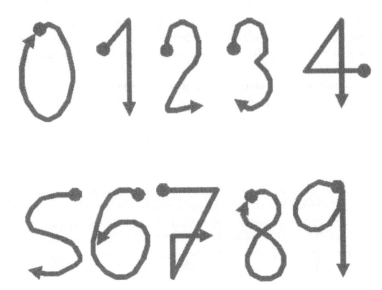

Fig. 1. The set of dynamic gestures for the experiment

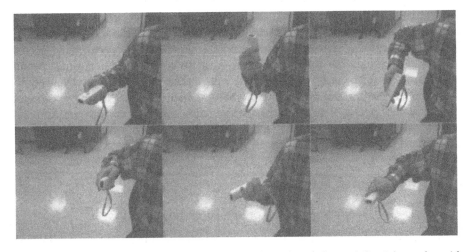

Fig. 2. From left to right and top to bottom: neutral, up, down, left, right and upside down static poses

of sensitivity. These three numbers can be visualized as a 3D vector a, that at rest has a magnitude of +1g in vertical direction downwards. While moving, the orientation of the vector vary depending on the roll and pitch of the device (not the yaw). The vector magnitude increases while moving, except when dropped, that makes the magnitude tend to zero.

In order to apply the kinetic pseudo-energy approach to get the starting and ending instants of a dynamic gesture, the vector magnitude can be exploited. It contains both the accelerations and decelerations during performances in a positive scalar magnitude that at rest has a value of 1. The mean value of its recent history can be visualized as the absolute value of the effective increment of the velocity magnitude, and therefore dynamic gestures occur while this mean value overcomes a certain threshold, taking into account its inertial delay. This way the gesture temporal variation, i.e. gesture, is represented with the normalized vector $u = (u_x, u_y, u_z) = a/|a|$, while $psE_k = |a|$.

Fig. 3 shows how the application of the kinetic pseudo-energy approach detects satisfactorily the execution of a dynamic gesture ($threshold = 1.2$). It can be also appreciated the delay to be taken into account to get the gesture properly.

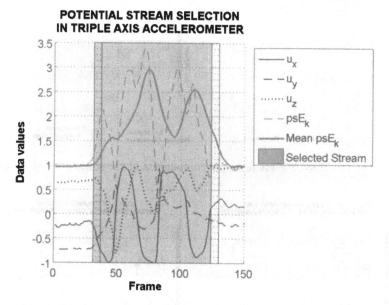

Fig. 3. The automatic determination of the start and end of a dynamic gesture

Fig. 4 and Fig. 5 show the three highest principal components (from PCA [19]) of the static and dynamic gesture databases respectively. It can be seen that in both cases the different performances for the same gestures tend to form well-defined clusters, which makes it easier to classify new performances correctly. We use PCA only for the 3D visualization of the data, that has more than three dimensions ($m \times n$ dimensions), not for data processing. In this case it is preferable not to compress data in order to maintain the details of the performances.

In order to test the classification performance, the Leave One Out training validation method [20] has been used with K-NN, SVM and Random Forest classifiers. Both K-NN and SVM obtain a recognition rate of 99 %, while the Random Forest obtains 55 % with the dynamic gestures database. The corresponding confusion matrices are shown in Fig. 6. The difference between K-NN

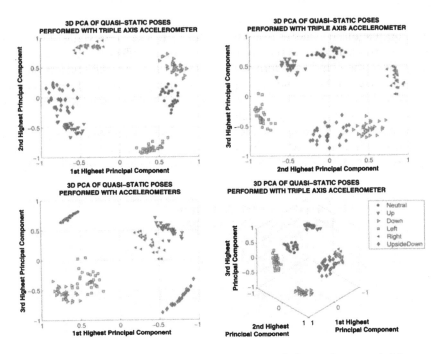

Fig. 4. The three highest principal components of the static poses database

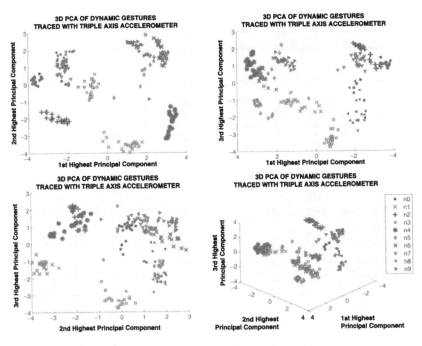

Fig. 5. The three highest principal components of the dynamic gestures database

Asigned Class	Real Class									
	0	1	2	3	4	5	6	7	8	9
0	20/20					1/20				
1		20/20								
2			20/20							
3				20/20						
4					20/20					1/20
5						19/20				
6							20/20			
7								20/20		
8									20/20	
9										19/20

Asigned Class	Real Class									
	0	1	2	3	4	5	6	7	8	9
0	19/20	2/20	3/20	5/20	8/20	8/20	12/20	13/20	15/20	12/20
1		18/20								
2			16/20		1/20	1/20		1/20		
3				14/20	2/20			1/20		
4					9/20					
5						10/20				
6						1/20	8/20			1/20
7								5/20		
8	1/20			1/20				1/20	4/20	
9			1/20							7/20

Fig. 6. On the top the confusion matrix of both K-NN and SVM. On the bottom the confusion matrix of Random Forest.

and SVM comes from the computation time during the training stage. K-NN needs 0.035" while SVM 10.277" in a Pentium 4 at 2.53 GHz and 512 RAM. In the case of the static gestures database K-NN achieves a recognition rate of 100 % due to the clear clusters that conform the poses.

5 Conclusions and Future Work

In this paper we have presented a new approach to automatically determine the starting and ending instants of human dynamic gestures. This approach uses the concept of pseudo-energy history for distinguishing static or quasi-static poses from dynamic actions. This way dynamic actions are delimited using data-flow's most recent kinetic status. If an action surpasses a certain historic kinetic threshold it can be guessed that a dynamic action has happened. Otherwise, the action is considered as static or quasi-static.

Along with this procedure, we also have presented a recognition method for both static or quasi-static and dynamic gestures. Movements are resampled to have a certain predefined number of frames using cubic splines. This makes possible to detect correctly gestures traced at different speeds, and also allows the different performances of the same gesture to conform well-defined clusters. This data treatment eases the posterior classification of new performances. This approach has been tested with a database of 200 dynamic gesture performances traced with a triple axis accelerometer, in order to recognize 10 different classes, obtaining a recognition rate of 99 %. In the case of static or quasi-static poses the recognition rate raises to 100 %. These results reveal its potential for HCI.

Future work will be focused in two main areas: (1) the improvement of the recognition procedure in order to distinguish cyclic gestures, and (2) the improvement of pseudo-energy history approach in order to handle transitions occurred among dynamic gestures.

Acknowledgments. This work has been subsidized by the SKILLS project *Multimodal Interfaces for Capturing and Transfer of Skill* funded by the European Union, FP6-IST-2005-035005, the Association of Friends of the University of Navarra (Amigos de la Universidad de Navarra), the Ministry of Education of Spain within the framework of the Torres Quevedo Program, and cofunded by the European Social Fund.

References

1. Min, B.W., Yoon, H.S., Soh, J., Ohashi, T., Ejima, T.: Visual recognition of static dynamic gesture: Gesture-driven editing system. Journal Of Visual Languages And Computing 10(3), 291–309 (1999)
2. Chang, C.C., Chen, J.J., Tai, W.K., Han, C.C.: New approach for static gesture recognition. Journal Of Information Science And Engineering 22(5), 1047–1057 (2006)
3. Essa, I.A., Pentland, A.P.: Coding, analysis, interpretation, and recognition of facial expressions. IEEE Transactions On Pattern Analysis And Machine Intelligence 19(7), 757–763 (1997)
4. Donato, G., Bartlett, M.S., Hager, J.C., Ekman, P.: Classifying facial actions. IEEE Transactions On Pattern Analysis And Machine Intelligence 21(10), 974–989 (1999)
5. Apple Inc. iPhone mobile phone at, http://www.apple.com/iphone/
6. Nintendo Wii^{TM} console at, http://www.wii.com/
7. Sony Ericsson W910i mobile phone at, http://www.sonyericsson.com/cws/products/mobilephones/overview/w910i/
8. Wren, C., Azarbayejani, A., Darrell, T., Pentland, A.: Pfinder: Real-time Tracking of the Human Body. In: IEEE Transactions on Pattern Analysis and Machine Intelligence (1997)
9. Theobalt, C., Magnor, M., Schueler, P., Seidel, H.P.: Combining 2D Feature Tracking and Volume Reconstruction for Online Video-Based Human Motion Capture. In: Proceedings of Pacific Graphics, Beijing, China, pp. 96–103 (2002)
10. Varona, J., Buades, J.M., Perales, F.J.: Hands and face tracking for VR applications. International Journal of Systems & Applications in Computer Graphics 29, 179–187 (2005)
11. Lee, H.-K., Kim, J.H.: An HMM-Based Threshold Model Approach for Gesture Recognition. IEEE Transactions on Pattern Analysis and Machine Intelligence 21(10), 961–973 (1999)
12. Rose, R.C.: Discriminant Wordspotting Techniques for Rejection Non-Vocabulary Utterances in Unconstrained Speech. In: Proceedings of the IEEE International Conference on Acoustics, Speech, and Signal Processing, San Francisco, USA, vol. 2, pp. 105–108 (1992)

13. Rabiner, L.R.: A tutorial on hidden Markov models and selected applications in speech recognition. Proceedings of the IEEE 77(2), 257–286 (1989)
14. Dasarathy, B.V.: KNN: Nearest Neighbor Pattern Classification Techniques. Edited collection. IEEE Press, California (1991)
15. Ibarguren, A., Maurtua, I., Sierra, B.: Recognition of sign language in real time through Data Gloves. In: Borrajo, D., Castillo, L., Corchado, J.M. (eds.) CAEPIA 2007. LNCS (LNAI), vol. 4788, pp. 307–316. Springer, Heidelberg (2007)
16. Analog Devices' iMEMS®acceletometers at, http://www.analog.com/
17. Shawe-Taylor, J., Cristianini, N.: Support Vector Machines and other kernel-based learning methods. Cambridge University Press, Cambridge (2000)
18. Breiman, L.: Random Forests. Machine Learning 45(1), 5–32 (2001)
19. Fukunaga, K.: Introduction to statistical pattern recognition. Academic Press Professional Inc., San Diego (1990)
20. Stone, M.: Cross-validation choice and assessment of statistical procedures. Journal of Royal Statistical Society 36, 111–147 (1974)

An Improved Algorithm for Estimating the ICA Model Concerning the Convergence Rate

Doru Constantin and Luminita State

University of Pitesti
Department of Computer Science
Address Str. Tg. din Vale, No.1, Romania
cdomanid@yahoo.com, radus@sunu.rnc.ro

Abstract. The aim of the present paper is to propose a estimation algorithm of the ICA model, an algorithm based on successive approximations. The convergence rate of the successive approximations method are substantiated for the bidimensional case, a case which presents interest from a practical point of view, and we want to establish the performances of the proposed algorithm to estimate the independent components. Comparative analysis is done and experimentally derived conclusions on the performance of the proposed method are drawn in the last section of the paper for signals recognition applications.

Keywords: Independent Component Analysis, Blind Source Separation, Numerical Method.

1 Introduction

A relevant issue which may occur in signal processing, mathematical statistical and neural networks is represented by necessity of obtaining adequate representations of multidimensional data. The problem can be formulated in terms of finding a function f such that the n dimensional transform defined by $s = f(x)$ possesses some desired properties, where x is a m dimensional random vector. Being given its computational simplicity, frequently the linear approach is attractive, that is the transform is

$$s = Wx \qquad (1)$$

where W is a matrix to be optimally determined from the point of view of a pre-established criterion.

There are a long series of methods and principles already proposed in the literature for solving the problem of fitting an adequate linear transform for multidimensional data [1,4], as for instance, Principal Component Analysis (PCA), factor analysis, projection methods and Independent Component Analysis (ICA).

The aim of Independent Component Analysis is to determine a transform such that the components $s_i, i = \overline{1..n}$ becomes statistically independent, or at least almost statistically independent. In order to find a suitable linear transform

F.J. Perales and R.B. Fisher (Eds.): AMDO 2008, LNCS 5098, pp. 400–408, 2008.

to assure that (1) $s_i, i = \overline{1..n}$ become 'nearly' statistically independent several methods have been developed so far. Some of them, as for instance Principal Component Analysis and factor analysis are second order approaches, that is they use exclusively the information contained by the covariance matrix of the random vector x, some of them, as for instance the projection methods and blind deconvolution are higher order methods that use an additional information to reduce the redundancies in the data. Independent Component Analysis has became one of the most promising approaches in this respect and, consists in the estimation of the generative model of the form $x = As$, where the $s = (s_1 s_2, \dots s_n)^T$ are supposed to be independent, and A is the mixing matrix $m \times n-$ dimensional of the model. The data model estimation in the framework of independent component analysis is stated in terms of a variational problem formulated on a given objective function.

The aim of the research reported in this paper is to introduce a new version of the FastICA algorithm; an algorithm that is based on secant iterations combined with successive approximations and to analyze the performances of the algorithm in signal applications.

2   Fixed-Point ICA Based on Iterations Method

2.1   The Standard FastICA Algorithm

In this part the ICA model and the standard FastICA algorithm are briefly exposed. The ICA model is state as $x = As$, where x is the observations vector and A is the mixing matrix of the original sources, s. The aim is to determine the sources, on the basis of x. One of the basic working assumption in estimation the ICA model is that the sources s are statistically independent and they have nongaussian distributions. This way the problem becomes to find the weighting matrix W (the demixing matrix), such that the transform $y = Wx$ gives suitable approximations of the independent sources.

In the following, the numerical estimation of the independent components is going to be obtained using the secant method combined with the successive approximation approaches, the variational problem being imposed on the negentropy taken as criterion function.

The negentropy is defined by:

$$I(y) = H(y_{gauss}) - H(y) \tag{2}$$

where $H(y) = -\int p_y(\eta) \log p_y(\eta) d\eta$ is the differential entropy of the random vector y.

Considering that that the Gaussian repartition is of largest differential entropy in the class of the repartitions having the same covariance matrix, the maximization of the negentropy (2) gives the best estimation of the ICA model. Although this approaches is well founded from information point of view the direct use of the expression (2) is not computationally tractable, and some approximations are needed instead. We use the approximation introduced in (Hyvarinen, 98):

$$I(y) = [E\{G(y)\} - E\{G(\nu)\}]^2 \tag{3}$$

where G is an nonquadratic function, v and y are Gaussian variables of zero mean and unit variance. Some of the most frequently used expressions of G are,

$$G_1(y) = \frac{1}{a_1} \log \cosh(a_1 y); \quad 1 \leq a_1 \leq 2, \quad G_2(y) = -\exp(-\frac{y^2}{2}); \quad G_3(y) = \frac{y^4}{4}$$

Note that the expressions of their first order derivatives are given by: $g_1(y) = \tanh(a_1 y)$; $g_2(y) = y \exp(-\frac{y^2}{2})$; $g_3(y) = y^3$, respectively.

The variational problem can be formulated as a constraint optimization problem as follows,

$$\max F(w), \quad \|w\|^2 = 1 \tag{4}$$

that is the objective function $F(w)$ has to be maximized on the unit sphere. In case the negentropy is taken as the objective function, we get,

$$F(w) = [E\{G(y)\} - E\{G(v)\}]^2 \tag{5}$$

where $y = w^T z$.

To solve the optimization problem from the (4) relation we write the Lagrange function using the Lagrange multiplications method:

$$L(w) = F(w) - \lambda(\|w\|^2 - 1) \tag{6}$$

The necessary conditions for the critical points are:

$$\frac{\partial L(w, \lambda)}{\partial w} = 0 \text{ and } \frac{\partial L(w, \lambda)}{\partial \lambda} = 0 \tag{7}$$

Applying (7) in the (6) relation we have:

$$\frac{\partial L(w, \lambda)}{\partial w} = \frac{\partial F(w)}{\partial w} - 2\lambda w = 0 \tag{8}$$

The expression of the gradient $\frac{\partial F(w)}{\partial w}$ is calculated like this:

$$\frac{\partial F(w)}{\partial w} = \frac{\partial [E\{G(y)\} - E\{G(v)\}]^2}{\partial w} = \tag{9}$$
$$= 2 * [E\{G(w^T z)\} - E\{G(v)\}] * [E\{zg(w^T z)\}]$$

and $\gamma = [E\{G(w^T z)\} - E\{G(v)\}]$ is a constant, because v is a Gaussian random variable. Thus we obtain:

$$\frac{\partial F(w)}{\partial w} = \gamma [E\{zg(w^T z)\}] \tag{10}$$

and it presents the gradient of the negentropy.

Replacing the (10) relation in (8) we obtain:

$$F^*(w) = E\{zg(w^T z)\} - \beta w = 0 \tag{11}$$

where β is a real constant, $\beta = E\left\{w_0^T z g(w_0^T z)\right\}$, where w_0 is the critical value of w.

The Newton method applied to (11) gives

$$w \leftarrow E\{zg\left(w^T z\right)\} - E\{g'\left(w^T z\right)\}w \tag{12}$$

The weighting vectors being normalized, we arrive at the following approximation scheme,

1. $w \leftarrow E\{zg\left(w^T z\right)\} - E\{g'\left(w^T z\right)\}w$
2. $w \leftarrow w/\|w\|$.

2.2   Successive Approximations for the ICA Model

We consider the following equation:

$$f(w) = 0 \tag{13}$$

where f is a function defined on R^n, $f : I \rightarrow R^n, I \subseteq R^n, n \in N^*$.

Since the case of defining f on R^2, presents a real interest from a practical point of view, further on we propose to substantiate the successive approximations for the bidimensional case, the extension to the general case being easily achieved by using the Pickard-Banach theorems.

Taking into consideration the case $n = 2$, the equation equivalent to (13) is:

$$w = \varphi(w) \tag{14}$$

and its roots are called fixed points of φ.

There is the iterations sequence build by:

$$w_{n+1} = \varphi(w_n), \quad n = 0, 1, 2, ... \tag{15}$$

where w_0 is an initial approximated value of the searched root.

Theorem 1. *If $\varphi : I_1 \times I_2 = I \rightarrow R^2, I_1, I_2 \subset R$ are compact domains and it has the following conditions:*

(α) $\forall w \in I \Rightarrow \varphi(w) \in I$ *and*
(β) $\exists q \in R, q \in [0, 1)$ *so that $\forall u_1, u_2 \in I$ the inequality is achieved:*

$$\|\varphi(u_1) - \varphi(u_2)\| \leq q\|u_1 - u_2\|$$

then we have:

1. *the $(w_n)_{n \in N}$ sequence generated by (15) is convergent;*
2. *$\overline{w} = \lim\limits_{n \to \infty} w_n$ is the unique root of the (13) equation on I.*

Proof (See Constantin, State, 2008)

Theorem 2. *Let the function φ previously defined, $\varphi \in C^{(p)}(I)$ and w^* a fixed point for φ. If the following conditions are satisfied:*

$$\varphi'(w^*) = ... = \varphi^{(p-1)}(w^*) = 0, \ \varphi^{(p)}(w^*) \neq 0$$

then we have the $(w_n)_{n \in N}$ sequence generated by (15) is convergent and the convergence rate is p.

Proof. As $\varphi'(w^*) = 0 < 1$, from the first theorem we obtain the convergence of the sequence $(w_n)_{n \in N}$. To determined the convergence rate, we develop the function into φ into Taylor' series:

$$\varphi(w) = \varphi(w^*) + \sum_{i=1}^{p-1} \frac{\varphi^{(i)}(w^*)}{i!} + \frac{\varphi^{(p)}(\xi)}{p!}(w - w^*) \tag{16}$$

where $\xi \in (w, w^*)$. Taking $w = w_k$ and from the theorem hypothesis, we obtain:

$$\frac{\|w_{k+1} - w^*\|}{\|w_k - w^*\|^p} = \frac{\varphi^{(p)}(\xi_k)}{p!}, \ \xi \in (w_k, w^*) \tag{17}$$

In the sequel, follow:

$$\lim_{k \to \infty} \frac{\|w_{k+1} - w^*\|}{\|w_k - w^*\|^p} = \frac{\varphi^{(p)}(w^*)}{p!} \tag{18}$$

and it results that the method have a values of the convergence rate equal with p.

Remark 1. The (β) condition can be replaced by: $\|\varphi'(w)\| \leq q < 1, \forall w \in I$ for the differentiable φ function.

Remark 2. If $f''(w^*) \neq 0$ the Newton method have a quadratically convergence, since:

$$F(w) = w - f(w)^{-1}f(w), \ F'(w) = \frac{f(w^*)f''(w^*)}{f'(w^*)^2} = 0, \ F''(w) = \frac{f''(w^*)}{f'(w^*)} \neq 0 \tag{19}$$

If $f''(w^*) = 0$ then the Newton method is likely to have the superior convergence rate, case that corresponds to w^* be a inflexion point.

Remark 3. As compared to the Newton method or the Secant method, the convergence rate of the iterative method (15) is at least of order two. Thus we obtain an iterative scheme resulting in an improved convergence rate in estimating the independent components.

A detailed version of the FastICA algorithm based on successive approximation is described in the following scheme.

The FastICA algorithm based on successive approximations

Step 1: Center the data to make its mean zero.

Step 2: Whiten the data z.

Step 3: Choose the number of independent components n and set counter $r \leftarrow 1$.

Step 4: Choose an initial guess of unit norm for w_r.

Step 5: Let

$$w_r \leftarrow w_r - \frac{1}{M} * \left[E \left\{ zg(w_r^T z) \right\} - \beta w_r \right] \tag{20}$$

where g is previously defined and M is the maximum value of the function $F^{*'}$.

Step 6: Do the orthogonalization transform:

$$w_r \leftarrow w_r - \sum_{j=1}^{r-1} (w_r^T w_j) w_j \tag{21}$$

Step 7: Let $w_r \leftarrow w_r / \|w_r\|$.

Step 8: If w_r has not converged ($< w_{n+1}, w_n > \nrightarrow 1$), go back to step 5.

Step 9: Set $r \leftarrow r + 1$. If $r \leq n$ then go to step 4.

3   Experimental Analysis

The assessment of the performances of the proposed algorithm for finding the independent components is achieved in problems of signals recognition. We define an absolute mean sum error (AbsMSE) for comparing the accuracy of matching between original signals and restored signals. Then AbsMSE is formulated as follows:

$$AbsMSE = \sum_{i=1}^{N} |s_i - s\_estimated_i| / N \tag{22}$$

where s_i and $s\_estimated_i$ represent the i-th pixel values for original and restored signals, respectively, and N is the total number of pixels.

All the presented tests include the recognition performances of the independent components using as an objective function the negentropy for which they used one at a time in the approximation the three functions adopted in the field [1].

In a comparative study the proposed method based on successive approximations combined with secant iterations has recognition performances of the original signals which are similar with the implemented methods, such as FastICA based on the secant method [2] or standard method.

3.1   Experimentally Derived Conclusions on the Performance of the Algorithm in the Case of the Mixtures of the Signals

Test I. We consider as observation data two signals which are mixed and recorded based on two independent components. In this first test, the original sources are signals generated using the Matlab functions, and the results obtained after applying the algorithm based on successive approximations show a recognition performance similar to the standard FastICA method based on the Newton and to the method FastICA method based on the secant method [2]. The source signals discovered by the algorithm, the mixed signals and the source signals generated by Matlab subjected to the analysis procedure in independent components are represented in figure 1. In the respective figure we can notice the marginal densities corresponding to the two signals as well as the joint density which is common to the mixtures for the source signals discovered by the algorithm, for the mixed signals and for the source signals, respectively.

The results of the test regarding the appliance of the SSAM algorithm are given in table 1.

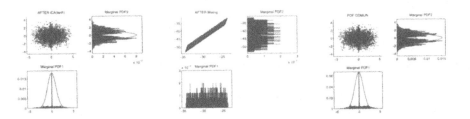

Fig. 1. Source Signals Discovered by the Algorithm (Left: 3 images), The Mixed Signals (Middle: 3 images) and Original Signals (Right: 3 images)

Test II. This test resembles the previously test with the difference that it uses, as original signals, the uniform distribution signals.

The figure 2 comprise the original source signals, the mixed signals and the source signals discovered by the algorithm for the uniform signals case.

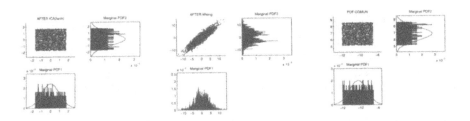

Fig. 2. Source Signals (uniform) Discovered by the Algorithm (Left: 3 images), The Mixed Signals (uniform) (Middle: 3 images) and Original Signals (uniform) (Right: 3 images)

Fig. 3. labelfig7 Original Faces Discovered by the Algorithm (Left: 2 images), The Mixed Faces for Face Recognition (Middle: 2 images) and Original Faces for Face Recognition (Right: 2 images)

The results obtained after the comparative study regarding the proposed method and other methods used in the estimation of the ICA model, are similar to the ones from the first test conform with table 1.

3.2 Experimentally Derived Conclusions on the Performance of the Algorithm in the Case of Image Signal

Test III. The achieved test refers to the capacity of the proposed algorithm of recognizing independent image faces from images of the mixed faces which can represent joint and superimposed faces as well as deteriorated images subjected to restoration.

In this test we considered again the bidimensional case with two mixed images over which we apply the deterioration algorithm of the original faces. The original image faces, the mixed image faces and the image faces discovered by the proposed algorithm are in figure 3. Just as the previously examples, the obtained results offer good recognition performances of the original faces, showing also in this case a qualitative superiority with respect to convergence speed in the recognition (the results are presented in table 1) compared with other used methods and anterior specified.

Table 1. AbsMSE of versions of the FastICA Algorithm for experimental tests

FastICA	Test I	Test I	Test I	Test II	Test II	Test II	TestIII	TestIII	TestIII
Basic Method	tanh (g_1)	exp (g_2)	kurt (g_3)	tanh (g_1)	exp (g_2)	kurt (g_3)	tanh (g_1)	exp (g_2)	kurt (g_3)
Newton	$1.0702*10^{-2}$	$1.0706*10^{-2}$	$1.0697*10^{-2}$	$2.3617*10^{-2}$	$2.3166*10^{-2}$	$2.4172*10^{-2}$	$4.493*10^{-3}$	$4.491*10^{-3}$	$5.813*10^{-3}$
Secant	$1.0716*10^{-2}$	$1.0682*10^{-2}$	$1.2793*10^{-2}$	$2.3271*10^{-2}$	$2.2754*10^{-2}$	$2.3181*10^{-2}$	$5.792*10^{-3}$	$5.741*10^{-3}$	$5.549*10^{-3}$
Successive Aproximations	$1.0706*10^{-2}$	$1.0695*10^{-2}$	$1.0699*10^{-2}$	$2.3295*10^{-2}$	$2.2981*10^{-2}$	$2.2996*10^{-2}$	$5.284*10^{-3}$	$5.352*10^{-3}$	$5.382*10^{-3}$

4 Summary and Conclusions

In this article we developed an algorithm for estimating the independent components based on a iterative scheme that uses the successive approximations method and we show that the convergence rate is superior compared with other methods. We derived a suitable algorithm and supplied a comparative analysis of its recognition capacities against the previously developed algorithm. In order to derive conclusive remarks the tests were performed on different signal samples.

References

1. Hyvarinen, A., Karhunen, J., Oja, E.: Independent Component Analysis. John Wiley & Sons, Chichester (2001)
2. Cho, Y.H., Hong, S.J., Park, S.M.: Face Recognition by Using Combined Method of Centroid Shift and Fixed-Point ICA Based on Secant Method. In: Proceedings of the Sixth International Conference on Intelligent Systems Design and Applications (ISDA 2006). IEEE Computer Society, Los Alamitos (2006)
3. State, L., Cocianu, C., Panayiotis, V., Constantin, D.: Principal directions - based algorthm for classification tasks. In: Proceedings of the Ninth International Symposium on Symbolic and Numeric Algorithms for Scientific Computing (SYNASC 2007), Timisoara, September 26-29,2007. IEEE Computer Society, Los Alamitos (2007)
4. Stone, J.V.: Independent Component Analysis. The MIT Press, Cambridge (2004)
5. Bartlett, M.S., Movellan, J.R., Sejnowski, T.J.: Face Recognition by Independent Component Analysis. IEEE Transactions on Neural Networks 13 (2002)

Automatic Adjustment of Rigs to Extracted Skeletons

Jorge E. Ramirez, Xavier Lligadas, and Antonio Susin

Universitat Politècnica de Catalunya
Barcelona, Spain
jramirez@lsi.upc.edu, xavier.lligadas@upc.edu, toni.susin@upc.edu
http://www.lsi.upc.edu/~moving/

Abstract. In the animation, the process of rigging a character is an elaborated and time consuming task. The rig is developed for a specific character, and it can not be reused in other meshes. In this paper we present a method to automatically adjust a human-like character rig to an arbitrary human-like 3D mesh, using a extracted skeleton obtained from the input mesh. Our method is based on the selection and extraction of feature points, to find an equivalence between an extracted skeleton and the animation rig.

Keywords: Animation, rig adjustment, skeletonization, thinning, voxelization.

1 Introduction

One of the most time consuming tasks in animation is character modeling, commonly when a character is animated a skeleton (rig) is created, this rig usually is adjusted to a specific 3D mesh. If the same rig and animation data wants to be used on a different mesh, an artist have to spend effort and time to adjust it to a new mesh. While the skeleton extraction is a well known problem ([4],[3])however the equivalence between the voxels or points, and their adjustment to an animation rig has not been explored as deeply as the skeletonization problem.

Our work take as a base the skeleton extraction, many approaches have emerged about how to solve this particular problem. In 2D this problem was solved using hexagonal sampling [14] as an alternative to the classic square sampling.

In 3D one of the most difunded are thinning algorithms ([4],[3],[11],[10]) which works by using a voxelized version of a model and removing voxels from the surface until an skeleton remains. In [13] it is used a Euclidean distance and Discrete medial surface to extract a 3D skeleton. A penalized algorithm [12] based in a modified dijkstra method is used for skeleton extraction, and a hybrid method [6] use a modified version of the thinning algorithm mixed with force fields to refine the process. Our work can be compared with the results obtained in [7] but this work is based on the embedding of a rig, instead of its adjustment to an extracted skeleton.

F.J. Perales and R.B. Fisher (Eds.): AMDO 2008, LNCS 5098, pp. 409–418, 2008.

The purpose of this paper is to reduce this adjustment task. In order to improve the adjustment process, we propose a method that automates the rigging process of a human like 3D mesh. Our method is composed by the next stages:

1. Model Voxelization: A 3D mesh is transformed into a set of voxels. This transformation is a discretization of the surfaces of the triangles of the mesh.
2. Skeleton extraction:Taking as a base the voxelizated model, we apply a skeleton extraction based on a secuencial thinning algorithm.
3. Points selection and their refinement: From the extracted skeleton we obtain and refine information about the input model; we also make an equivalence of points between the rig joints and the feature points of the extracted skeleton.
4. Scale and adjustment of joints: once we have made an equivalence of points we scale and adjust the joints of the rig to make them totally fit into the skeleton extracted from the mesh.

The skeleton adjust is a complex problem that depends on the input 3D mesh; to successfully apply this method we need to restrict the problem to the following conditions:

- The input 3D mesh has to be closed.
- The input must have an approximated fixed pose. In our particular the mesh needs to be stand up with the arms extended (T-pose).
- The 3D mesh has to have human like proportions.

Our method is based on a correct skeleton extraction to establish equivalences between feature points of the extracted skeleton and joints of the animation rig.

2   Model Voxelization

Voxelization is the process used to transform a closed 3d triangle mesh into to a voxel subset in a defined space [9], in general space voxelization is equivalent to a coordinate transformation and a map function to determine the vertex and faces position of our original model in voxel's space . Basically our voxelization process has been performed following the next steps:

1. Space Voxelization: We create a bounding box containing the model and then we subdivide it into voxels.
2. Mesh Voxelization: The vertex and faces of the triangular mesh are transformed into voxels.
3. Filling the voxelizated mesh: The empty voxelizated mesh is filled with voxels and transformed into a closed solid model.

Basically voxelizing a model is the transformation of the triangles to voxels. This task has been faced by different approaches like [3]. Our approach is based on the midpoint-line algorithm [1] extended to the 3D space. We have choose the midpoint-line algorithm because of its low processing cost, achieved by only using integers and additions to paint a line. For each triangle we transform their edges into voxels using the 3D midpoint-line algorithm, then we keep painting lines between edges until the entire triangle surface is filled. The voxels space struct is a simple list of bytes where a byte represent a voxel in the space, to move between voxels we rely on pointer arithmetic.

Once we have voxelizated the mesh, we get a set of surface voxels and a set of empty voxels within it. For the skeletization stage we need to fill the empty voxel set, the filling algorithm is an extension to 3D of the flood algorithm [1] used in image processing. When the model is voxelizated, a resolution space problem appears: if we are using low resolution (big voxel size) the map function will map some vertex to the same voxel. The problem emerges when the space between limbs or between a limb and the body of the mesh is lower than one voxel, in this particular case the voxelization process will merge two sections of the model. To solve this problem, we store three different voxels values: 0 for empty voxels, 1 for surface voxels and $n > 1$ for filled voxels. Only filled voxels will be used in the thinning process.

3   Skeleton Extraction

A skeleton is an object shape descriptor, in this paper the skeleton extraction is achieved by applying a thinning algorithm to an input 3D mesh. Basically a thinning algorithm is a process where the voxels that belongs to the surface (voxels where one or more of their faces are in contact with an empty voxel [8]) are deleted if the deletion does not affect the topology of the empty and filled voxels sets.

A voxel is a discretization of a point in a finite space[8], a simple point is a voxel whose removal does not change the topology of a voxel set. In this paper we are using $(26, 6)$ adjacency[8], where a black point is a voxel with a 0 as stored info and a white point is one voxel with value $n \geq 1$. As it was defined in section 2 we will work with voxels whose value is greater than 1. Most of the thinning algorithms are parallel as e.g. [10],[11], this kind of algorithms are useful if we have a large amount of data, in that case it is necessary to process the data using multiple processors. In our particular case the dimension of the discretized models are limited (see section 6),and altought we can implement this kind of algorithms with multi thread programming, we do prefer a more opti-mal algorithm (parallel algorithms generates latency due to the synchronization of subdivided tasks) to process the voxelizated model. The used algorithm is based on a secuencial version of the thinning algorithm[4] but with some added modifications to fit our needs and to optimize it.

In the thinning algorithm described in [4], the process is applied in 6 directions (*up,down,left,right,front* and *rear*) this stages of the algorithm are called *sub iterations*. Within each *sub iteration* a set of tests are applied to know if a voxel it is a deletion candidate. All deletion candidates are stored in a list.After the deletion candidate selection, the same tests done in the previous step are applied to the deletion candidates. If a voxel is still a deletion candidate after some of the voxels of the list were deleted, the voxel is deleted and his stored value will be set to 0.

We have modified the deletion candidates selection algorithm by adding a sorting process. In the sorting process the first positions of the deletion candidate list will be filled with highest delete direction value voxels, making the thinning a more robust process, obtaining a better approximation of the skeleton to the medial line of the model.

4   Points Selection and Their Refinement

From the voxelized skeleton extracted in section 3 we can find the correspondence between white points (voxels) and joints of an animation rig by using the white points neighborhood information.

4.1   Point Classification

A white point can be classified depending on the number of neighbors surrounding it:

- *End points*: Points which only have one neighbor. Normally this points represents the end of a model's limb..
- *Flow points*: Referees to point which have two neighbors. This points are part of a flow or a tubular segment in the skeleton.
- *Internal points*: Points with more than two neighbors. Points that give us information about the skeleton union segments.

Once we have classified the points, we can start to look for a correspondence between joints of an animation rig and the points within our extracted skeleton.

4.2   Animation Rig

Animation rig data is represented using a hierarchic model. The hierarchy is dependent on the data file format. Developing our approach, we decided to create a set of data structures to represent an animation rig, and left the hierarchy problem of a specific animation format to a separated module. In our structures we start with a joint as the root element,this root node is the model's gravity center. All the other joints will be represented as nodes, a node can have multiple child nodes(internal node), or it can have none(leaf node). A data structure that easily adapts to this kind of hierarchy is a tree with multiple child per nodes.

4.3   Internal Point Refinement

To classify the points of the extracted skeleton we have two options: check all the voxels in the space and classify all the points we find, or we can traverse only our skeleton points and classify them. We have developed a traversal algorithm that depends on the number of neighbors of a point:

Traversal algorithm

```
function traversal (p){
    inter<stack>;
    PUSH_STACK(inter,p);
```

```
while IS_NOT_EMPTY inter{
    neignum=GET_NEIGHBORHOOD(p);
    if(neignum >2){
        REG_INTERNAL_NODE(p);
        PUSH_STACK(inter,p);
    }
    else if(neignum = 1){
        REG_END_NODE(p);
        p=POP_STACK(inter);
    }
    else{
        REG_FLOW_NODE(p);
    }
    p=GET_FIRST_NEIGHBOR_LEFT(p);
}
}
```

Where the functions

- GET_NEIGHBORHOOD(p): Returns the numbers of neighbors of the point p.
- GET_FIRST_NEIGHBOR_LEFT(p):Returns the first unregistered neighbor of the point p.

Once the traversal has been done, we will have all the internal, end and flow nodes registered in a data structure. As the reader can see in figure 1 we will obtain multiple internal points, sometimes the distance between points will be smaller than the minimum limb length(the minimum length for the forearm is 0.146 of the height of the model [2]). This situation will difficult the correspondence process between the rig joints and the extracted skeleton points, that's happening because it is ambiguous which one of them has to be taken as the relevant point of the area. To overcome this problem we simplify a set of closer internal points into one, by identifying the point with higher number of neighbors and attracting the surrounding closer internal points to it (figure 1).

Fig. 1. Left: internal points of a extracted skeleton(diamonds). Right: single internal point after the refinement.

4.4   Point Correspondence

Once the skeleton is extracted from the voxelizated model, we have to deal with the problem of finding a correspondence between the skeleton points and the rig joints. To solve this problem we make some assumptions: the rig must have five joints as end nodes (if the rig is highly detailed it will have end nodes in the hands fingers and eyes of the model) this five end nodes will represent, feet, hands and head. Using our skeleton end points we will set a correspondence between the skeleton end points and the rig end joints. As a first step we have to find the orientation of our skeleton, to deal with this problem we will use an axis aligned bounding box to divide the space in eight parts (figure 2). If a skeleton is correctly orientated it will have more end points in the superior parts $(Q_{1-1} - Q_{1-4})$ of the bounding box and the feet end nodes will be placed in Q_{2-3} and Q_{2-4}. We made eight stacks to represent the bounding box parts, the end and internal points are stored in each stack depending of its position within the box. To assign the end points we follow the next steps:

- Head: Is assigned to the end point with the Y axis max value in the upper part of the bounding box stacks (Q_1 set).
- Right hand: Is assigned to the end point with the X axis min value in Q_{1-2} and Q_{1-3} stacks of the bounding box.
- Left hand: Is assigned to the end point with the X axis max value in Q_{1-1} and Q_{1-4} stacks of the bounding box.
- Left foot: Is assigned to the end point with Y axis min value in the Q_{2-4} stack of the bounding box.
- Right foot: Is assigned to the end point with Y axis min value in the Q_{2-3} stack of the bounding box.

5   Scale and Adjustment of Joints

To adjust a rig to an extracted skeleton it is necessary to choose an effective scale method. In our approach, instead of using the naive solution and only calculate a single scale factor for the rig, we have chosen scaling in parts to force the end and root points to fit into the extracted skeleton. Once the scaling has been done we apply an adjustment stage to the left internal joints of the rig, moving the scaled position to the closest voxel in the extracted skeleton.

5.1   Scaling in Parts

The scaling of the end and root points is a simple task when the correspondence of points has been done correctly. For each of the assigned points in section 4.4

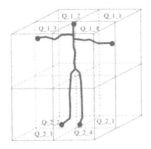

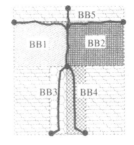

Fig. 2. Extracted skeleton encapsulated in a bounding box

Fig. 3. The bounding box used in the scale stage

Fig. 4. Left: an arm segment before adjustment. Right: arm segment after the adjustment.

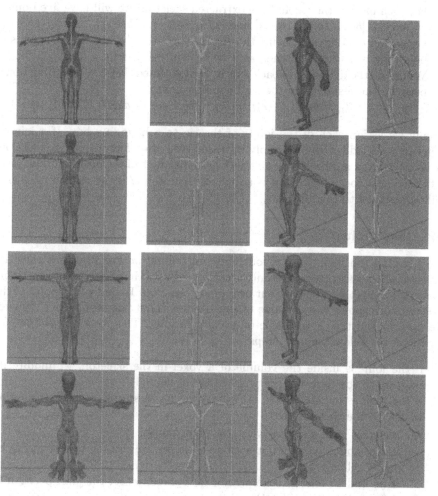

Fig. 5. Results of the skeleton adjust to a rig in different models. Rows: Woman Mid. Res.,Woman Low Res., Man Low Res.,Alien Low Res.

three scale factor are calculated, one for each coordinate. To make the calculation of the scale factors, we divide both the rig and the extracted model into five bounding boxes. The distributions of the bounding boxes are: four for the hands and feet (fig. 3) and one for all the points that are outside of these boxes.

The first four bounding boxes have one of its vertex placed over the root point (or joint depending of which set of boxes we are calculating) and its opposite vertex in one of the four limbs end points. The fifth bounding box is the bonding box that encapsulates the model, but its scale factors are mean factors calculated using the previous four bounding boxes scale factors.

The scale factors are calculated following the next steps:

- For each model (the rig and the extracted skeleton) we will have five bounding boxes ($[bbA_1, bbA_2..., bbA_5]$ and $[bbB_1, bbB_2, ..., bbB_5]$).
- For each bounding box we find the distance between the first and the opposite bounding box vertex for each axis: $bbA_1 = (dbbA_{1a}, dbbA_{1b}, dbbA_{1c})$.
- We divide the distances of each axis of the extracted skeleton bounding boxes between the distances of the rig bounding boxes:
  $sfbb_1 = (dbbB_{1a}/(dbbA_{1a} + \epsilon), dbbB_{1b}/(dbbA_{1b} + \epsilon), dbbB_{1c}/(dbbA_{1c} + \epsilon))$.

Finally we assign each of the joints of the rig to a bounding box. If a joint it is inside a bounding box we apply its associated scale factor over it, therefore the scale factors applied to a joint will be dependent of its position. The head is treated as a special case and is adjusted separately. All the remaining points will be assigned to the fifth box.

5.2   Joint Adjust

After scaling the joints to the root and end points, we are sure that they are adjusted to the extracted skeleton(the scaling adjust is implicitly), the remaining joints will probably be outside but near of our skeleton. To find which point of the skeleton correspond to every one of the joints without correspondence, spheres are used to find the closest skeleton point of a joint. The process is simple, for each joint we follow the next steps:

1. If the joint is inside the volume of a voxel in the skeleton, we modify its position to the center of the voxel in the skeleton.
2. If the joint is outside of the skeleton we start to search in the surrounding voxels for the closest one.
   - We start with a sphere with one voxel length.
   - If a neighbor point is not within the range, we rise the sphere radius by one voxel length.
   - If we find a skeleton voxel within the sphere, we set the joint position to the voxel position (fig. 4).
   - We iterate until we find a voxel to assign the joint.

6   Results

In this paper we have presented a method to adjust a rig to an arbitrary closed mesh. The results presented in this work (figure 5, table 1) depends directly on the resolution in voxels of the box encapsulating the model; For instance, if the resolution is lower than 100 voxels (in Y axis) the processing time will be reduced but the results may be inaccurate; on the other hand, if the resolution is higher than 200 voxels, the time will be considerably increased. The extracted skeleton will be a better shape descriptor, but the extra information increases the computation time, and in the best case scenario the extra information is ignored or may induce errors during the algorithm execution. Based on our experience, we believe that optimal resolution comprises from 121 to 149 voxels in the Y axis (the two remaining coordinates will be calculated based on model proportions) gives us the best results and computations times (about 6 seconds running as a maya plugin). Finally we have tested our method in four models(fig. 5): a human male and female in low resolution, a human female in medium resolution, and a human like character(alien) in low resolution. In the three human models we have obtained good results, but in the character like model, our method has failed because it has more than one end point in the feet. In the upper part of the body, the human like model, shows good results. Our tests were made on a laptop HP Turion 64 X2 with 2 gigas of RAM and Windows Xp.

Table 1. Results from the models in the figure 5

Model	Triangles	Resolution(voxels)	P. Time(sec.)
Woman Mid. Res.	28820	130×143×23	5.28006
Woman Low Res.	12944	129×127×25	3.29999
Man Low Res.	12944	129×127×25	3.389999
Alien Low Res.	11408	121×115×30	2.90999

7 Future Work

To add robustness and improve our method many things could be done. In the stage of voxelization we depend on the format of the meshes. At this moment we only can use single closed meshes, meshes composed of multiple sub meshes can not be solved at this moment but we believe that in the future this could be achieved. The correspondence stage is fundamental to obtain a satisfactory result. This stage can be improved so that it could deals with models that does not have the correct human proportions but that resemble the human body (toon characters). We have many ideas to expand this work, but we believe that adding a skinning process such as SSD or Radial Basis [5] to the mesh will be a valuable contribution. Also we would like to improve the joint adjustment; because, as it is shown in fig.5 the joint can be placed out of the articulation, causing odd effects during the mesh animation.

Acknowledgments

Authors are supported by grants from the "Consejo Nacional del Ciencia y Tecnologia" (CONACYT) MEX, TIN2007-67982-C02-01 ESP, "El comissionat per a universitats i recerca del departament d'innovació d'universitats i empreses de la Generalitat de Catalunya" and the European Social Fund, and we thank to our fellows of the LABSID for their valuable discussions.

References

1. Foley, van Dam, Feiner, H.: Computer Graphics: Principles and Practice. Addison Wesley, Reading (1996)
2. Plagenhoef, S.: Patterns of Human Motion. Prenctice-Hall, Inc., Englewood N.J (1971)
3. Brunner, D., Brunnett, G.: An extended concept of voxel neighborhoods for correct thinning in mesh segmentation. In: SCCG 2005: Proceedings of the 21st spring conference on Computer graphics, pp. 119–125. ACM Press, New York (2005)
4. Palágyi, K., Sorantin, E., Balogh, E., Kuba, A., Halmai, C., Erdohelyi, B., Hausegger, K.: A Sequential 3D Thinning Algorithm and Its Medical Applications. In: Insana, M.F., Leahy, R.M. (eds.) IPMI 2001. LNCS, vol. 2082, pp. 409–415. Springer, Heidelberg (2001)
5. Lewis, J.P., Cordner, M., Fong, N.: Pose Space Deformations: A Unified Approach to Shape Interpolation a nd Skeleton-Driven Deformation. In: Siggraph 2000, Computer Graphics Proceedings. ACM Press / ACM SIGGRAPH / Addison Wesley Longman, Washington (2000)
6. Liu, P.-C., Wu, F.-C., Ma, W.-C., Liang, R.-H., Ouhyoung, M.: Automatic Animation Skeleton Construction Using Repulsive Force Field. In: PG 2003: Proceedings of the 11th Pacific Conference on Computer Graphics and Applications, p. 409. IEEE Computer Society, Los Alamitos (2003)
7. Baran, I., Popović, J.: Automatic rigging and animation of 3D characters. In: SIGGRAPH 2007: ACM SIGGRAPH 2007 papers, ACM, San Diego (2007)
8. Bertrand, G.: A Boolean characterization of three-dimensional simple points. Pattern Recogn. Lett. 17(2), 115–124 (1994)
9. Cohen-Or, D., Kaufman, A.: Fundamentals of surface voxelization. Graph. Models Image Process 57(6), 453–461 (1995)
10. Lohou, C., Bertrand, G.: A 3D 12-subiteration thinning algorithm based on P-simple points. Discrete Appl. Math. 139(1-3), 171–195 (2004)
11. Palágyi, K., Kuba, A.: A 3D 6-subiteration thinning algorithm for extracting medial lines. Pattern Recogn. Lett. 19(7), 613–627 (1998)
12. Bitter, I., Kaufman, A.E., Sato, M.: Penalized-Distance Volumetric Skeleton Algorithm. IEEE Transactions on Visualization and Computer Graphics. 7(3), 195–206 (2001)
13. Wade, L., Parent, R.E.: Automated generation of control skeletons for use in animation. The Visual Computer. 18(2), 97–110 (2002)
14. Staunton, R.C.: An analysis of hexagonal thinning algorithms and skeletal shape representation. Pattern Recognition 29(7), 1131–1146 (1996)

Real-Time Recognition of Human Gestures for 3D Interaction

Antoni Jaume-i-Capó, Javier Varona, and Francisco J. Perales

Unitat de Gràfics i Visió per Ordinador
Departament de Ciències Matemàtiques i Informàtica
Universitat de les Illes Balears
Edifici Anselm Turmeda
Ctra. de Valldemossa km 7,5
(07122) Palma de Mallorca, Spain
{antoni.jaume,xavi.varona,paco.perales}@uib.es
http://dmi.uib.es/~ugiv/

Abstract. A fundamental natural interaction concept is not yet fully exploited in most of the existing human-computer interfaces. Recent technological advances have created the possibility to naturally and significantly enhance the interface perception by means of visual inputs, the so called Vision-Based Interaction (VBI). In this paper, we present a gesture recognition algorithm where the user's movements are obtained through a real-time vision-based motion capture system. Specifically, we focus on recognizing users motions with a particular mean, that is, a gesture. Defining an appropriate representation of the user's motions based on a temporal posture parameterization, we apply non-parametric techniques to learn and recognize the user's gestures in real-time. This scheme of recognition has been tested for controlling a classical computer videogame. The results obtained show an excellent performance in online classification and it allows the possibility to achieve a learning phase in real-time due to its computational simplicity.

Keywords: Vision-Based Gesture Recognition, Human-Computer Interaction, Non-Parametric Classification.

1 Introduction

Since computers first appeared, researchers have been conceiving forms of interaction between people and machines. Today human-computer interfaces are created in order to allow communication between humans and computers by means of a common set of physical or logical rules. Vision-based interfaces (VBI) use computer vision in order to sense and perceive the user and their actions within an HCI context [1]. In this sense, the idea of using body gestures as a means of interacting with computers is not new. The first notable system was Bolt's *Put That There* multimodal interface [2]. Bolt combined the use of speech recognition with pointing to move objects within a scene.

F.J. Perales and R.B. Fisher (Eds.): AMDO 2008, LNCS 5098, pp. 419–430, 2008.

The topic of human motion analysis has received great interest in the scientific community, mainly from biomechanics, computer graphics and computer vision researchers. From the computer vision community there are a lot of works that present several results in this field, for an exhaustive revision it is possible to read one of the most recent reviews on this topic [3]. From a human-computer interaction point of view, we are especially interested in obtaining user motions in order to recognize gestures that can be interpreted as system's events. In this sense, the approaches used for gesture recognition and analysis of human motion in general can be classified into three major categories: motion-based, appearance-based, and model-based. Motion-based approaches attempt to recognize the gesture directly from the motion without any structural information about the physical body [4,5]. Appearance-based approaches use two dimensional information such as gray scale images, edges or body silhouettes [6,7]. In contrast, model-based approaches focus on recovering the three dimensional configuration of articulated body parts [8,9,10]. However, model-based approaches are often difficult to apply to real-world applications. This fact is mainly due to the difficulty of capturing and tracking the requisite model parts, the user's body joints that take part in the considered gestures.

Usually, a partial solution can be to simplify the capture to a fewer body parts and using its temporal trajectories in order to recognize the gestures of interest [11]. For example, Rao et al. consider the problem of learning and recognizing actions performed by a human hand [12]. They target affine invariance and apply their method on real image sequences using skin color to find hands. They characterize a gesture by means of dynamic moments, which they define as maxima in the spatio-temporal curvature of the hand trajectory that is preserved from 3D to 2D. Their system does not require a model, in fact, it builds up its own model database by memorizing the input gestures. Another approach of hand-based gesture recognition methods use hand poses as gestures for navigating in virtual worlds [13]. Nevertheless, exploiting the sole 3D location of one or two hands is indeed not sufficient for the recognition of complex gestures in order to control interactive applications.

On the other hand, several techniques have been used for classification in gesture recognition systems. In the majority of approaches the temporal properties of the gesture are typically handled statistically using Hidden Markov Models (HMM), mainly due to the fact of directly using the image values [11]. However, these approaches are not applied in real-time because HMMs require a hard learning phase in order to tune all the model's parameters.

Our idea is to use the gesture recognition system in real-time, taking the advantage of having a robust estimation of the 3D positions of the user's body joints. In this paper, we present a gesture recognition system that takes into account all body limbs, involved in the considered gestures. The advantage of our system is that it is built over a motion capture system that recovers the body joints positions of the user's upper body in real-time. From the computed joints positions we make this data spatially invariant by normalizing limbs positions and sizes, only using the limbs orientations. From limbs orientations, the

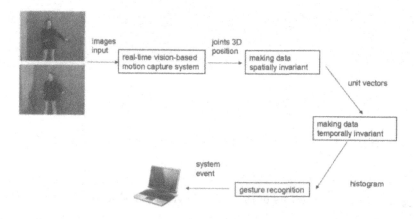

Fig. 1. System scheme

user posture is represented by an appropriate representation of all the limbs in a histogram. Cumulating the posture histograms we represent a gesture in a temporal invariant form. Finally, using this gesture representation, the performed gestures are classified for generating the desired computer events in real-time, see Figure 1.

This paper is organized as follows. The used real-time full-body motion capture system to obtain the user motions is presented in section 2. Next, in section 3, our human gesture representation is described. How the human gestures are recognized, is explained in section 4. The performance evaluation of our system in a real-time 3D interaction application and the obtained results are described in section 5. The obtained results are discussed in the last section to demonstrate the viability of this approach.

2   Human Motion Capture

In this work, the real-time constraint is very important due to our goal of using the captured motions as input for gesture recognition in a vision-based interface (VBI). In this sense, the motions of the user's limbs are extracted through a real-time vision-based motion capture system. Usually, locating all the user body joints in order to recover the user's posture is not possible with computer vision algorithms only. This is mainly due to the fact that most of the joints are occluded by clothes. Inverse Kinematic (IK) approaches can solve the body posture from their 3D position if we can clearly locate visible body parts such as face and hands. Therefore, these visible body parts (hereafter referred to as end-effectors) are automatically located in real-time and fed into an IK module, which in turn can provide a 3D feedback to the vision system (see Figure 2).

The only environmental constraint of the real-time vision-based motion capture system is that the user is located in an interactive space in front of a wide screen (such as a workbench), and that the background wall is covered with

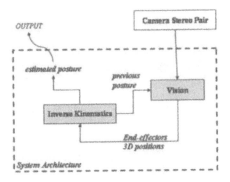

Fig. 2. General architecture of the real-time vision-based motion capture system

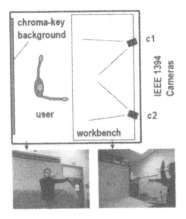

Fig. 3. Interactive space

chroma-key material, as it is shown in Figure 3. This system may work without chroma-key background; however, using it ensures a real-time response. This interactive space is instrumented with a stereo camera pair calibrated previously by means of an easy automatic process.

We apply chroma-keying, skin-color segmentation and 2D-tracking algorithms for each image of the stereo pair to locate the user's end-effectors in the scene. Then, we combine this result in a 3D-tracking algorithm to robustly estimate their 3D positions in the scene. Applying the Priority Inverse Kinematics algorithm with the 3D positions of the wrists as end-effectors, motion capture system recovers the 3D positions of each considered user joint. Detailed technical information on this system can be found in [14].

3   Human Gesture Representation

Using the computed 3D positions of the involved body joints, we address the main problems in the gesture recognition challenge: temporal, spatial and style variations between gestures. Temporal variations are due to different gesture speed between different users. Spatial variations are due to physical constraints of the human body such as different body sizes. Style variations are due to the personal way in which a user makes its movements. To cope with spatial variations we represent each body limb by means of a unit vector. Temporal variation is managed using a temporal gesture representation. Finally, the most difficult challenge, style variations, is solved by parameterizing the gestures of each user in an easy learning phase.

An appropriate posture representation for gesture recognition must cope spatial variations. In order to make data invariant to different body sizes, the first step is to change the reference system because the calibration process of the Vision-PIK algorithm defines the reference system. In our system we use a planar pattern for computing the intrinsic and extrinsic parameters of the camera stereo pair [15]. Using this approach, the coordinate system is placed in the world depending on the location of the calibration object, as it is shown in Figure 4. Therefore, joints' positions are referenced from an unknown world origin.

Fig. 4. Reference system alignment for unifying the joints' 3D positions reported by the vision-based motion capture system. Left: vision reference system. Right: user's centered reference system.

To solve this problem, the coordinate system is automatically aligned with the user's position and orientation in the first frame, as shown in Figure 4. The reference system origin is placed in the user's foot position. Next, the y-axis is aligned to the unit vector that joins the user's foot and back and the x-axis is aligned to the unit vector that joins the user's right shoulder and left shoulder, setting the y component to zero.

Once the reference system is aligned with the user position and orientation, joints 3D positions are environment independent because the reference origin is aligned with the user's body and does not depend on the calibration process. However, the data still depends on the size of the user's limbs. A possibility to make data size invariant is given by the use of motion information of the joints through Euler angles [16]. Nevertheless, in this case, motion information is unstable, i.e., small changes of these values could give wrong detections. Alternatively, we propose a representation of each body limb by means of a unit vector, which represents the limb orientation. Formally, the unit vector that represents the orientation of limb, l, defined by joints J_1 and J_2, $\boldsymbol{u}_l$, is computed as follows

$$\boldsymbol{u}_l = \frac{\mathbf{J}_2 - \mathbf{J}_1}{\|\mathbf{J}_2 - \mathbf{J}_1\|}, \tag{1}$$

where $\mathbf{J}_i = (x_i, y_i, z_i)$ is the i-th joint 3D-position in the user centered reference system. In this way, depending on the desired gesture alphabet, it is only necessary to compute the unit vector for the involved body limbs. This representation causes data to be independent from the user's size and it solves the spatial variations.

Once the motion capture data is spatially invariant, the next step is to represent the human posture. We build the posture representation by using unit vectors of the limbs involved in the gesture set. The idea is to represent the user's body posture as a feature vector composed by all the unit vectors of the user's limbs. Formally, the representation of the orientation of a limb, l, is

$$\mathbf{q}^l = (u_x^+, u_x^-, u_y^+, u_y^-, u_z^+, u_z^-), \tag{2}$$

where u_x^+ and u_x^- are respectively the positive and negative magnitudes of the x-component of unit vector, u_x, note that $u_x = u_x^+ - u_x^-$ and $u_x^+, u_x^- \geq 0$. The same applies for components u_y and u_z. In this way, the orientation components of the limb unit vector are half-wave rectified into six non-negative channels. Therefore, we build a histogram of limbs orientations which represents the complete user's limbs orientations. We propose two forms to build the histogram, see Figure 5.

The first one is by cumulative limbs orientations, see Equation 3,

$$\mathbf{q} = \sum_{l=1}^{n} \mathbf{q}^l, \tag{3}$$

and the second one is by linking limbs poses, see Equation 4,

$$\mathbf{q} = \{\mathbf{q}^l\}_{l=1..n}, \tag{4}$$

where n, in both cases, is the number of limbs involved in the gestures to recognize.

The main difference between the two representations depends on the considered gesture set. The cumulative representation is more robust to tracking errors, but the set of recognized gestures is much reduced. For example, the same movements of different limbs can not be distinguished. On the other hand, the linked representation allows the definition of more gestures, although it is more sensible to errors in the estimation of the limbs orientations.

Our approach represents gestures by means of a temporal representation of the user's postures. The reason for using posture information is that the postures directly define the gestures, even, in several cases, with only one posture it is

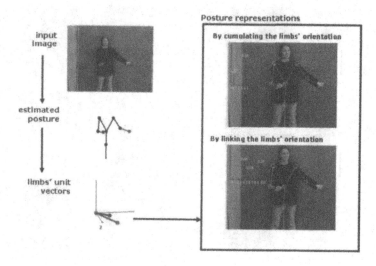

Fig. 5. Construction of the posture representation

possible to recognize a gesture. If we consider that a gesture is composed by several body postures, the gesture representation feature vector is composed by the cumulative postures involved in the gesture, that is

$$\hat{\mathbf{q}}_t = \frac{1}{T} \sum_{i=t-T}^{t} \mathbf{q}_i, \tag{5}$$

where t is the current frame and T is the gesture periodicity, and could be interpreted as a temporal window of cumulative postures. This process resumes the temporal variations of gestures by means of a detection of the periodicity of each user's gesture performance in order to fix the T value, that is, its temporal extent.

4   Human Gesture Recognition

An important goal of this work is that the human-computer interaction should be performed using natural gestures. As it has been shown in several experiments with children[17], a gesture is natural depending on the user experience. The key is to take advantage of the system overall possibility of working in real-time. For these reasons, before the recognition process starts the system asks the user to perform several of the allowable gestures in order to build a training set in real-time.

Therefore, previously to starting the game, the system asks the user randomly to make several isolated performances of each gesture. Performing several times the gestures in random order, the gesture models consider styles variations. This is a way to automatically build the training set. Besides, we have tested how

Fig. 6. Interpretations of the *rotation* gesture by different users

the users interpret each of the gestures, mainly the complex gestures, which are performed by different users in a completely different way, see Figure 6. This fact reinforces the idea of making user's specific gestures models. In order to complete the process, it is necessary to choose a distance for comparison between the current gesture, $\hat{\mathbf{q}}_t$, and a gesture model, $\hat{\mathbf{p}}$. We choose the Earth Mover's Distance (EMD), the measure of the amount of work necessary to transform one weighted point set into another. Moreover, it has been shown that bin-by-bin measures (e.g., L_p distance, normalized scalar product) are less robust than cross-bin measures (e.g., the Earth Mover's Distance (EMD), which allows features from different bins to be matched) for capturing perceptual dissimilarity between distributions [18].

5   Performance Evaluation

In order to test our gesture recognition approach, we have proposed playing a computer videogame interacting by means of body gestures with different users. In this case, the proposed game, a modified version of Tetris, allows users to use four different forms of control: *left, right, down* and *rotate*.

The present system has been implemented in Visual C++ using the OpenCV libraries [19] and it has been tested in a real-time interaction context on an AMD Athlon 2800 + 2.083 GHz under Windows XP. The images have been captured using two DFW-500 Sony cameras. The cameras provide 320 × 240 images at a capture rate of 30 frames per second.

To test the real-time, we have calculated the time used to recognize a gesture once the joints positions of the user have been obtained. The real time of

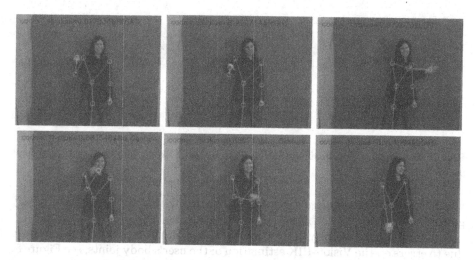

Fig. 7. Some visual results of gesture recognition. In the case of the rotate gesture, a sequence gesture is shown.

the vision-based motion capture system was tested in [14]. Including the gesture recognition step the frame rate is 21 frames per second. Therefore, we can conclude that our approach works near real-time.

For testing purposes, we acquired different sessions of different users while producing all the gestures during videogame. The game is manually controlled by a user in order to provide the immersive experience of really playing the game with its own gestures. This is the classical Wizard of Oz experiment [17]. At the moment, our dataset contains a training set where each user performs three times each form of control. After the training of the system, we evaluate its performance by testing the real behaviour of the recognition system. Specifically, the testing set is composed by 73 different gesture performances of the command set by three different users.

Table 1. Comparative results between the proposed posture representations

Posture Representation	Gestures	Correct	Wrong	Non Recognized	False Possitive
cumulated	73	**84.95%**	4.10%	10.95%	7.20%
linked	73	**87.69%**	2.73%	9.58%	4.18%

The results presented in Table 1 and in Figure 7 show that both representations obtain good results with a reasonable rate of correct recognition. Although, it should be considered that in this application the gesture set is reduced. Note that the linked representation is more accurate because the number of false positives is smaller than the cumulated representation, considering a false positive

Fig. 8. Recognition misclassifications due to errors of the Vision-PIK estimation of user's body joints

when the system recognizes a gesture although the user does not perform any gesture.

In addition, the majority of misclassifications and not recognized gestures are due to errors on the Vision-PIK estimation of the user's body joints, see Figure 8. In this case, in Table 1 it can be seen that the linked representation is again more robust to these feature extraction errors than the cumulated one.

6   Conclusions

We have shown the potential of the system through a user interface. In this sense, we have defined two appropriates gesture representation capable of coping with variations between gestures in different users and performances, also making recognition in real-time possible. Our approach is original and it could be extended to represent more complex gestures and human activities. In fact, hand-based gesture recognition can be approached with the presented representation by substituting the user's body posture with finger poses.

The complete system has been tested in a real-time application, a gesture-based videogame control, and the results obtained state that the presented approach for gesture recognition performs well. From these experiments, we can conclude that for the control of interactive applications with a reduced alphabet, the linked representation could alleviate the errors of the feature extraction step making the interface more robust. On the other hand, experiments have shown that, from a practical point of view, this technique of classification is appropriated for real world problems due to its simplicity in learning and on-line classification. Besides, the system adapts itself to each particular user's way of performing the gestures, avoiding a previous user's off-line training to learn the gestures that can be recognized by the system.

As future work, this approach can be extended to more complex gestures than the ones shown in the presented application adding more limbs to the gesture representation. It is important to point out that our approach needs further testing. Concretely, it should be tested in real sessions with more users. These sessions should test how the number of learning exemplars affects the recognition of gestures. Currently, we plan to use the recognized gesture in the

IK algorithm to improve its results using the on-line information of the gesture being performed.

Acknowledgements

This work has been supported by the Spanish M.E.C. under project TIN2007-67993 and the Ramon y Cajal fellowship of Dr. J. Varona.

References

1. Turk, M., Kolsch, M.: Perceptual interfaces. In: Emerging Topics in Computer Vision. Prentice Hall, Englewood Cliffs (2004)
2. Bolt, R.A.: 'put-that-there': Voice and gesture at the graphics interface. In: SIGGRAPH 1980: Proceedings of the 7th annual conference on Computer graphics and interactive techniques, pp. 262–270. ACM Press, New York (1980)
3. Moeslund, T.B., Hilton, A., Krüger, V.: A survey of advances in vision-based human motion capture and analysis. Computer Vision and Image Understanding 104(2–3), 90–126 (2006)
4. Bobick, A.F., Davis, J.W.: The recognition of human movement using temporal templates. IEEE Trans. Pattern Analysis and Machine Intelligence 23(3), 257–267 (2001)
5. Efros, A.A., Berg, A.C., Mori, G., Malik, J.: Recognizing action at a distance. In: Proceedings of International Conference on Computer Vision (ICCV 2003) (2003)
6. Starner, T., Weaver, J., Pentland, A.: Real-time american sign language recognition using desk andwearable computer based video. IEEE Trans. Pattern Analysis and Machine Intelligence 20(12), 1371–1375 (1998)
7. Elgammal, A., Shet, V., Yacoob, Y., Davis, L.: Learning dynamics for exemplar-based gesture recognition. In: Proceedings of Computer Vision and Pattern Recognition (CVPR 2003), pp. 571–578 (2003)
8. Kojima, A., Izumi, M., Tamura, T., Fukunaga, K.: Generating natural language description of human behavior from video images. In: Proceedings of 15th International Conference on Pattern Recognition, vol. 4, pp. 4728–4731 (2000)
9. Ren, H., Xu, G., Kee, S.: Subject-independent natural action recognition. In: Sixth IEEE International Conference on Automatic Face and Gesture Recognition, pp. 523–528 (2004)
10. Wang, L., Tan, T., Ning, H., Hu, W.: Silhouette analysis-based gait recognition for human identification. IEEE Transactions on Pattern Analysis and Machine Intelligence 25(12), 1505–1518 (2003)
11. Wu, Y., Huang, T.S.: Vision-based gesture recognition: A review. In: Braffort, A., Gibet, S., Teil, D., Gherbi, R., Richardson, J. (eds.) GW 1999. LNCS (LNAI), vol. 1739, pp. 103–115. Springer, Heidelberg (2000)
12. Rao, C., Yilmaz, A., Shah, M.: View-invariant representation and recognition of actions. International Journal of Computer Vision 50(2), 203–226 (2002)
13. O'Hagan, R.G., Zelinsky, A., Rougeaux, S.: Visual gesture interfaces for virtual environments. Interacting with Computers 14(3), 231–250 (2002)
14. Boulic, R., Varona, J., Unzueta, L., Peinado, M., Suescun, A., Perales, F.: Evaluation of on-line analytic and numeric inverse kinematics approaches driven by partial vision input. Virtual Reality (online) 10(1), 48–61 (2006)

15. Zhang, Z.: A flexible new technique for camera calibration. IEEE Transactions on Pattern Analysis and Machine Intelligence 22(11), 1330–1334 (2000)
16. Moeslund, T.B., Reng, L., Granum, E.: Finding motion primitives in human body gestures. In: Gesture in Human-Computer Interaction and Simulation: 6th International Gesture Workshop, pp. 133–144 (2006)
17. Höysniemi, J., Hämäläinen, P., Turkki, L., Rouvi, T.: Children's intuitive gestures in vision-based action games. Commun. ACM 48(1), 44–50 (2005)
18. Rubner, Y., Tomasi, C., Guibas, L.: The earth mover's distance as a metric for image retrieval. International Journal of Computer Vision 40(2), 99–121 (2000)
19. Bradski, G., Pisarevsky, V.: Intels computer vision library. In: Proceedings of Computer Vision and Pattern Recognition (CVPR 2000), vol. 2, pp. 796–797 (2000)

Effective Emotional Classification Combining Facial Classifiers and User Assessment

Isabelle Hupont[1], Sandra Baldassarri[2], Rafael Del Hoyo[1], and Eva Cerezo[2]

[1] Instituto Tecnológico de Aragón, Zaragoza (Spain)
{ihupont,rdelhoyo}@ita.es
[2] Departamento de Informática e Ingeniería de Sistemas,
Instituto de Investigación en Ingeniería de Aragón, Universidad de Zaragoza (Spain)
{sandra,ecerezo}@unizar.es

Abstract. An effective method for the automatic classification of facial expressions into emotional categories is presented. The system is able to classify the user facial expression in terms of the six Ekman's universal emotions (plus the neutral one), giving a membership confidence value to each emotional category. The method is capable of analysing any subject, male or female of any age and ethnicity. The classification strategy is based on a combination (weighted majority voting) of the five most used classifiers. Another significant difference with other works is that human assessment is taken into account in the evaluation of the results. The information obtained from the users classification makes it possible to verify the validity of our results and to increase the performance of our method.

Keywords: Facial Expressions, Emotional Classifiers, Multimodal Interfaces, Affective Computing

1 Introduction

Human computer intelligent interaction is an emerging field aimed at providing natural ways for humans to use computers as aids. It is argued that for a computer to be able to interact with humans it needs to have the communication skills of humans. One of these skills is the affective aspect of communication. Recent researches have focused on the development of virtual environments populated by 3D virtual characters capable of understanding the emotional state of the user and reacting accordingly. Addressing user's emotions in human-computer interaction significantly enhances the believability and lifelikeness of virtual humans [1].

The most expressive way humans display emotions is through facial expressions. Thus, the interpretation of facial expressions is the most followed method for achieving user's emotions detection. The process implies the extraction of facial expression information from the user's image or image sequence and the classification of that information into emotional categories. This paper focuses in the problem of classification, which involves the definition of the set of categories we want to deal with and the implementation of the categorization mechanisms.

F.J. Perales and R.B. Fisher (Eds.): AMDO 2008, LNCS 5098, pp. 431–440, 2008.

In the literature, facial expression analysers consider a set of characteristics extracted from the face (points or distances/angles between points) and use different methods of classification [2] in order to determine emotional categories. Most of the systems that work in real-time use a feature based representation of facial data for classification. The real-time methods that obtain better results are neural networks, rule-based expert systems, support vector machines (SVM) and Bayesian nets.

In the systems based on neuronal networks [3,4], the face expression is classified according to a categorization process "learned" by the neuronal network during the training phase.

Rule-based expert systems are also known as knowledge-based systems since they establish a set of rules based on the knowledge of an expert or on objective statistical observations. These systems have the advantage of being easily understood and implemented. They have been used in several works [5,6,7].

Support Vector Machines (SVM), instead, are a set of supervised learning methods used for classification that simultaneously minimize the empirical classification error and maximize the geometric margin; hence, they are also known as maximum margin classifiers. It has been only recently that this technique has been used for the classification of facial expressions [8,9].

Finally, Bayesian networks are directed acyclic graphs whose nodes represent variables, and whose arcs encode conditional dependences between the variables. Most of the algorithms that employ Bayesian networks use Hidden Markov Models [10,11].

There are other approaches for facial expression classification as the ones that use holistic face models; they often rely on Gabor filters [12] or Linear Discriminant Analysis [13], but they are very time consuming and they are not suited for real-time classification.

Regarding emotional categories, the classification proposed by Ekman [14] is the most followed one. It describes six universal basic emotions: joy, sadness, surprise, fear, disgust and anger. However, most existing approaches only consider a subset of these emotions and don't allow to represent a blend of them.

In this paper we present an effective method for the automatic classification of facial expressions into emotional categories based on a novel combination of existing classifiers. The system is able to classify the user emotion in terms of the six Ekman's universal emotions (plus the neutral one), giving a membership confidence value to each emotional category. The method is capable of analysing any subject, male or female of any age and ethnicity and takes into account emotional classification performed by humans to analyse the results.

The structure of the paper is the following: Section 2 discusses the selection of the facial features that are the inputs of the facial classifiers. In Section 3 the five different classifiers used are presented and the way these classifiers are combined is explained. Section 4 presents success rates and shows how users' assessment is used to analyse and improve results. Section 5 compares our results with the ones obtained with other methods. Finally, Section 6 is devoted to present the conclusions and future work.

2 Setting the Classifiers' Input: Extraction and Selection of Facial Information

It has been stated that all the necessary information for the recognition of expressions is contained in the deformation of a set of carefully selected characteristics of the eyes, mouth and eyebrows [14]. Making use of this property, and taken also other relevant works into account [5,6,15], we established the initial inputs of our classifiers to a set of distances and angles obtained from twenty characteristic facial points. In fact, the inputs will be the variations of these angles and distances with respect to the neutral face. The points are obtained thanks to a real-time facial feature tracking program presented elsewhere [16]. Figure 1 shows the correspondence of these points with those defined by the MPEG4 standard. The initial set of parameters obtained from these points is shown in Figure 2. In order to make the distances' values consistent (independently of the scale of the image, the distance to the camera, etc.), all the distances are normalized with respect to the distance between the eyes (MPEG4 Facial Animation Parameter Unit -FAPU- called "ESo"), which is a distance independent of the expression. The choice of angles for classification provides a size invariant classification and saves the effort of normalization.

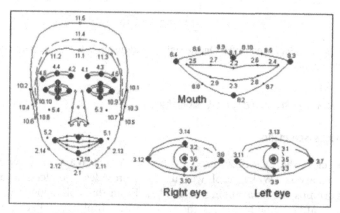

Fig. 1. Facial feature points according to MPEG4 standard

In other to determine the goodness and usefulness of the parameters, a study of the correlation between parameters was carried out using the data (distances and angles values) obtained from a training set of images. For this purpose, two different facial emotion databases have been used: the FG-NET database [17] that provides video sequences of 19 different Caucasian people; and the MMI Facial Expression Database [18] that holds 1280 videos of 43 different subjects from different races (Caucasian, Asian and Arabic). Both databases show the seven universal emotions of Ekman. A total of 1500 static frames were carefully selected from those databases to be use as training sets in the correlation study and in the tuning of the classifiers.

A study of the correlation matrix and dispersion diagrams between parameters was done. The idea was to determine the parameters most influential to the variable to predict (emotion) as well as to detect redundant parameters. From the obtained results, a set of important conclusions were extracted: a) Symmetrical distances (e.g. LD5 and RD5) are highly correlated and thus redundant; b) Distance D3 and angle A2 also present a high correlation value; c) Angles LA3 and RA3 are not influential for achieving the emotional classification. Therefore, from the initial set of parameters, we decided to work only with the most significant ones, marked in grey in Figure 2.

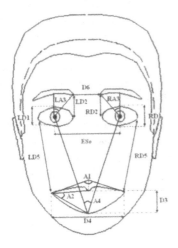

PARAMETER	MPEG4 FEATURE POINTS
LD1	distance(3.14,3.10)
RD1	distance(3.13,3.9)
LD2	distance(4.2,3.8)
RD2	distance(4.1,3.11)
D3	distance(8.1,8.2)
D4	distance(8.4,8.3)
LD5	distance(8.4,3.12)
RD5	distance(8.3,3.7)
D6	distance(4.2,4.1)
A1	angle(8.4,8.1,8.3)
A2	angle(8.1,8.4,8.2)
LA3	angle(4.4,3.6,4.2)
RA3	angle(4.1,3.5,4.3)
A4	angle(3.6,8.2,3.5)

Fig. 2. Facial parameters tested (left). On the right, relationship between the parameters and the MPEG4 feature points

3   A Novel Combination of Classifiers

3.1   Classifiers Selection

In order to select the classifiers used in this work, the Waikado Environment for Knowledge Analysis (Weka) tool was used. It provides a collection of machine learning algorithms for data mining tasks [19]. From this collection, five classifiers were selected after suitable tuning them: RIPPER, Multilayer Perceptron, SVM, Naive Bayes and C4.5. The selection was based on their widespread use as well as on the individual performance of their Weka implementation:

- RIPPER is a propositional "if...then..." rule-learner algorithm named "Repeated Incremental Pruning to Produce Error Reduction". The reason for having chosen this algorithm is the simplicity of its rules and its good performance, especially on large noisy datasets.
- Multilayer Perceptron is the most widely used neural network for classification tasks. The multilayer perceptron's power comes from its similarity to certain biological neural networks in the human brain, which is very useful for our working domain.
- The selection of the SVM classifier is due to the growing interest it arised in the literature in the last years.

- Naive Bayes is a simple probabilistic classifier based on applying Bayes' theorem with strong (naive) independence assumptions. Naive Bayes classifiers can be trained very efficiently in a supervised learning setting.
- C4.5 is also a rule-based classifier, but it is used to generate a decision tree. Its good performance is due to the use of the concept of Information Entropy to establish the classification mechanisms.

The classification results obtained for each classifier and emotion are shown in Table 1. These results are obtained from a 10-fold cross-validation test over the 1500 training images. Cross-validation measures the ability of the classifier to adapt itself to new data; this is why more realistic measurements are obtained. Therefore, values obtained with k-fold cross-validation are usually poorer that the ones obtained without cross-validation, as it can be observed in Table 2. This is an important issue when comparing classifiers' success rates.

Table 1. Success rates obtained for each classifier and each emotion with a 10-fold cross-validation test over the 1500 training images

	Disgust	Joy	Anger	Fear	Sadness	Neutral	Surprise
RIPPER	50.00%	85.70%	66.70%	48.10%	26.70%	80.00%	80.00%
SVM	76.50%	92.90%	55.60%	59.30%	40.00%	84.00%	82.20%
C4.5	58.80%	92.90%	66.70%	59.30%	30.00%	70.00%	73.30%
Naive Bayes	76.50%	85.70%	63.00%	85.20%	33.00%	86.00%	71.10%
Multilayer Perceptron	64.70%	92.90%	70.40%	63.00%	43.30%	86.00%	77.80%

Table 2. Success rates obtained for each classifier and each emotion without cross-validation test over the 1500 training images

	Disgust	Joy	Anger	Fear	Sadness	Neutral	Surprise
RIPPER	94.10%	100.00%	88.90%	85.20%	46.70%	86.00%	84.40%
SVM	94.10%	100.00%	77.80%	77.80%	70.00%	88.00%	93.30%
C4.5	91.20%	95.20%	92.60%	85.20%	93.30%	92.00%	91.10%
Naive Bayes	85.30%	90.50%	70.40%	85.20%	50.00%	92.00%	80.00%
Multilayer Perceptron	100.00%	100.00%	88.90%	100.00%	76.70%	100.00%	97.80%

3.2 Classifiers Combination

When dealing with matters of great importance, people often seek a second opinion before making a decision, sometimes a third and sometimes many more. In doing so, the individual opinions are weighted and combined through some thought process to reach a final decision that is presumably the most informed one. Following this idea, the combination of the outputs of several classifiers by averaging may reduce the risk of an unfortunate selection of a poorly performing classifier. The averaging may or may not beat the performance of the best classifier in the ensemble, but it certainly reduces the overall risk of making a particularly poor selection [20].

The classifier combination chosen follows a weighted majority voting strategy. The voted weights are assigned depending on the performance of each classifier for each emotion. To illustrate the combination strategy, let's imagine a simple case where only 2 classifiers are used and where the confusion matrix of each one of them is the given in Table 3.

Table 3. Confusion matrix of two classifiers (example)

Classifier 1

Emotion --> is classified as	Disgust	Joy	Anger	Fear	Sadness	Neutral	Surprise
Disgust	68.75%	6.25%	9.38%	3.13%	9.38%	3.13%	0.00%
Joy	6.98%	90.70%	0.00%	0.00%	0.00%	0.00%	2.33%
Anger	7.41%	0.00%	70.37%	0.00%	14.81%	7.41%	0.00%
Fear	10.34%	0.00%	0.00%	58.62%	3.45%	0.00%	27.59%
Sadness	17.39%	4.35%	4.35%	4.35%	56.52%	13.04%	0.00%
Neutral	0.00%	0.00%	7.02%	0.00%	15.79%	75.44%	1.75%
Surprise	0.00%	0.00%	0.00%	18.18%	0.00%	2.27%	79.55%

Classifier 2

Emotion --> is classified as	Disgust	Joy	Anger	Fear	Sadness	Neutral	Surprise
Disgust	57.78%	4.44%	11.11%	6.67%	11.11%	2.22%	6.67%
Joy	0.00%	100.00%	0.00%	0.00%	0.00%	0.00%	0.00%
Anger	9.52%	0.00%	71.43%	0.00%	14.29%	4.76%	0.00%
Fear	11.54%	0.00%	0.00%	61.54%	7.69%	3.85%	15.38%
Sadness	12.50%	0.00%	16.67%	0.00%	50.00%	20.83%	0.00%
Neutral	0.00%	1.85%	5.56%	0.00%	12.96%	77.78%	1.85%
Surprise	0.00%	0.00%	0.00%	17.39%	2.17%	0.00%	80.43%

When a classifier outputs a specific emotion, the row of its confusion matrix table corresponding to this emotion is selected. If the procedure is repeated for each classifier, a matrix of as many rows as classifiers studied and seven columns, corresponding to the seven emotions is created. The sum of the values present in each column of the matrix gives the score obtained by each emotion ("global output"). If the score result is divided by the number of classifiers, the average global output of the classifier is obtained.

For example, if classifier 1 outputs "disgust" and classifier 2 outputs "anger", the rows in grey in Table 3 is selected. From these data, the matrix shown in Table 4 is created. The sum of the columns allows to obtain the average global output for each emotion. As it can be seen, in the example the system detects emotions "anger" and "disgust" approximately with the same confidence value. This strategy has been applied to combine the five classifiers. Results obtained are presented in next section.

Table 4. Integrating the results of two classifiers (example)

C1 output	68.75%	6.25%	9.38%	3.13%	9.38%	3.13%	0.00%
C2 output	9.52%	0.00%	71.43%	0.00%	14.29%	4.76%	0.00%
Average global output	39.14%	3.13%	40.40%	1.56%	11.83%	3.94%	0.00%

4   Results: Success Rates and Human Assessment

The results obtained when applying the strategy explained in the previous section to combine the results of the five classifiers are shown in first row of Table 5. As it can be observed, the success rates for the neutral, joy and surprise emotions are very high (84.44%-95.23%). However, the system tends to confuse disgust with fear and fear with surprise; therefore, the performances for those emotions are slightly smaller. This is a problem that usually arises with these three emotions; this is why many classification works do not consider them. The showiest result of our classification is for sadness: it is confused with the neutral emotion in the 68% of the occasions, owing to the similarity of their facial expressions. Nevertheless, results can be considered positive, as the confusion matrices of two incompatible emotions (such as sadness and joy or joy and disgust) intermingle in less than the 0.2% of the occasions.

Table 5. Initial results obtained combining the five classifiers (first row) and after considering human assessment (second row)

Emotion	Joy	Surprise	Disgust	Anger	Sadness	Fear	Neutral
Initial results	95.23%	84.44%	79.41%	74.07%	30%	62.96%	92.00%
After human assessment	95.23%	91.11%	84.24%	77.78%	66.67%	92.59%	98.00%

In order to take into account the human factor in the evaluation of the results, 60 persons were told to classify the 1500 images of the database in terms of emotions. As a result, each one of the frames was classified by 10 different persons that were surveyed in 5 sessions of 50 images. With this information, the evaluation of results was repeated: the recognition was marked as "good" if the decision was coherent with the one taken by a human being. It is important to realize that, according to Bassili [21], a trained observer can correctly classify faces showing emotions with an average of 87%.

This kind of evaluation revision is really interesting and, as we will see, useful but it is not performed in other classification works. For example, in the image shown in Figure 3, the FG-NET database classifies it like "disgust" exclusively while the surveyed people recognized it as much "disgust" as "anger" and "sadness". Users' results are similar to our method, which obtains: 54.59% anger, 33.36% disgust, 12.15% sadness.

Fig. 3. Frame classified as "disgust" by the FG-NET database [17]

The results of considering users' assessment are shown in second row of Table 5. As it can be seen, the success ratios have considerably increased. Therefore, it can be concluded that the confusions of the algorithms go in the same direction than the users' ones: our classification strategy is appropriate and coherent with human classification.

5 Comparison with Other Methods

Table 6 compares the presented system, in the grey column, with other recent approaches with the same experimental proposal [5,8,11,3]. Many works do not detail if they have used or not cross-validation, so the direct comparison of results is not always possible. As it can be observed, our success rates are generally better. Besides, their confusion matrices uniformly distribute classification errors among all emotions: the probability of confusing joy with sadness, two incompatible emotions, is the same that the one of confusing joy with surprise. This is not the case in our method, as it has been explained in the previous section. It is also important to realize that the database used in this work is bigger than the used in the other ones (1500 images of 62 individuals of all races and genders), and therefore more universal.

Table 6. Classification rates of our method plus user assessment (in grey); and comparisons with the rates obtained by other recent approaches

		Combination of 5 classifiers + user assessment	Method of Hammal et al. [5]	Method of Datcu & Rothkrantz [8]	Method of Cohen et al. [11]	Method of Zhang et al. [3]
Type of classifier		combination	rule-based	SVM	Bayesian net (HMM)	neural network
Database		1500 frames, 62 subjects	630 frames, 8 subjects	474 frames	>40 subjects	213 frames, 9 japanese females
Validation strategy		10-fold cross-validation	hold-out method	2-fold cross-validation	leave-one-out cross-validation	10-fold cross-validation
User assesment		yes	no	no	no	yes
Success rates	Joy	95.23%	87.26%	72.64%	97.00%	90.10% The only available data is the overall recognition rate of the 6 + neutral universal emotions.
	Surprise	91.11%	84.44%	83.8%	85.00%	
	Disgust	88.24%	51.20%	80.35%	88.00%	
	Anger	77.78%	not recognized	75.86%	80.00%	
	Sadness	66.67%	not recognized	82.79%	85.00%	
	Fear	92.59%	not recognized	84.70%	93.00%	
	Neutral	98.00%	88.00%	not recognized	96.00%	

6 Conclusions and Future Work

This paper describes an effective method for the automatic classification of facial expressions. The method is based on the combination of the 5 classifiers most widely used in the literature. The combination strategy has been weighted majority voting. The classification results are obtained from a 10-fold cross-validation test over 1500 training images, and results are promising.

A comparison with other four recent works has been presented. The distinguishing features of our work are:

- the presented method is able to consider the six Ekman's emotions, plus the neutral one,
- it gives a confidence level for all classified emotions,
- the success rates are generally better,
- classification errors are not uniformly distributed: the confusion matrices of incompatible emotions intermingle in less than the 0.2% of the occasions,
- it has been tuned with a large database of individuals of all races and genders.

Another significant difference is the use of human assessment in the evaluation of the classification results. 60 persons were told to classify the 1500 images of the database in terms of emotions: our classification strategy has been proved to work in a similar way as human brain, leading to similar confusions.

Our emotional classifier is being used as a new multimodal input to Maxine [22], an engine developed by the group for managing 3D virtual scenarios and characters. Maxine focuses in the use of 3D characters to enrich user interaction in different application domains. User's emotion detection is a very useful input to develop affective computing strategies: the general vision is that if a user's emotion could be recognized by a computer, human-computer interaction would become more natural, enjoyable and productive. The computer could offer help and assistance to a confused user or try to cheer up a frustrated user, and hence react in more appropriate ways.

In the near future, we are considering new inputs to the system like adding information about the user's speech (frequency, volume, speed, etc.), introducing dynamic information (i.e. the evolution in the time of the evaluated facial parameters) or making a fuzzification of the input variables.

Acknowledgments. The authors wish to thank the Computer Graphics, Vision and Artificial Intelligence Group of the University of the Balearic Islands for providing us the real-time facial tracking module to test our classifier.

This work has been partially financed by the Spanish "Dirección General de Investigación", Nº TIN2007-63025 and by the Aragon Government through the WALQA agreement (ref. 2004/04/86) and the CTPP02/2006 project.

References

1. Boukricha, H., Becker, C., Wachsmuth, I.: Simulating Empathy for the Virtual Human Max. In: 2nd International Workshop on Emotion and Computing in conj. with the German Conference on Artificial Intelligence, Osnabrück, Germany, pp. 22–27 (2007)
2. Pantic, M., Rothkrantz, L.J.M.: Automatic Analysis of Facial Expressions: The State of the Art. Pattern Analysis and Machine Intelligence, IEEE Transactions 22(12), 1424–1445 (2000)
3. Zhang, Z., Lyons, M., Schuster, M., Akamatsu, S.: Comparison between Geometry-Based and Gabor Wavelets-Based Facial Expression Recognition Using Multi-Layer Perceptron. In: Proc. Int'l Conf. Automatic Face and Gesture Recognition, pp. 454–459 (1998)
4. Wallace, M., Raouzaiou, A., Tsapatsoulis, N., Kollias, S.: Facial Expression Classification Based on MPEG-4 FAPs: The Use of Evidence and Prior Knowledge for Uncertainty Removal. In: IEEE International Conference on Fuzzy Systems (FUZZ-IEEE), vol. 1, pp. 51–54 (2004)

5. Hammal, Z., Couvreur, L., Caplier, A., Rombaut, M.: Facial Expressions Recognition Based on the Belief Theory: Comparison with Diferent Classifiers. In: Proc. 13th International Conference on Image Analysis and Processing (2005)
6. Pantic, M., Rothkrantz, L.J.M.: Expert System for Automatic Analysis of Facial Expression. Image and Vision Computing J. 18(11), 881–905 (2000)
7. Cerezo, E., Hupont, I.: Emotional Facial Expression Classification for Multimodal Interfaces. In: Perales, F.J., Fisher, R.B. (eds.) AMDO 2006. LNCS, vol. 4069, pp. 405–413. Springer, Heidelberg (2006)
8. Datcu, D., Rothkrantz, L.J.M.: Facial Expression Recognition in still pictures and videos using Active Appearance Models. A comparison approach. In: Proceedings of the 2007 International Conference on Computer Systems and Technologies, vol. 285(112) (2007)
9. Qinzhen, X., Pinzheng, Z., Wenjiang, P., Luxi, Y., Zhenya, H.: A Facial Expression Recognition Approach Based on Confusion-Crossed Support Vector Machine Tree. In: International Conference on Intelligent Information Hiding and Multimedia Signal Processing, pp. 309–312 (2006)
10. Limin, M., Chelberg, D., Celenk, M.: Spatio-temporal modeling of facial expressions using Gabor-wavelets and hierarchical hidden Markov models. In: IEEE International Conference on Image Processing, vol. 2, pp. 57–60 (2005)
11. Cohen, I., Sebe, N., Garg, A., Chen, L.S., Huang, T.S.: Facial expression recognition from video sequences: temporal and static modeling. Computer Vision and Image Understanding 11(1-2), 160–187 (2003)
12. Duang-Duang, Y., Lian-Wen, J., Jun-Xun, Y., Li-Xin, Z., Jian-Cheng, H.: Facial expression recognition with Pyramid Gabor Features and Complete Kernel Fisher Linear Discriminant Analysis. International Journal of Information Technology 11(9), 91–100 (2005)
13. Edwards, G.J., Cootes, T.F., Taylor, C.J.: Face Recognition Using Active Appearance Models. In: Proc. European Conf. Computer Vision, vol. 2, pp. 581–695 (1998)
14. Ekman, P.: Facial Expression, the Handbook of Cognition and Emotion. John Wiley et Sons, Chichester (1999)
15. Esau, N., Wetzel, E., Kleinjohann, L., Keinjohann, B.: Real-time facial expression recognition using a fuzzy emotion model. In: IEEE International Fuzzy Systems Conference FUZZ-IEEE 2007, pp. 1–6 (2007)
16. Manresa-Yee, C., Varona, J., Perales, F.J.: Towards hands-free interfaces based on real-time robust facial gesture recognition. In: Perales, F.J., Fisher, R.B. (eds.) AMDO 2006. LNCS, vol. 4069, pp. 504–513. Springer, Heidelberg (2006)
17. FG-Net Database, http://www.mmk.ei.tum.de/~waf/fgnet/feedtum.html
18. Pantic, M., Valstar, M.F., Rademaker, R., Maat, L.: Web-based Database for Facial Expression Analysis. In: Proc. IEEE Int'l Conf. Multmedia and Expo. (2005)
19. Witten, I., Frank, E.: Data Mining: Practical machine learning tools and techniques, 2nd edn. Morgan Kaufmann, San Francisco (2005)
20. Polikar, R.: Ensemble Based Systems in Decision Making. IEEE Circuits and Systems Magazine 6(3), 21–45 (2006)
21. Bassili, J.N.: Emotion recognition: The role of facial movement and the relative importance of upper and lower areas of the face. Journal of Personality and Social Psychology 37, 2049–2059 (1997)
22. Cerezo, E., Baldassarri, S., Seron, F.: Interactive agents for multimodal emotional user interaction. In: IADIS Multi Conferences on Computer Science and Information Systems 2007, pp. 35–42 (2007)

Online and Offline Fingerprint Template Update Using Minutiae: An Experimental Comparison

Biagio Freni, Gian Luca Marcialis, and Fabio Roli

University of Cagliari
Department of Electrical and Electronic Engineering
Piazza d'Armi - I-09123 Cagliari (Italy)
{biagio.freni,marcialis,roli}@diee.unica.it

Abstract. Although the template fingerprint collected during the registration phase of personal verification systems can be considered in principle as representative of the subject identity, some recent works pointed out that it is not completely able to follow the intra-class variations of the fingerprint shape. Accordingly, making these systems adaptive to these variations is one of the most interesting problems, and is often called as the "template updating" problem. In this paper, two different approaches for fingerprint template updating are compared by experiments. The first one, already proposed in other works, relies on the concept of "online" template updating, that is, the fingerprint template is updated when the system is operating. As alternative, we propose the "offline" template update, which requires the collection of a representative batch of samples when the system is operating. They concur to the template updating when the system is offline, that is, it is not operating. Preliminary experiments carried out on the FVC data sets allow to point out some differences among the investigated approaches.

1 Introduction

Fingerprints [1] are the most used and popular among the biometric traits, for personal identification and verification. Several approaches have been proposed to fingerprint matching. The best ones are based on the so-called minutiae, that is, the terminations and bifurcations of the ridge lines [1]. The core of these verification systems, which allow to obtain good verification results as shown in several works [1], is the collection of one or more samples of each user's fingerprint, in order to extract a representative template, that is, a representative set of minutiae of the given subject. This is often performed during the so-called registration phase, in which the user, under the supervision of a human expert, put his finger on the electronic scanner surface for his fingerprint acquisition. It is easy to notice that this phase is expensive, especially when more samples must be collected. Further, the will of cooperating of the subject is crucial.

On the other hand, when the system is operating, a lot of fingerprint samples is captured, but, being out of a human expert supervision, they exhibit several differences. Moreover, intra-class variations of the fingerprint shape arise (due to

F.J. Perales and R.B. Fisher (Eds.): AMDO 2008, LNCS 5098, pp. 441–448, 2008.

scratches, increase of moisture or dryness, aging etc.), and the captured finger-prints can exhibit, over the time, minutiae sets different from that captured in the registration phase. Accordingly, recent works pointed out the need of making the current fingerprint verification systems adaptive to the above variations. This requirement can be realized by updating the template over the time [2,3,4].

We can currently subdivide the template update approaches in supervised and semi-supervised. The former [2] require, after a fixed period of time, a novel (supervised) registration phase in which fingerprint samples are collected. If necessary, the most representative samples among the collected ones can be selected. In [2], some clustering algorithms are proposed to this goal, as alternative to the manual selection.

The latter introduce the concept of semi-supervised template updating. In other words, the additional fingerprint samples are collected and pseudo-labelled during the verification phase and are exploited to update the template. The concept of sample pseudo-labeling relies on the decision of the verification system, and not on the explicit intervention of the human expert, thus justifying the term semi-supervised template updating. Hence, the labeling, that is, the association of the identity to the sample, is performed automatically, without the human contribute, making the template update process cheaper and feasible over frequent periods of time.

With regard to fingerprint template updating, methods in Refs. [3,4] try to update templates during the system operations. The claim is that these system can increase the reliability of templates without loss of time in additional registration phases. This can be realized by adopting algorithms aimed to the "fusion" of the input minutiae-set and the template minutiae-set. The output is a novel template, called "supertemplate", which should be more representative than the original template.

On the other hand, it is reasonable to hypothesise that, if a batch of unlabelled samples can be collected before updating, so increasing the centralization degree of the system, these samples could be exploited when the system is not operating. This approach can be called "offline template update".

In this paper, we compare online and offline approaches to fingerprint template updating by experiments on FVC2000 benchmark data sets [5]. Update is performed by adopting the fusion of minutiae-set proposed in [3] in order to generate a supertemplate, but also the use of multiple templates per client is investigated. Reported results allow to point out some interesting differences among the proposed methods.

The paper is organized as follows. Section 2 describes the online and offline systems to fingerprint template updating. Section 3 reports some experimental results. Section 4 draw some preliminary conclusions.

2   Offline and Online Fingerprint Template Updating

Let us consider a fingerprint verification system, with C enrolled users, also called "clients". For each client c, only one template is initially stored. Thus, the related gallery, T^c, is made up of only one template. No limit to the size of T^c is given in this paper, but it is worth noting that in real verification systems this size depends on the memory available and constraints in terms of verification time.

Proposed method is shown in pseudo-code form by Algorithm 1 for online template update and Algorithm 2 for offline template update.

In both algorithms, the boolean variable *buildSuperTemplate* is true if the system is constrained to work with only one template per class. Thus, a supertemplate, i.e. a sort of "average" minutiae set from those of samples inserted into the client's gallery, must be builded. Our supertemplate generation algorithm is the same proposed in Ref. [3].

Algorithm 1 works as follows. As a novel fingerprint is submitted to the system, features are extracted in order to generate an input feature set x. This set is compared with the template set of the claimed identity c. As well-known, the result of this comparison is a matching score, usually a real value into $[0, 1]$, which represents the degree of similarity among compared fingerprints. Function which outputs such a value is called $meanscore(x, T^c)$ in Algorithm 1. If this matching score exceeds a *threshold* value such that the probability of being impostor is low enough, the related input can be fused with existing template or added to the client's gallery. In the second case, as the size of T^c increases, multiple templates are available. Algorithm 1 stops according to a fixed criterion. This criterion depends on the particular context. For example, update can stop after a certain period of time is passed, or a certain number of verification attempts has been submitted, in order to test the system performance and monitor updated templates into each gallery.

Algorithm 2 works similarly to the previous one, with the difference that it is offline, i.e. works on a batch of unlabelled samples collected during system operations. This leads to the fact that it is possible to select, for each client, the sample exhibiting the highest matching score for update, among the ones with probability of being impostors low enough (line 6).

In our implementation of these algorithms:

1. Feature set x, and all templates in the union of clients galleries, namely, T, are represented by minutiae [1], which are terminations and bifurcations of fingerprint ridge lines. "String" algorithm has been implemented to match minutiae sets each others [1]. Further details can be found in [6];
2. *threshold* has been set to 1%FAR operational point, in order to have a low probability (1%) of introducing impostors into the gallery. A more conservative threshold was at zeroFAR, but in practical cases it allows to introduce a significantly smaller number of genuine users, thus slowing the performance increase of template update;
3. *threshold* can be evaluated only on T, which is the only "labelled" set available for this aim. In principle, *threshold* should be updated at each insertion of novel samples, but this increases computational time of updating, and it is not statistically significant. Therefore, we have chosen to update *threshold* after that at least one sample has been submitted for all clients (see Algorithm 1-2, lines 2-3).

Algorithm 1. Online Template Update

Require: {

    Let C be the number of clients

    Let M be the maximum number of template per client

    Let T^c the template gallery of class c

    Let $s = meanscore(x, T^c)$ be a function such that s is the average score of the input sample x on the template set T^c

    Let $buildSuperTemplate$ be a boolean variable which is true if a supertemplate must be builded

    Let $supert^c = fuse(T^c)$ be a supertemplate building function}

1: **repeat**
2:     $T = \cup_c T^c$
3:     Estimate $threshold$ on T
4:     **for** each client $c = 1..C$ **do**
5:         $x \Leftarrow i$ {where i is an input sample claiming c-th identity}
6:         $s = meanscore(x, T^c)$
7:         **if** $s > threshold$ **then**
8:             **if** $buildSuperTemplate$ **then**
9:                 $supert^c = fuse(T^c)$
10:                $T^c = \{supert^c\}$
11:             **else**
12:                $T^c = T^c \cup \{x\}$
13:             **end if**
14:         **end if**
15:     **end for**
16: **until** (stop criterion is not met)

---

3   Experimental Results

3.1   Data Sets

The FVC2000 data sets consist of four fingerprint databases (Db1-Db4) adopted for the Fingerprint Verification Competition held in 2000 [5]. Each one is made up of eight samples per 100 different fingers. The images of fingerprint impressions were collected with different sensors. In particular, the Db1 was acquired with a low-cost optical sensor (300x300 pixels), the Db2 with a low-cost capacitive sensor (256x364 pixels), the Db3 with another optical sensor (448x478 pixels) and for the Db4 a synthetic generator (240x320 pixels).

It is worth noting that, due to the small number of samples per client, FVC data sets are not fully appropriate for this task. In fact, template update algorithms should be tested on data sets with large number of samples per client, possibly captured at different periods of time [4]. On the other hand, FVC data sets exhibit large intra-class variations, thus can be useful for assessing a preliminary evaluation of template update algorithms, as done in Ref. [3].

Algorithm 2. Offline Template Update

Require: {
    Let C be the number of clients
    Let M be the maximum number of template per client
    Let X_c be the batch of unlabelled samples which claim to be the c-th client
    Let T^c the template gallery of client c
    Let $s = meanscore\,(x, T^c)$ be a function such that s is the average score of the
    input sample x on the template set T^c
    Let $buildSuperTemplate$ be a boolean variable which is true if a supertemplate
    must be builded
    Let $supert^c = fuse(T^c)$ be a supertemplate building function}
1: **repeat**
2:    $T = \cup_c T^c$
3:    Estimate $threshold$ on T
4:    **for** each client $c = 1..C$ **do**
5:      $X_{ct} = \{x \in X_c | meanscore(x, T^c) > threshold\}$
6:      $y = argmax_{x \in X_{ct}} meanscore(x, T^c)$
7:      $T^c = T^c \cup \{y\}$
8:      $X_c = X_c - \{y\}$
9:    **end for**
10:    $X_t = \cup_c X_{ct}$
11: **until** $(X_t \neq \phi)$
12: **if** $buildSuperTemplate$ **then**
13:    **for** each client $c = 1..C$ **do**
14:      $supert^c = fuse(T^c)$
15:      $T^c = \{supert^c\}$
16:    **end for**
17: **end if**

3.2   Experimental Protocol

We subdivided each data set in three partitions. The original labeled set is made up of one finger sample per subject. The set of unlabeled data is made up of six samples per subject and the test set, which we used for comparing the template updating approaches, is made up of one sample. We carried out seven experiments for each data set and averaged the results. In each experiment, the labeled set was always made up of the first sample, the test set was made up from the second to the eighth sample, and the unlabeled set was made up of the remaining six samples.

In online experiments, for each client a sample has been randomly chosen from the unlabelled set, with equal prior for genuine and impostors classes (on average, six genuine and seven impostors have been submitted for each client). In offline experiments, for each client, the same seven impostors used in the related online experiment have been considered with the six genuine samples, in order to make comparable reported results.

3.3   Results

First of all, we performed a study on the quality of images in FVC data sets. To this aim, we applied the NFIQ quality evaluation algorithm proposed by NIST [7]. NFIQ classifies fingerprint images in five cateogories: "Excellent", "Very good", "Good", "Fair", "Poor". In all cases, the majority of images fell in the first and second classes. This allowed to avoid the problem of image quality which could affect template update effectiveness [4], and to better focus on the pros and cons of investigated algorithms.

Figures 1(a-d) show the ROC curves obtained on the FVC2000 test sets. For each plot, five curves are shown: 1) "unimproved", which refers to the ROC curve obtained without template updating, 2) "online multiple templates", related to Algorithm 1 in which the variable $buildSuperTemplate \leftarrow FALSE$, 3) "online supertemplate", where $buildSuperTemplate \leftarrow TRUE$ in Algorithm 1, 4) "offline multiple templates" related to Algorithm 2 in which the variable $buildSuperTemplate \leftarrow FALSE$, 5) "offline supertemplate", where $buildSuperTemplate \leftarrow TRUE$ in Algorithm 2.

It is easy to see that all template update approaches have been effective with respect to the "unimproved" system.

By comparing offline curves each others, as well as online ones, it can be noticed that using multiple templates approach led to a better result than adopting a supertemplate, with the exception of FVC2000-Db4 data set. This can be explained as follows: (1) the minutiae sets "fusion" was dependent on the matching algorithm - "String" in this case. Finding a good alignment is an open issue, but it can be hypothesised that template update results can be improved; (2) performing fusion of templates "smoothed" the intra-class variations among them. In general, it is expected that using multiple templates is better than using only one (super)template. The exception of FVC2000-Db4 can be explained by hypothesising that intra-class variations were less evident in this data set, thus supertemplate avoided the redundancy of multiple templates.

Some interesting findings can be noticed by comparing online and offline algorithms each others. In the case of offline vs. online using supertemplate, the performance was quite similar, with a small superiority of the online approach. This result is remarkable, and points out a clear advantage of these approaches with respect to offline ones.

Things appear to change by considering online vs. offline using multiple templates. However, a clear superiority of the offline method appeared only for FVC2000-Db1 and Db2, whilst in the other ones online approach exhibited a better performance. This result and the previous one motivate further investigations on online and offline template update approaches.

3.4   Discussion on Results

Comparison of online and offline approaches must be done by considering:

- Performance achieved (ROC curves)
- Centralization degree of the system

- Memory available in smart cards or other supports embedding the personal information of each client
- Managing classification errors during update

In our opinion, the first requirement helps in evaluating the second one, whilst the third one can be referred to the particular technology adopted.

In fact, offline methods require that the centralized part of the system must capture, and store, over the time, a large number of queries. The template update process can be clearly separated from the verification phase. Using offline approaches derives from the hypothesis that the more samples are available, the more selective the template updating is (Algorithm 2). However, reported results showed that centralization is not always necessary.

Online approaches, which decrease the centralization degree of the system (since the update is performed at once), have shown to be effective on the adopted data sets, and exhibit a verification accuracy in some cases superior than that of offline approaches.

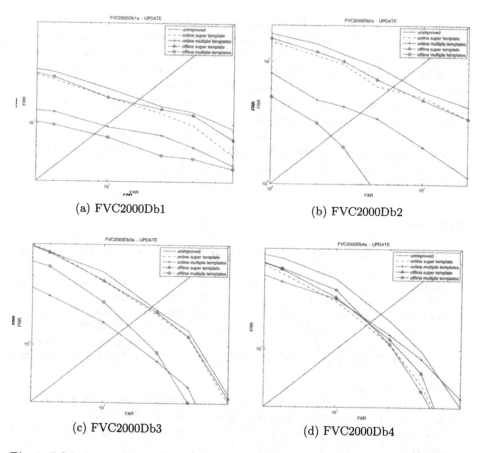

(a) FVC2000Db1

(b) FVC2000Db2

(c) FVC2000Db3

(d) FVC2000Db4

Fig. 1. ROC Curve of the offline and online algorithms on the four dataset FVC2000

A different problem is given by the choice of using multiple templates or a supertemplate. This is strongly dependent on the available technology (third item), and cannot be treated in this paper. Adopted algorithms do not take into account memory or verification time limitations, but this is a topic to be investigated.

The fourth item brings to a still open issue. In particular, how do classification errors (i.e. impostors with score higher than *threshold*) impact on the obtained galleries of templates when performing update? How much large are the security "breatches" caused by classification errors? This is a clear problem for current template update algorithms, especially for online ones. No solutions have been proposed so far. The common guideline is to set *threshold* high enough to reduce this problem. At current state of our knowledge, the human intervention should be taken into account in order to monitor the obtained galleries over certain periods of time.

4   Conclusions

In this paper, we started to investigate the differences of online and offline approaches to fingerprint template update in personal verification systems.

This preliminary experimentation has been performed on FVC2000 data sets, which are not fully suitable for the task, but have been already adopted for template update algorithms evaluation. Their images exhibit a high quality on average, thus help in studying the template update effectiveness under the hypothesis of cooperative user population.

It has been found that performance of offline and online approaches are comparable in some cases. In other cases, online approaches performed better than offline ones. This is a quite surprising result which is worthy to be better investigated in future works.

References

1. Maltoni, D., Maio, D., Jain, A.K., Prabhakar, S.: Handbook of fingerprint recognition. Springer, Heidelberg (2003)
2. Uludag, U., Ross, A., Jain, A.K.: Biometric template selection and update: a case study in fingerprints. Pattern Recognition 37(7), 1533–1542 (2004)
3. Jiang, X., Ser, W.: Online Fingerprint Template Improvement. IEEE Transactions on Pattern Analysis and Machine Intelligence 24(8), 1121–1126 (2002)
4. Ryu, C., Kim, H., Jain, A.K.: Template Adaptation based Fingerprint Verification. In: 18th ICPR 2006, vol. 4, pp. 582–585. IEEE Computer Society, Los Alamitos (2006)
5. http://bias.csr.unibo.it/fvc2000/
6. Jain, A.K., Hong, L., Bolle, R.: On-line Fingerprint Verification. IEEE Transactions on Pattern Analysis and Machine Intelligence 19(4), 302–314 (1997)
7. Tabassi, E., Wilson, C.L., Watson, C.I.: Fingerprint image quality, NIST Technical Report NISTIR 7151 (August 2004)

Users with Disabilities: Maximum Control with Minimum Effort

Julio Abascal

Laboratory of Human-Computer Interaction for Special Needs
University of the Basque Country-Euskal Herriko Unibertsitatea,
Manuel Lardizabal, 20018 Donostia. Spain
julio.abascal@ehu.es

Abstract. People with disabilities can benefit greatly from services provided by computers and robots. Access to remote communications and information as well as to interpersonal communication and environmental control are assisted by current ubiquitous computers, wired and wireless networks and intelligent environments. Sensory, physical or/and cognitive restrictions to interacting with computers can be avoided by means of alternative interaction devices and procedures. Nevertheless, alternative methods are usually much slower than standard communications, frequently leading users with disabilities into unbalanced or unsafe situations. Therefore, the main challenge of human-machine interaction systems that have to be used by people with disabilities is to obtain the maximum communication and control with the minimum physical and cognitive effort from the user. This lecture overviews the main techniques used to optimize the control and communication flow, resulting in higher user satisfaction and security.

1 Supportive Ambient Intelligence and Robotics

The advances in networking, computing and sensing technologies allow the design of intelligent environments able to give support to people located inside them. The Ambient Intelligence paradigm benefits from ubiquitous and wearable computers, communicated by wireless networks with static computers –which can be also connected to wired networks–, that are able to process enormous quantities of contextual information coming from networks of sensors. This technological infrastructure will allow the deployment of intelligent applications that proactively give support to the users.

Ambient Intelligence obviously provides an extraordinary opportunity to develop assistive environments for people with sensory, physical or cognitive restrictions due to aging, disability, illness, etc.

All these intelligent environments perform several supportive activities that are usually ignored by the user, such as adjusting the temperature, humidity, lights, etc., or verifying the safety of gas, electricity or water installations. In addition, intelligent environments have to communicate with the user to provide information or to request commands. The user interfaces are supposed to be as natural as possible, allowing a communication similar to the interaction between humans. That means that the

F.J. Perales and R.B. Fisher (Eds.): AMDO 2008, LNCS 5098, pp. 449–456, 2008.

system should be able to produce voice messages –and maybe to display some of them via wall screens or data glasses– and to recognize natural language and gestures. Some of these communication methods may not be appropriate for people with specific sensory or cognitive restrictions [1].

In a similar way, Mobile Robotics has experienced a notable development in recent years. For instance, sensors are more and more reliable and accurate at lower prices. In addition, processors are also more powerful and memory availability is larger and cheaper. For these reasons, it is possible nowadays to speak about "consumer robotics". Similarly to the evolution of personal computers, robots are finding new applications in the home, outside of the factories. One of the most promising fields among the non-industrial applications of robots is Assistive Robotics.

Assistive Robotics is proposing new ways of supporting people with motor restrictions to develop tasks that were previously impossible for them. Among the diverse applications that are being developed, assisted mobility and manipulation stand out.

Augmentative and Augmentative Mobility, AAM, (similarly to Augmentative and Alternative Communication[1]) attempts to provide people with methods and devices to enhance or restore their mobility. The application of the advancements in Mobile Robotics to AMM allowed the design of very advanced assisted mobility systems. Among them the most sophisticated are *smart wheelchairs*.

Smart wheelchairs are intended for people with severe motor restrictions that experience great difficulty in driving standard electric wheelchairs. They are usually provided with diverse types of sensors and embedded computers that receive information from the sensory system, handle the interaction with the user and control the motors through the power stage. The number and quality of the sensors determine the accuracy of the control. For this reason many experimental Smart Wheelchairs are provided with extremely advanced and expensive sensors that convert them into impressive mobile robots but are too expensive and sophisticated to be marketed.

The interaction between the user and the wheelchair is again a key factor. As previously mentioned, users of smart wheelchairs are people with severe motor restrictions that impede the use of standard input devices. Therefore, the design of interfaces for AAM has also to take into account specific guidelines to satisfy the needs of the users.

Another important human need is to manipulate objects in the surroundings. There are specific technologies applicable to people with severe motor disabilities or to people with amputations.

Articulated arms

The aim is the adaptation of articulated manipulators to allow people with severe hand movement restrictions to grasp and move objects. It is evident that is not possible just to use industrial robots at home. There are problems of size, height, security (the user and the robot share the work space), etc. For instance, to avoid the injuries caused by possible impacts, Casals proposed soft robots, even if they are less controllable that

---

[1] Augmentative and Alternative Communication (AAC) are extra ways of helping people who find it hard to communicate by speech or writing. More information in http://www.isaac-online.org/en/aac/what_is.html

the rigid ones [2]. Nevertheless, the most important barrier is human-robot interaction. Robots are designed to handle objects based on their position and orientation, using diverse types of coordinates. Users describe objects in terms of names, properties (colour, shape, size...), function, etc. Positions are usually related to other objects or to the room. It is not expected that a user should have to give the position, orientation and size of the object to be manipulated. Therefore, intelligent mediator applications are necessary to understand object description in natural language and to translate this into coordinates.

Prosthesis

The design of prosthetic hands and legs, based on robotic technologies has developed incredibly in recent years. They are used for a broad range of needs, but the most common are upper and lower limb substitution for amputees. However, even if the technology has improved considerably (allowing, for instance, the design of artificial tendons to perform fine-grained control of movements) the largest difficulty still resides in the control of the limb by the user. Some encouraging results have been obtained using the electric signals coming from the remaining nerves in recent amputees. Nevertheless, this technique seems not to be appropriate for older amputations, where the electric function of the nerves has been lost. Brain-computer interaction techniques are claimed as the best solution for limb control. Although huge progress has been made in this field, it is far from allowing reliable control of a complex hand prosthesis.

A special type of prosthesis is the exoskeleton. This is an external hard structure that helps the user to stand up and to make movements, to enhance coordination and strength, etc. Pons provides updated detailed information about *biomechatronic* exoskeletons in [3].

2 Requirements of the Human-Robot Interface

Some basic principles have to be taken into account in designing the interface to control both robotic assistant devices and intelligent environments. The first one is the rehabilitation goal. Numerous people with disabilities are able to enhance their cognitive abilities, personal attitudes and social integration when they are provided with adequate user interfaces. To this end the interface must encourage the use of all the capabilities of the user, and avoid taking decisions on behalf of the user when it is not absolutely necessary.

For instance, in the case of autonomous smart wheelchairs, they are able to automatically navigate requiring little or no interaction from the user. After the destination is somehow specified, the wheelchair is able to take all the necessary decisions to arrive at the selected place. Although this procedure is very convenient for people with extreme motor restrictions, many users have some remaining abilities that could be lost if they are not used. These abilities may even be enhanced when they are trained. Therefore the interface must facilitate, as much as possible, user participation in order to enhance their cognitive abilities, personal attitudes and social integration. In addition, the user must feel that he or she is the one who controls the device in order to avoid frustration and passivity That includes ease of switching between automatic/assisted/manual functioning.

Safety and reliability are also important requirements. Several of these systems interact with the environment in various ways that could be dangerous in the case of failure or malfunction. The designer must ensure that the system is safe, reliable and fault tolerant.

Another key issue is the final price. Inexpensive solutions are needed to prevent unaffordable systems. In the case of AAM, that means using cheap sensors (for example, infrared and ultrasonic sensors instead of laser, to measure distances). Currently processors are cheap and the inferior quality of the sensors can be balanced by a much greater processing capacity. Moreover, since most intelligent wheelchairs are built on commercial electric wheelchairs, carrying out any major changes in order to facilitate its future potential marketing by the industry without making large investments should be avoided.

3   Designing the Human-Device Interface

Let me mention three technological fields that can greatly enhance the quality of the result when they are used to design control interfaces.

3.1   Shared Control/Mixed Initiative

As has been previously mentioned, the goal of smart wheelchairs is to automate, as much as possible, the navigation operation, while leaving in the user's hands all those tasks that he or she is able to perform. This facilitates user rehabilitation by promoting his or her involvement and avoiding passivity. This kind of collaboration for control is called in mobile robotics *shared control*. In the shared control paradigm tasks are performed by both the user and the system in perfect harmony. Usually, the user performs the high level tasks (e.g. planning) and the system the low level ones, which are usually tedious or require a high degree of accuracy (e.g. driving). This means that the user is the one who makes decisions, except possibly in hazardous situations.

In the case of a smart wheelchair used by a person who only has problems in driving across difficult passages or avoiding obstacles, a scheme for shared control would be the following: the user normally drives the wheelchair and the system is programmed to take control only when an obstacle or a narrow space is detected. Even in this case user participation is still necessary. To cross a doorway, for instance, the user drives the wheelchair through it, but the system makes the required corrections in trajectory and speed to avoid collisions.

A recent field developed in the human-computer interaction area, called Mixed Initiative Interfaces, allows collaboration among the intelligent agents, the user being one of these. Its application may be very constructive in enhancing the design of control interfaces.

3.2   Adaptability

User physical and cognitive abilities may vary considerably over short periods of time due to fatigue, motivation, interest, attention, etc. Since these aspects can produce rather quick changes in the interaction, the interface should be able to adapt to people's physical and cognitive variations. User modelling techniques applied to user adapted interface design are the most appropriate way of coping with the changes in user performance.

User modelling requires the selection of relevant and observable parameters, such as reaction capacity, movement precision, etc., and the range of possible values for each of them. Diverse user profiles and stereotypes can be defined in function of the possible meaningful combinations of parameter values. Comparing actual parameters with the profiles allows the interface to make assumptions about the user.

For instance, the mentioned aim of facilitating user rehabilitation can be fulfilled if the user model includes information about the current user abilities, in order to allow the interface to give the decision to him or her when it is possible. Adaptability and user modelling are well established techniques that are being used successfully in several interaction fields [4].

3.3 Selection of the Navigational Paradigm

The design of the interface for assisted navigation, both in intelligent environments and by smart wheelchairs, may be highly influenced by the navigational paradigm. It is known that the interface plays a role of translator between both intelligent agents: the user and the system. The translation is easier when both of them share similar visions of the navigation task. Therefore, the design of the interface is highly conditioned by both the user's mental model of the task and the environment and the robot's navigation model. In the traditional approach, the robot performs the mapping, path planning, and driving tasks using maps. In this case, the interface has to assume that users have mental maps of the environment similar to the maps used by the system, and they are able to locate positions (especially the current one and the goal) in their mental maps.

The biologically inspired navigation model enables a more "natural" human-system interaction, similar to the one among humans. The behaviour-based approach to navigation is based on small processes, called behaviours, where each one is responsible for reading its own inputs and sensors, and decides on appropriate motor actions. When navigation is based on biological behaviour, the user and the robot share relative navigational concepts, such as "follow the corridor", "find the way out" etc., which are easier to be mentally processed by the user (since the users often do not have a structured mental map of the environment). In this case, the interface can also accept complex orders (such as "go to the library") which include many individual actions, or partial and relative descriptions of the way (such as "follow the corridor", "turn left", "find the window near the elevator", etc.) [5].

4 Input/Output Control Devices

As previously mentioned, the users with some motor disabilities may be severely restricted in handling the standard input devices, namely keyboard and mouse. For this reason, Assistive Technology researchers have developed several alternative control devices. These devices are adapted to the remaining capacities of each user. In general, they require lower dexterity, coordination or strength than the standard ones. Cook and Hussey (2001) [6] provide a comprehensive survey of Control interfaces for Assistive Technology.

For the case of smart wheelchairs, diverse human-wheelchair interaction systems have been proposed and tested. For instance, Rao et al. [7] propose a vision-based human interface that projects an image of the interface onto the lap tray of the smart wheelchair, monitored by an overhead video camera that picks up the user actions. This interface requires hand mobility and precision from the user. On the other hand, some authors, such as Simpson and Levine (1997) [8], have developed interesting voice interfaces for Smart Wheelchairs, but their application is quite limited because most users of smart wheelchairs have dysarthric speech that can be hardly recognized by current voice technology. Direct system-brain connection is being experimented for wheelchair driving. The results reported are promising for the long term, but currently allow quite limited driving exercises [9].

5   Enhancing the Communication Speed in Control Devices

The diverse alternatives for inputting commands in control interfaces require abilities that numerous wheel chair users do not have. People using smart wheelchairs usually have motor restrictions that limit hand movement, strength and precision. In addition, they may have problems in uttering commands clearly. For these cases, the most common way to produce commands is the use of one-touch scanning interfaces. There are diverse possibilities for arranging and scanning the selection set, and different mechanisms for activating the selected item, depending on the remaining capabilities of the user. For more details see Abascal, Gardeazabal and Garay (2004) [10].

Nevertheless, most alternative user interfaces are extremely slow when the user has to enter written text. That may happen, for instance, while providing the name of the destination to a smart wheelchair. In this section two proposals devoted to the enhancement of the communication speed are presented.

5.1   Word Prediction

The prediction of words is one of the most widely used techniques for increasing the rate in the Augmentative and Alternative Communication context. A predictor is a system that attempts to anticipate the next block of characters (letters, syllables, words, phrases, etc.) that the user wants to select, in order to reduce the effort and time for developing messages. In general, the prediction is based on the previously entered information and is possible because of the redundancy inherent to natural languages. In order to reduce the effort required, it is necessary to decrease the number of keystrokes needed to compose a message [11]. When the user enters a letter, the system analyzes the context and suggests the words most likely from this point. If the user does not accept any of the proposals, he or she may introduce a new letter and the prediction process is repeated. The system dynamically updates the frequency of use of words and includes new words in the dictionary.

When word prediction is used in control interfaces for navigation the hit rate is very high: usually only one or two selections are needed to produce the name of a destination. That is due to the small dictionary used for navigation proposals and to the dependence on the context. For instance, the TetraNauta [12] interface includes a system for predicting words to help the user when he or she must enter place names, destinations or similar strings in natural language, taking into account the frequency of letters and words and their context [13].

5.2 Scanning Period Adaptation

The scanning of the matrix containing the options is usually done at a fixed rate. During the period of time T that an option is selectable, the user requires some time to react, some time to select the item, and there is some remaining time. Evidently, T should be as short as possible to optimise the communication rate. When the selected T is too short, the user does not have enough time to react and produces frequent mistakes, slowing down the process. On the other hand, if T is too long, the unnecessary remaining time is large, also slowing down the process. Therefore, the best rate is obtained when the most appropriate T for each user is found. That is when the remaining time is very small, but not zero. Studies conducted with users have shown that for each specific user the time needed to react and activate the selected option changes over short periods of time due to diverse factors such as attention, fatigue, mood, interest, etc. For this reason there is not a permanent optimal T for each user, but a range where T varies with time between a maximum and a minimum. Therefore the best instantaneous selection rate would be obtained if the system could dynamically adapt T to the current reaction and selection capacity of the user. Abascal, Bonail, Cagigas, Garay and Gardeazabal (2008) proposed in [14] a scanning system based on a Fuzzy model that takes into account the current and average selection times to adapt the scanning period T to the present reaction time of the user. This system was implemented in the interface of the TetraNauta smart wheelchair.

6 Conclusions

The design of the control interface for both assistive robotic devices and intelligent environments requires the application of specific methodologies aimed at enhancing user control and communication, and decreasing the physical and cognitive effort needed to manage them. Therefore, to advance in human-machine interface design for people with disabilities it is crucial to go deeper into the application of well established methodologies, such as adaptability and user modelling, and to explore more recent paradigms, such as shared control and mixed initiative.

Acknowledgments

This work is partly based on the results of project AmbienNet developed with the support of the Spanish Ministry of Education and Science under the TIN2006-15617-C03-01 grant.

Bibliography

[1] Abascal, J., Civit, A., Falcó, J.L.: Threats and opportunities of rising technologies for Smart Houses. In: Accessibility for All CEN-CENELEC-ETSI Conference 2003, Nice (2003)

[2] Casals, A.: Assistant Robots. In: Casals, A. (ed.) Technological Aids for the Disabled. Societat Catalana de Technologia/Institut d'Estudis Catalans, Barcelona (1998)

[3] Pons, J.L. (ed.): Wearable Robots. Biomechatronic Exoskeletons, pp. 87–108. Wiley, Chichester (2008)

[4] Fink, J., Kobsa, A., Nill, A.: Adaptable and Adaptive Information Provision for All Users. Including Disabled and Elderly People. New Review of Hypermedia and Multimedia 4, 163–188 (1998)

[5] Abascal, J., Lazkano, E., Sierra, B.: Behavior-based Indoor Navigation. In: Cai, Y. (ed.) Ambient Intelligence for Scientific Discovery. LNCS (LNAI), vol. 3345, pp. 263–285. Springer, Heidelberg (2005)

[6] Cook, A.M., Hussey, S.: Assistive Technologies: Principles and Practice. In: Control interfaces for Assistive Technology, 2nd edn., ch. 6, Mosby (2001)

[7] Rao, R.S., Conn, K., Jung, S.H., Katupitiya, J., Kientz, T., Kumar, V., Ostrowski, J., Patel, S., Taylor, C.J.: Human robot interaction: application to smart wheelchairs. In: Procs of ICRA 2002. IEEE Int. Conf. on Robotics and Automation, vol. 4, pp. 3583–3588 (2002)

[8] Simpson, R.C., Levine, S.P.: Adaptive shared control of a smart wheelchair operated by voicecontrol. In: Proceedings of the 1997 IEEE/RSJ International Conference on Intelligent Robots and Systems, vol. 2(7-11), pp. 622–626 (1997)

[9] Millán José del, R.: Adaptive brain interfaces. Comms of the ACM 46(3) (2003)

[10] Abascal, J., Gardeazabal, L., Garay, N.: Optimisation of the Selection Set Features for Scanning Text Input. In: Miesenberger, K., Klaus, J., Zagler, W., Burger, D. (eds.) ICCHP 2004. LNCS, vol. 3118, pp. 788–795. Springer, Heidelberg (2004)

[11] Garay-Vitoria, N., Abascal, J.: Text Prediction Systems: A survey. Universal Access in the Information Society (UAIS) 4(3), 188–203 (2006)

[12] Vicente, S., Amaya, C., Díaz, F., Civit, A., Cagigas, D.: TetraNauta: A Intelligent Wheelchair for Users with Very Severe Mobility Restrictions. In: Procs. of the 2002 IEEE International Conference on Control Applications, pp. 778–783 (2002)

[13] Abascal, J., Cagigas, D., Garay, N., Gardeazabal, L.: Mobile Interface for a Smart Wheelchair. In: Paternó, F. (ed.) Mobile HCI 2002. LNCS, vol. 2411, pp. 373–377. Springer, Heidelberg (2002)

[14] Abascal, J., Bonail, B., Cagigas, D., Garay, N., Gardeazabal, L.: Trends in Adaptive Interface Design for Smart Wheelchairs. In: Lumsden, J. (ed.) Handbook of Research on User Interface Design and Evaluation for Mobile Technology. Idea Group Reference, Pennsylvania (2008)

Author Index

Lecture Notes in Computer Science

Sublibrary 6: Image Processing, Computer Vision, Pattern Recognition, and Graphics

For information about Vols. 1– 3948
please contact your bookseller or Springer

Vol. 4522: B.K. Ersbøll, K.S. Pedersen (Eds.), Image Analysis. XVIII, 989 pages. 2007.

Vol. 4485: F. Sgallari, A. Murli, N. Paragios (Eds.), Scale Space and Variational Methods in Computer Vision. XV, 931 pages. 2007.

Vol. 4478: J. Martí, J.M. Benedí, A.M. Mendonça, J. Serrat (Eds.), Pattern Recognition and Image Analysis, Part II. XXVII, 657 pages. 2007.

Vol. 4477: J. Martí, J.M. Benedí, A.M. Mendonça, J. Serrat (Eds.), Pattern Recognition and Image Analysis, Part I. XXVII, 625 pages. 2007.

Vol. 4472: M. Haindl, J. Kittler, F. Roli (Eds.), Multiple Classifier Systems. XI, 524 pages. 2007.

Vol. 4466: F.B. Sachse, G. Seemann (Eds.), Functional Imaging and Modeling of the Heart. XV, 486 pages. 2007.

Vol. 4418: A. Gagalowicz, W. Philips (Eds.), Computer Vision/Computer Graphics Collaboration Techniques. XV, 620 pages. 2007.

Vol. 4417: A. Kerren, A. Ebert, J. Meyer (Eds.), Human-Centered Visualization Environments. XIX, 403 pages. 2007.

Vol. 4391: Y. Stylianou, M. Faundez-Zanuy, A. Esposito (Eds.), Progress in Nonlinear Speech Processing. XII, 269 pages. 2007.

Vol. 4370: P.P. Lévy, B. Le Grand, F. Poulet, M. Soto, L. Darago, L. Toubiana, J.-F. Vibert (Eds.), Pixelization Paradigm. XV, 279 pages. 2007.

Vol. 4358: R. Vidal, A. Heyden, Y. Ma (Eds.), Dynamical Vision. IX, 329 pages. 2007.

Vol. 4338: P.K. Kalra, S. Peleg (Eds.), Computer Vision, Graphics and Image Processing. XV, 965 pages. 2006.

Vol. 4319: L.-W. Chang, W.-N. Lie (Eds.), Advances in Image and Video Technology. XXVI, 1347 pages. 2006.

Vol. 4292: G. Bebis, R. Boyle, B. Parvin, D. Koracin, P. Remagnino, A. Nefian, G. Meenakshisundaram, V. Pascucci, J. Zara, J. Molineros, H. Theisel, T. Malzbender (Eds.), Advances in Visual Computing, Part II. XXXII, 906 pages. 2006.

Vol. 4291: G. Bebis, R. Boyle, B. Parvin, D. Koracin, P. Remagnino, A. Nefian, G. Meenakshisundaram, V. Pascucci, J. Zara, J. Molineros, H. Theisel, T. Malzbender (Eds.), Advances in Visual Computing, Part I. XXXI, 916 pages. 2006.

Vol. 4245: A. Kuba, L.G. Nyúl, K. Palágyi (Eds.), Discrete Geometry for Computer Imagery. XIII, 688 pages. 2006.

Vol. 4241: R.R. Beichel, M. Sonka (Eds.), Computer Vision Approaches to Medical Image Analysis. XI, 262 pages. 2006.

Vol. 4225: J.F. Martínez-Trinidad, J.A. Carrasco Ochoa, J. Kittler (Eds.), Progress in Pattern Recognition, Image Analysis and Applications. XIX, 995 pages. 2006.

Vol. 4191: R. Larsen, M. Nielsen, J. Sporring (Eds.), Medical Image Computing and Computer-Assisted Intervention – MICCAI 2006, Part II. XXXVIII, 981 pages. 2006.

Vol. 4190: R. Larsen, M. Nielsen, J. Sporring (Eds.), Medical Image Computing and Computer-Assisted Intervention – MICCAI 2006, Part I. XXXVVIII, 949 pages. 2006.

Vol. 4179: J. Blanc-Talon, W. Philips, D. Popescu, P. Scheunders (Eds.), Advanced Concepts for Intelligent Vision Systems. XXIV, 1224 pages. 2006.

Vol. 4174: K. Franke, K.-R. Müller, B. Nickolay, R. Schäfer (Eds.), Pattern Recognition. XX, 773 pages. 2006.

Vol. 4170: J. Ponce, M. Hebert, C. Schmid, A. Zisserman (Eds.), Toward Category-Level Object Recognition. XI, 618 pages. 2006.

Vol. 4153: N. Zheng, X. Jiang, X. Lan (Eds.), Advances in Machine Vision, Image Processing, and Pattern Analysis. XIII, 506 pages. 2006.

Vol. 4142: A. Campilho, M. Kamel (Eds.), Image Analysis and Recognition, Part II. XXVII, 923 pages. 2006.

Vol. 4141: A. Campilho, M. Kamel (Eds.), Image Analysis and Recognition, Part I. XXVIII, 939 pages. 2006.

Vol. 4122: R. Stiefelhagen, J.S. Garofolo (Eds.), Multimodal Technologies for Perception of Humans. XII, 360 pages. 2007.

Vol. 4109: D.-Y. Yeung, J.T. Kwok, A. Fred, F. Roli, D. de Ridder (Eds.), Structural, Syntactic, and Statistical Pattern Recognition. XXI, 939 pages. 2006.

Vol. 4091: G.-Z. Yang, T. Jiang, D. Shen, L. Gu, J. Yang (Eds.), Medical Imaging and Augmented Reality. XIII, 399 pages. 2006.

Vol. 4073: A. Butz, B. Fisher, A. Krüger, P. Olivier (Eds.), Smart Graphics. XI, 263 pages. 2006.

Vol. 4069: F.J. Perales, R.B. Fisher (Eds.), Articulated Motion and Deformable Objects. XV, 526 pages. 2006.

Vol. 4057: J.P.W. Pluim, B. Likar, F.A. Gerritsen (Eds.), Biomedical Image Registration. XII, 324 pages. 2006.

Vol. 4046: S.M. Astley, M. Brady, C. Rose, R. Zwiggelaar (Eds.), Digital Mammography. XVI, 654 pages. 2006.

Vol. 4040: R. Reulke, U. Eckardt, B. Flach, U. Knauer, K. Polthier (Eds.), Combinatorial Image Analysis. XII, 482 pages. 2006.

Vol. 4035: T. Nishita, Q. Peng, H.-P. Seidel (Eds.), Advances in Computer Graphics. XX, 771 pages. 2006.

Vol. 3979: T.S. Huang, N. Sebe, M. Lew, V. Pavlović, M. Kölsch, A. Galata, B. Kisačanin (Eds.), Computer Vision in Human-Computer Interaction. XII, 121 pages. 2006.

Vol. 3954: A. Leonardis, H. Bischof, A. Pinz (Eds.), Computer Vision – ECCV 2006, Part IV. XVII, 613 pages. 2006.

Vol. 3953: A. Leonardis, H. Bischof, A. Pinz (Eds.), Computer Vision – ECCV 2006, Part III. XVII, 649 pages. 2006.

Vol. 3952: A. Leonardis, H. Bischof, A. Pinz (Eds.), Computer Vision – ECCV 2006, Part II. XVII, 661 pages. 2006.

Vol. 3951: A. Leonardis, H. Bischof, A. Pinz (Eds.), Computer Vision – ECCV 2006, Part I. XXXV, 639 pages. 2006.